Everyman, I will go with thee,
and be thy guide

Anthony Trollope

DOCTOR THORNE

Edited by
HUGH OSBORNE
University of Wales, Cardiff

Introduction by
JAMES KINCAID
University of Southern Carolina

EVERYMAN
J. M. DENT • LONDON
CHARLES E. TUTTLE
VERMONT

Consultant Editor for the Everyman Trollope series
David Skilton

Introduction, chronology and critical apparatus
© J. M. Dent 1997

First published in Everyman in 1908
This edition 1997

J. M. Dent
Orion Publishing Group
Orion House
5 Upper St Martin's Lane
London WC2H 9EA
and
Charles E. Tuttle Co. Inc.
28 South Main Street
Rutland, Vermont 05701, USA

Typeset by Setsystems Ltd, Saffron Walden, Essex
Printed in Great Britain by
The Guernsey Press Co. Ltd, Guernsey, C. I.

British Library Cataloguing-in-Publication Data
is available upon request.

ISBN 0 460 87604 X

CONTENTS

Note on the Author and Editors   vii
Note on the Text   ix
Chronology of Trollope's Life and Times   x
Introduction   xvii

DOCTOR THORNE

   VOLUME I

 1 The Greshams of Greshamsbury   3
 2 Long, Long Ago   18
 3 Dr Thorne   28
 4 Lessons from Courcy Castle   42
 5 Frank Gresham's First Speech   61
 6 Frank Gresham's Early Loves   71
 7 The Doctor's Garden   81
 8 Matrimonial Prospects   91
 9 Sir Roger Scatcherd   105
10 Sir Roger's Will   115
11 The Doctor Drinks His Tea   125
12 When Greek Meets Greek, Then Comes Tug of War 133
13 The Two Uncles   144
14 Sentence of Exile   153

   VOLUME II

15 Courcy   169
16 Miss Dunstable   177
17 The Election   187
18 The Rivals   201
19 The Duke of Omnium   216

20 The Proposal   224
21 Mr Moffat Falls into Trouble   232
22 Sir Roger is Unseated   246
23 Retrospective   254
24 Louis Scatcherd   263
25 Sir Roger Dies   275
26 War   290
27 Miss Thorne Goes on a Visit   300
28 The Doctor Hears Something to His Advantage   312
29 The Donkey Ride   323
30 Post Prandial   336

VOLUME III

31 The Small End of the Wedge   345
32 Mr Oriel   354
33 A Morning Visit   363
34 A Barouche and Four Arrives at Greshamsbury   374
35 Sir Louis Goes Out to Dinner   391
36 Will He Come Again?   400
37 Sir Louis Leaves Greshamsbury   408
38 De Courcy Precepts and De Courcy Practice   417
39 What the World Says About Blood   430
40 The Two Doctors Change Patients   440
41 Doctor Thorne Won't Interfere   449
42 What Can You Give in Return?   458
43 The Race of Scatcherd Becomes Extinct   471
44 Saturday Evening and Sunday Morning   481
45 Law Business in London   493
46 Our Pet Fox Finds a Tail   503
47 How the Bride Was Received, and Who Were Asked
    to the Wedding   514

Notes   529
Anthony Trollope and his Critics   553
Suggestions for Further Reading   561
Text Summary   563
Acknowledgements   567

NOTE ON THE AUTHOR AND EDITORS

ANTHONY TROLLOPE was born in London in 1817. The fourth surviving child of a failing barrister with a difficult personality and grandiose expectations, he spent a miserable childhood and youth. Because of his poverty he felt himself an outcast at Harrow and Winchester, where he was a scholastic failure. After his father went bankrupt, his mother supported the family by her writing. Through a family contact, Anthony was found a clerkship in the Post Office, and he was transferred to Ireland, where he became a reliable and energetic public servant. He married Rose Heseltine in 1844. Until retiring in 1897 he combined full-time Post Office work, reorganising large parts of the postal service of Great Britain, Ireland and the West Indies, with a huge literary output, and with life in society and on the hunting field. He published his first novel in 1847, but had only just become well known on his return to London in 1859. He was immensely popular in the 1860s, and made new efforts after 1870 to retain his market position. When he died in 1882 he had written nine volumes of stories and sketches, nine works of non-fiction and forty-seven novels, including two six-volume cycles, the *Chronicles of Barsetshire* and the Palliser novels. He journeyed extensively in Europe, North America, Australia, New Zealand and South Africa, writing fiction and factual books about his travels. His autobiography was published posthumously in 1883.

JAMES KINCAID is the Aerol Arnold Professor at the University of Southern California. He is author of *The Novels of Anthony Trollope* (1977), *Child-Loving: The Erotic Child and Victorian Culture* (1992) and *Annoying the Victorians* (1995) and has also edited various Victorian novels.

HUGH OSBORNE is Lecturer in English at the University of Wales, Cardiff. He has edited several editions of Victorian novels for Everyman Paperbacks, including *Wuthering Heights*, *The Mill on the Floss*, *Phineas Finn*, and co-edited, with David Skilton, *The Warden*, *Barchester Towers*, and *Can You Forgive Her?*.

NOTE ON THE TEXT

Trollope began writing *Doctor Thorne* on 20 October 1857, and completed it on 31 March 1858, while travelling in the Middle East, having departed for Alexandria at the end of January on Post Office business. The novel was first published in three volumes, in May 1858, by Chapman and Hall. Trollope revised the novel slightly for its re-issue by Chapman and Hall in 1878, as part of a uniform edition of the *Chronicles of Barsetshire*. This revised edition is used here. Several slight errors that persisted (*toga virile* instead of *toga virilis*, for instance, or 'si la jeunesse savante' instead of 'si la jeunesse savait') have been silently corrected. Various Victorianisms ('to-day, to-morrow', '&c') have also been adapted in accordance with modern usage.

CHRONOLOGY OF TROLLOPE'S LIFE

Year	Age	Life
1815		Born at Keppel St, Russell Square, London, on Monday 24 April
1823	8	Attends Harrow as a day boy until 1825
1825	10	Attends private school at Sunbury, Middlesex, until 1827
1827	12	Attends Winchester until 1830
1830	15	Returns to Harrow until 1834
1834	19	Family flees creditors to Belgium. Enters General Post Office as a clerk
1840	25	Suffers a serious illness
1841	26	Appointed surveyor's clerk in the Central District of Ireland

CHRONOLOGY OF HIS TIMES

Year	Artistic Context	Historical Events
1815	Austen, *Emma*	Battle of Waterloo
1817	Coleridge, *Biographia Literaria*	
1818	Scott, *The Heart of Midlothian* M. Shelley, *Frankenstein*	
1819		Peterloo massacre
1820	P. Shelley, *Prometheus Unbound*	Death of George III
1821	P. Shelley, *Defence of Poetry*	
1829		Catholic Emancipation Act passed
1830	Tennyson, *Poems, Chiefly Lyrical* Cobbett, *Rural Rides*	
1832		Reform Act passed
1833		Establishment of Oxford Movement
1837	Dickens, *Pickwick Papers*	Accession to throne of Victoria
1838	Carlyle, *Sartor Resartus* Dickens, *Nicholas Nickleby*	Emergence of Chartism
1840	Dickens, *The Old Curiosity Shop*	Introduction of the Penny Post
1841		Peel becomes Prime Minister
1842	Tennyson, *Poems in Two Volumes*	Collapse of Chartist movement

Year	Age	Life
1843	28	Starts to write *The Macdermots of Ballycloran* (pub. 1847)
1844	29	Marries Rose Heseltine (1821–1917)
1848	33	*The Kellys and the O'Kellys*
1850	35	*La Vendée*
1851	36	Tours of duty reorganising the posts in south-west England and Wales until 1852
1855	40	*The Warden*. Writes *The New Zealander* (pub. 1872)
1857	42	*Barchester Towers. The Three Clerks*
1858	43	Postal mission to Suez; *Doctor Thorne*. Reorganises postal routes in the West Indies
1859	44	*The Bertrams*. Becomes Surveyor of the Eastern District of England
1860	45	*Framley Parsonage* April 1860–April 1861. *Castle Richmond*
1861	46	*Orley Farm* March 1861–October 1862. *Brown, Jones and Robinson* August 1861–March 1862. Travels to USA
1862	47	*The Small House at Allington* September 1862–April 1864. *North America*
1863	48	*Rachel Ray*
1864	49	*Can You Forgive Her?* January 1864–August 1865
1865	50	*Miss Mackenzie. The Belton Estate* May 1865–January 1866
1866	51	*The Claverings* February 1866–May 1867. *Nina Balatka* July 1866–January 1867. *The Last Chronicle of Barset* December 1866–July 1867
1867	52	*Phineas Finn* October 1867–May 1869. *Linda Tressel* October 1867–May 1868. Edits *St Paul's Magazine* until 1870. Resigns from Post Office

Year	Artistic Context	Historical Events
1843	Dickens, *Martin Chuzzlewit*	Peel sends troops to Ireland
1844	Barrett, *Poems*	O'Connell tried for conspiracy
1846		Ireland devastated by famine Peel resigns after corn-law repeal
1847	Thackeray, *Vanity Fair*	
1848	E. Brontë, *Wuthering Heights* Macaulay, *History of England* Marx/Engels, *Communist Manifesto*	Revolution sweeps Europe
1850	Tennyson, *In Memoriam*	
1851		Opening of Great Exhibition
1852	Thackeray, *The History of Henry Esmond*	
1855	Dickens, *Little Dorrit*	Civil Service exams introduced
1857	Eliot, *Scenes of Clerical Life*	
1859	Eliot, *Adam Bede* Darwin, *The Origin of Species*	
1860	Dickens, *Great Expectations* Eliot, *The Mill on the Floss*	
1861	Eliot, *Silas Marner*	American Civil War begins
1862	Mill, *Utilitarianism*	Unification of Italy
1863	Thackeray dies	
1864	Browning, *Dramatis Personae*	
1865		American Civil War ends
1866	Swinburne, *Poems and Ballads* Eliot, *Felix Holt, The Radical*	Hyde Park riot
1867	Bagehot, *The English Constitution* Marx, *Das Kapital*	Second Reform Act passed

Year	Age	Life
1868	53	*He Knew He Was Right* October 1868–May 1869. Postal mission to USA. Stands unsuccessfully as Liberal candidate for Beverley
1869	54	*The Vicar of Bullhampton* July 1869–May 1870
1870	55	*Ralph the Heir* January 1870–July 1871. *Sir Harry Hotspur of Humblethwaite* May–December 1870
1871	56	*The Eustace Diamonds* July 1871–February 1873. Travels to Australia and New Zealand, May 1871–December 1872
1872	57	*The Golden Lion of Granpere* January–August
1873	58	*Lady Anna* April 1873–April 1874. *Phineas Redux* July 1873–January 1874. *Australia and New Zealand. Harry Heathcote*
1874	59	*The Way We Live Now* February 1874–September 1875
1875	60	*The Prime Minister* November 1875–June 1876. Travels to Australia and USA, March–October. Starts *An Autobiography* (compl. 1876, pub. 1883)
1876	61	*The American Senator* May 1876–July 1877
1877	62	*Is He Popenjoy?* October 1877–July 1878. Travels to South Africa
1878	63	*John Caldigate* April 1878–June 1879. *An Eye for an Eye* August 1878–June 1879. *South Africa*
1879	64	*Cousin Henry* March–May. *The Duke's Children* October 1879–July 1880. *Thackeray*
1880	65	*Dr Wortle's School* May–December
1881	66	*Ayala's Angel. The Fixed Period* October 1881–March 1882. *Marion Fay* December 1881–June 1882
1882	67	*Kept in the Dark* May–December. *Mr Scarborough's Family* May 1882–June 1883. *The Landleaguers* November 1882–October 1883. Dies 6 December, at Welbeck Street, Cavendish Square, London
1883		*An Autobiography*
1884		*An Old Man's Love*

Year	Artistic Context	Historical Events
1868	Collins, *The Moonstone* Browning, *The Ring and the Book*	
1869	Arnold, *Culture and Anarchy* Mill, *The Subjection of Women*	
1870	Dickens dies D. G. Rossetti, *Poems*	Franco-Prussian War Start of Irish Home Rule movement. Married Women's Property Act
1871	Darwin, *The Descent of Man*	
1872	Eliot, *Middlemarch*	
1874	Hardy, *Far From the Madding Crowd*	Irish Home Rule movement grows
1876	Eliot, *Daniel Deronda*	Victoria made Empress of India
1878	Swinburne, *Poems and Ballads: second series*	Congress of Berlin
1879	James, *Daisy Miller*	Irish National Land League formed
1880	Eliot dies	Charles Parnell tried for conspiracy
1881	James, *Portrait of a Lady* James, *Washington Square*	Land League outlawed
1884		Third Reform Act passed

INTRODUCTION

To enter into the world of *Doctor Thorne* (1858) is to find oneself immediately at the heart of the tradition of nineteenth-century realism, perhaps the most enduring of narrative practices. This tradition, with its minute particularity and respect for the intricacy of human psychology and the power of quotidian reality, is still so vital that modern readers are likely to be tricked into an easy familiarity. After all, many of the assumptions of the realist tradition animate modern films and television programmes. Trollope, who always thought of himself as a craftsman rather than a 'genius', would not have been displeased with the link with Hollywood celluloid, soap operas, even fly-on-the-wall documentaries. But beware of taking the comparison too seriously, for Trollope is the most subtle of realists, and *Doctor Thorne* is a deceptive land-mine of a novel. It may bring to mind daytime television, but it also evokes the fiction of two of Trollope's admirers, James and Tolstoy, deceptive realists themselves.

Doctor Thorne has always been a popular solo in Trollope's enduring hit, the Barsetshire series. It travels but a short distance from the famous cathedral town over to East Barsetshire, not so far that many of the old crowd from *Barchester Towers* (1857) can not be heard. Three later novels (*Framley Parsonage, the Small House at Allington, The Last Chronicle of Barset*) were to complete what to many readers is a series unmatched for the evocation of an English idyll, a vision of English life and landscape so unrushed and coherent as to draw into its bosom even those who have never seen anything like it or experienced first-hand its dukes, earls and country squires.

But we soon find that, for all its surface sunniness, *Doctor Thorne* is by no means as uncomplicated or undemanding as it may appear. For one thing, it initiates a playful rhetoric, a self-reflexive teasing of the reader that may recall not so much the simplicity of the idyll tradition as the duplicity of Sterne or

Nabokov. Trollope is fond of constructing narrators who pretend to be a little unsure of just how to get the story told.
Sometimes they simply throw up their hands (as the narrator of
Doctor Thorne does over legal issues in Ch. 45), draw attention
to the make-believe of the whole thing, open the story by
making fun of openings, and end it with pointed ridicule of
conclusions. This super-realism is subject to a sly mockery of
the conventions of realism itself.

   Doctor Thorne's busy narrator can disappear for pages at a
time, only to surface now and then for a friendly chat, making
readers suddenly aware that they have been pulled into a web of
conventional illusion. Remarkably, he not only hates the very
idea of plots, he lets it be known, openly teasing the reader's
natural interest in events and revealing what is going to happen
long before it does. The narrator opens *Doctor Thorne* by
saying that he is 'too old now to be hard-hearted' and will thus
allow the young hero and heroine to marry, thereby relieving
any anxiety about the novel's love interest, and, it might be
supposed, relieving the reader of any interest in the ensuing
events. If it is a boy-meets-girl novel that tells straight off that
boy-gets-girl, what is to keep anyone reading for the next five
hundred pages? A simple reason, and Trollope's own, is 'character', but it might also be that the reader becomes ensnared in
the sophisticated play of convention-busting, of sly reflexivity
that Trollope loves to exercise. For art like this, plots may seem
crude and distracting. In fact, for *Doctor Thorne*, Trollope
asked his brother for a plot, but used it without paying it much
heed. Though it is a sensational plot, he barely bothers to make
it credible, still less memorable. Perhaps no great novel has so
little going on, and what little there is of such slight importance
in the minds of readers.

   Doctor Thorne is compelling nonetheless, partly because it so
masterfully centres and shadows the heartfelt and moving
triumph of young love, the simplest story in the world and the
basis of all romantic comedy. 'Young people will be young,'
Lady Arabella says disapprovingly; 'And old people must be
old' (Ch. 26), responds the Doctor, slyly indicating that both he
and Lady Arabella are playing ancient roles in an ancient story
of how young love will always be opposed by age and will, just
as certainly, overcome any obstacle. Doctor Thorne is, as
Trollope tells us, the 'hero' of the work because he sees, as Lady

Arabella does not, just what sort of novel he is in, and he cooperates with the energies of the romantic comedy guiding it.

But these are not the only energies at work here, and Trollope's novel moves within the romantic comedy genre to explore not simply its pleasures but its ravages, not simply the rewards given to the young and pretty but the sacrifices exacted from their victims. Who pays for the party? At the dark, ironic edge of comedy stands the scapegoat, the figure whose expulsion from the community provides healing and festivity for the rest. This figure, the comic version of the tragic Oedipus or Hamlet, takes form in Shakespeare often as the refuser of festivity, the one who spoils the party, Malvolio in *Twelfth Night* being a prime example. Sometimes, however, the role of this ritual victim becomes so clearly realised and disturbing as to shift the tone altogether away from festivity; a common response, for example, to *The Merchant of Venice* and the focus, at least in modern performances, on Shylock. If we look too long at Shylock we sense that comedy defines itself as healthy only by locating or even constructing enemies, images of danger or disease it can then humiliate or cast out. Or kill.

When things become desperate for the comic community it may resort to homicide, at which point it risks leaving the world of comedy behind altogether, especially if the audience is allowed, even for a moment, to sympathize with the Shylock character, with the image of ritual sacrifice. In *Doctor Thorne* Trollope portrays just such a victim in Sir Roger Scatcherd, a fully sympathetic character of great power and ability, drawn against his will into a world that uses him ruthlessly and then leaves him with no prospect but death. At the centre of *Doctor Thorne*'s happy carnival is, surprisingly, Trollope's version of Shylock and a subtext of horror and even blood-letting, as though Count Dracula were loose in Barchester. Pastoral blessedness is mixed with Gothic Satanism, almost as if Edgar Allan Poe and Jane Austen were to have concocted a ghostly collaboration.

The solution to the economic problems of Greshamsbury and to the dilemma of how to get Frank and Mary together both lie with this tragic figure – burly, crude, alcoholic and recently knighted Sir Roger. Scatcherd has all the ability, all the energy, and most of the money that the established world so sorely lacks; so they take it from him. Reversing the usual story of the loud and vulgar newly-rich drowning out the delicate, Trollope shows how Scatcherd becomes increasingly displaced and exploited, alone with his bewilderment and his poison. Both he and his wife realise too late – though it is not clear there was ever a time they could have helped it – that their ascendancy has left them with nothing. Scatcherd may be 'the man for his time' (Ch. 9) his fortune coming from the new railways, but, for this hero, 'there was no sympathy; no tenderness of love; no retreat, save into himself, from the loud brass band of the outer world' (Ch. 22). He sees this with terrifying clarity: 'I'll tell you what, Thorne, when a man has made three hundred thousand pounds, there's nothing left for him but to die. It's all he's good for then' (Ch. 10). The dilemma he faces, the horror of his life, is, by a twist of the ingenious plot Trollope borrowed, made also the source of great happiness for others. It is a happiness rooted in sacrifice and darkness, originating in a rape and ending in an ambivalently tragic suicide, the blood sacrifice of the railroad king so that true 'blood' may be preserved.

And this is not the only darkness in Trollope's subversive novel. There is also the grimly ironic story of Scatcherd's son and heir, the pathetic (and pathetically named) Louis Philippe, who inherits nothing from his father but his alcoholism and who displays, in his wretched attempts to enter the world of rank, the helplessness of his father without any of the stern dignity or clarity of vision that had guarded the elder man from public humiliation. In some of the most gruellingly embarrassing scenes in literature, scenes the reader lives through in a kind of agony, Louis Philippe forces the Greshams and even Doctor Thorne to recognise what they are doing and what readers must do to reach the land of comic fulfilment.

It is a demanding task that Trollope demands of his hero: he must rescue not only his niece and the young squire but a whole world that seems about to crumble. The novel opens with a coming-of-age that threatens to be made a mockery, the beginning of the end of placid, gracious, rural England. No one seems able to resist the fresh, brash vulgarity, the tidal wave of new invention, new money, new power sweeping over the country like its major symbol, the railroad. At best the response of the old world seems feeble and confused: indeed, one is forced to wonder whether the old world is worth saving. At its worst it relaxes into the bestial decadence represented by the dinner at the Duke of Omnium's, where the graceful era of polite manners is replaced by the snorting feeding of 'hogs' (Ch. 19). The Gresham estate is being eaten away by irresponsibility, the De Courcy aristocrats are desperately trying to sell themselves to the highest bidder, and the only solid virtue seems lodged in the Doctor, an iconoclast Doctor, who stands aloof from all class allegiances.

But Doctor Thorne, along with his stubborn and heart-winning neice Mary, manages to irradiate this cold and dark world, to rescue the gentry and the estate, to preserve, at least for now, the old values and the old forms. The novel, in this sense, circles back to a time before its opening, to a time of true English pastoral: a world of benevolent landed squires, thriving rural economies, deferential workers, and a hearty respect for rank and blood. But there is a price to be paid, and *Doctor Thorne* draws much of its power from the almost brutal honesty with which it faces the cost of winning what finally is a class war. Indeed, class and class issues, along with the key terms associated with them – blood, money, land, the gentleman, responsibility – are so sharply foregrounded that any deconstructionist, new historian or Marxist will find ample material here. The terms are so complex and so very slippery that they slide away from even the most stable characters, like the Doctor. As a result, the reader is asked to regard as a hero the very figure whose steadfast ethical and social principles rest on quicksand.

That Trollope could have written a novel so intricate and seditious is surprising given that he had to fulfil the daily quota of pages he set himself under the most difficult circumstances. About a quarter of the way through the writing of *Doctor Thorne*, he was assigned by the Post Office to a project in Alexandria to arrange with the shrewd Nubar Bey a postal treaty with Egypt. On board ship, roaring at Nubar Bey about the speed of camels (Trollope insisted they could go much faster than he was being told), climbing pyramids, touring the Suez and the Holy Land, Trollope kept going steadily on his novel, writing about East Barsetshire amidst the whirling dervishes and the distractions of trying not to be just one more British tourist.

Yet that the novel could be written under such conditions is perhaps less surprising than Trollope's ability to become a successful writer from such rough-and-tumble, heart-piercing, demoralizing beginnings. Despite a childhood that makes Dickens's appear coddled, Trollope somehow found the resolve to write, and to write himself through a whole series of commercial failures before hitting on success, first a moderate success with *Barchester Towers*, and then the unmistakable real thing with *Doctor Thorne*. He must have looked back then at all the public-school bullies and the publishers who had scoffed at his early efforts, on all the pain and humiliation, the sense of being unworthy of the friendship of others, and felt a moment of unalloyed satisfaction. Only a brief moment, though: he finished *Doctor Thorne* one day and the very next began writing *The Bertrams*. Trollope, like the eponymous hero of his novel, was not one to bask in self-approval.

He might have been justified in some self-indulgence, given the skill and tact with which he had crafted *Doctor Thorne*, and not just its hero and heroine either but the full range of the cast, even (perhaps especially) the blocking characters. Often those we expect to detest we end by admiring, even to the point of wanting to be more in their company. This is especially true of Miss Dunstable, the Ointment of Lebanon heiress, who has every reason to be a comic type, a caricature, but who speaks instead with rare wit and unshakable aplomb. She is Sir Roger all over again, but she manages to protect herself, seeing quite clearly that the aristocrats are anxious to suck her blood and consequently keeping her veins to herself, while having a very good time of it and entertaining generously both the reader and all the good people in the novel. She represents just one example of Trollope's sly and disruptive way of playing with the reader's conventional expectations.

He does this too with Squire Gresham and, far more import-ant, his hen-pecking wife, Lady Arabella, a direct descendant of Jane Austen's Lady Catherine de Bourgh and an anticipation of Wilde's Miss Prism. But Trollope is writing something more than a comedy of manners here, and he makes the mother of the young squire oddly sympathetic in her drive to keep her son unpolluted by bad blood, i.e., Mary. Though we are asked to love Mary – and young Frank, too – Lady Arabella's point can also be seen. She loves her son and is, for all her henpeckery, justly worried about her husband's weakness, his inability to keep the estate from dissolving before their eyes. Lady Arabella is human, especially in her fears, and the narrator teases us into imagining that she is a hypochondriac, tied to the doctor only by fantasy-needs; but then ends a long paragraph of jokes with this shocking revelation: 'Now the complaint of which Lady Arabella was afraid, was cancer.' *Doctor Thorne* is a novel which allows no easy judgments, for Mary sees Lady Arabella's point too, and so does her uncle the Doctor. They see it, if possible, with more clarity and force than Lady Arabella and all the aristocratic De Courcys could ever muster. It is the deep respect Doctor and Mary Thorne hold for the principles that animate the aristocrats, that complicates their situation enormously and places on them the burden of playing both sides of the game. They need to make the best arguments the book has to offer on the importance of blood, on the preservation of rank; and then they need to find ways to counter, even subvert, those very arguments. The preservation of the aristocracy is too important to be left to the aristocrats; just as the traditions of old England are far too vital to be left to the old English.

So, like Prospero before him, the doctor must set about his heroic work of making a world that will be safe for the young lovers. Mediating between Greshamsbury and Sir Roger, Thorne is forever putting himself in impossible situations and finding a way out. He is outside of class, living resolutely in one world and holding passionate to the values of another. He has both the freedom and the odd chameleon ambivalence of the true artist, a somewhat grumpy artist, to be sure, but very soft on the inside, as Trollope's favourite heroes always are. He has about him an 'almost womanly tenderness' (Ch. 3), is devoted to children – 'he argued that the principal duty which a parent owed to a child was to make him happy' (Ch. 3) – and is dear to the reader not merely because of the clarity of his judgment or the depths of his courage, but because of the sweetness of his heart.

Doctor Thorne needs to haul out all the magic tricks he has in his bag to make things right for Frank and Mary, both of whom have about them more than a touch of the silly. Frank is especially prone to giddy posturings: 'I hate money' (Ch. 29); 'I don't care a straw for the world' (Ch. 39). Even his father, who is no fountainhead of wisdom, tells him he had better care some for the world, as it is hard to imagine living out of it. But Frank bumbles on, driven by his susceptibility and by hormonal ragings to fall in love with every decent-looking woman he meets. When he's not near the girl he loves, he really does love the girl he's near. Trollope cements our attachment to this scatter-hearted young man not by insisting on his inner strength but on his physical beauty. Over and over again Trollope's narrator, sometimes speaking as a woman, lets us know that Frank is simply stunning, irresistible.

Mary, on the other hand, has a large dose of what traditional male heroes usually have at least some of: courage and strength of character. Her outward appearance is essentially a matter of indifference: the narrator can even joke about it, and about our banal expectations: 'She is my heroine, and, as such, must necessarily be very beautiful.' 'But,' the narrator goes on, pounding home the point and the gender subversion, 'in truth, her mind and inner qualities' (Ch. 1) are what concern him and had better concern us. It is Mary who is tough and who knows what is at stake: nothing less than the preservation of Englishness: 'England is not yet a commercial country ... and let us hope that she will not soon become so. She might surely as well be called feudal England, or chivalrous England' (Ch. 1).

This devious novel directs its readers backward, towards that nostalgic pastoral idyll that was England. But it also makes us wonder if it is worth the trip. In order to get there it is necessary to play very rough, strew some corpses around. Trollope lets us know that this feudal England will not be around for long and maybe was not worth recalling in the first place. For now, however, we can take pleasure in what this deeply ambivalent novel does provide: the delight of comic hospitality and all it can offer, which includes forgiveness for Lady Arabella, a tentative confirmation of the doctor's beliefs, many happy nights for the young lovers, and, for us, the illusion, and that is all it may be, that something in this world can come to good.

DOCTOR THORNE

VOLUME I

CHAPTER I

The Greshams of Greshamsbury

Before the reader is introduced to the modest country medical practitioner who is to be the chief personage of the following tale, it will be well that he should be made acquainted with some particulars as to the locality in which, and the neighbours among whom, our doctor followed his profession.

There is a county in the west of England not so full of life, indeed, nor so widely spoken of as some of its manufacturing leviathan brethren in the north, but which is, nevertheless, very dear to those who know it well. Its green pastures, its waving wheat, its deep and shady and – let us add – dirty lanes, its paths and stiles, its tawny-coloured, well-built rural churches, its avenues of beeches, and frequent Tudor mansions, its constant county hunt, its social graces, and the general air of clanship which pervades it, has made it to its own inhabitants a favoured land of Goshen.* It is purely agricultural; agricultural in its produce, agricultural in its poor, and agricultural in its pleasures. There are towns in it, of course; dépôts from whence are brought seeds and groceries, ribbons and fire-shovels; in which markets are held and county balls are carried on; which return members to Parliament, generally – in spite of Reform Bills, past, present, and coming – in accordance with the dictates of some neighbouring land magnate:* from when emanate the country postmen, and where is located the supply of post-horses necessary for county visitings. But these towns add nothing to the importance of the county; they consist, with the exception of the assize town, of dull, all but death-like single streets. Each possesses two pumps, three hotels, ten shops, fifteen beer-houses, a beadle,* and a market-place.

Indeed, the town population of the county reckons for nothing when the importance of the county is discussed, with the exception, as before said, of the assize town, which is also a cathedral city. Herein is a clerical aristocracy, which is certainly not without its due weight. A resident bishop, a resident dean, an archdeacon, three or four resident prebendaries, and all their numerous chaplains, vicars, and ecclesiastical satellites, do make up a society sufficiently powerful to be counted as something by the county squirearchy. In other respects the greatness of Barsetshire depends wholly on the landed powers.

Barsetshire, however, is not now so essentially one whole as it was before the Reform Bill divided it. There is in these days an East Barsetshire, and there is a West Barsetshire; and people conversant with Barsetshire doings declare that they can already decipher some difference of feeling, some division of interests. The eastern moiety of the county is more purely Conservative than the western; there is, or was, a taint of Peelism* in the latter; and then, too, the residence of two such great Whig magnates as the Duke of Omnium and the Earl de Courcy in that locality in some degree overshadows and renders less influential the gentlemen who live near them.

It is to East Barsetshire that we are called. When the division above spoken of was first contemplated, in those stormy days in which gallant men were still combating reform ministers, if not with hope, still with spirit, the battle was fought by none more bravely than by John Newbold Gresham of Greshamsbury, the member for Barsetshire. Fate, however, and the Duke of Wellington* were adverse, and in the following Parliament John Newbold Gresham was only member for East Barsetshire.

Whether or not it was true, as stated at the time, that the aspect of the men with whom he was called on to associate at St Stephen's* broke his heart, it is not for us now to inquire. It is certainly true that he did not live to see the first year of the reformed Parliament brought to a close. The then Mr Gresham was not an old man at the time of his death, and his eldest son, Francis Newbold Gresham, was a very young man; but, notwithstanding his youth, and notwithstanding other grounds of objection which stood in the way of such preferment, and which must be explained, he was chosen in his father's place. The father's services had been too recent, too well appreciated, too thoroughly in unison with the feelings of those around him to allow of any other choice; and in this way young Frank Gresham found himself member for East Barsetshire, although the very men who elected him knew that they had but slender ground for trusting him with their suffrages.

Frank Gresham, though then only twenty-four years of age, was a married man, and a father. He had already chosen a wife, and by his choice had given much ground of distrust to the men of East Barsetshire. He had married no other than Lady Arabella de Courcy, the sister of the great Whig earl who lived at Courcy Castle in the west; that earl who not only had voted for the Reform Bill, but had been infamously active in bringing over other young peers so to vote, and whose name therefore stank in the nostrils of the staunch Tory squires of the county.

Not only had Frank Gresham so wedded, but having thus improperly and unpatriotically chosen a wife, he had added to his sin by becoming recklessly intimate with his wife's relations. It is true that he still called himself a Tory, belonged to the club of which his father had been one of the most honoured members, and in the days of the great battle got his head broken in a row, on the right side; but, nevertheless, it was felt by the good men, true and blue, of East Barsetshire, that a constant sojourner at Courcy Castle could not be regarded as a consistent Tory. When, however, his father died, that broken head served him in good stead: his sufferings in the cause were made the most of; these, in unison with his father's merits, turned the scale, and it was accordingly decided, at a meeting held at the George and Dragon at Barchester, that Frank Gresham should fill his father's shoes.

But Frank Gresham could not fill his father's shoes; they were too big for him. He did become member for East Barsetshire; but he was such a member – so lukewarm, so indifferent, so prone to associate with the enemies of the good cause, so little willing to fight the good fight,* that he soon disgusted those who most dearly loved the memory of the old squire.

De Courcy Castle in those days had great allurements for a young man, and all those allurements were made the most of to win over young Gresham. His wife, who was a year or two older than himself, was a fashionable woman, with thorough Whig tastes and aspirations, such as became the daughter of a great Whig earl; she cared for politics, or thought that she cared for them, more than her husband did: for a month or two previous to her engagement she had been attached to the Court, and had been made to believe that much of the policy of

England's rulers depended on the political intrigues of England's women. She was one who would fain be doing something if she only knew how, and the first important attempt she made was to turn her respectable young Tory husband into a second-rate Whig bantling. As this lady's character will, it is hoped, show itself in the following pages, we need not now describe it more closely.

It is not a bad thing to be son-in-law to a potent earl, member of Parliament for a county, and possessor of a fine old English seat, and a fine old English fortune. As a very young man, Frank Gresham found the life to which he was thus introduced agreeable enough. He consoled himself as best he might for the blue books* with which he was greeted by his own party, and took his revenge by consorting more thoroughly than ever with his political adversaries. Foolishly, like a foolish moth, he flew to the bright light, and, like the moths, of course he burnt his wings. Early in 1833 he had become a member of Parliament, and in the autumn of 1834 the dissolution came. Young members of three or four-and-twenty do not think much of dissolutions, forget the fancies of their constituents, and are too proud of the present to calculate much as to the future. So it was with Mr Gresham. His father had been member for Barsetshire all his life, and he looked forward to similar prosperity as though it were part of his inheritance; but he failed to take any of the steps which had secured his father's seat.

In the autumn of 1834 the dissolution came, and Frank Gresham, with his honourable lady wife and all the De Courcys at his back, found that he had mortally offended the county. To his great disgust another candidate was brought forward as a fellow to his late colleague, and though he manfully fought the battle, and spent ten thousand pounds in the contest, he could not recover his position. A high Tory, with a great Whig interest to back him, is never a popular person in England. No one can trust him, though there may be those who are willing to place him, untrusted, in high positions. Such was the case with Mr Gresham. There were many who were willing, for family considerations, to keep him in Parliament; but no one thought that he was fit to be there. The consequences were, that a bitter and expensive contest ensued. Frank Gresham, when twitted with being a Whig, foreswore the De Courcy family; and then, when ridiculed as having been thrown over by the Tories, foreswore his father's old friends. So between the two stools he fell to the ground, and, as a politician, he never again rose to his feet.

He never again rose to his feet; but twice again he made violent efforts to do so. Elections in East Barsetshire, from various causes, came quick upon each other in those days, and before he was eight-and-twenty years of age Mr Gresham had three times contested the county and been three times beaten. To speak the truth of him, his own spirit would have been satisfied with the loss of the first ten thousand pounds; but Lady Arabella was made of higher mettle. She had married a man with a fine place and a fine fortune; but she had nevertheless married a commoner and had in so far derogated from her high birth. She felt that her husband should be by rights a member of the House of Lords; but, if not, that it was at least essential that he should have a seat in the lower chamber. She would by degrees sink into nothing if she allowed herself to sit down, the mere wife of a mere country squire.

Thus instigated, Mr Gresham repeated the useless contest three times, and repeated it each time at a serious cost. He lost his money, Lady Arabella lost her temper, and things at Greshamsbury went on by no means as prosperously as they had done in the days of the old squire.

In the first twelve years of their marriage, children came fast into the nursery at Greshamsbury. The first that was born was a boy; and in those happy halcyon days, when the old squire was still alive, great was the joy at the birth of an heir to Greshamsbury; bonfires gleamed through the country-side, oxen were roasted whole, and the customary paraphernalia of joy usual to rich Britons on such occasions were gone through with wondrous éclat. But when the tenth baby, and the ninth little girl, was brought into the world, the outward show of joy was not so great.

Then other troubles came on. Some of these little girls were sickly, some very sickly. Lady Arabella had her faults, and they were such as were extremely detrimental to her husband's happiness and her own; but that of being an indifferent mother was not among them. She had worried her husband daily for years because he was not in Parliament, she had worried him because he would not furnish the house in Portman Square, she had worried him because he objected to have more people every winter at Greshamsbury Park than the house would hold; but now she changed her tune and worried him because Selina coughed, because Helena was hectic, because poor Sophy's spine was weak, and Matilda's appetite was gone.

Worrying from such causes was pardonable it will be said. So it was; but the manner was hardly pardonable. Selina's cough was certainly not fairly attributable to the old-fashioned furniture in Portman Square; nor would Sophy's spine have been materially benefited by her father having a seat in Parliament; and yet, to have heard Lady Arabella discussing those matters in family conclave, one would have thought that she would have expected such results.

As it was, her poor weak darlings were carried about from London to Brighton, from Brighton to some German baths, from the German baths back to Torquay, and thence – as regarded the four we have named – to that bourne from whence no further journey could be made* under the Lady Arabella's directions.

The one son and heir to Greshamsbury was named as his father, Francis Newbold Gresham. He would have been the hero of our tale had not that place been preoccupied by the village doctor. As it is, those who please may so regard him. It is he who is to be our favourite young man, to do the love scenes, to have his trials and his difficulties, and to win through them or not, as the case may be. I am too old now to be a hard-hearted author, and so it is probable that he may not die of a broken heart. Those who don't approve of a middle-aged bachelor country doctor as a hero, may take the heir to Greshamsbury in his stead, and call the book, if it so please them. 'The Loves and Adventures of Francis Newbold Gresham the younger.'

And Master Frank Gresham was not ill adapted for playing the part of a hero of this sort. He did not share his sisters' ill-health, and though the only boy of the family, he excelled all his sisters in personal appearance. The Greshams from time immemorial had been handsome. They were broad browed, blue eyed, fair haired, born with dimples in their chins, and that pleasant, aristocratic, dangerous curl of the upper lip which can equally express good humour or scorn. Young Frank was every inch a Gresham, and was the darling of his father's heart.

The De Courcys had never been plain. There was too much hauteur, too much pride, we may perhaps even fairly say, too much nobility in their gait and manners, and even in their faces, to allow of their being considered plain; but they were not a race nurtured by Venus or Apollo. They were tall and thin, with high cheek-bones, high foreheads, and large, dignified, cold eyes. The De Courcy girls had all good hair; and, as they also possessed easy manners and powers of talking, they managed to pass in the world for beauties till they were absorbed in the matrimonial market, and the world at large cared no longer whether they were beauties or not. The Misses Gresham were made in the De Courcy mould, and were not on this account the less dear to their mother.

The two eldest, Augusta and Beatrice, lived, and were apparently likely to live. The four next faded and died one after another – all in the same sad year – and were laid in the neat, new cemetery at Torquay. Then came a pair, born at one birth, weak, delicate, frail little flowers, with dark hair and dark eyes, and thin, long, pale faces, with long, bony hands, and long, bony feet, whom men looked on as fated to follow their sisters with quick steps. Hitherto, however, they had not followed them, nor had they suffered as their sisters had suffered; and some people at Greshamsbury attributed this to the fact that a change had been made in the family medical practitioner.

Then came the youngest of the flock, she whose birth we have said was not heralded with loud joy; for when she came into the world, four others, with pale temples, wan, worn cheeks, and skeleton, white arms, were awaiting permission to leave it.

Such was the family when, in the year 1854, the eldest son came of age. He had been educated at Harrow, and was now still at Cambridge; but, of course, on such a day as this he was at home. That coming of age must be a delightful time to a young man born to inherit broad acres and wide wealth. Those full-mouthed congratulations; those warm prayers with which his manhood is welcomed by the grey-haired seniors of the county; the affectionate, all but motherly caresses of neighbouring mothers who have seen him grow up from his cradle, of mothers who have daughters, perhaps, fair enough, and good enough, and sweet enough even for him; the soft-spoken, half-bashful, but tender greetings of the girls, who now, perhaps for the first time, call him by his stern family name, instructed by instinct rather than precept that the time has come when the familiar Charles or familiar John must by them be laid aside,

the 'lucky dogs,' and hints of silver spoons which are poured
into his ears as each young compeer slaps his back and bids him
live a thousand years and then never die; the shouting of the
tenantry, the good wishes of the old farmers who come up to
wring his hand, the kisses which he gets from the farmers' wives,
and the kisses which he gives to the farmers' daughters; all these
things must make the twenty-first birthday pleasant enough to a
young heir. To a youth, however, who feels that he is now liable
to arrest, and that he inherits no other privilege, the pleasure
may very possibly not be quite so keen.

The case with young Frank Gresham may be supposed to be
much nearer the former than the latter; but yet the ceremony of
his coming of age was by no means like that which fate had
accorded to his father. Mr Gresham was now an embarrassed
man, and though the world did not know it, or, at any rate, did
not know that he was deeply embarrassed, he had not the heart
to throw open his mansion and park and receive the county
with a free hand as though all things were going well with him.

Nothing was going well with him. Lady Arabella would allow
nothing near him or around him to be well. Everything with
him now turned to vexation; he was no longer a joyous, happy
man, and the people of East Barsetshire did not look for gala
doings on a grand scale when young Gresham came of age.

Gala doings, to a certain extent, there were there. It was in
July, and tables were spread under the oaks for the tenants.
Tables were spread, and meat, and beer, and wine were there,
and Frank, as he walked round and shook his guests by the
hand, expressed a hope that their relations with each other
might be long, close, and mutually advantageous.

We must say a few words now about the place itself.
Greshamsbury Park was a fine old English gentleman's seat –
was and is; but we can assert it more easily in past tense, as we
are speaking of it with reference to a past time. We have spoken
of Greshamsbury Park; there was a park so called, but the
mansion itself was generally known as Greshamsbury House,
and did not stand in the park. We may perhaps best describe it
by saying that the village of Greshamsbury consisted of one
long, straggling street, a mile in length, which in the centre
turned sharp round, so that one half of the street lay directly at
right angles to the other. In this angle stood Greshamsbury
House, and the gardens and grounds around it filled up the

space so made. There was an entrance with large gates at each end of the village, and each gate was guarded by the effigies of two huge pagans with clubs, such being the crest borne by the family; from each entrance a broad road, quite straight, running through to a majestic avenue of limes, led up to the house. This was built in the richest, perhaps we should rather say in the purest, style of Tudor architecture; so much so that, though Greshamsbury is less complete than Longleat, less magnificent than Hatfield* it may in some sense be said to be the finest specimen of Tudor architecture of which the country can boast.

It stands amid a multitude of trim gardens and stone-built terraces, divided one from another these to our eyes are not so attractive as that broad expanse of lawn by which our country houses are generally surrounded; but the gardens of Greshamsbury have been celebrated for two centuries, and any Gresham who would have altered them would have been considered to have destroyed one of the well-known landmarks of the family.

Greshamsbury Park – properly so called – spread far away on the other side of the village. Opposite to the two great gates leading up to the mansion were two smaller gates, the one opening on to the stables, kennels, and farmyard, and the other to the deer park. This latter was the principal entrance to the demesne, and a grand and picturesque entrance it was. The avenue of limes which on one side stretched up to the house, was on the other extended for a quarter of a mile, and then appeared to be terminated only by an abrupt rise in the ground. At the entrance there were four savages and four clubs, two to each portal, and what with the massive iron gates, surmounted by a stone wall, on which stood the family arms supported by two other club-bearers, the stone-built lodges, the Doric, ivy-covered columns which surrounded the circle, the four grim savages, and the extent of the space itself through which the high road ran, and which just abutted on the village, the spot was sufficiently significant of old family greatness.

Those who examined it more closely might see that under the arms was a scroll bearing the Gresham motto, and that the words were repeated in smaller letters under each of the savages. 'Gardez Gresham', had been chosen in the days of motto-choosing probably by some herald-at-arms as an appropriate legend for signifying the peculiar attributes of the family. Now, however, unfortunately, men were not of one mind as to the exact idea signified. Some declared, with much heraldic warmth, that it was an address to the savages, calling on them to take care of their patron; while others, with whom I myself am inclined to agree, averred with equal certainty that it was an advice to the people at large, especially to those inclined to rebel against the aristocracy of the county, that they should 'beware the Gresham'. The latter signification would betoken strength – so said the holders of this doctrine; the former weakness. Now the Greshams were ever a strong people, and never addicted to a false humility.

We will not pretend to decide the question. Alas! either construction was now equally unsuited to the family fortunes. Such changes had taken place in England since the Greshams had founded themselves that no savage could any longer in any way protect them; they must protect themselves like common folk, or live unprotected. Nor now was it necessary that any neighbour should shake in his shoes when the Gresham frowned. It would have been to be wished that the present Gresham himself could have been as indifferent to the frowns of some of his neighbours.

But the old symbols remained, and may such symbols long remain among us; they are still lovely and fit to be loved. They tell us of the true and manly feelings of other times; and to him who can read aright, they explain more fully, more truly than any written history can do, how Englishmen have become what they are. England is not yet a commercial country in the sense in which that epithet is used for her; and let us still hope that she will not soon become so. She might surely as well be called feudal England, or chivalrous England. If in western civilised Europe there does exist a nation among whom there are high signors, and with whom the owners of the land are the true aristocracy, the aristocracy that is trusted as being best and fittest to rule, that nation is the English. Choose out the ten leading men of each great European people. Choose them in France, in Austria, Sardinia, Prussia, Russia, Sweden, Denmark, Spain (?), and then select the ten in England whose names are best known as those of leading statesmen; the result will show in which country there still exists the closest attachment to, the sincerest trust in, the old feudal and now so-called landed interests.

England a commercial country! Yes; as Venice was. She may

excel other nations in commerce, but yet it is not that in which she most prides herself, in which she most excels. Merchants as such are not the first men among us; though it perhaps be open, barely open, to a merchant to become one of them. Buying and selling is good and necessary; it is very necessary, and may, possibly, be very good; but it cannot be the noblest work of man; and let us hope that it may not in our time be esteemed the noblest work of an Englishman.

Greshamsbury Park was very large; it lay on the outside of the angle formed by the village street, and stretched away on two sides without apparent limit or boundaries visible from the village road or house. Indeed, the ground on this side was so broken up into abrupt hills, and conical-shaped, oak-covered excrescences, which were seen peeping up through and over each other, that the true extent of the park was much magnified to the eye. It was very possible for a stranger to get into it and to find some difficulty in getting out again by any of its known gates; and such was the beauty of the landscape, that a lover of scenery would be tempted thus to lose himself.

I have said that on one side lay the kennels, and this will give me an opportunity of describing here one especial episode, a long episode, in the life of the existing squire. He had once represented his county in Parliament, and when he ceased to do so he still felt an ambition to be connected in some peculiar way with that county's greatness; he still desired that Gresham of Greshamsbury should be something more in East Barsetshire than Jackson of the Grange, or Baker of Mill Hill, or Bateson of Annesgrove. They were all his friends, and very respectable country gentlemen; but Mr Gresham of Greshamsbury should be more than this: even he had enough of ambition to be aware of such a longing. Therefore, when an opportunity occurred he took to hunting the county.

For this employment he was in every way well suited – unless it was in the matter of finance. Though he had in his very earliest manly years given such great offence by indifference to his family politics, and had in a certain degree fostered the ill-feeling by contesting the county in opposition to the wishes of his brother squires, nevertheless, he bore a loved and popular name. Men regretted that he should not have been what they wished him to be, that he should not have been such as was the old squire; but when they found that such was the case, that he could not be great among them as a politician, they were still willing that he should be great in any other way if there were county greatness for which he was suited. Now he was known as an excellent horseman, as a thorough sportsman, as one knowing in dogs, and tender-hearted as a sucking mother to a litter of young foxes; he had ridden in the county since he was fifteen, had a fine voice for a view hallo, knew every hound by name, and could wind a horn with sufficient music for all hunting purposes; moreover, he had come to his property, as was well known through all Barsetshire, with a clear income of fourteen thousand a year.

Thus, when some old worn-out master of hounds was run to ground, about a year after Mr Gresham's last contest for the county, it seemed to all parties to be a pleasant and rational arrangement that the hounds should go to Greshamsbury. Pleasant, indeed, to all except the Lady Arabella; and rational, perhaps, to all except the squire himself.

All this time he was already considerably encumbered. He had spent much more than he should have done, and so indeed had his wife, in those two splendid years in which they had figured as great among the great ones of the earth. Fourteen thousand a year ought to have been enough to allow a member of Parliament with a young wife and two or three children to live in London and keep up their country family mansion; but then the De Courcys were very great people, and Lady Arabella chose to live as she had been accustomed to do, and as her sister-in-law the countess lived: now Lord de Courcy had much more than fourteen thousand a year. Then came the three elections, with their vast attendant cost, and then those costly expedients to which gentlemen are forced to have recourse who have lived beyond their income, and find it impossible so to reduce their establishments as to live much below it. Thus when the hounds came to Greshamsbury, Mr Gresham was already a poor man.

Lady Arabella said much to oppose their coming; but Lady Arabella, though it could hardly be said of her that she was under her husband's rule, certainly was not entitled to boast that she had him under hers. She then made her first grand attack as to the furniture in Portman Square; and was then for the first time specially informed that the furniture there was not matter of much importance, as she would not in future be required to move her family to that residence during the London seasons. The sort of conversations which grew from such a commencement may be imagined. Had Lady Arabella worried her lord less, he might perhaps have considered with more coolness the folly of encountering so prodigious an increase to the expense of his establishment; had he not spent so much money in a pursuit which his wife did not enjoy, she might perhaps have been more sparing in her rebukes as to his indifference to her London pleasures. As it was, the hounds came to Greshamsbury, and Lady Arabella did go to London for some period in each year, and the family expenses were by no means lessened.

The kennels, however, were now again empty. Two years previous to the time at which our story begins, the hounds had been carried off to the seat of some richer sportsman. This was more felt by Mr Gresham than any other misfortune which he had yet incurred. He had been master of hounds for ten years, and that work he had at any rate done well. The popularity among his neighbours which he had lost as a politician he had regained as a sportsman, and he would fain have remained autocratic in the hunt, had it been possible. But he so remained much longer than he should have done, and at last they went away, not without signs and sounds of visible joy on the part of Lady Arabella.

But we have kept the Greshamsbury tenantry waiting under the oak-trees by far too long. Yes; when young Frank came of age there was still enough left at Greshamsbury, still means enough at the squire's disposal, to light one bonfire, to roast, whole in its skin, one bullock. Frank's virility came on him not quite unmarked, as that of the parson's son might do, or the son of the neighbouring attorney. It could still be reported in the Barsetshire Conservative *Standard* that 'The beards wagged all'* at Greshamsbury, now as they had done for many centuries on similar festivals. Yes; it was so reported. But this, like so many other such reports, had but a shadow of truth in it. 'They poured the liquor in,' certainly, those who were there; but the beards did not wag as they had been wont to wag in former years. Beards won't wag for the telling. The squire was at his wits' end for money, and the tenants one and all had so heard. Rents had been raised on them; timber had fallen fast; the lawyer on the estate was growing rich; tradesmen in Barchester, nay, in

Greshamsbury itself, were beginning to mutter; and the squire himself would not be merry. Under such circumstances the throats of a tenantry will still swallow, but their beards will not wag.

'I minds well,' said Farmer Oaklerath to his neighbour, 'when the squoire hisself comed of age. Lord love 'ee! there was fun going that day. There was more yale drank then than's been brewed at the big house these two years. T'old squoire was a one'er.'

'And I minds when squoire was borned; minds it well,' said an old farmer sitting opposite. 'Them was the days! it an't that long ago neither. Squoire a'nt come o' fifty yet; no, nor an't nigh it, though he looks it. Things be altered at Greemsbury' – such was the rural pronunciation – 'altered sadly, neebor Oaklerath. Well, well; I'll soon be gone, I will, and so it an't no use talking; but arter paying one pound fifteen for them acres for more nor fifty year, I didn't think I'd ever be axed for forty shilling.'

Such was the style of conversation which went on at the various tables. It had certainly been of a very different tone when the squire was born, when he came of age, and when, just two years subsequently, his son had been born. On each of these events similar rural fêtes had been given, and the squire himself had on these occasions been frequent among his guests. On the first, he had been carried round by his father, a whole train of ladies and nurses following. On the second, he had himself mixed in all the sports, the gayest of the gay, and each tenant had squeezed his way up to the lawn to get a sight of the Lady Arabella, who, as was already known, was to come from Courcy Castle to Greshamsbury to be their mistress. It was little they any of them cared now for the Lady Arabella. On the third, he himself had borne his child in his arms as his father had before borne him; he was then in the zenith of his pride, and though the tenantry whispered that he was somewhat less familiar with them than of yore, that he had put on somewhat too much of the De Courcy airs, still he was their squire, their master, the rich man in whose hand they lay. The old squire was then gone, and they were proud of the young member and his lady bride in spite of a little hauteur. None of them were proud of him now.

He walked once round among the guests, and spoke a few words of welcome at each table; and as he did so the tenants got up and bowed and wished health to the old squire, happiness to the young one, and prosperity to Greshamsbury; but, nevertheless, it was but a tame affair.

There were also other visitors, of the gentle sort, to do honour to the occasion; but not such swarms, not such a crowd at the mansion itself and at the houses of the neighbouring gentry as had always been collected on these former gala doings. Indeed, the party at Greshamsbury was not a large one, and consisted chiefly of Lady de Courcy and her suite. Lady Arabella still kept up, as far as she was able, her close connexion with Courcy Castle. She was there as much as possible, to which Mr Gresham never objected; and she took her daughters there whenever she could, though, as regarded the two elder girls, she was often interfered with by Mr Gresham, and not unfrequently by the girls themselves. Lady Arabella had a pride in her son, though he was by no means her favourite child. He was, however, the heir of Greshamsbury, of which fact she was disposed to make the most, and he was also a fine gainly open-hearted young man, who could not but be dear to any mother. Lady Arabella did love him dearly, though she felt a sort of disappointment in regard to him, seeing that he was not so much like a De Courcy as he should have been. She did love him dearly; and, therefore, when he came of age she got her sister-in-law and all the Ladies Amelia, Rosina, etc., to come to Greshamsbury; and she also, with some difficulty, persuaded the Honourable Georges and the Honourable Johns to be equally condescending. Lord de Courcy himself was in attendance at the Court – or said that he was – and Lord Porlock, the eldest son, simply told his aunt when he was invited that he never bored himself with those sort of things.

Then there were the Bakers, and the Batesons, and the Jacksons, who all lived near and returned home at night; there was the Reverend Caleb Oriel,* the High-Church rector, with his beautiful sister, Patience Oriel; there was Mr Yates Umbleby, the attorney and agent; and there was Dr Thorne, and the doctor's modest, quiet-looking little niece, Miss Mary.

CHAPTER II

Long, Long Ago

As Dr Thorne is our hero – or I should rather say my hero, a privilege of selecting for themselves in this respect being left to all my readers – and as Miss Mary Thorne is to be our heroine, a point on which no choice whatsoever is left to any one, it is necessary that they shall be introduced and explained and described in a proper, formal manner. I quite feel that an apology is due for beginning a novel with two long dull chapters full of description. I am perfectly aware of the danger of such a course. In so doing I sin against the golden rule which requires us all to put our best foot foremost, the wisdom of which is fully recognised by novelists, myself among the number. It can hardly be expected that any one will consent to go through with a fiction that offers so little of allurement in its first pages; but twist it as I will I cannot do otherwise. I find that I cannot make poor Mr Gresham hem or haw and turn himself uneasily in his arm-chair in a natural manner till I have said why he is uneasy. I cannot bring in my doctor speaking his mind freely among the bigwigs till I have explained that it is in accordance with his usual character to do so. This is unartistic on my part, and shows want of imagination as well as want of skill. Whether or not I can atone for these faults by straightforward, simple, plain story-telling – that, indeed, is very doubtful.

Dr Thorne belonged to a family in one sense as good, and at any rate as old, as that of Mr Gresham; and much older, he was apt to boast, than that of the De Courcys. This trait in his character is mentioned first, as it was the weakness for which he was most conspicuous. He was second cousin to Mr Thorne of Ullathorne, a Barsetshire squire living in the neighbourhood of Barchester, and who boasted that his estate had remained in his family, descending from Thorne to Thorne, longer than had been the case with any other estate or any other family in the county.*

But Dr Thorne was only a second cousin; and, therefore, though he was enticed to talk of the blood as belonging to some extent to himself, he had no right to lay claim to any position in the county other than such as he might win for himself if he chose to locate himself in it. This was a fact of which no one was more fully aware than our doctor himself. His father, who had been first cousin of a former Squire Thorne, had been a clerical dignitary in Barchester, but had been dead now many years. He had had two sons; one he had educated as a medical man, but the other, and the younger, whom he had intended for the Bar, had not betaken himself in any satisfactory way to any calling. This son had been first rusticated from Oxford, and then expelled; and thence returning to Barchester, had been the cause to his father and brother of much suffering.

Old Dr Thorne, the clergyman, died when the two brothers were yet young men, and left behind him nothing but some household and other property of the value of about two thousand pounds, which he bequeathed to Thomas, the elder son, much more than that having been spent in liquidating debts contracted by the younger. Up to that time there had been close harmony between the Ullathorne family and that of the clergy-man; but a month or two before the doctor's death – the period of which we are speaking was about two-and-twenty years before the commencement of our story – the then Mr Thorne of Ullathorne had made it understood that he would no longer receive at his house his cousin Henry, whom he regarded as a disgrace to the family.

Fathers are apt to be more lenient to their sons than uncles to their nephews, or cousins to each other. Dr Thorne still hoped to reclaim his black sheep, and thought that the head of his family showed an unnecessary harshness in putting an obstacle in his way of doing so. And if the father was warm in support of his profligate son, the young medical aspirant was warmer in support of his profligate brother. Dr Thorne, junior, was no roué himself, but perhaps, as a young man, he had not sufficient abhorrence of his brother's vices. At any rate, he stuck to him manfully; and when it was signified in the Close that Henry's company was not considered desirable at Ullathorne, Dr Thomas Thorne sent word to the squire that under such circumstances his visits there would also cease.

This was not very prudent, as the young Galen* had elected to establish himself in Barchester, very mainly in expectation of the help which his Ullathorne connexion would give him. This, however, in his anger he failed to consider; he was never known, either in early or in middle life, to consider in his anger those points which were probably best worth his consideration. This, perhaps, was of the less moment as his anger was of an unenduring kind, evaporating frequently with more celerity than he could get the angry words out of his mouth. With the Ullathorne people, however, he did establish a quarrel sufficiently permanent to be of vital injury to his medical prospects.

And then the father died, and the two brothers were left living together with very little means between them. At this time there were living, in Barchester, people of the name of Scatcherd. Of that family, as then existing, we have only to do with two, a brother and a sister. They were in a low rank of life, the one being a journeyman stone-mason, and the other an apprentice to a straw-bonnet maker; but they were, nevertheless, in some sort remarkable people. The sister was reputed in Barchester to be a model of female beauty of the strong and robuster cast, and had also a better reputation as being a girl of good character and honest, womanly conduct. Both of her beauty and of her reputation her brother was exceedingly proud, and he was the more so when he learnt that she had been asked in marriage by a decent master-tradesman in the city.

Roger Scatcherd had also a reputation, but not for beauty or propriety of conduct. He was known for the best stone-mason in the four counties, and as the man who could, on occasions, drink the most alcohol in a given time in the same localities. As a workman, indeed, he had higher repute even than this: he was not only a good and very quick stone-mason, but he had also a capacity of turning other men into good stone-masons: he had a gift of knowing what a man could and should do; and, by degrees, he taught himself what five, and ten, and twenty – latterly, what a thousand and two thousand men might accomplish among them: this, also, he did with very little aid from pen and paper, with which he was not, and never became, very conversant. He had also other gifts and other propensities. He could talk in a manner dangerous to himself and others; he could persuade without knowing that he did so; and being himself an extreme demagogue, in those noisy times just prior to the Reform Bill, he created a hubbub in Barchester of which he himself had had no previous conception.

Henry Thorne among his other bad qualities had one which his friends regarded as worse than all the others, and which perhaps justified the Ullathorne people in their severity. He loved to consort with low people. He not only drank – that might have been forgiven – but he drank in tap-rooms with vulgar drinkers; so said his friends, and so said his enemies. He denied the charge as being made in the plural number, and declared that his only low co-reveller was Roger Scatcherd. With Roger Scatcherd, at any rate, he associated, and became as democratic as Roger was himself. Now the Thornes of Ulla-thorne were of the very highest order of Tory excellence.

Whether or not Mary Scatcherd at once accepted the offer of the respectable tradesman, I cannot say. After the occurrence of certain events which must be here shortly told, she declared that she never had done so. Her brother averred that she most positively had. The respectable tradesman himself refused to speak on the subject.

It is certain, however, that Scatcherd, who had hitherto been silent enough about his sister in those social hours which he passed with his gentleman friend, boasted of the engagement when it was, as he said, made; and then boasted also of the girl's beauty. Scatcherd, in spite of his occasional intemperance, looked up in the world, and the coming marriage of his sister was, he thought, suitable to his own ambition for his family.

Henry Thorne had already heard of, and already seen, Mary Scatcherd; but hitherto she had not fallen in the way of his wickedness. Now, however, when he heard that she was to be decently married, the devil tempted him to tempt her. It boots not to tell all the tale. It came out clearly enough when all was told, that he made her most distinct promises of marriage; he even gave her such in writing; and having in this way obtained from her her company during some of her little holidays – her Sundays or summer evenings – he seduced her. Scatcherd accused him openly of having intoxicated her with drugs; and Thomas Thorne, who took up the case, ultimately believed the charge. It became known in Barchester that she was with child, and that the seducer was Henry Thorne.

Roger Scatcherd, when the news first reached him, filled himself with drink, and then swore that he would kill them both. With manly wrath, however, he set forth first against the man, and that with manly weapons. He took nothing with him but his fists and a big stick as he went in search of Henry Thorne.

The two brothers were then lodging together at a farm-house

close abutting on the town. This was not an eligible abode for a medical practitioner; but the young doctor had not been able to settle himself eligibly since his father's death; and wishing to put what constraint he could upon his brother, had so located himself. To this farm-house came Roger Scatcherd one sultry summer evening, his anger gleaming from his bloodshot eyes, and his rage heightened to madness by the rapid pace at which he had run from the city, and by the ardent spirits which were fermenting within him.

At the very gate of the farm-yard, standing placidly with his cigar in his mouth, he encountered Henry Thorne. He had thought of searching for him through the whole premises, of demanding his victim with loud exclamations, and making his way to him through all obstacles. In lieu of that, there stood the man before him.

'Well, Roger, what's in the wind?' said Henry Thorne.

They were the last words he ever spoke. He was answered by a blow from the blackthorn. A contest ensued, which ended in Scatcherd keeping his word – at any rate, as regarded the worst offender. How the fatal blow on the temples was struck was never exactly determined: one medical man said it might have been done in a fight with a heavy-headed stick; another thought that a stone had been used; a third suggested a stone-mason's hammer. It seemed, however, to be proved subsequently that no hammer was taken out, and Scatcherd himself persisted in declaring that he had taken in his hand no weapon but the stick. Scatcherd, however, was drunk; and even though he intended to tell the truth, may have been mistaken. There were, however, the facts that Thorne was dead; that Scatcherd had sworn to kill him about an hour previously; and that he had without delay accomplished his threat. He was arrested and tried for murder, all the distressing circumstances of the case came out on the trial: he was found guilty of man-slaughter, and sentenced to be imprisoned for six months. Our readers will probably think that the punishment was too severe.

Thomas Thorne and the farmer were on the spot soon after Henry Thome had fallen. The brother was at first furious for vengeance against his brother's murderer; but, as the facts came out, as he learnt what had been the provocation given, what had been the feelings of Scatcherd when he left the city, determined to punish him who had ruined his sister, his heart was changed.

Those were trying days for him. It behoved him to do what in him lay to cover his brother's memory from the obloquy which it deserved; it behoved him also to save, or to assist to save, from undue punishment the unfortunate man who had shed his brother's blood; and it behoved him also, at least so he thought, to look after that poor fallen one whose misfortunes were less merited than those either of his brother or of hers.

And he was not the man to get through these things lightly, or with as much ease as he perhaps might conscientiously have done. He would pay for the defence of the prisoner; he would pay for the defence of his brother's memory; and he would pay for the poor girl's comforts. He would do this, and he would allow no one to help him. He stood alone in the world, and insisted on so standing. Old Mr Thorne of Ullathorne offered again to open his arms to him; but he had conceived a foolish idea that his cousin's severity had driven his brother on to his bad career, and he would consequently accept no kindness from Ullathorne. Miss Thorne, the old squire's daughter – a cousin considerably older than himself, to whom he had at one time been much attached – sent him money; and he returned it to her under a blank cover. He had still enough for those unhappy purposes which he had in hand. As to what might happen afterwards, he was then mainly indifferent.

The affair made much noise in the county, and was inquired into closely by many of the county magistrates; by none more closely than by John Newbold Gresham, who was then alive. Mr Gresham was greatly taken with the energy and justice shown by Dr Thorne on the occasion; and when the trial was over, he invited him to Greshamsbury. The visit ended in the doctor establishing himself in that village.

We must return for a moment to Mary Scatcherd. She was saved from the necessity of encountering her brother's wrath, for that brother was under arrest for murder before he could get at her. Her immediate lot, however, was a cruel one. Deep as was her cause for anger against the man who had so inhumanly used her, still it was natural that she should turn to him with love rather than with aversion. To whom else could she in such plight look for love? When, therefore, she heard that he was slain, her heart sank within her; she turned her face to the wall, and laid herself down to die: to die a double death, for herself and the fatherless babe that was now quick within her.

But, in fact, life had still much to offer, both to her and to her child. For her it was still destined that she should, in a distant land, be the worthy wife of a good husband, and the happy mother of many children. For that embryo one it was destined – but that may not be so quickly told: to describe her destiny this volume has yet to be written.

Even in those bitterest days God tempered the wind to the shorn lamb.* Dr Thorne was by her bedside soon after the bloody tidings had reached her, and did for her more than either her lover or her brother could have done. When the baby was born, Scatcherd was still in prison, and had still three months' more confinement to undergo. The story of her great wrongs and cruel usage was much talked of, and men said that one who had been so injured should be regarded as having in nowise sinned at all.

One man, at any rate, so thought. At twilight, one evening, Thorne was surprised by a visit from a demure Barchester hardware dealer, whom he did not remember ever to have addressed before. This was the former lover of poor Mary Scatcherd. He had a proposal to make, and it was this: – if Mary would consent to leave the country at once, to leave it without notice from her brother, or talk or éclat on the matter, he would sell all that he had, marry her, and emigrate. There was but one other condition; she must leave her baby behind her. The hardware-man could find it in his heart to be generous, to be generous and true to his love; but he could not be generous enough to father the seducer's child.

'I could never abide it, sir, if I took it,' said he; 'and she, – why in course she would always love it the best.'

In praising his generosity, who can mingle any censure for such manifest prudence? He would still make her the wife of his bosom, defiled in the eyes of the world as she had been; but she must be to him the mother of his own children, not the mother of another's child.

And now again our doctor had a hard task to win through. He saw at once that it was his duty to use his utmost authority to induce the poor girl to accept such an offer. She liked the man; and here was opened to her a course which would have been most desirable, even before her misfortune. But it is hard to persuade a mother to part with her first babe; harder, perhaps, when the babe has been so fathered and so born than when the world has shone brightly on its earliest hours. She at first refused stoutly: she sent a thousand loves, a thousand thanks, profusest acknowledgements for his generosity to the man who showed her that he loved her so well; but Nature, she said, would not let her leave her child.

'And what will you do for her here, Mary?' said the doctor. Poor Mary replied to him with a deluge of tears.

'She is my niece,' said the doctor, taking up the tiny infant in his huge hands; 'she is already the nearest thing, the only thing I have in this world. I am her uncle, Mary. If you will go with this man I will be father to her and mother to her. Of what bread I eat, she shall eat; of what cup I drink, she shall drink. See, Mary, here is the Bible;' and he covered the book with his hand. 'Leave her to me, and by this word she shall be my child.'

The mother consented at last; left her baby with the doctor, married, and went to America. All this was consummated before Roger Scatcherd was liberated from jail. Some conditions the doctor made. The first was, that Scatcherd should not know that his sister's child was thus disposed of. Dr Thorne, in undertaking to bring up the baby, did not choose to encounter any tie with persons who might hereafter claim to be the girl's relations on the other side. Relations she would undoubtedly have had none had she been left to live or die as a workhouse bastard; but should the doctor succeed in life, should he ultimately be able to make this girl the darling of his own house, and then the darling of some other house, should she live and win the heart of some man whom the doctor might delight to call his friend and nephew; then relations might spring up whose ties would not be advantageous.

No man plumed himself on good blood more than Dr Thorne; no man had greater pride in his genealogical tree, and his hundred and thirty clearly proved descents from MacAdam; no man had a stronger theory as to the advantage held by men who have grandfathers over those who have none, or have none worth talking about. Let it not be thought that our doctor was a perfect charcater. No, indeed; most far from perfect. He had within him an inner, stubborn, self-admiring pride, which made him believe himself to be better and higher than those around him, and this from some unknown cause which he could hardly explain to himself. He had a pride in being a poor man of a high family; he had a pride in repudiating the very family of which he was proud; and he had a special pride in keeping his pride silently to himself. His father had been a Thorne, and his mother a Thorold. There was no better blood to be had in England. It was in the possession of such properties as these that he condescended to rejoice; this man, with a man's heart, a man's courage, and a man's humanity! Other doctors round the county had ditchwater in their veins; he could boast of a pure ichor,* to which that of the great Omnium family was but a muddy puddle. It was thus that he loved to excel his brother practitioners, he who might have indulged in the pride of excelling them both in talent and in energy! We speak now of his early days; but even in his maturer life, the man, though mellowed, was the same.

This was the man who now promised to take to his bosom as his own child a poor bastard whose father was already dead, and whose mother's family was such as the Scatcherds! It was necessary that the child's history should be known to none. Except to the mother's brother it was an object of interest to no one. The mother had for some short time been talked of; but now the nine-days' wonder was a wonder no longer. She went off to her far-away home; her husband's generosity was duly chronicled in the papers, and the babe was left untalked of and unknown.

It was easy to explain to Scatcherd that the child had not lived. There was a parting interview between the brother and sister in the jail, during which, with real tears and unaffected sorrow, the mother thus accounted for the offspring of her shame. Then she started, fortunate in her coming fortunes; and the doctor took with him his charge to the new country in which they were both to live. There he found for her a fitting home till she should be old enough to sit at his table and live in his bachelor house; and no one but old Mr Gresham knew who she was, or whence she had come.

Then Roger Scatcherd, having completed his six months' confinement, came out of prison.

Roger Scatcherd, though his hands were now red with blood, was to be pitied. A short time before the days of Henry Thorne's death he had married a young wife in his own class of life, and had made many resolves that henceforward his conduct should be such as might become a married man, and might not disgrace the respectable brother-in-law he was about to have given him.

Such was his condition when he first heard of his sister's plight. As has been said, he filled himself with drink and started off on the scent of blood.

During his prison days his wife had to support herself as she might. The decent articles of furniture which they had put together were sold; she gave up their little house, and, bowed down by misery, she also was brought near to death. When he was liberated he at once got work; but those who have watched the lives of such people know how hard it is for them to recover lost ground. She became a mother immediately after his liberation, and when her child was born they were in direst want; for Scatcherd was again drinking, and his resolves were blown to the wind.

The doctor was then living at Greshamsbury. He had gone over there before the day on which he undertook the charge of poor Mary's baby, and soon found himself settled as the Greshamsbury doctor. This occurred very soon after the birth of the young heir. His predecessor in this career had 'bettered' himself, or endeavoured to do so, by seeking the practice of some large town, and Lady Arabella, at a very critical time, was absolutely left with no other advice than that of a stranger, picked up, as she declared to Lady de Courcy, somewhere about Barchester jail, or Barchester court-house, she did not know which.

Of course Lady Arabella could not suckle the young heir herself. Ladies Arabella never can. They are gifted with the powers of being mothers, but not nursing-mothers. Nature gives them bosoms for show, but not for use. So Lady Arabella had a wet-nurse. At the end of six months the new doctor found that Master Frank was not doing quite so well as he should do; and after a little trouble it was discovered that the very excellent young woman who had been sent express from Courcy Castle to Greshamsbury – a supply being kept up on the lord's demesne for the family use – was fond of brandy. She was at once sent back to the castle, of course; and, as Lady de Courcy was too much in dudgeon to send another, Dr Thorne was allowed to procure one. He thought of the misery of Roger Scatcherd's wife, thought also of her health, and strength, and active habits; and thus Mrs Scatcherd became foster-mother to young Frank Gresham.

One other episode we must tell of past times. Previous to his

father's death, Dr Thorne was in love. Nor had he altogether
sighed and pleaded in vain; though it had not quite come to
that, that the young lady's friends, or even the young lady
herself, had actually accepted his suit. At that time his name
stood well in Barchester. His father was a prebendary; his
cousins and his best friends were the Thornes of Ullathorne, and
the lady, who shall be nameless, was not thought to be injudicious in listening to the young doctor. But when Henry Thorne
went so far astray, when the old doctor died, when the young
doctor quarrelled with Ullathorne, when the brother was killed
in a disgraceful quarrel, and it turned out that the physician had
nothing but his profession and no settled locality in which to
exercise it; then, indeed, the young lady's friends thought that
she *was* injudicious, and the young lady herself had not spirit
enough, or love enough, to be disobedient. In those stormy days
of the trial she told Dr Thorne, that perhaps it would be wise
that they should not see each other any more.

Dr Thorne, so counselled, at such a moment, – so informed
then, when he most required comfort from his love, at once
swore loudly that he agreed with her. He rushed forth with a
bursting heart, and said to himself that the world was bad, all
bad. He saw the lady no more; and, if I am rightly informed,
never again made matrimonial overtures to any one.

CHAPTER III

Dr Thorne

And thus Dr Thorne became settled for life in the little village of
Greshamsbury. As was then the wont with many country
practitioners, and as should be the wont with them all if they
consulted their own dignity a little less and the comforts of their
customers somewhat more, he added the business of a dispensing apothecary to that of physician.* In doing so, he was of
course much reviled. Many people around him declared that he
could not truly be a doctor, or, at any rate, a doctor to be so
called; and his brethren in the art living around him, though
they knew that his diplomas, degrees, and certificates were all

en règle,* rather countenanced the report. There was much about this newcomer which did not endear him to his own profession. In the first place he was a new-comer, and, as such, was of course to be regarded by other doctors as being *de trop.** Greshamsbury was only fifteen miles from Barchester, where there was a regular dépôt of medical skill, and but eight from Silverbridge, where a properly established physician had been in residence for the last forty years. Dr Thorne's predecessor at Greshamsbury had been a humble-minded general practitioner, gifted with a due respect for the physicians of the county; and he, though he had been allowed to physic the servants, and sometimes the children at Greshamsbury, had never had the presumption to put himself on a par with his betters.

Then, also, Dr Thorne, though a graduated physician, though entitled beyond all dispute to call himself a doctor, according to all the laws of the colleges, made it known to the East Barsetshire world, very soon after he had seated himself at Greshamsbury, that his rate of pay was to be seven-and-sixpence a visit within a circuit of five miles, with a proportionately increased charge at proportionately increased distances. Now there was something low, mean, unprofessional, and democratic in this; so, at least, said the children of Æsculapius* gathered together in conclave at Barchester. In the first place, it showed that this Thorne was always thinking of his money, like an apothecary, as he was; whereas, it would have behoved him, as a physician, had he had the feelings of a physician under his hat, to have regarded his own pursuits in a purely philosophical spirit, and to have taken any gain which might have accrued as an accidental adjunct to his station in life. A physician should take his fee without letting his left hand know what his right hand was doing; it should be taken without a thought, without a look, without a move of the facial muscles; the true physician should hardly be aware that the last friendly grasp of the hand had been made more precious by the touch of gold. Whereas, that fellow Thorne would lug out half a crown from his breeches pocket and give it in change for a ten-shilling piece. And then it was clear that this man had no appreciation of the dignity of a learned profession. He might constantly be seen compounding medicines in the shop, at the left hand of his front door; not making experiments philosophically in materia medica for the benefit of coming ages – which, if he did, he should have done in the seclusion of his study, far from profane eyes – but positively putting together common powders for rural bowels, or spreading vulgar ointments for agricultural ailments.

A man of this sort was not fit society for Dr Fillgrave of Barchester. That must be admitted. And yet he had been found to be fit society for the old squire of Greshamsbury, whose shoe-ribbons Dr Fillgrave would not have objected to tie; so high did the old squire stand in the county just previous to his death. But the spirit of the Lady Arabella was known by the medical profession of Barsetshire, and when that good man died it was felt that Thorne's short tenure of Greshamsbury favour was already over. The Barsetshire regulars were, however, doomed to disappointment. Our doctor had already contrived to endear himself to the heir; and though there was not even then much personal love between him and the Lady Arabella, he kept his place at the great house unmoved, not only in the nursery and in the bedrooms, but also at the squire's dining-table.

Now there was in this, it must be admitted, quite enough to make him unpopular among his brethren; and this feeling was soon shown in a marked and dignified manner. Dr Fillgrave, who had certainly the most respectable professional connexion in the county, who had a reputation to maintain, and who was accustomed to meet, on almost equal terms, the great medical baronets from the metropolis at the houses of the nobility – Dr Fillgrave declined to meet Dr Thorne in consultation. He exceedingly regretted, he said, most exceedingly, the necessity which he felt of doing so: he had never before had to perform so painful a duty; but, as a duty which he owed to his profession, he must perform it. With every feeling of respect for Lady ——, – a sick guest at Greshamsbury, – and for Mr Gresham, he must decline to attend in conjunction with Dr Thorne. If his services could be made available under any other circumstances, he would go to Greshamsbury as fast as post-horses could carry him.

Then, indeed, there was war in Barsetshire. If there was on Dr Thorne's cranium one bump more developed than another, it was that of combativeness.* Not that the doctor was a bully, or even pugnacious, in the usual sense of the word; he had no disposition to provoke a fight, no propense love of quarrelling; but there was that in him which would allow him to yield to no attack. Neither in argument nor in contest would he ever allow himself to be wrong; never at least to any one but to himself; and on behalf of his special hobbies, he was ready to meet the world at large.

It will therefore be understood, that when such a gauntlet was thus thrown in his very teeth by Dr Fillgrave, he was not slow to take it up. He addressed a letter to the Barsetshire Conservative *Standard*, in which he attacked Dr Fillgrave with some considerable acerbity. Dr Fillgrave responded in four lines, saying, that on mature consideration he had made up his mind not to notice any remarks that might be made on him by Dr Thorne in the public press. The Greshamsbury doctor then wrote another letter, more witty and much more severe than the last; and as this was copied into the Bristol, Exeter, and Gloucester papers, Dr Fillgrave found it very difficult to maintain the magnanimity of his reticence. It is sometimes becoming enough for a man to wrap himself in the dignified toga of silence, and proclaim himself indifferent to public attacks; but it is a sort of dignity which it is very difficult to maintain. As well might a man, when stung to madness by wasps, endeavour to sit in his chair without moving a muscle, as endure with patience and without reply the courtesies of a newspaper opponent. Dr Thorne wrote a third letter, which was too much for medical flesh and blood to bear. Dr Fillgrave answered it, not, indeed, in his own name, but in that of a brother doctor; and then the war raged merrily. It is hardly too much to say that Dr Fillgrave never knew another happy hour. Had he dreamed of what materials was made that young compounder of doses at Greshamsbury he would have met him in consultation, morning, noon, and night, without objection; but having begun the war, he was constrained to go on with it: his brethren would allow him no alternative. Thus he was continually being brought up to the fight, as a prize-fighter may be seen to be, who is carried up round after round, without any hope on his own part, and who, in each round, drops to the ground before the very wind of his opponent's blows.

But Dr Fillgrave, though thus weak himself, was backed in practice and in countenance by nearly all his brethren in the county. The guinea fee, the principle of *giving* advice and of selling no medicine, the great resolve to keep a distinct barrier between the physician and the apothecary, and, above all, the hatred of the contamination of a bill, were strong in the medical

mind of Barsetshire. Dr Thorne had the provincial medical
world against him, and so he appealed to the metropolis. The
Lancet took the matter up in his favour, but the *Journal of
Medical Science* was against him; the *Weekly Chirurgeon*, noted
for its medical democracy, upheld him as a medical prophet, but
the *Scalping Knife*,* a monthly periodical got up in dead opposition to the *Lancet*, showed him no mercy. So the war went on,
and our doctor, to a certain extent, became a noted character.

He had, moreover, other difficulties to encounter in his
professional career. It was something in his favour that he
understood his business; something that he was willing to labour
at it with energy; and resolved to labour at it conscientiously.
He had also other gifts, such as conversational brilliancy, an
aptitude for true good fellowship, firmness in friendship, and
general honesty of disposition, which stood him in stead as he
advanced in life. But, at his first starting, much that belonged to
himself personally was against him. Let him enter what house
he would, he entered it with a conviction, often expressed to
himself, that he was equal as a man to the proprietor, equal as a
human being to the proprietress. To age he would allow
deference, and to special recognised talent – at least, so he said;
to rank, also, he would pay that respect which was its clear
recognised prerogative; he would let a lord walk out of a room
before him if he did not happen to forget it; in speaking to a
duke he would address him as his Grace; and he would in no
way assume a familiarity with bigger men than himself, allowing
to the bigger man the privilege of making the first advances. But
beyond this he would admit that no man should walk the earth
with head higher than his own.

He did not talk of these things much; he offended no rank by
boasts of his own equality; he did not absolutely tell the Earl de
Courcy in words, that the privilege of dining at Courcy Castle
was to him no greater than the privilege of dining at Courcy
Parsonage; but there was that in his manner that told it. The
feeling in itself was perhaps good, and was certainly much
justified by the manner in which he bore himself to those below
him in rank; but there was folly in the resolution to run counter
to the world's recognized rules on such matters; and much
absurdity in his mode of doing so, seeing that at heart he was a
thorough Conservative. It is hardly too much to say that he
naturally hated a lord at first sight; but, nevertheless, he would

have expended his means, his blood, and spirit, in fighting for the upper house of Parliament.

Such a disposition, until it was thoroughly understood, did not tend to ingratiate him with the wives of the country gentlemen among whom he had to look for practice. And then, also, there was not much in his individual manner to recommend him to the favour of ladies. He was brusque, authoritative, given to contradiction, rough though never dirty in his personal belongings, and inclined to indulge in a sort of quiet raillery, which sometimes was not thoroughly understood. People did not always know whether he was laughing at them or with them; and some people were, perhaps, inclined to think that a doctor should not laugh at all when called in to act doctorially.

When he was known, indeed, when the core of the fruit had been reached, when the huge proportions of that loving, trusting heart had been learned, and understood, and appreciated, when that honesty had been recognised, that manly, and almost womanly tenderness had been felt, then, indeed, the doctor was acknowledged to be adequate to his profession. To trifling ailments he was too often brusque. Seeing that he accepted money for the cure of such, he should, we may say, have cured them without an offensive manner. So far he is without defence. But to real suffering no one found him brusque; no patient lying painfully on a bed of sickness ever thought him rough.

Another misfortune was, that he was a bachelor. Ladies think, and I, for one, think that ladies are quite right in so thinking, that doctors should be married men. All the world feels that a man when married acquires some of the attributes of an old woman – he becomes, to a certain extent, a motherly sort of being; he acquires a conversance with women's ways and women's wants, and loses the wilder and offensive sparks of his virility. It must be easier to talk to such a one about Matilda's stomach, and the growing pains in Fanny's legs, than to a young bachelor. This impediment also stood much in Dr Thorne's way during his first years at Greshamsbury.

But his wants were not at first great; and though his ambition was perhaps high, it was not of an impatient nature. The world was his oyster; but, circumstanced as he was, he knew it was not for him to open it with his lancet all at once.* He had bread to earn, which he must earn wearily; he had a character to make, which must come slowly; it satisfied his soul that, in addition to his immortal hopes, he had a possible future in this world to which he could look forward with clear eyes, and advance with a heart that would know no fainting.

On his first arrival at Greshamsbury he had been put by the squire into a house, which he still occupied when that squire's grandson came of age. There were two decent, commodious private houses in the village – always excepting the rectory, which stood grandly in its own grounds, and, therefore, was considered as ranking above the village residences – of these two Dr Thorne had the smaller. They stood exactly at the angle before described, on the outer side of it, and at right angles with each other. They both possessed good stables and ample gardens; and it may be as well to specify, that Mr Umbleby, the agent and lawyer to the estate, occupied the larger one.

Here Dr Thorne lived for eleven or twelve years, all alone; and then for ten or eleven more with his niece, Mary Thorne. Mary was thirteen when she came to take up her permanent abode as mistress of the establishment – or, at any rate, to act as the only mistress which the establishment possessed. This advent greatly changed the tenor of the doctor's ways.* He had been before pure bachelor; not a room in his house had been comfortably furnished: he at first commenced in a makeshift sort of way, because he had not at his command the means of commencing otherwise; and he had gone on in the same fashion, because the exact time had never come at which it was imperative in him to set his house in order. He had had no fixed hour for his meals, no fixed place for his books, no fixed wardrobe for his clothes. He had a few bottles of good wine in his cellar, and occasionally asked a brother bachelor to take a chop with him; but beyond this he had touched very little on the cares of housekeeping A slop-bowl full of strong tea, together with bread, and butter, and eggs, was produced for him in the morning, and he expected that at whatever hour he might arrive in the evening, some food should be presented to him wherewith to satisfy the cravings of nature; if, in addition to this, he had another slop-bowl of tea in the evening, he got all that he ever required, or all, at least, that he ever demanded.

But when Mary came, or rather when she was about to come, things were altogether changed at the doctor's. People had hitherto wondered – and especially Mrs Umbleby – how a gentleman like Dr Thorne could continue to live in so slovenly a manner; and now people again wondered, and again especially Mrs Umbleby, how the doctor could possibly think it necessary to put such a lot of furniture into his house because a little chit of a girl of twelve years of age was coming to live with him.

Mrs Umbleby had a great scope for her wonder. The doctor made a thorough revolution in his household, and furnished his house from the ground to the roof completely. He painted – for the first time since the commencement of his tenancy – he papered, he carpeted, and curtained, and mirrored, and linened, and blanketed, as though a Mrs Thorne with a good fortune were coming home tomorrow; and all for a girl of twelve years old. 'And how,' said Mrs Umbleby, to her friend Miss Gushing, 'how did he find out what to buy?' as though the doctor had been brought up like a wild beast, ignorant of the nature of tables and chairs, and with no more developed ideas of drawing-room drapery than an hippopotamus.

To the utter amazement of Mrs Umbleby and Miss Gushing, the doctor did it all very well. He said nothing about it to any one – he never did say much about such things – but he furnished his house well and discreetly; and when Mary Thorne came home from her school at Bath, to which she had been taken some six years previously, she found herself called upon to be the presiding genius of a perfect paradise.

It has been said that the doctor had managed to endear himself to the new squire before the old squire's death, and that, therefore, the change at Greshamsbury had had no professional ill effects upon him. Such was the case at the time; but, nevertheless, all did not go on smoothly in the Greshamsbury medical department. There was six or seven years' difference in age between Mr Gresham and the doctor, and, moreover, Mr Gresham was young for his age, and the doctor old; but, nevertheless, there was a very close attachment between them early in life. This was never thoroughly sundered, and, backed by this the doctor did maintain himself for some years before the fire of Lady Arabella's artillery. But drops falling, if they fall constantly, will bore through a stone.

Dr Thorne's pretensions, mixed with his subversive professional democratic tendencies, his seven-and-sixpenny visits, added to his utter disregard of Lady Arabella's airs, were too much for her spirit. He brought Frank through his first troubles, and that at first ingratiated her; he was equally successful with the early dietary of Augusta and Beatrice; but, as his success was obtained in direct opposition to the Courcy Castle nursery principles, this hardly did much in his favour. When the third daughter was born, he at once declared that she was a very weakly flower, and sternly forbade the mother to go to London. The mother, loving her babe, obeyed; but did not the less hate the doctor for the order, which she firmly believed was given at the instance and express dictation of Mr Gresham. Then another little girl came into the world, and the doctor was more imperative than ever as to the nursery rules and the excellence of country air. Quarrels were thus engendered, and Lady Arabella was taught to believe that this doctor of her husband's was after all no Solomon. In her husband's absence she sent for Dr Fillgrave, giving very express intimation that he would not have to wound either his eyes or dignity by encountering his enemy; and she found Dr Fillgrave a great comfort to her.

Then Dr Thorne gave Mr Gresham to understand that, under such circumstances, he could not visit professionally at Greshamsbury any longer. The poor squire saw there was no help for it, and though he still maintained his friendly connexion with his neighbour, the seven-and-sixpenny visits were at an end. Dr Fillgrave from Barchester, and the gentleman at Silverbridge, divided the responsibility between them, and the nursery principles of Courcy Castle were again in vogue at Greshamsbury.

So things went on for years, and those years were years of sorrow. We must not ascribe to our doctor's enemies the sufferings, and sickness, and deaths that occurred. The four frail little ones that died would probably have been taken had Lady Arabella been more tolerant of Dr Thorne. But the fact was, that they did die; and that the mother's heart then got the better of the woman's pride, and Lady Arabella humbled herself before Dr Thorne. She humbled herself, or would have done so, had the doctor permitted her. But he, with his eyes full of tears, stopped the utterance of her apology, took her two hands in his, pressed them warmly, and assured her that his joy in returning would be great, for the love that he bore to all that belonged to Greshamsbury. And so the seven-and-sixpenny visits were recommenced; and the great triumph of Dr Fillgrave came to an end.

Great was the joy in the Greshamsbury nursery when the

second change took place. Among the doctor's attributes, not hitherto mentioned, was an aptitude for the society of children. He delighted to talk to children, and to play with them. He would carry them on his back, three or four at a time, roll with them on the ground, race with them in the gardens, invent games for them, contrive amusements in circumstances which seemed quite adverse to all manner of delight; and, above all, his physic was not nearly so nasty as that which came from Silverbridge.

He had a great theory as to the happiness of children; and though he was not disposed altogether to throw over the precepts of Solomon* – always bargaining that he should, under no circumstances, be himself the executioner – he argued that the principal duty which a parent owed to a child was to make him happy. Not only was the man to be made happy – the future man, if that might be possible – but the existing boy was to be treated with equal favour; and his happiness, so said the doctor, was of much easier attainment.

'Why struggle after future advantage at the expense of present pain, seeing that the results were so very doubtful?' Many an opponent of the doctor had thought to catch him on the hip when so singular a doctrine was broached; but they were not always successful. 'What!' said his sensible enemies, 'is Johnny not to be taught to read because he does not like it?' 'Johnny must read by all means,' would the doctor answer; 'but is it necessary that he should not like it? If the preceptor have it in him, may not Johnny learn, not only to read, but to like to learn to read?'

'But', would say the enemies, 'children must be controlled.' 'And so must men also,' would say the doctor. 'I must not steal your peaches, nor make love to your wife, nor libel your character. Much as I might wish through my natural depravity to indulge in such vices, I am debarred from them without pain, and I may almost say without unhappiness.'

And so the argument went on, neither party convincing the other. But, in the meantime, the children of the neighbourhood became very fond of Dr Thorne.

Dr Thorne and the squire were still fast friends, but circumstances had occurred, spreading themselves now over a period of many years, which almost made the poor squire uneasy in the doctor's company. Mr Gresham owed a large sum of money, and he had, moreover, already sold a portion of his property. Unfortunately it had been the pride of the Greshams that their acres had descended from one to another without an entail, so that each possessor of Greshamsbury had had full power to dispose of the property as he pleased. Any doubt as to its going to the male heir had never hitherto been felt. It had occasionally been encumbered by charges for younger children; but these charges had been Liquidated, and the property had come down without any burden to the present squire. Now a portion of this had been sold, and it had been sold to a certain degree through the agency of Dr Thorne.

This made the squire an unhappy man. No man loved his family name and honour, his old family blazon and standing more thoroughly than he did: he was every whit a Gresham in heart; but his spirit had been weaker than that of his forefathers; and, in his days, for the first time, the Greshams were to go to the wall! Ten years before the beginning of our story it had been necessary to raise a large sum of money to meet and pay off pressing liabilities, and it was found that this could be done with more material advantage by selling a portion of the property than in any other way. A portion of it, about a third of the whole in value, was accordingly sold.

Boxall Hill lay half-way between Greshamsbury and Barchester, and was known as having the best partridge-shooting in the county; as having on it also a celebrated fox cover, Boxall Gorse, held in very high repute by Barsetshire sportsmen. There was not residence on the immediate estate, and it was altogether divided from the remainder of the Greshamsbury property. This, with many inward and outward groans, Mr Gresham permitted to be sold.

It was sold, and sold well, by private contract to a native of Barchester, who, having risen from the world's ranks, had made for himself great wealth. Somewhat of this man's character must hereafter be told; it will suffice to say that he relied for advice in money matters upon Dr Thorne, and that at Dr Thorne's suggestion he had purchased Boxall Hill, partridge-shooting and gorse cover all included. He had not only bought Boxall Hill, but had subsequently lent the squire large sums of money on mortgage, in all which transactions the doctor had taken part. It had therefore come to pass that Mr Gresham was not unfrequently called on to discuss his money affairs with Dr Thorne, and occasionally to submit to lectures and advice which might perhaps as well have been omitted.

So much for Dr Thorne. A few words must still be said about Miss Mary before we rush into our story; the crust will then have been broken, and the pie will be open to the guests. Little Miss Mary was kept at a farm-house till she was six; she was then sent to school at Bath, and transplanted to the doctor's newly furnished house a little more than six years after that. It must not be supposed that he had lost sight of his charge during her earlier years. He was much too well aware of the nature of the promise which he had made to the departing mother to do that. He had constantly visited his little niece, and long before the first twelve years of her life were over had lost all consciousness of his promise, and of his duty to the mother, in the stronger ties of downright personal love for the only creature that belonged to him.

When Mary came home the doctor was like a child in his glee. He prepared surprises for her with as much forethought and trouble as though he were contriving mines to blow up an enemy. He took her first into the shop, and then to the kitchen, thence to the dining-rooms, after that to his and her bedrooms, and so on till he came to the full glory of the new drawing-room, enhancing the pleasure by little jokes, and telling her that he should never dare to come into the last paradise without her permission, and not then till he had taken off his boots. Child as she was, she understood the joke, and carried it on like a little queen; and so they soon became the firmest of friends.

But though Mary was a queen, it was still necessary that she should be educated. Those were the earlier days in which Lady Arabella had humbled herself, and to show her humility she invited Mary to share the music-lessons of Augusta and Beatrice at the great house. A music-master from Barchester came over three times a week, and remained for three hours, and if the doctor chose to send his girl over, she could pick up what was going on without doing any harm. So said the Lady Arabella. The doctor, with many thanks and with no hesitation, accepted the offer, merely adding, that he had perhaps better settle separately with Signor Cantabili, the music-master. He was very much obliged to Lady Arabella for giving his little girl permission to join her lessons to those of the Miss Greshams.

It need hardly be said that the Lady Arabella was on fire at once. Settle with Signor Cantabili! No, indeed; she would do that; there must be no expense whatever incurred in such an arrangement on Miss Thorne's account! But here, as in most things, the doctor carried his point. It being the time of the lady's humility, she could not make as good a fight as she would otherwise have done; and thus she found, to her great disgust, that Mary Thorne was learning music in her schoolroom on equal terms, as regarded payment, with her own daughters. The arrangement having been made could not be broken, especially as the young lady in nowise made herself disagreeable; and more especially as the Miss Greshams themselves were very fond of her.

And so Mary Thorne learnt music at Greshamsbury, and with her music she learnt other things also: how to behave herself among girls of her own age; how to speak and talk as other young ladies do; how to dress herself, and how to move and walk. All which, she, being quick to learn, learnt without trouble at the great house. Something also she learnt of French, seeing that the Greshamsbury French governess was always in the room.

And then, some few years later, there came a rector, and a rector's sister; and with the latter Mary studied German, and French also. From the doctor himself she learnt much; the choice, namely, of English books for her own reading, and habits of thought somewhat akin to his own, though modified by the feminine softness of her individual mind.

And so Mary Thorne grew up and was educated. Of her personal appearance it certainly is my business as an author to say something. She is my heroine, and, as such, must necessarily be very beautiful; but, in truth, her mind and inner qualities are more clearly distinct to my brain than her outward form and features. I know that she was far from being tall, and far from being showy; that her feet and hands were small and delicate; that her eyes were bright when looked at, but not brilliant so as to make their brilliancy palpably visible to all around her; her hair was dark brown, and worn very plainly brushed from her forehead; her lips were thin, and her mouth, perhaps, in general inexpressive, but when she was eager in conversation it would show itself to be animated with curves of wondrous energy; and, quiet as she was in manner, sober and demure as was her usual settled appearance, she could talk, when the fit came on her, with an energy which in truth surprised those who did not know her; aye, and sometimes those who did. Energy! nay, it was occasionally a concentration of passion, which left her for the moment perfectly unconscious of all other cares but solicitude for that subject which she might then be advocating.

All her friends, including the doctor, had at times been made unhappy by this vehemence of character; but yet it was to that very vehemence that she owed it that all her friends so loved her. It had once nearly banished her in early years from the Greshamsbury schoolroom; and yet it ended in making her claim to remain there so strong, that Lady Arabella could no longer oppose it, even when she had the wish to do so.

A new French governess had lately come to Greshamsbury, and was, or was to be, a great pet with Lady Arabella, having all the great gifts with which a governess can be endowed, and being also a protégée from the castle. The castle, in Greshamsbury parlance, always meant that of Courcy. Soon after this a valued little locket belonging to Augusta Gresham was missing. The French governess had objected to its being worn in the schoolroom, and it had been sent up to the bedroom by a young servant-girl, the daughter of a small farmer on the estate. The locket was missing, and after a while, a considerable noise in the matter having been made, was found, by the diligence of the governess, somewhere among the belongings of the English servant. Great was the anger of Lady Arabella, loud were the protestations of the girl, mute the woe of her father, piteous the tears of her mother, inexorable the judgement of the Greshamsbury world. But something occurred, it matters now not what, to separate Mary Thorne in opinion from that world at large. Out she then spoke, and to her face accused the governess of the robbery. For two days Mary was in disgrace almost as deep as that of the farmer's daughter. But she was neither quiet nor dumb in her disgrace. When Lady Arabella would not hear her, she went to Mr Gresham. She forced her uncle to move in the matter. She gained over to her side, one by one, the potentates of the parish, and ended by bringing Mam'selle Larron down on her knees with a confession of the facts. From that time Mary Thorne was dear to the tenantry of Greshamsbury; and specially dear at one small household, where a rough-spoken father of a family was often heard to declare, that for Miss Mary Thorne he'd face man or magistrate, duke or devil.

And so Mary Thorne grew up under the doctor's eye, and at the beginning of our tale she was one of the guests assembled at Greshamsbury on the coming of age of the heir, she herself having then arrived at the same period of her life.

CHAPTER IV

Lessons from Courcy Castle

It was the first of July, young Frank Gresham's birthday, and the London season was not yet over; nevertheless, Lady de Courcy had managed to get down into the country to grace the coming of age of the heir, bringing with her all the Ladies Amelia, Rosina, Margaretta, and Alexandrina, together with such of the Honourable Johns and Georges as could be collected for the occasion.

The Lady Arabella had contrived this year to spend ten weeks in town, which, by a little stretching, she made to pass for the season; and had managed, moreover, at last to refurnish, not ingloriously, the Portman Square drawing-room. She had gone up to London under the pretext, imperatively urged, of Augusta's teeth – young ladies' teeth are not unfrequently of value in this way, – and having received authority for a new carpet, which was really much wanted, had made such dexterous use of that sanction as to run up an upholsterer's bill of six or seven hundred pounds. She had of course had her carriage and horses; the girls of course had gone out; it had been positively necessary to have a few friends in Portman Square; and, altogether, the ten weeks had not been unpleasant, and not inexpensive.

For a few confidential minutes before dinner, Lady de Courcy and her sister-in-law sat together in the latter's dressing-room, discussing the unreasonableness of the squire, who had expressed himself with more than ordinary bitterness as to the folly – he had probably used some stronger word – of these London proceedings.

'Heavens!' said the countess, with much eager animation; 'what can the man expect? What does he wish you to do?'

'He would like to sell the house in London, and bury us all here for ever. Mind, I was there only for ten weeks.'

'Barely time for the girls to get their teeth properly looked at! But, Arabella, what does he say?' Lady de Courcy was very anxious to learn the exact truth of the matter, and ascertain, if she could, whether Mr Gresham was really as poor as he pretended to be.

'Why, he said yesterday that he would have no more going to town at all; that he was barely able to pay the claims made on him, and keep up the house here, and that he would not – '

'Would not what?' asked the countess.

'Why, he said that he would not utterly ruin poor Frank.'

'Ruin Frank!'

'That's what he said.'

'But, surely, Arabella, it is not so bad as that? What possible reason can there be for him to be in debt?'

'He is always talking of those elections.'

'But, my dear, Boxall Hill paid all that off. Of course Frank will not have such an income as there was when you married into the family; we all know that. And whom will he have to thank but his father? But Boxall Hill paid all those debts, and why should there be any difficulty now?'

'It was those nasty dogs, Rosina,' said the Lady Arabella, almost in tears.

'Well, I for one never approved of the hounds coming to Greshamsbury. When a man has once involved his property he should not incur any expenses that are not absolutely necessary. That is a golden rule which Mr Gresham ought to have remembered. Indeed, I put it to him nearly in those very words; but Mr Gresham never did, and never will receive with common civility anything that comes from me.'

'I know, Rosina, he never did; and yet where would he have been but for the De Courcys?' So exclaimed, in her gratitude, the Lady Arabella; to speak truth, however, but for the De Courcys, Mr Gresham might have been at this moment on the top of Boxall Hill, monarch of all he surveyed.

'As I was saying,' continued the countess, 'I never approved of the hounds coming to Greshamsbury; but yet, my dear, the hounds can't have eaten up everything. A man with ten thousand a year ought to be able to keep hounds; particularly as he had a subscription.'

'He says the subscription was little or nothing.'

'That's nonsense, my dear. Now, Arabella, what does he do with his money? that's the question. Does he gamble?'

'Well,' said Lady Arabella, very slowly, 'I don't think he does.' If the squire did gamble he must have done it very slyly, for he rarely went away from Greshamsbury, and certainly very few men looking like gamblers were in the habit of coming thither as guests. 'I don't think he does gamble.' Lady Arabella put her emphasis on the word gamble, as though her husband, if he might perhaps be charitably acquitted of that vice, was certainly guilty of every other known in the civilised world.

'I know he used,' said Lady de Courcy, looking very wise, and rather suspicious. She certainly had sufficient domestic reasons for disliking the propensity; 'I know he used; and when a man begins, he is hardly ever cured.'

'Well, if he does, I don't know it,' said the Lady Arabella.

'The money, my dear, must go somewhere. What excuse does he give when you tell him you want this and that – all the common necessaries of life, that you have always been used to?'

'He gives no excuse; sometimes he says the family is so large.'

'Nonsense! Girls cost nothing; there's only Frank, and he can't have cost anything yet. Can he be saving money to buy back Boxall Hill?'

'Oh, no!' said the Lady Arabella, quickly. 'He is not saving anything; he never did, and never will save, though he is so stingy to me. He is hard pushed for money; I know that.'

'Then where has it gone?' said the Countess de Courcy, with a look of stern decision.

'Heaven only knows! Now Augusta is to be married, I must of course have a few hundred pounds. You should have heard how he groaned when I asked him for it. Heaven only knows where the money goes!' And the injured wife wiped a piteous tear from her eye with her fine dress cambric handkerchief. 'I have all the sufferings and privations of a poor man's wife, but I have none of the consolations. He has no confidence in me; he never tells me anything; he never talks to me about his affairs. If he talks to any one it is to that horrid doctor.'

'What, Dr Thorne?' Now the Countess de Courcy hated Dr Thorne with a holy hatred.

'Yes, Dr Thorne. I believe that he knows everything; and advises everything, too. Whatever difficulties poor Gresham may have, I do believe Dr Thorne has brought them about. I do believe it, Rosina.'

'Well, that is surprising. Mr Gresham, with all his faults, is a gentleman; and how he can talk about his affairs with a low apothecary like that, I, for one, cannot imagine. Lord de Courcy has not always been to me all that he should have been; far from it.' And Lady de Courcy thought over in her mind injuries of a much graver description than any that her sister-in-law had ever suffered; 'but I have never known anything like that at Courcy Castle. Surely Umbleby knows all about it, doesn't he?'

'Not half so much as the doctor,' said Lady Arabella.

The countess shook her head slowly: the idea of Mr Gresham, a country gentleman of good estate like him, making a confidant of a country doctor was too great a shock for her nerves; and for a while she was constrained to sit silent before she could recover herself.

'One thing at any rate is certain, Arabella,' said the countess, as soon as she found herself again sufficiently composed to offer counsel in a properly dictatorial manner. 'One thing at any rate is certain; if Mr Gresham be involved so deeply as you say, Frank has but one duty before him. He must marry money. The heir of fourteen thousand a year may indulge himself in looking for blood, as Mr Gresham did, my dear' – it must be understood that there was very little compliment in this, as the Lady Arabella had always conceived herself to be a beauty – 'or for beauty, as some men do,' continued the countess, thinking of the choice that the present Earl de Courcy had made; 'but Frank must marry money. I hope he will understand this early: do make him understand this before he makes a fool of himself; when a man thoroughly understands this, when he knows what his circumstances require, why, the matter becomes easy to him. I hope that Frank understands that he has no alternative. In his position he must marry money.'

But, alas! alas! Frank Gresham had already made a fool of himself.

'Well, my boy, I wish you joy with all my heart,' said the Honourable John, slapping his cousin on the back, as he walked round to the stable-yard with him before dinner, to inspect a setter puppy of peculiarly fine breed which had been sent to Frank as a birthday present. 'I wish I were an elder son; but we can't all have that luck.'

'Who wouldn't sooner be the younger son of an earl than the eldest son of a plain squire?' said Frank, wishing to say something civil in return for his cousin's civility.

'I wouldn't for one,' said the Honourable John. 'What chance have I? There's Porlock's as strong as a horse; and then George comes next. And the governor's good for these twenty years.' And the young man sighed as he reflected what small hope there was that all those who were nearest and dearest to him should die out of his way, and leave him to the sweet enjoyment of an earl's coronet and fortune. 'Now, you're sure of your game some day; and as you've no brothers, I suppose the squire'll let you do pretty well what you like. Besides, he's not so strong as my governor, though he's younger.'

Frank had never looked at his fortune in this light before, and was so slow and green that he was not much delighted at the prospect now that it was offered to him. He had always, however, been taught to look to his cousins, the De Courcys, as men with whom it would be very expedient that he should be intimate; he therefore showed no offence, but changed the conversation.

'Shall you hunt with the Barsetshires this next season, John? I hope you will; I shall.'

'Well, I don't know. It's very slow. It's all tillage here, or else woodland. I rather fancy I shall go to Leicestershire when the partridge-shooting is over. What sort of a lot do you mean to come out with, Frank?'

Frank became a little red as he answered, 'Oh, I shall have two,' he said; 'that is, the mare I have had these two years, and the horse my father gave me this morning.'

'What! only those two? and the mare is nothing more than a pony.'

'She is fifteen hands,' said Frank, offended.

'Well, Frank, I certainly would not stand that,' said the Honourable John. 'What, go out before the county with one untrained horse and a pony; and you the heir to Greshamsbury!'

'I'll have him so trained before November,' said Frank, 'that nothing in Barsetshire shall stop him. Peter says' – Peter was the Greshamsbury stud-groom – 'that he tucks up his hind legs beautifully.'

'But who the deuce would think of going to work with one horse; or two either, if you insist on calling the old pony a

huntress? I'll put you up to a trick, my lad: if you stand that
you'll stand anything; and if you don't mean to go in leading-
strings all your life, now is the time to show it. There's young
Baker – Harry Baker, you know – he came of age last year, and
he has as pretty a string of nags as any one would wish to set
eyes on; four hunters and a hack. Now, if old Baker has four
thousand a year it's every shilling he has got.'

This was true, and Frank Gresham, who in the morning had
been made so happy by his father's present of a horse, began to
feel that hardly enough had been done for him. It was true that
Mr Baker had only four thousand a year; but it was also true
that he had no other child than Harry Baker; that he had no
great establishment to keep up; that he owed a shilling to no
one; and, also, that he was a great fool in encouraging a mere
boy to ape all the caprices of a man of wealth. Nevertheless, for
a moment Frank Gresham did feel that, considering his position,
he was being treated rather unworthily.

'Take the matter in your own hands, Frank,' said the Honourable John, seeing the impression that he had made. 'Of course
the governor knows very well that you won't put up with such
a stable as that. Lord bless you! I have heard that when he
married my aunt, and that was when he was about your age, he
had the best stud in the whole county; and then he was in
Parliament before he was three-and-twenty.'

'His father, you know, died when he was very young,' said
Frank.

'Yes; I know he had a stroke of luck that doesn't fall to every
one; but – '

Young Frank's face grew dark now instead of red. When his
cousin submitted to him the necessity of having more than two
horses for his own use he could listen to him; but when the same
monitor talked of the chance of a father's death as a stroke of
luck, Frank was too much disgusted to be able to pretend to
pass it over with indifference. What! was he thus to think of his
father, whose face was always lighted up with pleasure when his
boy came near him, and so rarely bright at any other time?
Frank had watched his father closely enough to be aware of this;
he knew how his father delighted in him; he had had cause to
guess that his father had many troubles, and that he strove hard
to banish the memory of them when his son was with him. He
loved his father truly, purely, and thoroughly, liked to be with

him, and would be proud to be his confidant. Could he then
listen quietly while his cousin spoke of the chance of his father's
death as a stroke of luck?

'I shouldn't think it a stroke of luck, John. I should think it
the greatest misfortune in the world.'

It is so difficult for a young man to enumerate sententiously a
principle of morality, or even an expression of ordinary good
feeling, without giving himself something of a ridiculous air,
without assuming something of mock grandeur!

'Oh, of course, my dear fellow,' said the Honourable John,
laughing; 'that's a matter of course. We all understand that
without saying it. Porlock, of course, would feel exactly the
same about the governor; but if the governor were to walk, I
think Porlock would console himself with the thirty thousand a
year.'

'I don't know what Porlock would do; he's always quarrelling
with my uncle, I know. I only spoke of myself; I never quarrelled
with my father, and I hope I never shall.'

'All right, my lad of wax, all right. I dare say you won't be
tried; but if you are, you'll find before six months are over, that
it's a very nice thing to be master of Greshamsbury.'

'I'm sure I shouldn't find anything of the kind.'

'Very well, so be it. You wouldn't do as young Hatherly did,
at Hatherly Court, in Gloucestershire, when his father kicked
the bucket. You know Hatherly, don't you?'

'No; I never saw him.'

'He's Sir Frederick now, and has, or had, one of the finest
fortunes in England, for a commoner; the most of it is gone
now. Well, when he heard of his governor's death, he was in
Paris, but he went off to Hatherly as fast as special train and
post-horses would carry him, and got there just in time for the
funeral. As he came back to Hatherly Court from the church,
they were putting up the hatchment over the door, and Master
Fred saw that the undertakers had put at the bottom "Resurgam". You know what that means?'

'Oh, yes,' said Frank.

'"I'll come back again."' said the Honourable John, constru-
ing the Latin for the benefit of his cousin. '"No," said Fred
Hatherly, looking up at the hatchment; "I'm blessed if you do,
old gentleman. That would be too much of a joke; I'll take care
of that." So he got up at night, and he got some fellows with

him, and they climbed up and painted out "Resurgam", and they painted into its place, "Requiescat in pace"; which means, you know, "you'd a great deal better stay where you are". Now I call that good. Fred Hatherly did that as sure as – as sure as – as sure as anything.'

Frank could not help laughing at the story, especially at his cousin's mode of translating the undertaker's mottoes;* and then they sauntered back from the stables into the house to dress for dinner.

Dr Thorne had come to the house somewhat before dinner-time, at Mr Gresham's request, and was now sitting with the squire in his own book-room – so called – while Mary was talking to some of the girls upstairs.

'I must have ten or twelve thousand pounds; ten at the very least,' said the squire, who was sitting in his usual armchair, close to his littered table, with his head supported on his hand, looking very unlike the father of an heir to a noble property, who had that day come of age.

It was the first of July, and of course there was no fire in the grate; but, nevertheless, the doctor was standing with his back to the fireplace, with his coat-tails over his arms, as though he were engaged, now in summer as he so often was in winter, in talking, and roasting his hinder person at the same time.

'Twelve thousand pounds! it's a very large sum of money.'

'I said ten,' said the squire.

'Ten thousand pounds is a large sum of money. There is no doubt he'll let you have it. Scatcherd will let you have it; but I know he'll expect to have the title-deeds.'

'What! for ten thousand pounds?' said the squire. 'There is not a registered debt against the property but his own and Armstrong's.'

'But his own is very large already.'

'Armstrong's is nothing; about four-and-twenty thousand pounds.'

'Yes; but he comes first, Mr Gresham.'

'Well, what of that? To hear you talk, one would think that there was nothing left of Greshamsbury. What's four-and-twenty thousand pounds? Does Scatcherd know what the rent-roll is?'

'Oh, yes, he knows it well enough: I wish he did not.'

'Well, then, why does he make such a bother about a few thousand pounds? The title-deeds, indeed!'

'What he means is, that he must have ample security to cover what he has already advanced before he goes on. I wish to goodness you had no further need to borrow. I did think that things were settled last year.'

'Oh, if there's any difficulty, Umbleby will get it for me.'

'Yes; and what will you have to pay for it?'

'I'd sooner pay double than be talked to in this way,' said the squire, angrily, and, as he spoke, he got up hurriedly from his chair, thrust his hands into his trousers-pockets, walked quickly to the window, and immediately walking back again, threw himself once more into his chair.

'There are some things a man cannot bear, doctor,' said he, beating the devil's tattoo* on the floor with one of his feet, 'though God knows I ought to be patient now, for I am made to bear a good many such things. You had better tell Scatcherd that I am obliged to him for his offer, but that I will not trouble him.'

The doctor during this little outburst had stood quite silent with his back to the fireplace and his coat-tails hanging over his arms; but though his voice said nothing, his face said much. He was very unhappy; he was greatly grieved to find that the squire was so soon again in want of money, and greatly grieved also to find that this want had made him so bitter and unjust. Mr Gresham had attacked him; but as he was determined not to quarrel with Mr Gresham, he refrained from answering.

The squire also remained silent for a few minutes; but he was not endowed with the gift of silence, and was soon, as it were, compelled to speak again.

'Poor Frank!' said he. 'I could yet be easy about everything if it were not for the injury I have done him. Poor Frank!'

The doctor advanced a few paces from off the rug, and taking his hand out of his pocket, he laid it gently on the squire's shoulder. 'Frank will do very well yet,' said he. 'It is not absolutely necessary that a man should have fourteen thousand pounds a year to be happy.'

'My father left me the property entire, and I should leave it entire to my son; – but you don't understand this.'

The doctor did understand the feeling fully. The fact, on the other hand, was that, long as he had known him, the squire did not understand the doctor.

'I would you could, Mr Gresham,' said the doctor, 'so that your mind might be happier; but that cannot be, and, therefore, I say again, that Frank will do very well yet, although he will not inherit fourteen thousand pounds a year; and I would have you say the same thing to yourself.'

'Ah! you don't understand it,' persisted the squire. 'You don't know how a man feels when he – Ah, well! it's no use my troubling you with what cannot be mended. I wonder whether Umbleby is about the place anywhere?'

The doctor was again standing with his back against the chimney-piece, and with his hands in his pockets.

'You did not see Umbleby as you came in?' again asked the squire.

'No, I did not; and if you will take my advice you will not see him now; at any rate with reference to this money.'

'I tell you I must get it from some one; you say Scatcherd won't let me have it.'

'No, Mr Gresham; I did not say that.'

'Well, you said what was as bad. Augusta is to be married in September, and the money must be had. I have agreed to give Moffat six thousand pounds, and he is to have the money down in hard cash.'

'Six thousand pounds,' said the doctor. 'Well, I suppose that is not more than your daughter should have. But then, five times six are thirty; thirty thousand pounds will be a large sum to make up.'

The father thought to himself that his younger girls were but children, and that the trouble of arranging their marriage portions might well be postponed a while. Sufficient for the day is the evil thereof.*

'That Moffat is a griping, hungry fellow,' said the squire. 'I suppose Augusta likes him; and, as regards money, it is a good match.'

'If Miss Gresham loves him, that is everything. I am not in love with him myself; but then, I am not a young lady.'

'The De Courcys are very fond of him. Lady de Courcy says that he is a perfect gentleman, and thought very much of in London.'

'Oh! if Lady de Courcy says that, of course it's all right,' said

the doctor, with a quiet sarcasm, that was altogether thrown
away on the squire.

The squire did not like any of the De Courcys; especially, he
did not like Lady de Courcy; but still he was accessible to a
certain amount of gratification in the near connexion which he
had with the earl and countess; and when he wanted to support
his family greatness, would sometimes weakly fall back upon
the grandeur of Courcy Castle. It was only when talking to his
wife that he invariably snubbed the pretensions of his noble
relatives.

The two men after this remained silent for a while; and then
the doctor, renewing the subject for which he had been summoned into the book-room, remarked, that as Scatcherd was
now in the country – he did not say, was now at Boxall Hill, as
he did not wish to wound the squire's ears – perhaps he had
better go and see him, and ascertain in what way this affair of
the money might be arranged. There was no doubt, he said, that
Scatcherd would supply the sum required at a lower rate of
interest than that at which it could be procured through
Umbleby's means.

'Very well,' said the squire, 'I'll leave it in your hands, then. I
think ten thousand pounds will do. And now I'll dress for
dinner.' And then the doctor left him.

Perhaps the reader will suppose after this that the doctor had
some pecuniary interest of his own in arranging the squire's
loans; or, at any rate, he will think that the squire must have so
thought. Not in the least; neither had he any such interest, nor
did the squire think that he had any. What Dr Thorne did in
this matter he did for love; what Dr Thorne did in this matter
the squire well knew was done for love. But the squire of
Greshamsbury was a great man at Greshamsbury; and it
behoved him to maintain the greatness of his squirehood when
discussing his affairs with the village doctor. So much he had at
any rate learnt from his contact with the De Courcys.

And the doctor – proud, arrogant, contradictory, headstrong
as he was – why did he bear to be thus snubbed? Because he
knew that the squire of Greshamsbury, when struggling with
debt and poverty, required an indulgence for his weakness. Had
Mr Gresham been in easy circumstances, the doctor would by
no means have stood so placidly with his hands in his pockets,
and have had Mr Umbleby thus thrown in his teeth. The doctor

loved the squire, loved him as his own oldest friend; but he loved him ten times better as being in adversity than he could ever have done had things gone well at Greshamsbury in his time.

While this was going on downstairs, Mary was sitting upstairs with Beatrice Gresham in the schoolroom. The old schoolroom, so called, was now a sitting-room, devoted to the use of the grown-up young ladies of the family, whereas one of the old nurseries was now the modern schoolroom. Mary well knew her way to this sanctum, and, without asking any questions, walked up to it when her uncle went to the squire. On entering the room she found that Augusta and the Lady Alexandrina were also there, and she hesitated for a moment at the door.

'Come in, Mary,' said Beatrice, 'you know my cousin Alexandrina.' Mary came in, and having shaken hands with her two friends, was bowing to the lady, when the lady condescended, put out her noble hand, and touched Miss Thorne's fingers.

Beatrice was Mary's friend, and many heart-burnings and much mental solicitude did that young lady give to her mother by indulging in such a friendship. But Beatrice, with some faults, was true at heart, and she persisted in loving Mary Thorne in spite of the hints which her mother so frequently gave as to the impropriety of such an affection.

Nor had Augusta any objection to the society of Miss Thorne. Augusta was a strong-minded girl, with much of the De Courcy arrogance, but quite as well inclined to show it in opposition to her mother as in any other form. To her alone in the house did Lady Arabella show much deference. She was now going to make a suitable match with a man of large fortune, who had been procured for her as an eligible *parti* by her aunt, the countess. She did not pretend, had never pretended, that she loved Mr Moffat, but she knew, she said, that in the present state of her father's affairs such a match was expedient. Mr Moffat was a young man of very large fortune, in Parliament, inclined to business, and in every way recommendable. He was not a man of birth, to be sure; that was to be lamented; – in confessing that Mr Moffat was not a man of birth, Augusta did not go so far as to admit that he was the son of a tailor; such, however, was the rigid truth in this matter – he was not a man of birth, that was to be lamented; but in the present state of affairs at Greshamsbury, she understood well that it was her duty to postpone her own feelings in some respect. Mr Moffat would bring fortune; she would bring blood and connexion. And as she so said, her bosom glowed with strong pride to think that she would be able to contribute so much more towards the proposed future partnership than her husband would do.

'Twas thus that Miss Gresham spoke of her match to her dear friends, her cousins the De Courcys for instance, to Miss Oriel, her sister Beatrice, and even to Mary Thorne. She had no enthusiasm, she admitted, but she thought she had good judgement. She thought she had shown good judgement in accepting Mr Moffat's offer, though she did not pretend to any romance of affection. And, having so said, she went to work with considerable mental satisfaction, choosing furniture, carriages, and clothes, not extravagantly as her mother would have done, not in deference to the sterner dictates of the latest fashion as her aunt would have done, with none of the girlish glee in new purchases which Beatrice would have felt, but with sound judgement. She bought things that were rich, for her husband was to be rich, and she meant to avail herself of his wealth; she bought things that were fashionable, for she meant to live in the fashionable world; but she bought what was good, and strong, and lasting, and worth its money.

Augusta Gresham had perceived early in life that she could not obtain success either as an heiress or as a beauty, nor could she shine as a wit; she therefore fell back on such qualities as she had, and determined to win the world as a strong-minded, useful woman. That which she had of her own was blood; having that, she would in all ways do what in her lay to enhance its value. Had she not possessed it, it would to her mind have been the vainest of pretences.

When Mary came in, the wedding preparations were being discussed. The number and names of the bridesmaids were being settled, the dresses were on the tapis, the invitadons to be given were talked over. Sensible as Augusta was, she was not above such feminine cares; she was, indeed, rather anxious that the wedding should go off well. She was a little ashamed of her tailor's son, and therefore anxious that things should be as brilliant as possible.

The bridesmaids' names had just been written on a card as Mary entered the room. There were the Ladies Amelia, Rosina, Margaretta, and Alexandrina of course at the head of it; then came Beatrice and the twins; then Miss Oriel, who, though only a parson's sister, was a person of note, birth, and fortune. After this there had been here a great discussion whether or not there should be any more. If there were to be one more there must be two. Now Miss Moffat had expressed a direct wish, and Augusta, though she would much rather have done without her, hardly knew how to refuse. Alexandrina – we hope we may be allowed to drop the 'lady', for the sake of brevity, for the present scene only – was dead against such an unreasonable request. 'We none of us know her, you know; and it would not be comfortable.' Beatrice strongly advocated the future sister-in-law's acceptance into the bevy: she had her own reasons; she was pained that Mary Thorne should not be among the number, and if Miss Moffat were accepted, perhaps Mary might be brought in as her colleague.

'If you have Miss Moffat,' said Alexandrina, 'you must have dear little Pussy, too; and I really think that Pussy is too young; it will be troublesome.' Pussy was the youngest Miss Gresham, who was now only eight years old, and whose real name was Nina.

'Augusta,' said Beatrice, speaking with some slight hesitation, some soupçon of doubt, before the high authority of her noble cousin, 'if you do have Miss Moffat would you mind asking Mary Thorne to join her? I think Mary would like it, because, you see, Patience Oriel is to be one; and we have known Mary much longer than we have known Patience.'

Then out and spake the Lady Alexandrina.

'Beatrice, dear, if you think of what you are asking, I am sure you will see that it would not do; would not do at all. Miss Thorne is a very nice girl, I am sure; and, indeed, what little I have seen of her I highly approve. But, after all, who is she? Mamma, I know, thinks that Arabella has been wrong to let her be here so much, but – '

Beatrice became rather red in the face, and, in spite of the dignity of her cousin, was preparing to defend her friend.

'Mind, I am not saying a word against Miss Thorne.'

'If I am married before her, she shall be one of my brides-maids,' said Beatrice.

'That will probably depend on circumstances,' said the Lady Alexandrina; I find that I cannot bring my courteous pen to drop the title. 'But Augusta is very peculiarly situated. Mr

Moffat is, you see, not of the very highest birth; and, therefore, she should take care that on her side every one about her is well born.'

'Then you cannot have Miss Moffat,' said Beatrice.

'No; I would not if I could help it,' said the cousin.

'But the Thornes are as good a family as the Greshams,' said Beatrice. She had not quite courage to say, as good as the De Courcys.

'I dare say they are; and if this was Miss Thorne of Ullathorne, Augusta probably would not object to her. But can you tell me who Miss Mary Thorne is?'

'She is Dr Thorne's niece.'

'You mean that she is called so; but do you know who her father was, or who her mother was? I, for one, must own I do not. Mamma, I believe, does, but – '

At this moment the door opened gently, and Mary Thorne entered the room.

It may easily be conceived, that while Mary was making her salutations the three other young ladies were a little cast back. The Lady Alexandrina, however, quickly recovered herself, and, by her inimitable presence of mind and facile grace of manner, soon put the matter on a proper footing.

'We were discussing Miss Gresham's marriage,' said she; 'I am sure I may mention to an acquaintance of so long standing as Miss Thorne, that the first of September has been now fixed for the wedding.'

Miss Gresham! Acquaintance of so long standing! Why, Mary and Augusta Gresham had for years, we will hardly say now for how many, passed their mornings together in the same school-room; had quarrelled and squabbled, and caressed and kissed, and been all but as sisters to each other. Acquaintance, indeed! Beatrice felt that her ears were tingling, and even Augusta was a little ashamed. Mary, however, knew that the cold words had come from a De Courcy, and not from a Gresham, and did not, therefore, resent them.

'So it's settled, Augusta, is it?' said she; 'the first of September. I wish you joy with all my heart,' and coming round, she put her arm over Augusta's shoulder and kissed her. The Lady Alexandrina could not but think that the doctor's niece uttered her congratulations very much as though she were speaking to an equal; very much as though she had a father and mother of her own.

'You will have delicious weather,' continued Mary. 'September, and the beginning of October, is the nicest time of the year. If I were going honeymooning it is just the time of year I would choose.'

'I wish you were, Mary,' said Beatrice.

'So do not I, dear, till I have found some decent sort of a body to honeymoon along with me. I won't stir out of Greshamsbury till I have sent you off before me, at any rate. And where will you go, Augusta?'

'We have not settled that,' said Augusta. 'Mr Moffat talks of Paris.'

'Who ever heard of going to Paris in September?' said the Lady Alexandrina.

'Or who ever heard of the gentleman having anything to say on the matter?' said the doctor's niece. 'Of course Mr Moffat will go wherever you are pleased to take him.'

The Lady Alexandrina was not pleased to find how completely the doctor's niece took upon herself to talk, and sit, and act at Greshamsbury as though she was on a par with the young ladies of the family. That Beatrice should have allowed this would not have surprised her; but it was to be expected that Augusta would have shown better judgement.

'These things require some tact in their management; some delicacy when high interests are at stake,' said she. 'I agree with Miss Thorne in thinking that, in ordinary circumstances, with ordinary people, perhaps, the lady should have her way. Rank, however, has its drawbacks, Miss Thorne, as well as its privileges.'

'I should not object to the drawbacks,' said the doctor's niece, 'presuming them to be of some use; but I fear I might fail in getting on so well with the privileges.'

The Lady Alexandrina looked at her as though not fully aware whether she intended to be pert. In truth, the Lady Alexandrina was rather in the dark on the subject. It was almost impossible, it was incredible, that a fatherless, motherless, doctor's niece should be pert to an earl's daughter at Greshamsbury, seeing that that earl's daughter was the cousin of the Miss Greshams. And yet the Lady Alexandrina hardly knew what other construction to put on the words she had just heard.

It was at any rate clear to her that it was not becoming that she should just then stay any longer in that room. Whether she intended to be pert or not, Miss Mary Thorne was, to say the least, very free. The De Courcy ladies knew what was due to them – no ladies better; and, therefore, the Lady Alexandrina made up her mind at once to go to her own bedroom.

'Augusta,' she said, rising slowly from her chair with much stately composure, 'it is nearly time to dress; will you come with me? We have a great deal to settle, you know.'

So she swam out of the room, and Augusta, telling Mary that she would see her again at dinner, swam – no, tried to swim – after her. Miss Gresham had had great advantages; but she had not been absolutely brought up at Courcy Castle, and could not as yet quite assume the Courcy style of swimming.

'There,' said Mary, as the door closed behind the rustling muslins of the ladies. 'There, I have made an enemy for ever, perhaps two; that's satisfactory.'

'And why have you done it, Mary? When I am fighting your battles behind your back, why do you come and upset it all by making the whole family of the De Courcys dislike you? In such a matter as that, they'll all go together.'

'I am sure they will,' said Mary; 'whether they would be equally unanimous in a case of love and charity, that, indeed, is another question.'

'But why should you try to make my cousin angry; you that ought to have so much sense? Don't you remember what you were saying yourself the other day, of the absurdity of combating pretences which the world sanctions?'

'I do, Trichy, I do; don't scold me now. It is so much easier to preach than to practise. I do so wish I was a clergyman.'

'But you have done so much harm, Mary.'

'Have I?' said Mary, kneeling down on the ground at her friend's feet. 'If I humble myself very low; if I kneel through the whole evening in a corner; if I put my neck down and let all your cousins trample on it, and then your aunt, would not that make atonement? I would not object to wearing sackcloth, either; and I'd eat a little ashes – or, at any rate, I'd try.'

'I know you're very clever, Mary; but still I think you're a fool. I do, indeed.'

'I am a fool, Trichy, I do confess it; and am not a bit clever: but don't scold me; you see how humble I am; not only humble but umble,* which I look upon to be the comparative, or, indeed, superlative degree. Or perhaps there are four degrees; humble, umble, stumble, tumble; and then, when one is absolutely in the dirt at their feet, perhaps these big people won't wish one to stoop any further.'

'Oh, Mary!'

'And, oh, Trichy! you don't mean to say I mayn't speak out before you. There, perhaps you'd like to put your foot on my neck.' And then she put her head down to the foot-stool and kissed Beatrice's foot.

'I'd like, if I dared, to put my hand on your cheek and give you a good slap for being such a goose.'

'Do; do, Trichy: you shall tread on me, or slap me, or kiss me; whichever you like.'

'I can't tell you how vexed I am,' said Beatrice; 'I wanted to arrange something.'

'Arrange something! What? arrange what? I love arranging. I fancy myself qualified to be an arranger-general in female matters. I mean pots and pans, and such like. Of course I don't allude to extraordinary people and extraordinary circumstances that require tact, and delicacy, and drawbacks, and that sort of thing.'

'Very well, Mary.'

'But it's not very well; it's very bad if you look like that. Well, my pet, there, I won't. I won't allude to the noble blood of your noble relatives either in joke or in earnest. What is it you want to arrange, Trichy?'

'I want you to be one of Augusta's bridesmaids.'

'Good heavens, Beatrice! Are you mad? What! Put me, even for a morning, into the same category of finery as the noble brood from Courcy Castle!'

'Patience is to be one.'

'But that is no reason why Impatience should be another, and I should be very impatient under such honours. No, Trichy; joking apart, do not think of it. Even if Augusta wished it I should refuse. I should be obliged to refuse. I, too, suffer from pride; a pride quite as unpardonable as that of others: I could not stand with your four lady-cousins behind your sister at the altar. In such a galaxy they would be the stars, and I – '

'Why, Mary, all the world knows that you are prettier than any of them!'

'I am all the world's very humble servant. But, Trichy, I should not object if I were as ugly as the veiled prophet and they all as beautiful as Zuleika.* The glory of that galaxy will be held to depend not on its beauty, but on its birth. You know how they would look at me; how they would scorn me; and there, in church, at the altar, with all that is solemn round us, I could not return their scorn as I might do elsewhere. In a room I'm not a bit afraid of them all.' And Mary was again allowing herself to be absorbed by that feeling of indomitable pride, of antagonism to the pride of others, which she herself in her cooler moments was the first to blame.

'You often say, Mary, that that sort of arrogance should be despised and passed over without notice.'

'So it should, Trichy. I tell you that as the clergyman tells you to hate riches. But though the clergyman tells you so, he is not the less anxious to get rich himself.'

'I particularly wish you to be one of Augusta's bridesmaids.'

'And I particularly wish to decline the honour; which honour has not been, and will not be, offered to me. No, Trichy. I will not be Augusta's bridesmaid, but – but – but –'

'But what, dearest?'

'But, Trichy, when some one else is married, when the new wing has been built to a house that you know of –'

'Now, Mary, hold your tongue, or you know you'll make me angry.'

'I do so like to see you angry. And when that time comes, when that wedding does take place, then I will be a bridesmaid, Trichy. Yes! even though I am not invited. Yes! though all the De Courcys in Barsetshire should tread upon me and obliterate me. Though I should be as dust among the stars, though I should creep up in calico among their satins and lace, I will nevertheless be there; close, close to the bride; to hold something for her, to touch her dress, to feel that I am near her, to – to – to –' and she threw her arms round her companion, and kissed her over and over again. 'No, Trichy; I won't be Augusta's bridesmaid; I'll bide my time for bridesmaiding.'

What protestations Beatrice made against the probability of such an event as was foreshadowed in her friend's promise we will not now repeat. The afternoon was advancing, and the ladies also had to dress for dinner, to do honour to the young heir.

CHAPTER V

Frank Gresham's First Speech

We have said, that over and above those assembled in the house, there came to the Greshamsbury dinner on Frank's birthday the Jacksons of the Grange, consisting of Mr and Mrs Jackson; the Batesons from Annesgrove, viz., Mr and Mrs Bateson, and Miss Bateson, their daughter – an unmarried lady of about fifty; the Bakers of Mill Hill, father and son; and Mr Caleb Oriel, the rector, with his beautiful sister, Patience. Dr Thorne, and his niece Mary, we count among those already assembled at Greshamsbury.

There was nothing very magnificent in the number of the guests thus brought together to do honour to young Frank; but he, perhaps, was called on to take a more prominent part in the proceedings, to be made more of a hero than would have been the case had half the county been there. In that case the importance of the guests would have been so great that Frank would have got off with a half-muttered speech or two; but now he had to make a separate oration to every one, and very weary work he found it.

The Batesons, Bakers, and Jacksons were very civil; no doubt the more so from an unconscious feeling on their part, that as the squire was known to be a little out at elbows as regards money, any deficiency on their part might be considered as owing to the present state of affairs at Greshamsbury. Fourteen thousand a year will receive honour; in that case there is no doubt, and the man absolutely possessing it is not apt to be suspicious as to the treatment he may receive; but the ghost of fourteen thousand a year is not always so self-assured. Mr Baker, with his moderate income, was a very much richer man than the squire; and, therefore, he was peculiarly forward in congratulating Frank on the brilliancy of his prospects.

Poor Frank had hardly anticipated what there would be to do, and before dinner was announced he was very tired of it. He had no warmer feeling for any of his grand cousins than a very ordinary cousinly love; and he had resolved, forgetful of birth and blood, and all those gigantic considerations which, now that manhood had come upon him, he was bound always to bear in mind, – he had resolved to sneak out to dinner comfortably with Mary Thorne if possible; and if not with Mary, then with his other love, Patience Oriel.

Great, therefore, was his consternation at finding that, after being kept continually in the foreground for half an hour before dinner, he had to walk out to the dining-room with his aunt the countess, and take his father's place for the day at the bottom of the table.

'It will now depend altogether upon yourself, Frank, whether you maintain or lose that high position in the county which has been held by the Greshams for so many years,' said the countess, as she walked through the spacious hall, resolving to lose no time in teaching to her nephew that great lesson which it was so imperative that he should learn.

Frank took this as an ordinary lecture, meant to inculcate general good conduct, such as old bores of aunts are apt to inflict on youthful victims in the shape of nephews and nieces.

'Yes,' said Frank; 'I suppose so; and I mean to go along all square, aunt, and no mistake. When I get back to Cambridge, I'll read like bricks.'

His aunt did not care two straws about his reading. It was not by reading that the Greshams of Greshamsbury had held their heads up in the county, but by having high blood and plenty of money. The blood had come naturally to this young man; but it behoved him to look for the money in a great measure himself. She, Lady de Courcy, could doubtless help him; she might probably be able to fit him with a wife who would bring her money to match his birth. His reading was a matter in which she could in no way assist him: whether his taste might lead him to prefer books or pictures, or dogs and horses, or turnips in drills, or old Italian plates and dishes, was a matter which did not much signify; with which it was not at all necessary that his noble aunt should trouble herself.

'Oh! you are to go to Cambridge again, are you? Well, if your father wishes it; – though very little is ever gained now by a university connexion.'

'I am to take my degree in October, aunt; and I am determined, at any rate, that I won't be plucked.'

'Plucked!'

'No; I won't be plucked. Baker was plucked last year, and all because he got into the wrong set at John's. He's an excellent fellow if you knew him. He got among a set of men who did nothing but smoke and drink beer. Malthusians, we call them.'

'Malthusians!'

'"Malt," you know, aunt, and "use"; meaning that they drink beer.* So poor Harry Baker got plucked. I don't know that a fellow's any the worse; however, I won't get plucked.'

By this time the party had taken their place round the long board, Mr Gresham sitting at the top, in the place usually occupied by the Lady Arabella. She, on the present occasion, sat next to her son on the one side, as the countess did on the other. If, therefore, Frank now went astray, it would not be from want of proper leading.

'Aunt, will you have some beef?' said he, as soon as the soup and fish had been disposed of, anxious to perform the rites of hospitality now for the first time committed to his charge.

'Do not be in a hurry, Frank,' said his mother; 'the servants will – '

'Oh! ah! I forgot; there are cutlets and those sort of things. My hand is not in yet for this work, aunt. Well, as I was saying about Cambridge – '

'Is Frank to go back to Cambridge, Arabella?' said the countess to her sister-in-law, speaking across her nephew.

'So his father seems to say.'

'Is it not a waste of time?' asked the countess.

'You know I never interfere,' said the Lady Arabella; 'I never liked the idea of Cambridge myself, at all. All the De Courcys were Christchurch men; but the Greshams, it seems, were always at Cambridge.'

'Would it not be better to send him abroad at once?'

'Much better, I should think,' said the Lady Arabella: 'but you know I never interfere: perhaps you would speak to Mr Gresham.'

The countess smiled grimly, and shook her head with a decidedly negative shake. Had she said out loud to the young man, 'Your father is such an obstinate, pig-headed, ignorant fool, that it is no use speaking to him; it would be wasting fragrance on the desert air,'* she could not have spoken more plainly. The effect on Frank was this: that he said to himself, speaking quite as plainly as Lady de Courcy had spoken by her shake of the face, 'My mother and aunt are always down on the governor, always; but the more they are down on him the more

I'll stick to him. I certainly will take my degree: I will read like bricks; and I'll begin tomorrow.'

'Now will you take some beef, aunt?' This was said out loud.

The Countess de Courcy was very anxious to go on with her lesson without loss of time; but she could not, while surrounded by guests and servants, enunciate the great secret: 'You must marry money, Frank; that is your one great duty; that is the matter to be borne steadfastly in your mind.' She could not now, with sufficient weight and impress of emphasis, pour this wisdom into his ears; the more especially as he was standing up to his work of carving, and was deep to his elbows in horse-radish, fat, and gravy. So the countess sat silent while the banquet proceeded.

'Beef, Harry?' shouted out the young heir to his friend Baker. 'Oh! but I see it isn't your turn yet. I beg your pardon, Miss Bateson,' and he sent to that lady a pound and a half of excellent meat, cut out with great energy in one slice, about half an inch thick.

And so the banquet went on.

Before dinner Frank had found himself obliged to make numerous small speeches in answer to the numerous individual congratulations of his friends; but these were as nothing to the one great accumulated onus of an oration which he had long known that he should have to sustain after the cloth was taken away. Some one of course would propose his health, and then there would be a clatter of voices, ladies and gentlemen, men and girls; and when that was done he would find himself standing on his legs, with the room about him, going round and found and round.

Having had a previous hint of this, he had sought advice from his cousin, the Honourable George, whom he regarded as a dab at speaking; at least, so he had heard the Honourable George say of himself.

'What the deuce is a fellow to say, George, when he stands up after the clatter is done?'

'Oh, it's the easiest thing in life,' said the cousin. 'Only remember this: you mustn't get astray; that is what they call presence of mind, you know. I'll tell you what I do, and I'm often called up, you know; at our agriculturals I always propose the farmers' daughters: well, what I do is this – I keep my eye steadfastly fixed on one of the bottles, and never move it.'

'On one of the bottles!' said Frank; 'wouldn't it be better if I made a mark of some old covey's head? I don't like looking at the table.'

'The old covey'd move, and then you'd be done; besides, there isn't the least use in the world in looking up. I've heard people say, who go to those sort of dinners every day of their lives, that whenever anything witty is said, the fellow who says it is sure to be looking at the mahogany.'

'Oh, you know I shan't say anything witty; I'll be quite the other way.'

'But there's no reason you shouldn't learn the manner. That's the way I succeeded. Fix your eye on one of the bottles, put your thumbs in your waistcoat-pockets; stick out your elbows, bend your knees a little, and then go ahead.'

'Oh, ah! go ahead; that's very well; but you can't go ahead if you haven't got any steam.'

'A very little does it. There can be nothing so easy as your speech. When one has to say something new every year about the farmers' daughters, why one has to use one's brains a bit. Let's see; how will you begin? Of course you'll say that you are not accustomed to this sort of thing; that the honour conferred upon you is too much for your feelings; that the bright array of beauty and talent around you quite overpowers your tongue, and all that sort of thing. Then declare you're a Gresham to the backbone.'

'Oh, they know that.'

'Well, tell them again. Then of course you must say something about us; or you'll have the countess as black as Old Nick.'

'About my aunt, George? What on earth can I say about her when she's there herself before me?'

'Before you! of course; that's just the reason. Oh, say any lie you can think of; you must say something about us. You know we've come down from London on purpose.'

Frank, in spite of the benefit he was receiving from his cousin's erudition, could not help wishing in his heart that they had all remained in London; but this he kept to himself. He thanked his cousin for his hints, and though he did not feel that the trouble of his mind was completely cured, he began to hope that he might go through the ordeal without disgracing himself.

Nevertheless, he felt rather sick at heart when Mr Baker got up to propose the toast as soon as the servants were gone. The servants, that is, were gone officially; but they were there in a body, men and women, nurses, cooks, and ladies' maids, coachmen, grooms, and footmen, standing in the two doorways to hear what Master Frank would say. The old housekeeper headed the maids at one door, standing boldly inside the room; and the butler controlled the men at the other, marshalling them back with a drawn corkscrew.

Mr Baker did not say much; but what he did say, he said well. They had all seen Frank Gresham grow up from a child; and were now required to welcome as a man amongst them one who was so well qualified to carry on the honour of that loved and respected family. His young friend, Frank, was every inch a Gresham. Mr Baker omitted to make mention of the infusion of De Courcy blood, and the countess, therefore, drew herself up on her chair and looked as though she were extremely bored. He then alluded tenderly to his own long friendship with the present squire, Francis Newbold Gresham the elder; and sat down, begging them to drink health, prosperity, long life, and an excellent wife to their dear young friend, Francis Newbold Gresham the younger.

There was a great jingling of glasses, of course; made the merrier and the louder by the fact that the ladies were still there as well as the gentlemen. Ladies don't drink toasts frequently; and, therefore, the occasion coming rarely was the more enjoyed. 'God bless you, Frank!' 'Your good health, Frank!' 'And especially a good wife, Frank!' 'Two or three of them, Frank!' 'Good health and prosperity to you, Mr Gresham!' 'More power to you, Frank, my boy!' 'May God bless and preserve you, my dear boy!' and then a merry, sweet, eager voice, from the far end of the table, 'Frank! Frank! do look at me; pray do, Frank; I am drinking your health in real wine; ain't I, papa?' Such were the addresses which greeted Mr Francis Newbold Gresham the younger as he essayed to rise upon his feet for the first time since he had come to man's estate.

When the clatter was at an end, and he was fairly on his legs, he cast a glance before him on the table, to look for a decanter. He had not much liked his cousin's theory of sticking to the bottle; nevertheless, in the difficulty of the moment, it was well to have any system to go by. But, as misfortune would have it, though the table was covered with bottles, his eye could not catch one. Indeed, his eye at first could catch nothing, for the things swam before him, and the guests all seemed to dance in their chairs.

Up he got, however, and commenced his speech. As he could not follow his preceptor's advice as touching the bottle, he adopted his own crude plan of 'making a mark of some old covey's head', and therefore looked dead at the doctor.

'Upon my word, I am very much obliged to you, gentlemen and ladies, ladies and gentlemen I should say, for drinking my health, and doing me so much honour, and all that sort of thing. Upon my word I am. Especially to Mr Baker. I don't mean you, Harry, you're not Mr Baker.'

'As much as you're Mr Gresham, Master Frank.'

'But I am not Mr Gresham; and I don't mean to be for many a long year if I can help it; not at any rate till we have had another coming of age here.'

'Bravo, Frank; and whose will that be?'

'That will be my son, and a very fine lad he will be; and I hope he'll make a better speech than his father. Mr Baker said I was every inch a Gresham. Well, I hope I am.' Here the countess began to look cold and angry. 'I hope the day will never come when my father won't own me for one.'

'There's no fear, no fear,' said the doctor, who was almost put out of countenance by the orator's intense gaze. The countess looked colder and more angry, and muttered something to herself about a bear-garden.

'Gardez Gresham; eh? Harry! mind that when you're sticking in a gap and I'm coming after you. Well, I am sure I am very much obliged to you for the honour you have all done me, especially the ladies, who don't do this sort of thing on ordinary occasions. I wish they did; don't you, doctor? And talking of ladies, my aunt and cousins have come all the way from London to hear me make this speech, which certainly is not worth the trouble; but, all the same, I am very much obliged to them.' And he looked round and made a little bow at the countess. 'And so I am to Mr and Mrs Jackson, and Mr and Mrs and Miss Bateson, and Mr Baker – I'm not at all obliged to you, Harry – and to Mr Oriel and Miss Oriel, and to Mr Umbleby, and to Dr Thorne, and to Mary – I beg her pardon, I mean Miss Thorne.' And then he sat down, amid the loud plaudits of the company, and a string of blessings which came from the servants behind him.

After this, the ladies rose and departed. As she went, Lady Arabella kissed her son's forehead, and then his sisters kissed him, and one or two of his lady-cousins; and then Miss Bateson shook him by the hand. 'Oh, Miss Bateson,' said he, 'I thought the kissing was to go all round.' So Miss Bateson laughed and went her way; and Patience Oriel nodded at him, but Mary Thorne, as she quietly left the room, almost hidden among the extensive draperies of the grander ladies, hardly allowed her eyes to meet his.

He got up to hold the door for them as they passed; and, as they went, he managed to take Patience by the hand; he took her hand and pressed it for a moment, but dropped it quickly, in order that he might go through the same ceremony with Mary, but Mary was too quick for him.

'Frank,' said Mr Gresham, as soon as the door was closed, 'bring your glass here, my boy'; and the father made room for his son close beside himself. 'The ceremony is over now, so you may leave your place of dignity.' Frank sat himself down where he was told, and Mr Gresham put his hand on his son's shoulder and half caressed him, while the tears stood in his eyes. 'I think the doctor is right, Baker, I think he'll never make us ashamed of him.'

'I am sure he never will,' said Mr Baker.

'I don't think he ever will,' said Dr Thorne.

The tones of the men's voices were very different. Mr Baker did not care a straw about it; why should he? He had an heir of his own as well as the squire; one also who was the apple of *his* eye. But the doctor, – he did care; he had a niece, to be sure, whom he loved, perhaps as well as these men loved their sons; but there was room in his heart also for young Frank Gresham.

After this small exposé of feeling they sat silent for a moment or two. But silence was not dear to the heart of the Honourable John, and so he took up the running.

'That's a niceish nag you gave Frank this morning,' said he to his uncle. 'I was looking at him before dinner. He is a Monsoon,* isn't he?'

'Well, I can't say I know how he was bred,' said the squire. 'He shows a good deal of breeding.'

'He's a Monsoon, I'm sure,' said the Honourable John. 'They've all those ears, and that peculiar dip in the back. I suppose you gave a goodish figure for him?'

'Not so very much,' said the squire.

'He's a trained hunter, I suppose?'

'If not, he soon will be,' said the squire.

'Let Frank alone for that,' said Harry Baker.

'He jumps beautifully, sir,' said Frank. 'I haven't tried him myself, but Peter made him go over the bar two or three times this morning.'

The Honourable John was determined to give his cousin a helping hand, as he considered it. He thought that Frank was very ill used in being put off with so incomplete a stud, and thinking also that the son had not spirit enough to attack his father himself on the subject, the Honourable John determined to do it for him.

'He's the making of a very nice horse, I don't doubt. I wish you had a string like him, Frank.'

Frank felt the blood rush to his face. He would not for worlds have his father think that he was discontented, or otherwise than pleased with the present he had received that morning. He was heartily ashamed of himself in that he had listened with a certain degree of complacency to his cousin's tempting; but he had no idea that the subject would be repeated – and then repeated, too, before his father, in a manner to vex him on such a day as this, before such people as were assembled there. He was very angry with his cousin, and for a moment forgot all his hereditary respect for a De Courcy.

'I tell you what, John,' said he, 'do you choose your day, some day early in the season, and come out on the best thing you have, and I'll bring, not the black horse, but my old mare; and then do you try and keep near me. If I don't leave you at the back of God-speed before long, I'll give you the mare and the horse too.'

The Honourable John was not known in Barsetshire as one of the most forward of its riders. He was a man much addicted to hunting, as far as the get-up of the thing was concerned; he was great in boots and breeches; wondrously conversant with bits and bridles; he had quite a collection of saddles; and patronised every newest invention for carrying spare shoes, sandwiches, and flasks of sherry. He was prominent at the cover side; – some people, including the master of the hounds, thought him perhaps a little too loudly prominent; he affected a familiarity with the dogs, and was on speaking acquaintance with every man's horse.

But when the work was cut out, when the pace began to be sharp, when it behoved a man either to ride or visibly to decline to ride, then – so at least said they who had not the De Courcy interest quite closely at heart – then, in those heart-stirring moments, the Honourable John was too often found deficient.

There was, therefore, a considerable laugh at his expense when Frank, instigated to his innocent boast by a desire to save his father, challenged his cousin to a trial of prowess. The Honourable John was not, perhaps, as much accustomed to the ready use of his tongue as was his honourable brother, seeing that it was not his annual business to depict the glories of the farmers' daughters; at any rate, on this occasion he seemed to be at some loss for words: he shut up, as the slang phrase goes, and made no further allusion to the necessity of supplying young Gresham with a proper string of hunters.

But the old squire had understood it all; had understood the meaning of his nephew's attack; had thoroughly understood also the meaning of his son's defence, and the feeling which had actuated it. He also had thought of the stableful of horses which had belonged to himself when he came of age; and of the much more humble position which his son would have to fill than that which *his* father had prepared for him. He thought of this, and was sad enough, though he had sufficient spirit to hide from his friends around him the fact, that the Honourable John's arrow had not been discharged in vain.

'He shall have Champion,' said the father to himself. 'It is time for me to give it up.'

Now Champion was one of two fine old hunters which the squire kept for his own use. And it might have been said of him now, at the period of which we are speaking, that the only really happy moments of his life were those which he spent in the field. So much as to its being time for him to give it up.

CHAPTER VI

Frank Gresham's Early Loves

It was, we have said, the first of July, and such being the time of the year, the ladies, after sitting in the drawing-room for half an hour or so, began to think that they might as well go through the drawing-room windows on to the lawn. First one slipped out a little way, and then another; and then they got on to the lawn; and then they talked of their hats; till, by degrees, the younger ones of the party, and at last the elder also, found themselves dressed for walking.

The windows, both of the drawing-room and the dining-room, looked out on to the lawn; and it was only natural that the girls should walk from the former to the latter. It was only natural that they, being there, should tempt their swains to come to them by the sight of their broad-brimmed hats and evening dresses; and natural, also, that the temptation should not be resisted. The squire, therefore, and the elder male guests soon found themselves alone round their wine.

'Upon my word, we were enchanted by your eloquence, Mr Gresham, were we not?' said Miss Oriel, turning to one of the De Courcy girls who was with her.

Miss Oriel was a very pretty girl; a little older than Frank Gresham, – perhaps a year or so. She had dark hair, large round dark eyes, a nose a little too broad, a pretty mouth, a beautiful chin, and, as we have said before, a large fortune; – that is, moderately large – let us say twenty thousand pounds, there or thereabouts. She and her brother had been living at Greshamsbury for the last two years, the living having been purchased for him – such were Mr Gresham's necessities – during the lifetime of the last old incumbent. Miss Oriel was in every respect a nice neighbour; she was good-humoured, lady-like, lively, neither too clever nor too stupid, belonging to a good family, sufficiently fond of this world's good things, as became a pretty young lady so endowed, and sufficiently fond also, of the other world's good things, as became the mistress of a clergyman's house.

'Indeed, yes,' said the Lady Margaretta. 'Frank is very eloquent. When he described our rapid journey from London, he nearly moved me to tears. But well as he talks, I think he carves better.'

'I wish you'd had to do it, Margaretta; both the carving and talking.'

'Thank you, Frank; you're very civil.'

'But there's one comfort, Miss Oriel; it's over now, and done. A fellow can't be made to come of age twice.'

'But you'll take your degree, Mr Gresham; and then, of course, there'll be another speech; and then you'll get married, and then there will be two or three more.'

'I'll speak at your wedding, Miss Oriel, long before I do at my own.'

'I shall not have the slightest objection. It will be so kind of you to patronise my husband.'

'But, by Jove, will he patronise me? I know you'll marry some awful bigwig, or some terribly clever fellow; won't she, Margaretta?'

'Miss Oriel was saying so much in praise of you before you came out,' said Margaretta, 'that I began to think that her mind was intent on remaining at Greshamsbury all her life.'

Frank blushed, and Patience laughed. There was but a year's difference in their age; Frank, however, was still a boy, though Patience was fully a woman.

'I am ambitious, Lady Margaretta,' said she. 'I own it; but I am moderate in my ambition. I do love Greshamsbury, and if Mr Gresham had a younger brother, perhaps, you know – '

'Another just like myself, I suppose,' said Frank.

'Oh, yes. I could not possibly wish for any change.'

'Just as eloquent as you are, Frank,' said the Lady Margaretta.

'And as good a carver,' said Patience.

'Miss Bateson has lost her heart to him for ever, because of his carving,' said the Lady Margaretta.

'But perfection never repeats itself,' said Patience.

'Well, you see, I have not got any brothers,' said Frank; 'so all I can do is to sacrifice myself.'

'Upon my word, Mr Gresham, I am under more than ordinary obligations to you; I am, indeed,' and Miss Oriel stood still in the path, and made a very graceful curtsy. 'Dear me! only think, Lady Margaretta, that I should be honoured with an offer from the heir the very moment he is legally entitled to make one.'

'And done with so much gallantry, too,' said the other;

'expressing himself quite willing to postpone any views of his own for your advantage.'

'Yes,' said Patience; 'that's what I value so much: had he loved me now, there would have been no merit on his part; but a sacrifice you know – '

'Yes, ladies are so fond of such sacrifices. Frank, upon my word, I had no idea you were so very excellent at making speeches.'

'Well,' said Frank, 'I shouldn't have said sacrifice, that was a slip; what I meant was – '

'Oh, dear me,' said Patience, 'wait a minute; now we are going to have a regular declaration. Lady Margaretta, you haven't got a scent-bottle, have you? And if I should faint, where's the garden-chair?'

'Oh, but I'm not going to make a declaration at all,' said Frank.

'Are you not? Oh! Now, Lady Margaretta, I appeal to you; did you not understand him to say something very particular?'

'Certainly, I thought nothing could be plainer,' said the Lady Margaretta.

'And so, Mr Gresham, I am to be told, that after all it means nothing,' said Patience, putting her handkerchief up to her eyes.

'It means that you are an excellent hand at quizzing a fellow like me.'

'Quizzing! No; but you are an excellent hand at deceiving a poor girl like me. Well, remember I have got a witness; here is Lady Margaretta, who heard it all. What a pity it is that my brother is a clergyman. You calculated on that, I know; or you would never have served me so.'

She said so just as her brother had joined them, or rather just as he had joined Lady Margaretta de Courcy; for her ladyship and Mr Oriel walked on in advance by themselves. Lady Margaretta had found it rather dull work, making a third in Miss Oriel's flirtation with her cousin; the more so as she was quite accustomed to take a principal part herself in all such transactions. She therefore not unwillingly walked on with Mr Oriel. Mr Oriel, it must be conceived, was not a common, everyday parson, but had points about him which made him quite fit to associate with an earl's daughter. And as it was known that he was not a marrying man, having very exalted ideas on that point connected with his profession,* the Lady

Margaretta, of course, had the less objection to trust herself alone with him.

But directly she was gone, Miss Oriel's tone of banter ceased. It was very well making a fool of a lad of twenty-one when others were by; but there might be danger in it when they were alone together.

'I don't know any position on earth more enviable than yours, Mr Gresham,' she said, quite soberly and earnestly; 'how happy you ought to be!'

'What, in being laughed at by you, Miss Oriel, for pretending to be a man, when you choose to make out that I am only a boy? I can bear being laughed at pretty well generally, but I can't say that your laughing at me makes me feel so happy as you say I ought to be.'

Frank was evidently of an opinion totally different from that of Miss Oriel. Miss Oriel, when she found herself *tête-à-tête* with him, thought it was time to give over flirting; Frank, however, imagined that it was just the moment for him to begin. So he spoke and looked very languishing, and put on him quite the airs of an Orlando.*

'Oh, Mr Gresham, such good friends as you and I may laugh at each other, may we not?'

'You may do what you like, Miss Oriel: beautiful women I believe always may; but you remember what the spider said to the fly, "That which is sport to you, may be death to me."'* Anyone looking at Frank's face as he said this, might well have imagined that he was breaking his very heart for love of Miss Oriel. Oh, Master Frank! Master Frank! if you act thus in the green leaf, what will you do in the dry?*

While Frank Gresham was thus misbehaving himself, and going on as though to him belonged the privilege of falling in love with pretty faces, as it does to ploughboys and other ordinary people, his great interests were not forgotten by those guardian saints who were so anxious to shower down on his head all manner of temporal blessings.

Another conversation had taken place in the Greshamsbury gardens, in which nothing light had been allowed to present itself; nothing frivolous had been spoken. The countess, the Lady Arabella, and Miss Gresham had been talking over Greshamsbury affairs, and they had latterly been assisted by the Lady Amelia, than whom no De Courcy ever born was more wise, more solemn, more prudent, or more proud. The ponderosity of her qualifications for nobility was sometimes too much even for her mother, and her devotion to the peerage was such, that she would certainly have declined a seat in heaven if offered to her without the promise that it should be in the upper house.

The subject first discussed had been Augusta's prospects. Mr Moffat had been invited to Courcy Castle, and Augusta had been taken thither to meet him, with the express intention on the part of the countess, that they should be man and wife. The countess had been careful to make it intelligible to her sister-in-law and niece, that though Mr Moffat would do excellently well for a daughter of Greshamsbury, he could not be allowed to raise his eyes to a female scion of Courcy Castle.

'Not that we personally dislike him,' said the Lady Amelia; 'but rank has its drawbacks, Augusta.' As the Lady Amelia was now somewhat nearer forty than thirty, and was still allowed to walk

In maiden meditation, fancy free,*

it may be presumed that in her case rank had been found to have serious drawbacks.

To this Augusta said nothing in objection. Whether desirable by a De Courcy or not, the match was to be hers, and there was no doubt whatever as to the wealth of the man whose name she was to take: the offer had been made, not to her, but to her aunt; the acceptance had been expressed, not by her, but by her aunt. Had she thought of recapitulating in her memory all that had ever passed between Mr Moffat and herself, she would have found that it did not amount to more than the most ordinary conversation between chance partners in a ballroom. Nevertheless, she was to be Mrs Moffat. All that Mr Gresham knew of him was, that when he met the young man for the first and only time in his life, he found him extremely hard to deal with in the matter of money. He had insisted on having ten thousand pounds with his wife, and at last refused to go on with the match unless he got six thousand pounds. This latter sum the poor squire had undertaken to pay him.

Mr Moffat had been for a year or two MP for Barchester; having been assisted in his views on that ancient city by all the De Courcy interest. He was a Whig, of course. Not only had Barchester, departing from the light of other days, returned a

Whig member of Parliament, but it was declared, that at the next election, now near at hand, a Radical would be sent up, a man pledged to the ballot, to economies of all sorts, one who would carry out Barchester politics in all their abrupt, obnoxious, pestilent virulence. This was one Scatcherd, a great railway contractor, a man who was a native of Barchester, who had bought property in the neighbourhood, and who had achieved a sort of popularity there and elsewhere by the violence of his democratic opposition to the aristocracy. According to this man's political tenets, the Conservatives should be laughed at as fools, but the Whigs should be hated as knaves.

Mr Moffat was now coming down to Courcy Castle to look after his electioneering interests, and Miss Gresham was to return with her aunt to meet him. The countess was very anxious that Frank should also accompany them. Her great doctrine, that he must marry money, had been laid down with authority and received without doubt. She now pushed it further, and said that no time should be lost; that he should not only marry money, but do so very early in life; there was always danger in delay. The Greshams – of course she alluded only to the males of the family – were foolishly soft-hearted; no one could say what might happen. There was that Miss Thorne always at Greshamsbury.

This was more than the Lady Arabella could stand. She protested that there was at least no ground for supposing that Frank would absolutely disgrace his family.

Still the countess persisted: 'Perhaps not,' she said; 'but when young people of perfectly different ranks were allowed to associate together, there was no saying what danger might arise. They all knew that old Mr Bateson – the present Mr Bateson's father – had gone off with the governess; and young Mr Everbeery, near Taunton, had only the other day married a cook-maid.'

'But Mr Everbeery was always drunk, aunt,' said Augusta, feeling called upon to say something for her brother.

'Never mind, my dear; these things do happen, and they are very dreadful.'

'Horrible!' said the Lady Amelia; 'diluting the best blood of the country, and paving the way for revolutions.' This was very grand; but, nevertheless, Augusta could not but feel that she perhaps might be about to dilute the blood of her coming children in marrying the tailor's son. She consoled herself by trusting that, at any rate, she paved the way for no revolutions.

'When a thing is so necessary,' said the countess, 'it cannot be done too soon. Now, Arabella, I don't say that anything will come of it; but it may: Miss Dunstable is coming down to us next week. Now, we all know that when old Dunstable died last year, he left over two hundred thousand to his daughter.'

'It is a great deal of money, certainly,' said Lady Arabella.

'It would pay off everything, and a great deal more,' said the countess.

'It was ointment,* was it not, aunt?' said Augusta.

'I believe so, my dear; something called the ointment of Lebanon, or something of that sort: but there's no doubt about the money.'

'But how old is she, Rosina?' asked the anxious mother.

'About thirty, I suppose; but I don't think that much signifies.'

'Thirty,' said Lady Arabella, rather dolefully. 'And what is she like? I think that Frank already begins to like girls that are young and pretty.'

'But surely, aunt,' said the Lady Amelia, 'now that he has come to man's discretion, he will not refuse to consider all that he owes to his family. A Mr Gresham of Greshamsbury has a position to support.' The De Courcy scion spoke these last words in the sort of tone that a parish clergyman would use, in warning some young farmer's son that he should not put himself on an equal footing with the ploughboys.

It was at last decided that the countess should herself convey to Frank a special invitation to Courcy Castle, and that when she got him there, she should do all that lay in her power to prevent his return to Cambridge, and to further the Dunstable marriage.

'We did think of Miss Dunstable for Porlock, once,' she said, naïvely: 'but when we found that it wasn't much over two hundred thousand, why, that idea fell to the ground.' The terms on which the De Courcy blood might be allowed to dilute itself were, it must be presumed, very high indeed.

Augusta was sent off to find her brother, and to send him to the countess in the small drawing-room. Here the countess was to have her tea, apart from the outer common world, and here, without interruption, she was to teach her great lesson to her nephew.

Augusta did find her brother, and found him in the worst of bad society – so at least the stern De Courcys would have thought. Old Mr Bateson and the governess, Mr Everbeery and his cook's diluted blood, and ways paved for revolutions, all presented themselves to Augusta's mind when she found her brother walking with no other company than Mary Thorne, and walking with her, too, in much too close proximity.

How he had contrived to be off with the old love and so soon on with the new, or rather, to be off with the new love and again on with the old,* we will not stop to inquire. Had Lady Arabella, in truth, known all her son's doings in this way, could she have guessed how very nigh he had approached to the iniquity of old Mr Bateson, and to the folly of young Mr Everbeery, she would in truth have been in a hurry to send him off to Courcy Castle and Miss Dunstable. Some days before the commencement of our story, young Frank had sworn in sober earnest – in what he intended for his most sober earnest, his most earnest sobriety – that he loved Mary Thorne with a love for which words could find no sufficient expression – with a love that could never die, never grow dim, never become less, which no opposition on the part of others could extinguish, which no opposition on her part should repel; that he might, could, would, and should have her for his wife, and that if she told him she didn't love him, he would –

'Oh, oh! Mary; do you love me? Don't you love me? Won't you love me? Say you will. Oh, Mary, dearest Mary, will you? won't you? do you? don't you? Come now, you have a right to give a fellow an answer.'

With such eloquence had the heir of Greshamsbury, when not yet twenty-one years of age, attempted to possess himself of the affections of the doctor's niece. And yet three days afterwards he was quite ready to flirt with Miss Oriel.

If such things are done in the green wood, what will be done in the dry?

And what had Mary said when these fervent protestations of an undying love had been thrown at her feet? Mary, it must be remembered, was very nearly of the same age as Frank; but, as I and others have so often said before, 'Women grow on the sunny side of the wall.'* Though Frank was only a boy, it behoved Mary to be something more than a girl. Frank might be allowed, without laying himself open to much just reproach, to throw all of what he believed to be his heart into a protestation of what he believed to be love; but Mary was in duty bound to be more thoughtful, more reticent, more aware of the facts of their position, more careful of her own feelings, and more careful also of his.

And yet she could not put him down as another young lady might put down another young gentleman. It is very seldom that a young man, unless he be tipsy, assumes an unwelcome familiarity in his early acquaintance with any girl; but when acquaintance has been long and intimate, familiarity must follow as a matter of course. Frank and Mary had been so much together in his holidays, had so constantly consorted together as boys and girls, that, as regarded her, he had not that innate fear of a woman which represses a young man's tongue; and she was so used to his good-humour, his fun, and high jovial spirits, and was, withal, so fond of them and him, that it was very difficult for her to mark with accurate feeling, and stop with reserved brow, the shade of change from a boy's liking to a man's love.

And Beatrice, too, had done harm in this matter. With a spirit painfully unequal to that of her grand relatives, she had quizzed Mary and Frank about their early flirtations. This she had done; but had instinctively avoided doing so before her mother and sister, and had thus made a secret of it, as it were, between herself, Mary, and her brother; – had given currency, as it were, to the idea that there might be something serious between the two. Not that Beatrice had ever wished to promote a marriage between them, or had even thought of such a thing. She was girlish, thoughtless, imprudent, inartistic, and very unlike a De Courcy. Very unlike a De Courcy she was in all that; but, nevertheless, she had the De Courcy veneration for blood, and, more than that, she had the Gresham feeling joined to that of the De Courcys. The Lady Amelia would not for worlds have had the De Courcy blood defiled; but gold she thought could not defile. Now Beatrice was ashamed of her sister's marriage, and had often declared, within her own heart, that nothing could have made her marry a Mr Moffat.

She had said so also to Mary, and Mary had told her that she was right. Mary also was proud of blood, was proud of her uncle's blood, and the two girls had talked together in all the warmth of girlish confidence, of the great glories of family traditions and family honours. Beatrice had talked in utter ignorance as to her friend's birth; and Mary, poor Mary, she had talked, being as ignorant; but not without a strong suspicion that, at some future time, a day of sorrow would tell her some fearful truth.

On one point Mary's mind was strongly made up. No wealth, no mere worldly advantage could make any one her superior. If she were born a gentlewoman, then was she fit to match with any gentleman. Let the most wealthy man in Europe pour all his wealth at her feet, she could, if so inclined, give him back at any rate more than that. That offered at her feet she knew would never tempt her to yield up the fortress of her heart, the guardianship of her soul, the possession of her mind; not that alone, nor that, even, as any possible slightest fraction of a make-weight.

If she were born a gentlewoman! And then came to her mind those curious questions; what makes a gentleman? what makes a gentlewoman? What is the inner reality, the spiritualized quintessence of that privilege in the world which men call rank, which forces the thousands and hundreds of thousands to bow down before the few elect? What gives, or can give it, or should give it?

And she answered the question. Absolute, intrinsic, acknowledged, individual merit must give it to its possessor, let him be whom, and what, and whence he might. So far the spirit of democracy was strong within her. Beyond this it could be had but by inheritance, received as it were second-hand, or twenty-second-hand. And so far the spirit of aristocracy was strong within her. All this she had, as may be imagined, learnt in early years from her uncle; and all this she was at great pains to teach Beatrice Gresham, the chosen of her heart.

When Frank declared that Mary had a right to give him an answer, he meant that he had a right to expect one. Mary acknowledged this right, and gave it to him.

'Mr Gresham,' she said.

'Oh, Mary; Mr Gresham!'

'Yes, Mr Gresham. It must be Mr Gresham after that. And, moreover, it must be Miss Thorne as well.'

'I'll be shot if it shall, Mary.'

'Well; I can't say that I shall be shot if it be not so; but if it be not so, if you do not agree that it shall be so, I shall be turned out of Greshamsbury.'

'What! you mean my mother?' said Frank.

'Indeed, I mean no such thing,' said Mary, with a flash from her eye that made Frank almost start. 'I mean no such thing. I mean you, not your mother. I am not in the least afraid of Lady Arabella; but I am afraid of you.'

'Afraid of me, Mary!'

'Miss Thorne; pray, pray remember. It must be Miss Thorne. Do not turn me out of Greshamsbury. Do not separate me from Beatrice. It is you that will drive me out; no one else. I could stand my ground against your mother – I feel I could; but I cannot stand against you if you treat me otherwise than – than – '

'Otherwise than what? I want to treat you as the girl I have chosen from all the world as my wife.'

'I am sorry you should so soon have found it necessary to make a choice. But, Mr Gresham, we must not joke about this at present. I am sure you would not willingly injure me; but if you speak to me, or of me, again in that way, you will injure me, injure me so much that I shall be forced to leave Greshamsbury in my own defence. I know you are too generous to drive me to that.'

And so the interview had ended. Frank, of course, went upstairs to see if his new pocket-pistols were all ready, properly cleaned, loaded, and capped, should he find, after a few days' experience, that prolonged existence was unendurable.

However, he managed to live through the subsequent period; doubtless with the view of preventing any disappointment to his father's guests.

CHAPTER VII

The Doctor's Garden

Mary had contrived to quiet her lover with considerable propriety of demeanour. Then came on her the somewhat harder task of quieting herself. Young ladies, on the whole, are perhaps quite as susceptible of the softer feelings as young gentlemen are. Now Frank Gresham was handsome, amiable, by no means a fool in intellect, excellent in heart; and he was, moreover, a gentleman, being the son of Mr Gresham of Greshamsbury. Mary had been, as it were, brought up to love him. Had aught but good happened to him, she would have cried as for a brother. It must not therefore be supposed that when Frank Gresham told her that he loved her, she had not heard it altogether unconcerned.

He had not, perhaps, made his declaration with that propriety of language in which such scenes are generally described as being carried on. Ladies may perhaps think that Mary should have been deterred, by the very boyishness of his manner, from thinking at all seriously on the subject. His 'will you, won't you – do you, don't you?' does not sound like the poetic raptures of a highly inspired lover. But, nevertheless, there had been warmth, and a reality in it not in itself repulsive; and Mary's anger – anger? no, not anger – her objections to the declaration were probably not based on the absurdity of her lover's language.

We are inclined to think that these matters are not always discussed by mortal lovers in the poetically passionate phraseology which is generally thought to be appropriate for their description. A man cannot well describe that which he has never seen nor heard; but the absolute words and acts of one such scene did once come to the author's knowledge. The couple were by no means plebeian, or below the proper standard of high bearing and high breeding; they were a handsome pair, living among educated people, sufficiently given to mental pursuits, and in every way what a pair of polite lovers ought to be. The all-important conversation passed in this wise. The site of the passionate scene was the seashore, on which they were walking, in autumn.

Gentleman. 'Well, Miss – , the long and the short of it is this: here I am; you can take me or leave me.'

Lady – scratching a gutter on the sand with her parasol, so as to allow a little salt water to run out of one hole into another. 'Of course, I know that's all nonsense.'

Gentleman. 'Nonsense! By Jove, it isn't nonsense at all: come, Jane; here I am: come, at any rate you can say something.'

Lady. 'Yes, I suppose I can say something.'

Gentleman. 'Well, which is it to be; take me or leave me?'

Lady – very slowly, and with a voice perhaps hardly articulate, carrying on, at the same time, her engineering works on a wider scale. 'Well, I don't exactly want to leave you.'

And so the matter was settled: settled with much propriety and satisfaction; and both the lady and gentleman would have thought, had they ever thought about the matter at all, that this, the sweetest moment of their lives, had been graced by all the poetry by which such moments ought to be hallowed.*

When Mary had, as she thought, properly subdued young Frank, the offer of whose love she, at any rate, knew was, at such a period of his life, an utter absurdity, then she found it necessary to subdue herself. What happiness on earth could be greater than the possession of such a lover, had the true possession been justly and honestly within her reach? What man could be more lovable than such a man as would grow from such a boy? And then, did she not love him, – love him already, without waiting for any change? Did she not feel that there was that about him, about him and about herself, too, which might so well fit them for each other? It would be so sweet to be the sister of Beatrice, the daughter of the squire, to belong to Greshamsbury as a part and parcel of itself.

But though she could not restrain these thoughts, it never for a moment occurred to her to take Frank's offer in earnest. Though she was a grown woman, he was still a boy. He would have to see the world before he settled in it, and would change his mind about woman half a score of times before he married. Then, too, though she did not like the Lady Arabella, she felt that she owed something, if not to her kindness, at least to her forbearance; and she knew, felt inwardly certain, that she would be doing wrong, that the world would say she was doing wrong, that her uncle would think her wrong, if she endeavoured to take advantage of what had passed.

She had not for an instant doubted; not for a moment had she contemplated it as possible that she should ever become Mrs Gresham because Frank had offered to make her so; but, nevertheless, she could not help thinking of what had occurred – of thinking of it, most probably much more than Frank did himself.

A day or two afterwards, on the evening before Frank's birthday, she was alone with her uncle, walking in the garden behind their house, and she then essayed to question him, with the object of learning if she were fitted by her birth to be the

wife of such a one as Frank Gresham. They were in the habit of
walking there together when he happened to be at home of a
summer's evening. This was not often the case, for his hours of
labour extended much beyond those usual to the upper working
world, the hours, namely, between breakfast and dinner; but
those minutes that they did thus pass together, the doctor
regarded as perhaps the pleasantest of his life.

'Uncle,' said she, after a while, 'what do you think of this
marriage of Miss Gresham's?'

'Well, Minnie' – such was his name of endearment for her – 'I
can't say I have thought much about it, and I don't suppose
anybody else has either.'

'She must think about it, of course; and so must he, I suppose.'

'I'm not sure of that. Some folks would never get married if
they had to trouble themselves with thinking about it.'

'I suppose that's why you never got married, uncle?'

'Either that, or thinking of it too much. One is as bad as the
other.'

Mary had not contrived to get at all near her point as yet; so
she had to draw off, and after a while begin again.

'Well, I have been thinking about it, at any rate, uncle.'

'That's very good of you; that will save me the trouble: and
perhaps save Miss Gresham too. If you have thought it over
thoroughly, that will do for all.'

'I believe Mr Moffat is a man of no family.'

'He'll mend in that point, no doubt, when he has got a wife.'

'Uncle, you're a goose: and what is worse, a very provoking
goose.'

'Niece, you're a gander; and what is worse, a very silly gander.
What is Mr Moffat's family to you and me? Mr Moffat has that
which ranks above family honours. He is a very rich man.'

'Yes,' said Mary, 'I know he is rich; and a rich man I suppose
can buy everything – except a woman that is worth having.'

'A rich man can buy anything,' said the doctor; 'not that I
meant to say that Mr Moffat has bought Miss Gresham. I have
no doubt that they will suit each other very well,' he added with
an air of decisive authority, as though he had finished the
subject.

But his niece was determined not to let him pass so. 'Now,
uncle,' said she, 'you know you are pretending to a great deal of

worldly wisdom, which, after all, is not wisdom at all in your eyes.'

'Am I?'

'You know you are: and as for the impropriety of discussing Miss Gresham's marriage – '

'I did not say it was improper.'

'Oh, yes, you did; of course such things must be discussed. How is one to have an opinion if one does not get it by looking at the things which happen around us?'

'Now I am going to be blown up,' said Dr Thorne.

'Dear uncle, do be serious with me.'

'Well, then, seriously, I hope Miss Gresham will be very happy as Mrs Moffat.'

'Of course you do: so do I. I hope it as much as I can hope what I don't at all see ground for expecting.'

'People constantly hope without any such ground.'

'Well, then, I'll hope in this case. But, uncle – '

'Well, my dear?'

'I want your opinion, truly and really. If you were a girl – '

'I am perfectly unable to give any opinion founded on so strange an hypothesis.'

'Well; but if you were a marrying man.'

'The hypothesis is quite as much out of my way.'

'But, uncle, I am a girl, and perhaps I may marry; – or at any rate think of marrying some day.'

'The latter alternative is certainly possible enough.'

'Therefore, in seeing a friend take such a step, I cannot but speculate on the matter as though I were myself in her place. If I were Miss Gresham, should I be right?'

'But, Minnie, you are not Miss Gresham.'

'No, I am Mary Thorne; it is a very different thing, I know. I suppose *I* might marry any one without degrading myself.'

It was almost ill-natured of her to say this; but she had not meant to say it in the sense which the sounds seemed to bear. She had failed in being able to bring her uncle to the point she wished by the road she had planned, and in seeking another road, she had abruptly fallen into unpleasant places.*

'I should be very sorry that my niece should think so,' said he; 'and am sorry, too, that she should say so. But, Mary, to tell the truth, I hardly know at what you are driving. You are, I think, not so clear minded – certainly, not so clear worded – as is usual with you.'

'I will tell you, uncle;' and, instead of looking up into his face, she turned her eyes down on the green lawn beneath their feet.

'Well, Minnie, what is it?' and he took both her hands in his.

'I think that Miss Gresham should not marry Mr Moffat. I think so because her family is high and noble, and because his is low and ignoble. When one has an opinion on such matters, one cannot but apply it to things and people around one; and having applied my opinion to her, the next step naturally is to apply it to myself. Were I Miss Gresham, I would not marry Mr Moffat though he rolled in gold. I know where to rank Miss Gresham. What I want to know is, where I ought to rank myself?'

They had been standing when she commenced her last speech; but as she finished it, the doctor moved on again, and she moved with him. He walked on slowly without answering her; and she, out of her full mind, pursued aloud the tenor of her thoughts.

'If a woman feels that she would not lower herself by marrying in a rank beneath herself, she ought also to feel that she would not lower a man that she might love by allowing him to marry into a rank beneath his own – that is, to marry her.'

'That does not follow,' said the doctor quickly. 'A man raises a woman to his own standard, but a woman must take that of the man she marries.'

Again they were silent, and again they walked on, Mary holding her uncle's arm with both her hands. She was determined however to come to the point, and after considering for a while how best she might do it, she ceased to beat any longer about the bush, and asked him a plain question.

'The Thornes are as good a family as the Greshams, are they not?'

'In absolute genealogy they are, my dear. That is, when I choose to be an old fool and talk of such matters in a sense different from that in which they are spoken of by the world at large, I may say that the Thornes are as good, or perhaps better, than the Greshams; but I should be sorry to say so seriously to any one. The Greshams now stand much higher in the county than the Thornes do.'

'But they are of the same class.'

'Yes, yes; Wilfred Thorne, of Ullathorne, and our friend the squire here, are of the same class.'

'But, uncle, I and Augusta Gresham – are we of the same class?'

'Well, Minnie, you would hardly have me boast that I am of the same class with the squire – I, a poor country doctor?'

'You are not answering me fairly, dear uncle; dearest uncle, do you not know that you are not answering me fairly? You know what I mean. Have I a right to call the Thornes of Ullathorne my cousins?'

'Mary, Mary, Mary!' said he, after a minute's pause, still allowing his arm to hang loose, that she might hold it with both her hands. 'Mary, Mary, Mary I would that you had spared me this!'

'I could not have spared it to you for ever, uncle.'

'I would that you could have done so; I would that you could!'

'It is over now, uncle: it is told now; I will grieve you no more. Dear, dear, dearest! I should love you more than ever now; I would, I would, I would if that were possible. What should I be but for you? What must I have been but for you?' And she threw herself on his breast, and clinging with her arms round his neck, kissed his forehead, cheeks, and lips.

There was nothing more then said on the subject between them. Mary asked no further question, nor did the doctor volunteer further information. She would have been most anxious to ask about her mother's history had she dared to do so; but she did not dare to ask; she could not bear to be told that her mother had been, perhaps was, a worthless woman. That she was truly a daughter of a brother of the doctor, that she did know. Little as she had heard of her relatives in her early youth, few as had been the words which had fallen from her uncle in her hearing as to her parentage, she did know this, that she was the daughter of Henry Thorne, a brother of the doctor and a son of the old prebendary. Trifling little things that had occurred, accidents which could not be prevented, had told her this; but not a word had ever passed any one's lips as to her mother. The doctor, when speaking of his youth, had spoken of her father; but no one had spoken of her mother. She had long known that she was a child of a Thorne; now she knew also that she was no cousin of the Thornes of Ullathorne; no cousin, at least, in the world's ordinary language, no niece indeed of her uncle, unless by his special permission that she should be so.

When the interview was over, she went up alone to the drawing-room, and there she sat thinking. She had not been there long before her uncle came up to her. He did not sit down, or even take off the hat which he still wore; but coming close to her, and still standing, he spoke thus: –

'Mary, after what has passed I should be very unjust and very cruel not to tell you one thing more than you have now learned. Your mother was unfortunate in much, not in everything; but the world, which is very often stern in such matters, never judged her to have disgraced herself. I tell you this, my child, in order that you may respect her memory;' and so saying, he again left her without giving her time to speak a word.

What he then told her he had told her in mercy. He felt what must be her feelings when she reflected that she had to blush for her mother; that not only could she not speak of her mother, but that she might hardly think of her with innocence; and to mitigate such sorrow as this, and also to do justice to the woman whom his brother had so wronged, he had forced himself to reveal so much as is stated above.

And then he walked slowly by himself, backwards and forwards through the garden, thinking of what he had done with reference to this girl, and doubting whether he had done wisely and well. He had resolved, when first the little infant was given over to his charge, that nothing should be known of her or by her as to her mother. He was willing to devote himself to this orphan child of his brother, this last chance seedling of his father's house; but he was not willing so to do this as to bring himself in any manner into familiar contact with the Scatcherds. He had boasted to himself that he, at any rate, was a gentleman; and that she, if she were to live in his house, sit at his table, and share his hearth, must be a lady. He would tell no lie about her; he would not to any one make her out to be aught other or aught better than she was; people would talk about her of course, only let them not talk to him; he conceived of himself – and the conception was not without due ground – that should any do so, he had that within him which would silence them. He would never claim for this little creature – thus brought into the world without a legitimate position in which to stand – he would never claim for her any station that would not properly be her own. He would make for her a station as best he could. As he might sink or swim, so should she.

So he had resolved; but things had arranged themselves, as they often do, rather than been arranged by him. During ten or twelve years no one had heard of Mary Thorne; the memory of Henry Thorne and his tragic death had passed away; the knowledge that an infant had been born whose birth was connected with that tragedy, a knowledge never widely spread, had faded down into utter ignorance. At the end of these twelve years, Dr Thorne had announced, that a young niece, a child of a brother long since dead, was coming to live with him. As he had contemplated, no one spoke to him; but some people did no doubt talk among themselves. Whether or not the exact truth was surmised by any, it matters not to say; with absolute exactness, probably not; with great approach to it, probably yes. By one person, at any rate, no guess whatever was made; no thought relative to Dr Thorne's niece ever troubled him; no idea that Mary Scatcherd had left a child in England ever occurred to him; and that person was Roger Scatcherd, Mary's brother.

To one friend, and one only, did the doctor tell the whole truth, and that was to the squire. 'I have told you,' said the doctor, 'partly that you may know that the child has no right to mix with your children if you think much of such things. Do you, however, see to this. I would rather that no one else should be told.'

No one else had been told; and the squire had 'seen to it,' by accustoming himself to look at Mary Thorne running about the house with his own children as though she were one of the same brood. Indeed, the squire had always been fond of Mary, had personally noticed her, and, in the affair of Mam'selle Larron, had declared that he would have her placed at once on the bench of magistrates; – much to the disgust of the Lady Arabella.

And so things had gone on and on, and had not been thought of with much downright thinking; till now, when she was one-and-twenty years of age, his niece came to him, asking as to her position, and inquiring in what rank of life she was to look for a husband.

And so the doctor walked backwards and forwards through his garden, slowly, thinking now with some earnestness what if, after all, he had been wrong about his niece? What if by endeavouring to place her in the position of a lady, he had falsely so placed her, and robbed her of all legitimate position?

What if there was no rank of life to which she could now properly attach herself?

And then, how had it answered, that plan of his of keeping her all to himself? He, Dr Thorne, was still a poor man; the gift of saving money had not been his; he had ever had a comfortable house for her to live in, and, in spite of Doctors Fillgrave, Century, Rerechild, and others, had made from his profession an income sufficient for their joint wants; but he had not done as others do: he had no three or four thousand pounds in the Three per Cents., on which Mary might live in some comfort when he should die. Late in life he had insured his life for eight hundred pounds; and to that, and that only, had he to trust for Mary's future maintenance. How had it answered, then, this plan of letting her be unknown to, and undreamed of by, those who were as near to her on her mother's side as he was on the father's? On that side, though there had been utter poverty, there was now absolute wealth.

But when he took her to himself, had he not rescued her from the very depths of the lowest misery: from the degradation of the workhouse; from the scorn of honest-born charity-children; from the lowest of this world's low conditions? Was she not now the apple of his eye, his one great sovereign comfort – his pride, his happiness, his glory? Was he to make her over, to make any portion of her over to others, if, by doing so, she might be able to share the wealth, as well as the coarse manners and uncouth society of her at present unknown connexions? He, who had never worshipped wealth on his own behalf; he, who had scorned the idol of gold, and had ever been teaching her to scorn it; was he now to show that his philosophy had all been false as soon as the temptation to do so was put in his way?

But yet, what man would marry this bastard child, without a sixpence, and bring not only poverty, but ill blood also on his own children? It might be very well for him, Dr Thorne; for him whose career was made, whose name, at any rate, was his own; for him who had a fixed standing-ground in the world; it might be well for him to indulge in large views of a philosophy antagonistic to the world's practice; but had he a right to do it for his niece? What man would marry a girl so placed? For those among whom she might have legitimately found a level, education had now utterly unfitted her. And then, he well knew that she would never put out her hand in token of love to any one without telling all she knew and all she surmised as to her own birth.

And that question of this evening; had it not been instigated by some appeal to her heart? Was there not already within her breast some cause for disquietude which had made her so pertinacious? Why else had she told him then, then for the first time, that she did not know where to rank herself? If such appeal had been made to her, it must have come from young Frank Gresham. What, in such case, would it behove him to do? Should he pack up his all, his lancet-cases, pestle and mortar, and seek anew fresh ground in a new world, leaving behind a huge triumph to those learned enemies of his, Fillgrave, Century, and Rerechild? Better that than remain at Greshamsbury at the cost of his child's heart and pride.

And so he walked slowly backwards and forwards through his garden, meditating these things painfully enough.

CHAPTER VIII

Matrimonial Prospects

It will of course be remembered that Mary's interview with the other girls at Greshamsbury took place some two or three days subsequently to Frank's generous offer of his hand and heart. Mary had quite made up her mind that the whole thing was to be regarded as a folly, and that it was not to be spoken of to any one; but yet her heart was sore enough. She was full of pride, and yet she knew she must bow her neck to the pride of others. Being, as she was herself, nameless, she could not but feel a stern, unflinching antagonism, the antagonism of a democrat, to the pretensions of others who were blessed with that of which she had been deprived. She had this feeling; and yet, of all things that she coveted, she most coveted that, for glorying in which, she was determined to heap scorn on others. She said to herself, proudly, that God's handiwork was the inner man, the inner woman, the naked creature animated by a living soul; that all other adjuncts were but man's clothing for the creature; all others, whether stitched by tailors or contrived by kings. Was it not within her capacity to do as nobly, to love as truly, to worship her God in heaven with as perfect a faith, and her god on earth with as leal a troth, as though blood had descended to her purely through scores of purely born progenitors? So to herself she spoke; and yet, as she said it, she knew that were she a man, such a man as the heir of Greshamsbury should be, nothing should tempt her to sully her children's blood by mating herself with any one that was base born. She felt that were she an Augusta Gresham, no Mr Moffat, let his wealth be what it might, should win her hand unless he too could tell of family honours and a line of ancestors.

And so, with a mind at war with itself, she came forth armed to do battle against the world's prejudices, those prejudices she herself still loved so well.

And was she to give up her old affections, her feminine loves, because she found that she was cousin to nobody? Was she no longer to pour out her heart to Beatrice Gresham with all the girlish volubility of an equal? Was she to be severed from Patience Oriel, and banished – or rather was she to banish herself – from the free place she had maintained in the various youthful female conclaves held within that parish of Greshamsbury?

Hitherto, what Mary Thorne would say, what Miss Thorne suggested in such or such a matter, was quite as frequently asked as any opinion from Augusta Gresham – quite as frequently, unless when it chanced that any of the De Courcy girls were at the house. Was this to be given up? These feelings had grown up among them since they were children, and had not hitherto been questioned among them. Now they were questioned by Mary Thorne. Was she in fact to find that her position had been a false one, and must be changed?

Such had been her feelings when she protested that she would not be Augusta Gresham's bridesmaid, and offered to put her neck beneath Beatrice's foot; when she drove the Lady Margaretta out of the room, and gave her own opinion as to the proper grammatical construction of the word humble; such also had been her feelings when she kept her hand so rigidly to herself while Frank held the dining-room door open for her to pass through.

'Patience Oriel,' said she to herself, 'can talk to him of her father and mother: let Patience take his hand; let her talk to him;' and then, not long afterwards, she saw that Patience did talk to him; and seeing it, she walked along silent, among some of the old people, and with much effort did prevent a tear from falling down her cheek.

But why was the tear in her eye? Had she not proudly told Frank that his love-making was nothing but a boy's silly rhapsody? Had she not said so while she had yet reason to hope that her blood was as good as his own? Had she not seen at a glance that his love tirade was worthy of ridicule, and of no other notice? And yet there was a tear now in her eye because this boy, whom she had scolded from her, whose hand, offered in pure friendship, she had just refused, because he, so rebuffed by her, had carried his fun and gallantry to one who would be less cross to him!

She could hear as she was walking, that while Lady Margaretta was with them, their voices were loud and merry; and her sharp ear could also hear, when Lady Margaretta left them, that Frank's voice became low and tender. So she walked on, saying nothing, looking straight before her, and by degrees separating herself from all the others.

The Greshamsbury grounds were on one side somewhat too closely hemmed in by the village. On this side was a path running the length of one of the streets of the village; and far down the path, near to the extremity of the gardens, and near also to a wicket-gate which led out into the village, and which could be opened from the inside, was a seat, under a big yew-tree, from which, through a breach in the houses, might be seen the parish church, standing in the park on the other side. Hither Mary walked alone, and here she seated herself, determined to get rid of her tears and their traces before she again showed herself to the world.

'I shall never be happy here again,' she said to herself; 'never. I am no longer one of them, and I cannot live among them unless I am so.' And then an idea came across her mind that she hated Patience Oriel; and then, instantly another idea followed it – quick as such thoughts are quick – that she did not hate Patience Oriel at all; that she liked her, nay, loved her; that Patience Oriel was a sweet girl; and that she hoped the time would come when she might see her the lady of Greshamsbury. And then the tear, which had been no whit controlled, which indeed had now made itself master of her, came to a head, and, bursting through the floodgates of the eye, came rolling down, and in its fall, wetted her hand as it lay on her lap. 'What a fool! what an idiot! what an empty-headed cowardly fool I am!' said she, springing up from the bench on her feet.

As she did so, she heard voices close to her, at the little gate. They were those of her uncle and Frank Gresham.

'God bless you, Frank!' said the doctor, as he passed out of the grounds. 'You will excuse a lecture, won't you, from so old a friend? – though you are a man now, and discreet, of course, by Act of Parliament.'

'Indeed I will, doctor,' said Frank. 'I will excuse a longer lecture than that from you.'

'At any rate it won't be tonight,' said the doctor, as he disappeared. 'And if you see Mary, tell her that I am obliged to go; and that I will send Janet down to fetch her.'

Now Janet was the doctor's ancient maid-servant.

Mary could not move on without being perceived; she therefore stood still till she heard the click of the door, and then began walking rapidly back to the house by the path which had brought her thither. The moment, however, that she did so, she found that she was followed; and in a very few minutes Frank was alongside of her.

'Oh, Mary!' said he, calling to her, but not loudly, before he quite overtook her, 'how odd that I should come across you just when I have a message for you! and why are you all alone?'

Mary's first impulse was to reiterate her command to him to call her no more by her Christian name; but her second impulse told her that such an injunction at the present moment would not be prudent on her part. The traces of her tears were still there; and she well knew that a very little, the slightest show of tenderness on his part, the slightest effort on her own to appear indifferent, would bring down more than one other such intruder. It would, moreover, be better for her to drop all outward sign that she remembered what had taken place. So long, then, as he and she were at Greshamsbury together, he should call her Mary if he pleased. He would soon be gone; and while he remained, she would keep out of his way.

'Your uncle has been obliged to go away to see an old woman at Silverbridge.'

'At Silverbridge! why, he won't be back all night. Why could not the old woman send for Dr Century?'

'I suppose she thought two old women could not get on well together.'

Mary could not help smiling. She did not like her uncle going off so late on such a journey; but it was always felt as a triumph when he was invited into the strongholds of his enemies.

'And Janet is to come over for you. However, I told him it was quite unnecessary to disturb another old woman, for that I should of course see you home.'

'Oh, no, Mr Gresham; indeed you'll not do that.'

'Indeed, and indeed, I shall.'

'What! on this great day, when every lady is looking for you, and talking of you. I suppose you want to set the countess against me for ever. Think, too, how angry Lady Arabella will be if you are absent on such an errand as this.'

'To hear you talk, Mary, one would think that you were going to Silverbridge yourself.'

'Perhaps I am.'

'If I did not go with you, some of the other fellows would. John, or George –'

'Good gracious, Frank! Fancy either of the Mr De Courcys walking home with me!'

She had forgotten herself, and the strict propriety on which she had resolved, in the impossibility of forgoing her little joke against the De Courcy grandeur; she had forgotten herself, and had called him Frank in her old, former, eager, free tone of voice; and then, remembering she had done so, she drew herself up, bit her lips, and determined to be doubly on her guard for the future.

'Well, it shall be either one of them or I,' said Frank: 'perhaps you would prefer my cousin George to me?'

'I should prefer Janet to either, seeing that with her I should not suffer the extreme nuisance of knowing that I was a bore.'

'A bore! Mary, to me?'

'Yes, Mr Gresham, a bore to you. Having to walk home through the mud with village young ladies is boring. All gentlemen feel it to be so.'

'There is no mud; if there were you would not be allowed to walk at all.'

'Oh! village young ladies never care for such things, though fashionable gentlemen do.'

'I would carry you home, Mary, if it would do you a service,' said Frank, with considerable pathos in his voice.

'Oh, dear me! pray do not, Mr Gresham. I should not like it at all,' said she: 'a wheelbarrow would be preferable to that.'

'Of course. Anything would be preferable to my arm, I know.'

'Certainly; anything in the way of a conveyance. If I were to act baby, and you were to act nurse, it really would not be comfortable for either of us.'

Frank Gresham felt disconcerted, though he hardly knew why. He was striving to say something tender to his lady-love; but every word that he spoke she turned into joke. Mary did not answer him coldly or unkindly; but, nevertheless, he was displeased. One does not like to have one's little offerings of sentimental service turned into burlesque when one is in love in earnest. Mary's jokes had appeared so easy too; they seemed to come from a heart so little troubled. This, also, was cause of vexation to Frank. If he could but have known all, he would, perhaps, have been better pleased.

He determined not to be absolutely laughed out of his tenderness. When, three days ago, he had been repulsed, he had gone away owning to himself that he had been beaten; owning so much, but owning it with great sorrow and much shame. Since that he had come of age; since that he had made speeches, and speeches had been made to him; since that he had gained courage by flirting with Patience Oriel. No faint heart ever won a fair lady, as he was well aware; he resolved, therefore, that his heart should not be faint, and that he would see whether the fair lady might not be won by becoming audacity.

'Mary,' said he, stopping in the path – for they were now near the spot where it broke out upon the lawn, and they could already hear the voices of the guests – 'Mary, you are unkind to me.'

'I am not aware of it, Mr Gresham; but if I am, do not you retaliate. I am weaker than you, and in your power; do not you, therefore, be unkind to me.'

'You refused my hand just now,' continued he. 'Of all the people here at Greshamsbury, you are the only one that has not wished me joy; the only one – '

'I do wish you joy; I will wish you joy; there is my hand,' and she frankly put out her ungloved hand. 'You are quite man enough to understand me: there is my hand; I trust you to use it only as it is meant to be used.'

He took it in his and pressed it cordially, as he might have done that of any other friend in such a case; and then – did not drop it as he should have done. He was not a St Anthony,* and it was most imprudent in Miss Thorne to subject him to such a temptation.

'Mary,' said he; 'dear Mary! dearest Mary! if you did but know how I love you!'

As he said this, holding Miss Thorne's hand, he stood on the pathway with his back towards the lawn and house, and, therefore, did not at first see his sister Augusta, who had just at that moment come upon them. Mary blushed up to her straw hat, and, with a quick jerk, recovered her hand. Augusta saw the motion, and Mary saw that Augusta had seen it.

From my tedious way of telling it, the reader will be led to imagine that the hand-squeezing had been protracted to a duration quite incompatible with any objection to such an arrangement on the part of the lady; but the fault is all mine: in no part hers. Were I possessed of a quick spasmodic style of narrative,* I should have been able to include it all – Frank's misbehaviour, Mary's immediate anger, Augusta's arrival, and keen, Argus-eyed* inspection, and then Mary's subsequent misery – in five words and half a dozen dashes and inverted commas. The thing should have been so told; for, to do Mary justice, she did not leave her hand in Frank's a moment longer than she could help herself.

Frank, feeling the hand withdrawn, and hearing, when it was too late, the step on the gravel, turned sharply round. 'Oh, it's you, is it, Augusta? Well, what do you want?'

Augusta was not naturally very ill-natured, seeing that in her veins the high De Courcy blood was somewhat tempered by an admixture of the Gresham attributes; nor was she predisposed to make her brother her enemy by publishing to the world any of his little tender peccadilloes; but she could not but bethink herself of what her aunt had been saying as to the danger of any such encounters as that she had just now beheld; she could not but start at seeing her brother thus, on the very brink of the precipice of which the countess had specially forewarned her mother. She, Augusta, was, as she well knew, doing her duty by her family in marrying a tailor's son for whom she did not care a chip, seeing the tailor's son was possessed of untold wealth. Now when one member of a household is making a struggle for a family, it is painful to see the benefit of that struggle negatived by the folly of another member. The future Mrs Moffat did feel aggrieved by the fatuity of the young heir, and, consequently, took upon herself to look as much like her Aunt De Courcy as she could do.

'Well, what is it?' said Frank, looking rather disgusted. 'What makes you stick your chin up and look in that way?' Frank had hitherto been rather a despot among his sisters, and forgot that the eldest of them was now passing altogether from under his sway to that of the tailor's son.

'Frank,' said Augusta, in a tone of voice which did honour to the great lessons she had lately received, 'Aunt De Courcy wants to see you immediately in the small drawing-room;' and, as she said so, she resolved to say a few words of advice to Miss Thorne as soon as her brother should have left them.

'In the small drawing-room, does she? Well, Mary, we may as well go together, for I suppose it is tea-time now.'

'You had better go at once, Frank,' said Augusta; 'the countess will be angry if you keep her waiting. She has been expecting you these twenty minutes. Mary Thorne and I can return together.'

There was something in the tone in which the words, 'Mary Thorne,' were uttered, which made Mary at once draw herself up. 'I hope,' said she, 'that Mary Thorne will never be any hindrance to either of you.'

Frank's ear had also perceived that there was something in the tone of his sister's voice not boding comfort to Mary; he perceived that the De Courcy blood in Augusta's veins was already rebelling against the doctor's niece on his part, though it had condescended to submit itself to the tailor's son on her own part.

'Well, I am going,' said he; 'but look here, Augusta, if you say one word of Mary – '

Oh, Frank! Frank! you boy, you very boy! you goose, you silly goose! Is that the way you make love, desiring one girl not to tell of another, as though you were three children, tearing your frocks and trousers in getting through the same hedge together? Oh, Frank! Frank! you, the full-blown heir of Greshambury? You, a man already endowed with a man's discretion? You, the forward rider, that did but now threaten young Harry Baker and the Honourable John to eclipse them by prowess in the field? You, of age? Why, thou canst not as yet have left thy mother's apron-string!

'If you say one word of Mary – '

So far had he got in his injunction to his sister, but further than that, in such a case, was he never destined to proceed. Mary's indignation flashed upon him, striking him dumb long before the sound of her voice reached his ears; and yet she spoke as quick as the words would come to her call, and somewhat loudly too.

'Say one word of Mary, Mr Gresham! And why should she not say as many words of Mary as she may please? I must tell you all now, Augusta! and I must also beg you not to be silent for my sake. As far as I am concerned, tell it to whom you please. This is the second time your brother – '

'Mary, Mary,' said Frank, deprecating her loquacity.

'I beg your pardon, Mr Gresham; you have made it necessary that I should tell your sister all. He has now twice thought it well to amuse himself by saying to me words which it was ill-natured in him to speak, and – '

'Ill-natured, Mary!'

'Ill-natured in him to speak,' continued Mary, 'and to which it would be absurd for me to listen. He probably does the same to others,' she added, being unable in heart to forget that sharpest of her wounds, that flirtation of his with Patience Oriel; 'but to me it is almost cruel. Another girl might laugh at him, or listen to him, as she would choose; but I can do neither. I shall now keep away from Greshamsbury, at any rate till he has left it; and, Augusta, I can only beg you to understand, that, as far as I am concerned, there is nothing which may not be told to all the world.'

And, so saying, she walked on a little in advance of them, as proud as a queen. Had Lady de Courcy herself met her at that moment, she would almost have felt herself forced to shrink out of the pathway. 'Not say a word of me!' she repeated to herself, but still out loud. 'No word need be left unsaid on my account; none, none.'

Augusta followed her, dumbfounded at her indignation; and Frank also followed, but not in silence. When his first surprise at Mary's great anger was over, he felt himself called upon to say some word that might tend to exonerate his lady-love; and some word also of protestation as to his own purpose.

'There is nothing to be told, nothing, at least, of Mary,' he said, speaking to his sister; 'but of me, you may tell this, if you choose to disoblige your brother – that I love Mary Thorne with all my heart; and that I will never love any one else.'

By this time they had reached the lawn, and Mary was able to turn away from the path which led up to the house. As she left them she said in a voice, now low enough, 'I cannot prevent him from talking nonsense, Augusta; but you will bear me witness, that I do not willingly hear it.' And, so saying, she started off almost in a run towards a distant part of the gardens, in which she saw Beatrice.

Frank, as he walked up to the house with his sister, endeavoured to induce her to give him a promise that she would tell no tales as to what she had heard and seen.

'Of course, Frank, it must be all nonsense,' she had said; 'and you shouldn't amuse yourself in such a way.'

'Well, but, Guss, come, we have always been friends; don't let us quarrel just when you are going to be married.' But Augusta would make no promise.

Frank, when he reached the house, found the countess waiting for him, sitting in the little drawing-room by herself, – somewhat impatiently. As he entered he became aware that there was some peculiar gravity attached to the coming interview. Three persons, his mother, one of his younger sisters, and the Lady Amelia, each stopped him to let him know that the countess was waiting; and he perceived that a sort of guard was kept upon the door to save her ladyship from any undesirable intrusion.

The countess frowned at the moment of his entrance, but soon smoothed her brow, and invited him to take a chair ready prepared for him opposite to the elbow of the sofa on which she was leaning. She had a small table before her, on which was her teacup, so that she was able to preach to him nearly as well as though she had been ensconced in a pulpit.

'My dear Frank,' said she, in a voice thoroughly suitable to the importance of the communication, 'you have today come of age.'

Frank remarked that he understood that such was the case, and added that, 'that was the reason of all the fuss.'

'Yes; you have today come of age. Perhaps I should have been glad to see such an occasion noticed at Greshamsbury with some more suitable signs of rejoicing.'

'Oh, aunt! I think we did it all very well.'

'Greshamsbury, Frank, is, or at any rate ought to be, the seat of the first commoner in Barsetshire.'

'Well; so it is. I am quite sure there isn't a better fellow than father anywhere in the county.'

The countess sighed. Her opinion of the poor squire was very different from Frank's. 'It is no use now,' said she, 'looking back to that which cannot be cured. The first commoner in Barsetshire should hold a position – I will not of course say equal to that of a peer.'

'Oh dear, no; of course not,' said Frank; and a bystander might have thought that there was a touch of satire in his tone.

'No, not equal to that of a peer; but still of very paramount importance. Of course my first ambition is bound up in Porlock.'

'Of course,' said Frank, thinking how very weak was the staff on which his aunt's ambition rested; for Lord Porlock's youthful career had not been such as to give unmitigated satisfaction to his parents.

'Is bound up in Porlock:' and then the countess plumed herself; but the mother sighed. 'And next to Porlock, Frank, my anxiety is about you.'

'Upon my honour, aunt, I am very much obliged. I shall be all right, you'll see.'

'Greshamsbury, my dear boy, is not now what it used to be.

'Isn't it?' asked Frank.

'No, Frank; by no means. I do not wish to say a word to you against your father. It may, perhaps, have been his misfortune, rather than his fault – '

'She is always down on the governor; always,' said Frank to himself; resolving to stick bravely to the side of the house to which he had elected to belong.

'But there is the fact, Frank, too plain to us all; Greshamsbury is not what it was. It is your duty to restore it to its former importance.'

'My duty!' said Frank, rather puzzled.

'Yes, Frank, your duty. It all depends on you now. Of course you know that your father owes a great deal of money.'

Frank muttered something. Tidings had in some shape

reached his ears that his father was not comfortably circumstanced as regarded money.

'And then, he has sold Boxall Hill. It cannot be expected that Boxall Hill shall be repurchased, as some horrid man, a railway maker, I believe – '

'Yes; that's Scatcherd.'

'Well, he has built a house there I'm told; so I presume that it cannot be bought back: but it will be your duty, Frank, to pay all the debts that there are on the property, and to purchase what, at any rate, will be equal to Boxall Hill.'

Frank opened his eyes wide and stared at his aunt, as though doubting much whether or no she were in her right mind. He pay off the family debts! He buy up property of four thousand pounds a year! He remained, however, quite quiet, waiting the elucidation of the mystery.

'Frank, of course you understand me.'

Frank was obliged to declare, that just at the present moment he did not find his aunt so clear as usual.

'You have but one line of conduct left you, Frank: your position, as heir to Greshamsbury, is a good one; but your father has unfortunately so hampered you with regard to money, that unless you set the matter right yourself, you can never enjoy that position. Of course you must marry money.'

'Marry money!' said he, considering for the first time that in all probability Mary Thorne's fortune would not be extensive. 'Marry money!'

'Yes, Frank. I know no man whose position so imperatively demands it; and luckily for you, no man can have more facility for doing so. In the first place you are very handsome.'

Frank blushed like a girl of sixteen.

'And then, as the matter is made plain to you at so early an age, you are not of course hampered by any indiscreet tie; by any absurd engagement.'

Frank blushed again; and then saying to himself, 'How much the old girl knows about it!' felt a little proud of his passion for Mary Thorne, and of the declaration he had made to her.

'And your connexion with Courcy Castle,' continued the countess, now carrying up the list of Frank's advantages to its great climax, 'will make the matter so easy for you, that, really, you will hardly have any difficulty.'

Frank could but say how much obliged he felt to Courcy Castle and its inmates.

'Of course I would not wish to interfere with you in any underhand way, Frank; but I will tell you what has occurred to me. You have heard, probably, of Miss Dunstable?'

'The daughter of the ointment of Lebanon man?'

'And of course you know that her fortune is immense,' continued the countess, not deigning to notice her nephew's allusion to the ointment. 'Quite immense when compared with the wants and position of any commoner. Now she is coming to Courcy Castle, and I wish you to come and meet her.'

'But, aunt, just at this moment I have to read for my degree like anything. I go up, you know, in October.'

'Degree!' said the countess. 'Why, Frank, I am talking to you of your prospects in life, of your future position, of that on which everything hangs, and you tell me of your degree!'

Frank, however, obstinately persisted that he must take his degree, and that he should commence reading hard at six a.m. tomorrow morning.

'You can read just as well at Courcy Castle. Miss Dunstable will not interfere with that said his aunt, who knew the expediency of yielding occasionally; 'but I must beg you will come over and meet her. You will find her a most charming young woman, remarkably well educated I am told, and – '

'How old is she?' asked Frank.

'I really cannot say exactly,' said the countess; 'but it is not, I imagine, matter of much moment.'

'Is she thirty?' asked Frank, who looked upon an unmarried woman of that age as quite an old maid.

'I dare say she may be about that age,' said the countess, who regarded the subject from a very different point of view.

'Thirty!' said Frank out loud, but speaking, nevertheless, as though to himself.

'It is a matter of no moment,' said his aunt, almost angrily. 'When the subject itself is of such vital importance, objections of no real weight should not be brought into view. If you wish to hold up your head in the country; if you wish to represent your county in Parliament, as has been done by your father, your grandfather, and your great-grandfathers; if you wish to keep a house over your head, and to leave Greshamsbury to your son after you, you must marry money. What does it signify whether Miss Dunstable be twenty-eight or thirty? She has got money; and if you marry her, you may then consider that your position in life is made.'

Frank was astonished at his aunt's eloquence; but, in spite of that eloquence, he made up his mind that he would not marry Miss Dunstable. How could he, indeed, seeing that his troth was already plighted to Mary Thorne in the presence of his sister? This circumstance, however, he did not choose to plead to his aunt, so he recapitulated any other objections that presented themselves to his mind.

In the first place, he was so anxious about his degree that he could not think of marrying at present; then he suggested that it might be better to postpone the question till the season's hunting should be over; he declared that he could not visit Courcy Castle till he got a new suit of clothes home from the tailor; and ultimately remembered that he had a particular engagement to go fly-fishing with Mr Oriel on that day week.

None, however, of these valid reasons were sufficiently potent to turn the countess from her point.

'Nonsense, Frank,' said she, 'I wonder that you can talk of fly-fishing when the prosperity of Greshamsbury is at stake. You will go with Augusta and myself to Courcy Castle tomorrow.'

'Tomorrow, aunt!' he said, in the tone in which a condemned criminal might make his ejaculation on hearing that a very near day had been named for execution. 'Tomorrow!'

'Yes, we return tomorrow, and shall be happy to have your company. My friends, including Miss Dunstable, come on Thursday. I am quite sure you will like Miss Dunstable. I have settled all that with your mother, so we need say nothing further about it. And now, good night, Frank.'

Frank, finding that there was nothing more to be said, took his departure, and went out to look for Mary. But Mary had gone home with Janet half an hour since, so he betook himself to his sister Beatrice.

'Beatrice,' said he, 'I am to go to Courcy Castle tomorrow.'

'So I heard mamma say.'

'Well; I only came of age today, and I will not begin by running counter to them. But I tell you what, I won't stay above a week at Courcy Castle for all the De Courcys in Barsetshire. Tell me, Beatrice, did you ever hear of a Miss Dunstable?'

CHAPTER IX

Sir Roger Scatcherd

Enough has been said in this narrative to explain to the reader that Roger Scatcherd, who was whilom a drunken stone-mason in Barchester, and who had been so prompt to avenge the injury done to his sister, had become a great man in the world. He had become a contractor, first for little things, such as half a mile or so of a railway embankment, or three or four canal bridges, and then a contractor for great things, such as Government hospitals, locks, docks, and quays, and had latterly had in his hands the making of whole lines of railway.

He had been occasionally in partnership with one man for one thing, and then with another for another; but had, on the whole, kept his own interests to himself, and now at the time of our story, he was a very rich man.

And he had acquired more than wealth. There had been a time when the Government wanted the immediate performance of some extraordinary piece of work, and Roger Scatcherd had been the man to do it. There had been some extremely necessary bit of a railway to be made in half the time that such work would properly demand, some speculation to be incurred requiring great means and courage as well, and Roger Scatcherd had been found to be the man for the time. He was then elevated for the moment to the dizzy pinnacle of a newspaper hero, and became one of those 'whom the king delighteth to honour.'* He went up one day to Court to kiss Her Majesty's hand, and came down to his new grand house at Boxall Hill, Sir Roger Scatcherd, Bart.

'And now, my lady,' said he, when he explained to his wife the high state to which she had been called by his exertions and the Queen's prerogative, 'let's have a bit of dinner and a drop of som'at hot.' Now the drop of som'at hot signified a dose of alcohol sufficient to send three ordinary men very drunk to bed.

While conquering the world Roger Scatcherd had not conquered his old bad habits. Indeed, he was the same man at all points that he had been when formerly seen about the streets of Barchester with his stone-mason's apron tucked up round his waist. The apron he had abandoned, but not the heavy promi-

nent thoughtful brow, with the wildly flashing eye beneath it.
He was still the same good companion, and still also the same
hard-working hero. In this only had he changed, that now he
would work, and some said equally well, whether he were drunk
or sober. Those who were mostly inclined to make a miracle of
him – and there was a school of worshippers ready to adore him
as their idea of a divine, superhuman, miracle-moving, inspired
prophet – declared that his wondrous work was best done, his
calculations most quickly and most truly made, that he saw with
most accurate eye into the far-distant balance of profit and loss,
when he was under the influence of the rosy god.* To these
worshippers his breakings-out, as his periods of intemperance
were called in his own set, were his moments of peculiar
inspiration – his divine frenzies, in which he communicated
most closely with those deities who preside over trade transactions; his Eleusinian mysteries,* to approach him in which was
permitted only to a few of the most favoured.

'Scatcherd has been drunk this week past,' they would say
one to another, when the moment came at which it was to be
decided whose offer should be accepted for constructing a
harbour to hold all the commerce of Lancashire, or to make a
railway from Bombay to Canton. 'Scatcherd has been drunk this
week past: I am told that he has taken over three gallons of
brandy.' And then they felt sure that none but Scatcherd would
be called upon to construct the dock or make the railway.

But be this as it may, be it true or false that Sir Roger was
most efficacious when in his cups, there can be no doubt that he
could not wallow for a week in brandy, six or seven times every
year, without in great measure injuring, and permanently injuring, the outward man. Whatever immediate effect such symposiums might have on the inner mind – symposiums indeed
they were not; posiums* I will call them, if I may be allowed;
for in latter life, when he drank heavily, he drank alone –
however little for evil, or however much for good the working
of his brain might be affected, his body suffered greatly. It was
not that he became feeble or emaciated, old-looking or inactive,
that his hand shook, or that his eye was watery; but that in the
moments of his intemperance his life was often not worth a
day's purchase. The frame which God had given to him was
powerful beyond the power of ordinary men; powerful to act in
spite of these violent perturbations; powerful to repress and

conquer the qualms and headaches and inward sicknesses to which the votaries of Bacchus are ordinarily subject; but this power was not without its limit. If encroached on too far, it would break and fall and come asunder, and then the strong man would at once become a corpse.

Scatcherd had but one friend in the world. And, indeed, this friend was no friend in the ordinary acceptance of the word. He neither ate with him nor drank with him, nor even frequently talked with him. Their pursuits in life were wide asunder. Their tastes were all different. The society in which each moved very seldom came together. Scatcherd had nothing in unison with this solitary friend; but he trusted him, and he trusted no other living creature on God's earth.

He trusted this man; but even him he did not trust thoroughly; not at least as one friend should trust another. He believed that this man would not rob him; would probably not lie to him; would not endeavour to make money of him; would not count him up or speculate on him, and make out a balance of profit and loss; and, therefore, he determined to use him. But he put no trust whatever in his friend's counsel, in his modes of thought; none in his theory, and none in his practice. He disliked his friend's counsel, and, in fact, disliked his society, for his friend was somewhat apt to speak to him in a manner approaching to severity. Now Roger Scatcherd had done many things in the world, and made much money; whereas his friend had done but few things, and made no money. It was not to be endured that the practical, efficient man should be taken to task by the man who proved himself to be neither practical nor efficient; not to be endured, certainly, by Roger Scatcherd, who looked on men of his own class as the men of the day, and on himself as by no means the least among them.

The friend was our friend Dr Thorne.

The doctor's first acquaintance with Scatcherd has been already explained. He was necessarily thrown into communication with the man at the time of the trial, and Scatcherd then had not only sufficient sense, but sufficient feeling also to know that the doctor behaved very well. This communication had in different ways been kept up between them. Soon after the trial Scatcherd had begun to rise, and his first savings had been intrusted to the doctor's care. This had been the beginning of a pecuniary connexion which had never wholly ceased, and which had led to the purchase of Boxall Hill, and to the loan of large sums of money to the squire.

In another way also there had been a close alliance between them, and one not always of a very pleasant description. The doctor was, and long had been, Sir Roger's medical attendant, and, in his unceasing attempts to rescue the drunkard from the fate which was so much to be dreaded, he not unfrequently was driven into a quarrel with his patient.

One thing further must be told of Sir Roger. In politics he was as violent a Radical as ever, and was very anxious to obtain a position in which he could bring his violence to bear. With this view he was about to contest his native borough of Barchester, in the hope of being returned in opposition to the De Courcy candidate; and with this object he had now come down to Boxall Hill.

Nor were his claims to sit for Barchester such as could be despised. If money were to be of avail, he had plenty of it, and was prepared to spend it; whereas, rumour said that Mr Moffat was equally determined to do nothing so foolish. Then again, Sir Roger had a sort of rough eloquence, and was able to address the men of Barchester in language that would come home to their hearts, in words that would endear him to one party while they made him offensively odious to the other; but Mr Moffat could make neither friends nor enemies by his eloquence. The Barchester roughs called him a dumb dog that could not bark, and sometimes sarcastically added that neither could he bite. The De Courcy interest, however, was at his back, and he had also the advantage of possession. Sir Roger, therefore, knew that the battle was not to be won without a struggle.

Dr Thorne got safely back from Silverbridge that evening, and found Mary waiting to give him his tea. He had been called there to a consultation with Dr Century, that amiable old gentleman having so far fallen away from the high Fillgrave tenets as to consent to the occasional endurance of such degradation.

The next morning he breakfasted early, and, having mounted his strong iron-grey cob, started for Boxall Hill. Not only had he there to negotiate the squire's further loan, but also to exercise his medical skill. Sir Roger having been declared contractor for cutting a canal from sea to sea, through the Isthmus of Panama,* had been making a week of it; and the result was that Lady Scatcherd had written rather peremptorily to her husband's medical friend.

The doctor consequently trotted off to Boxall Hill on his iron-grey cob. Among his other merits was that of being a good horseman, and he did much of his work on horseback. The fact that he occasionally took a day with the East Barsetshires, and that when he did so he thoroughly enjoyed it, had probably not failed to add something to the strength of the squire's friendship.

'Well, my lady, how is he? Not much the matter, I hope?' said the doctor, as he shook hands with the titled mistress of Boxall Hill in a small breakfast-parlour in the rear of the house. The showrooms of Boxall Hill were furnished most magnificently, but they were set apart for company; and as the company never came – seeing that they were never invited – the grand rooms and the grand furniture were not of much material use to Lady Scatcherd.

'Indeed then, doctor, he's just bad enough,' said her ladyship, not in a very happy tone of voice; 'just bad enough. There's been a some'at at the back of his head, rapping, and rapping, and rapping; and if you don't do something, I'm thinking it will rap him too hard yet.'

'Is he in bed?'

'Why, yes, he is in bed; for when he was first took he couldn't very well help hisself, so we put him to bed. And then, he don't seem to be quite right yet about the legs, so he hasn't got up; but he's got that Winterbones with him to write for him, and when Winterbones is there, Scatcherd might as well be up for any good that bed'll do him.'

Mr Winterbones was confidential clerk to Sir Roger. That is to say, he was a writing-machine of which Sir Roger made use to do certain work which could not well be adjusted without some such contrivance. He was a little, withered, dissipated, broken-down man, whom gin and poverty had nearly burnt to a cinder, and dried to an ash. Mind he had none left, nor care for earthly things, except the smallest modicum of substantial food, and the largest allowance of liquid sustenance. All that he had ever known he had forgotten, except how to count up figures and to write: the results of his counting and his writing never stayed by him from one hour to another; nay, not from one folio to another. Let him, however, be adequately screwed up with gin, and adequately screwed down by the presence of his master, and then no amount of counting and writing would be too much for him. This was Mr Winterbones, confidential clerk to the great Sir Roger Scatcherd.

'We must send Winterbones away, I take it,' said the doctor.

'Indeed, doctor, I wish you would. I wish you'd send him to Bath, or anywhere else out of the way. There is Scatcherd, he takes brandy; and there is Winterbones, he takes gin; and it'd puzzle a woman to say which is worst, master or man.'

It will be seen from this, that Lady Scatcherd and the doctor were on very familiar terms as regarded her little domestic inconveniences.

'Tell Sir Roger I am here, will you?' said the doctor.

'You'll take a drop of sherry before you go up?' said the lady.

'Not a drop, thank you,' said the doctor.

'Or, perhaps, a little cordial?'

'Not a drop of anything, thank you; I never do, you know.'

'Just a thimbleful of this?' said the lady, producing from some recess under the sideboard a bottle of brandy; 'just a thimbleful? It's what he takes himself.'

When Lady Scatcherd found that even this argument failed, she led the way to the great man's bedroom.

'Well, doctor! well, doctor! well, doctor!' was the greeting with which our son of Galen was saluted some time before he entered the sick-room. His approaching step was heard, and thus the *ci-devant** Barchester stonemason saluted his coming friend. The voice was loud and powerful, but not clear and sonorous. What voice that is nurtured on brandy can ever be clear? It had about it a peculiar huskiness, a dissipated guttural tone, which Thorne immediately recognised, and recognised as being more marked, more guttural, and more husky than heretofore.

'So you've smelt me out, have you, and come for your fee? Ha! ha! ha! Well, I have had a sharpish bout of it, as her ladyship there no doubt has told you. Let her alone to make the worst of it. But, you see, you're too late, man. I've bilked the old gentleman again, without troubling you.'

'Any way, I'm glad you're something better, Scatcherd.'

'Something! I don't know what you call something. I never was better in my life. Ask Winterbones there.'

'Indeed, now, Scatcherd, you ain't; you're bad enough if you only knew it. And as for Winterbones, he has no business here up in your bedroom, which stinks of gin so, it does. Don't you believe him, doctor; he ain't well, nor yet nigh well.'

Winterbones, when the above ill-natured allusion was made to the aroma coming from his libations, might be seen to deposit surreptitiously beneath the little table at which he sat, the cup with which he had performed them.

The doctor, in the meantime, had taken Sir Roger's hand on the pretext of feeling his pulse, but was drawing quite as much information from the touch of the sick man's skin, and the look of the sick man's eye.

'I think Mr Winterbones had better go back to the London office,' said he. 'Lady Scatcherd will be your best clerk for some little time, Sir Roger.'

'Then I'll be d – if Mr Winterbones does anything of the kind,' said he; 'so there's an end of that.'

'Very well,' said the doctor. 'A man can die but once. It is my duty to suggest measures for putting off the ceremony as long as possible. Perhaps, however, you may wish to hasten it.'

'Well, I am not very anxious about it, one way or the other,' said Scatcherd. And as he spoke there came a fierce gleam from his eye, which seemed to say – 'If that's the bugbear with which you wish to frighten me, you will find that you are mistaken.'

'Now, doctor, don't let him talk that way, don't,' said Lady Scatcherd, with her handkerchief to her eyes.

'Now, my lady, do you cut it; cut at once,' said Sir Roger, turning hastily round to his better-half; and his better-half, knowing that the province of a woman is to obey, did cut it. But as she went she gave the doctor a pull by the coat sleeve, so that thereby his healing faculties might be sharpened to the very utmost.

'The best woman in the world, doctor; the very best,' said he, as the door closed behind the wife of his bosom.

'I'm sure of it,' said the doctor.

'Yes, till you find a better one,' said Scatcherd. 'Ha! ha! ha! but good or bad, there are some things which a woman can't understand, and some things which she ought not to be let to understand.'

'It's natural she should be anxious about your health, you know.'

'I don't know that,' said the contractor. 'She'll be very well off. All that whining won't keep a man alive, at any rate.'

There then was a pause, during which the doctor continued his medical examination. To this the patient submitted with a bad grace, but still he did submit.

'We must turn over a new leaf, Sir Roger; indeed we must.'

'Bother,' said Sir Roger.

'Well, Scatcherd; I must do my duty to you, whether you like it or not.'

'That is to say, I am to pay you for trying to frighten me.'

'No human nature can stand such shocks as these much longer.'

'Winterbones,' said the contractor, turning to his clerk, 'go down, go down, I say; but don't be out of the way. If you go to the public-house, by G – , you may stay there for me. When I take a drop, – that is if I ever do, it does not stand in the way of work.' So Mr Winterbones, picking up his cup again, and concealing it in some way beneath his coat flap, retreated out of the room, and the two friends were alone.

'Scatcherd,' said the doctor, 'you have been as near your God, as any man ever was who afterwards ate and drank in this world.'

'Have I, now?' said the railway hero, apparently somewhat startled.

'Indeed you have; indeed you have.'

'And now I'm all right again?'

'All right! How can you be all right, when you know that your limbs refuse to carry you? All right! why the blood is still beating round your brain with a violence that would destroy any other brain but yours.'

'Ha! ha! ha!' laughed Scatcherd. He was very proud of thinking himself to be differently organised from other men. 'Ha! ha! ha! Well, and what am I to do now?'

The whole of the doctor's prescription we will not give at length. To some of his ordinances Sir Roger promised obedience; to others he objected violently, and to one or two he flatly refused to listen. The great stumbling-block was this, that total abstinence from business for two weeks was enjoined; and that it was impossible, so Sir Roger said, that he should abstain for two days.

'If you work,' said the doctor, 'in your present state, you will certainly have recourse to the stimulus of drink; and if you drink, most assuredly you will die.'

'Stimulus! Why, do you think I can't work without Dutch courage?'

'Scatcherd, I know that there is brandy in the room at this moment, and that you have been taking it within these two hours.'

'You smell that fellow's gin,' said Scatcherd.

'I feel the alcohol working within your veins,' said the doctor, who still had his hand on his patient's arm.

Sir Roger turned himself roughly in the bed so as to get away from his Mentor,* and then he began to threaten in his turn.

'I'll tell you what it is, doctor; I've made up my mind, and I'll do it. I'll send for Fillgrave.'

'Very well,' said he of Greshamsbury, 'send for Fillgrave. Your case is one in which even he can hardly go wrong.'

'You think you can hector me, and do as you like because you had me under your thumb in other days. You're a very good fellow, Thorne, but I ain't sure that you are the best doctor in all England.'

'You may be sure I am not; you may take me for the worst if you will. But while I am here as your medical adviser, I can only tell you the truth to the best of my thinking. Now the truth is this, that another bout of drinking will in all probability kill you; and any recourse to stimulus in your present condition may do so.'

'I'll send for Fillgrave – '

'Well, send for Fillgrave, only do it at once. Believe me at any rate in this, that whatever you do, you should do at once. Oblige me in this; let Lady Scatcherd take away that brandy bottle till Dr Fillgrave comes.'

'I'm d – if I do. Do you think I can't have a bottle of brandy in my room without swigging?'

'I think you'll be less likely to swig it if you can't get at it.'

Sir Roger made another angry turn in his bed as well as his half-paralysed limbs would let him; and then, after a few moments' peace, renewed his threats with increased violence.

'Yes; I'll have Fillgrave over here. If a man be ill, really ill, he should have the best advice he can get. I'll have Fillgrave, and I'll have that other fellow from Silverbridge to meet him. What's his name? – Century.'

The doctor turned his head away; for though the occasion

was serious, he could not help smiling at the malicious vengeance with which his friend proposed to gratify himself.

'I will; and Rerechild too. What's the expense? I suppose five or six pound apiece will do it; eh, Thorne?'

'Oh, yes; that will be liberal I should say. But, Sir Roger, will you allow me to suggest what you ought to do? I don't know how far you may be joking –'

'Joking!' shouted the baronet; 'you tell a man he's dying and joking in the same breath. You'll find I'm not joking.'

'Well, I dare say not. But if you have not full confidence in me –'

'I have no confidence in you at all.'

'Then why not send to London? Expense is no object to you.'

'It is an object; a great object.'

'Nonsense! Send to London for Sir Omicron Pie: send for some man whom you will really trust when you see him.'

'There's not one of the lot I'd trust as soon as Fillgrave. I've known Fillgrave all my life, and I trust him. I'll send for Fillgrave and put my case in his hands. If any one can do anything for me, Fillgrave is the man.'

'Then in God's name send for Fillgrave,' said the doctor. 'And now goodbye, Scatcherd; and as you do send for him, give him a fair chance. Do not destroy yourself by more brandy before he comes.'

'That's my affair, and his; not yours,' said the patient.

'So be it: give me your hand, at any rate, before I go. I wish you well through it, and when you are well, I'll come and see you.'

'Good-bye – good-bye; and look here, Thorne, you'll be talking to Lady Scatcherd downstairs, I know; now, no nonsense. You understand me, eh? no nonsense, you know.'

CHAPTER X

Sir Roger's Will

Dr Thorne left the room and went downstairs, being fully aware that he could not leave the house without having some communication with Lady Scatcherd. He was no sooner within the passage than he heard the sick man's bell ring violently; and then the servant, passing him on the staircase, received orders to send a mounted messenger immediately to Barchester. Dr Fillgrave was to be summoned to come as quickly as possible to the sick man's room, and Mr Winterbones was to be sent up to write the note.

Sir Roger was quite right in supposing that there would be some words between the doctor and her ladyship. How, indeed, was the doctor to get out of the house without such, let him wish it ever so much? There were words; and these were protracted, while the doctor's cob was being ordered round, till very many were uttered which the contractor would probably have regarded as nonsense.

Lady Scatcherd was no fit associate for the wives of English baronets; – was no doubt by education and manners much better fitted to sit in their servants' halls; but not on that account was she a bad wife or a bad woman. She was painfully, fearfully anxious for that husband of hers, whom she honoured and worshipped, as it behoved her to do, above all other men. She was fearfully anxious as to his life, and faithfully believed, that if any man could prolong it, it was that old and faithful friend whom she had known to be true to her lord since their early married troubles.

When, therefore, she found that he had been dismissed, and that a stranger was to be sent for in his place, her heart sank low within her.

'But, doctor,' she said, with her apron up to her eyes, 'you ain't going to leave him, are you?'

Dr Thorne did not find it easy to explain to her ladyship that medical etiquette would not permit him to remain in attendance on her husband, after he had been dismissed and another physician called in his place.

'Etiquette!' said she, crying. 'What's etiquette to do with it when a man is a-killing hisself with brandy?'

'Fillgrave will forbid that quite as strongly as I can do.'

'Fillgrave!' said she. 'Fiddlestick! Fillgrave, indeed!'

Dr Thorne could almost have embraced her for the strong feeling of thorough confidence on the one side, and thorough distrust on the other, which she contrived to throw into those few words.

'I'll tell you what, doctor; I won't let the messenger go. I'll bear the brunt of it. He can't do much now he ain't up, you know. I'll stop the boy; we won't have no Fillgraves here.'

This, however, was a step to which Dr Thorne would not assent. He endeavoured to explain to the anxious wife, that after what had passed he could not tender his medical services till they were again asked for.

'But you can slip in as a friend, you know; and then by degrees you can come round him, eh? can't you now, doctor? And as to the payment – '

All that Dr Thorne said on the subject may easily be imagined. And in this way, and in partaking of the lunch which was forced upon him, an hour had nearly passed between his leaving Sir Roger's bedroom and putting his foot into the stirrup. But no sooner had the cob begun to move on the gravel-sweep before the house, than one of the upper windows opened, and the doctor was summoned to another conference with the sick man.

'He says you are to come back, whether or no,' said Mr Winterbones, screeching out of the window, and putting all his emphasis on the last words.

'Thorne! Thorne! Thorne!' shouted the sick man from his sick-bed, so loudly that the doctor heard him, seated as he was on horseback out before the house.

'You're to come back, whether or no,' repeated Winterbones, with more emphasis, evidently conceiving that there was a strength of injunction in that 'whether or no' which would be found quite invincible.

Whether actuated by these magic words, or by some internal process of thought, we will not say; but the doctor did slowly, and as though unwillingly, dismount again from his steed, and slowly retrace his steps into the house.

'It is no use,' said he to himself, 'for that messenger has already gone to Barchester.'

'I have sent for Dr Fillgrave,' were the first words which the contractor said to him when he again found himself by the bedside.

'Did you call me back to tell me that?' said Thorne, who now really felt angry at the impertinent petulance of the man before him: 'you should consider, Scatcherd, that my time may be of value to others, if not to you.'

'Now don't be angry, old fellow,' said Scatcherd, turning to him, and looking at him with a countenance quite different from any that he had shown that day: a countenance in which there was a show of manhood, – some show also of affection. 'You ain't angry now because I've sent for Fillgrave?'

'Not in the least,' said the doctor, very complacently. 'Not in the least. Fillgrave will do you as much good as I can do for you.'

'And that's none at all, I suppose; eh, Thorne?'

'That depends on yourself. He will do you good if you will tell him the truth, and will then be guided by him. Your wife, your servant, any one can be as good a doctor to you as either he or I; as good, that is, in the main point. But you have sent for Fillgrave now; and of course you must see him. I have much to do, and you must let me go.'

Scatcherd, however, would not let him go, but held his hand fast. 'Thorne,' said he, 'if you like it, I'll make them put Fillgrave under the pump directly he comes here. I will indeed, and pay all the damage myself.'

This was another proposition to which the doctor could not consent; but he was utterly unable to refrain from laughing. There was an earnest look of entreaty about Sir Roger's face as he made the suggestion; and, joined to this, there was a gleam of comic satisfaction in his eye which seemed to promise, that if he received the least encouragement he would put his threat into execution. Now our doctor was not inclined to taking any steps towards subjecting his learned brother to pump discipline; but he could not but admit to himself that the idea was not a bad one.

'I'll have it done, I will, by heavens! if you'll only say the word,' protested Sir Roger.

But the doctor did not say the word, and so the idea passed off.

'You shouldn't be testy with a man when he's ill,' said

Scatcherd, still holding the doctor's hand, of which he had again got possession; 'specially not an old friend; and specially again when you've been a-blowing of him up.'

It was not worth the doctor's while to aver that the testiness had all been on the other side, and that he had never lost his good-humour; so he merely smiled, and asked Sir Roger if he could do anything further for him.

'Indeed you can, doctor; and that's why I sent for you, – why I sent for you yesterday. Get out of the room, Winterbones,' he then said, gruffly, as though he were dismissing from his chamber a dirty dog. Winterbones, not a whit offended, again hid his cup under his coat-tail and vanished.

'Sit down, Thorne, sit down,' said the contractor, speaking quite in a different manner from any that he had yet assumed. 'I know you're in a hurry, but you must give me half an hour. I may be dead before you can give me another; who knows?'

The doctor of course declared that he hoped to have many a half-hour's chat with him for many a year to come.

'Well, that's as may be. You must stop now, at any rate. You can make the cob pay for it, you know.'

The doctor took a chair and sat down. Thus entreated to stop, he had hardly any alternative but to do so.

'It wasn't because I'm ill that I sent for you, or rather let her ladyship send for you. Lord bless you, Thorne; do you think I don't know what it is that makes me like this? When I see that poor wretch, Winterbones, killing himself with gin, do you think I don't know what's coming to myself as well as him?'

'Why do you take it then? Why do you do it? Your life is not like his. Oh, Scatcherd! Scatcherd!' and the doctor prepared to pour out the flood of his eloquence in beseeching this singular man to abstain from his well-known poison.

'Is that all you know of human nature, doctor? Abstain. Can you abstain from breathing, and live like a fish does under water?'

'But Nature has not ordered you to drink, Scatcherd.'

'Habit is second nature, man; and a stronger nature than the first. And why should I not drink? What else has the world given me for all that I have done for it? What other resource have I? What other gratification?'

'Oh, my God! Have you not unbounded wealth? Can you not do anything you wish? be anything you choose?'

'No,' and the sick man shrieked with an energy that made him audible all through the house. 'I can do nothing that I would choose to do; be nothing that I would wish to be! What can I do? What can I be? What gratification can I have except the brandy bottle? If I go among gentlemen, can I talk to them? If they have anything to say about a railway, they will ask me a question: if they speak to me beyond that, I must be dumb. If I go among my workmen, can they talk to me? No; I am their master, and a stern master. They bob their heads and shake in their shoes when they see me. Where are my friends? Here!' said he, and he dragged a bottle from under his very pillow. 'Where are my amusements? Here!' and he brandished the bottle almost in the doctor's face. 'Where is my one resource, my one gratification, my only comfort after all my toils? Here, doctor; here, here, here!' and, so saying, he replaced his treasure beneath his pillow.

There was something so horrifying in this, that Dr Thorne shrank back amazed, and was for a moment unable to speak.

'But, Scatcherd,' he said at last; 'surely you would not die for such a passion as that?'

'Die for it? Aye, would I. Live for it while I can live; and die for it when I can live no longer. Die for it! What is that for a man to do? Do not men die for a shilling a day? What is a man the worse for dying? What can I be the worse for dying? A man can die but once, you said just now. I'd die ten times for this.'

'You are speaking now either in madness, or else in folly, to startle me.'

'Folly enough, perhaps, and madness enough, also. Such a life as mine makes a man a fool, and makes him mad, too. What have I about me that I should be afraid to die? I'm worth three hundred thousand pounds; and I'd give it all to be able to go to work tomorrow with a hod and mortar, and have a fellow clap his hand upon my shoulder, and say: "Well, Roger, shall us have that 'ere other halfpint this morning?" I'll tell you what, Thorne, when a man has made three hundred thousand pounds, there's nothing left for him but to die. It's all he's good for then. When money's been made, the next thing is to spend it. Now the man who makes it has not the heart to do that.'

The doctor, of course, in hearing all this, said something of a tendency to comfort and console the mind of his patient. Not that anything he could say would comfort or console the man;

but that it was impossible to sit there and hear such fearful truths – for as regarded Scatcherd they were truths – without making some answer.

'This is as good as a play, isn't it, doctor?' said the baronet. 'You didn't know how I could come out like one of those actor fellows. Well, now, come; at last I'll tell you why I have sent for you. Before that last burst of mine I made my will.'

'You had a will made before that.'

'Yes, I had. That will is destroyed. I burnt it with my own hand, so that there should be no mistake about it. In that will I had named two executors, you and Jackson. I was then partner with Jackson in the York and Yeovil Grand Central. I thought a deal of Jackson then. He's not worth a shilling now.'

'Well, I'm exactly in the same category.'

'No, you're not. Jackson is nothing without money; but money'll never make you.'

'No, nor I shan't make money,' said the doctor.

'No, you never will. Nevertheless, there's my other will, there, under that desk there; and I've put you in as sole executor.'

'You must alter that, Scatcherd; you must indeed; with three hundred thousand pounds to be disposed of, the trust is far too much for any one man: besides you must name a younger man; you and I are of the same age, and I may die the first.'

Now, doctor, doctor, no humbug; let's have no humbug from you. Remember this: if you're not true, you're nothing.'

'Well, but, Scatcherd – '

'Well, but, doctor, there's the will, it's already made. I don't want to consult you about that. You are named as executor, and if you have the heart to refuse the act when I'm dead, why, of course you can do so.'

The doctor was no lawyer, and hardly knew whether he had any means of extricating himself from this position in which his friend was determined to place him.

'You'll have to see that will carried out, Thorne. Now I'll tell you what I have done.'

'You're not going to tell me how you've disposed of your property?'

'Not exactly; at least not all of it. One hundred thousand I've left in legacies, including, you know, what Lady Scatcherd will have.'

'Have you not left the house to Lady Scatcherd?'

'No; what the devil would she do with a house like this? She doesn't know how to live in it now she has got it. I have provided for her; it matters not how. The house and the estate, and the remainder of my money, I have left to Louis Philippe.'

'What! two hundred thousand pounds?' said the doctor.

'And why shouldn't I leave two hundred thousand pounds to my son, even to my eldest son if I had more than one? Does not Mr Gresham leave all his property to his heir? Why should not I make an eldest son as well as Lord de Courcy or the Duke of Omnium? I suppose a railway contractor ought not to be allowed an eldest son by Act of Parliament! Won't my son have a title to keep up? And that's more than the Greshams have among them.'

The doctor explained away what he said as well as he could. He could not explain that what he had really meant was this, that Sir Roger Scatcherd's son was not a man fit to be trusted with the entire control of an enormous fortune.

Sir Roger Scatcherd had but one child; that child which had been born in the days of his early troubles, and had been dismissed from his mother's breast in order that the mother's milk might nourish the young heir of Greshamsbury. The boy had grown up, but had become strong neither in mind nor body. His father had determined to make a gentleman of him, and had sent him to Eton and to Cambridge. But even this receipt, generally as it is recognised, will not make a gentleman. It is hard, indeed, to define what receipt will do so, though people do have in their own minds some certain undefined, but yet tolerably correct ideas on the subject. Be that as it may, two years at Eton, and three terms at Cambridge, did not make a gentleman of Louis Philippe Scatcherd.

Yes; he was christened Louis Philippe, after the King of the French.* If one wishes to look out in the world for royal nomenclature, to find children who have been christened after kings and queens, or the uncles and aunts of kings and queens, the search should be made in the families of democrats. None have so servile a deference for the very nail-parings of royalty; none feel so wondering an awe at the exaltation of a crowned head; none are so anxious to secure to themselves some shred or fragment that has been consecrated by the royal touch. It is the distance which they feel to exist between themselves and the throne which makes them covet the crumbs of majesty, the odds and ends and chance splinters of royalty.

There was nothing royal about Louis Philippe Scatcherd but his name. He had now come to man's estate, and his father, finding the Cambridge receipt to be inefficacious, had sent him abroad to travel with a tutor. The doctor had from time to time heard tidings of this youth; he knew that he had already shown symptoms of his father's vices, but no symptoms of his father's talents; he knew that he had begun life by being dissipated, without being generous; and that at the age of twenty-one he had already suffered from delirium tremens.

It was on this account that he had expressed disapprobation, rather than surprise, when he heard that his father intended to bequeath the bulk of his large fortune to the uncontrolled will of this unfortunate boy.

'I have toiled for my money hard, and I have a right to do as I like with it. What other satisfaction can it give me?'

The doctor assured him that he did not at all mean to dispute this.

'Louis Philippe will do well enough, you'll find,' continued the baronet, understanding what was passing within his companion's breast. 'Let a young fellow sow his wild oats while he is young, and he'll be steady enough when he grows old.'

'But what if he never lives to get through the sowing?' thought the doctor to himself. 'What if that wild-oats operation is carried on in so violent a manner as to leave no strength in the soil for the produce of a more valuable crop?' It was of no use saying this however, so he allowed Scatcherd to continue.

'If I'd had a free fling when I was a youngster, I shouldn't have been so fond of the brandy bottle now. But any way, my son shall be my heir. I've had the gumption to make the money, but I haven't the gumption to spend it. My son, however, shall be able to ruffle* it with the best of them. I'll go bail he shall hold his head higher than ever young Gresham will be able to hold his. They are much of the same age, as well I have cause to remember; – and so has her ladyship there.'

Now the fact was, that Sir Roger Scatcherd felt in his heart no special love for young Gresham; but with her ladyship it might almost be a question whether she did not love the youth whom she had nursed almost as well as that other one who was her own proper offspring.

'And will you not put any check on thoughtless expenditure? If you live ten or twenty years, as we hope you may, it will become unnecessary; but in making a will, a man should always remember he may go off suddenly.'

'Especially if he goes to bed with a brandy bottle under his head; eh, doctor? But, mind, that's a medical secret, you know; not a word of that out of the bedroom.'

Dr Thorne could but sigh. What could he say on such a subject to such a man as this?

'Yes, I have put a check upon his expenditure. I will not let his daily bread depend on any man; I have therefore left him five hundred a year at his own disposal, from the day of my death. Let him make what ducks and drakes of that he can.'

'Five hundred a year certainly is not much,' said the doctor.

'No; nor do I want to keep him to that. Let him have whatever he wants if he sets about spending it properly. But the bulk of the property – this estate of Boxall Hill, and the Greshamsbury mortgage, and those other mortgages – I have tied up in this way: they shall be all his at twenty-five; and up to that age it shall be in your power to give him what he wants. If he shall die without children before he shall be five-and-twenty years of age, they are all to go to Mary's eldest child.'

Now Mary was Sir Roger's sister, the mother, therefore, of Miss Thorne, and, consequently, the wife of the respectable ironmonger who went to America, and the mother of a family there.

'Mary's eldest child!' said the doctor, feeling that the perspiration had nearly broken out on his forehead, and that he could hardly control his feelings. 'Mary's eldest child! Scatcherd, you should be more particular in your description, or you will leave your best legacy to the lawyers.'

'I don't know, and never heard the name of one of them.'

'But do you mean a boy or a girl?'

'They may be all girls for what I know, or all boys; besides, I don't care which it is. A girl would probably do best with it. Only you'd have to see that she married some decent fellow; you'd be her guardian.'

'Pooh, nonsense,' said the doctor. 'Louis will be five-and-twenty in a year or two.'

'In about four years.'

'And for all that's come and gone yet, Scatcherd, you are not going to leave us yourself quite as soon as all that.'

'Not if I can help it, doctor; but that's as may be.'

'The chances are ten to one that such a clause in your will will never come to bear.'

'Quite so, quite so. If I die, Louis Philippe won't; but I thought it right to put in something to prevent his squandering it all before he comes to his senses.'

'Oh! quite right, quite right. I think I would have named a later age than twenty-five.'

'So would not I. Louis Philippe will be all right by that time. That's my lookout. And now, doctor, you know my will; and if I die tomorrow, you will know what I want you to do for me.'

'You have merely said the eldest child, Scatcherd?'

'That's all; give it here, and I'll read it to you.'

'No, no; never mind. The eldest child! You should be more particular, Scatcherd; you should, indeed. Consider what an enormous interest may have to depend on those words.'

'Why, what the devil could I say? I don't know their names; never even heard them. But the eldest is the eldest, all the world over. Perhaps I ought to say the youngest, seeing that I am only a railway contractor.'

Scatcherd began to think that the doctor might now as well go away and leave him to the society of Winterbones and the brandy; but, much as our friend had before expressed himself in a hurry, he now seemed inclined to move very leisurely. He sat there by the bedside, resting his hands on his knees, and gazing unconsciously at the counterpane. At last he gave a deep sigh, and then he said, 'Scatcherd, you must be more particular in this. If I am to have anything to do with it, you must, indeed, be more explicit.'

'Why, how the deuce can I be more explicit? Isn't her eldest living child plain enough, whether he be Jack, or she be Gill?'

'What did your lawyer say to this, Scatcherd?'

'Lawyer! You don't suppose I let my lawyer know what I was putting. No; I got the form and the paper, and all that from him, and had him here, in one room, while Winterbones and I did it in another. It's all right enough. Though Winterbones wrote it, he did it in such a way he did not know what he was writing.'

The doctor sat a while longer, still looking at the counterpane, and then got up to depart. 'I'll see you again soon,' said he; 'tomorrow, probably.'

'Tomorrow!' said Sir Roger, not at all understanding why Dr Thorne should talk of returning so soon. 'Tomorrow! why I ain't so bad as that, man, am I? If you come so often as that you'll ruin me.'

'Oh, not as a medical man; not as that; but about this will, Scatcherd. I must think it over; I must, indeed.'

'You need not give yourself the least trouble in the world about my will till I'm dead; not the least. And who knows – may be, I may be settling your affairs yet; eh, doctor? looking after your niece when you're dead and gone, and getting a husband for her, eh? Ha! ha! ha!'

And then, without further speech, the doctor went his way.

CHAPTER XI

The Doctor Drinks His Tea

The doctor got on his cob and went his way, returning duly to Greshamsbury. But, in truth, as he went he hardly knew whither he was going, or what he was doing. Sir Roger had hinted that the cob would be compelled to make up for lost time by extra exertion on the road; but the cob had never been permitted to have his own way as to pace more satisfactorily than on the present occasion. The doctor, indeed, hardly knew that he was on horseback, so completely was he enveloped in the cloud of his own thoughts.

In the first place, that alternative which it had become him to put before the baronet as one unlikely to occur – that of the speedy death of both father and son – was one which he felt in his heart of hearts might very probably come to pass.

'The chances are ten to one that such a clause will never be brought to bear.' This he had said partly to himself, so as to ease the thoughts which came crowding on his brain; partly, also, in pity for the patient and the father. But now that he thought the matter over, he felt that there were no such odds. Were not the odds the other way? Was it not almost probable that both these men might be gathered to their long account within the next four years? One, the elder, was a strong man, indeed; one who might yet live for years to come if he would but give himself fair play. But then, he himself protested, and protested with a truth too surely grounded, that fair play to himself was beyond his own power to give. The other, the younger, had everything against him. Not only was he a poor, puny creature, without physical strength, one of whose life a friend could never feel sure under any circumstances, but he also was already addicted to his father's vice; he also was already killing himself with alcohol.

And then, if these two men did die within the prescribed period, if this clause in Sir Roger's will were brought to bear, if it should become his, Dr Thorne's, duty to see that clause carried out, how would he be bound to act? That woman's eldest child was his own niece, his adopted bairn, his darling, the pride of his heart, the cynosure of his eye,* his child also, his own Mary. Of all his duties on this earth, next to that one great duty to his God and conscience, was his duty to her. What, under these circumstances, did his duty to her require of him?

But then, that one great duty, that duty which she would be the first to expect from him; what did that demand of him? Had Scatcherd made his will without saying what its clauses were, it seemed to Thorne that Mary must have been the heiress, should that clause become necessarily operative. Whether she were so or not would at any rate be for lawyers to decide. But now the case was very different. This rich man had confided in him, and would it not be a breach of confidence, an act of absolute dishonesty – an act of dishonesty both to Scatcherd and to that far-distant American family, to that father who, in former days, had behaved so nobly, and to that eldest child of his, would it not be gross dishonesty to them all if he allowed this man to leave a will by which his property might go to a person never intended to be his heir?

Long before he had arrived at Greshamsbury his mind on this point had been made up. Indeed, it had been made up while sitting there by Scatcherd's bedside. It had not been difficult to make up his mind to so much; but then, his way out of this dishonesty was not so easy for him to find. How should he set this matter right so as to inflict no injury on his niece, and no sorrow on himself – if that indeed could be avoided?

And then other thoughts crowded on his brain. He had always professed – professed at any rate to himself and to her – that of all the vile objects of a man's ambition, wealth, wealth merely for its own sake, was the vilest. They, in their joint school of inherent philosophy, had progressed to ideas which they might find it not easy to carry out, should they be called on by events to do so. And if this would have been difficult to either when acting on behalf of self alone, how much more difficult when one might have to act for the other! This difficulty had now come to the uncle. Should he, in this emergency, take upon himself to fling away the golden chance which might accrue to his niece if Scatcherd should be encouraged to make her partly his heir?

'He'd want her to go and live there – to live with him and his wife. All the money in the Bank of England would not pay her for such misery,' said the doctor to himself, as he slowly rode into his own yard.

On one point, and one only, had he definitely made up his mind. On the following day he would go over again to Boxall Hill, and would tell Scatcherd the whole truth. Come what might, the truth must be the best. And so, with some gleam of comfort, he went into the house, and found his niece in the drawing-room with Patience Oriel.

'Mary and I have been quarrelling,' said Patience. 'She says the doctor is the greatest man in a village; and I say the parson is, of course.'

'I only say that the doctor is the most looked after,' said Mary. 'There's another horrid message for you to go to Silverbridge, uncle. Why can't that Dr Century manage his own people?'

'She says,' continued Miss Oriel, 'that if a parson was away for a month, no one would miss him; but that a doctor is so precious that his very minutes are counted.'

'I am sure uncle's are. They begrudge him his meals. Mr Oriel never gets called away to Silverbridge.'

'No; we in the Church manage our parish arrangements better than you do. We don't let strange practitioners in among our flocks because the sheep may chance to fancy them. Our sheep have to put up with our spiritual doses whether they like them or not. In that respect we are much the best off. I advise you, Mary, to marry a clergyman, by all means.'

'I will when you marry a doctor,' said she.

'I am sure nothing on earth would give me greater pleasure,' said Miss Oriel, getting up and curtsying very low to Dr Thorne; 'but I am not quite prepared for the agitation of an offer this morning, so I'll run away.'

And so she went; and the doctor, getting on his other horse, started again for Silverbridge, wearily enough. 'She's happy now where she is,' said he to himself, as he rode along. 'They all treat her there as an equal at Greshamsbury. What though she be no cousin to the Thornes of Ullathorne. She has found her place there among them all, and keeps it on equal terms with the best of them. There is Miss Oriel; her family is high; she is rich, fashionable, a beauty, courted by every one; but yet she does not look down on Mary. They are equal friends together. But how would it be if she were taken to Boxall Hill, even as a recognised niece of the rich man there? Would Patience Oriel and Beatrice Gresham go there after her? Could she be happy there as she is in my house here, poor though it be? It would kill her to pass a month with Lady Scatcherd and put up with that man's humours, to see his mode of life, to be dependent on him, to belong to him.' And then the doctor, hurrying on to Silverbridge, again met Dr Century at the old lady's bedside, and having made his endeavours to stave off the inexorable coming of the grim visitor, again returned to his own niece and his own drawing-room.

'You must be dead, uncle,' said Mary, as she poured out his tea for him, and prepared the comforts of that most comfortable meal – tea, dinner, and supper, all in one. 'I wish Silverbridge was fifty miles off.'

'That would only make the journey worse; but I am not dead yet, and, what is more to the purpose, neither is my patient.' And as he spoke he contrived to swallow a jorum of scalding tea, containing in measure somewhat near a pint. Mary, not a whit amazed at this feat, merely refilled the jorum without any observation; and the doctor went on stirring the mixture with his spoon, evidently oblivious that any ceremony had been performed by either of them since the first supply had been administered to him.

When the clatter of knives and forks was over, the doctor turned himself to the hearthrug, and putting one leg over the other, he began to nurse it as he looked with complacency at his third cup of tea, which stood untasted beside him. The fragments of the solid banquet had been removed, but no sacrilegious hand had been laid on the teapot and cream jug.

'Mary,' said he, 'suppose you were to find out tomorrow morning that, by some accident, you had become a great heiress, would you be able to suppress your exultation?'

'The first thing I'd do, would be to pronounce a positive edict that you should never go to Silverbridge again; at least without a day's notice.'

'Well, and what next? what would you do next?'

'The next thing – the next thing would be to send to Paris for a French bonnet exactly like the one Patience Oriel had on. Did you see it?'

'Well, I can't say I did; bonnets are invisible now; besides, I never remark anybody's clothes, except yours.'

'Oh! do look at Miss Oriel's bonnet the next time you see her. I cannot understand why it should be so, but I am sure of this – no English fingers could put together such a bonnet as that; and I am nearly sure that no French fingers could do it in England.'

'But you don't care so much about bonnets, Mary!' This the doctor said as an assertion; but there was, nevertheless, somewhat of a question involved in it.

'Don't I, though?' said she. 'I do care very much about bonnets; especially since I saw Patience this morning. I asked her how much it cost – guess.'

'Oh! I don't know – a pound!'

'A pound, uncle!'

'What! a great deal more? Ten pounds?'

'Oh, uncle!'

'What! more than ten pounds? Then I don't think even Patience Oriel ought to give it.'

'No, of course she would not; but, uncle, it really cost a hundred francs!'

'Oh! a hundred francs; that's four pounds, isn't it? Well, and how much did your last bonnet cost?'

'Mine! oh, nothing – five and ninepence, perhaps; I trimmed it myself. If I were left a great fortune, I'd send to Paris tomorrow; no, I'd go myself to Paris to buy a bonnet, and I'd take you with me to choose it.'

The doctor sat silent for a while meditating about this, during which he unconsciously absorbed the tea beside him; and Mary again replenished his cup.

'Come, Mary,' said he at last, 'I'm in a generous mood; and as I am rather more rich than usual, we'll send to Paris for a French bonnet. The going for it must wait a while longer I am afraid.'

'You're joking.'

'No, indeed. If you know the way to send – that I must confess would puzzle me; but if you'll manage the sending, I'll manage the paying; and you shall have a French bonnet.'

'Uncle!' said she, looking up at him.

'Oh, I'm not joking; I owe you a present, and I'll give you that.'

'And if you do, I'll tell you what I'll do with it. I'll cut it into fragments, and burn them before your face. Why, uncle, what do you take me for? You're not a bit nice tonight to make such an offer as that to me; not a bit, not a bit.' And then she came over from her seat at the tea-tray and sat down on a foot-stool close at his knee. 'Because I'd have a French bonnet if I had a large fortune, is that a reason why I should like one now? If you were to pay four pounds for a bonnet for me, it would scorch my head every time I put it on.'

'I don't see that: four pounds would not ruin me. However, I don't think you'd look a bit better if you had it; and, certainly, I should not like to scorch these locks,' and putting his hand upon her shoulders, he played with her hair.

'Patience has a pony-phaeton, and I'd have one if I were rich; and I'd have all my books bound as she does; and, perhaps, I'd give fifty guineas for a dressing-case.'

'Fifty guineas!'

'Patience did not tell me; but so Beatrice says. Patience showed it to me once, and it is a darling. I think I'd have the dressing-case before the bonnet. But, uncle – '

'Well?'

'You don't suppose I want such things?'

'Not improperly. I am sure you do not.'

'Not properly, or improperly; not much, or little. I covet many things; but nothing of that sort. You know, or should know, that I do not. Why did you talk of buying a French bonnet for me?'

Dr Thorne did not answer this question, but went on nursing his leg.

'After all,' said he, 'money is a fine thing.'

'Very fine, when it is well come by,' she answered; 'that is, without detriment to the heart or soul.'

'I should be a happier man if you were provided for as is Miss Oriel. Suppose, now, I could give you up to a rich man who would be able to insure you against all wants?'

'Insure me against all wants! Oh, that would be a man. That would be selling me, wouldn't it, uncle? Yes, selling me; and the price you would receive would be freedom from future apprehensions as regards me. It would be a cowardly sale for you to make; and then, as to me – me the victim. No, uncle; you must bear the misery of having to provide for me – bonnets and all. We are all in the same boat, and you shan't turn me overboard.'

'But if I were to die, what would you do then?'

'And if I were to die, what would you do? People must be bound together. They must depend on each other. Of course, misfortunes may come; but it is cowardly to be afraid of them beforehand. You and I are bound together, uncle; and though you say these things to tease me, I know you do not wish to get rid of me.'

'Well, well; we shall win through, doubtless; if not in one way, then in another.'

'Win through! Of course we shall; who doubts our winning? but, uncle – '

'But, Mary.'

'Well?'

'You haven't got another cup of tea, have you?'

'Oh, uncle! you have had five.'

'No, my dear! not five; only four – only four, I assure you; I have been very particular to count. I had one while I was – '

'Five, uncle; indeed and indeed.'

'Well, then, as I hate the prejudice which attaches luck to an odd number, I'll have a sixth to show that I am not superstitious.'

While Mary was preparing the sixth jorum, there came a knock at the door. Those late summonses were hateful to Mary's ear, for they were usually the forerunners of a midnight ride through the dark lanes to some farmer's house. The doctor had been in the saddle all day, and, as Janet brought the note into the room, Mary stood up as though to defend her uncle from any further invasion on his rest.

'A note from the house, miss,' said Janet: now 'the house', in Greshamsbury's parlance, always meant the squire's mansion.

'No one ill at the house, I hope,' said the doctor, taking the note from Mary's hand. 'Oh – ah – yes; it's from the squire – there's nobody ill: wait a minute, Janet, and I'll write a line. Mary, lend me your desk.'

The squire, anxious as usual for money, had written to ask what success the doctor had had in negotiating the new loan with Sir Roger. The fact, however, was, that in his visit at Boxall Hill, the doctor had been altogether unable to bring on the carpet the matter of his loan. Subjects had crowded themselves in too quickly during that interview – those two interviews at Sir Roger's bedside; and he had been obliged to leave without even alluding to the question.

'I must at any rate go back now,' said he to himself. So he wrote to the squire, saying that he was to be at Boxall Hill again on the following day, and that he would call at the house on his return.

'That's settled, at any rate,' said he.

'What's settled?' said Mary.

'Why, I must go to Boxall Hill again tomorrow. I must go early, too, so we'd better be off to bed. Tell Janet I must breakfast at half-past seven.'

'You couldn't take me, could you? I should so like to see that Sir Roger.'

'To see Sir Roger! Why, he's ill in bed.'

'That's an objection, certainly; but some day, when he's well, could not you take me over? I have the greatest desire to see a man like that; a man who began with nothing and has now more than enough to buy the whole parish of Greshamsbury.'

'I don't think you'd like him at all.'

'Why not? I am sure I should; I am sure I should like him, and Lady Scatcherd, too. I heard you say that she is an excellent woman.'

'Yes, in her way; and he, too, is good in his way; but they are neither of them in your way: they are extremely vulgar –'

'Oh! I don't mind that; that would make them more amusing; one doesn't go to those sort of people for polished manners.'

'I don't think you'd find the Scatcherds pleasant acquaintances at all,' said the doctor, taking his bed-candle, and kissing his niece's forehead as he left the room.

CHAPTER XII

When Greek Meets Greek, then Comes Tug of War*

The doctor, that is our doctor, had thought nothing more of the message which had been sent to that other doctor, Dr Fillgrave; nor in truth did the baronet. Lady Scatcherd had thought of it, but her husband during the rest of the day was not in a humour which allowed her to remind him that he would soon have a new physician on his hands; so she left the difficulty to arrange itself, waiting in some little trepidation till Dr Fillgrave should show himself.

It was well that Sir Roger was not dying for want of his assistance, for when the message reached Barchester, Dr Fillgrave was some five or six miles out of town, at Plumptead; and as he did not get back till late in the evening, he felt himself necessitated to put off his visit to Boxall Hill till the next morning. Had he chanced to have been made acquainted with that little conversation about the pump, he would probably have postponed it even yet a while longer.

He was, however, by no means sorry to be summoned to the bedside of Sir Roger Scatcherd. It was well known at Barchester, and very well known to Dr Fillgrave, that Sir Roger and Dr Thorne were old friends. It was very well known to him also, that Sir Roger, in all his bodily ailments, had hitherto been contented to entrust his safety to the skill of his old friend. Sir Roger was in his way a great man, and much talked of in Barchester, and rumour had already reached the ears of the Barchester Galen, that the great railway contractor was ill. When, therefore, he received a peremptory summons to go over to Boxall Hill, he could not but think that some pure light had broken in upon Sir Roger's darkness, and taught him at last where to look for true medical accomplishment.

And then, also, Sir Roger was the richest man in the county, and to county practitioners a new patient with large means is a godsend; how much greater a godsend when he be not only acquired, but taken also from some rival practitioner, need hardly be explained.

Dr Fillgrave, therefore, was somewhat elated when, after a very early breakfast, he stepped into the post-chaise which was to carry him to Boxall Hill. Dr Fillgrave's professional advancement had been sufficient to justify the establishment of a brougham, in which he paid his ordinary visits round Barchester; but this was a special occasion, requiring special speed, and about to produce no doubt a special guerdon,* and therefore a pair of post-horses were put into request.

It was hardly yet nine when the post-boy somewhat loudly rang the bell at Sir Roger's door; and then Dr Fillgrave, for the first time, found himself in the new grand hall of Boxall Hill House.

'I'll tell my lady,' said the servant, showing him into the grand dining-room; and there for some fifteen or twenty minutes Dr Fillgrave walked up and down the length of the Turkey carpet all alone.

Dr Fillgrave was not a tall man, and was perhaps rather more inclined to corpulence than became his height. In his stocking-feet, according to the usually received style of measurement, he was five feet five; and he had a little round abdominal protuberance, which an inch and a half added to the heels of his boots hardly enabled him to carry off as well as he himself would have wished. Of this he was apparently conscious, and it gave to him an air of not being entirely at his ease. There was, however, a personal dignity in his demeanour, a propriety in his gait, and an air of authority in his gestures which should prohibit one from stigmatizing those efforts at altitude as a failure. No doubt he did achieve much; but, nevertheless, the effort would occasionally betray itself, and the story of the frog and the ox* would irresistibly force itself into one's mind at those moments when it most behoved Dr Fillgrave to be magnificent.

But if the bulgy roundness of his person and the shortness of his legs in any way detracted from his personal importance, these trifling defects were, he was well aware, more than atoned for by the peculiar dignity of his countenance. If his legs were short, his face was not; if there was any undue preponderance below the waistcoat, all was in due symmetry above the necktie.

His hair was grey, not grizzled nor white, but properly grey; and stood up straight from off his temples on each side with an unbending determination of purpose. His whiskers, which were of an admirable shape, coming down and turning gracefully at the angle of his jaw, were grey also, but somewhat darker than his hair. His enemies in Barchester declared that their perfect shade was produced by a leaden comb. His eyes were not brilliant, but were very effective, and well under command. He was rather short-sighted, and a pair of eye-glasses was always on his nose, or in his hand. His nose was long, and well pronounced, and his chin, also, was sufficiently prominent; but the great feature of his face was his mouth. The amount of secret medical knowledge of which he could give assurance by the pressure of those lips was truly wonderful. By his lips, also, he could be most exquisitely courteous, or most sternly forbidding. And not only could he be either the one or the other; but he could at his will assume any shade of difference between the two, and produce any mixture of sentiment.

When Dr Fillgrave was first shown into Sir Roger's dining-room, he walked up and down the room for a while with easy, jaunty step, with his hands joined together behind his back, calculating the price of the furniture, and counting the heads which might be adequately entertained in a room of such noble proportions; but in seven or eight minutes an air of impatience might have been seen to suffuse his face. Why could he not be shown up into the sick man's room? What necessity could there be for keeping him there, as though he were some apothecary with a box of leeches in his pocket? He then rang the bell, perhaps a little violently. 'Does Sir Roger know that I am here?' he said to the servant. 'I'll tell my lady,' said the man, again vanishing.

For five minutes more he walked up and down, calculating no longer the value of the furniture, but rather that of his own importance. He was not wont to be kept waiting in this way; and though Sir Roger Scatcherd was at present a great and a rich man, Dr Fillgrave had remembered him a very small and a very poor man. He now began to think of Sir Roger as the stone-mason, and to chafe somewhat more violently at being so kept by such a man.

When one is impatient, five minutes is as the duration of all time, and a quarter of an hour is eternity. At the end of twenty minutes the step of Dr Fillgrave up and down the room had become very quick, and he had just made up his mind that he would not stay there all day to the serious detriment, perhaps fatal injury, of his other expectant patients. His hand was again on the bell, and was about to be used with vigour, when the door opened and Lady Scatcherd entered.

The door opened and Lady Scatcherd entered; but she did so very slowly, as though she were afraid to come into her own dining-room. We must go back a little and see how she had been employed during those twenty minutes.

'Oh laws!' Such had been her first exclamation on hearing that the doctor was in the dining-room. She was standing at the time with her housekeeper in a small room in which she kept her linen and jam, and in which, in company with the same housekeeper, she spent the happiest moments of her life.

'Oh laws! now, Hannah, what shall we do?'

'Send 'un up at once to the master, my lady! let John take 'un up.'

'There'll be such a row in the house, Hannah; I know there will.'

'But sure-ly didn't he send for 'un? Let the master have the row himself, then; that's what I'd do, my lady, added Hannah, seeing that her ladyship still stood trembling in doubt, biting her thumb-nail.

'You couldn't go up to the master yourself, could you now, Hannah?' said Lady Scatcherd in her most persuasive tone.

'Why no,' said Hannah, after a little deliberation; 'no, I'm afeard I couldn't.'

'Then I must just face it myself.' And up went the wife to tell her lord that the physician for whom he had sent had come to attend his bidding.

In the interview which then took place the baronet had not indeed been violent, but he had been very determined. Nothing on earth, he said, should induce him to see Dr Fillgrave and offend his dear old friend Thorne.

'But, Roger,' said her ladyship, half crying, or rather pretending to cry in her vexation, 'what shall I do with the man? How shall I get him out of the house?'

'Put him under the pump,' said the baronet; and he laughed his peculiar low guttural laugh, which told so plainly of the havoc which brandy had made in his throat.

'That's nonsense, Roger; you know I can't put him under the pump. Now you are ill, and you'd better see him just for five minutes. I'll make it all right with Dr Thorne.'

'I'll be d – if I do, my lady.' All the people about Boxall Hill called poor Lady Scatcherd 'my lady,' as if there was some excellent joke in it; and so, indeed, there was.

'You know you needn't mind nothing he says, nor yet take nothing he sends: and I'll tell him not to come no more. Now do'ee see him, Roger.'

But there was no coaxing Roger over now, or indeed ever: he was a wilful, headstrong, masterful man; a tyrant always, though never a cruel one; and accustomed to rule his wife and household as despotically as he did his gangs of workmen. Such men it is not easy to coax over.

'You go down and tell him I don't want him, and won't see him, and that's an end of it. If he chose to earn his money, why didn't he come yesterday when he was sent for? I'm well now, and don't want him; and what's more, I won't have him. Winterbones, lock the door.'

So Winterbones, who during this interview had been at work at his little table, got up to lock the door, and Lady Scatcherd had no alternative but to pass through it before the last edict was obeyed.

Lady Scatcherd, with slow step, went downstairs and again sought counsel with Hannah, and the two, putting their heads together, agreed that the only cure for the present evil was to be found in a good fee. So Lady Scatcherd, with a five-pound note in her hand, and trembling in every limb, went forth to encounter the august presence of Dr Fillgrave.

As the door opened, Dr Fillgrave dropped the bell-rope which was in his hand, and bowed low to the lady. Those who knew the doctor well, would have known from his bow that he was not well pleased; it was as much as though he said, 'Lady Scatcherd, I am your most obedient humble servant; at any rate it appears that it is your pleasure to treat me as such.'

Lady Scatcherd did not understand all this; but she perceived at once that the man was angry.

'I hope Sir Roger does not find himself worse,' said the doctor. 'The morning is getting on; shall I step up and see him?'

'Hem! ha! oh! Why, you see, Dr Fillgrave, Sir Roger finds hisself vastly better this morning, vastly so.'

'I'm very glad to hear it, very; but as the morning is getting on, shall I step up to see Sir Roger?'

'Why, Dr Fillgrave, sir, you see, he finds hisself so much hisself this morning, that he a'most thinks it would be a shame to trouble you.'

'A shame to trouble me!' This was a sort of shame which Dr Fillgrave did not at all comprehend. 'A shame to trouble me! Why, Lady Scatcherd – '

Lady Scatcherd saw that she had nothing for it but to make the whole matter intelligible. Moreover, seeing that she appreciated more thoroughly the smallness of Dr Fillgrave's person than she did the peculiar greatness of his demeanour, she began to be a shade less afraid of him than she had thought she should have been.

'Yes, Dr Fillgrave; you see, when a man like he gets well, he can't abide the idea of doctors: now yesterday, he was all for sending for you; but today he comes to hisself, and don't seem to want no doctor at all.'

Then did Dr Fillgrave seem to grow out of his boots, so suddenly did he take upon himself sundry modes of expansive attitude; – to grow out of his boots and to swell upwards, till his angry eyes almost looked down on Lady Scatcherd, and each erect hair bristled up towards the heavens.

'This is very singular, very singular, Lady Scatcherd; very singular, indeed; very singular; quite unusual. I have come here from Barchester, at some considerable inconvenience, at some very considerable inconvenience, I may say, to my regular patients; and – and – and – I don't know that anything so very singular ever occurred to me before.' And then Dr Fillgrave, with a compression of his lips which almost made the poor woman sink into the ground, moved towards the door.

Then Lady Scatcherd bethought her of her great panacea. 'It isn't about the money, you know, doctor,' said she; 'of course Sir Roger don't expect you to come here with posthorses for nothing.' In this, by the by, Lady Scatcherd did not stick quite close to veracity, for Sir Roger, had he known it, would by no means have assented to any payment; and the note which her ladyship held in her hand was taken from her own private purse. 'It ain't at all about the money, doctor;' and then she tendered the bank-note, which she thought would immediately make all things smooth.

Now Dr Fillgrave dearly loved a five-pound fee. What physician is so unnatural as not to love it? He dearly loved a five-pound fee; but he loved his dignity better. He was angry also; and like all angry men, he loved his grievance. He felt that he had been badly treated; but if he took the money he would throw away his right to indulge any such feeling. At that moment his outraged dignity and his cherished anger were worth more to him than a five-pound note. He looked at it with wishful but still averted eyes, and then sternly refused the tender.

'No, madam,' said he; 'no, no;' and with his right hand raised with his eye-glasses in it, he motioned away the tempting paper. 'No; I should have been happy to have given Sir Roger the benefit of any medical skill I may have, seeing that I was specially called in – '

'But, doctor; if the man's well, you know – '

'Oh, of course; if he's well, and does not choose to see me, there's an end of it. Should he have any relapse, as my time is valuable, he will perhaps oblige me by sending elsewhere. Madam, good morning. I will, if you will allow me, ring for my carriage – that is, post-chaise.'

'But, doctor, you'll take the money; you must take the money; indeed you'll take the money,' said Lady Scatcherd, who had now become really unhappy at the idea that her husband's unpardonable whim had brought this man with post-horses all the way from Barchester, and that he was to be paid nothing for his time nor costs.

'No, madam, no. I could not think of it. Sir Roger, I have no doubt, will know better another time. It is not a question of money; not at all.'

'But it is a question of money, doctor; and you really shall, you must.' And poor Lady Scatcherd, in her anxiety to acquit herself at any rate of any pecuniary debt to the doctor, came to personal close quarters with him, with the view of forcing the note into his hands.

'Quite impossible, quite impossible,' said the doctor, still cherishing his grievance, and valiantly rejecting the root of all evil. 'I shall not do anything of the kind, Lady Scatcherd.'

'Now doctor, do'ee; to oblige me.'

'Quite out of the question.' And so, with his hands and hat behind his back, in token of his utter refusal to accept any pecuniary accommodation of his injury, he made his way backwards to the door, her ladyship perseveringly pressing him in front. So eager had been the attack on him, that he had not waited to give his order about the post-chaise, but made his way at once towards the hall.

'Now, do'ee take it, do'ee,' pressed Lady Scatcherd.

'Utterly out of the question,' said Dr Fillgrave, with great deliberation, as he backed his way into the hall. As he did so, of course he turned round, – and he found himself almost in the arms of Dr Thorne.

As Burley must have glared at Bothwell when they rushed together in that dread encounter on the mountain side;* as Achilles may have glared at Hector* when at last they met, each resolved to test in fatal conflict the prowess of the other, so did Dr Fillgrave glare at his foe from Greshamsbury, when, on turning round on his exalted heel, he found his nose on a level with the top button of Dr Thorne's waistcoat.

And here, if it be not too tedious, let us pause a while to recapitulate and add up the undoubted grievances of the Barchester practitioner. He had made no effort to ingratiate himself into the sheepfold of that other shepherd-dog; it was not by his seeking that he was now at Boxall Hill; much as he hated Dr Thorne, full sure as he felt of that man's utter ignorance, of his incapacity to administer properly even a black dose,* of his murdering propensities, and his low, mean, unprofessional style of practice; nevertheless, he had done nothing to undermine him with these Scatcherds. Dr Thorne might have sent every mother's son at Boxall Hill to his long account, and Dr Fillgrave would not have interfered; – would not have interfered unless specially and duly called upon to do so.

But he had been specially and duly called on. Before such a step was taken some words must undoubtedly have passed on the subject between Thorne and the Scatcherds. Thorne must have known what was to be done. Having been so called, Dr Fillgrave had come – had come all the way in a post-chaise – had been refused admittance to the sick man's room, on the plea that the sick man was no longer sick; and just as he was about to retire feeless – for the want of the fee was not the less a grievance from the fact of its having been tendered and refused – feeless, dishonoured, and in dudgeon, he encountered this other doctor – this very rival whom he had been sent to supplant;

he encountered him in the very act of going to the sick man's room.

What mad fanatic Burley, what god-succoured insolent Achilles, ever had such cause to swell with wrath as at that moment had Dr Fillgrave? Had I the pen of Molière, I could fitly tell of such medical anger,* but with no other pen can it be fitly told. He did swell, and when the huge bulk of his wrath was added to his natural proportions, he loomed gigantic before the eyes of the surrounding followers of Sir Roger.

Dr Thorne stepped back three steps and took his hat from his head, having, in the passage from the hall-door to the dining-room, hitherto omitted to do so. It must be borne in mind that he had no conception whatever that Sir Roger had declined to see the physician for whom he had sent; none whatever that that physician was now about to return, feeless, to Barchester.

Dr Thorne and Dr Fillgrave were doubtless well-known enemies. All the world of Barchester, and all that portion of the world of London which is concerned with the lancet and the scalping-knife, were well aware of this: they were continually writing against each other; continually speaking against each other; but yet they had never hitherto come to that positive personal collision which is held to justify a cut direct. They very rarely saw each other; and when they did meet, it was in some casual way in the streets of Barchester or elsewhere, and on such occasions their habit had been to bow with very cold propriety.

On the present occasion, Dr Thorne of course felt that Dr Fillgrave had the whiphand of him; and, with a sort of manly feeling on such a point, he conceived it to be most compatible with his own dignity to show, under such circumstances, more than his usual courtesy – something, perhaps, amounting almost to cordiality. He had been supplanted, *quoad* doctor, in the house of this rich, eccentric, railway baronet, and he would show that he bore no malice on that account.

So he smiled blandly as he took off his hat, and in a civil speech he expressed a hope that Dr Fillgave had not found his patient to be in any very unfavourable state.

Here was an aggravation to the already lacerated feelings of the injured man. He had been brought thither to be scoffed and scorned at, that he might be a laughing-stock to his enemies, and food for mirth to the vile-minded. He swelled with noble anger till he would have burst, had it not been for the opportune padding of his frock-coat.

'Sir,' said he; 'sir:' and he could hardly get his lips open to give vent to the tumult of his heart. Perhaps he was not wrong; for it may be that his lips were more eloquent than would have been his words.

'What's the matter?' said Dr Thorne, opening his eyes wide, and addressing Lady Scatcherd over the head and across the hairs of the irritated man below him. 'What on earth is the matter? Is anything wrong with Sir Roger?'

'Oh, laws, doctor!' said her ladyship. 'Oh, laws; I'm sure it ain't my fault. Here's Dr Fillgrave in a taking, and I'm quite ready to pay him, – quite. If a man gets paid, what more can he want?' And she again held out the five-pound note over Dr Fillgrave's head.

What more, indeed, Lady Scatcherd, can any of us want, if only we could keep our tempers and feelings a little in abeyance? Dr Fillgrave, however, could not so keep his; and, therefore, he did want something more, though at the present moment he could have hardly said what.

Lady Scatcherd's courage was somewhat resuscitated by the presence of her ancient trusty ally; and, moreover, she began to conceive that the little man before her was unreasonable beyond all conscience in his anger, seeing that that for which he was ready to work had been offered to him without any work at all.

'Madam,' said he, again turning round at Lady Scatcherd, 'I was never before treated in such a way in any house in Barsetshire – never – never.'

'Good heavens, Dr Fillgrave!' said he of Greshamsbury, 'what is the matter?'

'I'll let you know what is the matter, sir,' said he, turning round again as quickly as before. 'I'll let you know what is the matter. I'll publish this, sir, to the medical world;' and as he shrieked out the words of the threat, he stood on tiptoes and brandished his eye-glasses up almost into his enemy's face.

'Don't be angry with Dr Thorne,' said Lady Scatcherd. 'Any ways, you needn't be angry with him. If you must be angry with anybody –'

'I shall be angry with him, madam,' ejaculated Dr Fillgrave, making another sudden demi-pirouette. 'I am angry with him –

or, rather, I despise him;' and completing the circle, Dr Fillgrave again brought himself round in full front of his foe.

Dr Thorne raised his eyebrows and looked inquiringly at Lady Scatcherd; but there was a quiet sarcastic motion round his mouth which by no means had the effect of throwing oil on the troubled waters.

'I'll publish the whole of this transaction to the medical world, Dr Thorne – the whole of it; and if that has not the effect of rescuing the people of Greshamsbury out of your hands, then – then – then, I don't know what will. Is my carriage – that is, post-chaise there?' and Dr Fillgrave, speaking very loudly, turned majestically to one of the servants.

'What have I done to you, Dr Fillgrave,' said Dr Thorne, now absolutely laughing, 'that you should determine to take my bread out of my mouth? I am not interfering with your patient. I have come here simply with reference to money matters appertaining to Sir Roger.'

'Money matters! Very well – very well; money matters. That is your idea of medical practice! Very well – very well. Is my post-chaise at the door? I'll publish it all to the medical world – every word – every word of it, every word of it.'

'Publish what, you unreasonable man?'

'Man! sir; whom do you call a man? I'll let you know whether I'm a man – post-chaise there!'

'Don't 'ee call him names now, doctor; don't 'ee, pray don't'ee,' said Lady Scatcherd.

By this time they had all got somewhat nearer the hall-door; but the Scatcherd retainers were too fond of the row to absent themselves willingly at Dr Fillgrave's bidding, and it did not appear that any one went in search of the post-chaise.

'Man! sir; I'll let you know what it is to speak to me in that style. I think, sir, you hardly know who I am.'

'All that I know of you at present is, that you are my friend Sir Roger's physician, and I cannot conceive what has occurred to make you so angry.' And as he spoke, Dr Thorne looked carefully at him to see whether that pump-discipline had in truth been applied. There were no signs whatever that cold water had been thrown upon Dr Fillgrave.

'My post-chaise – is my post-chaise there? The medical world shall know all; you may be sure, sir, the medical world shall know it all;' and thus, ordering his post-chaise, and threatening

Dr Thorne with the medical world, Dr Fillgrave made his way to the door.

But the moment he put on his hat he resumed. 'No, madam,' said he. 'No; it is quite out of the question: such an affair is not to be arranged by such means. I'll publish it all to the medical world – post-chaise there!' and then, using all his force, he flung as far as he could into the hall a light bit of paper. It fell at Dr Thorne's feet, who, raising it, found that it was a five-pound note.

'I put it into his hat just while he was in his tantrum,' said Lady Scatcherd. 'And I thought that perhaps he would not find it till he got to Barchester. Well, I wish he'd been paid, certainly, although Sir Roger wouldn't see him;' and in this manner Dr Thorne got some glimpse of understanding into the cause of the great offence.

'I wonder whether Sir Roger will see *me*,' said he, laughing.

CHAPTER XIII

The Two Uncles

'Ha! ha! ha! Ha! ha! ha!' laughed Sir Roger, lustily, as Dr Thorne entered the room. 'Well, if that ain't rich, I don't know what is. Ha! ha! ha! But why did they not put him under the pump, doctor?'

The doctor, however, had too much tact, and too many things of importance to say, to allow of his giving up much time to the discussion of Dr Fillgrave's wrath. He had come determined to open the baronet's eyes as to what would be the real effect of his will, and he had also to negotiate a loan for Mr Gresham, if that might be possible. Dr Thorne therefore began about the loan, that being the easier subject, and found that Sir Roger was quite clearheaded as to his money concerns, in spite of his illness. Sir Roger was willing enough to lend Mr Gresham more money – six, eight, ten, twenty thousand; but then, in doing so, he should insist on obtaining possession of the title-deeds.

'What! the title-deeds of Greshamsbury for a few thousand pounds?' said the doctor.

'I don't know whether you call ninety thousand pounds a few thousands; but the debt will about amount to that.'

'Ah! that's the old debt.'

'Old and new together, of course; every shilling I lend more weakens my security for what I have lent before.'

'But you have the first claim, Sir Roger.'

'I ought to be first and last to cover such a debt as that. If he wants further accommodation, he must part with his deeds, doctor.'

The point was argued backwards and forwards for some time without avail, and the doctor then thought it well to introduce the other subject.

'Well, Sir Roger, you're a hard man.'

'No I ain't,' said Sir Roger; 'not a bit hard; that is, not a bit too hard. Money is always hard. I know I found it hard to come by; and there is no reason why Squire Gresham should expect to find me so very soft.'

'Very well; there is an end of that. I thought you would have done as much to oblige me, that is all.'

'What! take bad security to oblige you?'

'Well, there's an end of that.'

'I'll tell you what; I'll do as much to oblige a friend as any one. I'll lend you five thousand pounds, you yourself, without security at all, if you want it.'

'But you know I don't want it; or, at any rate, shan't take it.'

'But to ask me to go on lending money to a third party, and he over head and ears in debt, by way of obliging you, why, it's a little too much.'

'Well, there's an end of it. Now I've something to say to you about that will of yours.'

'Oh! that's settled.'

'No, Scatcherd; it isn't settled. It must be a great deal more settled before we have done with it, as you'll find when you hear what I have to tell you.'

'What you have to tell me!' said Sir Roger, sitting up in bed; 'and what have you to tell me?'

'Your will says your sister's eldest child.'

'Yes; but that's only in the event of Louis Philippe dying before he is twenty-five.'

'Exactly; and now I know something about your sister's eldest child, and, therefore, I have come to tell you.'

'You know something about Mary's eldest child?'

'I do, Scatcherd; it is a strange story, and maybe it will make you angry. I cannot help it if it does so. I should not tell you this if I could avoid it; but as I do tell you, for your sake, as you will see, and not for my own, I must implore you not to tell my secret to others.'

Sir Roger now looked at him with an altered countenance. There was something in his voice of the authoritative tone of other days, something in the doctor's look which had on the baronet the same effect which in former days it had sometimes had on the stone-mason.

'Can you give me a promise, Scatcherd, that what I tell you shall not be repeated?'

'A promise! Well, I don't know what it's about, you know. I don't like promises in the dark.'

'Then I must leave it to your honour; for what I have to say must be said. You remember my brother, Scatcherd?'

Remember his brother! thought the rich man to himself. The name of the doctor's brother had not been alluded to between them since the days of that trial; but still it was impossible but that Scatcherd should well remember him.

'Yes, yes; certainly. I remember your brother,' said he. 'I remember him well; there's no doubt about that.'

'Well, Scatcherd,' and, as he spoke, the doctor laid his hand with kindness on the other's arm, 'Mary's eldest child was my brother's child as well.'

'But there is no such child living,' said Sir Roger; and, in his violence, as he spoke he threw from off him the bedclothes, and tried to stand upon the floor. He found, however, that he had no strength for such an effort, and was obliged to remain leaning on the bed and resting on the doctor's arm.

'There was no such child ever lived,' said he. 'What do you mean by this?'

Dr Thorne would say nothing further till he had got the man into bed again. This he at last effected, and then went on with the story in his own way.

'Yes, Scatcherd, that child is alive; and for fear that you should unintentionally make her your heir, I have thought it right to tell you this.'

'A girl, is it?'

'Yes, a girl.'

'And why should you want to spite her? If she is Mary's child, she is your brother's child also. If she is my niece, she must be your niece too. Why should you want to spite her? Why should you try to do her such a terrible injury?'

'I do not want to spite her.'

'Where is she? Who is she? What is she called? Where does she live?'

The doctor did not at once answer all these questions. He had made up his mind that he would tell Sir Roger that this child was living, but he had not as yet resolved to make known all the circumstances of her history. He was not even yet quite aware whether it would be necessary to say that this foundling orphan was the cherished darling of his own house.

'Such a child is, at any rate, living,' said he; 'of that I give you my assurance; and under your will, as now worded, it might come to pass that that child should be your heir. I do not want to spite her, but I should be wrong to let you make your will without such knowledge, seeing that I am possessed of it myself.'

'But where is the girl?'

'I do not know that that signifies.'

'Signifies! Yes; it does signify a great deal. But, Thorne, Thorne, now that I remember it, now that I can think of things, it was – was it not you yourself who told me that the baby did not live?'

'Very possibly.'

'And was it a lie that you told me?'

'If so, yes. But it is no lie that I tell you now.'

'I believed you then, Thorne; then, when I was a poor broken-down day-labourer, lying in jail, rotting there; but I tell you fairly, I do not believe you now. You have some scheme in this.'

'Whatever scheme I may have, you can frustrate by making another will. What can I gain by telling you this? I only do so to induce you to be more explicit in naming your heir.'

They both remained silent for a while, during which the baronet poured out from his hidden resource a glass of brandy, and swallowed it.

'When a man is taken aback suddenly by such tidings as these, he must take a drop of something, eh, doctor?'

Dr Thorne did not see the necessity; but the present, he felt, was no time for arguing the point.

'Come, Thorne, where is the girl? You must tell me that. She is my niece, and I have a right to know. She shall come here, and I will do something for her. By the Lord! I would as soon she had the money as any one else, if she is anything of a good 'un; – some of it, that is. Is she a good 'un?'

'Good!' said the doctor, turning away his face. 'Yes; she is good enough.'

'She must be grown up now. None of your light skirts, eh?'

'She is a good girl,' said the doctor, somewhat loudly and sternly. He could hardly trust himself to say much on this point.

'Mary was a good girl, a very good girl, till' – and Sir Roger raised himself up in his bed with his fist clenched, as though he were again about to strike that fatal blow at the farm-yard gate. 'But, come, it's no good thinking of that; you behaved well and manly, always. And so poor Mary's child is alive; at least, you say so.'

'I say so, and you may believe it. Why should I deceive you?'

'No, no; I don't see why. But then why did you deceive me before?'

To this the doctor chose to make no answer, and again there was silence for a while.

'What do you call her, doctor?'

'Her name is Mary.'

'The prettiest woman's name going; there's no name like it,' said the contractor, with an unusual tenderness in his voice. 'Mary – yes; but Mary what? What other name does she go by?'

Here the doctor hesitated.

'Mary Scatcherd – eh?'

'No. Not Mary Scatcherd.'

'Not Mary Scatcherd! Mary what, then? You, with your d – pride, wouldn't let her be called Mary Thorne, I know.'

This was too much for the doctor. He felt that there were tears in his eyes, so he walked away to the window to dry them, unseen. Had he had fifty names, each more sacred than the other, the most sacred of them all would hardly have been good enough for her.

'Mary what, doctor? Come, if the girl is to belong to me, if I am to provide for her, I must know what to call her, and where to look for her.'

'Who talked of your providing for her?' said the doctor, turning angrily round at the rival uncle. 'Who said that she was to belong to you? She will be no burden to you; you are only told of this that you may not leave your money to her without knowing it. She is provided for – that is, she wants nothing; she will do well enough; you need not trouble yourself about her.'

'But if she's Mary's child, Mary's child in real truth, I will trouble myself about her. Who else should do so? For the matter of that, I'd as soon say her as any of those others in America. What do I care about blood? I shan't mind her being a bastard. That is to say, of course, if she's decently good. Did she ever get any kind of teaching; book-learning or anything of that sort?'

Dr Thorne at this moment hated his friend the baronet with almost a deadly hatred; that he, rough brute as he was – for he was a rough brute – that he should speak in such language of the angel who gave to that home in Greshamsbury so many of the joys of Paradise – that he should speak of her as in some degree his own, that he should inquire doubtingly as to her attributes and her virtues. And then the doctor thought of her Italian and French readings, of her music, of her nice books, and sweet lady ways, of her happy companionship with Patience Oriel, and her dear, bosom friendship with Beatrice Gresham. He thought of her grace, and winning manners, and soft, polished, feminine beauty; and, as he did so, he hated Sir Roger Scatcherd, and regarded him with loathing, as he might have regarded a wallowing hog.

At last a light seemed to break in upon Sir Roger's mind. Dr Thorne, he perceived, did not answer his last question. He perceived, also, that the doctor was affected with some more than ordinary emotion. Why should it be that this subject of Mary Scatcherd's child moved him so deeply? Sir Roger had never been at the doctor's house at Greshamsbury, had never seen Mary Thorne, but he had heard that there lived with the doctor some young female relative; and thus a glimmering light seemed to come in upon Sir Roger's bed.

He had twitted the doctor with his pride; had said that it was impossible that the girl should be called Mary Thorne. What if she were so called? What if she were now warming herself at the doctor's hearth?

'Well, come, Thorne, what is it you call her? Tell it out, man. And, look you, if it's your name she bears, I shall think more of you, a deal more than ever I did yet. Come, Thorne, I'm her uncle too. I have a right to know. She is Mary Thorne, isn't she?'

The doctor had not the hardihood nor the resolution to deny it. 'Yes,' said he, 'that is her name; she lives with me.'

'Yes, and lives with all those grand folks at Greshamsbury too. I have heard of that.'

'She lives with me, and belongs to me, and is as my daughter.'

'She shall come over here. Lady Scatcherd shall have her to stay with her. She shall come to us. And as for my will, I'll make another. I'll – '

'Yes, make another will – or else alter that one. But as to Miss Thorne coming here – '

'What! Mary – '

'Well, Mary. As to Mary Thorne coming here, that I fear will not be possible. She cannot have two homes. She has cast her lot with one of her uncles, and she must remain with him now.'

'Do you mean to say she must never have any relation but one?'

'But one such as I am. She would not be happy over here. She does not like new faces. You have enough depending on you; I have but her.'

'Enough! why, I have only got Louis Philippe. I could provide for a dozen girls.'

'Well, well, well, we will not talk about that.'

'Ah! but, Thorne, you have told me of this girl now, and I cannot but talk of her. If you wished to keep the matter dark, you should have said nothing about it. She is my niece as much as yours. And, Thorne, I loved my sister Mary quite as well as you loved your brother; quite as well.'

Any one who might now have heard and seen the contractor would have hardly thought him to be the same man who, a few hours before, was urging that the Barchester physician should be put under the pump.

'You have your son, Scatcherd. I have no one but that girl.'

'I don't want to take her from you. I don't want to take her; but surely there can be no harm in her coming here to see us. I can provide for her, Thorne, remember that. I can provide for her without reference to Louis Philippe. What are ten or fifteen thousand pounds to me? Remember that, Thorne.'

Dr Thorne did remember it. In that interview he remembered many things, and much passed through his mind on which he felt himself compelled to resolve somewhat too suddenly. Would he be justified in rejecting, on behalf of Mary, the offer of pecuniary provision which this rich relative seemed so well inclined to make? Or, if he accepted it, would he in truth be studying her interests? Scatcherd was a self-willed, obstinate man – now indeed touched by an unwonted tenderness; but he was one to whose lasting tenderness Dr Thorne would be very unwilling to trust his darling. He did resolve, that on the whole he should best discharge his duty, even to her, by keeping her to himself, and rejecting, on her behalf, any participation in the baronet's wealth. As Mary herself had said, 'some people must be bound together;' and their destiny, that of himself and his niece, seemed to have so bound them. She had found her place at Greshamsbury, her place in the world; and it would be better for her now to keep it, than to go forth and seek another that would be richer, but at the same time less suited to her.

'No, Scatcherd,' he said at last, 'she cannot come here; she would not be happy here, and, to tell you the truth, I do not wish her to know that she has other relatives.'

'Ah! she would be ashamed of her mother, you mean, and of her mother's brother too, eh? She's too fine a lady, I suppose, to take me by the hand and give me a kiss, and call me her uncle? I and Lady Scatcherd would not be grand enough for her, eh?'

'You may say what you please, Scatcherd: I of course cannot stop you.'

'But I don't know how you'll reconcile what you are doing to your conscience. What right can you have to throw away the girl's chance, now that she has a chance? What fortune can you give her?'

'I have done what little I could,' said Thorne, proudly.

'Well, well, well, well, I never heard such a thing in my life; never. Mary's child, my own Mary's child, and I'm not to see her! But, Thorne, I tell you what! I will see her. I'll go over to her, I'll go to Greshamsbury, and tell her who I am, and what I can do for her. I tell you fairly I will. You shall not keep her away from those who belong to her, and can do her a good turn. Mary's daughter; another Mary Scatcherd! I almost wish she were called Mary Scatcherd! Is she like her, Thorne? Come, tell me that; is she like her mother?'

'I do not remember her mother; at least not in health.'

'Not remember her! ah, well. She was the handsomest girl in Barchester, anyhow. That was given up to her. Well, I didn't ever think to be talking of her again. Thorne, you cannot but expect that I shall go over and see Mary's child?'

'Now, Scatcherd, look here,' and the doctor, coming away from the window, where he had been standing, sat himself down by the bedside, 'you must not come over to Greshamsbury.'

'Oh! but I shall.'

'Listen to me, Scatcherd. I do not want to praise myself in any way; but when that girl was an infant, six months old, she was like to be a thorough obstacle to her mother's fortune in life. Tomlinson was willing to marry your sister, but he would not marry the child too. Then I took the baby, and I promised her mother that I would be to her as a father. I have kept my word as fairly as I have been able. She has sat at my hearth, and drunk of my cup, and been to me as my own child. After that, I have a right to judge what is best for her. Her life is not like your life, and her ways are not as your ways – '

'Ah, that is just it; we are too vulgar for her.'

'You may take it as you will,' said the doctor, who was too much in earnest to be in the least afraid of offending his companion. 'I have not said so; but I do say that you and she are unlike in your way of living.'

'She wouldn't like an uncle with a brandy bottle under his head, eh?'

'You could not see her without letting her know what is the connexion between you; of that I wish to keep her in ignorance.'

'I never knew any one yet who was ashamed of a rich connexion. How do you mean to get a husband for her, eh?'

'I have told you of her existence,' continued the doctor, not appearing to notice what the baronet had last said, 'because I found it necessary that you should know the fact of your sister having left this child behind her; you would otherwise have made a will different from that intended, and there might have been a lawsuit, and mischief and misery when we are gone. You must perceive that I have done this in honesty to you; and you yourself are too honest to repay me by taking advantage of this knowledge to make me unhappy.'

'Oh, very well, doctor. At any rate, you are a brick, I will say that. But I'll think of all this, I'll think of it; but it does startle me to find that poor Mary has a child living so near to me.'

'And now, Scatcherd, I will say good-bye. We part friends, don't we?'

'Oh, but doctor, you ain't going to leave me so. What am I to do? What doses shall I take? How much brandy may I drink? May I have a grill for dinner? D – me, doctor, you have turned Fillgrave out of the house. You mustn't go and desert me.'

Dr Thorne laughed, and then, sitting himself down to write medically, gave such prescriptions and ordinances as he found to be necessary. They amounted but to this: that the man was to drink, if possible, no brandy; and if that were not possible, then as little as might be.

This having been done, the doctor again proceeded to take his leave; but when he got to the door he was called back. 'Thorne! Thorne! About that money for Mr Gresham; do what you like, do just what you like. Ten thousand, is it? Well, he shall have it. I'll make Winterbones write about it at once. Five per cent., isn't it? No, four and a half. Well, he shall have ten thousand more.'

'Thank you, Scatcherd, thank you, I am really very much obliged to you, I am indeed. I wouldn't ask it if I were not sure your money is safe. Good-bye, old fellow, and get rid of that bedfellow of yours,' and again he was at the door.

'Thorne,' said Sir Roger, once more. 'Thorne, just come back for a minute. You wouldn't let me send a present, would you, – fifty pounds or so, – just to buy a few flounces?'

The doctor contrived to escape without giving a definite answer to this question; and then, having paid his compliments to Lady Scatcherd, remounted his cob and rode back to Greshamsbury.

CHAPTER XIV

Sentence of Exile

Dr Thorne did not at once go home to his own house. When he reached the Greshamsbury gates, he sent his horse to its own stable by one of the people at the lodge, and then walked on to the mansion. He had to see the squire on the subject of the forthcoming loan, and he had also to see Lady Arabella.

The Lady Arabella, though she was not personally attached to the doctor with quite so much warmth as some others of her family, still had reasons of her own for not dispensing with his visits to the house. She was one of his patients, and a patient fearful of the disease with which she was threatened. Though she thought the doctor to be arrogant, deficient as to properly submissive demeanour towards herself, an instigator to marital parsimony in her lord, one altogether opposed to herself and her interests in Greshamsbury politics, nevertheless, she did feel trust in him as a medical man. She had no wish to be rescued out of his hands by any Dr Fillgrave, as regarded that complaint of hers, much as she may have desired, and did desire, to sever him from all Greshamsbury councils in all matters not touching the healing art.

Now the complaint of which the Lady Arabella was afraid, was cancer: and her only present confidant in this matter was Dr Thorne.

The first of the Greshamsbury circle whom he saw was Beatrice, and he met her in the garden.

'Oh, doctor,' said she, 'where has Mary been this age? She has not been up here since Frank's birthday.'

'Well, that was only three days ago. Why don't you go down and ferret her out in the village?'

'So I have done. I was there just now, and found her out. She was out with Patience Oriel. Patience is all and all with her now. Patience is all very well, but if they throw me over – '

'My dear Miss Gresham, Patience is and always was a virtue.'

'A poor, beggarly, sneaking virtue after all, doctor. They should have come up, seeing how deserted I am here. There's absolutely nobody left.'

'Has Lady de Courcy gone?'

'Oh, yes! All the De Courcys have gone. I think, between ourselves, Mary stays away because she does not love them too well. They have all gone, and have taken Augusta and Frank with them.'

'Has Frank gone to Courcy Castle?'

'Oh, yes; did not you hear? There was rather a fight about it. Master Frank wanted to get off, and was as hard to catch as an eel, and then the countess was offended; and papa said he didn't see why Frank was to go if he didn't like it. Papa is very anxious about his degree, you know.'

The doctor understood it all as well as though it had been described to him at full length. The countess had claimed her prey, in order that she might carry him off to Miss Dunstable's golden embrace. The prey, not yet old enough and wise enough to connect the worship of Plutus with that of Venus,* had made sundry futile feints and dodges in the vain hope of escape. Then the anxious mother had enforced the De Courcy behests with all a mother's authority; but the father, whose ideas on the subject of Miss Dunstable's wealth had probably not been consulted, had, as a matter of course, taken exactly the other side of the question. The doctor did not require to be told all this in order to know how the battle had raged. He had not yet heard of the great Dunstable scheme; but he was sufficiently acquainted with Greshamsbury tactics to understand that the war had been carried on somewhat after this fashion.

As a rule, when the squire took a point warmly to heart, he was wont to carry his way against the De Courcy interest. He could be obstinate enough when it so pleased him, and had before now gone so far as to tell his wife, that her thrice-noble sister-in-law might remain at home at Courcy Castle – or, at any rate, not come to Greshamsbury – if she could not do so without striving to rule him and every one else when she got there. This had of course been repeated to the countess, who had merely replied to it by a sisterly whisper, in which she sorrowfully intimated that some men were born brutes, and always would remain so.

'I think they all are,' the Lady Arabella had replied; wishing, perhaps, to remind her sister-in-law that the breed of brutes was as rampant in West Barsetshire as in the eastern division of the county.

The squire, however, had not fought on this occasion with all his vigour. There had, of course, been some passages between him and his son, and it had been agreed that Frank should go for a fortnight to Courcy Castle.

'We mustn't quarrel with them, you know, if we can help it,' said the father; 'and, therefore, you must go sooner or later.'

'Well, I suppose so; but you don't know how dull it is, governor.'

'Don't I?' said Mr Gresham.

'There's a Miss Dunstable to be there; did you ever hear of her, sir?'

'No, never.'

'She's a girl whose father used to make ointment, or something of that sort.'

'Oh, yes, to be sure; the ointment of Lebanon. He used to cover all the walls in London. I haven't heard of him this year past.'

'No; that's because he's dead. Well, she carries on the ointment now, I believe; at any rate, she has got all the money. I wonder what she's like.'

'You'd better go and see,' said the father, who now began to have some inkling of an idea why the two ladies were so anxious to carry his son off to Courcy Castle at this exact time. And so Frank had packed up his best clothes, given a last fond look at the new black horse, repeated his last special injunctions to Peter, and had then made one of the stately *cortège* which proceeded through the county from Greshamsbury to Courcy Castle.

'I am very glad of that, very,' said the squire, when he heard that the money was to be forthcoming. 'I shall get it on easier terms from him than elsewhere; and it kills me to have continual bother about such things.' And Mr Gresham, feeling that that difficulty was tided over for a time, and that the immediate pressure of little debts would be abated, stretched himself on his easy chair as though he were quite comfortable; – one may say almost elated.

How frequent it is that men on their road to ruin feel elation such as this! A man signs away a moiety of his substance; nay, that were nothing; but a moiety of the substance of his children; he puts his pen to the paper that ruins him and them; but in doing so he frees himself from a score of immediate little pestering, stinging troubles: and, therefore, feels as though fortune had been almost kind to him.

The doctor felt angry with himself for what he had done when he saw how easily the squire adapted himself to this new loan. 'It will make Scatcherd's claim upon you very heavy,' said he.

Mr Gresham at once read all that was passing through the doctor's mind. 'Well, what else can I do?' said he. 'You wouldn't have me allow my daughter to lose this match for the sake of a few thousand pounds? It will be well at any rate to have one of them settled. Look at that letter from Moffat.'

The doctor took the letter and read it. It was a long, wordy, ill-written rigmarole, in which that amorous gentleman spoke with much rapture of his love and devotion for Miss Gresham; but at the same time declared, and most positively swore, that the adverse cruelty of his circumstances was such, that it would not allow him to stand up like a man at the hymeneal altar until six thousand pounds hard cash had been paid down at his banker's.

'It may be all right,' said the squire; 'but in my time gentlemen were not used to write such letters as that to each other.'

The doctor shrugged his shoulders. He did not know how far he would be justified in saying much, even to his friend the squire, in dispraise of his future son-in-law.

'I told him that he should have the money; and one would have thought that that would have been enough for him. Well: I suppose Augusta likes him. I suppose she wishes the match; otherwise, I would give him such an answer to that letter as should startle him a little.'

'What settlement is he to make?' said Thorne.

'Oh, that's satisfactory enough; couldn't be more so; a thousand a year and the house at Wimbledon for her; that's all very well. But such a lie, you know, Thorne. He's rolling in money, and yet he talks of this beggarly sum as though he couldn't possibly stir without it.'

'If I might venture to speak my mind,' said Thorne.

'Well?' said the squire, looking at him earnestly.

'I should be inclined to say that Mr Moffat wants to cry off, himself.'

'Oh, impossible; quite impossible. In the first place, he was so very anxious for the match. In the next place, it is such a great thing for him. And then, he would never dare; you see, he is dependent on the De Courcys for his seat.'

'But suppose he loses his seat?'

'But there is not much fear of that, I think. Scatcherd may be a very fine fellow, but I think they'll hardly return him at Barchester.'

'I don't understand much about it,' said Thorne; 'but such things do happen.'

'And you believe that this man absolutely wants to get off the match; absolutely thinks of playing such a trick as that on my daughter; – on me?'

'I don't say he intends to do it; but it looks to me as though he were making a door for himself, or trying to make a door: if so, your having the money will stop him there.'

'But, Thorne, don't you think he loves the girl? If I thought not –'

The doctor stood silent for a moment, and then he said, 'I am not a love-making man myself, but I think that if I were much in love with a young lady I should not write such a letter as that to her father.'

'By heavens! If I thought so,' said the squire – 'but, Thorne, we can't judge of those fellows as one does of gentlemen; they are so used to making money, and seeing money made, that they have an eye to business in everything.'

'Perhaps so, perhaps so,' muttered the doctor, showing very evidently that he still doubted the warmth of Mr Moffat's affection.

'The match was none of my making, and I cannot interfere now to break it off: it will give her a good position in the world; for, after all, money goes a great way, and it is something to be in Parliament. I can only hope she likes him. I do truly hope she likes him;' and the squire also showed by the tone of his voice that, though he might hope that his daughter was in love with her intended husband, he hardly conceived it to be possible that she should be so.

And what was the truth of the matter? Miss Gresham was no more in love with Mr Moffat than you are – oh, sweet, young, blooming beauty! Not a whit more; not, at least, in your sense of the word, nor in mine. She had by no means resolved within her heart that of all the men whom she had ever seen, or ever could see, he was far away the nicest and best. That is what you will do when you are in love, if you be good for anything. She had no longing to sit near to him – the nearer the better; she had no thought of his taste and his choice when she bought her ribbons and bonnets; she had no indescribable desire that all her female friends should be ever talking to her about him. When she wrote to him, she did not copy her letters again and again, so that she might be, as it were, ever speaking to him; she took no special pride in herself because he had chosen her to be his life's partner. In point of fact, she did not care one straw about him.

And yet she thought she loved him; was, indeed, quite confident that she did so; told her mother that she was sure

Gustavus would wish this, she knew Gustavus would like that, and so on; but as for Gustavus himself, she did not care a chip for him.

She was in love with her match just as farmers are in love with wheat at eighty shillings a quarter, or shareholders – innocent gudgeons* – with seven and a half per cent. interest on their paid-up capital. Eighty shillings a quarter, and seven and a half per cent interest, such were the returns which she had been taught to look for in exchange for her young heart; and, having obtained them, or being thus about to obtain them, why should not her young heart be satisfied? Had she not sat herself down obediently at the feet of her lady Gamaliel,* and should she not be rewarded? Yes, indeed, she shall be rewarded.

And then the doctor went to the lady. On their medical secrets we will not intrude; but there were other matters bearing on the course of our narrative, as to which Lady Arabella found it necessary to say a word or so to the doctor; and it is essential that we should know what was the tenor of those few words so spoken.

How the aspirations, and instincts, and feelings of a household become changed as the young birds begin to flutter with feathered wings, and have half-formed thoughts of leaving the parental nest! A few months back, Frank had reigned almost autocratic over the lesser subjects of the kingdom of Greshamsbury. The servants, for instance, always obeyed him, and his sisters never dreamed of telling anything which he directed should not be told. All his mischief, all his troubles, and all his loves were confided to them, with the sure conviction that they would never be made to stand in evidence against him.

Trusting to this well-ascertained state of things, he had not hesitated to declare his love for Miss Thorne before his sister Augusta. But his sister Augusta had now, as it were, been received into the upper house; having duly received, and duly profited by the lessons of her great instructress, she was now admitted to sit in conclave with the higher powers: her sympathies, of course, became changed, and her confidence was removed from the young and giddy and given to the ancient and discreet. She was as a schoolboy, who, having finished his schooling, and being fairly forced by necessity into the stern bread-earning world, undertakes the new duties of tutoring. Yesterday he was taught, and fought, of course, against the schoolmaster; today he teaches, and fights as keenly for him. So it was with Augusta Gresham, when, with careful brow, she whispered to her mother that there was something wrong between Frank and Mary Thorne.

'Stop it at once, Arabella: stop it at once,' the countess had said; 'that, indeed, will be ruin. If he does not marry money, he is lost. Good heavens the doctor's niece! A girl that nobody knows where she comes from!'

'He's going with you tomorrow, you know,' said the anxious mother.

'Yes; and that is so far well: if he will be led by me, the evil may be remedied before he returns; but it is very, very hard to lead young men. Arabella, you must forbid that girl to come to Greshamsbury again on any pretext whatever. The evil must be stopped at once.'

'But she is here so much as a matter of course.'

'Then she must be here as a matter of course no more: there has been folly, very great folly, in having her here. Of course she would turn out to be a designing creature with such temptation before her; with such a prize within her reach, how could she help it?'

'I must say, aunt, she answered him very properly,' said Augusta.

'Nonsense,' said the countess; 'before you, of course she did. Arabella, the matter must not be left to the girl's propriety. I never knew the propriety of a girl of that sort to be fit to be depended upon yet. If you wish to save the whole family from ruin, you must take steps to keep her away from Greshamsbury now at once. Now is the time; now that Frank is to be away. Where so much, so very much depends on a young man's marrying money, not one day ought to be lost.'

Instigated in this manner, Lady Arabella resolved to open her mind to the doctor, and to make it intelligible to him that, under present circumstances, Mary's visits at Greshamsbury had better be discontinued. She would have given much, however, to have escaped this business. She had in her time tried one or two falls with the doctor, and she was conscious that she had never yet got the better of him: and then she was in a slight degree afraid of Mary herself. She had a presentiment that it would not be so easy to banish Mary from Greshamsbury: she was not sure that that young lady would not boldly assert her right to her place in the school-room; appeal loudly to the squire, and, perhaps, declare her determination of marrying the heir, out before them all. The squire would be sure to uphold her in that, or in anything else.

And then, too, there would be the greatest difficulty in wording her request to the doctor; and Lady Arabella was sufficiently conscious of her own weakness to know that she was not always very good at words. But the doctor, when hard pressed, was never at fault: he could say the bitterest things in the quietest tone, and Lady Arabella had a great dread of these bitter things. What, also, if he should desert her himself; withdraw from her his skill and knowledge of her bodily wants and ailments now that he was so necessary to her? She had once before taken to that measure of sending to Barchester for Dr Fillgrave, but it had answered with her hardly better than with Sir Roger and Lady Scatcherd.

When, therefore, Lady Arabella found herself alone with the doctor, and called upon to say out her say in what best language she could select for the occasion, she did not feel to be very much at her ease. There was that about the man before her which cowed her, in spite of her being the wife of the squire, the sister of an earl, a person quite acknowledged to be of the great world, and the mother of the very important young man whose affections were now about to be called in question. Nevertheless, there was the task to be done, and with a mother's courage she essayed it.

'Dr Thorne,' said she, as soon as their medical conference was at an end, 'I am very glad you came over today, for I had something special which I wanted to say to you:' so far she got, and then stopped; but, as the doctor did not seem inclined to give her any assistance, she was forced to flounder on as best she could.

'Something very particular, indeed. You know what a respect and esteem, and I may say affection, we all have for you,' – here the doctor made a low bow – 'and I may say for Mary also;' here the doctor bowed himself again. 'We have done what little we could to be pleasant neighbours, and I think you'll believe me when I say that I am a true friend to you and dear Mary – '

The doctor knew that something very unpleasant was coming, but he could not at all guess what might be its nature. He felt, however, that he must say something; so he expressed a hope that he was duly sensible of all the acts of kindness he had ever received from the squire and the family at large.

'I hope, therefore, my dear doctor, you won't take amiss what I am going to say.'

'Well, Lady Arabella, I'll endeavour not to do so.'

'I am sure I would not give any pain if I could help it, much less to you. But there are occasions, doctor, in which duty must be paramount; paramount to all other considerations, you know; and, certainly, this occasion is one of them.'

'But what is the occasion, Lady Arabella?'

'I'll tell you, doctor. You know what Frank's position is?'

'Frank's position! as regards what?'

'Why, his position in life; an only son, you know.'

'Oh, yes; I know his position in that respect; an only son, and his father's heir; and a very fine fellow he is. You have but one son, Lady Arabella, and you may well be proud of him.

Lady Arabella sighed. She did not wish at the present moment to express herself as being in any way proud of Frank. She was desirous rather, on the other hand, of showing that she was a good deal ashamed of him; only not quite so much ashamed of him as it behoved the doctor to be of his niece.

'Well, perhaps so; yes,' said Lady Arabella, 'he is, I believe, a very good young man, with an excellent disposition; but, doctor, his position is very precarious; and he is just at that time of life when every caution is necessary.'

To the doctor's ears, Lady Arabella was now talking of her son as a mother might of her infant when whooping-cough was abroad or croup imminent. 'There is nothing on earth the matter with him, I should say,' said the doctor. 'He has every possible sign of perfect health.'

'Oh, yes; his health! Yes, thank God, his health is good; that is a great blessing.' And Lady Arabella thought of her four flowerets that had already faded. 'I am sure I am most thankful to see him growing up so strong. But it is not that I mean, doctor.'

'Then what is it, Lady Arabella?'

'Why, doctor, you know the squire's position with regard to money matters?'

Now the doctor undoubtedly did know the squire's position with regard to money matters, – knew it much better than did Lady Arabella; but he was by no means inclined to talk on that subject to her ladyship. He remained quite silent, therefore, although Lady Arabella's last speech had taken the form of a question. Lady Arabella was a little offended at this want of freedom on his part, and became somewhat sterner in her tone – a thought less condescending in her manner.

'The squire has unfortunately embarrassed the property, and Frank must look forward to inherit it with very heavy encumbrances; I fear very heavy indeed, though of what exact nature I am kept in ignorance.'

Looking at the doctor's face, she perceived that there was no probability whatever that her ignorance would be enlightened by him.

'And, therefore, it is highly necessary that Frank should be very careful.'

'As to his private expenditure, you mean?' said the doctor.

'No; not exactly that: though of course he must be careful as to that, too; that's of course. But that is not what I mean, doctor; his only hope of retrieving his circumstances is by marrying money.'

'With every other conjugal blessing that a man can have, I hope he may have that also.' So the doctor replied with imperturbable face; but not the less did he begin to have a shade of suspicion of what might be the coming subject of the conference. It would be untrue to say that he had ever thought it probable that the young heir should fall in love with his niece; that he had ever looked forward to such a chance, either with complacency or with fear; nevertheless, the idea had of late passed through his mind. Some word that had fallen from Mary, some closely watched expression of her eye, or some quiver in her lip when Frank's name was mentioned, had of late made him involuntarily think that such might not be impossible; and then, when the chance of Mary becoming the heiress to so large a fortune had been forced upon his consideration, he had been unable to prevent himself from building happy castles in the air, as he rode slowly home from Boxall Hill. But not a whit the more on that account was he prepared to be untrue to the squire's interest, or to encourage a feeling which must be distasteful to all the squire's friends.

'Yes, doctor; he must marry money.'

'And worth, Lady Arabella; and a pure feminine heart; and youth and beauty. I hope he will marry them all.'

Could it be possible, that in speaking of a pure feminine heart, and youth and beauty, and such like gewgaws, the doctor was thinking of his niece? Could it be that he had absolutely made up his mind to foster and encourage this odious match?

The bare idea made Lady Arabella wrathful, and her wrath gave her courage. 'He must marry money, or he will be a ruined man. Now, doctor, I am informed that things – words that is – have passed between him and Mary which never ought to have been allowed.'

And now also was the doctor wrathful. 'What things? what words?' said he, appearing to Lady Arabella as though he rose in his anger nearly a foot in altitude before her eyes. 'What has passed between them? and who says so?'

'Doctor, there have been love-makings, you may take my word for it; love-makings of a very, very, very advanced description.'

This, the doctor could not stand. No, not for Greshamsbury and its heir; not for the squire and all his misfortunes; not for Lady Arabella and the blood of all the De Courcys could he stand quiet and hear Mary thus accused. He sprang up another foot in height, and expanded equally in width as he flung back the insinuation.

'Who says so? Whoever says so, whoever speaks of Miss Thorne in such language, says what is not true. I will pledge my word – '

'My dear doctor, my dear doctor, what took place was quite clearly heard; there was no mistake about it, indeed.'

'What took place? What was heard?'

'Well, then, I don't want, you know, to make more of it than can be helped. The thing must be stopped, that is all.'

'What thing? Speak out, Lady Arabella. I will not have Mary's conduct impugned by innuendoes. What is it that the eavesdroppers have heard?'

'Dr Thorne, there have been no eavesdroppers.'

'And no talebearers either? Will your ladyship oblige me by letting me know what is the accusation which you bring against my niece?'

'There has been most positively an offer made, Dr Thorne.'

'And who made it?'

'Oh, of course I am not going to say but what Frank must

have been very imprudent. Of course he has been to blame. There has been fault on both sides, no doubt.'

'I utterly deny it. I positively deny it. I know nothing of the circumstances; have heard nothing about it – '

'Then of course you can't say,' said Lady Arabella.

'I know nothing of the circumstance; have heard nothing about it,' continued Dr Thorne; 'but I do know my niece, and am ready to assert that there has not been fault on both sides. Whether there has been any fault on any side, that I do not yet know.'

'I can assure you, Dr Thorne, that an offer was made by Frank; such an offer cannot be without its allurements to a young lady circumstanced like your niece.'

'Allurements!' almost shouted the doctor, and, as he did so, Lady Arabella stepped back a pace or two, retreating from the fire which shot out of his eyes. 'But the truth is, Lady Arabella, you do not know my niece. If you will have the goodness to let me understand what it is that you desire I will tell you whether I can comply with your wishes.'

'Of course it will be very inexpedient that the young people should be thrown together again; – for the present, I mean.'

'Well!'

'Frank has now gone to Courcy Castle; and he talks of going from thence to Cambridge. But he will doubtless be here, backwards and forwards; and perhaps it will be better for all parties – safer, that is, doctor – if Miss Thorne were to discontinue her visits to Greshamsbury for a while.'

'Very well!' thundered out the doctor. 'Her visits to Greshamsbury shall be discontinued.'

'Of course, doctor, this won't change the intercourse between us; between you and the family.'

'Not change it!' said he. 'Do you think that I will break bread in a house from whence she has been ignominiously banished? Do you think that I can sit down in friendship with those who have spoken of her as you have now spoken? You have many daughters; what would you say if I accused one of them as you have accused her?'

'Accused, doctor! No, I don't accuse her. But prudence, you know, does sometimes require us – '

'Very well; prudence requires you to look after those who

belong to you; and prudence also requires me to look after my one lamb. Good morning, Lady Arabella.'

'But, doctor, you are not going to quarrel with us? You will come when we want you; eh! won't you?'

Quarrel! quarrel with Greshamsbury! Angry as he was, the doctor felt that he could ill bear to quarrel with Greshamsbury. A man past fifty cannot easily throw over the ties that have taken twenty years to form, and wrench himself away from the various close ligatures with which, in such a period, he has become bound. He could not quarrel with the squire; he could ill bear to quarrel with Frank; though he now began to conceive that Frank had used him badly, he could not do so; he could not quarrel with the children, who had almost been born into his arms; nor even with the very walls, and trees, and grassy knolls with which he was so dearly intimate. He could not proclaim himself an enemy to Greshamsbury; and yet he felt that fealty to Mary required of him that, for the present, he should put on an enemy's guise.

'If you want me, Lady Arabella, and send for me, I will come to you; otherwise I will, if you please, share the sentence which has been passed on Mary. I will now wish you good morning.' And then, bowing low to her, he left the room and the house, and sauntered slowly away to his own home.

What was he to say to Mary? He walked very slowly down the Greshamsbury avenue, with his hands clasped behind his back, thinking over the whole matter; thinking of it, or rather trying to think of it. When a man's heart is warmly concerned in any matter, it is almost useless for him to endeavour to think of it. Instead of thinking, he gives play to his feelings, and feeds his passion by indulging it. 'Allurements!' he said to himself, repeating Lady Arabella's words. 'A girl circumstanced like my niece! How utterly incapable is such a woman as that to understand the mind, and heart, and soul of such a one as Mary Thorne!' And then his thoughts recurred to Frank. 'It has been ill done of him; ill done of him: young as he is, he should have had feeling enough to have spared me this. A thoughtless word has been spoken which will now make her miserable!' And then, as he walked on, he could not divest his mind of the remembrance of what had passed between him and Sir Roger. What if, after all, Mary should become the heiress to all that money? What, if she should become, in fact, the owner of Greshamsbury? for indeed it seemed too possible that Sir Roger's heir would be the owner of Greshamsbury.

The idea was one which he disliked to entertain, but it would recur to him again and again. It might be, that a marriage between his niece and the nominal heir to the estate might be of all matches the best for young Gresham to make. How sweet would be the revenge, how glorious the retaliation on Lady Arabella, if, after what had now been said, it should come to pass that all the difficulties of Greshamsbury should be made smooth by Mary's love, and Mary's hand! It was a dangerous subject on which to ponder; and, as he sauntered down the road, the doctor did his best to banish it from his mind, – not altogether successfully.

But as he went he again encountered Beatrice. 'Tell Mary I went to her today,' said she, 'and that I expect her up here tomorrow. If she does not come, I shall be savage.'

'Do not be savage,' said he, putting out his hand, 'even though she should not come.'

Beatrice immediately saw that his manner with her was not playful, and that his face was serious. 'I was only in joke,' said she; 'of course I was only joking. But is anything the matter? Is Mary ill?'

'Oh, no; not ill at all; but she will not be here tomorrow, nor probably for some time. But, Miss Gresham, you must not be savage with her.'

Beatrice tried to interrogate him, but he would not wait to answer her questions. While she was speaking he bowed to her in his usual old-fashioned courteous way, and passed on out of hearing. 'She will not come up for some time,' said Beatrice to herself. 'Then mamma must have quarrelled with her.' And at once in her heart she acquitted her friend of all blame in the matter, whatever it might be, and condemned her mother unheard.

The doctor, when he arrived at his own house, had in nowise made up his mind as to the manner in which he would break the matter to Mary; but by the time that he had reached the drawing-room, he had made up his mind to this, that he would put off the evil hour till the morrow. He would sleep on the matter – lie awake on it, more probably – and then at breakfast, as best he could, tell her what had been said of her.

Mary that evening was more than usually inclined to be

playful. She had not been quite certain till the morning, whether Frank had absolutely left Greshamsbury, and had, therefore, preferred the company of Miss Oriel to going up to the house. There was a peculiar cheerfulness about her friend Patience, a feeling of satisfaction with the world and those in it, which Mary always shared when with her; and now she had brought home to the doctor's fireside, in spite of her young troubles, a smiling face, if not a heart altogether happy.

'Uncle,' she said at last, 'what makes you so sombre? Shall I read to you?'

'No; not tonight, dearest.'

'Why, uncle; what is the matter?'

'Nothing, nothing.'

'Ah, but it is something, and you shall tell me;' and, getting up, she came over to his armchair, and leant over his shoulder.

He looked at her for a minute in silence, and then, getting up from his chair, passed his arm round her waist, and pressed her closely to his heart.

'My darling!' he said, almost convulsively. 'My best, own, truest darling!' and Mary, looking up into his face, saw that the big tears were running down his cheeks.

But still he told her nothing that night.

END OF VOLUME I

CHAPTER XV

Courcy

When Frank Gresham expressed to his father an opinion that
Courcy Castle was dull, the squire, as may be remembered, did
not pretend to differ from him. To men such as the squire, and
such as the squire's son, Courcy Castle was dull. To what class
of men it would not be dull the author is not prepared to say;
but it may be presumed that the De Courcys found it to their
liking, or they would have made it other than it was.

The castle itself was a huge brick pile, built in the days of
William III,* which, though they were grand days for the
construction of the Constitution, were not very grand for
architecture of a more material description. It had, no doubt, a
perfect right to be called a castle, as it was entered by a castle-
gate which led into a court, the porter's lodge for which was
built as it were into the wall; there were attached to it also two
round, stumpy adjuncts, which were, perhaps properly, called
towers, though they did not do much in the way of towering;
and, moreover, along one side of the house, over what would
otherwise have been the cornice, there ran a castellated parapet,
through the assistance of which, the imagination no doubt was
intended to supply the muzzles of defiant artillery. But any
artillery which would have so presented its muzzle must have
been very small, and it may be doubted whether even a bowman
could have obtained shelter there.

The grounds about the castle were not very inviting, nor, as
grounds, very extensive; though, no doubt, the entire domain
was such as suited the importance of so puissant a nobleman as
Earl de Courcy. What, indeed, should have been the park was
divided out into various large paddocks. The surface was flat
and unbroken; and though there were magnificent elm-trees
standing in straight lines, like hedgerows, the timber had not

that beautiful, wild, scattered look which generally gives the great charm to English scenery.

The town of Courcy – for the place claimed to rank as a town – was in many particulars like the castle. It was built of dingy-red brick – almost more brown than red – and was solid, dull-looking, ugly, and comfortable. It consisted of four streets, which were formed by two roads crossing each other, making at the point of junction a centre for the town. Here stood the Red Lion; had it been called the brown lion, the nomenclature would have been more strictly correct; and here, in the old days of coaching, some life had been wont to stir itself at those hours in the day and night when the Freetraders, Tallyhoes, and Royal Mails* changed their horses. But now there was a railway station a mile and a half distant, and the moving life of the town of Courcy was confined to the Red Lion omnibus, which seemed to pass its entire time in going up and down between the town and the station, quite unembarrassed by any great weight of passengers.

There were, so said the Courcyites when away from Courcy, excellent shops in the place; but they were not the less accustomed, when at home among themselves, to complain to each other of the vile extortion with which they were treated by their neighbours. The ironmonger, therefore, though he loudly asserted that he could beat Bristol in the quality of his wares in one direction, and undersell Gloucester in another, bought his tea and sugar on the sly in one of those larger towns; and the grocer, on the other hand, equally distrusted the pots and pans of home production. Trade, therefore, at Courcy, had not thriven since the railway had opened: and, indeed, had any patient inquirer stood at the cross through one entire day, counting the customers who entered the neighbouring shops, he might well have wondered that any shops in Courcy could be kept open.

And how changed has been the bustle of that once noisy inn to the present death-like silence of its green courtyard! There, a lame ostler crawls about with his hands thrust into the capacious pockets of his jacket, feeding on memory. That weary pair of omnibus jades, and three sorry posters, are all that now grace those stables where horses used to be stalled in close contiguity by the dozen; where twenty grains apiece, abstracted from every feed of oats consumed during the day, would have afforded a daily quart to the lucky pilferer.

Come, my friend, and discourse with me. Let us know what are thy ideas of the inestimable benefits which science has conferred on us in these, our latter days.* How dost thou, among others, appreciate railways and the power of steam, telegraphs, telegrams, and our new expresses? But indifferently, you say. 'Time was I've zeed vifteen pair o' 'osses go out of this 'ere yard in vour-and-twenty hour; and now there be'ant vifteen, no, not ten, in vour-and-twenty days! There was the duik – not this 'un; he be'ant no gude; but this 'un's vather – why, when he'd come down the road, the cattle did be-a-going, vour days an end. Here'd be the tooter and the young gen'lemen, and the governess and the young leddies, and then the servants – they'd be al'ays the grandest folk of all – and then the duik and the doochess – Lord love' ee, zur; the money did fly in them days! But now – ' and the feeling of scorn and contempt which the lame ostler was enabled by his native talent to throw into that word, 'now,' was quite as eloquent against the power of steam as anything that has been spoken at dinners, or written in pamphlets by the keenest admirers of latter-day lights.

'Why, luke at this 'ere town,' continued he of the seise,* 'the grass be a-growing in the very streets; – that can't be no gude. Why, luke'ee here, zur; I do be a'standing at this 'ere gateway, just this way, hour arfter hour, and my heyes is hopen, mostly; – I zees who's a-coming and who's a-going. Nobody's a-coming and nobody's a-going; that can't be no gude. Luke at that there homnibus; why, darn me – ' and now, in his eloquence at this peculiar point, my friend became more loud and powerful than ever – 'why, darn me, if maister harns enough with that there bus to put hiron on them there osses' feet, I'll – be – blowed!' And as he uttered this hypothetical denunciation on himself he spoke very slowly, bringing out every word as it were separately, and lowering himself at his knees at every sound, moving at the same time his right hand up and down. When he had finished, he fixed his eyes upon the ground, pointing downwards, as if there was to be the site of his doom if the curse that he had called down upon himself should ever come to pass: and then, waiting no further converse, he hobbled away, melancholy, to his deserted stables.

Oh, my friend! my poor lame friend! it will avail nothing to tell thee of Liverpool and Manchester; of the glories of Glasgow, with her flourishing banks; of London, with its third million of inhabitants; of the great things which commerce is doing for this nation of thine! What is commerce to thee, unless it be a commerce in posting on that worn-out, all but useless great western turnpike-road? There is nothing left for thee but to be carted away as rubbish – for thee and for many of us in these now prosperous days; oh, my melancholy, care-ridden friend!

Courcy Castle was certainly a dull place to look at, and Frank, in his former visits, had found that the appearance did not belie the reality. He had been but little there when the earl had been at Courcy; and as he had always felt from his childhood a peculiar distaste to the governance of his aunt the countess, this perhaps may have added to his feeling of dislike. Now, however, the castle was to be fuller than he had ever before known it; the earl was to be at home; there was some talk of the Duke of Omnium coming for a day or two, though that seemed doubtful; there was some faint doubt of Lord Porlock; Mr Moffat, intent on the coming election – and also, let us hope, on his coming bliss – was to be one of the guests; and there also was to be the great Miss Dunstable.

Frank, however, found that those grandees were not expected quite immediately. 'I might go back to Greshamsbury for three or four days as she is not to be here,' he said naïvely to his aunt, expressing, with tolerable perspicuity, his feeling, that he regarded his visit to Courcy Castle quite as a matter of business. But the countess would hear of no such arrangement. Now that she had got him, she was not going to let him fall back into the perils of Miss Thorne's intrigues, or even of Miss Thorne's propriety. 'It is quite essential,' she said, 'that you should be here a few days before her, so that she may see that you are at home.' Frank did not understand the reasoning; but he felt himself unable to rebel, and he therefore remained there, comforting himself, as best he might, with the eloquence of the Honourable George, and the sporting humours of the Honourable John.

Mr Moffat's was the earliest arrival of any importance. Frank had not hitherto made the acquaintance of his future brotherin-law, and there was, therefore, some little interest in the first interview. Mr Moffat was shown into the drawing-room before the ladies had gone up to dress, and it so happened that Frank was there also. As no one else was in the room but his sister and two of his cousins, he had expected to see the lovers rush into each other's arms. But Mr Moffat restrained his ardour, and Miss Gresham seemed contented that he should do so.

He was a nice, dapper man, rather above the middle height, and good-looking enough had he had a little more expression in his face. He had dark hair, very nicely brushed, small black whiskers, and a small black moustache. His boots were excellently well made, and his hands were very white. He simpered gently as he took hold of Augusta's fingers, and expressed a hope that she had been quite well since last he had had the pleasure of seeing her. Then he touched the hands of the Lady Rosina and the Lady Margaretta.

'Mr Moffat, allow me to introduce you to my brother?'

'Most happy, I'm sure,' said Mr Moffat, again putting out his hand, and allowing it to slip through Frank's grasp, as he spoke in a pretty, mincing voice: 'Lady Arabella quite well? – and your father, and sisters? Very warm, isn't it? – quite hot in town, I do assure you.'

'I hope Augusta likes him,' said Frank to himself, arguing on the subject exactly as his father had done; 'but for an engaged lover he seems to me to have a very queer way with him.' Frank, poor fellow! who was of a coarser mould, would, under such circumstances, have been all for kissing – sometimes, indeed, even under other circumstances.

Mr Moffat did not do much towards improving the conviviality of the castle. He was, of course, a good deal intent upon his coming election, and spent much of his time with Mr Nearthewinde, the celebrated parliamentary agent. It behoved him to be a good deal at Barchester, canvassing the electors and undermining, by Mr Nearthewinde's aid, the mines for blowing him out of his seat, which were daily being contrived by Mr Closerstil, on behalf of Sir Roger. The battle was to be fought on the internecine principle, no quarter being given or taken on either side; and of course this gave Mr Moffat as much as he knew how to do.

Mr Closerstil was well known to be the sharpest man at his business in all England, unless the palm should be given to his great rival Mr Nearthewinde; and in this instance he was to be assisted in the battle by a very clever young barrister, Mr Romer, who was an admirer of Sir Roger's career in life. Some people in

Barchester, when they saw Sir Roger, Closerstil, and Mr Romer
saunter down the High Street, arm in arm, declared that it was
all up with poor Moffat; but others, in whose head the bump of
veneration* was strongly pronounced, whispered to each other
that great shibboleth* the name of the Duke of Omnium – and
mildly asserted it to be impossible that the duke's nominee
should be thrown out.

Our poor friend the squire did not take much interest in the
matter, except in so far that he liked his son-in-law to be in
Parliament. Both the candidates were in his eye equally wrong
in their opinions. He had long since recanted those errors of his
early youth, which had cost him his seat for the county, and had
abjured the De Courcy politics. He was staunch enough as a
Tory now that his being so would no longer be of the slightest
use to him; but the Duke of Omnium, and Lord de Courcy, and
Mr Moffat were all Whigs; Whigs, however, differing altogether
in politics from Sir Roger, who belonged to the Manchester
school,* and whose pretensions, through some of those inscru-
table twists in modern politics which are quite unintelligible to
the minds of ordinary men outside the circle, were on this
occasion secretly favoured by the high Conservative party.

How Mr Moffat, who had been brought into the political
world by Lord de Courcy, obtained all the weight of the duke's
interest I never could exactly learn. For the duke and the earl
did not generally act as twin-brothers on such occasions.

There is a great difference in Whigs. Lord de Courcy was a
Court Whig, following the fortunes, and enjoying, when he
could get it, the sunshine of the throne. He was a sojourner at
Windsor, and a visitor at Balmoral. He delighted in gold sticks,
and was never so happy as when holding some cap of maintenance or spur of precedence with due dignity and acknowledged
grace in the presence of all the Court. His means had been
somewhat embarrassed by early extravagance; and, therefore,
as it was to his taste to shine, it suited him to shine at the cost
of the Court rather than at his own.

The Duke of Omnium was a Whig of a very different calibre.
He rarely went near the presence of majesty, and when he did
do so, he did it merely as a disagreeable duty incident to his
position. He was very willing that the Queen should be queen
so long as he was allowed to be Duke of Omnium. Nor had he
begrudged Prince Albert any of his honours till he was called

Prince Consort.* Then, indeed, he had, to his own intimate friends, made some remark in three words, not flattering to the discretion of the Prime Minister. The Queen might be queen so long as he was Duke of Omnium. Their revenues were about the same, with the exception, that the duke's were his own, and he could do what he liked with them. This remembrance did not unfrequently present itself to the duke's mind. In person, he was a plain, thin man, tall, but undistinguished in appearance, except that there was a gleam of pride in his eye which seemed every moment to be saying, 'I am the Duke of Omnium.' He was unmarried, and, if report said true, a great debauchee; but if so he had always kept his debaucheries decently away from the eyes of the world, and was not, therefore, open to that loud condemnation which should fall like a hailstorm round the ears of some more open sinners.

Why these two mighty nobles put their heads together in order that the tailor's son should represent Barchester in Parliament, I cannot explain. Mr Moffat was, as has been said, Lord de Courcy's friend; and it may be that Lord de Courcy was able to repay the duke for his kindness, as touching Barchester, with some little assistance in the county representation.

The next arrival was that of the Bishop of Barchester; a meek, good, worthy man, much attached to his wife, and somewhat addicted to his ease. She, apparently, was made in a different mould, and by her energy and diligence atoned for any want in those qualities which might be observed in the bishop himself. When asked his opinion, his lordship would generally reply by saying – 'Mrs Proudie and I think so and so.' But before that opinion was given, Mrs Proudie would take up the tale, and she, in her more concise manner, was not wont to quote the bishop as having at all assisted in the consideration of the subject. It was well known in Barsetshire that no married pair consorted more closely or more tenderly together; and the example of such conjugal affection among persons in the upper classes is worth mentioning, as it is believed by those below them, and too often with truth, that the sweet bliss of connubial reciprocity is not so common as it should be among the magnates of the earth.*

But the arrival even of the bishop and his wife did not make the place cheerful to Frank Gresham, and he began to long for Miss Dunstable; in order that he might have something to do. He could not get on at all with Mr Moffat. He had expected that the man would at once have called him Frank, and that he would have called the man Gustavus; but they did not even get beyond Mr Moffat and Mr Gresham. 'Very hot in Barchester today, very,' was the nearest approach to conversation which Frank could attain with him; and as far as he, Frank, could see, Augusta never got much beyond it. There might be *tête-à-tête* meetings between them, but, if so, Frank could not detect when they took place; and so, opening his heart at last to the Honourable George, for the want of a better confidant, he expressed his opinion that his future brother-in-law was a muff.*

'A muff – I believe you too. What do you think now? I have been with him and Nearthewinde in Barchester these three days past, looking up the electors' wives and daughters, and that kind of thing.'

'I say, if there is any fun in it you might as well take me with you.'

'Oh, there is not much fun; they are mostly so slobbered and dirty. A sharp fellow is Nearthewinde, and knows what he is about well.'

'Does he look up the wives and daughters too?'

'Oh, he goes on every tack, just as it's wanted. But there was Moffat, yesterday, in a room behind the milliner's shop near Cuthbert's Gate; I was with him. The woman's husband is one of the choristers and an elector, you know and Moffat went to look for his vote. Now, there was no one there when we got there but the three young women, the wife, that is, and her two girls – very pretty women they are too.'

'I say, George, I'll go and get that chorister's vote for Moffat; I ought to do it as he's to be my brother-in-law.'

'But what do you think Moffat said to the women?'

'Can't guess – he didn't kiss any of them, did he?'*

'Kiss any of them? No; but he begged to give them his positive assurance as a gentleman, that if he was returned to Parliament he would vote for an extension of the franchise, and the admission of the Jews into Parliament.'

'Well, he is a muff!' said Frank.

CHAPTER XVI

Miss Dunstable

At last the great Miss Dunstable came. Frank, when he heard that the heiress had arrived, felt some slight palpitation at his heart. He had not the remotest idea in the world of marrying her; indeed, during the last week past, absence had so heightened his love for Mary Thorne that he was more than ever resolved that he would never marry any one but her. He knew that he had made her a formal offer of his hand, and that it behoved him to keep to it, let the charms of Miss Dunstable be what they might; but, nevertheless, he was prepared to go through a certain amount of courtship, in obedience to his aunt's behests, and he felt a little nervous at being brought up in that way, face to face, to do battle with two hundred thousand pounds.

'Miss Dunstable has arrived,' said his aunt to him, with great complacency, on his return from an electioneering visit to the beauties of Barchester which he made with his cousin George on the day after the conversation which was repeated at the end of the last chapter. 'She has arrived, and is looking remarkably well; she has quite a *distingué* air, and will grace any circle to which she may be introduced. I will introduce you before dinner, and you can take her out.'

'I couldn't propose to her tonight, I suppose?' said Frank, maliciously.

'Don't talk nonsense, Frank,' said the countess, angrily. 'I am doing what I can for you, and taking an infinity of trouble to endeavour to place you in an independent position; and now you talk nonsense to me.'

Frank muttered some sort of an apology, and then went to prepare himself for the encounter.

Miss Dunstable, though she had come by the train, had brought with her her own carriage, her own horses, her own coachman and footman, and her own maid, of course. She had also brought with her half a score of trunks, full of wearing apparel; some of them nearly as rich as that wonderful box which was stolen a short time since from the top of a cab.* But she brought all these things, not in the least because she wanted them herself, but because she had been instructed to do so.

Frank was a little more than ordinarily careful in dressing. He spoilt a couple of white neckties before he was satisfied, and was rather fastidious as to the set of his hair. There was not much of the dandy about him in the ordinary meaning of the word; but he felt that it was incumbent on him to look his best, seeing what it was expected that he should now do. He certainly did not mean to marry Miss Dunstable; but as he was to have a flirtation with her, it was as well that he should do so under the best possible auspices.

When he entered the drawing-room he perceived at once that the lady was there. She was seated between the countess and Mrs Proudie; and mammon, in her person, was receiving worship from the temporalities and spiritualities of the land. He tried to look unconcerned, and remained in the farther part of the room, talking with some of his cousins; but he could not keep his eye off the future possible Mrs Frank Gresham; and it seemed as though she was as much constrained to scrutinise him as he felt to scrutinise her.

Lady de Courcy had declared that she was looking extremely well, and had particularly alluded to her *distingué* appearance. Frank at once felt that he could not altogether go along with his aunt in this opinion. Miss Dunstable might be very well; but her style of beauty was one which did not quite meet with his warmest admiration.

In age she was about thirty; but Frank, who was no great judge in such matters, and who was accustomed to have very young girls round him, at once put her down as being ten years older. She had a very high colour, very red cheeks, a large mouth, big white teeth, a broad nose, and bright, small, black eyes. Her hair also was black and bright, but very crisp and strong, and was combed close round her face in small crisp black ringlets. Since she had been brought out into the fashionable world some one of her instructors in fashion had given her to understand that curls were not the thing. 'They'll always pass muster,' Miss Dunstable had replied, 'when they are done up with banknotes.' It may therefore be presumed that Miss Dunstable had a will of her own.

'Frank,' said the countess, in the most natural and unpremeditated way, as soon as she caught her nephew's eye, 'come here. I want to introduce you to Miss Dunstable.' The introduction was then made. 'Mrs Proudie, would you excuse me? I must positively go and say a few words to Mrs Barlow, or the poor woman will feel herself huffed;' and, so saying, she moved off, leaving the coast clear for Master Frank.

He of course slipped into his aunt's place, and expressed a hope that Miss Dunstable was not fatigued by her journey.

'Fatigued!' said she, in a voice rather loud, but very good-humoured, and not altogether unpleasing; 'I am not to be fatigued by such a thing as that. Why, in May we came through all the way from Rome to Paris without sleeping – that is, without sleeping in a bed – and we were upset three times out of the sledges coming over the Simplon. It was such fun! Why, I wasn't to say tired even then.'

'All the way from Rome to Paris!' said Mrs Proudie – in a tone of astonishment, meant to flatter the heiress – 'and what made you in such a hurry?'

'Something about money matters,' said Miss Dunstable, speaking rather louder than usual. 'Something to do with the ointment. I was selling the business just then.'

Mrs Proudie bowed, and immediately changed the conversation. 'Idolatry is, I believe, more rampant than ever in Rome,' said she; 'and I fear there is no such thing at all as Sabbath observances.'

'Oh, not the least,' said Miss Dunstable, with rather a joyous air; 'Sundays and week-days are all the same there.'

'How very frightful!' said Mrs Proudie.

'But it's a delicious place. I do like Rome, I must say. And as for the Pope, if he wasn't quite so fat he would be the nicest old fellow in the world. Have you been in Rome, Mrs Proudie?'

Mrs Proudie sighed as she replied in the negative, and declared her belief that danger was to be apprehended from such visits.

'Oh! – ah! – the, malaria – of course – yes; if you go at the wrong time; but nobody is such a fool as that now.'

'I was thinking of the soul, Miss Dunstable,' said the lady-bishop, in her peculiar, grave tone. 'A place where there are no Sabbath observances –

'And have you been at Rome, Mr Gresham?' said the young lady, turning almost abruptly round to Frank, and giving a somewhat uncivilly cold shoulder to Mrs Proudie's exhortation. She, poor lady, was forced to finish her speech to the Honourable George, who was standing near to her. He having an idea that bishops and all their belongings, like other things appertaining to religion, should, if possible, be avoided; but if that were not possible, should be treated with much assumed gravity, immediately put on a long face, and remarked that – 'it was a deuced shame: for his part he always liked to see people go quiet on Sundays. The parsons had only one day out of seven, and he thought they were fully entitled to that.' Satisfied with which, or not satisfied, Mrs Proudie had to remain silent till dinner-time.

'No,' said Frank; 'I never was in Rome. I was in Paris once, and that's all.' And then, feeling a not unnatural anxiety as to the present state of Miss Dunstable's worldly concerns, he took an opportunity of falling back on that part of the conversation which Mrs Proudie had exercised so much tact in avoiding.

'And was it sold?' said he.

'Sold! what sold?'

'You were saying about the business – that you came back without going to bed because of selling the business.'

'Oh! – the ointment. No; it was not sold. After all, the affair did not come off, and I might have remained and had another roll in the snow. Wasn't it a pity?'

'So,' said Frank to himself, 'if I should do it, I should be owner of the ointment of Lebanon: how odd!' And then he gave her his arm and handed her down to dinner.

He certainly found that the dinner was less dull than any other he had sat down to at Courcy Castle. He did not fancy that he should ever fall in love with Miss Dunstable; but she certainly was an agreeable companion. She told him of her tour, and the fun she had in her journeys; how she took a physician with her for the benefit of her health, whom she generally was forced to nurse; of the trouble it was to her to look after and wait upon her numerous servants; of the tricks she played to bamboozle people who came to stare at her; and, lastly, she told him of a lover who followed her from country to country, and was now in hot pursuit of her, having arrived in London the evening before she left.

'A lover?' said Frank, somewhat startled by the suddenness of the confidence.

'A lover – yes – Mr Gresham; why should I not have a lover?'

'Oh! – no – of course not. I dare say you have a good many.'

'Only three or four, upon my word; that is, only three or four that I favour. One is not bound to reckon the others, you know.'

'No, they'd be too numerous. And so you have three whom

you favour, Miss Dunstable;' and Frank sighed, as though he intended to say that the number was too many for his peace of mind.

'Is not that quite enough? But of course I change them sometimes;' and she smiled on him very good-naturedly. 'It would be very dull if I were always to keep the same.'

'Very dull, indeed,' said Frank, who did not quite know what to say.

'Do you think the countess would mind my having one or two of them here if I were to ask her?'

'I am quite sure she would,' said Frank, very briskly. 'She would not approve of it at all; nor should I.'

'You – why, what have you to do with it?'

'A great deal – so much so that I positively forbid it; but, Miss Dunstable – '

'Well, Mr Gresham?'

'We will contrive to make up for the deficiency as well as possible, if you will permit us to do so. Now for myself – '

'Well, for yourself?'

At this moment the countess gleamed her accomplished eye round the table, and Miss Dunstable rose from her chair as Frank was preparing his attack, and accompanied the other ladies into the drawing-room.

His aunt, as she passed him, touched his arm lightly with her fan, so lightly that the action was perceived by no one else. But Frank well understood the meaning of the touch, and appreciated the approbation which it conveyed. He merely blushed however at his own dissimulation; for he felt more certain than ever that he would never marry Miss Dunstable, and he felt nearly equally sure that Miss Dunstable would never marry him.

Lord de Courcy was now at home; but his presence did not add much hilarity to the claret-cup. The young men, however, were very keen about the election, and Mr Nearthewinde, who was one of the party, was full of the most sanguine hopes.

'I have done one good at any rate,' said Frank; 'I have secured the chorister's vote.'

'What! Bagley?' said Nearthewinde. 'The fellow kept out of my way, and I couldn't see him.'

'I haven't exactly seen him,' said Frank; 'but I've got his vote all the same.'

'What! by a letter?' said Mr Moffat.

'No, not by a letter,' said Frank, speaking rather low as he looked at the bishop and the earl; 'I got a promise from his wife: I think he's a little in the henpecked line.'

'Ha – ha – ha!' laughed the good bishop, who, in spite of Frank's modulation of his voice, had overheard what had passed. 'Is that the way you manage electioneering matters in our cathedral city? Ha – ha – ha!' The idea of one of his choristers being in the henpecked line was very amusing to the bishop.

'Oh, I got a distinct promise,' said Frank, in his pride; and then added incautiously, 'but I had to order bonnets for the whole family.'

'Hush-h-h-h-h!' said Mr Nearthewinde, absolutely flabbergasted by such imprudence on the part of one of his client's friends. 'I am quite sure that your order had no effect, and was intended to have no effect on Mr Bagley's vote.'

'Is that wrong?' said Frank; 'upon my word I thought that it was quite legitimate.'

'One should never admit anything in electioneering matters, should one?' said George, turning to Mr Nearthewinde.

'Very little, Mr de Courcy; very little indeed – the less the better. It's hard to say in these days what is wrong and what is not. Now, there's Reddypalm, the publican, the man who has the Brown Bear. Well, I was there of course: he's a voter, and if any man in Barchester ought to feel himself bound to vote for a friend of the duke's, he ought. Now, I was so thirsty when I was in that man's house that I was dying for a glass of beer; but for the life of me I didn't dare order one.'

'Why not?' said Frank, whose mind was only just beginning to be enlightened by the great doctrine of purity of election as practised in English provincial towns.

'Oh, Closerstil had some fellow looking at me; why, I can't walk down that town without having my very steps counted. I like sharp fighting myself, but I never go so sharp as that.'

'Nevertheless, I got Bagley's vote,' said Frank, persisting in praise of his own electioneering prowess; 'and you may be sure of this, Mr Nearthewinde, none of Closerstil's men were looking at me when I got it.'

'Who'll pay for the bonnets, Frank?' said George, whispering to him.

'Oh, I'll pay for them if Moffat won't. I think I shall keep an account there; they seem to have good gloves and those sort of things.'

'Very good, I have no doubt,' said George.

'I suppose your lordship will be in town soon after the meeting of Parliament?' said the bishop, questioning the earl.

'Oh! yes; I suppose I must be there. I am never allowed to remain very long in quiet. It is a great nuisance; but it is too late to think of that now.'

'Men in high places, my lord, never were, and never will be, allowed to consider themselves. They burn their torches not in their own behalf,' said the bishop, thinking, perhaps, as much of himself as he did of his noble friend. 'Rest and quiet are the comforts of those who have been content to remain in obscurity.'

'Perhaps so,' said the earl, finishing his glass of claret with an air of virtuous resignation. 'Perhaps so.' His own martyrdom, however, had not been severe, for the rest and quiet of home had never been peculiarly satisfactory to his tastes. Soon after this they all went to the ladies.

It was some little time before Frank could find an opportunity of recommencing his allotted task with Miss Dunstable. She got into conversation with the bishop and some other people, and, except that he took her teacup and nearly managed to squeeze one of her fingers as he did so, he made very little further progress till towards the close of the evening.

At last he found her so nearly alone as to admit of his speaking to her in his low confidential voice.

'Have you managed that matter with my aunt?' said he.

'What matter?' said Miss Dunstable; and her voice was not low, nor particularly confidential.

'About those three or four gentlemen whom you wish her to invite here.'

'Oh! my attendant knights! no, indeed; you gave me such very slight hope of success; besides, you said something about my not wanting them.'

'Yes, I did: I really think they'd be quite unnecessary. If you should want any one to defend you –'

'At these coming elections, for instance.'

'Then, or at any other time, there are plenty here who will be ready to stand up for you.'

'Plenty! I don't want plenty: one good lance in the olden days was always worth more than a score of ordinary men-at-arms.'

'But you talked about three or four.'

'Yes; but then you see, Mr Gresham, I have never yet found the one good lance – at least, not good enough to suit my ideas of true prowess.'

What could Frank do but declare that he was ready to lay his own in rest, now and always in her behalf? His aunt had been quite angry with him, and had thought that he turned her into ridicule, when he spoke of making an offer to her guest that very evening; and yet here he was so placed that he had hardly an alternative. Let his inward resolution to abjure the heiress be ever so strong, he was now in a position which allowed him no choice in the matter. Even Mary Thorne could hardly have blamed him for saying, that so far as his own prowess went, it was quite at Miss Dunstable's service. Had Mary been looking on, she, perhaps, might have thought that he could have done so with less of that look of devotion which he threw into his eyes.

'Well, Mr Gresham, that's very civil – very civil indeed,' said Miss Dunstable. 'Upon my word, if a lady wanted a true knight she might do worse than trust to you. Only I fear that your courage is of so exalted a nature that you would be ever ready to do battle for any beauty who might be in distress – or, indeed, who might not. You could never confine your valour to the protection of one maiden.'

'Oh, yes! but I would though, if I liked her,' said Frank. 'There isn't a more constant fellow in the world than I am in that way – you try me, Miss Dunstable.'

'When young ladies make such trials as that, they sometimes find it too late to go back if the trial doesn't succeed, Mr Gresham.'

'Oh, of course there's always some risk. It's like hunting; there would be no fun if there was no danger.'

'But if you get a tumble one day you can retrieve your honour the next; but a poor girl, if she once trusts a man who says that he loves her, has no such chance. For myself, I would never listen to a man unless I'd known him for seven years at least.'

'Seven years!' said Frank, who could not help thinking that in seven years' time Miss Dunstable would be almost an old woman. 'Seven days is enough to know any person.'

'Or perhaps seven hours; eh, Mr Gresham?'

'Seven hours – well, perhaps seven hours, if they happen to be a good deal together during the time.'

'There's nothing after all like love at first sight, is there, Mr Gresham?'

Frank knew well enough that she was quizzing him, and could not resist the temptation he felt to be revenged on her. 'I am sure it's very pleasant,' said he; 'but as for myself, I have never experienced it.'

'Ha, ha, ha!' laughed Miss Dunstable. 'Upon my word, Mr Gresham, I like you amazingly. I didn't expect to meet anybody down here that I should like half so much. You must come and see me in London, and I'll introduce you to my three knights,' and so saying, she moved away and fell into conversation with some of the higher powers.

Frank felt himself to be rather snubbed, in spite of the strong expression which Miss Dunstable had made in his favour. It was not quite clear to him that she did not take him for a boy. He was, to be sure, avenged on her for that by taking her for a middle-aged woman; but, nevertheless, he was hardly satisfied with himself. 'I might give her a heartache yet,' said he to himself; 'and she might find afterwards that she was left in the lurch with all her money.' And so he retired, solitary, into a far part of the room, and began to think of Mary Thorne. As he did so, and as his eyes fell upon Miss Dunstable's stiff curls, he almost shuddered.

And then the ladies retired. His aunt, with a good-natured smile on her face, came to him as she was leaving the room, the last of the bevy, and putting her hand on his arm, led him out into a small unoccupied chamber which opened from the grand saloon.

'Upon my word, Master Frank,' said she, 'you seem to be losing no time with the heiress. You have quite made an impression already.'

'I don't know much about that, aunt,' said he, looking rather sheepish.

'Oh, I declare you have; but, Frank, my dear boy, you should not precipitate these sort of things too much. It is well to take a little more time: it is more valued; and perhaps, you know, on the whole – '

Perhaps Frank might know; but it was clear that Lady de

Courcy did not: at any rate, she did not know how to express herself. Had she said out her mind plainly, she would probably have spoken thus: 'I want you to make love to Miss Dunstable, certainly; or at any rate to make an offer to her; but you need not make a show of yourself and of her, too, by doing it so openly as all that.' The countess, however, did not want to reprimand her obedient nephew, and therefore did not speak out her thoughts.

'Well?' said Frank, looking up into her face.

'Take a *leetle* more time – that is all, my dear boy; slow and sure, you know;' so the countess again patted his arm and went away to bed.

'Old fool!' muttered Frank to himself, as he returned to the room where the men were still standing. He was right in this: she was an old fool, or she would have seen that there was no chance whatever that her nephew and Miss Dunstable should become man and wife.

'Well, Frank,' said the Honourable John; 'so you're after the heiress already.'

'He won't give any of us a chance,' said the Honourable George. 'If he goes on in that way she'll be Mrs Gresham before a month is over. But, Frank, what will she say of your manner of looking for Barchester votes?'

'Mr Gresham is certainly an excellent hand at canvassing,' said Mr Nearthewinde; 'only a little too open in his manner of proceeding.'

'I got that chorister for you at any rate,' said Frank. 'And you would never have had him without me.'

'I don't think half so much of the chorister's vote as that of Miss Dunstable,' said the Honourable George: 'that's the interest that is really worth the looking after.'

'But, surely,' said Mr Moffat, 'Miss Dunstable has no property in Barchester?' Poor man! his heart was so intent on his election that he had not a moment to devote to the claims of love.

CHAPTER XVII

The Election

And now the important day of the election had arrived, and some men's hearts beat quickly enough. To be or not to be a member of the British Parliament is a question of very considerable moment in a man's mind. Much is often said of the great penalties which the ambitious pay for enjoying this honour; of the tremendous expenses of elections; of the long, tedious hours of unpaid labour: of the weary days passed in the House; but, nevertheless, the prize is one very well worth the price paid for it – well worth any price that can be paid for it short of wading through dirt and dishonour.

No other great European nation has anything like it to offer to the ambition of its citizens; for in no other great country of Europe, not even in those which are free, has the popular constitution obtained, as with us, true sovereignty and power of rule. Here it is so; and when a man lays himself out to be a member of Parliament, he plays the highest game and for the highest stakes which the country affords.

To some men, born silver-spooned, a seat in Parliament comes as a matter of course. From the time of their early manhood they hardly know what it is not to sit there; and the honour is hardly appreciated, being too much a matter of course. As a rule, they never know how great a thing it is to be in Parliament; though, when reverses occasionally will come, they fully feel how dreadful it is to be left out.

But to men aspiring to be members, or to those who having been once fortunate have again to fight the battle without assurance of success, the coming election must be matter of dread concern. Oh, how delightful to hear that the long-talked-of rival has declined the contest, and that the course is clear! or to find by a short canvass that one's majority is safe, and the pleasures of crowing over an unlucky, friendless foe quite secured!

No such gratification as this filled the bosom of Mr Moffat on the morning of the Barchester election. To him had been brought no positive assurance of success by his indefatigable agent, Mr Nearthewinde. It was admitted on all sides that the contest would be a very close one and Mr Nearthewinde would not do more than assert that they ought to win unless things went very wrong with them.

Mr Nearthewinde had other elections to attend to, and had not been remaining at Courcy Castle ever since the coming of Miss Dunstable: but he had been there, and at Barchester, as often as possible, and Mr Moffat was made greatly uneasy by reflecting how very high the bill would be.

The two parties had outdone each other in the loudness of their assertions, that each would on his side conduct the election in strict conformity to law. There was to be no bribery. Bribery! who, indeed, in these days would dare to bribe; to give absolute money for an absolute vote, and pay for such an article in downright palpable sovereigns? No. Purity was much too ramp-ant for that, and the means of detection too well understood. But purity was to be carried much further than this. There should be no treating; no hiring of two hundred voters to act as messengers at twenty shillings a day in looking up some four hundred other voters; no bands were to be paid for; no carriages furnished; no ribbons supplied. British voters were to vote, if vote they would, for the love and respect they bore to their chosen candidate. If so actuated, they would not vote, they might stay away; no other inducement would be offered.

So much was said loudly – very loudly – by each party; but, nevertheless, Mr Moffat, early in these election days, began to have some misgivings about the bill. The proclaimed arrange-ment had been one exactly suitable to his taste; for Mr Moffat loved his money. He was a man in whose breast the ambition of being great in the world, and of joining himself to aristocratic people was continually at war with the great cost which such tastes occasioned. His last election had not been a cheap triumph. In one way or another money had been dragged from him for purposes which had been to his mind unintelligible; and when, about the middle of his first session, he had, with much grumbling, settled all demands, he had questioned with himself whether his whistle was worth its cost.

He was therefore a great stickler for purity of election; although, had he considered the matter, he should have known that with him money was his only passport into that Elysium in which he had lived for two years. He probably did not consider it; for when, in those canvassing days immediately preceding the election, he had seen that all the beer-houses were open, and half the population was drunk, he had asked Mr Nearthewinde whether this violation of the treaty was taking place only on the part of his opponent, and whether, in such case, it would not be duly noticed with a view to a possible future petition.

Mr Nearthewinde assured him triumphantly that half at least of the wallowing swine were his own especial friends; and that somewhat more than half of the publicans of the town were eagerly engaged in fighting his, Mr Moffat's, battle. Mr Moffat groaned, and would have expostulated had Mr Nearthewinde been willing to hear him. But that gentleman's services had been put into requisition by Lord de Courcy rather than by the candidate. For the candidate he cared but little. To pay the bill would be enough for him. He, Mr Nearthewinde, was doing his business as he well knew how to do it; and it was not likely that he should submit to be lectured by such as Mr Moffat on a trumpery score of expense.

It certainly did appear on the morning of the election as though some great change had been made in that resolution of the candidates to be very pure. From an early hour rough bands of music were to be heard in every part of the usually quiet town; carts and gigs, omnibuses and flys, all the old carriages from all the inn-yards, and every vehicle of any description which could be pressed into the service were in motion; if the horses and post-boys were not to be paid for by the candidates, the voters themselves were certainly very liberal in their mode of bringing themselves to the poll. The election district of the city of Barchester extended for some miles on each side of the city, so that the omnibuses and flys had enough to do. Beer was to be had at the public-houses, almost without question, by all who chose to ask for it; and rum and brandy were dispensed to select circles within the bars with equal profusion. As for ribbons, the mercers' strops must have been emptied of that article, as far as scarlet and yellow were concerned. Scarlet was Sir Roger's colour, while the friends of Mr Moffat were decked with yellow. Seeing what he did see, Mr Moffat might well ask whether there had not been a violation of the treaty of purity!

At the time of this election there was some question whether England should go to war* with all her energy; or whether it would not be better for her to save her breath to cool her porridge, and not meddle more than could be helped with

foreign quarrels. The last view of the matter was advocated by
Sir Roger,* and his motto of course proclaimed the merits of
domestic peace and quiet. 'Peace abroad and a big loaf at home,'
was consequently displayed on four or five huge scarlet banners,
and carried waving over the heads of the people. But Mr Moffat
was a staunch supporter of the Government, who were already
inclined to be belligerent, and 'England's honour' was therefore
the legend under which he selected to do battle. It may, however,
be doubted whether there was in all Barchester one inhabitant –
let alone one elector – so fatuous as to suppose that England's
honour was in any special manner dear to Mr Moffat; or that
he would be a whit more sure of a big loaf than he was now,
should Sir Roger happily become a member of the legislature.

And then the fine arts were resorted to, seeing that language
fell short in telling all that was found necessary to be told. Poor
Sir Roger's failing as regards the bottle was too well known;
and it was also known that, in acquiring his title, he had not
quite laid aside the rough mode of speech which he had used in
early years. There was, consequently, a great daub painted up
on sundry walls, on which a navvy, with a pimply, bloated face,
was to be seen standing on a railway bank, leaning on a spade
holding a bottle in one hand, while he invited a comrade to
drink. 'Come, Jack, shall us have a drop of some'at short?' were
the words coming out of the navvy's mouth; and under this was
painted in huge letters,

THE LAST NEW BARONET

But Mr Moffat hardly escaped on easier terms. The trade by
which his father had made his money was as well known as that
of the railway contractor; and every possible symbol of tailor-
dom was displayed in graphic portraiture on the walls and
hoardings of the city. He was drawn with his goose,* with his
scissors, with his needle, with his tapes; he might be seen
measuring, cutting, stitching, pressing, carrying home his
bundle, and presenting his little bill; and under each of these
representations was repeated his own motto, 'England's
honour.'

Such were the pleasant little amenities with which the people
of Barchester greeted the two candidates who were desirous of
the honour of serving them in Parliament.

'The polling went on briskly and merrily. There were somewhat above nine hundred registered voters, of whom the greater portion recorded their votes early in the day. At two o'clock, according to Sir Roger's committee, the numbers were as follows: –

Scatcherd   275
Moffat   268

Whereas, by the light afforded by Mr Moffat's people, they stood in a slightly different ratio to each other, being written thus:

Moffat   277
Scatcherd   269

This naturally heightened the excitement, and gave additional delight to the proceedings. At half-past two it was agreed by both sides that Mr Moffat was ahead; the Moffatites claiming a majority of twelve, and the Scatcherdites allowing a majority of one. But by three o'clock sundry good men and true, belonging to the railway interest, had made their way to the booth in spite of the efforts of a band of roughs from Courcy, and Sir Roger was again leading, by ten or a dozen, according to his own showing.

One little transaction which took place in the earlier part of the day deserves to be recorded. There was in Barchester an honest publican – honest as the world of publicans goes – who not only was possessed of a vote, but possessed also of a son who was a voter. He was one Reddypalm, and in former days, before he had learned to appreciate the full value of an Englishman's franchise, he had been a declared Liberal and an early friend of Roger Scatcherd's. In latter days he had governed his political feelings with more decorum, and had not allowed himself to be carried away by such foolish fervour as he had evinced in his youth. On this special occasion, however, his line of conduct was so mysterious as for a while to baffle even those who knew him best.

His house was apparently open in Sir Roger's interest. Beer, at any rate, was flowing there as elsewhere; and scarlet ribbons going in – not perhaps, in a state of perfect steadiness – came out more unsteady than before. Still had Mr Reddypalm been deaf to the voice of that charmery,* Closerstil, though he had charmed with all his wisdom. Mr Reddypalm had stated, first his unwillingness to vote at all: – he had, he said, given over politics, and was not inclined to trouble his mind again with the subject; then he had spoken of his great devotion to the Duke of Omnium, under whose grandfathers his grandfather had been bred: Mr Nearthewinde had, as he said, been with him, and proved to him beyond a shadow of a doubt that it would show the deepest ingratitude on his part to vote against the duke's candidate.

Mr Closerstil thought he understood all this, and sent more, and still more men to drink beer. He even caused – taking infinite trouble to secure secrecy in the matter – three gallons of British brandy to be ordered and paid for as the best French. But, nevertheless, Mr Reddypalm made no sign to show that he considered that the right thing had been done. On the evening before the election he told one of Mr Closerstil's confidential men, that he had thought a good deal about it, and that he believed he should be constrained by his conscience to vote for Mr Moffat.

We have said that Mr Closerstil was accompanied by a learned friend of his, one Mr Romer, a barrister, who was greatly interested for Sir Roger, and who, being a strong Liberal, was assisting in the canvass with much energy. He, hearing how matters were likely to go with this conscientious publican, and feeling himself peculiarly capable of dealing with such delicate scruples, undertook to look into the case in hand. Early, therefore, on the morning of the election, he sauntered down the cross street in which hung out the sign of the Brown Bear, and, as he expected, found Mr Reddypalm near his own door.

Now it was quite an understood thing that there was to be no bribery. This was understood by no one better than by Mr Romer, who had, in truth, drawn up many of the published assurances to that effect. And, to give him his due, he was fully minded to act in accordance with these assurances. The object of all the parties was to make it worth the voters' while to give their votes; but to do so without bribery. Mr Romer had repeatedly declared that he would have nothing to do with any illegal practising; but he had also declared that, as long as all was done according to law, he was ready to lend his best efforts to assist Sir Roger. How he assisted Sir Roger, and adhered to the law, will now be seen.

Oh, Mr Romer! Mr Romer! is it not the case with thee that

thou 'wouldst not play false and yet wouldst wrongly win'?*
Not in electioneering, Mr Romer, any more than in other
pursuits, can a man touch pitch and not be defiled; as thou,
innocent as thou art, wilt soon learn to thy terrible cost.

'Well, Reddypalm,' said Mr Romer, shaking hands with him.
Mr Romer had not been equally cautious as Nearthewinde, and
had already drunk sundry glasses of ale at the Brown Bear, in
the hope of softening the stern Bearwarden. 'How is it to be
today? Which is to be the man?'

'If any one knows that, Mr Romer, you must be the man. A
poor numbskull like me knows nothing of them matters. How
should I? All I looks to, Mr Romer, is selling a trifle of drink
now and then – selling it, and getting paid for it, you know, Mr
Romer.'

'Yes, that's important, no doubt. But come, Reddypalm, such
an old friend of Sir Roger as you are, a man he speaks of as one
of his intimate friends, I wonder how you can hesitate about it.
Now with another man, I should think that he wanted to be
paid for voting – '

'Oh, Mr Romer! – fie – fie – fie!'

'I know it's not the case with you. It would be an insult to
offer you money, even if money were going. I should not
mention this, only as money is not going, neither on our side
nor on the other, no harm can be done.'

'Mr Romer, if you speak of such a thing you'll hurt me. I
know the value of an Englishman's franchise too well to wish to
sell it. I would not demean myself so low; no, not though five-
and-twenty pound a vote was going, as there was in the good
old times – and that's not so long ago neither.'

'I am sure you wouldn't, Reddypalm; I'm sure you wouldn't.
But an honest man like you should stick to old friends. Now,
tell me,' and putting his arm through Reddypalm's, he walked
with him into the passage of his own house; 'Now, tell me – is
there anything wrong? It's between friends, you know. Is there
anything wrong?'

'I wouldn't sell my vote for untold gold,' said Reddypalm,
who was perhaps aware that untold gold would hardly be
offered to him for it.

'I am sure you would not,' said Mr Romer.

'But,' said Mr Reddypalm, 'a man likes to be paid his little
bill.'

'Surely, surely,' said the barrister.

'And I did say two years since, when your friend Mr Closerstil brought a friend of his down to stand here – it wasn't Sir Roger then – but when he brought a friend of his down, and when I drew two or three hogsheads of ale on their side, and when my bill was questioned and only half-settled, I did say that I wouldn't interfere with no election no more. And no more I will, Mr Romer, – unless it be to give a quiet vote for the nobleman under whom I and mine always lived respectable.'

'Oh!' said Mr Romer.

'A man do like to have his bill paid, you know, Mr Romer.'

Mr Romer could not but acknowledge that this was a natural feeling on the part of an ordinary mortal publican.

'It goes agin the grain with a man not to have his little bill paid, and specially at election time,' again urged Mr Reddypalm.

Mr Romer had not much time to think about it; but he knew well that matters were so nearly balanced, that the votes of Mr Reddypalm and his son were of inestimable value.

'If it's only about your bill,' said Mr Romer, 'I'll see to have that settled. I'll speak to Closerstil about that.'

'All right!' said Reddypalm, seizing the young barrister's hand and shaking it warmly; 'all right!' And late in the afternoon, when a vote or two became matter of intense interest, Mr Reddypalm and his son came up to the hustings and boldly tendered theirs for their old friend, Sir Roger.

There was a great deal of eloquence heard in Barchester on that day. Sir Roger had by this time so far recovered as to be able to go through the dreadfully hard work of canvassing and addressing the electors from eight in the morning till near sunset. A very perfect recovery, most men will say. Yes; a perfect recovery as regarded the temporary use of his faculties, both physical and mental; though it may be doubted whether there can be any permanent recovery from such disease as his. What amount of brandy he consumed to enable him to perform this election work, and what lurking evil effect the excitement might have on him – of these matters no record was kept in the history of those proceedings.

Sir Roger's eloquence was of a rough kind; but not perhaps the less operative on those for whom it was intended. The aristocracy of Barchester consisted chiefly of clerical dignitaries, bishops, deans, prebendaries, and such like: on them and theirs it was not probable that anything said by Sir Roger would have much effect. Those men would either abstain from voting, or vote for the railway hero, with the view of keeping out the De Courcy candidate. Then came the shopkeepers, who might also be regarded as a stiffnecked generation, impervious to election-eering eloquence. They would, generally, support Mr Moffat. But there was an inferior class of voters, ten-pound freeholders,* and such like, who, at this period, were somewhat given to have an opinion of their own, and over them it was supposed that Sir Roger did obtain some power by his gift of talking.

'Now, gentlemen, will you tell me this,' said he, bawling at the top of his voice from off the portico which graced the door of the Dragon of Wantly, at which celebrated inn Sir Roger's committee sat: – 'Who is Mr Moffat, and what has he done for us? There have been some picture-makers about the town this week past. The Lord knows who they are; I don't. These clever fellows do tell you who I am, and what I've done. I ain't very proud of the way they've painted me, though there's something about it I ain't ashamed of either. See here,' and he held up on one side of him one of the great daubs of himself – 'just hold it there till I can explain it,' and he handed the paper to one of his friends. 'That's me,' said Sir Roger, putting up his stick, and pointing to the pimply-nosed representation of himself.

'Hurrah! Hur-r-r-rah more power to you – we all know who you are, Roger. You're the boy! When did you get drunk last?' Such-like greetings, together with a dead cat which was flung at him from the crowd, and which he dextrously parried with his stick, were the answers which he received to this exordium.

'Yes,' said he, quite undismayed by this little missile which had so nearly reached him: 'that's me. And look here; this brown, dirty-looking broad streak here is intended for a railway; and that thing in my hand – not the right hand; I'll come to that presently – '

'How about the brandy, Roger?'

'I'll come to that presently. I'll tell you about the brandy in good time. But that thing in my left hand is a spade. Now, I never handled a spade, and never could; but, boys, I handled a chisel and mallet; and many a hundred block of stone has come out smooth from under that hand;' and Sir Roger lifted up his great broad palm wide open.

'So you did, Roger, and well we minds it.'

'The meaning, however, of that spade is to show that I made that railway. Now I'm very much obliged to those gentlemen over at the White Horse for putting up this picture of me. It's a true picture, and it tells you who I am. I did make that railway. I have made thousands of miles of railway; I am making thousands of miles of railways – some in Europe, some in Asia, some in America. It's a true picture,' and he poked his stick through it and held it up to the crowd. 'A true picture: but for that spade and that railway, I shouldn't be now here asking your votes; and, when next February comes, I shouldn't be sitting in Westminster to represent you, as, by God's grace, I certainly will do. That tells you who I am. But now, will you tell me who Mr Moffat is?'

'How about the brandy, Roger?'

'Oh, yes, the brandy! I was forgetting that and the little speech that is coming out of my mouth – a deal shorter speech, and a better one than what I am making now. Here, in the right hand you see is a brandy bottle. Well, boys, I'm not a bit ashamed of that; as long as a man does his work – and the spade shows that – it's only fair he should have something to comfort him. I'm always able to work, and few men work much harder. I'm always able to work, and no man has a right to expect more of me. I never expect more than that from those who work with me.'

'No more you don't, Roger: a little drop's very good, ain't it, Roger? Keeps the cold from the stomach, eh, Roger?'

'Then as to this speech, "Come, Jack, let's have a drop of some'at short." Why, that's a good speech, too. When I do drink I like to share with a friend; and I don't care how humble that friend is.'

'Hurrah! more power. That's true, too, Roger; may you never be without a drop to wet your whistle.'

'They say I'm the last new baronet. Well, I ain't ashamed of that; not a bit. When will Mr Moffat get himself made a baronet? No man can truly say I'm too proud of it. I have never stuck myself up; no, nor stuck my wife up either: but I don't see much to be ashamed of because the bigwigs chose to make a baronet of me.'

'Nor, no more thee h'ant, Roger. We'd all be barrownites if so be we knew the way.'

'But now, having polished off this bit of a picture, let me ask you who Mr Moffat is? There are pictures enough about him, too; though Heaven knows where they all come from. I think Sir Edwin Landseer* must have done this one of the goose; it is so deadly natural. Look at it; there he is. Upon my word, whoever did that ought to make his fortune at some of these exhibitions. Here he is again with a big pair of scissors. He calls himself "England's honour;" what the deuce England's honour has to do with tailoring, I can't tell you: perhaps Mr Moffat can. But mind you, my friends, I don't say anything against tailoring: some of you are tailors, I dare say.'

'Yes, we be,' said a little squeaking voice from out of the crowd.

'And a good trade it is. When I first knew Barchester there were tailors here who could lick any stone-mason in the trade; I say nothing against tailors. But it isn't enough for a man to be a tailor unless he's something else along with it. You're not so fond of tailors that you'll send one up to Parliament merely because he is a tailor.'

'We won't have no tailors. No; nor yet no cabbaging.* Take a go of brandy, Roger; you're blown.'

'No, I'm not blown yet. I've a deal more to say about Mr Moffat before I shall be blown. What has he done to entitle him to come here before you and ask you to send him to Parliament? Why; he isn't even a tailor. I wish he were. There's always some good in a fellow who knows how to earn his own bread. But he isn't a tailor; he can't even put a stitch in towards mending England's honour. His father was a tailor; not a Barchester tailor, mind you, so as to give him any claim on your affections; but a London tailor. Now the question is, do you want to send the son of a London tailor up to Parliament to represent you?'

'No, we don't; nor yet we won't neither.'

'I rather think not. You've had him once, and what has he done for you? Has he said much for you in the House of Commons? Why, he's so dumb a dog that he can't bark even for a bone. I'm told it's quite painful to hear him fumbling and mumbling and trying to get up a speech there over at the White Horse. He doesn't belong to the city; he hasn't done anything for the city; and he hasn't the power to do anything for the city. Then, why on earth does he come here? I'll tell you. The Earl de Courcy brings him. He's going to marry the Earl de Courcy's niece; for they say he's very rich – this tailor's son – only they do say also that he doesn't much like to spend his money. He's going to marry Lord de Courcy's niece, and Lord de Courcy wishes that his nephew should be in Parliament. There, that's the claim which Mr Moffat has here on the people of Barchester. He's Lord de Courcy's nominee, and those who feel themselves bound hand and foot, heart and soul, to Lord de Courcy, had better vote for him. Such men have my leave. If there are enough of such at Barchester to send him to Parliament, the city in which I was born must be very much altered since I was a young man.'

And so finishing his speech, Sir Roger retired within, and recruited himself in the usual manner.

Such was the flood of eloquence at the Dragon of Wantley. At the White Horse, meanwhile, the friends of the De Courcy interest were treated perhaps to sounder political views; though not expressed in periods so intelligibly fluent as those of Sir Roger.

Mr Moffat was a young man, and there was no knowing to what proficiency in the Parliamentary gift of public talking he might yet attain; but hitherto his proficiency was not great. He had, however, endeavoured to make up by study for any want of readiness of speech, and had come to Barchester daily, for the last four days, fortified with a very pretty harangue, which he had prepared for himself in the solitude of his chamber. On the three previous days matters had been allowed to progress with tolerable smoothness, and he had been permitted to deliver himself of his elaborate eloquence with few other interruptions than those occasioned by his own want of practice. But on this, the day of days, the Barchesterian roughs were not so complaisant. It appeared to Mr Moffat, when he essayed to speak, that he was surrounded by enemies rather than friends; and in his heart he gave great blame to Mr Nearthewinde for not managing matters better for him.

'Men of Barchester,' he began, in a voice which was every now and then preternaturally loud, but which, at each fourth or fifth word, gave way from want of power, and descended to its natural weak tone. 'Men of Barchester – electors and non-electors – '

'We is hall electors; hall on us, my young kiddy.'

'Electors and non-electors, I now ask your suffrages, not for the first time – '

'Oh! we've tried you. We know what you're made on. Go on, Snip; don't you let 'em put you down.'

'I've had the honour of representing you in Parliament for the last two years, and – '

'And a deuced deal you did for us, didn't you?'

'What could you expect from the ninth part of a man?* Never mind, Snip – go on; don't you be put out by any of them. Stick to your wax and thread like a man – like the ninth part of a man – go on a little faster, Snip.'

'For the last two years – and – and – ' Here Mr Moffat looked round to his friends for some little support, and the Honourable George, who stood close behind him, suggested that he had gone through it like a brick.

'And – and I went through it like a brick,' said Mr Moffat, with the gravest possible face, taking up, in his utter confusion, the words that were put into his mouth.

'Hurray! – so you did – you're the real brick. Well done, Snip; go it again with the wax and thread!'

'I am a thorough-paced reformer,' continued Mr Moffat, somewhat reassured by the effect of the opportune words which his friend had whispered into his ear. 'A thorough-paced reformer – a thorough-paced reformer – '

'Go on, Snip. We all know what that means.'

'A thorough-paced reformer – '

'Never mind your paces, man; but get on. Tell us something new. We're all reformers, we are.'

Poor Mr Moffat was a little thrown back. It wasn't so easy to tell these gentlemen anything new, harassed as he was at this moment; so he looked back at his honourable supporter for some further hint. 'Say something about their daughters,' whispered George, whose own flights of oratory were always on that subject. Had he counselled Mr Moffat to say a word or two about the tides, his advice would not have been less to the purpose.

'Gentlemen,' he began again – 'you all know that I am a thorough-paced reformer – '

'Oh! drat your reform. He's a dumb dog. Go back to your goose, Snippy; you never were made for this work. Go to Courcy Castle and reform that.'

Mr Moffat, grieved in his soul, was becoming inextricably bewildered by such *facetiæ* as these, when an egg – and it may be feared not a fresh egg – flung with unerring precision, struck him on the open part of his well-plaited shirt, and reduced him to speechless despair.

An egg is a means of delightful support when properly administered; but it is not calculated to add much spirit to a man's eloquence, or to ensure his powers of endurance, when supplied in the manner above described. Men there are, doubtless, whose tongues would not be stopped even by such an argument as this; but Mr Moffat was not one of them. As the insidious fluid trickled down beneath his waistcoat, he felt that all further powers of coaxing the electors out of their votes, by words flowing from his tongue sweeter than honey, was for that occasion denied to him. He could not be self-confident, energetic, witty, and good-humoured with a rotten egg drying in through his clothes. He was forced, therefore, to give way, and with sadly disconcerted air retired from the open window at which he had been standing.

It was in vain that the Honourable George, Mr Nearthewinde, and Frank endeavoured again to bring him to the charge. He was like a beaten prize-fighter, whose pluck has been cowed out of him, and who, if he stands up, only stands up to fall. Mr Moffat got sulky also, and when he was pressed, said that Barchester and the people in it might be d – . 'With all my heart,' said Mr Nearthewinde. 'That wouldn't have any effect on their votes.'

But, in truth, it mattered very little whether Mr Moffat spoke, or whether he didn't speak. Four o'clock was the hour for closing the poll, and that was now fast coming. Tremendous exertions had been made about half-past three, by a safe emissary sent from Nearthewinde, to prove to Mr Reddypalm that all manner of contingent advantages would accrue to the Brown Bear if it should turn out that Mr Moffat should take his seat for Barchester. No bribe was, of course, offered or even hinted at. The purity of Barchester was not contaminated during the day by one such curse as this. But a man, and a publican, would be required to do some great deed in the public line; to open some colossal tap; to draw beer for the million; and no one would be so fit as Mr Reddypalm – if only it might turn out that Mr Moffat should, in the coming February, take his seat as member for Barchester.

But Mr Reddypalm was a man of humble desires, whose

ambitions soared no higher than this – that his little bills should be duly settled. It is wonderful what love an innkeeper has for his bill in its entirety. An account, with a respectable total of five or six pounds, is brought to you, and you complain but of one article; that fire in the bedroom was never lighted; or that second glass of brandy and water never called for. You desire to have the shilling expunged, and all your host's pleasure in the whole transaction is destroyed. Oh! my friends, pay for the brandy and water, though you never drank it; suffer the fire to pass, though it never warmed you. Why make a good man miserable for such a trifle?

It became notified to Reddypalm with sufficient clearness that his bill for the past election should be paid without further question; and, therefore, at five o'clock the Mayor of Barchester proclaimed the results of the contest in the following figures:

Scatcherd   378
Moffat   376

Mr Reddypalm's two votes had decided the question. Mr Nearthewinde immediately went up to town; and the dinner party at Courcy Castle that evening was not a particularly pleasant meal.

This much, however, had been absolutely decided before the yellow committee concluded their labour at the White Horse: there should be a petition. Mr Nearthewinde had not been asleep, and already knew something of the manner in which Mr Reddypalm's mind had been quieted.

CHAPTER XVIII

The Rivals

The intimacy between Frank and Miss Dunstable grew and prospered. That is to say, it prospered as an intimacy, though perhaps hardly as a love affair. There was a continued succession of jokes between them, which no one else in the castle under-stood; but the very fact of there being such a good understanding between them rather stood in the way of, than assisted, that consummation which the countess desired. People, when they are in love with each other, or even when they pretend to be, do not generally show it by loud laughter. Nor is it frequently the case that a wife with two hundred thousand pounds can be won without some little preliminary despair. Now there was no despair at all about Frank Gresham.

Lady de Courcy, who thoroughly understood that portion of the world in which she herself lived, saw that things were not going quite as they should do, and gave much and repeated advice to Frank on the subject. She was the more eager in doing this, because she imagined Frank had done what he could to obey her first precepts. He had not turned up his nose at Miss Dunstable's curls, nor found fault with her loud voice: he had not objected to her as ugly, nor even shown any dislike to her age. A young man who had been so amenable to reason was worthy of further assistance; and so Lady de Courcy did what she could to assist him.

'Frank, my dear boy,' she would say, 'you are a little too noisy, I think. I don't mean for myself, you know; I don't mind it. But Miss Dunstable would like it better if you were a little more quiet with her.'

'Would she, aunt?' said Frank, looking demurely up into the countess's face. 'I rather think she likes fun and noise, and that sort of thing. You know she's not very quiet herself.'

'Ah! – but Frank, there are times, you know, when that sort of thing should be laid aside. Fun, as you call it, is all very well in its place. Indeed, no one likes it better than I do. But that's not the way to show admiration. Young ladies like to be admired; and if you'll be a little more soft-mannered with Miss Dunstable, I'm sure you'll find it will answer better!'

And so the old bird taught the young bird how to fly – very needlessly – for in this matter of flying, Nature gives her own lessons thoroughly; and the ducklings will take the water, even though the maternal hen warn them against the perfidious element never so loudly.

Soon after this, Lady de Courcy began to be not very well pleased in the matter. She took it into her head that Miss Dunstable was sometimes almost inclined to laugh at her; and on one or two occasions it almost seemed as though Frank was joining Miss Dunstable in doing so. The fact indeed was, that Miss Dunstable was fond of fun; and, endowed as she was with all the privileges which two hundred thousand pounds may be supposed to give to a young lady, did not very much care at whom she laughed. She was able to make a tolerably correct guess at Lady de Courcy's plan towards herself; but she did not for a moment think that Frank had any intention of furthering his aunt's views. She was, therefore, not at all ill-inclined to have her revenge upon the countess.

'How very fond your aunt is of you!' she said to him one wet morning, as he was sauntering through the house; now laughing, and almost romping with her – then teasing his sister about Mr Moffat – and then bothering his lady-cousins out of all their propriety.

'Oh, very!' said Frank: 'she is a dear, good woman, is my Aunt De Courcy.'

'I declare she takes more notice of you and your doings than of any of your cousins. I wonder they ain't jealous.'

'Oh! they're such good people. Bless me, they'd never be jealous.'

'You are so much younger than they are, that I suppose she thinks you want more of her care.'

'Yes; that's it. You see she's fond of having a baby to nurse.'

'Tell me, Mr Gresham, what was it she was saying to you last night? I know we had been misbehaving ourselves dreadfully. It was all your fault; you would make me laugh so.'

'That's just what I said to her.'

'She was talking about me, then?'

'How on earth should she talk of any one else as long as you are here? Don't you know that all the world is talking about you?'

'Is it? – dear me, how kind! But I don't care a straw about any world just at present but Lady de Courcy's world. What did she say?'

'She said you were very beautiful – '

'Did she? – how good of her!'

'No; I forgot. It – it was I that said that; and she said – what was it she said? She said, that after all, beauty was but skin deep – and that she valued you for your virtues and prudence rather than your good looks.'

'Virtues and prudence! She said I was prudent and virtuous?'

'Yes.'

'And you talked of my beauty? That was so kind of you! You didn't either of you say anything about other matters?'

'What other matters?'

'Oh! I don't know. Only some people are sometimes valued rather for what they've got than for any good qualities belonging to themselves intrinsically.'

'That can never be the case with Miss Dunstable; especially not at Courcy Castle,' said Frank, bowing easily from the corner of the sofa over which he was leaning.

'Of course not,' said Miss Dunstable; and Frank at once perceived that she spoke in a tone of voice differing much from that half-bantering, half-good-humoured manner that was customary with her. 'Of course not: any such idea would be quite out of the question at Courcy Castle; quite out of the question with Lady de Courcy.' She paused a moment, and then added in a tone different again, and unlike any that he had yet heard from her: – 'It is, at any rate, out of the question with Mr Frank Gresham – of that I am quite sure.'

Frank ought to have understood her, and have appreciated the good opinion which she intended to convey; but he did not entirely do so. He was hardly honest himself towards her; and he could not at first perceive that she intended to say that she thought him so. He knew very well that she was alluding to her own huge fortune, and was alluding also to the fact that people of fashion sought her because of it; but he did not know that she intended to express a true acquittal as regarded him of any such baseness.

And did he deserve to be acquitted? Yes, upon the whole he did; – to be acquitted of that special sin. His desire to make Miss Dunstable temporarily subject to his sway arose, not from a hankering after her fortune, but from an ambition to get the better in a contest in which other men around him seemed to be failing.

For it must not be imagined that, with such a prize to be struggled for, all others stood aloof and allowed him to have his own way with the heiress, undisputed. The chance of a wife with two hundred thousand pounds is a godsend which comes in a man's life too seldom to be neglected, let that chance be never so remote.

Frank was the heir to a large embarrassed property; and, therefore, the heads of families, putting their wisdoms together, had thought it most meet that this daughter of Plutus should, if possible, fall to his lot. But not so thought the Honourable George; and not so thought another gentleman who was at that time an inmate of Courcy Castle.

These suitors perhaps somewhat despised their young rival's efforts. It may be that they had sufficient worldly wisdom to know that so important a crisis of life is not settled among quips and jokes, and that Frank was too much in jest to be in earnest. But be that as it may, his love-making did not stand in the way of their love-making; nor his hopes, if he had any, in the way of their hopes.

The Honourable George had discussed this matter with the Honourable John in a properly fraternal manner. It may be that John had also an eye to the heiress; but, if so, he had ceded his views to his brother's superior claims; for it came about that they understood each other very well, and John favoured George with salutary advice on the occasion.

'If it is to be done at all, it should be done very sharp,' said John.

'As sharp as you like,' said George. 'I'm not the fellow to be studying three months in what attitude I'll fall at a girl's feet.'

'No: and when you are there you mustn't take three months more to study how you'll get up again. If you do it at all, you must do it sharp,' repeated John, putting great stress on his advice.

'I have said a few soft words to her already, and she didn't seem to take them badly,' said George.

'She's no chicken, you know,' remarked John; 'and with a woman like that, beating about the bush never does any good. The chances are she won't have you – that's of course; plums like that don't fall into a man's mouth merely for shaking the tree. But it's possible she may; and if she will, she's as likely to take you today as this day six months. If I were you I'd write her a letter.'

'Write her a letter – eh?' said George, who did not altogether dislike the advice, for it seemed to take from his shoulders the burden of preparing a spoken address. Though he was so glib in speaking about the farmers' daughters, he felt that he should have some little difficulty in making known his passion to Miss Dunstable by word of mouth.

'Yes; write a letter. If she'll take you at all, she'll take you that way; half the matches going are made up by writing letters. Write her a letter and get it put on her dressing-table.' George said that he would, and so he did.

George spoke quite truly when he hinted that he had said a few soft things to Miss Dunstable. Miss Dunstable, however, was accustomed to hear soft things. She had been carried much about in society among fashionable people since, on the settlement of her father's will, she had been pronounced heiress to all the ointment of Lebanon; and many men had made calculations respecting her similar to those which were now animating the brain of the Honourable George de Courcy. She was already quite accustomed to being the target at which spendthrifts and the needy rich might shoot their arrows: accustomed to being so shot at, and tolerably accustomed to protect herself without making scenes in the world, or rejecting the advantageous establishments offered to her with any loud expressions of disdain. The Honourable George, therefore, had been permitted to say soft things very much as a matter of course.

And very little more outward fracas arose from the correspondence which followed than had arisen from the soft things so said. George wrote the letter, and had it duly conveyed to Miss Dunstable's bed-chamber. Miss Dunstable duly received it, and had her answer conveyed back discreetly to George's hands. The correspondence ran as follows: –

'COURCY CASTLE, Aug. – , 185–.
'My dearest Miss Dunstable,

'I cannot but flatter myself that you must have perceived from my manner that you are not indifferent to me. Indeed, indeed, you are not. I may truly say, and swear' (these last strong words had been put in by the special counsel of the Honourable John), 'that if ever a man loved a woman truly, I truly love you. You may think it very odd that I should say this in a letter instead of speaking it out before your face; but your powers of raillery are so great' ('touch her up about her wit' had been the advice of the Honourable John) 'that I am all but afraid to encounter them. Dearest, dearest Martha – oh do not blame me for so addressing you! – if you will trust your happiness to me you shall never find that you have been deceived. My ambition shall be to make you shine in that circle which you are so well qualified to adorn, and to see you firmly fixed in that sphere of fashion for which all your tastes adapt you.

'I may safely assert – and I do assert it with my hand on my heart – that I am actuated by no mercenary motives. Far be it from me to marry any woman – no, not a princess – on account of her money. No marriage can be happy without mutual affection; and I do fully trust – no, not trust, but hope – that there may be such between you and me, dearest Miss Dunstable. Whatever settlements you might propose, I should accede to. It is you, your sweet person, that I love, not your money.

'For myself, I need not remind you that I am the second son of my father; and that, as such, I hold no inconsiderable station in the world. My intention is to get into Parliament, and to make a name for myself, if I can, among those who shine in the House of Commons. My elder brother, Lord Porlock, is, as you are aware, unmarried; and we all fear that the family honours are not likely to be perpetuated by him, as he has all manner of troublesome liaisons which will probably prevent his settling in life. There is nothing at all of that kind in my way. It will indeed be a delight to place a coronet on the head of my lovely Martha: a coronet which can give no fresh grace to her, but which will be so much adorned by her wearing it.

'Dearest Miss Dunstable, I shall wait with the utmost impatience for your answer; and now, burning with hope that it may not be altogether unfavourable to my love, I beg permission to sign myself

'Your own most devoted,
'George de Courcy.'

The ardent lover had not to wait long for an answer from his mistress. She found this letter on her toilet-table one night as she went to bed. The next morning she came down to breakfast and met her swain with the most unconcerned air in the world; so much so that he began to think, as he munched his toast with rather a shamefaced look, that the letter on which so much was to depend had not yet come safely to hand. But his suspense was not of a prolonged duration. After breakfast, as was his wont, he went out to the stables with his brother and Frank Gresham; and while there, Miss Dunstable's man, coming up to him, touched his hat, and put a letter into his hand.

Frank, who knew the man, glanced at the letter and looked at his cousin; but he said nothing. He was, however, a little jealous, and felt that an injury was done to him by any correspondence between Miss Dunstable and his cousin George.

Miss Dunstable's reply was as follows; and it may be remarked that it was written in a very clear and well-penned hand, and one which certainly did not betray much emotion of the heart: –

'My dear Mr de Courcy,

'I am sorry to say that I had not perceived from your manner that you entertained any peculiar feelings towards me; as, had I done so, I should at once have endeavoured to put an end to them. I am much flattered by the way in which you speak of me; but I am in too humble a position to return your affection; and can, therefore, only express a hope that you may be soon able to eradicate it from your bosom. A letter is a very good way of making an offer, and as such I do not think it at all odd; but I certainly did not expect such an honour last night. As to my raillery, I trust it has never yet hurt you. I can assure you it never shall. I hope you will soon have a worthier ambition than that to which you allude; for I am well aware that no attempt will ever make me shine anywhere.

'I am quite sure you have had no mercenary motives: such motives in marriage are very base, and quite below your name and lineage. Any little fortune that I may have must be a matter of indifference to one who looks forward, as you do, to put a coronet on his wife's brow. Nevertheless, for the sake of the family, I trust that Lord Porlock, in spite of his obstacles, may live to do the same for a wife of his own some of these days. I am glad to hear that there is nothing to interfere with your own prospects of domestic felicity.

'Sincerely hoping that you may be perfectly successful in your proud ambition to shine in Parliament, and regretting extremely that I cannot share that ambition with you, I beg to subscribe myself, with very great respect,

'Your sincere well-wisher,
'Martha Dunstable.'

The Honourable George, with that modesty which so well became him, accepted Miss Dunstable's reply as a final answer to his little proposition, and troubled her with no further courtship. As he said to his brother John, no harm had been done, and he might have better luck next time. But there was an inmate of Courcy Castle who was somewhat more pertinacious in his search after love and wealth. This was no other than Mr Moffat: a gentleman whose ambition was not satisfied by the cares of his Barchester contest, or the possession of one affianced bride.

Mr Moffat was, as we have said, a man of wealth; but we all know, from the lessons of our early youth, how the love of money increases and gains strength by its own success. Nor was he a man of so mean a spirit as to be satisfied with mere wealth. He desired also place and station, and gracious countenance among the great ones of the earth. Hence had come his adherence to the De Courcys; hence his seat in Parliament; and hence, also, his perhaps ill-considered match with Miss Gresham.

There is no doubt but that the privilege of matrimony offers opportunities to money-loving young men which ought not to be lightly abused. Too many young men marry without giving any consideration to the matter whatever. It is not that they are indifferent to money, but that they recklessly miscalculate their own value, and omit to look around and see how much is done by those who are more careful. A man can be young but once, and, except in cases of a special interposition of Providence, can marry but once. The chance once thrown away may be said to be irrecoverable! How, in after-life, do men toil and turmoil through long years to attain some prospect of doubtful advancement! Half that trouble, half that care, a tithe of that circumspection would, in early youth, have probably secured to them the enduring comfort of a wife's wealth.

You will see men labouring night and day to become bank directors; and even a bank direction may only be the road to ruin. Others will spend years in degrading subserviency to obtain a niche in a will; and the niche, when at last obtained and enjoyed, is but a sorry payment for all that has been endured. Others, again, struggle harder still, and go through even deeper waters: they make the wills for themselves, forge stock-shares, and fight with unremitting, painful labour to appear to be the thing that they are not. Now, in many of these cases, all this might have been spared had the men made adequate use of those opportunities which youth and youthful charms afford once – and once only. There is no road to wealth so easy and respectable as that of matrimony; that is, of course, provided that the aspirant declines the slow course of honest work. But then, we can so seldom put old heads on young shoulders!

In the case of Mr Moffat, we may perhaps say that a specimen was produced of this bird, so rare in the land.* His shoulders were certainly young, seeing that he was not yet six-and-twenty; but his head had ever been old. From the moment when he was first put forth to go alone – at the age of twenty-one – his life had been one calculation how he could make the most of himself. He had allowed himself to be betrayed into no folly by an unguarded heart; no youthful indiscretion had marred his prospects. He had made the most of himself. Without wit, or depth, or any mental gift – without honesty of purpose or industry for good work – he had been for two years sitting member for Barchester; was the guest of Lord de Courcy; was engaged to the eldest daughter of one of the best commoners' families in England; and was, when he first began to think of Miss Dunstable, sanguine that his re-election to Parliament was secure.

When, however, at this period he began to calculate what his position in the world really was, it occurred to him that he was doing an ill-judged thing in marrying Miss Gresham. Why marry a penniless girl – for Augusta's trifle of a fortune was not a penny in his estimation – while there was Miss Dunstable in the world to be won? His own six or seven thousand a year, quite unembarrassed as it was, was certainly a great thing; but what might he not do if to that he could add the almost fabulous wealth of the great heiress? Was she not here, put absolutely in his path? Would it not be a wilful throwing away of a chance not to avail himself of it? He must, to be sure, lose the De Courcy friendship; but if he should then have secured his Barchester seat for the usual term of a parliamentary session, he might be able to spare that. He would also, perhaps, encounter some Gresham enmity: this was a point on which he did think more than once: but what will not a man encounter for the sake of two hundred thousand pounds?

It was thus that Mr Moffat argued with himself, with much prudence, and brought himself to resolve that he would at any rate become a candidate for the great prize. He also, therefore, began to say his soft things; and it must be admitted that he said them with more considerate propriety than had the Honourable

George. Mr Moffat had an idea that Miss Dunstable was not a fool, and that in order to catch her he must do more than endeavour to lay salt on her tail, in the guise of flattery. It was evident to him that she was a bird of some cunning, not to be caught by an ordinary gin, such as those commonly in use with the Honourable Georges of Society.

It seemed to Mr Moffat, that though Miss Dunstable was so sprightly, so full of fun, and so ready to chatter on all subjects, she well knew the value of her own money, and of her position as dependent on it: he perceived that she never flattered the countess, and seemed to be no whit absorbed by the titled grandeur of her host's family. He gave her credit, therefore, for an independent spirit: and an independent spirit in his estimation was one that placed its sole dependence on a respectable balance at its banker's.

Working on these ideas, Mr Moffat commenced operations in such manner that his overtures to the heiress should not, if unsuccessful, interfere with the Greshamsbury engagement. He began by making common cause with Miss Dunstable: their positions in the world, he said to her, were very closely similar. They had both risen from the lower class by the strength of honest industry: they were both now wealthy, and had both hitherto made such use of their wealth as to induce the highest aristocracy of England to admit them into their circles.

'Yes, Mr Moffat,' had Miss Dunstable remarked; 'and if all that I hear be true, to admit you into their very families.'

At this Mr Moffat slightly demurred. He would not affect, he said, to misunderstand what Miss Dunstable meant. There had been something said on the probability of such an event; but he begged Miss Dunstable not to believe all that she heard on such subjects.

'I do not believe much,' said she; 'but I certainly did think that that might be credited.'

Mr Moffat then went on to show how it behoved them both, in holding out their hands half-way to meet the aristocratic overtures that were made to them, not to allow themselves to be made use of. The aristocracy, according to Mr Moffat, were people of a very nice sort; the best acquaintance in the world; a portion of mankind to be noticed by whom should be one of the first objects in life of the Dunstables and Moffats. But the Dunstables and Moffats should be very careful to give little or nothing in return. Much, very much in return, would be looked for. The aristocracy, said Mr Moffat, were not a people to allow the light of their countenance to shine forth without looking for a *quid pro quo*, for some compensating value. In all their intercourse with the Dunstables and Moffats, they would expect a payment. It was for the Dunstables and Moffats to see that, at any rate, they did not pay more for the article they got than its market value.

The way in which she, Miss Dunstable, and he, Mr Moffat, would be required to pay would be by taking each of them some poor scion of the aristocracy in marriage; and thus expending their hard-earned wealth in procuring high-priced pleasures for some well-born pauper. Against this, peculiar caution was to be used. Of course, the further induction to be shown was this: that people so circumstanced should marry among themselves; the Dunstables and the Moffats each with the other, and not tumble into the pitfalls prepared for them.

Whether these great lessons had any lasting effect on Miss Dunstable's mind may be doubted. Perhaps she had already made up her mind on the subject which Mr Moffat so well discussed. She was older than Mr Moffat, and, in spite of his two years of parliamentary experience, had perhaps more knowledge of the world with which she had to deal. But she listened to what he said with complacency; understood his object as well as she had that of his aristocratic rival; was no whit offended; but groaned in her spirit as she thought of the wrongs of Augusta Gresham.

But all this good advice, however, would not win the money for Mr Moffat without some more decided step; and that step he soon decided on taking, feeling assured that what he had said would have its due weight with the heiress.

The party at Courcy Castle was now soon about to be broken up. The male De Courcys were going down to a Scotch mountain. The female De Courcys were to be shipped off to an Irish castle. Mr Moffat was to go up to town to prepare his petition. Miss Dunstable was again about to start on a foreign tour in behalf of her physician and attendants; and Frank Gresham was at last to be allowed to go to Cambridge; that is to say, unless his success with Miss Dunstable should render such a step on his part quite preposterous.

'I think you may speak now, Frank,' said the countess. 'I

really think you may: you have known her now for a consider-able time; and, as far as I can judge, she is very fond of you.'

'Nonsense, aunt,' said Frank; 'she doesn't care a button for me.'

'I think differently; and lookers-on, you know, always under-stand the game best. I suppose you are not afraid to ask her.'

'Afraid!' said Frank, in a tone of considerable scorn. He almost made up his mind that he would ask her to show that he was not afraid. His only obstacle to doing so was, that he had not the slightest intention of marrying her.

There was to be but one other great event before the party broke up, and that was a dinner at the Duke of Omnium's. The duke had already declined to come to Courcy; but he had in a measure atoned for this by asking some of the guests to join a great dinner which he was about to give to his neighbours.

Mr Moffat was to leave Courcy Castle the day after the dinner-party, and he therefore determined to make his great attempt on the morning of that day. It was with some difficulty that he brought about an opportunity; but at last he did so, and found himself alone with Miss Dunstable in the walks of Courcy Park.

'It is a strange thing, is it not,' said he, recurring to his old view of the same subject, 'that I should be going to dine with the Duke of Omnium – the richest man, they say, among the whole English aristocracy?'

'Men of that kind entertain everybody, I believe, now and then,' said Miss Dunstable, not very civilly.

'I believe they do; but I am not going as one of the every-bodies. I am going from Lord de Courcy's house with some of his own family. I have no pride in that – not the least; I have more pride in my father's honest industry. But it shows what money does in this country of ours.'

'Yes, indeed; money does a great many queer things.' In saying this Miss Dunstable could not but think that money had done a very queer thing in inducing Miss Gresham to fall in love with Mr Moffat.

'Yes; wealth is very powerful: here we are, Miss Dunstable, the most honoured guests in this house.'

'Oh! I don't know about that; you may be, for you are a member of Parliament, and all that – '

'No; not a member now, Miss Dunstable.'

'Well, you will be, and that's all the same; but I have no such title to honour, thank God.'

They walked on in silence for a little while, for Mr Moffat hardly knew how to manage the business he had in hand. 'It is quite delightful to watch these people,' he said at last: 'now they accuse us of being tuft-hunters.'*

'Do they?' said Miss Dunstable. 'Upon my word I didn't know that anybody ever so accused me.'

'I didn't mean you and me personally.'

'Oh! I'm glad of that.'

'But that is what the world says of persons of our class. Now it seems to me that the toadying is all on the other side. The countess here does toady you, and so do the young ladies.'

'Do they? if so, upon my word I didn't know it. But, to tell the truth, I don't think much of such things. I live mostly to myself, Mr Moffat.'

'I see that you do, and I admire you for it; but, Miss Dunstable, you cannot always live so,' and Mr Moffat looked at her in a manner which gave her the first intimation of his coming burst of tenderness.

'That's as may be, Mr Moffat,' said she.

He went on beating about the bush for some time – giving her to understand how necessary it was that persons situated as they were should live either for themselves or for each other, and that, above all things, they should beware of falling into the mouths of voracious aristocratic lions who go about looking for prey – till they came to a turn in the grounds; at which Miss Dunstable declared her determination of going in. She had walked enough, she said. As by this time Mr Moffat's immediate intentions were becoming visible she thought it prudent to retire. 'Don't let me take you in, Mr Moffat; but my boots are a little damp, and Dr Easyman will never forgive me if I do not hurry in as fast as I can.'

'Your feet damp? – I hope not: I do hope not,' said he, with a look of the greatest solicitude.

'Oh! it's nothing to signify; but it's well to be prudent, you know. Good morning, Mr Moffat.'

'Miss Dunstable!'

'Eh – yes!' and Miss Dunstable stopped in the grand path. 'I won't let you return with me, Mr Moffat, because I know you were not coming in so soon.'

'Miss Dunstable; I shall be leaving this tomorrow.'

'Yes; and I go myself the day after.'

'I know it. I am going to town and you are going abroad. It may be long – very long – before we meet again.'

'About Easter,' said Miss Dunstable; 'that is, if the doctor doesn't knock up on the road.'

'And I had, had wished to say something before we part for so long a time. Miss Dunstable – '

'Stop! – Mr Moffat. Let me ask you one question. I'll hear anything that you have got to say, but on one condition: that is, that Miss Augusta Gresham shall be by while you say it. Will you consent to that?'

'Miss Augusta Gresham,' said he, 'has no right to listen to my private conversation.'

'Has she not, Mr Moffat? then I think she should have. I, at any rate, will not so far interfere with what I look on as her undoubted privileges as to be a party to any secret in which she may not participate.'

'But, Miss Dunstable – '

'And to tell you fairly, Mr Moffat, any secret that you do tell me, I shall most undoubtedly repeat to her before dinner. Good morning, Mr Moffat; my feet are certainly a little damp, and if I stay a moment longer, Dr Easyman will put off my foreign trip for at least a week.' And so she left him standing alone in the middle of the gravel-walk.

For a moment or two Mr Moffat consoled himself in his misfortune by thinking how he might best avenge himself on Miss Dunstable. Soon, however, such futile ideas left his brain. Why should he give over the chase because the rich galleon had escaped him on this, his first cruise in pursuit of her? Such prizes were not to be won so easily. Her present objection clearly consisted in his engagement to Miss Gresham, and in that only. Let that engagement be at an end, notoriously and publicly broken off, and this objection would fall to the ground. Yes; ships so richly freighted were not to be run down in one summer morning's plain sailing. Instead of looking for his revenge on Miss Dunstable, it would be more prudent in him – more in keeping with his character – to pursue his object, and overcome such difficulties as he might find in his way.

CHAPTER XIX

The Duke of Omnium

The Duke of Omnium was, as we have said, a bachelor. Not the less on that account did he on certain rare gala days entertain the beauty of the county at his magnificent rural seat, or the female fashion of London in Belgrave Square; but on this occasion the dinner at Gatherum Castle* for such was the name of his mansion – was to be confined to the lords of the creation. It was to be one of those days on which he collected round his board all the notables of the county, in order that his popularity might not wane, or the established glory of his hospitable house become dim.

On such an occasion it was not probable that Lord de Courcy would be one of the guests. The party, indeed, who went from Courcy Castle was not large, and consisted of the Honourable George, Mr Moffat, and Frank Gresham. They went in a tax-cart, with a tandem horse,* driven very knowingly by George de Courcy; and the fourth seat on the back of the vehicle was occupied by a servant, who was to look after the horses at Gatherum.

The Honourable George drove either well or luckily, for he reached the duke's house in safety; but he drove very fast. Poor Miss Dunstable! what would have been her lot had anything but good happened to that vehicle, so richly freighted with her three lovers! They did not quarrel as to the prize, and all reached Gatherum Castle in good-humour with each other.

The castle was a new building of white stone, lately erected at an enormous cost by one of the first architects of the day. It was an immense pile, and seemed to cover ground enough for a moderate-sized town. But, nevertheless, report said that when it was completed, the noble owner found that he had no rooms to live in; and that, on this account, when disposed to study his own comfort, he resided in a house of perhaps one-tenth the size, built by his grandfather in another county.

Gatherum Castle would probably be called Italian in its style of architecture;* though it may, I think, be doubted whether any such edifice, or anything like it, was ever seen in any part of Italy. It was a vast edifice; irregular in height – or it appeared to be so – having long wings on each side too high to be passed over by the eye as mere adjuncts to the mansion, and a portico so large as to make the house behind it look like another building of a greater altitude. This portico was supported by Ionic columns,* and was in itself doubtless a beautiful structure. It was approached by a flight of steps, very broad and very grand; but, as an approach by a flight of steps hardly suits an Englishman's house, to the immediate entrance of which it is necessary that his carriage should drive, there was another front door in one of the wings which was commonly used. A carriage, however, could on very stupendously grand occasions – the visits, for instance, of queens and kings, and royal dukes – be brought up under the portico; as the steps had been so constructed as to admit of a road, with a rather stiff ascent, being made close in front of the wing up into the very porch.

Opening from the porch was the grand hall, which extended up to the top of the house. It was magnificent, indeed; being decorated with many-coloured marbles, and hung round with various trophies of the house of Omnium; banners were there, and armour; the sculptured busts of many noble progenitors; full-length figures in marble of those who had been especially prominent; and every monument of glory that wealth, long years, and great achievements could bring together. If only a man could but live in his hall and be for ever happy there! But the Duke of Omnium could not live happily in his hall; and the fact was, that the architect, in contriving this magnificent entrance for his own honour and fame, had destroyed the duke's house as regards most of the ordinary purposes of residence.

Nevertheless, Gatherum Castle is a very noble pile; and, standing as it does on an eminence, has a very fine effect when seen from many a distant knoll and verdant-wooded hill.

At seven o'clock Mr de Courcy and his friends got down from their drag at the smaller door – for this was no day on which to mount up under the portico; nor was that any suitable vehicle to have been entitled to such honour. Frank felt some excitement a little stronger than that usual to him at such moments, for he had never yet been in company with the Duke of Omnium; and he rather puzzled himself to think on what points he would talk to the man who was the largest landowner in that county in which he himself had so great an interest. He, however, made up his mind that he would allow the duke to choose his own subjects; merely reserving to himself the right of pointing out how deficient in gorse covers was West Barsetshire – that being the duke's division.

They were soon divested of their coats and hats, and, without entering on the magnificence of the great hall, were conducted through rather a narrow passage into rather a small drawing-room – small, that is, in proportion to the number of gentlemen there assembled. There might be about thirty, and Frank was inclined to think that they were almost crowded. A man came forward to greet them when their names were announced; but our hero at once knew that he was not the duke; for this man was fat and short, whereas the duke was thin and tall.

There was a great hubbub going on; for everybody seemed to be talking to his neighbour; or, in default of a neighbour, to himself. It was clear that the exalted rank of their host had put very little constraint on his guests' tongues, for they chatted away with as much freedom as farmers at an ordinary.*

'Which is the duke?' as last Frank contrived to whisper to his cousin.

'Oh; – he's not here,' said George; 'I suppose he'll be in presently. I believe he never shows till just before dinner.'

Frank, of course, had nothing further to say; but he already began to feel himself a little snubbed: he thought that the duke, duke though he was, when he asked people to dinner should be there to tell them that he was glad to see them.

More people flashed into the room, and Frank found himself rather closely wedged in with a stout clergyman of his acquaintance. He was not badly off, for Mr Athill was a friend of his own, who had held a living near Greshamsbury. Lately, however, at the lamented decease of Dr Stanhope – who had died of apoplexy at his villa in Italy* – Mr Athill had been presented with the better preferment of Eiderdown, and had, therefore, removed to another part of the county. He was somewhat of a *bon-vivant*, and a man who thoroughly understood dinner-parties; and with much good nature he took Frank under his special protection.

'You stick to me, Mr Gresham,' he said, 'when we go into the dining-room. I'm an old hand at the duke's dinners, and know how to make a friend comfortable as well as myself.'

'But why doesn't the duke come in?' demanded Frank.

'He'll be here as soon as dinner is ready,' said Mr Athill. 'Or, rather, the dinner will be ready as soon as he is here. I don't care, therefore, how soon he comes.'

Frank did not understand this, but he had nothing to do but to wait and see how things went.

He was beginning to be impatient, for the room was now nearly full, and it seemed evident that no other guests were coming; when suddenly a bell rang, and a gong was sounded, and at the same instant a door that had not yet been used flew open, and a very plainly dressed, plain, tall man entered the room. Frank at once knew that he was at last in presence of the Duke of Omnium.

But his grace, late as he was in commencing the duties as host, seemed in no hurry to make up for lost time. He quietly stood on the rug, with his back to the empty grate, and spoke one or two words in a very low voice to one or two gentlemen who stood nearest to him. The crowd, in the meanwhile, became suddenly silent. Frank, when he found that the duke did not come and speak to him, felt that he ought to go and speak to the duke; but no one else did so, and when he whispered his surprise to Mr Athill, that gentleman told him that this was the duke's practice on all such occasions.

'Fothergill,' said the duke – and it was the only word he had yet spoken out loud – 'I believe we are ready for dinner.' Now Mr Fothergill was the duke's land-agent, and he it was who had greeted Frank and his friends at their entrance.

Immediately the gong was again sounded, and another door leading out of the drawing-room into the dining-room was opened. The duke led the way, and then the guests followed. 'Stick close to me, Mr Gresham,' said Athill, 'we'll get about the middle of the table, where we shall be cosy – and on the other side of the room, out of this dreadful draught – I know the place well, Mr Gresham; stick to me.'

Mr Athill, who was a pleasant, chatty companion, had hardly seated himself, and was talking to Frank as quickly as he could, when Mr Fothergill, who sat at the bottom of the table, asked him to say grace. It seemed to be quite out of the question that the duke should take any trouble with his guests whatever. Mr Athill consequently dropped the word that he was speaking, and uttered a prayer – if it was a prayer – that they might all have grateful hearts for that which God was about to give them.

If it was a prayer! As far as my own experience goes, such

utterances are seldom prayers, seldom can be prayers. And if not prayers, what then? To me it is unintelligible that the full tide of glibbest chatter can be stopped at a moment in the midst of profuse good living, and the Giver thanked becomingly in words of heartfelt praise. Setting aside for the moment what one daily hears and sees, may not one declare that a change so sudden is not within the compass of the human mind? But then, to such reasoning one cannot but add what one does hear and see; one cannot but judge of the ceremony by the manner in which one sees it performed – uttered, that is – and listened to. Clergymen there are – one meets them now and then – who endeavour to give to the dinner-table grace some of the solemnity of a church ritual, and what is the effect? Much the same as though one were to be interrupted for a minute in the midst of one of our church liturgies to hear a drinking-song.

And will it be argued, that a man need be less thankful because, at the moment of receiving, he utters no thanksgiving? or will it be thought that a man is made thankful because what is called a grace is uttered after dinner? It can hardly be imagined that any one will so argue, or so think.

Dinner-graces are, probably, the last remaining relic of certain daily services[1] which the Church in olden days enjoined: nones, complines, and vespers* were others. Of the nones and complines we have happily got quit; and it might be well if we could get rid of the dinner-graces also. Let any man ask himself whether, on his own part, they are acts of prayer and thanksgiving – and if not that, what then?

When the large party entered the dining-room one or two gentlemen might be seen to come in from some other door and set themselves at the table near to the duke's chair. These were guests of his own, who were staying in the house, his particular friends, the men with whom he lived: the others were strangers whom he fed, perhaps once a year, in order that his name might be known in the land as that of one who distributed food and wine hospitably through the county. The food and wine, the attendance also, and the view of the vast repository of plate he vouchsafed willingly to his county neighbours; – but it was

[1] It is, I know, alleged that graces are said before dinner, because our Saviour uttered a blessing before his last supper. I cannot say that the idea of such analogy is pleasing to me.

beyond his good nature to talk to them. To judge by the present appearance of most of them, they were quite as well satisfied to be left alone.

Frank was altogether a stranger there, but Mr Athill knew every one at the table.

'That's Apjohn,' said he: 'don't you know Mr Apjohn, the attorney from Barchester? he's always here; he does some of Fothergill's law business, and makes himself useful. If any fellow knows the value of a good dinner, he does. You'll see that the duke's hospitality will not be thrown away upon him.'

'It's very much thrown away upon me, I know,' said Frank, who could not at all put up with the idea of sitting down to dinner without having been spoken to by his host.

'Oh, nonsense!' said his clerical friend; 'you'll enjoy yourself amazingly by and by. There is not such champagne in any other house in Barsetshire; and then the claret – ' And Mr Athill pressed his lips together, and gently shook his head, meaning to signify by the motion that the claret of Gatherum Castle was sufficient atonement for any penance which a man might have to go through in his mode of obtaining it.

'Who's that funny little man sitting there, next but one to Mr de Courcy? I never saw such a queer fellow in my life.'

'Don't you know old Bolus? Well, I thought every one in Barsetshire knew Bolus; you especially should do so, as he is such a dear friend of Dr Thorne.'

'A dear friend of Dr Thorne?'

'Yes; he was apothecary at Scarington in the old days, before Dr Fillgrave came into vogue. I remember when Bolus was thought to be a very good sort of a doctor.'

'Is he – is he – ' whispered Frank, 'is he by way of a gentleman?'

'Ha! ha! ha! Well, I suppose we must be charitable, and say that he is quite as good, at any rate, as many others there are here – ' and Mr Athill, as he spoke, whispered into Frank's ear, 'You see, there's Finnie here, another Barchester attorney. Now, I really think where Finnie goes Bolus may go too.'*

'The more the merrier, I suppose,' said Frank.

'Well, something a little like that. I wonder why Thorne is not here? I'm sure he was asked.'

'Perhaps he did not particularly wish to meet Finnie and

Bolus. Do you know, Mr Athill, I think he was quite right not
to come. As for myself, I wish I was anywhere else.'

'Ha! ha! ha! You don't know the duke's ways yet; and what's
more, you're young, you happy fellow! But Thorne should have
more sense; he ought to show himself here.'

The gormandising was now going on at a tremendous rate.
Though the volubility of their tongues had been for a while
stopped by the first shock of the duke's presence, the guests
seemed to feel no such constraint upon their teeth. They fed,
one may almost say, rabidly, and gave their orders to the
servants in an eager manner; much more impressive than that
usual at smaller parties. Mr Apjohn, who sat immediately
opposite to Frank, had, by some well-planned manœuvre,
contrived to get before him the jowl of a salmon; but, unfortunately, he was not for a while equally successful in the article of
sauce. A very limited portion – so at least thought Mr Apjohn –
had been put on his plate; and a servant, with a huge sauce
tureen, absolutely passed behind his back inattentive to his
audible requests. Poor Mr Apjohn in his despair turned round
to arrest the man by his coat-tails; but he was a moment too
late, and all but fell backwards on the floor. As he righted
himself he muttered an anathema, and looked with a face of
mute anguish at his plate.

'Anything the matter, Apjohn?' said Mr Fothergill, kindly,
seeing the utter despair written on the poor man's countenance;
'can I get anything for you?'

'The sauce!' said Mr Apjohn, in a voice that would have
melted a hermit; and as he looked at Mr Fothergill, he pointed
at the now distant sinner, who was dispensing his melted
ambrosia at least ten heads upwards, away from the unfortunate
supplicant.

Mr Fothergill, however, knew where to look for balm for
such wounds, and in a minute or two Mr Apjohn was employed
quite to his heart's content.

'Well,' said Frank to his neighbour, 'it may be very well once
in a way; but I think that on the whole Dr Thorne is right.'

'My dear Mr Gresham, see the world on all sides,' said Mr
Athill, who had also been somewhat intent on the gratification
of his own appetite, though with an energy less evident than
that of the gentleman opposite. 'See the world on all sides if you

have an opportunity; and, believe me, a good dinner now and then is a very good thing'

'Yes; but I don't like eating it with hogs.'

'Whish – h! softly, softly, Mr Gresham, or you'll disturb Mr Apjohn's digestion. Upon my word, he'll want it all before he has done. Now, I like this kind of thing once in a way.'

'Do you?' said Frank, in a tone that was almost savage.

'Yes; indeed I do. One sees so much character. And after all, what harm does it do?'

'My idea is that people should live with those whose society is pleasant to them.'

'Live – yes, Mr Gresham – I agree with you there. It wouldn't do for me to live with the Duke of Omnium; I shouldn't understand, or probably approve, his ways. Nor should I, perhaps, much like the constant presence of Mr Apjohn. But now and then – once in a year or so – I do own I like to see them both. Here's the cup; now whatever you do, Mr Gresham, don't pass the cup without tasting it.'

And so the dinner passed on, slowly enough as Frank thought, but all too quickly for Mr Apjohn. It passed away, and the wine came circulating freely. The tongues again were loosed, the teeth being released from their labours, and under the influence of the claret the duke's presence was forgotten.

But very speedily the coffee was brought. 'This will soon be over now,' said Frank, to himself, thankfully; for, though he by no means despised good claret, he had lost his temper too completely to enjoy it at the present moment. But he was much mistaken; the farce as yet was only at its commencement. The duke took his cup of coffee, and so did the few friends who sat close to him, but the beverage did not seem to be in great request with the majority of the guests. When the duke had taken his modicum, he rose up and silently retired, saying no word and making no sign. And then the farce commenced.

'Now, gentlemen,' said Mr Fothergill, cheerily, 'we are all right. Apjohn, is there claret there? Mr Bolus, I know you stick to the Madeira; you are quite right, for there isn't much of it left, and my belief is there'll never be more like it.'

And so the duke's hospitality went on, and the duke's guests drank merrily for the next two hours.

'Shan't we see any more of him?' asked Frank.

'Any more of whom?' said Mr Athill.

'Of the duke?'

'Oh, no; you'll see no more of him. He always goes when the coffee comes. It's brought in as an excuse. We've had enough of the light of his countenance* to last till next year. The duke and I are excellent friends; have been so these fifteen years; but I never see more of him than that.'

'I shall go away,' said Frank.

'Nonsense. Mr de Courcy and your other friend won't stir for this hour yet.'

'I don't care. I shall walk on, and they may catch me. I may be wrong; but it seems to me that a man insults me when he asks me to dine with him and never speaks to me. I don't care if he be ten times Duke of Omnium; he can't be more than a gentleman, and as such I am his equal.' And then, having thus given vent to his feelings in somewhat high-flown language, he walked forth and trudged away along the road towards Courcy.

Frank Gresham had been born and bred a Conservative, whereas the Duke of Omnium was well known as a consistent Whig. There is no one so devoutly resolved to admit of no superior as your Conservative, born and bred, no one so inclined to high domestic despotism as your through-going consistent old Whig.

When he had proceeded about six miles, Frank was picked up by his friends; but even then his anger had hardly cooled.

'Was the duke as civil as ever when you took your leave of him?' said he to his cousin George, as he took his seat on the drag.

'The juke has jeuced jude wine – lem me tell you that, old fella,' hiccupped out the Honourable George, as he touched up the leader under the flank.

CHAPTER XX

The Proposal

And now the departures from Courcy Castle came rapidly one after another, and there remained but one more evening before Miss Dunstable's carriage was to be packed. The countess, in the early moments of Frank's courtship, had controlled his ardour and checked the rapidity of his amorous professions; but as days, and at last weeks, wore away, she found that it was necessary to stir the fire which she had before endeavoured to slacken.

'There will be nobody here tonight but our own circle,' said she to him, 'and I really think you should tell Miss Dunstable what your intentions are. She will have fair ground to complain of you if you do not.'

Frank began to feel that he was in a dilemma. He had commenced making love to Miss Dunstable partly because he liked the amusement, and partly from a satirical propensity to quiz his aunt by appearing to fall into her scheme. But he had overshot the mark, and did not know what answer to give when he was thus called upon to make a downright proposal. And then, although he did not care two rushes about Miss Dunstable in the way of love, he nevertheless experienced a sort of jealousy when he found that she appeared to be indifferent to him, and that she corresponded the meanwhile with his cousin George. Though all their flirtations had been carried on on both sides palpably by way of fun, though Frank had told himself ten times a day that his heart was true to Mary Thorne, yet he had an undefined feeling that it behoved Miss Dunstable to be a little in love with him. He was not quite at ease in that she was not a little melancholy now that his departure was so nigh; and, above all, he was anxious to know what were the real facts about that letter. He had in his own breast threatened Miss Dunstable with a heartache; and now, when the time for their separation came, he found that his own heart was the more likely to ache of the two.

'I suppose I must say something to her, or my aunt will never be satisfied,' said he to himself as he sauntered into the little drawing-room on that last evening. But at the very time he was ashamed of himself, for he knew that he was going to ask badly.

His sister and one of his cousins were in the room, but his aunt, who was quite on the alert, soon got them out of it, and Frank and Miss Dunstable were alone.

'So all our fun and all our laughter is come to an end,' said she, beginning the conversation. 'I don't know how you feel, but for myself I really am a little melancholy at the idea of parting;'

and she looked up at him with her laughing black eyes, as though she never had, and never could have a care in the world.

'Melancholy! oh, yes; you look so,' said Frank, who really did feel somewhat lackadaisically sentimental.

'But how thoroughly glad the countess must be that we are both going,' continued she. 'I declare we have treated her most infamously. Ever since we've been here we've had all the amusement to ourselves. I've sometimes thought she would turn me out of the house.'

'I wish with all my heart she had.'

'Oh, you cruel barbarian! why on earth should you wish that?'

'That I might have joined you in your exile. I hate Courcy Castle, and should have rejoiced to leave – and – and – '

'And what?'

'And I love Miss Dunstable, and should have doubly, trebly rejoiced to leave it with her.'

Frank's voice quivered a little as he made this gallant profession; but still Miss Dunstable only laughed the louder. 'Upon my word, of all my knights you are by far the best behaved,' said she, 'and say much the prettiest things.' Frank became rather red in the face, and felt that he did so. Miss Dunstable was treating him like a boy. While she pretended to be so fond of him she was only laughing at him, and corresponding the while with his cousin George. Now Frank Gresham already entertained a sort of contempt for his cousin, which increased the bitterness of his feelings. Could it really be possible that George had succeeded while he had utterly failed; that his stupid cousin had touched the heart of the heiress while she was playing with him as with a boy?

'Of all your knights! Is that the way you talk to me when we are going to part? When was it, Miss Dunstable, that George de Courcy became one of them?'

Miss Dunstable for a while looked serious enough. 'What makes you ask that?' said she. 'What makes you inquire about Mr de Courcy?'

'Oh, I have eyes, you know, and can't help seeing. Not that I see, or have seen anything that I could possibly help.'

'And what have you seen, Mr Gresham?'

'Why, I know you have been writing to him.'

'Did he tell you so?'

'No; he did not tell me; but I know it.'

For a moment she sat silent, and then her face again resumed its usual happy smile. 'Come, Mr Gresham, you are not going to quarrel with me, I hope, even if I did write a letter to your cousin. Why should I not write to him? I correspond with all manner of people I'll write to you some of these days if you'll let me, and will promise to answer my letters.'

Frank threw himself back on the sofa on which he was sitting, and, in doing so, brought himself somewhat nearer to his companion than he had been; he then drew his hand slowly across his forehead, pushing back his thick hair, and as he did so he sighed somewhat plaintively.

'I do not care,' said he, 'for the privilege of correspondence on such terms. If my cousin George is to be a correspondent of yours also, I will give up my claim.'

And then he sighed again, so that it was piteous to hear him. He was certainly an arrant puppy, and an egregious ass into the bargain; but then, it must be remembered in his favour that he was only twenty-one, and that much had been done to spoil him. Miss Dunstable did remember this, and therefore abstained from laughing at him.

'Why, Mr Gresham, what on earth do you mean? In all human probability I shall never write another line to Mr de Courcy; but, if I did, what possible harm could it do you?'

'Oh, Miss Dunstable! you do not in the least understand what my feelings are.'

'Don't I? Then I hope I never shall. I thought I did. I thought they were the feelings of a good, true-hearted friend; feelings that I could sometimes look back upon with pleasure as being honest when so much that one meets is false. I have become very fond of you, Mr Gresham, and I should be sorry to think that I did not understand your feelings.'

This was almost worse and worse. Young ladies like Miss Dunstable – for she was still to be numbered in the category of young ladies – do not usually tell young gentlemen that they are very fond of them. To boys and girls they may make such a declaration. Now Frank Gresham regarded himself as one who had already fought his battles, and fought them not without glory;* he could not therefore endure to be thus openly told by Miss Dunstable that she was very fond of him.

'Fond of me, Miss Dunstable! I wish you were.'

'So I am – very.'

'You little know how fond I am of you, Miss Dunstable,' and he put out his hand to take hold of hers. She then lifted up her own, and slapped him lightly on the knuckles.

'And what can you have to say to Miss Dunstable that can make it necessary that you should pinch her hand? I tell you fairly, Mr Gresham, if you make a fool of yourself, I shall come to a conclusion that you are all fools, and that it is hopeless to look out for any one worth caring for.'

Such advice as this, so kindly given, so wisely meant, so clearly intelligible, he should have taken and understood, young as he was. But even yet he did not do so.

'A fool of myself! Yes; I suppose I must be a fool if I have so much regard for Miss Dunstable as to make it painful to me to know that I am to see her no more: a fool: yes, of course I am a fool – a man is always a fool when he loves.'

Miss Dunstable could not pretend to doubt his meaning any longer; and was determined to stop him, let it cost what it would. She now put out her hand, not over white, and, as Frank soon perceived, gifted with a very fair allowance of strength.

'Now, Mr Gresham,' said she, 'before you go any further you shall listen to me. Will you listen to me for a moment without interrupting me?'

Frank was of course obliged to promise that he would do so.

'You are going – or rather you were going, for I shall stop you – to make to me a profession of love.'

'A profession!' said Frank making a slight unsuccessful effort to get his hand free.

'Yes; a profession – a false profession, Mr Gresham, – a false profession – a false profession. Look into your heart – into your heart of hearts I know you at any rate have a heart; look into it closely Mr Gresham, you know you do not love me; not as a man should love the woman whom he swears to love.'

Frank was taken aback. So appealed to he found that he could not any longer say that he did love her. He could only look into her face with all his eyes, and sit there listening to her.

'How is it possible that you should love me? I am Heaven knows how many years your senior. I am neither young nor beautiful, nor have I been brought up as she should be whom you in time will really love and make your wife. I have nothing that should make you love me; but – but, I am rich.'

'It is not that,' said Frank, stoutly, feeling himself imperatively called upon to utter something in his own defence.

'Ah, Mr Gresham, I fear it is that. For what other reason can you have laid your plans to talk in this way to such a woman as I am?'

'I have laid no plans,' said Frank, now getting his hand to himself. 'At any rate, you wrong me there, Miss Dunstable.'

'I like you so well – nay, love you, if a woman may talk of love in the way of friendship – that if money, money alone would make you happy, you should have it heaped on you. If you want it, Mr Gresham, you shall have it.'

'I have never thought of your money,' said Frank, surlily.

'But it grieves me,' continued she, 'it does grieve me, to think that you, you, you – so young, so gay, so bright – that you should have looked for it in this way. From others I have taken it just as the wind that whistles;' and now two big slow tears escaped from her eyes, and would have rolled down her rosy cheeks, were it not that she brushed them off with the back of her hand.

'You have utterly mistaken me, Miss Dunstable,' said Frank.

'If I have, I will humbly beg your pardon,' said she. 'But – but – but – '

'You have; indeed you have.'

'How can I have mistaken you? Were you not about to say that you loved me; to talk absolute nonsense; to make me an offer? If you were not, if I have mistaken you indeed, I will beg your pardon.'

Frank had nothing further to say in his own defence. He had not wanted Miss Dunstable's money – that was true; but he could not deny that he had been about to talk that absolute nonsense of which she spoke with so much scorn.

'You would almost make me think that there are none honest in this fashionable world of yours. I well know why Lady de Courcy has had me here: how could I help knowing it? She has been so foolish in her plans that ten times a day she has told her own secret. But I have said to myself twenty times, that if she were crafty, you were honest.'

'And am I dishonest?'

'I have laughed in my sleeve to see how she played her game, and to hear others around playing theirs; all of them thinking that they could get the money of the poor fool who had come at their beck and call; but I was able to laugh at them as long as I thought that I had one true friend to laugh with me. But one cannot laugh with all the world against one.'

'I am not against you, Miss Dunstable.'

'Sell yourself for money! why, if I were a man I would not sell one jot of liberty for mountains of gold. What! tie myself in the heyday of my youth to a person I could never love, for a price! perjure myself, destroy myself – and not only myself, but her also, in order that I might live idly! Oh, heavens! Mr Gresham! can it be that the words of such a woman as your aunt have sunk so deeply in your heart; have blackened you so foully as to make you think of such vile folly as this? Have you forgotten your soul, your spirit, your man's energy, the treasure of your heart? And you, so young! For shame, Mr Gresham! for shame – for shame!'

Frank found the task before him by no means an easy one. He had to make Miss Dunstable understand that he had never had the slightest idea of marrying her, and that he had made love to her merely with the object of keeping his hand in for the work as it were; with that object, and the other equally laudable one of interfering with his cousin George.

And yet there was nothing for him but to get through this task as best he might. He was goaded to it by the accusations which Miss Dunstable brought against him; and he began to feel, that though her invectives against him might be bitter when he had told the truth, they could not be so bitter as those she now kept hinting at under her mistaken impression as to his views. He had never had any strong propensity for money-hunting; but now that offence appeared in his eyes abominable, unmanly, and disgusting. Any imputation would be better than that.

'Miss Dunstable, I never for a moment thought of doing what you accuse me of; on my honour, I never did. I have been very foolish – very wrong – idiotic, I believe; but I have never intended that.'

'Then, Mr Gresham, what did you intend?'

This was rather a difficult question to answer; and Frank was not very quick in attempting it. 'I know you will not forgive me,' he said at last; 'and, indeed, I do not see how you can. I don't know how it came about; but this is certain, Miss

Dunstable; I have never for a moment thought about your fortune; that is, thought about it in the way of coveting it.'

'You never thought of making me your wife, then?'

'Never,' said Frank, looking boldly into her face.

'You never intended really to propose to go with me to the altar, and then make yourself rich by one great perjury?'

'Never for a moment,' said he.

'You have never gloated over me as the bird of prey gloats over the poor beast that is soon to become carrion beneath its claws? You have not counted me out as equal to so much land, and calculated on me as a balance at your banker's? Ah, Mr Gresham,' she continued, seeing that he stared as though struck almost with awe by her strong language; 'you little guess what a woman situated as I am has to suffer.'

'I have behaved badly to you, Miss Dunstable, and I beg your pardon; but I have never thought of your money.'

'Then we will be friends again, Mr Gresham, won't we? It is so nice to have a friend like you. There, I think I understand it now; you need not tell me.'

'It was half by way of making a fool of my aunt,' said Frank, in an apologetic tone

'There is merit in that, at any rate,' said Miss Dunstable. 'I understand it all now; you thought to make a fool of me in real earnest. Well, I can forgive that; at any rate it is not mean.'

It may be, that Miss Dunstable did not feel much acute anger at finding that this young man had addressed her with words of love in the course of an ordinary flirtation, although that flirtation had been unmeaning and silly. This was not the offence against which her heart and breast had found peculiar cause to arm itself; this was not the injury from which she had hitherto experienced suffering.

At any rate, she and Frank again became friends, and, before the evening was over, they perfectly understood each other. Twice during this long *tête-à-tête* Lady de Courcy came into the room to see how things were going on, and twice she went out almost unnoticed. It was quite clear to her that something uncommon had taken place, was taking place, or would take place; and that should this be for weal or for woe, no good could now come from her interference. On each occasion, therefore, she smiled sweetly on the pair of turtle-doves, and glided out of the room as quietly as she had glided into it.

But at last it became necessary to remove them; for the world had gone to bed. Frank, in the meantime, had told to Miss Dunstable all his love for Mary Thorne, and Miss Dunstable had enjoined him to be true to his vows. To her eyes there was something of heavenly beauty in young, true love – of beauty that was heavenly because it had been unknown to her.

'Mind you let me hear, Mr Gresham,' said she. 'Mind you do; and, Mr Gresham, never, never forget her for one moment; not for one moment, Mr Gresham.'

Frank was about to swear that he never would – again, when the countess, for the third time, sailed into the room.

'Young people,' said she, 'do you know what o'clock it is?'

'Dear me, Lady de Courcy, I declare it is past twelve; I really am ashamed of myself. How glad you will be to get rid of me tomorrow!'

'No, no, indeed we shan't; shall we, Frank?' and so Miss Dunstable passed out.

Then once again the aunt tapped her nephew with her fan. It was the last time in her life that she did so. He looked up in her face, and his look was enough to tell her that the acres of Greshamsbury were not to be reclaimed by the ointment of Lebanon.

Nothing further on the subject was said. On the following morning Miss Dunstable took her departure, not much heeding the rather cold words of farewell which her hostess gave her; and on the following day Frank started for Greshamsbury.

CHAPTER XXI

Mr Moffat Falls into Trouble

We will now, with the reader's kind permission, skip over some months in our narrative. Frank returned from Courcy Castle to Greshamsbury, and having communicated to his mother – much in the same manner as he had to the countess – the fact that his mission had been unsuccessful, he went up after a day or two to Cambridge. During his short stay at Greshamsbury he did not even catch a glimpse of Mary. He asked for her, of course, and was told that it was not likely that she would be at the house just at present. He called at the doctor's, but she was denied to him there: 'she was out,' Janet said, – 'probably with Miss Oriel.' He went to the parsonage and found Miss Oriel at home; but Mary had not been seen that morning. He then returned to the house; and, having come to the conclusion that she had not thus vanished into air, otherwise than by preconcerted arrangement, he boldly taxed Beatrice on the subject.

Beatrice looked very demure; declared that no one in the house had quarrelled with Mary; confessed that it had been thought prudent that she should for a while stay away from Greshamsbury; and, of course, ended by telling her brother everything, including all the scenes that had passed between Mary and herself.

'It is out of the question your thinking of marrying her, Frank,' said she. 'You must know that nobody feels it more strongly than poor Mary herself;' and Beatrice looked the very personification of domestic prudence.

'I know nothing of the kind,' said he, with the headlong imperative air that was usual with him in discussing matters with his sisters. 'I know nothing of the kind. Of course I cannot say what Mary's feelings may be: a pretty life she must have had of it among you. But you may be sure of this, Beatrice, and so may my mother, that nothing on earth shall make me give her up – nothing.' And Frank, as he made the protestation, strengthened his own resolution by thinking of all the counsel that Miss Dunstable had given him.

The brother and sister could hardly agree, as Beatrice was dead against the match. Not that she would not have liked Mary Thorne for a sister-in-law, but that she shared to a certain degree the feeling which was now common to all the Greshams – that Frank must marry money. It seemed, at any rate, to be imperative that he should either do that or not marry at all. Poor Beatrice was not very mercenary in her views: she had no wish to sacrifice her brother to any Miss Dunstable; but yet she felt, as they all felt – Mary Thorne included – that such a match as that, of the young heir with the doctor's niece, was not to be thought of; – not to be spoken of as a thing that was in any way possible. Therefore, Beatrice, though she was Mary's great friend, though she was her brother's favourite sister, could give

Frank no encouragement. Poor Frank! circumstances had made but one bride possible to him: he must marry money.

His mother said nothing to him on the subject: when she learnt that the affair with Miss Dunstable was not to come off, she merely remarked that it would perhaps be best for him to return to Cambridge as soon as possible. Had she spoken her mind out, she would probably have also advised him to remain there as long as possible. The countess had not omitted to write to her when Frank left Courcy Castle; and the countess's letter certainly made the anxious mother think that her son's education had hardly yet been completed. With this secondary object, but with that of keeping him out of the way of Mary Thorne in the first place, Lady Arabella was now quite satisfied that her son should enjoy such advantages as an education completed at the university might give him.

With his father Frank had a long conversation; but, alas! the gist of his father's conversation was this, that it behoved him, Frank, to marry money. The father, however, did not put it to him in the cold, callous way in which his lady-aunt had done, and his lady-mother. He did not bid him go and sell himself to the first female he could find possessed of wealth. It was with inward self-reproaches, and true grief of spirit, that the father told the son that it was not possible for him to do as those may do who are born really rich, or really poor.

'If you marry a girl without a fortune, Frank, how are you to live?' the father asked, after having confessed how deep he himself had injured his own heir.

'I don't care about money, sir,' said Frank. 'I shall be just as happy as if Boxall Hill had never been sold. I don't care a straw about that sort of thing.'

'Ah! my boy; but you will care: you will soon find that you do care.'

'Let me go into some profession. Let me go to the Bar. I am sure I could earn my own living. Earn it! of course I could, why not I as well as all others? I should like of all things to be a barrister.'

There was much more of the same kind, in which Frank said all that he could think of to lessen his father's regrets. In their conversation not a word was spoken about Mary Thorne. Frank was not aware whether or no his father had been told of the great family danger which was dreaded in that quarter. That he had been told, we may surmise, as Lady Arabella was not wont to confine the family dangers to her own bosom. Moreover, Mary's presence had, of course, been missed. The truth was, that the squire had been told, with great bitterness, of what had come to pass, and all the evil had been laid at his door. He it had been who had encouraged Mary to be regarded almost as a daughter of the house of Greshamsbury: he it was who taught that odious doctor – odious in all but his aptitude for good doctoring – to think himself a fit match for the aristocracy of the county. It had been his fault, this great necessity that Frank should marry money; and now it was his fault that Frank was absolutely talking of marrying a pauper.

By no means in quiescence did the squire hear these charges brought against him. The Lady Arabella, in each attack, got quite as much as she gave, and, at last, was driven to retreat in a state of headache, which she declared to be chronic; and which, so she assured her daughter Augusta, must prevent her from having any more lengthened conversations with her lord – at any rate for the next three months. But though the squire may be said to have come off on the whole as victor in these combats they did not perhaps have, on that account, the less effect upon him. He knew it was true that he had done much towards ruining his son; and he also could think of no other remedy than matrimony. It was Frank's doom, pronounced even by the voice of his father, that he must marry money.

And so Frank went off again to Cambridge, feeling himself, as he went, to be a much lesser man in Greshamsbury estimation than he had been some two months earlier, when his birthday had been celebrated. Once during his short stay at Greshamsbury he had seen the doctor; but the meeting had been anything but pleasant. He had been afraid to ask after Mary; and the doctor had been too diffident of himself to speak of her. They had met casually on the road, and, though each in his heart loved the other, the meeting had been anything but pleasant.

And so Frank went back to Cambridge; and, as he did so, he stoutly resolved that nothing should make him untrue to Mary Thorne. 'Beatrice,' said he, on the morning he went away, when she came into his room to superintend his packing – 'Beatrice, if she ever talks about me – '

'Oh, Frank, my darling Frank, don't think of it – it is madness; she knows it is madness.'

'Never mind; if she ever talks about me, tell her that the last word I said was, that I would never forget her. She can do as she likes.'

Beatrice made no promise, never hinted that she would give the message; but it may be taken for granted that she had not been long in company with Mary Thorne before she did give it.

And then there were other troubles at Greshamsbury. It had been decided that Augusta's marriage was to take place in September; but Mr Moffat had, unfortunately, been obliged to postpone the happy day. He himself had told Augusta – not, of course, without protestations as to his regret – and had written to this effect to Mr Gresham. 'Electioneering matters, and other troubles had,' he said, 'made this peculiarly painful postponement absolutely necessary.'

Augusta seemed to bear her misfortune with more equanimity than is, we believe, usual with young ladies under such circumstances. She spoke of it to her mother in a very matter-of-fact way, and seemed almost contented at the idea of remaining at Greshamsbury till February; which was the time now named for the marriage. But Lady Arabella was not equally well satisfied, nor was the squire.

'I half believe that fellow is not honest,' he had once said out loud before Frank, and thus set Frank a-thinking of what dishonesty in the matter it was probable that Mr Moffat might be guilty, and what would be the fitting punishment for such a crime. Nor did he think on the subject in vain; especially after a conference on the matter which he had with his friend Harry Baker. This conference took place during the Christmas vacation.

It should be mentioned, that the time spent by Frank at Courcy Castle had not done much to assist him in his views as to an early degree, and that it had at last been settled that he should stay up at Cambridge another year. When he came home at Christmas he found that the house was not peculiarly lively. Mary was absent on a visit with Miss Oriel. Both these young ladies were staying with Miss Oriel's aunt, in the neighbourhood of London; and Frank soon learnt that there was no chance that either of them would be home before his return. No message had been left for him by Mary – none at least had been left with Beatrice; and he began in his heart to accuse her of coldness and perfidy; – not, certainly, with much justice, seeing that she had never given him the slightest encouragement.

The absence of Patience Oriel added to the dullness of the place. It was certainly hard upon Frank that all the attraction of the village should be removed to make way and prepare for his return – harder, perhaps, on them; for, to tell the truth, Miss Oriel's visit had been entirely planned to enable her to give Mary a comfortable way of leaving Greshamsbury during the time that Frank should remain at home. Frank thought himself cruelly used. But what did Mr Oriel think when doomed to eat his Christmas pudding alone, because the young squire would be unreasonable in his love? What did the doctor think, as he sat solitary by his deserted hearth – the doctor, who no longer permitted himself to enjoy the comforts of the Greshamsbury dining-table? Frank hinted and grumbled; talked to Beatrice of the determined constancy of his love, and occasionally consoled himself by a stray smile from some of the neighbouring belles. The black horse was made perfect; the old grey pony was by no means discarded; and much that was satisfactory was done in the sporting line. But still the house was dull, and Frank felt that he was the cause of its being so. Of the doctor he saw but little: he never came to Greshamsbury unless to see Lady Arabella as doctor, or to be closeted with the squire. There were no social evenings with him; no animated confabulations at the doctor's house; no discourses between them, as there had wont to be, about the merits of the different covers, and the capacities of the different hounds. These were dull days on the whole for Frank; and sad enough, we may say, for our friend the doctor.

In February, Frank again went back to college; having settled with Harry Baker certain affairs which weighed on his mind. He went back to Cambridge, promising to be home on the 20th of the month, so as to be present at his sister's wedding. A cold and chilling time had been named for these hymeneal joys, but one not altogether unsuited to the feelings of the happy pair. February is certainly not a warm month; but with the rich it is generally a cosy, comfortable time. Good fires, winter cheer, groaning tables, and warm blankets, make a fictitious summer, which, to some tastes, is more delightful than the long days and the hot sun. And some marriages are especially winter matches. They depend for their charm on the same substantial attractions: instead of heart beating to heart in sympathetic unison, purse chinks to purse. The rich new furniture of the new abode is looked to instead of the rapture of a pure embrace. The new carriage is depended on rather than the new heart's companion; and the first bright gloss, prepared by the upholsterer's hands, stands in lieu of the rosy tints which young love lends to his true votaries.

Mr Moffat had not spent his Christmas at Greshamsbury. That eternal election petition, those eternal lawyers, the eternal care of his well-managed wealth, forbade him the enjoyment of any such pleasures. He could not come to Greshamsbury for Christmas, nor yet for the festivities of the new year; but now and then he wrote prettily worded notes, sending occasionally a silver-gilt pencil-case, or a small brooch, and informed Lady Arabella that he looked forward to the 20th of February with great satisfaction. But, in the meanwhile, the squire became anxious, and at last went up to London; and Frank, who was at Cambridge, bought the heaviest-cutting whip to be found in that town, and wrote a confidential letter to Harry Baker.

Poor Mr Moffat! It is well known that none but the brave deserve the fair;* but thou, without much excuse for bravery, had secured for thyself one who, at any rate, was fair enough for thee. Would it not have been well hadst thou looked into thyself to see what real bravery might be in thee, before thou hadst prepared to desert this fair one thou hadst already won? That last achievement, one may say, did require some special courage.

Poor Mr Moffat! It is wonderful that as he sat in that gig, going to Gatherum Castle, planning how he would be off with Miss Gresham and afterwards on with Miss Dunstable,* it is wonderful that he should not then have cast his eye behind him, and looked at that stalwart pair of shoulders which were so close to his own back. As he afterwards pondered on his scheme while sipping the duke's claret, it is odd that he should not have observed the fiery pride of purpose and power of wrath which was so plainly written on that young man's brow: or, when he matured, and finished, and carried out his purpose, that he did not think of that keen grasp which had already squeezed his own hand with somewhat too warm a vigour, even in the way of friendship.

Poor Mr Moffat! it is probable that he forgot to think of Frank at all as connected with his promised bride; it is probable that he looked forward only to the squire's violence and the enmity of the house of Courcy; and that he found from inquiry at his heart's pulses, that he was man enough to meet these. Could he have guessed what a whip Frank Gresham would have bought at Cambridge – could he have divined what a letter would have been written to Harry Baker – it is probable, nay, we think we may say certain, that Miss Gresham would have become Mrs Moffat.

Miss Gresham, however, never did become Mrs Moffat. About two days after Frank's departure for Cambridge – it is just possible that Mr Moffat was so prudent as to make himself aware of the fact – but just two days after Frank's departure, a very long, elaborate, and clearly explanatory letter was received at Greshamsbury. Mr Moffat was quite sure that Miss Gresham and her very excellent parents would do him the justice to believe that he was not actuated, etc., etc., etc. The long and the short of this was, that Mr Moffat signified his intention of breaking off the match without offering any intelligible reason.

Augusta again bore her disappointment well: not, indeed, without sorrow and heartache, and inward, hidden tears; but still well. She neither raved, nor fainted, nor walked about by moonlight alone. She wrote no poetry, and never once thought of suicide. When, indeed, she remembered the rosy-tinted lining, the unfathomable softness of that Long-acre carriage, her spirit did for one moment give way; but, on the whole, she bore it as a strong-minded woman and a De Courcy should do.

But both Lady Arabella and the squire were greatly vexed. The former had made the match, and the latter, having consented to it, had incurred deeper responsibilities to enable him to bring it about. The money which was to have been given to Mr Moffat was still to the fore; but alas! how much, how much that he could ill spare, had been thrown away on bridal preparations! It is, moreover, an unpleasant thing for a gentleman to have his daughter jilted; perhaps peculiarly so to have her jilted by a tailor's son.

Lady Arabella's woe was really piteous. It seemed to her as though cruel fate were heaping misery after misery upon the wretched house of Greshamsbury. A few weeks since things were going on so well with her! Frank then was all but the accepted husband of almost untold wealth – so, at least, she was informed by her sister-in-law – whereas, Augusta was the accepted wife of wealth, not indeed untold, but of dimensions quite sufficiently respectable to cause much joy in the telling. Where now were her golden hopes? Where now the splendid future of her poor duped children? Augusta was left to pine alone; and Frank, in a still worse plight, insisted on maintaining his love for a bastard and a pauper.

For Frank's affair she had received some poor consolation by laying all the blame on the squire's shoulders. What she had then said was now repaid to her with interest; for not only had she been the maker of Augusta's match, but she had boasted of the deed with all a mother's pride.

It was from Beatrice that Frank had obtained his tidings. This last resolve on the part of Mr Moffat had not altogether been unsuspected by some of the Greshams, though altogether unsuspected by the Lady Arabella. Frank had spoken of it as a possibility to Beatrice, and was not quite unprepared when the information reached him. He consequently bought his big-cutting whip, and wrote his confidential letter to Harry Baker.

On the following day Frank and Harry might have been seen, with their heads nearly close together, leaning over one of the tables in the large breakfast-room at the Tavistock Hotel in Covent Garden. The ominous whip, to the handle of which Frank had already made his hand well accustomed, was lying on the table between them; and ever and anon Harry Baker would take it up and feel its weight approvingly. Oh, Mr Moffat! poor Mr Moffat! go not out into the fashionable world today; above all, go not to that club of thine in Pall Mall; but, oh! especially go not there, as is thy wont to do, at three o'clock in the afternoon!

With much care did those two young generals lay their plans of attack. Let it not for a moment be thought that it was ever in the minds of either of them that two men should attack one. But it was thought that Mr Moffat might be rather coy in coming out from his seclusion to meet the proffered hand of his once intended brother-in-law when he should see that hand armed with a heavy whip. Baker, therefore, was content to act as a decoy duck, and remarked that he might no doubt also make himself useful in restraining the public mercy, and, probably, in controlling the interference of policemen.

'It will be deuced hard if I can't get five or six shies at him,' said Frank, again clutching his weapon almost spasmodically.

Oh, Mr Moffat! five or six shies with such a whip, and such an arm! For myself, I would sooner join in a second Balaclava gallop* than encounter it.

At ten minutes before four these two heroes might be seen walking up Pall Mall, towards the —— Club. Young Baker walked with an eager disengaged air. Mr Moffat did not know his appearance; he had, therefore, no anxiety to pass along unnoticed. But Frank had in some mysterious way drawn his hat very far over his forehead, and had buttoned his shooting-coat up round his chin. Harry had recommended to him a great-coat, in order that he might the better conceal his face; but Frank had found that the great-coat was an encumbrance to his arm. He put it on, and when thus clothed he had tried the whip, he found that he cut the air with much less potency than in the lighter garment. He contented himself, therefore, with looking down on the pavement as he walked along, letting the long point of the whip stick up from his pocket, and flattering himself that even Mr Moffat would not recognise him at the first glance. Poor Mr Moffat! If he had but had the chance!

And now, having arrived at the front of the club, the two friends for a moment separate: Frank remains standing on the pavement, under the shade of the high stone area-railing, while Harry jauntily skips up three steps at a time, and with a very civil word of inquiry of the hall porter, sends in his card to Mr Moffat –

MR HENRY BAKER

Mr Moffat, never having heard of such a gentleman in his life, unwittingly comes out into the hall, and Harry, with his sweetest smile, addresses him.

Now the plan of the campaign had been settled in this wise: Baker was to send into the club for Mr Moffat, and invite that gentleman down into the street. It was probable that the invitation might be declined; and it had been calculated in such case that the two gentlemen would retire for parley into the strangers' room, which was known to be immediately opposite the hall door. Frank was to keep his eye on the portals, and if he found that Mr Moffat did not appear as readily as might be desired, he also was to ascend the steps and hurry into the strangers' room. Then, whether he met Mr Moffat there or elsewhere, or wherever he might meet him, he was to greet him with all the friendly vigour in his power, while Harry disposed of the club porters.

But fortune, who ever favours the brave, specially favoured Frank Gresham on this occasion. Just as Harry Baker had put his card into the servant's hand, Mr Moffat, with his hat on, prepared for the street, appeared in the hall; Mr Baker addressed him with his sweetest smile, and begged the pleasure of saying a word or two as they descended into the street. Had not Mr Moffat been going thither it would have been very improbable that he should have done so at Harry's instance. But, as it was, he merely looked rather solemn at his visitor – it was his wont to look solemn – and continued the descent of the steps.

Frank, his heart leaping the while, saw his prey, and retreated two steps behind the area-railing, the dread weapon already well poised in his hand. Oh! Mr Moffat! Mr Moffat! if there be any goddess to interfere in thy favour, let her come forward now without delay; let her now bear thee off on a cloud if there be one to whom thou art sufficiently dear! But there is no such goddess.

Harry smiled blandly till they were well on the pavement, saying some nothing, and keeping the victim's face averted from the avenging angel; and then, when the raised hand was sufficiently nigh, he withdrew two steps towards the nearest lamp-post. Not for him was the honour of the interview; – unless, indeed, succouring policemen might give occasion for some gleam of glory.

But succouring policemen were no more to be come by than goddesses. Where were ye, men, when that savage whip fell about the ears of the poor ex-legislator? In Scotland Yard, sitting dozing on your benches, or talking soft nothings to the housemaids round the corner; for ye were not walking on your beats, nor standing at coign of vantage, to watch the tumults of the day. But had ye been there what could ye have done? Had Sir Richard himself* been on the spot Frank Gresham would still, we may say, have had his five shies at that unfortunate one.

When Harry Baker quickly seceded from the way, Mr Moffat at once saw his fate before him. His hair doubtless stood on end, and his voice refused to give the loud screech with which he sought to invoke the club. An ashy paleness suffused his cheeks, and his tottering steps were unable to bear him away in flight. Once, and twice, the cutting whip came down across his

back. Had he been wise enough to stand still and take his
thrashing in that attitude, it would have been well for him. But
men so circumstanced have never such prudence. After two
blows he made a dash at the steps, thinking to get back into the
club; but Harry, who had by no means reclined in idleness
against the lamp-post, here stopped him: 'You had better go
back into the street,' said Harry; 'indeed you had,' giving him a
shove from the second step.

Then of course Frank could not do other than hit him
anywhere. When a gentleman is dancing about with much
energy it is hardly possible to strike him fairly on his back. The
blows, therefore, came now on his legs and now on his head;
and Frank unfortunately got more than his five or six shies
before he was interrupted.

The interruption however came, all too soon for Frank's idea
of justice. Though there be no policemen to take part in a
London row, there are always others ready enough to do so;
amateur policemen, who generally sympathise with the wrong
side, and, in nine cases out of ten, expend their generous energy
in protecting thieves and pickpockets. When it was seen with
what tremendous ardour that dread weapon fell about the ears
of the poor undefended gentleman, interference there was at
last, in spite of Harry Baker's best endeavours, and loudest
protestations.

'Do not interrupt them, sir,' said he; 'pray do not. It is a
family affair, and they will neither of them like it.'

In the teeth, however, of these assurances, rude people did
interfere, and after some nine or ten shies Frank found himself
encompassed by the arms, and encumbered by the weight, of a
very stout gentleman, who hung affectionately about his neck
and shoulders; whereas, Mr Moffat was already receiving consolation from two motherly females, sitting in a state of syncope
on the good-natured knees of a fishmonger's apprentice.

Frank was thoroughly out of breath: nothing came from his
lips but half-muttered expletives and unintelligible denuncia-
tions of the iniquity of his foe. But still he struggled to be at him
again. We all know how dangerous is the taste of blood; how
cruelty will become a custom even with the most tender-hearted.
Frank felt that he had hardly fleshed his virgin lash: he thought,
almost with despair, that he had not yet at all succeeded as
became a man and a brother; his memory told him of but one

or two slight touches that had gone well home to the offender.
He made a desperate effort to throw off that incubus round his
neck and rush again to the combat.

'Harry – Harry; don't let him go – don't let him go,' he barely
articulated.

'Do you want to murder the man, sir; to murder him?' said
the stout gentleman over his shoulder, speaking solemnly into
his very ear.

'I don't care,' said Frank, struggling manfully but uselessly.
'Let me out, I say; I don't care – don't let him go, Harry,
whatever you do.'

'He has got it pretty tidily,' said Harry; 'I think that will
perhaps do for the present.'

By this time there was a considerable concourse. The club
steps were crowded with the members; among whom there were
many of Mr Moffat's acquaintance. Policemen also now flocked
up, and the question arose as to what should be done with the
originators of the affray. Frank and Harry found that they were
to consider themselves under a gentle arrest, and Mr Moffat, in
a fainting state, was carried into the interior of the club.

Frank, in his innocence, had intended to have celebrated this
little affair when it was over by a slight repast and a bottle of
claret with his friend, and then to have gone back to Cambridge
by the mail train. He found, however, that his schemes in this
respect were frustrated. He had to get bail to attend at Marlborough Street police-office should he be wanted within the next
two or three days; and was given to understand that he would
be under the eye of the police, at any rate until Mr Moffat
should be out of danger.

'Out of danger!' said Frank to his friend with a startled look.
'Why, I hardly got at him.' Nevertheless, they did have their
slight repast, and also their bottle of claret.

On the second morning after this occurrence, Frank was again
sitting in that public room at the Tavistock, and Harry was
again sitting opposite to him. The whip was not now so
conspicuously produced between them, having been carefully
packed up and put away among Frank's other travelling properties. They were so sitting, rather glum, when the door swung
open, and a heavy, quick step was heard advancing towards
them. It was the squire; whose arrival there had been momentarily expected.

'Frank,' said he – 'Frank, what on earth is all this?' and as he spoke he stretched out both his hands, the right to his son and the left to his friend.

'He has given a blackguard a licking, that is all,' said Harry.

Frank felt that his hand was held with a peculiarly warm grasp; and he could not but think that his father's face, raised though his eyebrows were – though there was on it an intended expression of amazement and, perhaps, regret – nevertheless, he could not but think that his father's face looked kindly at him.

'God bless my soul, my dear boy! what have you done to the man?'

'He's not a ha-porth the worse, sir,' said Frank, still holding his father's hand.

'Oh, isn't he!' said Harry, shrugging his shoulders 'He must be made of some very tough article then.'

'But, my dear boys, I hope there's no danger. I hope there's no danger.'

'Danger!' said Frank, who could not yet induce himself to believe that he had been allowed a fair chance with Mr Moffat.

'Oh, Frank! Frank! how could you be so rash? In the middle of Pall Mall, too. Well! well! well! All the women down at Greshamsbury will have it that you have killed him.'

'I almost wish I had,' said Frank.

'Oh, Frank! Frank! But now tell me – '

And then the father sat well pleased while he heard, chiefly from Harry Baker, the full story of his son's prowess. And then they did not separate without another slight repast and another bottle of claret.

Mr Moffat retired into the country for a while, and then went abroad; having doubtless learnt that the petition was not likely to give him a seat for the city of Barchester. And this was the end of the wooing with Miss Gresham.

CHAPTER XXII

Sir Roger is Unseated

After this, little occurred at Greshamsbury, or among Greshamsbury people, which it will be necessary for us to record. Some notice was, of course, taken of Frank's prolonged absence from his college; and tidings, perhaps exaggerated tidings, of what had happened in Pall Mall were not slow to reach the High Street of Cambridge. But that affair was gradually hushed up; and Frank went on with his studies.

He went back to his studies; it then being an understood arrangement between him and his father that he should not return to Greshamsbury till the summer vacation. On this occasion, the squire and Lady Arabella had, strange to say, been of the same mind. They both wished to keep their son away from Miss Thorne; and both calculated, that at his age and with his disposition, it was not probable that any passion would last out a six months' absence. 'And when the summer comes it will be an excellent opportunity for us to go abroad,' said Lady Arabella. 'Poor Augusta will require some change to renovate her spirits.'

To this last proposition the squire did not assent. It was, however, allowed to pass over; and this much was fixed, that Frank was not to return home till midsummer.

It will be remembered that Sir Roger Scatcherd had been elected as sitting member for the city of Barchester; but it will also be remembered that a petition against his return was threatened. Had that petition depended solely on Mr Moffat, Sir Roger's seat no doubt would have been saved by Frank Gresham's cutting whip. But such was not the case. Mr Moffat had been put forward by the De Courcy interest; and that noble family with its dependents was not to go to the wall because Mr Moffat had had a thrashing. No; the petition was to go on; and Mr Nearthewinde declared, that no petition in his hands had half so good a chance of success. 'Chance, no, but certainty,' said Mr Nearthewinde; for Mr Nearthewinde had learnt something with reference to that honest publican and the payment of his little bill.

The petition was presented and duly backed; the recognizances were signed, and all the proper formalities formally executed; and Sir Roger found that his seat was in jeopardy. His return had been a great triumph to him; and, unfortunately, he had celebrated that triumph as he had been in the habit of celebrating most of the very triumphant occasions of his life. Though he was then hardly yet recovered from the effects of his last attack, he indulged in another violent drinking bout; and, strange to say, did so without any immediate visible bad effects.

In February he took his seat amidst the warm congratulations of all men of his own class, and early in the month of April his case came on for trial. Every kind of electioneering sin known to the electioneering world was brought to his charge; he was accused of falseness, dishonesty, and bribery of every sort: he had, it was said in the paper of indictment, bought votes, obtained them by treating, carried them off by violence, conquered them by strong drink, polled them twice over, counted those of dead men, stolen them, forged them, and created them by every possible, fictitious contrivance: there was no description of wickedness appertaining to the task of procuring votes of which Sir Roger had not been guilty, either by himself or by his agents. He was quite horrorstruck at the list of his own enormities. But he was somewhat comforted when Mr Closerstil told him that the meaning of it all was that Mr Romer, the barrister, had paid a former bill due to Mr Reddypalm, the publican.

'I fear he was indiscreet, Sir Roger; I really fear he was. Those young men always are. Being energetic, they work like horses; but what's the use of energy without discretion, Sir Roger?'

'But, Mr Closerstil, I knew nothing about it from first to last.'

'The agency can be proved, Sir Roger,' said Mr Closerstil, shaking his head. And then there was nothing further to be said on the matter.

In these days of snow-white purity all political delinquency is abominable in the eyes of – British politicians; but no delinquency is so abominable as that of venality at elections.* The sin of bribery is damnable. It is the one sin for which, in the House of Commons, there can be no forgiveness. When discovered, it should render the culprit liable to political death, without hope of pardon. It is treason against a higher throne than that on which the Queen sits. It is a heresy which requires an *auto-da-fé*.* It is pollution to the whole House, which can

only be cleansed by a great sacrifice. Anathema maranatha!*
out with it from amongst us, even though the half of our heart's
blood be poured forth in the conflict! Out with it, and for ever!

Such is the language of patriotic members with regard to
bribery; and doubtless, if sincere, they are in the right. It is a
bad thing, certainly, that a rich man should buy votes; bad also
that a poor man should sell them. By all means let us repudiate
such a system with heartfelt disgust.

With heartfelt disgust, if we can do so, by all means; but not
with disgust pretended only and not felt in the heart at all. The
laws against bribery at elections are now so stringent that an
unfortunate candidate may easily become guilty, even though
actuated by the purest intentions. But not the less on that
account does any gentleman, ambitious of the honour of serving
his country in Parliament, think it necessary as a preliminary
measure to provide a round sum of money at his banker's. A
candidate must pay for no treating, no refreshments, no band of
music; he must give neither ribbons to the girls nor ale to the
men. If a huzza be uttered in his favour, it is at his peril; it may
be necessary for him to prove before a committee that it was the
spontaneous result of British feeling in his favour, and not the
purchased result of British beer. He cannot safely ask any one
to share his hotel dinner. Bribery hides itself now in the most
impalpable shapes, and may be effected by the offer of a glass
of sherry. But not the less on this account does a poor man find
that he is quite unable to overcome the difficulties of a contested
election.

We strain at our gnats with a vengeance, but we swallow our
camels with ease.* For what purpose is it that we employ those
peculiarly safe men of business – Messrs Nearthewinde and
Closerstil – when we wish to win our path through all obstacles
into that sacred recess, if all be so open, all so easy, all so much
above board? Alas! the money is still necessary, is still prepared,
or at any rate expended. The poor candidate of course knows
nothing of the matter till the attorney's bill is laid before him,
when all danger of petitions has passed away. He little dreamed
till then, not he, that there had been banquetings and junketings,
secret doings and deep drinkings at his expense. Poor candidate!
Poor member! Who was so ignorant as he! 'Tis true he has paid
such bills before; but 'tis equally true that he specially begged
his managing friend, Mr Nearthewinde, to be very careful that

all was done according to law! He pays the bill, however, and on the next election will again employ Mr Nearthewinde.

Now and again, at rare intervals, some glimpse into the inner sanctuary does reach the eyes of ordinary mortal men without; some slight accidental peep into those mysteries from whence all corruption has been so thoroughly expelled; and then, how delightfully refreshing is the sight, when, perhaps, some ex-member, hurled from his paradise like a fallen peri,* reveals the secret of that pure heaven, and, in the agony of his despair, tells us all that it cost him to sit for through those few halcyon years!

But Mr Nearthewinde is a safe man, and easy to be employed with but little danger. All these stringent bribery laws only enhance the value of such very safe men as Mr Nearthewinde. To him, stringent laws against bribery are the strongest assurance of valuable employment. Were these laws of a nature to be evaded with ease, any indifferent attorney might manage a candidate's affairs and enable him to take his seat with security.

It would have been well for Sir Roger if he had trusted solely to Mr Closerstil; well also for Mr Romer had he never fished in those troubled waters. In due process of time the hearing of the petition came on, and then who so happy, sitting at his ease at his London Inn, blowing his cloud from a long pipe, with measureless content, as Mr Reddypalm? Mr Reddypalm was the one great man of that contest. All depended on Mr Reddypalm; and well he did his duty.

The result of the petition was declared by the committee to be as follows: – that Sir Roger's election was null and void – that the election altogether was null and void – that Sir Roger had, by his agent, been guilty of bribery in obtaining a vote by the payment of a bill alleged to have been previously refused payment – that Sir Roger himself knew nothing about it; – this is always a matter of course; – but that Sir Roger's agent, Mr Romer, had been wittingly guilty of bribery with reference to the transaction above described. Poor Sir Roger! Poor Mr Romer!

Poor Mr Romer indeed! His fate was perhaps as sad as well might be, and as foul a blot to the purism of these very pure times in which we live. Not long after those days, it so happening that some considerable amount of youthful energy and *quidnunc** ability were required to set litigation afloat at Hong-Kong, Mr Romer was sent thither as the fittest man for such work, with rich assurance of future guerdon. Who so happy then as Mr Romer! But even among the pure there is room for envy and detraction. Mr Romer had not yet ceased to wonder at new worlds, as he skimmed among the islands of that southern ocean, before the edict had gone forth for his return. There were men sitting in that huge court of Parliament on whose breasts it lay as an intolerable burden, that England should be represented among the antipodes by one who had tampered with the purity of the franchise. For them there was no rest till this great disgrace should be wiped out and atoned for. Men they were of that calibre, that the slightest reflection on them of such a stigma seemed to themselves to blacken their own character. They could not break bread with satisfaction till Mr Romer was recalled. He was recalled, and of course ruined – and the minds of those just men were then at peace.

To any honourable gentleman who really felt his brow suffused with a patriotic blush, as he thought of his country dishonoured by Mr Romer's presence at Hong-Kong – to any such gentleman, if any such there were, let all honour be given, even though the intensity of his purity may create amazement to our less finely organised souls. But if no such blush suffused the brow of any honourable gentleman; if Mr Romer was recalled from quite other feelings – what then in lieu of honour shall we allot to those honourable gentlemen who were most concerned?'

Sir Roger, however, lost his seat, and, after three months of the joys of legislation, found himself reduced by a terrible blow to the low level of private life.

And the blow to him was very heavy. Men but seldom tell the truth of what is in them, even to their dearest friends; they are ashamed of having feelings, or rather of showing that they are troubled by any intensity of feeling. It is the practice of the time to treat all pursuits as though they were only half important to us, as though in what we desire we were only half in earnest. To be visibly eager seems childish, and is always bad policy; and men, therefore, nowadays, though they strive as hard as ever in the service of ambition – harder than ever in that of mammon – usually do so with a pleasant smile on, as though after all they were but amusing themselves with the little matter in hand.

Perhaps it had been so with Sir Roger in those electioneering days when he was looking for votes. At any rate, he had spoken of this seat in Parliament as but a doubtful good. 'He was willing, indeed, to stand, having been asked; but the thing would interfere wonderfully with his business; and then, what did he know about Parliament? Nothing on earth: it was the maddest scheme, but, nevertheless, he was not going to hang back when called upon – he had always been rough and ready when wanted, – and there he was now ready as ever, and rough enough too, God knows.'

'Twas thus that he had spoken of his coming parliamentary honours; and men had generally taken him at his word. He had been returned, and this success had been hailed as a great thing for the cause and class to which he belonged. But men did not know that his inner heart was swelling with triumph, and that his bosom could hardly contain his pride as he reflected that the poor Barchester stone-mason was now the representative in Parliament of his native city. And so, when his seat was attacked, he still laughed and joked. 'They were welcome to it for him,' he said; 'he could keep it or want it; and of the two, perhaps, the want of it would come most convenient to him. He did not exactly think that he had bribed any one; but if the bigwigs chose to say so, it was all one to him. He was rough and ready, now as ever,' etc., etc.

But when the struggle came, it was to him a fearful one; not the less fearful because there was no one, no, not one friend in all the world, to whom he could open his mind and speak out honestly what was in his heart. To Dr Thorne he might perhaps have done so had his intercourse with the doctor been sufficiently frequent; but it was only now and again when he was ill, or when the squire wanted to borrow money, that he saw Dr Thorne. He had plenty of friends, heaps of friends in the parliamentary sense; friends who talked about him, and lauded him at public meetings; who shook hands with him on platforms, and drank his health at dinners; but he had no friend who could sit with him over his own hearth in true friendship, and listen to, and sympathise with, and moderate the sighings of the inner man. For him there was no sympathy; no tenderness of love; no retreat, save into himself, from the loud brass band of the outer world.

The blow hit him terribly hard. It did not come altogether unexpectedly, and yet, when it did come, it was all but unendurable. He had made so much of the power of walking into that august chamber, and sitting shoulder to shoulder in legislative equality with the sons of dukes and the curled darlings of the nation.* Money had given him nothing, nothing but the mere feeling of brute power: with his three hundred thousand pounds he had felt himself to be no more palpably near to the goal of his ambition than when he had chipped stones for three shillings and sixpence a day. But when he was led up and introduced at that table, when he shook the old premier's hand on the floor of the House of Commons, when he heard the honourable member for Barchester alluded to in grave debate as the greatest living authority on railway matters, then, indeed, he felt that he had achieved something.

And now this cup was ravished from his lips, almost before it was tasted. When he was first told as a certainty that the decision of the committee was against him, he bore up against the misfortune like a man. He laughed heartily, and declared himself well rid of a very profitless profession; cut some little joke about Mr Moffat and his thrashing, and left on those around him an impression that he was a man so constituted, so strong in his own resolves, so steadily pursuant of his own work, that no little contentions of this kind could affect him. Men admired his easy laughter, as, shuffling his half-crowns with both his hands in his trousers-pockets, he declared that Messrs Romer and Reddypalm were the best friends he had known for this many a day.

But not the less did he walk out from the room in which he was standing a broken-hearted man. Hope could not buoy him up as she may do other ex-members in similarly disagreeable circumstances. He could not afford to look forward to what further favours parliamentary future might have in store for him after a lapse of five or six years. Five or six years! Why, his life was not worth four years' purchase; of that he was perfectly aware: he could not now live without the stimulus of brandy; and yet, while he took it, he knew he was killing himself. Death he did not fear; but he would fain have wished, after his life of labour, to have lived, while yet he could live, in the blaze of that high world to which for a moment he had attained.

He laughed loud and cheerily as he left his parliamentary friends, and, putting himself into the train, went down to Boxall Hill. He laughed loud and cheerily; but he never laughed again. It had not been his habit to laugh much at Boxall Hill. It was there he kept his wife, and Mr Winterbones, and the brandy bottle behind his pillow. He had not often there found it necessary to assume that loud and cheery laugh.

On this occasion he was apparently well in health when he got home; but both Lady Scatcherd and Mr Winterbones found him more than ordinarily cross. He made an affectation at sitting very hard to business, and even talked of going abroad to look at some of his foreign contracts. But even Winterbones found that his patron did not work as he had been wont to do; and at last, with some misgivings, he told Lady Scatcherd that he feared that everything was not right.

'He's always at it, my lady, always,' said Mr Winterbones.

'Is he?' said Lady Scatcherd, well understanding what Mr Winterbones' allusion meant.

'Always, my lady. I never saw nothing like it. Now, there's me – I can always go my half-hour when I've had my drop; but he, why, he don't go ten minutes, not now.'

This was not cheerful to Lady Scatcherd; but what was the poor woman to do? When she spoke to him on any subject he only snarled at her; and now that the heavy fit was on him, she did not dare even to mention the subject of his drinking. She had never known him so savage in his humour as he was now, so bearish in his habits, so little inclined to humanity, so determined to rush headlong down, with his head between his legs, into the bottomless abyss.

She thought of sending for Dr. Thorne; but she did not know under what guise to send for him, – whether as doctor or as friend: under neither would he now be welcome; and she well knew that Sir Roger was not the man to accept in good part either a doctor or a friend who might be unwelcome. She knew that this husband of hers, this man who, with all his faults, was the best of her friends, whom of all she loved best – she knew that he was killing himself, and yet she could do nothing. Sir Roger was his own master, and if kill himself he would, kill himself he must.

And kill himself he did. Not indeed by one sudden blow. He did not take one huge dose of his consuming poison and then fall dead upon the floor. It would perhaps have been better for himself, and better for those around him, had he done so. No; the doctors had time to congregate around his bed; Lady Scatcherd was allowed a period of nurse-tending; the sick man was able to say his last few words and bid adieu to his portion of the lower world with dying decency. As these last words will have some lasting effect upon the surviving personages of our story, the reader must be content to stand for a short while by the side of Sir Roger's sick-bed, and help us to bid him Godspeed on the journey which lies before him.

CHAPTER XXIII

Retrospective

It was declared in the early pages of this work that Dr Thorne was to be our hero; but it would appear very much as though he had latterly been forgotten. Since that evening when he retired to rest without letting Mary share the grievous weight which was on his mind, we have neither seen nor heard aught of him.

It was then full midsummer, and it is now early spring: and during the intervening months the doctor had not had a happy time of it. On that night, as we have before told, he took his niece to his heart; but he could not then bring himself to tell her that which it was so imperative she should know. Like a coward, he would put off the evil hour till the next morning, and thus robbed himself of his night's sleep.

But when the morning came the duty could not be postponed. Lady Arabella had given him to understand that his niece would no longer be a guest at Greshamsbury; and it was quite out of the question that Mary, after this, should be allowed to put her foot within the gate of the domain without having learnt what Lady Arabella had said. So he told it her before breakfast, walking round their little garden, she with her hand in his.

He was perfectly thunderstruck by the collected – nay, cool way in which she received his tidings. She turned pale, indeed; he felt also that her hand somewhat trembled in his own, and he perceived that for a moment her voice shook; but no angry word escaped her lip, nor did she even deign to repudiate the charge, which was, as it were, conveyed in Lady Arabella's request. The doctor knew, or thought he knew – nay, he did know – that Mary was wholly blameless in the matter: that she had at least given no encouragement to any love on the part of the young heir; but, nevertheless, he had expected that she would avouch her own innocence. This, however, she by no means did.

'Lady Arabella is quite right,' she said, 'quite right; if she has any fear of that kind, she cannot be too careful.'

'She is a selfish, proud women,' said the doctor; 'quite indifferent to the feelings of others; quite careless how deeply she may hurt her neighbours, if, in doing so, she may possibly benefit herself.'

'She will not hurt me, uncle, nor yet you. I can live without going to Greshamsbury.'

'But it is not to be endured that she should dare to cast an imputation upon my darling.'

'On me, uncle? She casts no imputation on me. Frank has been foolish: I have said nothing of it, for it was not worth while to trouble you. But as Lady Arabella chooses to interfere, I have no right to blame her. He has said what he should not have said; he has been foolish. Uncle, you know I could not prevent it.'

'Let her send him away then, not you; let her banish him.'

'Uncle, he is her son. A mother can hardly send her son away so easily: could you send me away, uncle?'

He merely answered her by twining his arm round her waist and pressing her to his side. He was well sure that she was badly treated; and yet now that she so unaccountably took Lady Arabella's part, he hardly knew how to make this out plainly to be the case.

'Besides, uncle, Greshamsbury is in a manner his own; how can he be banished from his father's house? No, uncle; there is an end of my visits there. They shall find that I will not thrust myself in their way.'

And then Mary, with a calm brow and steady gait, went in and made the tea.

And what might be the feelings of her heart when she so sententiously told her uncle that Frank had been foolish? She was of the same age with him; as impressible, though more powerful in hiding such impressions, – as all women should be; her heart was as warm, her blood as full of life, her innate desire for the companionship of some much-loved object as strong as his. Frank had been foolish in avowing his passion. No such folly as that could be laid at her door. But had she been proof against the other folly? Had she been able to walk heart-whole by his side while he chatted his commonplaces about love? Yes,

they are commonplaces when we read of them in novels;
common enough, too, to some of us when we write them; but
they are by no means commonplace when first heard by a young
girl in the rich, balmy fragrance of a July evening stroll.

Nor are they commonplaces when so uttered for the first or
second time at least, or perhaps the third. 'Tis a pity that so
heavenly a pleasure should pall upon the senses.

If it was so that Frank's folly had been listened to with a
certain amount of pleasure, Mary did not even admit so much
to herself. But why should it have been otherwise? Why should
she have been less prone to love than he was? Had he not
everything which girls do love? which girls should love? which
God created noble, beautiful, all but godlike, in order that
women, all but goddesslike, might love? To love thoroughly,
truly, heartily, with her whole body, soul, heart, and strength;
should not that be counted for a merit in a woman? And yet we
are wont to make a disgrace of it. We do so most unnaturally,
most unreasonably; for we expect our daughters to get themselves married off our hands. When the period of that step
comes, then love is proper enough; but up to that – before that
– as regards all those preliminary passages which must, we
suppose, be necessary – in all those it becomes a young lady to
be icy-hearted as a river-god in winter.

> O whistle and I'll come to you, my lad!
> O whistle and I'll come to you, my lad!
> Tho' father and mither and a' should go mad,
> O whistle and I'll come to you, my lad!*

This is the kind of love which a girl should feel before she
puts her hand proudly in that of her lover, and consents that
they two shall be made one flesh.

Mary felt no such love as this. She, too, had some inner
perception of that dread destiny by which it behoved Frank
Gresham to be forewarned. She, too – though she had never
heard so much said in words – had an almost instinctive
knowledge that his fate required him to marry money. Thinking
over this in her own way, she was not slow to convince herself
that it was out of the question that she should allow herself to
love Frank Gresham. However well her heart might be inclined
to such a feeling, it was her duty to repress it. She resolved,

therefore, to do so; and she sometimes flattered herself that she had kept her resolution.

These were bad times for the doctor, and bad times for Mary too. She had declared that she could live without going to Greshamsbury; but she did not find it so easy. She had been going to Greshamsbury all her life, and it was as customary with her to be there as at home. Such old customs are not broken without pain. Had she left the place it would have been far different; but, as it was, she daily passed the gates, daily saw and spoke to some of the servants, who knew her as well as they did the young ladies of the family – was in hourly contact, as it were, with Greshamsbury. It was not only that she did not go there, but that every one knew that she had suddenly discontinued doing so. Yes, she could live without going to Greshamsbury; but for some time she had but a poor life of it. She felt, nay, almost heard, that every man and woman, boy and girl, in the village was telling his and her neighbour that Mary Thorne no longer went to the house because of Lady Arabella and the young squire.

But Beatrice, of course, came to her. What was she to say to Beatrice? The truth! Nay, but it is not always so easy to say the truth, even to one's dearest friends.

'But you'll come up now he has gone?' said Beatrice.

'No, indeed,' said Mary, 'that would hardly be pleasant to Lady Arabella, nor to me either. No, Trichy, dearest; my visits to dear old Greshamsbury are done, done, done: perhaps in some twenty years' time I may be walking about the lawn with your brother, and discussing our childish days – that is, always, if the then Mrs Gresham shall have invited me.'

'How can Frank have been so wrong, so unkind, so cruel?' said Beatrice.

This, however, was a light in which Miss Thorne did not take any pleasure in discussing the matter. Her ideas of Frank's fault, and unkindness, and cruelty, were doubtless different from those of his sister. Such cruelty was not unnaturally excused in her eyes by many circumstances which Beatrice did not fully understand. Mary was quite ready to go hand in hand with Lady Arabella and the rest of the Greshamsbury folk in putting an end, if possible, to Frank's passion: she would give no one a right to accuse her of assisting to ruin the young heir; but she

could hardly bring herself to admit that he was so very wrong –
no, nor yet even so very cruel.

And then the squire came to see her, and this was a yet harder
trial than the visit of Beatrice. It was so difficult for her to speak
to him that she could not but wish him away; and yet, had he
not come, had he altogether neglected her, she would have felt
it to be unkind. She had ever been his pet, had always received
kindness from him.

'I am sorry for all this, Mary; very sorry,' said he, standing
up, and holding both her hands in his.

'It can't be helped, sir,' said she, smiling.

'I don't know,' said he; 'I don't know – it ought to be helped
somehow – I am quite sure you have not been to blame.'

'No,' said she, very quietly, as though the position was one
quite a matter of course. 'I don't think I have been very much to
blame. There will be misfortunes sometimes when nobody is to
blame.'

'I do not quite understand it all,' said the squire; 'but if Frank
–'

'Oh! we will not talk about him,' said she, still laughing
gently.

'You can understand, Mary, how dear he must be to me; but
if –'

'Mr Gresham, I would not for worlds be the cause of any
unpleasantness between you and him.'

'But I cannot bear to think that we have banished you, Mary.'

'It cannot be helped. Things will all come right in time.'

'But you will be so lonely here.'

'Oh! I shall get over that. Here, you know, Mr Gresham, "I
am monarch of all I survey;"* and there is a great deal in that.'

The squire did not quite catch her meaning, but a glimmering
of it did reach him. It was competent to Lady Arabella to banish
her from Greshamsbury; it was within the sphere of the squire's
duties to prohibit his son from an imprudent match; it was for
the Greshams to guard their Greshamsbury treasure as best they
could within their own territories; but let them beware that they
did not attack her on hers. In obedience to the first expression
of their wishes, she had submitted herself to this public mark of
their disapproval because she had seen at once, with her clear
intellect, that they were only doing that which her conscience
must approve. Without a murmur, therefore, she consented to

be pointed at as the young lady who had been turned out of Greshamsbury because of the young squire. She had no help for it. But let them take care that they did not go beyond that. Outside those Greshamsbury gates she and Frank Gresham, she and Lady Arabella met on equal terms; let them each fight their own battle.

The squire kissed her forehead affectionately and took his leave, feeling, somehow, that he had been excused and pitied, and made much of; whereas he had called on his young neighbour with the intention of excusing, and pitying, and making much of her. He was not quite comfortable as he left the house; but, nevertheless, he was sufficiently honest-hearted to own to himself that Mary Thorne was a fine girl. Only that it was so absolutely necessary that Frank should marry money – and only, also, that poor Mary was such a birthless foundling in the world's esteem – only, but for these things, what a wife she would have made for that son of his!

To one person only did she talk freely on the subject, and that one was Patience Oriel; and even with her the freedom was rather of the mind than of the heart. She never said a word of her feeling with reference to Frank, but she said much of her position in the village, and of the necessity she was under to keep out of the way.

'It is very hard,' said Patience, 'that the offence should be all with him, and the punishment all with you.'

'Oh! as for that,' said Mary, laughing, 'I will not confess to any offence, nor yet to any punishment; certainly not to any punishment.'

'It comes to the same thing in the end.'

'No, not so, Patience; there is always some little sting of disgrace in punishment: now I am not going to hold myself as in the least disgraced.'

'But, Mary, you must meet the Greshams sometimes.'

'Meet them! I have not the slightest objection on earth to meet all, or any of them. They are not a whit dangerous to me, my dear. 'Tis I that am the wild beast, and 'tis they that must avoid me,' and then she added, after a pause – slightly blushing – 'I have not the slightest objection even to meet him if chance brings him in my way. Let them look to that. My undertaking goes no further than this, that I will not be seen within their gates.'

But the girls so far understood each other that Patience undertook, rather than promised, to give Mary what assistance she could; and, despite Mary's bravado, she was in such a position that she much wanted the assistance of such a friend as Miss Oriel.

After an absence of some six weeks, Frank, as we have seen, returned home. Nothing was said to him, except by Beatrice, as to these new Greshamsbury arrangements; and he, when he found Mary was not at the place, went boldly to the doctor's house to seek her. But it has been seen, also, that she discreetly kept out of his way. This she had thought fit to do when the time came, although she had been so ready with her boast that she had no objection on earth to meet him.

After that there had been the Christmas vacation, and Mary had again found discretion to be the better part of valour. This was doubtless disagreeable enough. She had no particular wish to spend her Christmas with Miss Oriel's aunt instead of at her uncle's fireside. Indeed, her Christmas festivities had hitherto always been kept at Greshamsbury, the doctor and herself having made a part of the family circle there assembled. This was out of the question now; and perhaps the absolute change to old Miss Oriel's house was better for her than the lesser change to her uncle's drawing-room. Besides, how could she have demeaned herself when she met Frank in their parish church? All this had been fully understood by Patience, and, therefore, had this Christmas visit been planned.

And then this affair of Frank and Mary Thorne ceased for a while to be talked of at Greshamsbury, for that other affair of Mr Moffat and Augusta monopolised the rural attention. Augusta, as we have said, bore it well, and sustained the public gaze without much flinching. Her period of martyrdom, however, did not last long, for soon the news arrived of Frank's exploit in Pall Mall; and then the Greshamsburyites forgot to think much more of Augusta, being fully occupied in thinking of what Frank had done.

The tale, as it was first told, declared that Frank had followed Mr Moffat up into his club; had dragged him thence into the middle of Pall Mall, and had then slaughtered him on the spot. This was by degrees modified till a sobered fiction became generally prevalent, that Mr Moffat was lying somewhere, still alive, but with all his bones in a general state of compound fracture. This adventure again brought Frank into the ascendant, and restored to Mary her former position as the Greshamsbury heroine.

'One cannot wonder at his being very angry,' said Beatrice, discussing the matter with Mary – very imprudently.

'Wonder – no; the wonder would have been if he had not been angry. One might have been quite sure that he would have been angry enough.'

'I suppose it was not absolutely right for him to beat Mr Moffat,' said Beatrice, apologetically.

'Not right, Trichy? I think it was very right.'

'Not to beat him so very much, Mary!'

'Oh, I suppose a man can't exactly stand measuring how much he does these things. I like your brother for what he has done, and I say so frankly – though I suppose I ought to eat my tongue out before I should say such a thing, eh, Trichy?'

'I don't know that there's any harm in that,' said Beatrice, demurely. 'If you both liked each other there would be no harm in that – if that were all.'

'Wouldn't there?' said Mary, in a low tone of bantering satire; 'that is so kind, Trichy, coming from you – from one of the family, you know.'

'You are well aware, Mary, that if I could have my wishes – '

'Yes: I am well aware what a paragon of goodness you are. If you could have your way I should be admitted into heaven again; shouldn't I? Only with this proviso, that if a stray angel should ever whisper to me with bated breath, mistaking me, perchance, for one of his own class, I should be bound to close my ears to his whispering, and remind him humbly that I was only a poor mortal. You would trust me so far, wouldn't you, Trichy?'

'I would trust you in any way, Mary. But I think you are unkind in saying such things to me.'

'Into whatever heaven I am admitted, I will go only on this understanding: that I am to be as good an angel as any of those around me.'

'But, Mary dear, why do you say this to me?'

'Because – because – because – ah me! Why, indeed, but because I have no one else to say it to. Certainly not because you have deserved it.'

'It seems as though you were finding fault with me.'

'And so I am; how can I do other than find fault? How can I help being sore? Trichy, you hardly realise my position; you hardly see how I am treated; how I am forced to allow myself to be treated without a sign of complaint. You don't see it all. If you did, you would not wonder that I should be sore.'

Beatrice did not quite see it all; but she saw enough of it to know that Mary was to be pitied; so, instead of scolding her friend for being cross, she threw her arms round her and kissed her affectionately.

But the doctor all this time suffered much more than his niece did. He could not complain out loudly; he could not aver that his pet lamb had been ill treated; he could not even have the pleasure of openly quarrelling with Lady Arabella; but not the less did he feel it to be most cruel that Mary should have to live before the world as an outcast, because it had pleased Frank Gresham to fall in love with her.

But his bitterness was not chiefly against Frank. That Frank had been very foolish he could not but acknowledge; but it was a kind of folly for which the doctor was able to find excuse. For Lady Arabella's cold propriety he could find no excuse.

With the squire he had spoken no word on the subject up to this period of which we are now writing. With her ladyship he had never spoken on it since that day when she had told him that Mary was to come no more to Greshamsbury. He never now dined or spent his evenings at Greshamsbury, and seldom was to be seen at the house, except when called in professionally. The squire, indeed, he frequently met; but he either did so in the village, or out on horseback, or at his own house.

When the doctor first heard that Sir Roger had lost his seat, and had returned to Boxall Hill, he resolved to go over and see him. But the visit was postponed from day to day, as visits are postponed which may be made any day, and he did not in fact go till he was summoned there somewhat peremptorily. A message was brought to him one evening to say that Sir Roger had been struck by paralysis, and that not a moment was to be lost.

'It always happens at night,' said Mary, who had more sympathy for the living uncle whom she did know, than for that other dying uncle whom she did not know.

'What matters? – there – just give me my scarf. In all probability I may not be home tonight – perhaps not till late tomorrow. God bless you, Mary!' and away the doctor went on his cold bleak ride to Boxall Hill.

'Who will be his heir?' As the doctor rode along, he could not quite rid his mind of this question. The poor man now about to die had wealth enough to make many heirs. What if his heart should have softened towards his sister's child! What if Mary should be found in a few days to be possessed of such wealth that the Greshams should be again happy to welcome her at Greshamsbury!

The doctor was not a lover of money – and he did his best to get rid of such pernicious thoughts. But his longings, perhaps, were not so much that Mary should be rich, as that she should have the power of heaping coals of fire upon the heads of those people who had so injured her.*

CHAPTER XXIV

Louis Scatcherd

When Dr Thorne reached Boxall Hill he found Mr Rerechild from Barchester there before him. Poor Lady Scatcherd, when her husband was stricken by the fit, hardly knew in her dismay what adequate steps to take. She had, as a matter of course, sent for Dr Thorne; but she had thought that in so grave a peril the medical skill of no one man could suffice. It was, she knew, quite out of the question for her to invoke the aid of Dr Fillgrave, whom no earthly persuasion would have brought to Boxall Hill; and as Mr Rerechild was supposed in the Barchester world to be second – though at a long interval – to that great man, she had applied for his assistance.

Now Mr Rerechild was a follower and humble friend of Dr Fillgrave; and was wont to regard anything that came from the Barchester doctor as sure light from the lamp of Æsculapius. He could not therefore be other than an enemy of Dr Thorne. But he was a prudent, discreet man, with a long family, averse to professional hostilities, as knowing that he could make more by medical friends than medical foes, and not at all inclined to take up any man's cudgel to his own detriment. He had, of course, heard of that dreadful affront which had been put upon his friend, as had all the 'medical world' – all the medical world at least of Barsetshire; and he had often expressed his sympathy with Dr Fillgrave and his abhorrence of Dr Thorne's anti-professional practices. But now that he found himself about to be brought in contact with Dr Thorne, he reflected that the Galen of Greshamsbury was at any rate equal in reputation to him of Barchester; that the one was probably on the rise, whereas the other was already considered by some as rather antiquated; and he therefore wisely resolved that the present would be an excellent opportunity for him to make a friend of Dr Thorne.

Poor Lady Scatcherd had an inkling that Dr Fillgrave and Mr Rerechild were accustomed to row in the same boat, and she was not altogether free from fear that there might be an outbreak. She therefore took an opportunity before Dr Thome's arrival to deprecate any wrathful tendency.

'Oh, Lady Scatcherd! I have the greatest respect for Dr Thorne,' said he; 'the greatest possible respect: a most skilful practitioner – something brusque certainly, and perhaps a little obstinate. But what then? we have all our faults, Lady Scatcherd.'

'Oh – yes; we all have, Mr Rerechild; that's certain.'

'There's my friend Fillgrave – Lady Scatcherd. He cannot bear anything of that sort. Now I think he's wrong, and so I tell him.' Mr Rerechild was in error here; for he had never yet ventured to tell Dr Fillgrave that he was wrong in anything. 'We must bear and forbear, you know. Dr Thorne is an excellent man – in his way very excellent, Lady Scatcherd.'

This little conversation took place after Mr Rerechild's first visit to his patient: what steps were immediately taken for the relief of the sufferer we need not describe. They were doubtless well intended, and were, perhaps, as well adapted to stave off the coming evil day as any that Dr Fillgrave, or even the great Sir Omicron Pie might have used.

And then Dr Thorne arrived.

'Oh, doctor! doctor!' exclaimed Lady Scatcherd, almost hanging round his neck in the hall. 'What are we to do? What are we to do? He's very bad.'

'Has he spoken?'

'No; nothing like a word: he has made one or two muttered

sounds; but, poor soul, you could make nothing of it – oh, doctor! doctor! he has never been like this before.'

It was easy to see where Lady Scatcherd placed any such faith as she might still have in the healing art. 'Mr Rerechild is here and has seen him,' she continued. 'I thought it best to send for two, for fear of accidents. He has done something – I don't know what. But, doctor, do tell me the truth now; I look to you to tell me the truth.'

Dr Thorne then went up and saw his patient; and had he literally complied with Lady Scatcherd's request, he might have told her at once that there was no hope. As, however, he had not the heart to do this, he mystified the case as doctors so well know how to do, and told her that 'there was cause to fear, great cause for fear; he was sorry to say, very great cause for much fear.'

Dr Thorne promised to stay that night there, and, if possible, the following night also; and then Lady Scatcherd became troubled in her mind as to what she should do with Mr Rerechild. He also declared, with much medical humanity, that, let the inconvenience be what it might, he too would stay the night. 'The loss,' he said, 'of such a man as Sir Roger Scatcherd was of such paramount importance as to make other matters trivial. He would certainly not allow the whole weight to fall on the shoulders of his friend Dr Thorne: he also would stay at any rate that night by the sick man's bedside. By the following morning some change might be expected.'

'I say, Dr Thorne,' said her ladyship, calling the doctor into the housekeeping-room, in which she and Hannah spent any time that they were not required upstairs; 'just come in, doctor: you couldn't tell him we don't want him any more, could you?'

'Tell whom?' said the doctor.

'Why – Mr Rerechild: mightn't he go away, do you think?'

Dr Thorne explained that Mr Rerechild certainly might go away if he pleased; but that it would by no means be proper for one doctor to tell another to leave the house. And so Mr Rerechild was allowed to share the glories of the night.

In the meantime the patient remained speechless; but it soon became evident that Nature was using all her efforts to make one final rally. From time to time he moaned and muttered as though he was conscious, and it seemed as though he strove to speak. He gradually became awake, at any rate to suffering, and

Dr Thorne began to think that the last scene would be postponed for yet a while longer.

'Wonderful strong constitution – eh, Dr Thorne? wonderful!' said Mr Rerechild.

'Yes; he has been a strong man.'

'Strong as a horse, Dr Thorne. Lord, what that man would have been if he had given himself a chance! You know his constitution of course.'

'Yes; pretty well. I've attended him for many years.'

'Always drinking, I suppose; always at it – eh?'

'He has not been a temperate man, certainly.'

'The brain, you see, clean gone – and not a particle of coating left to the stomach; and yet what a struggle he makes – interesting case, isn't it?'

'It's very sad to see such an intellect so destroyed.'

'Very sad, very sad indeed. How Fillgrave would have liked to have seen this case. He is a clever man, is Fillgrave – in his way, you know.'

'I'm sure he is,' said Dr Thorne.

'Not that he'd make anything of a case like this now – he's not, you know, quite – quite – perhaps not quite up to the new time of day, if one may say so.'

'He has had a very extensive provincial practice,' said Dr Thorne.

'Oh, very – very; and made a tidy lot of money too, has Fillgrave. He's worth six thousand pounds, I suppose; now that's a good deal of money to put by in a little town like Barchester.'

'Yes, indeed.'

'What I say to Fillgrave is this – keep your eyes open; one should never be too old to learn – there's always something new worth picking up. But, no – he won't believe that. He can't believe that any new ideas can be worth anything. You know a man must go to the wall in that way – eh, doctor?'

And then again they were called to their patient. 'He's doing finely, finely,' said Mr Rerechild to Lady Scatcherd. 'There's a fair ground to hope he'll rally; fair ground, is there not, doctor?'

'Yes, he'll rally; but how long that may last, that we can hardly say.'

'Oh, no, certainly not, certainly not – that is not with any certainty; but still he's doing finely, Lady Scatcherd, considering everything.'

'How long will you give him, doctor?' said Mr Rerechild to his new friend when they were again alone. 'Ten days? I say ten days, or from that to a fortnight, not more; but I think he'll struggle on ten days.'

'Perhaps so,' said the doctor. 'I should not like to say exactly to a day.'

'No, certainly not. We cannot say exactly to a day; but I say ten days; as for anything like a recovery, that you know – '

'Is out of the question,' said Dr Thorne, gravely.

'Quite so, quite so; coating of the stomach clean gone, you know; brain destroyed: did you observe the periporollida? – never saw them so swelled before: now when the periporollida are swollen like that – '

'Yes, very much; it's always the case when paralysis has been brought about by intemperance.'

'Always, always; I have remarked that always; the periporollida in such cases are always extended; most interesting case, isn't it? I do wish Fillgrave could have seen it. But, I believe you and Fillgrave don't quite – eh?'

'No, not quite,' said Dr Thorne; who, as he thought of his last interview with Dr Fillgrave, and of that gentleman's exceeding anger as he stood in the hall below, could not keep himself from smiling, sad as the occasion was.

Nothing would induce Lady Scatcherd to go to bed; but the two doctors agreed to lie down, each in a room on one side of the patient. How was it possible that anything but good should come to him, being so guarded? 'He is going on finely, Lady Scatcherd, quite finely,' were the last words Mr Rerechild said as he left the room.

And then Dr Thorne, taking Lady Scatcherd's hand and leading her out into another chamber, told her the truth.

'Lady Scatcherd,' said he, in his tenderest voice – and his voice could be very tender when occasion required it – 'Lady Scatherd, do not hope; you must not hope; it would be cruel to bid you do so.'

'Oh, doctor! oh, doctor!'

'My dear friend, there is no hope.'

'Oh, Dr Thorne!' said the wife, looking wildly up into her

companion's face, though she hardly yet realised the meaning of what he said, although her senses were half stunned by the blow.

'Dear Lady Scatcherd, is it not better that I should tell you the truth?'

'Oh, I suppose so; oh yes, oh yes; ah me! ah me! ah me!' And then she began rocking herself backwards and forwards on her chair, with her apron up to her eyes. 'What shall I do? what shall I do?'

'Look to Him, Lady Scatcherd, who only can make such grief endurable.'

'Yes, yes, yes; I suppose so. Ah me! ah me! But, Dr Thorne, there must be some chance – isn't there any chance? That man says that he's going on so well.'

'I fear there is no chance – as far as my knowledge goes there is no chance.'

'Then why does that chattering magpie tell such lies to a woman? Ah me! ah me! ah me! oh, doctor! doctor! what shall I do? what shall I do?' and poor Lady Scatcherd, fairly overcome by her sorrow, burst out crying like a great school-girl.

And yet what had her husband done for her that she should thus weep for him? Would not her life be much more blessed when this cause of all her troubles should be removed from her? Would she not then be a free woman instead of a slave? Might she not then expect to begin to taste the comforts of life? What had that harsh tyrant of hers done that was good or serviceable for her? Why should she thus weep for him in paroxysms of truest grief?

We hear a good deal of jolly widows; and the slanderous raillery of the world tells much of conjugal disturbances as a cure for which women will look forward to a state of widowhood with not unwilling eyes. The raillery of the world is very slanderous. In our daily jests we attribute to each other vices of which neither we, nor our neighbours, nor our friends, nor even our enemies are ever guilty. It is our favourite parlance to talk of the family troubles of Mrs Green on our right, and to tell how Mrs Young on our left is strongly suspected of having raised her hand to her lord and master. What right have we to make these charges? What have we seen in our own personal walks through life to make us believe that women are devils? There may possibly have been a Xantippe here and there, but

Imogenes* are to be found under every bush. Lady Scatcherd, in spite of the life she had led, was one of them.

'You should send a message up to London for Louis,' said the doctor.

'We did that, doctor: we did that today – we sent up a telegraph. Oh me! oh me! poor boy, what will he do? I shall never know what to do with him, never! never!' And with such sorrowful wailings she sat rocking herself through the long night, every now and then comforting herself by the performance of some menial service in the sick man's room.

Sir Roger passed the night much as he had passed the day, except that he appeared gradually to be growing nearer to a state of consciousness. On the following morning they succeeded at last in making Mr Rerechild understand that they were not desirous of keeping him longer from his Barchester practice; and at about twelve o'clock Dr Thorne also went, promising that he would return in the evening, and again pass the night at Boxall Hill.

In the course of the afternoon Sir Roger once more awoke to his senses, and when he did so his son was standing at his bedside. Louis Philippe Scatcherd – or as it may be more convenient to call him, Louis – was a young man just of the age of Frank Gresham. But there could hardly be two youths more different in their appearance. Louis, though his father and mother were both robust persons, was short and slight, and now of a sickly frame. Frank was a picture of health and strength; but, though manly in disposition, was by no means precocious either in appearance or manners. Louis Scatcherd looked as though he was four years the other's senior. He had been sent to Eton when he was fifteen, his father being under the impression that this was the most ready and best-recognised method of making him a gentleman. Here he did not altogether fail as regarded the coveted object of his becoming the companion of gentlemen. He had more pocket-money than any other lad in the school, and was possessed also of a certain effrontery which carried him ahead among boys of his own age. He gained, therefore, a degree of éclat, even among those who knew, and very frequently said to each other, that young Scatcherd was not fit to be their companion except on such open occasions as those of cricket-matches and boat-races. Boys, in this respect, are at least as exclusive as men, and understand as well the difference between an inner and an outer circle. Scatcherd had many companions at school who were glad enough to go up to Maidenhead with him in his boat; but there was not one among them who would have talked to him of his sister.

Sir Roger was vastly proud of his son's success, and did his best to stimulate it by lavish expenditure at the Christopher, whenever he could manage to run down to Eton. But this practice, though sufficiently unexceptionable to the boys, was not held in equal delight by the masters. To tell the truth, neither Sir Roger nor his son were favourites with these stern custodians. At last it was felt necessary to get rid of them both; and Louis was not long in giving them an opportunity, by getting tipsy twice in one week. On the second occasion he was sent away, and he and Sir Roger, though long talked of, were seen no more at Eton.

But the universities were still open to Louis Philippe, and before he was eighteen he was entered as a gentleman-commoner at Trinity. As he was, moreover, the eldest son of a baronet, and had almost unlimited command of money, here also he was enabled for a while to shine.

To shine! but very fitfully; and one may say almost with a ghastly glare. The very lads who had eaten his father's dinners at Eton, and shared his four-oar at Eton, knew much better than to associate with him at Cambridge now that they had put on the *toga virilis*.* They were still as prone as ever to fun, frolic, and devilry – perhaps more so even than ever, seeing that more was in their power; but they acquired an idea that it behoved them to be somewhat circumspect as to the men with whom their pranks were perpetrated. So, in those days, Louis Scatcherd was coldly looked on by his whilom Eton friends.

But young Scatcherd did not fail to find companions at Cambridge also. There are few places indeed in which a rich man cannot buy companionship. But the set with whom he lived at Cambridge were the worst of the place. They were fast, slang men, who were fast and slang, and nothing else – men who imitated grooms in more than their dress, and who looked on the customary heroes of race-courses as the highest lords of the ascendant* upon earth. Among those at college young Scatcherd did shine as long as such lustre was permitted to him. Here, indeed, his father, who had striven only to encourage him at

Eton, did strive somewhat to control him. But that was not now easy. If he limited his son's allowance, he only drove him to do his debauchery on credit. There were plenty to lend money to the son of the great millionaire; and so, after eighteen months' trial of a university education, Sir Roger had no alternative but to withdraw his son from his *alma mater.**

What was he then to do with him? Unluckily it was considered quite unnecessary to take any steps towards enabling him to earn his bread. Now nothing on earth can be more difficult than bringing up well a young man who has not to earn his own bread, and who has no recognised station among other young men similarly circumstanced. Juvenile dukes, and sprouting earls, find their duties and their places as easily as embryo clergymen and sucking barristers. Provision is made for their peculiar positions: and, though they may possibly go astray, they have a fair chance given to them of running within the posts. The same may be said of such youths as Frank Gresham. There are enough of them in the community to have made it necessary that their well-being should be a matter of care and forethought. But there are but few men turned out in the world in the position of Louis Scatcherd; and, of those few, but very few enter the real battle of life under good auspices.

Poor Sir Roger, though he had hardly time with all his multitudinous railways to look into this thoroughly, had a glimmering of it. When he saw his son's pale face, and paid his wine bills, and heard of his doings in horseflesh, he did know that things were not going well; he did understand that the heir to a baronetcy and a fortune of some ten thousand a year might be doing better. But what was he to do? He could not watch over his boy himself; so he took a tutor for him and sent him abroad.

Louis and the tutor got as far as Berlin, with what mutual satisfaction to each other need not be specially described. But from Berlin Sir Roger received a letter in which the tutor declined to go on any further in the task which he had undertaken. He found that he had no influence over his pupil, and he could not reconcile it to his conscience to be the spectator of such a life as that which Mr Scatcherd led. He had no power in inducing Mr Scatcherd to leave Berlin; but he would remain there himself till he should hear from Sir Roger. So Sir Roger had to leave the huge Government works which he was then erecting on the southern coast, and hurry off to Berlin to see what could be done with young Hopeful.

The young Hopeful was by no means a fool; and in some matters was more than a match for his father. Sir Roger, in his anger, threatened to cast him off without a shilling. Louis, with mixed penitence and effrontery, reminded him that he could not change the descent of the title; promised amendment; declared that he had done only as do other young men of fortune; and hinted that the tutor was a strait-laced ass. The father and the son returned together to Boxall Hill, and three months afterwards Mr Scatcherd set up for himself in London.

And now his life, if not more virtuous, was more crafty that it had been. He had no tutor to watch his doings and complain of them, and he had sufficient sense to keep himself from absolute pecuniary ruin. He lived, it is true, where sharpers and blacklegs* had too often opportunities of plucking him; but, young as he was, he had been sufficiently long about the world to take care he was not openly robbed; and as he was not openly robbed, his father, in a certain sense, was proud of him.

Tidings however came – came at least in those last days – which cut Sir Roger to the quick; tidings of vice in the son which the father could not but attribute to his own example. Twice the mother was called up to the sick-bed of her only child, while he lay raving in that horrid madness by which the outraged mind avenges itself on the body! Twice he was found raging in *delirium tremens*, and twice the father was told that a continuance of such life must end in an early death.

It may easily be conceived that Sir Roger was not a happy man. Lying there with that brandy bottle beneath his pillow, reflecting in his moments of rest that that son of his had his brandy bottle also beneath his pillow, he could hardly have been happy. But he was not a man to say much about his misery. Though he could restrain neither himself nor his heir, he could endure in silence; and in silence he did endure, till, opening his eyes to the consciousness of death, he at last spoke a few words to the only friend he knew.

Louis Scatcherd was not a fool, nor was he naturally, perhaps, of a depraved disposition; but he had to reap the fruits of the worst education which England was able to give him. There were moments in his life when he felt that a better, a higher, nay, a much happier career was open to him than that which he had prepared himself to lead. Now and then he would reflect what money and rank might have done for him; he would look with wishful eyes to the proud doings of others of his age; would dream of quiet joys, of a sweet wife, of a house to which might be asked friends who were neither jockeys nor drunkards; he would dream of such things in his short intervals of constrained sobriety; but the dream would only serve to make him moody.

This was the best side of his character; the worst, probably, was that which was brought into play by the fact that he was not a fool. He would have had a better chance of redemption in this world – perhaps also in another – had he been a fool. As it was, he was no fool: he was not to be done, not he; he knew, no one better, the value of a shilling; he knew, also, how to keep his shillings, and how to spend them. He consorted much with blacklegs and suchlike, because blacklegs were to his taste. But he boasted daily, nay, hourly to himself, and frequently to those around him, that the leeches who were stuck round him could draw but little blood from him. He could spend his money freely; but he would so spend it that he himself might reap the gratification of the expenditure. He was acute, crafty, knowing, and up to every damnable dodge practised by men of the class with whom he lived. At one-and-twenty he was that most odious of all odious characters – a close-fisted reprobate.

He was a small man, not ill-made by Nature, but reduced to unnatural tenuity by dissipation – a corporeal attribute of which he was apt to boast, as it enabled him, as he said, to put himself up at 7 st. 7 lb. without any 'd —— nonsense of not eating and drinking.' The power, however, was one of which he did not often avail himself, as his nerves were seldom in a fit state for riding. His hair was dark red, and he wore red moustaches, and a great deal of red beard beneath his chin, cut in a manner to make him look like an American. His voice also had a Yankee twang, being a cross between that of an American trader and an English groom; and his eyes were keen and fixed, and cold and knowing.

Such was the son whom Sir Roger saw standing at his bedside when first he awoke to consciousness. It must not be supposed that Sir Roger looked at him with our eyes. To him he was an only child, the heir of his wealth, the future bearer of his title; the most heart-stirring remembrancer of those other days, when he had been so much a poorer, and so much a happier man. Let that boy be bad or good, he was all Sir Roger had; and the father was still able to hope, when others thought that all ground for hope was gone.

The mother also loved her son with a mother's natural love; but Louis had ever been ashamed of his mother, and had, as far as possible, estranged himself from her. Her heart, perhaps, fixed itself with almost a warmer love on Frank Gresham, her foster-son. Frank she saw but seldom, but when she did see him he never refused her embrace. There was, too, a joyous, genial lustre about Frank's face which always endeared him to women, and made his former nurse regard him as the pet creation of the age. Though she but seldom interfered with any monetary arrangement of her husband's, yet once or twice she had ventured to hint that a legacy left to the young squire would make her a happy woman. Sir Roger, however, on these occasions had not appeared very desirous of making his wife happy.

'Ah, Louis! is that you?' ejaculated Sir Roger, in tones hardly more than half-formed: afterwards, in a day or two that is, he fully recovered his voice; but just then he could hardly open his jaws, and spoke almost through his teeth. He managed, however, to put out his hand and lay it on the counterpane, so that his son could take it.

'Why, that's well, governor,' said the son; 'you'll be as right as a trivet in a day or two – eh, governor?'

The 'governor' smiled with a ghastly smile. He already pretty well knew that he would never again be 'right,' as his son called it, on that side the grave. It did not, moreover, suit him to say much just at that moment, so he contented himself with holding his son's hand. He lay still in this position for a moment, and then, turning round painfully on his side, endeavoured to put his hand to the place where his dire enemy usually was concealed. Sir Roger, however, was too weak now to be his own master; he was at length, though too late, a captive in the hands of nurses and doctors, and the bottle had now been removed.

Then Lady Scatcherd came in, and seeing that her husband was no longer unconscious, she could not but believe that Dr Thorne had been wrong; she could not but think that there must be some ground for hope. She threw herself on her knees at the bedside, bursting into tears as she did so, and taking Sir Roger's hand in hers covered it with kisses.

'Bother!' said Sir Roger.

She did not, however, long occupy herself with the indulgence of her feelings; but going speedily to work, produced such sustenance as the doctors had ordered to be given when the patient might awake. A breakfast-cup was brought to him, and a few drops were put into his mouth; but he soon made it manifest that he would take nothing more of a description so perfectly innocent.

'A drop of brandy – just a little drop,' said he, half-ordering, and half-entreating.

'Ah, Roger!' said Lady Scatcherd.

'Just a little drop, Louis,' said the sick man, appealing to his son.

'A little will be good for him; bring the bottle, mother,' said the son.

After some altercation the brandy bottle was brought, and Louis, with what he thought a very sparing hand, proceeded to pour about half a wine-glassful into the cup. As he did so, Sir Roger, weak as he was, contrived to shake his son's arm, so as greatly to increase the dose.

'Ha! ha! ha!' laughed the sick man, and then greedily swallowed the dose.

CHAPTER XXV

Sir Roger Dies

That night the doctor stayed at Boxall Hill, and the next night; so that it became a customary thing for him to sleep there during the latter part of Sir Roger's illness. He returned home daily to Greshamsbury; for he had his patients there, to whom he was as necessary as to Sir Roger, the foremost of whom was Lady Arabella. He had, therefore, no slight work on his hands, seeing that his nights were by no means wholly devoted to rest.

Mr Rerechild had not been much wrong as to the remaining space of life which he had allotted to the dying man. Once or twice Dr Thorne had thought that the great original strength of his patient would have enabled him to fight against death for a somewhat longer period; but Sir Roger would give himself no chance. Whenever he was strong enough to have a will of his own, he insisted on having his very medicine mixed with brandy; and in the hours of the doctor's absence, he was too often successful in his attempts.

'It does not much matter,' Dr Thorne had said to Lady Scatcherd. 'Do what you can to keep down the quantity, but do not irritate him by refusing to obey. It does not much signify now.' So Lady Scatcherd still administered the alcohol, and he from day to day invented little schemes for increasing the amount, over which he chuckled with ghastly laughter.

Two or three times during these days Sir Roger essayed to speak seriously to his son; but Louis always frustrated him. He either got out of the room on some excuse, or made his mother interfere on the score that so much talking would be bad for his father. He already knew with tolerable accuracy what was the purport of his father's will, and by no means approved of it; but as he could not now hope to induce his father to alter it so as to make it more favourable to himself, he conceived that no conversation on matters of business could be of use to him.

'Louis,' said Sir Roger, one afternoon to his son; 'Louis, I have not done by you as I ought to have done – I know that now.'

'Nonsense, governor; never mind about that now; I shall do well enough, I dare say. Besides, it isn't too late; you can make it twenty-three years instead of twenty-five, if you like it.'

'I do not mean as to money, Louis. There are things besides money which a father ought to look to.'

'Now, father, don't fret yourself – I'm all right; you may be sure of that.'

'Louis, it's that accursed brandy – it's that that I'm afraid of: you see me here, my boy, how I'm lying here now.'

'Don't you be annoying yourself, governor; I'm all right – quite right; and as for you, why, you'll be up and about yourself in another month or so.'

'I shall never be off this bed, my boy, till I'm carried into my coffin, on those chairs there. But I'm not thinking of myself, Louis, but you; think what you may have before you if you can't avoid that accursed bottle.'

'I'm all right, governor; right as a trivet. It's very little I take, except at an odd time or so.'

'Oh, Louis! Louis!'

'Come, father, cheer up; this sort of thing isn't the thing for you at all. I wonder where mother is: she ought to be here with the broth; just let me go, and I'll see for her.'

The father understood it all. He saw that it was now much beyond his faded powers to touch the heart or conscience of such a youth as his son had become. What now could he do for his boy except die? What else, what other benefit, did his son require of him but to die; to die so that his means of dissipation might be unbounded? He let go the unresisting hand which he held, and, as the young man crept out of the room, he turned his face to the wall. He turned his face to the wall and held bitter commune with his own heart. To what had he brought himself? To what had he brought his son? Oh, how happy would it have been for him could he have remained all his days a working stone-mason in Barchester! How happy could he have died as such, years ago! Such tears as those which wet that pillow are the bitterest which human eyes can shed.

But while they were dropping, the memoir of his life was in quick course of preparation. It was, indeed, nearly completed, with considerable detail. He had lingered on four days longer than might have been expected, and the author had thus had more than usual time for the work. In these days a man is nobody unless his biography is kept so far posted up that it may be ready for the national breakfast-table on the morning after his demise. When it chances that the dead hero is one who was taken in his prime of life, of whose departure from among us the most far-seeing biographical scribe can have no prophetic inkling, this must be difficult. Of great men, full of years, who are ripe for the sickle, who in the course of Nature must soon fall, it is of course comparatively easy for an active compiler to have his complete memoir ready on his desk. But in order that the idea of omnipresent and omniscient information may be kept up, the young must be chronicled as quickly as the old. In some cases this task must, one would say, be difficult. Nevertheless, it is done.

The memoir of Sir Roger Scatcherd was progressing favourably. In this it was told how fortunate had been his life; how, in his case, industry and genius combined had triumphed over the difficulties which humble birth and deficient education had thrown in his way; how he had made a name among England's great men; how the Queen had delighted to honour him, and nobles had been proud to have him for a guest at their mansions. Then followed a list of all the great works which he had achieved, of the railroads, canals, docks, harbours, jails, and hospitals which he had constructed. His name was held up as an example to the labouring classes of his countrymen, and he was pointed at as one who had lived and died happy – ever happy, said the biographer, because ever industrious.* And so a great moral question was inculcated. A short paragraph was devoted to his appearance in Parliament; and unfortunate Mr Romer was again held up to disgrace, for the thirtieth time, as having been the means of depriving our legislative councils of the great assistance of Sir Roger's experience.

'Sir Roger', said the biographer in his concluding passage, 'was possessed of an iron frame; but even iron will yield to the repeated blows of the hammer. In the latter years of his life he was known to overtask himself; and at length the body gave way, though the mind remained firm to the last. The subject of this memoir was only fifty-nine when he was taken from us.'

And thus Sir Roger's life was written, while the tears were yet falling on his pillow at Boxall Hill. It was a pity that a proof-sheet could not have been sent to him. No man was vainer of his reputation, and it would have greatly gratified him to know that posterity was about to speak of him in such terms – to speak of him with a voice that would be audible for twenty-four hours.

Sir Roger made no further attempt to give counsel to his son. It was too evidently useless. The old dying lion felt that the lion's power had already passed from him, and that he was helpless in the hands of the young cub who was so soon to inherit the wealth of the forest. But Dr Thorne was more kind to him. He had something yet to say as to his worldly hopes and worldly cares; and his old friend did not turn a deaf ear to him.

It was during the night that Sir Roger was most anxious to talk, and most capable of talking. He would lie through the day in a state half-comatose; but towards evening he would rouse himself, and by midnight he would be full of fitful energy. One night, as he lay wakeful and full of thought, he thus poured forth his whole heart to Dr Thorne.

'Thorne,' said he, 'I told you all about my will, you know.'

'Yes,' said the other; 'and I have blamed myself greatly that I have not again urged you to alter it. Your illness came too suddenly, Scatcherd; and then I was averse to speak of it.'

'Why should I alter it? It is a good will; as good as I can make. Not but that I have altered it since I spoke to you. I did it that day after you left me.'

'Have you definitely named your heir in default of Louis?'

'No – that is, yes – I had done that before; I have said Mary's eldest child: I have not altered that.'

'But, Scatcherd, you must alter it.'

'Must! well then I won't; but I'll tell you what I have done, I have added a postscript – a codicil they call it – saying that you, and you only, know who is her eldest child. Winterbones and Jack Martin have witnessed that.'

Dr Thorne was going on to explain how very injudicious such an arrangement appeared to be; but Sir Roger would not listen to him. It was not about that that he wished to speak to him. To him it was matter of but minor interest who might inherit his money if his son should die early; his care was solely for his son's welfare. At twenty-five the heir might make his own will – might bequeath all this wealth according to his own fancy. Sir Roger would not bring himself to believe that his son could follow him to the grave in so short a time.

'Never mind that, doctor, now; but about Louis; you will be his guardian, you know.'

'Not his guardian. He is more than of age.'

'Ah! but doctor, you will be his guardian. The property will not be his till he be twenty-five. You will not desert him?'

'I will not desert him; but I doubt whether I can do much for him – what can I do, Scatcherd?'

'Use the power that a strong man has over a weak one. Use the power that my will will give you. Do for him as you would for a son of your own if you saw him going in bad courses. Do as a friend should do for a friend that is dead and gone. I would do so for you, doctor, if our places were changed.'

'What I can do, that I will do,' said Thorne, solemnly, taking as he spoke the contractor's hand in his own with a tight grasp.

'I know you will; I know you will. Oh! doctor, may you never feel as I do now! May you on your death-bed have no dread as I have, as to the fate of those you will leave behind you!'

Dr Thorne felt that he could not say much in answer to this. The future fate of Louis Scatcherd was, he could not but own to himself, greatly to be dreaded. What good, what happiness, could be presaged for such a one as he was? What comfort could he offer to the father? And then he was called on to compare, as it were, the prospects of this unfortunate with those of his own darling; to contrast all that was murky, foul, and disheartening, with all that was perfect; to liken Louis Scatcherd to the angel who brightened his own hearthstone. How could he answer such an appeal?

He said nothing; but merely tightened his grasp of the other's hand, to signify that he would do, as best he could, all that was asked of him. Sir Roger looked up sadly into the doctor's face, as though expecting some word of consolation. There was no comfort, no consolation to come to him!

'For three or four years he must greatly depend upon you,' continued Sir Roger.

'I will do what I can,' said the doctor. 'What I can do I will do. But he is not a child, Scatcherd: at his age he must stand or fall mainly by his own conduct. The best thing for him will be to marry.'

'Exactly; that's just it, Thorne: I was coming to that. If he would marry, I think he would do well yet, for all that has come and gone. If he married, of course you would let him have the command of his own income.'

'I will be governed entirely by your wishes: under any circumstances his income will, as I understand, be quite sufficient for him, married or single.'

'Ah? – but, Thorne, I should like to think he should shine with the best of them. For what have I made the money if not for that? Now if he marries – decently, that is – some woman you know that can assist him in the world, let him have what he wants. It is not to save the money that I put it into your hands.'

'No, Scatcherd; not to save the money, but to save him. I think that while you are yet with him you should advise him to marry.'

'He does not care a straw for what I advise, not one straw. Why should he? How can I tell him to be sober when I have been a beast all my life myself? How can I advise him? That's where it is! it is that that now kills me. Advise! Why, when I speak to him he treats me like a child.'

'He fears that you are too weak, you know: he thinks that you should not be allowed to talk.'

'Nonsense! he knows better; you know better. Too weak! what signifies? Would I not give all that I have of strength at one blow if I could open his eyes to see as I see but for one minute?' And the sick man raised himself up in his bed as though he were actually going to expend all that remained to him of vigour in the energy of a moment.

'Gently, Scatcherd; gently. He will listen to you yet; but do not be so unruly.'

'Thorne, you see that bottle there? Give me half a glass of brandy.'

The doctor turned round in his chair; but he hesitated in doing as he was desired.

'Do as I ask you, doctor. It can do no harm now; you know that well enough. Why torture me now?'

'No, I will not torture you; but you will have water with it?'

'Water! No; the brandy by itself. I tell you I cannot speak without it. What's the use of canting now? You know it can make no difference.'

Sir Roger was right. It could make no difference; and Dr Thorne gave him the half glass of brandy.

'Ah, well; you've a stingy hand, doctor; confounded stingy. You don't measure your medicines out in such light doses.'

'You will be wanting more before morning, you know.'

'Before morning! indeed I shall; a pint or so before that. I remember the time, doctor, when I have drunk to my own cheek* above two quarts between dinner and breakfast! aye, and worked all the day after it!'

'You have been a wonderful man, Scatcherd, very wonderful.'

'Aye, wonderful! well, never mind. It's over now. But what was I saying? – about Louis, doctor; you'll not desert him?'

'Certainly not.'

'He's not strong; I know that. How should he be strong, living as he has done? Not that it seemed to hurt me when I was his age.'

'You had the advantage of hard work.'

'That's it. Sometimes I wish that Louis had not a shilling in the world; that he had to trudge about with an apron round his waist as I did. But it's too late now to think of that. If he would only marry, doctor.'

Dr Thorne again expressed an opinion that no step would be so likely to reform the habits of the young heir as marriage; and repeated his advice to the father to implore his son to take a wife.

'I'll tell you what, Thorne,' said he. And then, after a pause, he went on. 'I have not half told you as yet what is on my mind; and I'm nearly afraid to tell it; though, indeed, don't know why I should be.'

'I never knew you afraid of anything yet,' said the doctor, smiling gently.

'Well, then, I'll not end by turning coward. Now, doctor, tell the truth to me; what do you expect me to do for that girl of yours that we were talking of – Mary's child?'

There was a pause for a moment, for Thorne was slow to answer him.

'You would not let me see her, you know, though she is my niece as truly as she is yours.'

'Nothing,' at last said the doctor, slowly. 'I expect nothing. I would not let you see her, and therefore I expect nothing.'

'She will have it all if poor Louis should die,' said Sir Roger.

'If you intend it so you should put her name into the will,' said the other. 'Not that I ask you or wish you to do so. Mary, thank God, can do without wealth.'

'Thorne, on one condition I will put her name into it. I will alter it all on one condition. Let the two cousins be man and wife – let Louis marry poor Mary's child.'

The proposition for a moment took away the doctor's breath, and he was unable to answer. Not for all the wealth of India would he have given up his lamb to that young wolf, even though he had had the power to do so. But that lamb – lamb though she was – had, as he well knew, a will of her own on such a matter. What alliance could be more impossible, thought he to himself, than one between Mary Thorne and Louis Scatcherd!

'I will alter it all if you will give me your hand upon it that you will do your best to bring about this marriage. Everything shall be his on the day he marries her; and should he die unmarried, it shall all then be hers by name. Say the word, Thorne, and she shall come here at once. I shall yet have time to see her.'

But Dr Thorne did not say the word; just at the moment he said nothing, but he slowly shook his head.

'Why not, Thorne?'

'My friend, it is impossible.'

'Why impossible?'

'Her hand is not mine to dispose of, nor is her heart.'

'Then let her come over herself.'

'What! Scatcherd, that the son might make love to her while the father is so dangerously ill! Bid her come to look for a rich husband! That would not be seemly, would it?'

'No; not for that: let her come merely that I may see her; that we may all know her. I will leave the matter then in your hands if you will promise me to do your best.'

'But, my friend, in this matter I cannot do my best. I can do nothing. And, indeed, I may say at once, that it is altogether out of the question. I know*'

'What do you know?' said the baronet, turning on him almost angrily. 'What can you know to make you say that this is impossible? Is she a pearl of such price that a man may not win her?'

'She is a pearl of great price.'*

'Believe me, doctor, money goes far in winning such pearls.'

'Perhaps so: I know little about it. But this I do know, that money will not win her. Let us talk of something else; believe me it is useless for us to think of this.'

'Yes; if you set your face against it obstinately. You must think very poorly of Louis if you suppose that no girl can fancy him.'

'I have not said so, Scatcherd.'

'To have the spending of ten thousand a year, and be a baronet's lady! Why, doctor, what is it you expect for this girl?'

'Not much, indeed; not much. A quiet heart and a quiet home; not much more.'

'Thorpe, if you will be ruled by me in this, she shall be the most topping woman in this county.'

'My friend, my friend, why thus grieve me? Why should you thus harass yourself? I tell you it is impossible. They have never seen each other; they have nothing, and can have nothing in common; their tastes, and wishes, and pursuits are different. Besides, Scatcherd, marriages never answer that are so made; believe me, it is impossible.'

The contractor threw himself back on his bed, and lay for some ten minutes perfectly quiet; so much so that the doctor began to think that he was sleeping. So thinking, and wearied with watching, Dr Thorne was beginning to creep quietly from the room, when his companion again roused himself, almost with vehemence.

'You won't do this thing for me, then?' said he.

'Do it! It is not for you or me to do such things as that. Such things must be left to those concerned themselves.'

'You will not even help me?'

'Not in this thing, Sir Roger.'

'Then, by—, she shall not under any circumstances ever have a shilling of mine. Give me some of that stuff there,' and he again pointed to the brandy bottle which stood ever within his sight.

The doctor poured out and handed to him another small modicum of spirit.

'Nonsense, man; fill the glass. I'll stand no nonsense now. I'll be master in my own house to the last. Give it here, I tell you. Ten thousand devils are tearing me within. You – you could have comforted me; but you would not. Fill the glass I tell you.'

'I should be killing you were I to do it.'

'Killing me! killing me! you are always talking of killing me. Do you suppose that I am afraid to die? Do not I know how soon it is coming? Give me the brandy, I say, or I will be out across the room to fetch it.'

'No, Scatcherd. I cannot give it to you; not while I am here. Do you remember how you were engaged this morning?' – he had that morning taken the sacrament from the parish clergyman – 'you would not wish to make me guilty of murder, would you?'

'Nonsense! You are talking nonsense; habit is second nature. I tell you I shall sink without it. Why, you know I always get it directly your back is turned. Come, I will not be bullied in my own house; give me that bottle, I say!' – and Sir Roger essayed, vainly enough, to raise himself from the bed.

'Stop, Scatcherd; I will give it to you – I will help you. It may be that habit is second nature.' Sir Roger in his determined energy had swallowed, without thinking of it, the small quantity which the doctor had before poured out for him, and still held the empty glass within his hand. This the doctor now took and filled nearly to the brim.

'Come, Thorne, a bumper; a bumper for this once. "Whatever

the drink, it a bumper must be." You stingy fellow! I would not treat you so. Well – well.'

'It's as full as you can hold it, Scatcherd.'

'Try me; try me! my hand is a rock; at least at holding liquor.' And then he drained the contents of the glass, which were sufficient in quantity to have taken away the breath from any ordinary man.

'Ah, I'm better now. But, Thorne, I do love a full glass, ha! ha! ha!'

There was something frightful, almost sickening, in the peculiar hoarse guttural tone of his voice. The sounds came from him as though steeped in brandy, and told, all too plainly, the havoc which the alcohol had made. There was a fire too about his eyes which contrasted with his sunken cheeks: his hanging jaw, unshorn beard, and haggard face were terrible to look at. His hands and arms were hot and clammy, but so thin and wasted! Of his lower limbs the lost use had not returned to him, so that in all his efforts at vehemence he was controlled by his own want of vitality. When he supported himself, half-sitting against the pillows, he was in a continual tremor; and yet, as he boasted, he could still lift his glass steadily to his mouth. Such now was the hero of whom that ready compiler of memoirs had just finished his correct and succinct account.

After he had had his brandy, he sat glaring a while at vacancy, as though he was dead to all around him, and was thinking – thinking – thinking of things in the infinite distance of the past.

'Shall I go now,' said the doctor, 'and send Lady Scatcherd to you?'

'Wait a while, doctor; just one minute longer. So you will do nothing for Louis then?'

'I will do everything for him that I can do.'

'Ah, yes! everything but the one thing that will save him. Well, I will not ask you again. But remember, Thorne, I shall alter my will tomorrow.'

'Do so by all means; you may well alter it for the better. If I may advise you, you will have down your own business attorney from London. If you will let me send he will be here before tomorrow night.'

'Thank you for nothing, Thorne: I can manage that matter myself. Now leave me; but remember, you have ruined that girl's fortune.'

The doctor did leave him, and went not altogether happy to his room. He could not but confess to himself that he had, despite himself as it were, fed himself with hope that Mary's future might be made more secure, aye, and brighter too, by some small unheeded fraction broken off from the huge mass of her uncle's wealth. Such hope, if it had amounted to hope, was now all gone. But this was not all, nor was this the worst of it. That he had done right in utterly repudiating all idea of a marriage between Mary and her cousin – of that he was certain enough; that no earthly consideration would have induced Mary to plight her troth to such a man – that, with him, was as certain as doom. But how far had he done right in keeping her from the sight of her uncle? How could he justify it to himself if he had thus robbed her of her inheritance, seeing that he had done so from a selfish fear lest she, who was now all his own, should be known to the world as belonging to others rather than to him? He had taken upon him on her behalf to reject wealth as valueless; and yet he had no sooner done so than he began to consume his hours with reflecting how great to her would be the value of wealth. And thus, when Sir Roger told him, as he left the room, that he had ruined Mary's fortune, he was hardly able to bear the taunt with equanimity.

On the next morning, after paying his professional visit to his patient, and satisfying himself that the end was now drawing near with steps terribly quickened, he went down to Greshamsbury.

'How long is this to last, uncle?' said his niece, with sad voice, as he again prepared to return to Boxall Hill.

'Not long, Mary; do not begrudge him a few more hours of life.'

'No, I did not, uncle. I will say nothing more about it. Is his son with him?' And then, perversely enough, she persisted in asking numerous questions about Louis Scatcherd.

'Is he likely to marry, uncle?'

'I hope so, my dear.'

'Will he be so very rich?'

'Yes; ultimately he will be very rich.'

'He will be a baronet, will he not?'

'Yes, my dear.'

'What is he like, uncle?'

'Like – I never know what a young man is like. He is like a man with red hair.'

'Uncle, you are the worst hand in describing I ever knew. If I'd seen him for five minutes, I'd be bound to make a portrait of him; and you, if you were describing a dog, you'd only say what colour his hair was.'

'Well, he's a little man.'

'Exactly, just as I should say that Mrs Umbleby had a red-haired little dog. I wish I had known these Scatcherds, uncle. I do so admire people that can push themselves in the world. I wish I had known Sir Roger.'

'You will never know him now, Mary.'

'I suppose not. I am so sorry for him. Is Lady Scatcherd nice?'

'She's an excellent woman.'

'I hope I may know her some day. You are so much there now, uncle; I wonder whether you ever mention me to them. If you do, tell her from me how much I grieve for her.'

That same night Dr Thorne again found himself alone with Sir Roger. The sick man was much more tranquil, and apparently more at ease than he had been on the preceding night. He said nothing about his will, and not a word about Mary Thorne; but the doctor knew that Winterbones and a notary's clerk from Barchester had been in the bedroom a great part of the day; and, as he knew also that the great man of business was accustomed to do his most important work by the hands of such tools as these, he did not doubt but that the will had been altered and remodelled. Indeed, he thought it more than probable, that when it was opened it would be found to be wholly different in its provisions from that which Sir Roger had already described.

'Louis is clever enough,' he said, 'sharp enough, I mean. He won't squander the property.'

'He has good natural abilities,' said the doctor.

'Excellent, excellent,' said the father. 'He may do well, very well, if he can only be kept from this;' and Sir Roger held up the empty wine-glass which stood by his bedside. 'What a life he may have before him! – and to throw it away for this!' and as he spoke he took the glass and tossed it across the room. 'Oh, doctor! would that it were all to begin again!'

'We all wish that, I dare say, Scatcherd.'

'No, you don't wish it. You ain't worth a shilling, and yet you regret nothing. I am worth half a million in one way or the other, and I regret everything – everything – everything!'

'You should not think in that way, Scatcherd; you need not think so. Yesterday you told Mr Clarke that you were comfortable in your mind.' Mr Clarke was the clergyman who had visited him.

'Of course I did. What else could I say when he asked me? It wouldn't have been civil to have told him that his time and words were all thrown away. But, Thorne, believe me, when a man's heart is sad – sad – sad to the core, a few words from a parson at the last moment will never make it all right.'

'May He have mercy on you, my friend! – if you will think of Him, and look to Him, He will have mercy on you.'

'Well – I will try, doctor; but would that it were all to do again. You'll see to the old woman for my sake, won't you?'

'What, Lady Scatcherd?'

'Lady Devil! If anything angers me now it is that "ladyship" – her to be my lady! Why, when I came out of jail that time, the poor creature had hardly a shoe to her foot. But it wasn't her fault, Thorne; it was none of her doing. She never asked for any such nonsense.'

'She has been an excellent wife, Scatcherd; and what is more, she is an excellent woman. She is, and ever will be, one of my dearest friends.'

'Thank'ee, doctor, thank'ee. Yes; she has been a good wife – better for a poor man than a rich one; but then, that was what she was born to. You won't let her be knocked about by them, will you, Thorne?'

Dr Thorne again assured him, that as long as he lived Lady Scatcherd should never want one true friend; in making this promise, however, he managed to drop all allusion to the obnoxious title.

'You'll be with him as much as possible, won't you?' again asked the baronet, after lying quite silent for a quarter of an hour.

'With whom?' said the doctor, who was then all but asleep.

'With my poor boy; with Louis.'

'If he will let me, I will,' said the doctor.

'And, doctor, when you see a glass at his mouth, dash it down; thrust it down, though you thrust out the teeth with it. When you see that, Thorne, tell him of his father – tell him what his father might have been but for that; tell him how his father died like a beast, because he could not keep himself from drink.'

These, reader, were the last words spoken by Sir Roger Scatcherd. As he uttered them he rose up in bed with the same vehemence which he had shown on the former evening. But in the very act of doing so he was again struck by paralysis, and before nine on the following morning all was over.

'Oh, my man – my own, own man!' exclaimed the widow, remembering in the paroxysm of her grief nothing but the loves of their early days; 'the best, the brightest, the cleverest of them all!'

Some weeks after this Sir Roger was buried, with much pomp and ceremony, within the precincts of Barchester Cathedral; and a monument was put up to him soon after, in which he was portrayed as smoothing a block of granite with a mallet and chisel; while his eagle eye, disdaining such humble work, was fixed upon some intricate mathematical instrument above him. Could Sir Roger have seen it himself, he would probably have declared, that no workman was ever worth his salt who looked one way while he rowed another.

Immediately after the funeral the will was opened, and Dr Thorne discovered that the clauses of it were exactly identical with those which his friend had described to him some months back. Nothing had been altered; nor had the document been unfolded since that strange codicil was added, in which it was declared that Dr Thorne knew – and only Dr Thorne – who was the eldest child of the testator's only sister. At the same time, however, a joint executor with Dr Thorne had been named – one Mr Stock, a man of railway fame – and Dr Thorne himself was made a legatee to the humble extent of a thousand pounds. A life income of a thousand pounds a year was left to Lady Scatcherd.

CHAPTER XXVI

War

We need not follow Sir Roger to his grave, nor partake of the baked meats which were furnished for his funeral banquet.* Such men as Sir Roger Scatcherd are always well buried, and we have already seen that his glories were duly told to posterity in the graphic diction of his sepulchral monument. In a few days the doctor had returned to his quiet home, and Sir Louis found himself reigning at Boxall Hill in his father's stead – with, however, a much diminished sway, and, as he thought it, but a poor exchequer. We must soon return to him and say something of his career as a baronet; but for the present, we may go back to our more pleasant friends at Greshamsbury.

But our friends at Greshamsbury had not been making themselves pleasant – not so pleasant to each other as circumstances would have admitted. In those days which the doctor had felt himself bound to pass, if not altogether at Boxall Hill, yet altogether away from his own home, so as to admit of his being as much as possible with his patient, Mary had been thrown more than ever with Patience Oriel, and almost more than ever with Beatrice Gresham. As regarded Mary, she would doubtless have preferred the companionship of Patience, though she loved Beatrice far the best; but she had no choice. When she went to the parsonage Beatrice came there also, and when Patience came to the doctor's house Beatrice either accompanied or followed her. Mary could hardly have rejected their society, even had she felt it wise to do so. She would in such case have been all alone, and her severance from the Greshamsbury house and household, from the big family in which she had for so many years been almost at home, would have made such solitude almost unendurable.

And then these two girls both knew – not her secret; she had no secret – but the little history of her ill-treatment. They knew that though she had been blameless in this matter, yet she had been the one to bear the punishment; and, as girls and bosom friends, they could not but sympathise with her, and endow her with heroic attributes; make her, in fact, as we are doing, their little heroine for the nonce. This was, perhaps, not serviceable for Mary; but it was far from being disagreeable.

The tendency to finding matter for hero-worship in Mary's endurance was much stronger with Beatrice than with Miss Oriel. Miss Oriel was the elder, and naturally less afflicted with the sentimentation of romance. She had thrown herself into Mary's arms because she had seen that it was essentially necessary for Mary's comfort that she should do so. She was anxious to make her friend smile, and to smile with her. Beatrice was quite as true in her sympathy; but she rather wished that she and Mary might weep in unison, shed mutual tears, and break their hearts together.

Patience had spoken of Frank's love as a misfortune, of his conduct as erroneous, and to be excused only by his youth, and had never appeared to surmise that Mary also might be in love as well as he. But to Beatrice the affair was a tragic difficulty, admitting of no solution; a Gordian knot, not to be cut;* a misery now and for ever. She would always talk about Frank when she and Mary were alone; and, to speak the truth, Mary did not stop her as she perhaps should have. As for a marriage between them, that was impossible; Beatrice was well sure of that: it was Frank's unfortunate destiny that he must marry money – money, and, as Beatrice sometimes thoughtlessly added, cutting Mary to the quick, – money and family also. Under such circumstances a marriage between them was quite impossible; but not the less did Beatrice declare, that she would have loved Mary as her sister-in-law had it been possible; and how worthy Frank was of a girl's love, had such love been permissible.

'It is so cruel,' Beatrice would say; 'so very, very cruel. You would have suited him in every way.'

'Nonsense, Trichy; I should have suited him in no possible way at all; nor he me.'

'Oh, but you would – exactly. Papa loves you so well.'

'And mamma; that would have been so nice.'

'Yes; and mamma, too – that is, had you had a fortune,' said the daughter, naïvely. 'She always liked you personally, always.'

'Did she?'

'Always. And we all love you so.'

'Especially Lady Alexandrina.'

'That would not have signified, for Frank cannot endure the De Courcys himself.'

'My dear, it does not matter one straw whom your brother can endure or not endure just at present. His character is to be formed, and his tastes, and his heart also.'

'Oh, Mary! – his heart.'

'Yes, his heart; not the fact of his having a heart. I think he has a heart; but he himself does not yet understand it.'

'Oh, Mary! you do not know him.'

Such confessions were not without danger to poor Mary's comfort. It came soon to be the case that she looked rather for this sort of sympathy from Beatrice, than for Miss Oriel's pleasant but less piquant gaiety.

So the days of the doctor's absence were passed, and so also the first week after his return. During this week it was almost daily necessary that the squire should be with him. The doctor was now the legal holder of Sir Roger's property, and, as such, the holder also of all the mortgages on Mr Gresham's property; and it was natural that they should be much together. The doctor would not, however, go up to Greshamsbury on any other than medical business; and it therefore became necessary that the squire should be a good deal at the doctor's house.

Then the Lady Arabella became unhappy in her mind. Frank, it was true, was away at Cambridge, and had been successfully kept out of Mary's way since the suspicion of danger had fallen upon Lady Arabella's mind. Frank was away, and Mary was systematically banished, with due acknowledgment from all the powers in Greshamsbury. But this was not enough for Lady Arabella as long as her daughter still habitually consorted with the female culprit, and as long as her husband consorted with the male culprit. It seemed to Lady Arabella at this moment as though, in banishing Mary from the house, she had in effect banished herself from the most intimate of the Greshamsbury social circles. She magnified in her own mind the importance of the conferences between the girls, and was not without some fear that the doctor might be talking the squire over into very dangerous compliance.

She resolved, therefore, on another duel with the doctor. In the first she had been pre-eminently and unexpectedly successful. No young sucking dove could have been more mild than that terrible enemy whom she had for years regarded as being too puissant for attack. In ten minutes she had vanquished him, and succeeded in banishing both him and his niece from the house without losing the value of his services. As is always the case with us, she had begun to despise the enemy she had conquered, and to think that the foe, once beaten, could never rally.

Her object was to break off all confidential intercourse between Beatrice and Mary, and to interrupt, as far as she could do it, that between the doctor and the squire. This, it may be said, could be more easily done by skilful management within her own household. She had, however, tried that and failed. She had said much to Beatrice as to the imprudence of her friendship with Mary, and she had done this purposely before the squire; injudiciously however, – for the squire had immediately taken Mary's part, and had declared that he had no wish to see a quarrel between his family and that of the doctor; that Mary Thorne was in every way a good girl, and an eligible friend for his own child; and had ended by declaring, that he would not have Mary persecuted for Frank's fault. This had not been the end, nor nearly the end of what had been said on the matter at Greshamsbury; but the end, when it came, came in this wise, that Lady Arabella determined to say a few more words to the doctor as to the expediency of forbidding familiar intercourse between Mary and any of the Greshamsbury people.

With this view Lady Arabella absolutely bearded the lion in his den, the doctor in his shop. She had heard that both Mary and Beatrice were to pass a certain afternoon at the parsonage, and took the opportunity of calling at the doctor's house. A period of many years had passed since she had last so honoured that abode. Mary, indeed, had been so much one of her own family that the ceremony of calling on her had never been thought necessary; and thus, unless Mary had been absolutely ill, there would have been nothing to bring her ladyship to the house. All this she knew would add to the importance of the occasion, and she judged it prudent to make the occasion as important as it might well be.

She was so far successful that she soon found herself *tête à tête* with the doctor in his own study. She was no whit dismayed by the pair of human thigh-bones which lay close to his hand, and which, when he was talking in that den of his own, he was in the constant habit of handling with much energy; nor was she frightened out of her propriety even by the little child's skull which grinned at her from off the chimney-piece.

'Doctor,' she said, as soon as the first complimentary greetings were over, speaking in her kindest and most would-be-confidential tone, 'Doctor, I am still uneasy about that boy of mine, and I have thought it best to come to you at once, and tell you freely what I think.'

The doctor bowed, and said that he was very sorry that she should have any cause of uneasiness about his young friend Frank.

'Indeed, I am very uneasy, doctor; and having, as I do have, such reliance on your prudence, and such perfect confidence in your friendship, I have thought it best to come and speak to you openly:' thereupon the Lady Arabella paused, and the doctor bowed again.

'Nobody knows so well as you do the dreadful state of the squire's affairs.'

'Not so very dreadful; not so very dreadful,' said the doctor, mildly: 'that is, as far as I know.'

'Yes they are, doctor; very dreadful; very dreadful indeed. You know how much he owes to this young man: I do not, for the squire never tells anything to me; but I know that it is a very large sum of money; enough to swamp the estate and ruin Frank. Now I call that very dreadful.'

'No, no, not ruin him, Lady Arabella; not ruin him, I hope.'

'However, I did not come to talk to you about that. As I said before, I know nothing of the squire's affairs, and, as a matter of course, I do not ask you to tell me. But I am sure you will agree with me in this, that, as a mother, I cannot but be interested about my only son,' and Lady Arabella put her cambric handkerchief to her eyes.

'Of course you are; of course you are,' said the doctor; 'and, Lady Arabella, my opinion of Frank is such, that I feel sure that he will do well;' and, in his energy, Dr Thorne brandished one of the thigh-bones almost in the lady's face.

'I hope he will; I am sure I hope he will. But, doctor, he has such dangers to contend with; he is so warm and impulsive that I fear his heart will bring him into trouble. Now, you know, unless Frank marries money he is lost.'

The doctor made no answer to this last appeal, but as he sat and listened a slight frown came across his brow.

'He must marry money, doctor. Now we have, you see, with your assistance, contrived to separate him from dear Mary – '

'With my assistance, Lady Arabella! I have given no assistance, nor have I meddled in the matter; nor will I.'

'Well, doctor, perhaps not meddled; but you agreed with me, you know, that the two young people had been imprudent.'

'I agreed to no such thing, Lady Arabella; never, never. I not only never agreed that Mary had been imprudent, but I will not agree to it now, and will not allow any one to assert it in my presence without contradicting it:' and then the doctor worked away at the thigh-bones in a manner that did rather alarm her ladyship.

'At any rate, you thought that the young people had better be kept apart.'

'No; neither did I think that: my niece, I felt sure, was safe from danger. I knew that she would do nothing that would bring either her or me to shame.'

'Not to shame,' said the lady, apologetically, as it were, using the word perhaps not exactly in the doctor's sense.

'I felt no alarm for her,' continued the doctor, 'and desired no change. Frank is your son, and it is for you to look to him. You thought proper to do so by desiring Mary to absent herself from Greshamsbury.'

'Oh no, no, no!' said Lady Arabella

'But you did, Lady Arabella; and as Greshamsbury is your home, neither I nor my niece had any ground of complaint. We acquiesced, not without much suffering, but we did acquiesce; and you, I think, can have no ground of complaint against us.'

Lady Arabella had hardly expected that the doctor would reply to her mild and conciliatory exordium with so much sternness. He had yielded so easily to her on the former occasion. She did not comprehend that when she uttered her sentence of exile against Mary, she had given an order which she had the power of enforcing; but that obedience to that order had now placed Mary altogether beyond her jurisdiction. She was, therefore, a little surprised, and for a few moments overawed by the doctor's manner; but she soon recovered herself, remembering, doubtless, that fortune favours none but the brave.

'I make no complaint, Dr Thorne,' she said, assuming a tone more befitting a De Courcy than that hitherto used, 'I make no complaint either as regards you or Mary.'

'You are very kind, Lady Arabella.'

'But I think that it is my duty to put a stop, a peremptory stop to anything like a love affair between my son and your niece.'

'I have not the least objection in life. If there is such a love affair, put a stop to it – that is, if you have the power.'

Here the doctor was doubtless imprudent. But he had begun to think that he had yielded sufficiently to the lady; and he had begun to resolve, also, that though it would not become him to encourage even the idea of such a marriage, he would make Lady Arabella understand that he thought his niece quite good enough for her son, and that the match, if regarded as imprudent, was to be regarded as equally imprudent on both sides. He would not suffer that Mary and her heart and feelings and interest should be altogether postponed to those of the young heir; and, perhaps, he was unconsciously encouraged in this determination by the reflection that Mary herself might perhaps become a young heiress.

'It is my duty,' said Lady Arabella, repeating her words with even a stronger De Courcy intonation; 'and your duty also, Dr Thorne.'

'My duty!' said he, rising from his chair and leaning on the table with the two thigh-bones. 'Lady Arabella, pray understand at once, that I repudiate any such duty, and will have nothing whatever to do with it.'

'But you do not mean to say that you will encourage this unfortunate boy to marry your niece?'

'The unfortunate boy, Lady Arabella – whom, by the by, I regard as a very fortunate young man – is your son, not mine. I shall take no steps about his marriage, either one way or the other.'

'You think it right, then, that your niece should throw herself in his way?'

'Throw herself in his way! What would you say if I came up to Greshamsbury and spoke to you of your daughters in such language? What would my dear friend, Mr Gresham say, if some neighbour's wife should come and so speak to him? I will tell you what he would say: he would quietly beg her to go back to her own home and meddle only with her own matters.'

This was dreadful to Lady Arabella. Even Dr Thorne had never before dared thus to lower her to the level of common humanity, and liken her to any other wife in the country-side.

Moreover, she was not quite sure whether he, the parish doctor, was not desiring her, the earl's daughter, to go home and mind her own business. On this first point, however, there seemed to be room for doubt, of which she gave herself the benefit.

'It would not become me to argue with you, Dr Thorne,' she said.

'Not at least on this subject,' said he.

'I can only repeat that I mean nothing offensive to our dear Mary; for whom, I think I may say, I have always shown almost a mother's care.'

'Neither am I, nor is Mary, ungrateful for the kindness she has received at Greshamsbury.'

'But I must do my duty: my own children must be my first consideration.'

'Of course they must, Lady Arabella; that's of course.'

'And, therefore, I have called on you to say that I think it is imprudent that Beatrice and Mary should be so much together.'

The doctor had been standing during the latter part of this conversation, but now he began to walk about, still holding the two bones like a pair of dumb-bells.

'God bless my soul!' he said; 'God bless my soul Why, Lady Arabella, do you suspect your own daughter as well as your own son? Do you think that Beatrice is assisting Mary in preparing this wicked clandestine marriage? I tell you fairly, Lady Arabella, the present tone of your mind is such that I cannot understand it.'

'I suspect nobody, Dr Thorne; but young people will be young.'

'And old people must be old, I suppose; the more's the pity Lady Arabella, Mary is the same to me as my own daughter, and owes me the obedience of a child; but as I do not disapprove of your daughter Beatrice as an acquaintance for her, but rather, on the other hand, regard with pleasure their friendship, you cannot expect that I should take any steps to put an end to it.'

'But suppose it should lead to renewed intercourse between Frank and Mary?'

'I have no objection. Frank is a very nice young fellow, gentlemanlike in his manners, and neighbourly in his disposition.'

'Doctor Thorne – '

'Lady Arabella – '

'I cannot believe that you really intend to express a wish – '

'You are quite right. I have not intended to express any wish; nor do I intend to do so. Mary is at liberty, within certain bounds – which I am sure she will not pass – to choose her own friends. I think she has not chosen badly as regards Miss Beatrice Gresham; and should she even add Frank Gresham to the number – '

'Friends! why they were more than friends; they were declared lovers!'

'I doubt that, Lady Arabella, because I have not heard of it from Mary. But even were it so, I do not see why I should object.'

'Not object!'

'As I said before, Frank is, to my thinking, an excellent young man. Why should I object?'

'Dr Thorne!' said her ladyship, now also rising from her chair in a state of too evident perturbation.

'Why should I object? It is for you, Lady Arabella, to look after your lambs; for me to see that, if possible, no harm shall come to mine. If you think that Mary is an improper acquaintance for your children, it is for you to guide them; for you and for their father. Say what you think fit to your own daughter; but pray understand, once for all, that I will allow no one to interfere with my niece.'

'Interfere!' said Lady Arabella, now absolutely confused by the severity of the doctor's manner.

'I will allow no one to interfere with her; no one, Lady Arabella. She has suffered very greatly from imputations which you have most unjustly thrown on her. It was, however, your undoubted right to turn her out of your house if you thought fit; – though, as a woman who had known her for so many years, you might, I think, have treated her with more forbearance. That, however, was your right, and you exercised it. There your privilege stops; yes, and must stop, Lady Arabella. You shall not persecute her here, on the only spot of ground she can call her own.'

'Persecute her, Doctor Thorne! You do not mean to say that I have persecuted her?'

'Ah! but I do mean to say so. You do persecute her, and would continue to do so did I not defend her. It is not sufficient that she is forbidden to enter your domain – and so forbidden with the knowledge of all the country round but you must come here also with the hope of interrupting all the innocent pleasures of her life. Fearing lest she should be allowed even to speak of your son, to hear a word of him through his own sister, you would put her in prison, tie her up, keep her from the light of day – '

'Doctor Thorne! how can you – '

But the doctor was not to be interrupted.

'It never occurs to you to tie him up, put him in prison. No; he is the heir to Greshamsbury; he is your son, an earl's grandson. It is only natural, after all, that he should throw a few foolish words at the doctor's niece. But she! it is an offence not to be forgiven on her part that she should, however unwillingly, have been forced to listen to them! Now understand me, Lady Arabella; if any of your family come to my house I shall be delighted to welcome them: if Mary should meet any of them elsewhere I shall be delighted to hear of it. Should she tell me tomorrow that she was engaged to marry Frank, I should talk over the matter with her, quite coolly, solely with a view to her interest, as would be my duty; feeling, at the same time, that Frank would be lucky in having such a wife. Now you know my mind, Lady Arabella. It is so I should do my duty; – you can do yours as you may think fit.'

Lady Arabella had by this time perceived that she was not destined on this occasion to gain any great victory. She, how-ever, was angry as well as the doctor. It was not the man's vehemence that provoked her so much as his evident determi-nation to break down the prestige of her rank, and place her on a footing in no respect superior to his own. He had never before been so audaciously arrogant; and, as she moved towards the door, she determined in her wrath that she would never again have confidential intercourse with him in any relation of life whatsoever.

'Dr Thorne,' said she, 'I think you have forgotten yourself. You must excuse me if I say that after what has passed I–I–I – '

'Certainly,' said he, fully understanding what she meant; and bowing low as he opened first the study-door, then the front door, then the garden-gate.

And then Lady Arabella stalked off, not without full obser-vation from Mrs Yates Umbleby and her friend Miss Gushing, who lived close by.

CHAPTER XXVII

Miss Thorne Goes on a Visit

And now began the unpleasant things at Greshamsbury of which we have here told. When Lady Arabella walked away from the doctor's house she resolved that, let it cost what it might, there should be war to the knife* between her and him. She had been insulted by him – so at least she said to herself, and so she was prepared to say to others also – and it was not to be borne that a De Courcy should allow her parish doctor to insult her with impunity. She would tell her husband with all the dignity that she could assume, that it had now become absolutely necessary that he should protect his wife by breaking entirely with his unmannered neighbour; and, as regarded the young members of her family, she would use the authority of a mother, and absolutely forbid them to hold any intercourse with Mary Thorne. So resolving, she walked quickly back to her own house.

The doctor, when left alone, was not quite satisfied with the part he had taken in the interview. He had spoken from impulse rather than from judgement, and, as is generally the case with men who do so speak, he had afterwards to acknowledge to himself that he had been imprudent. He accused himself probably of more violence than he had really used, and was therefore unhappy; but, nevertheless, his indignation was not at rest. He was angry with himself; but not on that account the less angry with Lady Arabella. She was cruel, overbearing, and unreasonable; cruel in the most cruel of manners, so he thought; but not on that account was he justified in forgetting the forbearance due from a gentleman to a lady. Mary, however, had owed much to the kindness of this woman, and, therefore, Dr Thorne felt that he should have forgiven much.

Thus the doctor walked about his room, much disturbed; now accusing himself for having been so angry with Lady Arabella, and then feeding his own anger by thinking of her misconduct.

The only immediate conclusion at which he resolved was this, that it was unnecessary that he should say anything to Mary on the subject of her ladyship's visit. There was, no doubt, sorrow enough in store for his darling; why should he aggravate it?

Lady Arabella would doubtless not stop now in her course; but why should he accelerate the evil which she would doubtless be able to effect?

Lady Arabella, when she returned to the house, allowed no grass to grow under her feet. As she entered the house she desired that Miss Beatrice should be sent to her directly she returned; and she desired also, that as soon as the squire should be in his room a message to that effect might be immediately brought to her.

'Beatrice,' she said, as soon as the young lady appeared before her, and in speaking she assumed her firmest tone of authority, 'Beatrice, I am sorry, my dear, to say anything that is unpleasant to you, but I must make it a positive request that you will for the future drop all intercourse with Dr Thorne's family.'

Beatrice, who had received Lady Arabella's message immediately on entering the house, and had run upstairs imagining that some instant haste was required, now stood before her mother rather out of breath, holding her bonnet by the strings.

'Oh, mamma!' she exclaimed, 'what on earth has happened?'

'My dear,' said the mother, 'I cannot really explain to you what has happened; but I must ask you to give me your positive assurance that you will comply with my request.'

'You don't mean that I am not to see Mary any more?'

'Yes I do, my dear; at any rate, for the present. When I tell you that your brother's interest imperatively demands it, I am sure that you will not refuse me.'

Beatrice did not refuse, but she did not appear too willing to comply. She stood silent, leaning against the end of a sofa and twisting her bonnet-strings in her hand.

'Well, Beatrice – '

'But, mamma, I don't understand.'

Lady Arabella had said that she could not exactly explain: but she found it necessary to attempt to do so.

'Dr Thorne has openly declared to me that a marriage between poor Frank and Mary is all that he could desire for his niece. After such unparalleled audacity as that, even your father will see the necessity of breaking with him.'

'Dr Thorne! Oh, mamma, you must have misunderstood him.'

'My dear, I am not apt to misunderstand people; especially when I am so much in earnest as I was in talking to Dr Thorne.'

'But, mamma, I know so well what Mary herself thinks about it.'

'And I know what Dr Thorne thinks about it; he, at any rate, has been candid in what he has said; there can be no doubt on earth that he has spoken his true thoughts; there can be no reason to doubt him: of course such a match would be all that he could wish'

'Mamma, I feel sure that there is some mistake.'

'Very well, my dear. I know that you are infatuated about these people, and that you are always inclined to contradict what I say to you; but, remember, I expect that you will obey me when I tell you not to go to Dr Thorne's house any more.'

'But, mamma –'

'I expect you to obey me, Beatrice. Though you are so prone to contradict, you have never disobeyed me; and I fully trust that you will not do so now.'

Lady Arabella had begun by exacting, or trying to exact a promise, but as she found that this was not forthcoming, she thought it better to give up the point without a dispute. It might be that Beatrice would absolutely refuse to pay this respect to her mother's authority, and then where would she have been?

At this moment a servant came up to say that the squire was in his room, and Lady Arabella was opportunely saved the necessity of discussing the matter further with her daughter. 'I am now,' she said, 'going to see your father on the same subject; you may be quite sure, Beatrice, that I should not willingly speak to him on any matter relating to Dr Thorne did I not find it absolutely necessary to do so.'

This Beatrice knew was true, and she did therefore feel convinced that something terrible must have happened.

While Lady Arabella opened her budget the squire sat quite silent, listening to her with apparent respect. She found it necessary that her description to him should be much more elaborate than that which she had vouchsafed to her daughter, and, in telling her grievance, she insisted most especially on the personal insult which had been offered to herself.

'After what has now happened,' said she, not quite able to repress a tone of triumph as she spoke, 'I do expect, Mr Gresham, that you will – will –'

'Will what, my dear?'

'Will at least protect me from the repetition of such treatment.'

'You are not afraid that Dr Thorne will come here to attack you? As far as I can understand, he never comes near the place, unless when you send for him.'

'No; I do not think that he will come to Greshamsbury any more. I believe I have put a stop to that.'

'Then what is it, my dear, that you want me to do?'

Lady Arabella paused a minute before she replied. The game which she now had to play was not very easy; she knew, or thought she knew, that her husband, in his heart of hearts, much preferred his friend to the wife of his bosom, and that he would, if he could, shuffle out of noticing the doctor's iniquities. It behoved her, therefore, to put them forward in such a way that they must be noticed.

'I suppose, Mr Gresham, you do not wish that Frank should marry the girl?'

'I do not think that there is the slightest chance of such a thing; and I am quite sure that Dr Thorne would not encourage it.'

'But I tell you. Mr Gresham, that he says that he will encourage it.'

'Oh, you have misunderstood him.'

'Of course; I always misunderstand everything. I know that. I misunderstood it when I told you how you would distress yourself if you took those nasty hounds.'

'I have had other troubles more expensive than the hounds,' said the poor squire, sighing.

'Oh, yes; I know what you mean; a wife and family are expensive, of course. It is a little too late now to complain of that.'

'My dear, it is always too late to complain of any troubles when they are no longer to be avoided. We need not, therefore, talk any more about the hounds at present.'

'I do not wish to speak of them, Mr Gresham.'

'Nor I.'

'But I hope you will not think me unreasonable if I am anxious to know what you intend to do about Dr Thorne.'

'To do?'

'Yes; I suppose you will do something: you do not wish to see your son marry such a girl as Mary Thorne.'

'As far as the girl herself is concerned,' said the squire, turning rather red, 'I am not sure that he could do much better. I know nothing whatever against Mary. Frank, however, cannot afford to make such a match. It would be his ruin.'

'Of course it would; utter ruin: he never could hold up his head again. Therefore it is I ask, What is it you intend to do?'

The squire was bothered. He had no intention whatever of doing anything, and no belief in his wife's assertion as to Dr Thorne's iniquity. But he did not know how to get her out of the room. She asked him the same question over and over again, and on each occasion urged on him the heinousness of the insult to which she personally had been subjected; so that at last he was driven to ask her what it was she wished him to do.

'Well, then, Mr Gresham, if you ask me, I must say, that I think you should abstain from any intercourse with Dr Thorne whatever.'

'Break off all intercourse with him?'

'Yes.'

'What do you mean? He has been turned out of this house, and I'm not to go to see him at his own.'

'I certainly think that you ought to discontinue your visits to Dr Thorne altogether.'

'Nonsense, my dear; absolute nonsense.'

'Nonsense! Mr Gresham it is nonsense. As you speak in that way, I must let you know plainly what I feel. I am endeavouring to do my duty by my son. As you justly observe, such a marriage as this would be utter ruin to him. When I found that the young people were actually talking of being in love with each other, making vows and all that sort of thing, I did think it time to interfere. I did not, however, turn them out of Greshamsbury, as you accuse me of doing. In the kindest possible manner – '

'Well – well – well; I know all that. There, they are gone, and that's enough. I don't complain; surely that ought to be enough.'

'Enough! Mr Gresham. No; it is not enough. I find that, in spite of what has occurred, the closest intimacy exists between the two families; that poor Beatrice, who is so very young, and not so prudent as she should be, is made to act as a go-between; and when I speak to the doctor, hoping that he will assist me in preventing this, he not only tells me that he means to encourage Mary in her plans, but positively insults me to my face, laughs at me for being an earl's daughter, and tells me – yes, he absolutely told me – to get out of his house.'

Let it be told with some shame as to the squire's conduct, that his first feeling on hearing this was one of envy – of envy and regret that he could not make the same uncivil request. Not that he wished to turn his wife absolutely out of his house; but he would have been very glad to have had the power of dismissing her summarily from his own room. This, however, was at present impossible; so he was obliged to make some mild reply.

'You must have mistaken him, my dear. He could not have intended to say that.'

'Oh! of course, Mr Gresham. It is all a mistake, of course. It will be a mistake, only a mistake when you find your son married to Mary Thorne.'

'Well, my dear, I cannot undertake to quarrel with Dr Thorne.' This was true; for the squire could hardly have quarrelled with Dr Thorne, even had he wished it.

'Then I think it right to tell you that I shall. And, Mr Gresham, I did not expect much co-operation from you; but I did think that you would have shown some little anger when you heard that I had been so ill-treated. I shall, however, know how to take care of myself; and I shall continue to do the best I can to protect Frank from these wicked intrigues.'

So saying, her ladyship arose and left the room, having succeeded in destroying the comfort of all our Greshamsbury friends. It was very well for the squire to declare that he would not quarrel with Dr Thorne, and of course he did not do so. But he, himself, had no wish whatever that his son should marry Mary Thorne; and as a falling drop will hollow a stone, so did the continual harping of his wife on the subject give rise to some amount of suspicion in his own mind. Then as to Beatrice, though she had made no promise that she would not again visit Mary, she was by no means prepared to set her mother's authority altogether at defiance; and she also was sufficiently uncomfortable.

Dr Thorne said nothing of the matter to his niece, and she, therefore, would have been absolutely bewildered by Beatrice's absence, had she not received some tidings of what had taken place at Greshamsbury through Patience Oriel. Beatrice and Patience discussed the matter fully, and it was agreed between them that it would be better that Mary should know what

sterner orders respecting her had gone forth from the tyrant at
Greshamsbury, and that she might understand that Beatrice's
absence was compulvery. Patience was thus placed in this
position, that on one day she walked and talked with Beatrice,
and on the next with Mary; and so matters went on for a while
at Greshamsbury – not very pleasantly.

Very unpleasantly and very uncomfortably did the months of
May and June pass away. Beatrice and Mary occasionally met,
drinking tea together at the parsonage, or in some other of the
ordinary meetings of country society; but there were no more
confidentially distressing confidential discourses, no more whispering of Frank's name, no more sweet allusions to the inexpe-
diency of a passion, which, according to Beatrice's views, would
have been so delightful had it been expedient.

The squire and doctor also met constantly; there were unfortunately many subjects on which they were obliged to meet.
Louis Philippe – or Sir Louis as we must call him – though he
had no power over his own property, was wide awake to all the
coming privileges of ownership, and he would constantly point
out to his guardian the manner in which, according to his ideas,
the most should be made of it. The young baronet's ideas of
good taste were not of the most refined description, and he did
not hesitate to tell Dr Thorne that his, the doctor's, friendship
with Mr Gresham must be no bar to his, the baronet's, interest.
Sir Louis also had his own lawyer, who gave Dr Thorne to
understand that, according to his ideas, the sum due on Mr
Gresham's property was too large to be left on its present
footing; the title-deeds, he said, should be surrendered or the
mortgage foreclosed. All this added to the sadness which now
seemed to envelop the village of Greshamsbury.

Early in July, Frank was to come home. The manner in which
the comings and goings of 'poor Frank' were allowed to disturb
the arrangements of all the ladies, and some of the gentlemen,
of Greshamsbury was most abominable. And yet it can hardly
be said to have been his fault. He would have been only too well
pleased had things been allowed to go on after their old fashion.
Things were not allowed so to go on. At Christmas Miss Oriel
had submitted to be exiled, in order that she might carry Mary
away from the presence of the young Bashaw,* an arrangement
by which all the winter festivities of the poor doctor had been

thoroughly sacrificed; and now it began to be said that some similar plan for the summer must be suggested.

It must not be supposed that any direction to this effect was conveyed either to Mary or to the doctor. The suggestion came from them, and was mentioned only to Patience. But Patience, as a matter of course, told Beatrice, and Beatrice told her mother, somewhat triumphantly, hoping thereby to convince the she-dragon of Mary's innocence. Alas! she-dragons are not easily convinced of the innocence of any one. Lady Arabella quite coincided in the propriety of Mary's being sent off, – whither she never inquired, – in order that the coast might be clear for 'poor Frank;' but she did not a whit the more abstain from talking of the wicked intrigues of those Thornes. As it turned out, Mary's absence caused her to talk the more.

The Boxall Hill property, including the house and furniture, had been left to the contractor's son; it being understood that the property would not be at present in his own hands, but that he might inhabit the house if he chose to do so. It would thus be necessary for Lady Scatcherd to find a home for herself, unless she could remain at Boxall Hill by her son's permission. In this position of affairs the doctor had been obliged to make a bargain between them. Sir Louis did wish to have the comfort, or perhaps the honour, of a country house; but he did not wish to have the expense of keeping it up. He was also willing to let his mother live at the house; but not without a consideration. After a prolonged degree of haggling, terms were agreed upon; and a few weeks after her husband's death, Lady Scatcherd found herself alone at Boxall Hill – alone as regards society in the ordinary sense, but not quite alone as concerned her ladyship, for the faithful Hannah was still with her.

The doctor was of course often at Boxall Hill, and never left it without an urgent request from Lady Scatcherd that he would bring his niece over to see her. Now Lady Scatcherd was no fit companion for Mary Thorne, and though Mary had often asked to be taken to Boxall Hill, certain considerations had hitherto induced the doctor to refuse the request; but there was that about Lady Scatcherd, – a kind of homely honesty of purpose, an absence of all conceit as to her own position, and a strength of womanly confidence in the doctor as her friend, which by degrees won upon his heart. When, therefore, both he and Mary felt that it would be better for her again to absent herself for a while from Greshamsbury, it was, after much deliberation, agreed that she should go on a visit to Boxall Hill.

To Boxall Hill, accordingly, she went, and was received almost as a princess. Mary had all her life been accustomed to women of rank, and had never habituated herself to feel much trepidation in the presence of titled grandees; but she had prepared herself to be more than ordinarily submissive to Lady Scatcherd. Her hostess was a widow, was not a woman of high birth, was a woman of whom her uncle spoke well; and, for all these reasons, Mary was determined to respect her, and pay to her every consideration. But when she was settled down in the house she found it almost impossible to do so. Lady Scatcherd treated her as a farmer's wife might have treated some convalescent young lady who had been sent to her charge for a few weeks, in order that she might benefit by the country air. Her ladyship could hardly bring herself to sit still and eat her dinner tranquilly in her guest's presence. And then nothing was good enough for Mary. Lady Scatcherd besought her, almost with tears, to say what she liked best to eat and drink; and was in despair when Mary declared she didn't care, that she liked anything, and that she was in nowise particular in such matters.

'A roast fowl, Miss Thorne?'

'Very nice, Lady Scatcherd.'

'And bread sauce?'

'Bread sauce – yes; oh, yes – I like bread sauce,' – and poor Mary tried hard to show a little interest.

'And just a few sausages. We make them all in the house, Miss Thorne; we know what they are. And mashed potatoes – do you like them best mashed or baked?'

Mary, finding herself obliged to vote, voted for mashed potatoes.

'Very well. But, Miss Thorne, if you would like boiled fowl better, with a little bit of ham, you know, I do hope you'll say so. And there's lamb in the house, quite beautiful; now do 'ee say something; do 'ee, Miss Thorne.'

So invoked, Mary felt herself obliged to say something, and declared for the roast fowl and sausages; but she found it very difficult to pay much outward respect to a person who would pay so much outward respect to her. A day or two after her arrival it was decided that she should ride about the place on a donkey; she was accustomed to riding, the doctor having generally taken care that one of his own horses should, when required, consent to carry a lady; but there was no steed at Boxall Hill that she could mount; and when Lady Scatcherd had offered to get a pony for her, she had willingly compromised matters by expressing the delight she would have in making a campaign on a donkey. Upon this, Lady Scatcherd had herself set off in quest of the desired animal, much to Mary's horror; and did not return till the necessary purchase had been effected. Then she came back with the donkey close at her heels, almost holding its collar, and stood there at the hall-door till Mary came to approve.

'I hope she'll do. I don't think she'll kick,' said Lady Scatcherd, patting the head of her purchase quite triumphantly.

'Oh, you are so kind, Lady Scatcherd. I'm sure she'll do quite nicely; she seems to be very quiet,' said Mary.

'Please, my lady, it's a he,' said the boy who held the halter.

'Oh! a he, is it?' said her ladyship; 'but the he-donkeys are quite as quiet as the shes, ain't they?'

'Oh, yes, my lady; a deal quieter, all the world over, and twice as useful.'

'I'm so glad of that, Miss Thorne,' said Lady Scatcherd, her eyes bright with joy.

And so Mary was established with her donkey, who did all that could be expected from an animal in his position.

'But, dear Lady Scatcherd,' said Mary, as they sat together at the open drawing-room window the same evening, 'you must not go on calling me Miss Thorne; my name is Mary, you know. Won't you call me Mary?' and she came and knelt at Lady Scatcherd's feet, and took hold of her, looking up into her face.

Lady Scatcherd's cheeks became rather red, as though she was somewhat ashamed of her position.

'You are so very kind to me,' continued Mary, 'and it seems so cold to hear you call me Miss Thorne.'

'Well, Miss Thorne, I'm sure I'd call you anything to please you. Only I didn't know whether you'd like it from me. Else I do think Mary is the prettiest name in all the language.'

'I should like it very much.'

'My dear Roger always loved that name better than any other; ten times better. I used to wish sometimes that I'd been called Mary.'

'Did he! Why?'

'He once had a sister called Mary; such a beautiful creature! I declare I sometimes think you are like her.'

'Oh, dear! then she must have been beautiful indeed,' said Mary, laughing.

'She was very beautiful. I just remember her – oh, so beautiful! she was quite a poor girl, you know; and so was I then. Isn't it odd that I should have to be called "my lady" now? Do you know, Miss Thorne – '

'Mary! Mary! 'said her guest.

'Ah, yes; but somehow, I hardly like to make so free; but, as I was saying, I do so dislike being called "my lady:" I always think the people are laughing at me; and so they are.'

'Oh, nonsense!'

'Yes, they are though: poor dear Roger, he used to call me "my lady" just to make fun of me; I didn't mind it so much from him. But, Miss Thorne – '

'Mary, Mary, Mary.'

'Ah, well! I shall do it in time. But, Miss – Mary, ha! ha! ha! never mind, let me alone. But what I want to say is this: do you think I could drop it? Hannah says, that if I go the right way about it she is sure I can.'

'Oh! but, Lady Scatcherd, you shouldn't think of such a thing.'

'Shouldn't I now?'

'Oh, no; for your husband's sake you should be proud of it. He gained great honour, you know.'

'Ah, well,' said she, sighing after a short pause; 'if you think it will do him any good, of course I'll put up with it. And then I know Louis would be mad if I talked of such a thing. But, Miss Thorne, dear, a woman like me don't like to have to be made a fool of all the days of her life if she can help it.'

'But, Lady Scatcherd,' said Mary, when this question of the title had been duly settled, and her ladyship made to understand that she must bear the burden for the rest of her life, 'but, Lady Scatcherd, you were speaking of Sir Roger's sister; what became of her?'

'Oh, she did very well at last, as Sir Roger did himself; but in early life she was very unfortunate – just at the time of my marriage with dear Roger – ,' and then, just as she was about to commence so much as she knew of the history of Mary Scatcherd, she remembered that the author of her sister-in-law's misery had been a Thorne, a brother of the doctor; and, therefore, as she presumed, a relative of her guest; and suddenly she became mute.

'Well,' said Mary; 'just as you were married, Lady Scatcherd?'

Poor Lady Scatcherd had very little worldly knowledge, and did not in the least know how to turn the conversation or escape from the trouble into which she had fallen. All manner of reflections began to crowd upon her. In her early days she had known very little of the Thornes, nor had she thought much of them since, except as regarded her friend the doctor; but at this moment she began for the first time to remember that she had never heard of more than two brothers in the family. Who then could have been Mary's father? She felt at once that it would be improper for her to say anything as to Henry Thorne's terrible faults and sudden fate; – improper, also, to say more about Mary Scatcherd; but she was quite unable to drop the matter otherwise than abruptly, and with a start.

'She was very unfortunate, you say, Lady Scatcherd?'

'Yes, Miss Thorne; Mary, I mean – never mind me – I shall do it in time. Yes, she was; but now I think of it, I had better say nothing more about it. There are reasons, and I ought not to have spoken of it. You won't be provoked with me, will you?'

Mary assured her that she would not be provoked, and of course asked no more questions about Mary Scatcherd; nor did she think much more about it. It was not so however with her ladyship, who could not keep herself from reflecting that the old clergyman in the Close at Barchester certainly had but two sons, one of whom was now the doctor at Greshamsbury, and the other of whom had perished so wretchedly at the gate of that farmyard. Who then was the father of Mary Thorne?

The days passed very quietly at Boxall Hill. Every morning Mary went out on her donkey, who justified by his demeanour and all that had been said in his praise; then she would read or draw, then walk with Lady Scatcherd, then dine, then walk again; and so the days passed quietly away. Once or twice a week the doctor would come over and drink his tea there, riding home in the cool of the evening. Mary also received one visit from her friend Patience.

So the days passed quietly away till the tranquillity of the house was suddenly broken by tidings from London. Lady Scatcherd received a letter from her son, contained in three lines, in which he intimated that on the following day he meant to honour her with a visit. He had intended, he said, to have gone to Brighton with some friends; but as he felt himself a little out of sorts, he would postpone his marine trip and do his mother the grace of spending a few days with her.

This news was not very pleasant to Mary, by whom it had been understood, as it had also by her uncle, that Lady Scatcherd would have the house to herself; but as there were no means of preventing the evil, Mary could only inform the doctor, and prepare herself to meet Sir Louis Scatcherd.

CHAPTER XXVIII

The Doctor Hears Something to His Advantage

Sir Louis Scatcherd had told his mother that he was rather out of sorts, and when he reached Boxall Hill it certainly did not appear that he had given any exaggerated statement of his own maladies. He certainly was a good deal out of sorts. He had had more than one attack of delirium tremens since his father's death, and had almost been at death's door.

Nothing had been said about this by Dr Thorne at Boxall Hill; but he was by no means ignorant of his ward's state. Twice he had gone up to London to visit him; twice he had begged him to go down into the country and place himself under his mother's care. On the last occasion, the doctor had threatened him with all manner of pains and penalties: with pains, as to his speedy departure from this world and all its joys; and with penalties, in the shape of poverty if that departure should by any chance be retarded. But these threats had at the moment been in vain, and the doctor had compromised matters by inducing Sir Louis to promise that he would go to Brighton. The baronet, however, who was at length frightened by some renewed attack, gave up his Brighton scheme, and, without any notice to the doctor, hurried down to Boxall Hill.

Mary did not see him on the first day of his coming, but the doctor did. He received such intimation of the visit as enabled him to be at the house soon after the young man's arrival; and, knowing that his assistance might be necessary, he rode over to Boxall Hill. It was a dreadful task to him, this of making the same fruitless endeavour for the son that he had made for the father, and in the same house. But he was bound by every consideration to perform the task. He had promised the father that he would do for the son all that was in his power; and he had, moreover, the consciousness, that should Sir Louis succeed in destroying himself, the next heir to all the property was his own niece, Mary Thorne.

He found Sir Louis in a low, wretched, miserable state. Though he was a drunkard as his father was, he was not at all such a drunkard as was his father. The physical capacities of the men were very different. The daily amount of alcohol which the father had consumed would have burnt up the son in a week; whereas, though the son was continually tipsy, what he swallowed would hardly have had an injurious effect upon the father.

'You are all wrong, quite wrong,' said Sir Louis, petulantly; 'it isn't that at all. I have taken nothing this week past – literally nothing. I think it's the liver.'

Dr Thorne wanted no one to tell him what was the matter with his ward. It was his liver; his liver, and his head, and his stomach, and his heart. Every organ in his body had been destroyed, or was in course of destruction. His father had killed himself with brandy; the son, more elevated in his tastes, was doing the same thing with curaçoa, maraschino, and cherry-bounce.*

'Sir Louis,' said the doctor – he was obliged to be much more punctilious with him than he had been with the contractor – 'the matter is in your own hands entirely: if you cannot keep your lips from that accursed poison, you have nothing in this world to look forward to; nothing, nothing!'

Mary proposed to return with her uncle to Greshamsbury, and he was at first well inclined that she should do so. But this idea was overruled, partly in compliance with Lady Scatcherd's entreaties, and partly because it would have seemed as though they had both thought the presence of its owner had made the house an unfit habitation for decent people. The doctor therefore returned, leaving Mary there; and Lady Scatcherd busied herself between her two guests.

On the next day Sir Louis was able to come down to a late dinner, and Mary was introduced to him. He had dressed himself in his best array; and as he had – at any rate for the present moment – been frightened out of his libations, he was prepared to make himself as agreeable as possible. His mother waited on him almost as a slave might have done; but she seemed to do so with the fear of a slave rather than the love of a mother. She was fidgety in her attentions, and worried him by endeavouring to make her evening sitting-room agreeable.

But Sir Louis, though he was not very sweetly behaved under these manipulations from his mother's hands, was quite complaisant to Miss Thorne; nay, after the expiration of a week he was almost more than complaisant. He piqued himself on his gallantry, and now found that, in the otherwise dull seclusion of Boxall Hill, he had a good opportunity of exercising it. To do him justice it must be admitted that he would not have been incapable of a decent career had he stumbled upon some girl who could have loved him before he stumbled upon his maraschino bottle. Such might have been the case with many a lost rake. The things that are bad are accepted because the things that are good do not come easily in his way. How many a miserable father reviles with bitterness of spirit the low tastes of his son, who has done nothing to provide his child with higher pleasures!

Sir Louis – partly in the hopes of Mary's smiles, and partly frightened by the doctor's threats – did, for a while, keep himself within decent bounds. He did not usually appear before Mary's eyes till three or four in the afternoon; but when he did come forth, he came forth sober and resolute to please. His mother was delighted, and was not slow to sing his praises; and even the doctor, who now visited Boxall Hill more frequently than ever, began to have some hopes.

One constant subject, I must not say of conversation, on the part of Lady Scatcherd, but rather of declamation, had hitherto been the beauty and manly attributes of Frank Gresham. She had hardly ceased to talk to Mary of the infinite good qualities of the young squire, and especially of his prowess in the matter of Mr Moffat, Mary had listened to all this eloquence, not perhaps with inattention, but without much reply. She had not been exactly sorry to hear Frank talked about; indeed, had she been so minded, she could herself have said something on the same subject; but she did not wish to take Lady Scatcherd altogether into her confidence, and she had been unable to say much about Frank Gresham without doing so. Lady Scatcherd had, therefore, gradually conceived the idea that her darling was not a favourite with her guest.

Now, therefore, she changed the subject; and, as her own son was behaving with such unexampled propriety, she dropped Frank and confined her eulogies to Louis. He had been a little wild, she admitted; young men so often were so; but she hoped that it was now over.

'He does still take a little drop of those French drinks in the morning,' said Lady Scatcherd, in her confidence; for she was too honest to be false, even in her own cause. 'He does do that, I know: but that's nothing, my dear, to swilling all day; and everything can't be done at once, can it, Miss Thorne?'

On this subject Mary found her tongue loosened. She could not talk about Frank Gresham, but she could speak with hope to the mother of her only son. She could say that Sir Louis was still very young; that there was reason to trust that he might now reform; that his present conduct was apparently good; and that he appeared capable of better things. So much she did say; and the mother took her sympathy for more than it was worth.

On this matter, and on this matter perhaps alone, Sir Louis and Lady Scatcherd were in accord. There was much to recommend Mary to the baronet; not only did he see her to be beautiful, and perceive her to be attractive and ladylike; but she was also the niece of the man who, for the present, held the purse-strings of his wealth. Mary, it is true, had no fortune. But Sir Louis knew that she was acknowledged to be a lady; and he was ambitious that his 'lady' should be a lady. There was also much to recommend Mary to the mother, to any mother; and thus it came to pass, that Miss Thorne had no obstacle between her and the dignity of being Lady Scatcherd the second; – no obstacle whatever, if only she could bring herself to wish it.

It was some time – two or three weeks, perhaps – before Mary's mind was first opened to this new brilliancy in her prospects. Sir Louis at first was rather afraid of her, and did not declare his admiration in any very determined terms. He certainly paid her many compliments which, from any one else, she would have regarded as abominable. But she did not expect great things from the baronet's taste: she concluded that he was only doing what he thought a gentleman should do; and she was willing to forgive much for Lady Scatcherd's sake.

His first attempts were, perhaps, more ludicrous than passionate. He was still too much an invalid to take walks, and Mary was therefore saved from his company in her rambles; but he had a horse of his own at Boxall Hill, and had been advised to ride by the doctor. Mary also rode – on a donkey only, it is true – but Sir Louis found himself bound in gallantry to accompany her. Mary's steed had answered every expectation, and proved himself very quiet; so quiet that, without the admonition of a cudgel behind him, he could hardly be persuaded into the demurest trot. Now, as Sir Louis's horse was of a very different mettle, he found it rather difficult not to step faster than his inamorata; and, let him struggle as he would, was generally so far ahead as to be debarred the delights of conversation.

When for the second time he proposed to accompany her, Mary did what she could to hinder it. She saw that he had been rather ashamed of the manner in which his companion was mounted, and she herself would have enjoyed her ride much more without him. He was an invalid, however; it was necessary to make much of him, and Mary did not absolutely refuse his offer.

'Lady Scatcherd,' said he, as they were standing at the door previous to mounting – he always called his mother Lady Scatcherd – 'why don't you have a horse for Miss Thorne? This donkey is – is – really is, so very – very – can't go at all, you know?'

Lady Scatcherd began to declare that she would willingly have got a pony if Mary would have let her do so.

'Oh, no, Lady Scatcherd; not on any account. I do like the donkey so much – I do indeed.'

'But he won't go,' said Sir Louis. 'And for a person who rides like you, Miss Thorne – such a horsewoman you know – why, you know, Lady Scatcherd, it's positively ridiculous; d— absurd, you know.'

And then, with an angry look at his mother, he mounted his horse, and was soon leading the way down the avenue.

'Miss Thorne,' said he, pulling himself up at the gate, 'if I had known that I was to be so extremely happy as to have found you here, I would have brought you down the most beautiful creature, an Arab. She belongs to my friend Jenkins; but I wouldn't have stood at any price in getting her for you. By Jove! if you were on that mare, I'd back you, for style and appearance, against anything in Hyde Park.'

The offer of this sporting wager, which naturally would have been very gratifying to Mary, was lost upon her, for Sir Louis had again unwittingly got on in advance, but he stopped himself in time to hear Mary again declare her passion was a donkey.

'If you could only see Jenkins's little mare, Miss Thorne! Only say the word, and she shall be down here before the week's out. Price shall be no obstacle – none whatever. By Jove, what a pair you would be!'

This generous offer was repeated four or five times; but on each occasion Mary only half heard what was said, and on each occasion the baronet was far too much in advance to hear Mary's reply. At last he recollected that he wanted to call on one of the tenants, and begged his companion to allow him to ride on.

'If you at all dislike being left alone, you know – '

'Oh dear no, not at all, Sir Louis. I am quite used to it.'

'Because I don't care about it, you know; only I can't make this horse of mine walk the same pace as that brute.'

'You mustn't abuse my pet, Sir Louis.'

'It's a d— shame on my mother's part,' said Sir Louis, who, even when in his best behaviour, could not quite give up his ordinary mode of conversation. 'When she was fortunate enough to get such a girl as you to come and stay with her, she ought to have had something proper for her to ride upon; but I'll look to it as soon as I am a little stronger, you see if I don't;' and, so saying, Sir Louis trotted off, leaving Mary in peace with her donkey.

Sir Louis had now been living cleanly and forswearing sack* for what was to him a very long period, and his health felt the good effects of it. No one rejoiced at this more cordially than did the doctor. To rejoice at it was with him a point of conscience. He could not help telling himself now and again that, circumstanced as he was, he was most specially bound to take joy in any sign of reformation which the baronet might show. Not to do so would be almost tantamount to wishing that he might die in order that Mary might inherit his wealth; and, therefore, the doctor did with all his energy devote himself to the difficult task of hoping and striving that Sir Louis might yet live to enjoy what was his own. But the task was altogether a difficult one, for as Sir Louis became stronger in health, so also did he become more exorbitant in his demands on the doctor's patience, and more repugnant to the doctor's tastes.

In his worst fits of disreputable living he was ashamed to apply to his guardian for money; and in his worst fits of illness he was, through fear, somewhat patient under his doctor's hands; but just at present he had nothing of which to be ashamed, and was not at all patient.

'Doctor,' – said he, one day, at Boxall Hill – 'how about those Greshamsbury title-deeds?'

'Oh, that will all be properly settled between my lawyer and your own.'

'Oh – ah – yes; no doubt the lawyers will settle it: settle it with a fine bill of costs, of course. But, as Finnie says,' – Finnie was Sir Louis's legal adviser – 'I have got a tremendously large interest at stake in this matter; eighty thousand pounds is no joke. It ain't everybody that can shell out eighty thousand pounds when they're wanted; and I should like to know how the thing's going on. I've a right to ask, you know; eh, doctor?'

'The title-deeds of a large portion of the Greshamsbury estate will be placed with the mortgage-deeds before the end of next month.'

'Oh, that's all right. I choose to know about these things; for though my father did make such a con – found – ed will, that's no reason I shouldn't know how things are going.'

'You shall know everything that I know, Sir Louis.'

'And now, doctor, what are we to do about money?'

'About money?'

'Yes; money, rhino, ready! "put money in your purse,* and cut a dash;" eh, doctor? Not that I want to cut a dash. No, I'm going on the quiet line altogether now: I've done with all that sort of thing.'

'I'm heartily glad of it; heartily,' said the doctor.

'Yes, I'm not going to make way for my far-away cousin yet; not if I know it, at least. I shall soon be all right now, doctor; shan't I?'

'"All right" is a long word, Sir Louis. But I do hope you will be all right in time, if you will live with decent prudence. You shouldn't take that filth in the morning though.'

'Filth in the morning! That's my mother, I suppose! That's

her ladyship! She's been talking, has she? Don't you believe her, doctor. There's not a young man in Barsetshire is going more regular, all right within the posts, than I am.'

The doctor was obliged to acknowledge that there did seem to be some improvement.

'And now, doctor, how about money? Eh?'

Doctor Thorne, like other guardians similarly circumstanced, began to explain that Sir Louis had already had a good deal of money, and had begun also to promise that more should be forthcoming in the event of good behaviour, when he was somewhat suddenly interrupted by Sir Louis.

'Well, now, I'll tell you what, doctor; I've got a bit of news for you; something that I think will astonish you.'

The doctor opened his eyes, and tried to look as though ready to be surprised.

'Something that will really make you look about; and something, too, that will be very much to the hearer's advantage, – as the newspaper advertisements say.'

'Something to my advantage?' said the doctor.

'Well, I hope you'll think so. Doctor, what would you think now of my getting married?'

'I should be delighted to hear it – more delighted that I can express; that is, of course, if you were to marry well. It was your father's most eager wish that you should marry early.'

'That's partly my reason,' said the young hypocrite. 'But then, if I marry I must have an income fit to live on; eh, doctor?'

The doctor had some fear that his interesting protégé was desirous of a wife for the sake of the income, instead of desiring the income for the sake of the wife. But let the cause be what it would, marriage would probably be good for him; and he had no hesitation, therefore, telling him, that if he married well, he should be put in possession of sufficient income to maintain the new Lady Scatcherd in a manner becoming her dignity.

'As to marrying well,' said Sir Louis, 'you, I take it, will be the last man, doctor, to quarrel with my choice.'

'Shall I?' said the doctor, smiling.

'Well, you won't disapprove, I guess, as the Yankee says. What would you think of Miss Mary Thorne?'

It must be said in Sir Louis's favour that he had probably no idea whatever of the estimation in which such young ladies as Mary Thorne are held by those who are nearest and dearest to them. He had no sort of conception that she was regarded by her uncle as an inestimable treasure, almost too precious to be rendered up to the arms of any man; and infinitely beyond any price in silver and gold, baronets' incomes of eight or ten thousand a year, and such coins usually current in the world's markets. He was a rich man and a baronet, and Mary was an unmarried girl without a portion. In Sir Louis's estimation he was offering everything, and asking for nothing. He certainly had some idea that girls were apt to be coy, and required a little wooing in the shape of presents, civil speeches – perhaps kisses also. The civil speeches he had, he thought, done, and imagined that they had been well received. The other things were to follow; an Arab pony, for instance, – and the kisses probably with it; and then all these difficulties would be smoothed.

But he did not for a moment conceive that there would be any difficulty with the uncle. How should there be? Was he not a baronet with ten thousand a year coming to him? Had he not everything which fathers want for portionless daughters, and uncles for dependent nieces? Might he not well inform the doctor that he had something to tell him for his advantage?

And yet, to tell the truth, the doctor did not seem to be overjoyed when the announcement was first made to him. He was by no means overjoyed. On the contrary, even Sir Louis could perceive his guardian's surprise was altogether unmixed with delight.

What a question was this that was asked him! What would he think of a marriage between Mary Thorne – his Mary and Sir Louis Scatcherd? Between the alpha of the whole alphabet, and him whom he could not but regard as almost the omega! Think of it! Why he would think of it as though a lamb and a wolf were to stand at the altar together. Had Sir Louis been a Hottentot, or an Esquimaux, the proposal could not have astonished him more. The two persons were so totally of a different class, that the idea of the one falling in love with the other had never occurred to him. 'What would you think of Miss Mary Thorne?' Sir Louis had asked; and the doctor, instead of answering him with ready and pleased alacrity, stood silent, thunderstruck with amazement.

'Well, wouldn't she be a good wife?' said Sir Louis, rather in a tone of disgust at the evident disapproval shown at his choice. 'I thought you'd have been so delighted.'

'Mary Thorne!' ejaculated the doctor at last. 'Have you spoken to my niece about this, Sir Louis?'

'Well, I have, and yet I haven't; I haven't, and yet in a manner I have.'

'I don't understand you,' said the doctor.

'Why, you see, I haven't exactly popped to her yet; but I have been doing the civil; and if she's up to snuff, as I take her to be, she knows very well what I'm after by this time.'

Up to snuff! Mary Thorne, his Mary, up to snuff! To snuff too of such a very disagreeable description!

'I think, Sir Louis, that you are in mistake about this. I think you will find that Mary will not be disposed to avail herself of the great advantages – for great they undoubtedly are – which you are able to offer to your intended wife. If you will take my advice you will give up thinking of Mary. She would not suit you.'

'Not suit me! Oh, but I think she just would. She's got no money, you mean?'

'No, I did not mean that. It will not signify to you whether your wife has money or not. You need not look for money. But you should think of some one more nearly of your own temperament. I am quite sure that my niece would refuse you.'

These last words the doctor uttered with much emphasis. His intention was to make the baronet understand that the matter was quite hopeless, and to induce him if possible to drop it on the spot. But he did not know Sir Louis; he ranked him too low in the scale of human beings, and gave him no credit for any strength of character. Sir Louis in his way did love Mary Thorne; and could not bring himself to believe that Mary did not, or at any rate would not soon return his passion. He was, moreover, sufficiently obstinate, firm we ought perhaps to say, – for his pursuit in this case was certainly not an evil one, – and he at once made up his mind to succeed in spite of the uncle.

'If she consents, however, you will do so too?' asked he.

'It is impossible she should consent,' said the doctor.

'Impossible! I don't see anything at all impossible. But if she does?'

'But she won't.'

'Very well, – that's to be seen. But just tell me this; if she does, will you consent?'

'The stars would fall first. It's all nonsense. Give it up, my dear friend; believe me you are only preparing unhappiness for yourself;' and the doctor put his hand kindly on the young man's arm. 'She will not, cannot accept such an offer.'

'Will not! cannot!' said the baronet, thinking over all the reasons which in his estimation could possibly be inducing the doctor to be so hostile to his views, and shaking the hand off his arm. 'Will not! cannot! But come, doctor, answer my question fairly. If she'll have me for better or worse, you won't say aught against it; will you?'

'But she won't have you; why should you give her and yourself the pain of a refusal?'

'Oh, as for that, I must stand my chance like another. And as for her, why d—, doctor, you wouldn't have me believe that any young lady thinks it so very dreadful to have a baronet with ten thousand pounds a year at her feet, specially when that same baronet ain't very old, nor yet particularly ugly. I ain't so green as that, doctor.'

'I suppose she must go through it, then,' said the doctor, musing.

'But, Dr Thorne, I did look for a kinder answer from you, considering all that you say so often about your great friendship for my father. I did think you'd at any rate answer me when I asked you a question!'

But the doctor did not want to answer that special question. Could it be possible that Mary should wish to marry this odious man, could such a state of things be imagined to be the case, he would not refuse his consent, infinitely as he would be disgusted by her choice. But he would not give Sir Louis any excuse for telling Mary that her uncle approved of so odious a match.

'I cannot say that in any case I should approve of such a marriage, Sir Louis. I cannot bring myself to say so; for I know it would make you both miserable. But on that matter my niece will choose wholly for herself.'

'And about the money, doctor?'

'If you marry a decent woman you shall not want the means of supporting her decently,' and so saying the doctor walked away, leaving Sir Louis to his meditations.

CHAPTER XXIX

The Donkey Ride

Sir Louis, when left to himself, was slightly dismayed and somewhat discouraged; but he was not induced to give up his object. The first effort of his mind was made in conjecturing what private motive Dr Thorne could possibly have in wishing to debar his niece from marrying a rich young baronet. That the objection was personal to himself, Sir Louis did not for a moment imagine. Could it be that the doctor did not wish that his niece should be richer, and grander, and altogether bigger than himself? Or was it possible that his guardian was anxious to prevent him from marrying from some view to the reversion of the large fortune? That there was some such reason, Sir Louis was well sure; but let it be what it might, he would get the better of the doctor. 'He knew,' so he said to himself, 'what stuff girls were made of. Baronets did not grow like blackberries.' And so, assuring himself with such philosophy, he determined to make his offer.

The time he selected for doing this was the hour before dinner; but on the day on which his conversation with the doctor had taken place, he was deterred by the presence of a strange visitor. To account for this strange visit it will be necessary that we should return to Greshamsbury for a few minutes.

Frank, when he returned home for his summer vacation, found that Mary had again flown; and the very fact of her absence added fuel to the fire of his love, more perhaps than even her presence might have done. For the flight of the quarry ever adds eagerness to the pursuit of the huntsman. Lady Arabella, moreover, had a bitter enemy; a foe, utterly opposed to her side in the contest, where she had once fondly looked for her staunchest ally. Frank was now in the habit of corresponding with Miss Dunstable, and received from her most energetic admonitions to be true to the love which he had sworn. True to it he resolved to be; and therefore, when he found that Mary was flown, he resolved to fly after her.

He did not, however, do this till he had been in a measure provoked to it by the sharp-tongued cautions and blunted irony of his mother. It was not enough for her that she had banished

Mary out of the parish, and made Dr Thorne's life miserable; not enough that she harassed her husband with harangues on the constant subject of Frank's marrying money, and dismayed Beatrice with invectives against the iniquity of her friend. The snake was so but scotched;* to kill it outright she must induce Frank utterly to renounce Miss Thorne.

This task she essayed, but not exactly with success. 'Well, mother,' said Frank at last, turning very red, partly with shame, and partly with indignation, as he made the frank avowal, 'since you will press me about it, I tell you fairly that my mind is made up to marry Mary sooner or later, if – '

'Oh, Frank! good heavens! you wicked boy; you are saying this purposely to drive me distracted.'

'If,' continued Frank, not attending to his mother's interjections, 'if she will consent.'

'Consent!' said Lady Arabella. 'Oh, heavens!' and falling into the corner of the sofa, she buried her face in her handkerchief.

'Yes, mother, if she will consent. And now that I have told you so much, it is only just that I should tell you this also; that as far as I can see at present I have no reason to hope that she will do so.'

'Oh, Frank, the girl is doing all she can to catch you!' said Lady Arabella, – not prudently.

'No, mother; there you wrong her altogether; wrong her most cruelly.'

'You ungracious, wicked boy! you call me cruel!'

'I don't call you cruel; but you do wrong her cruelly, most cruelly. When I have spoken to her about this – for I have spoken to her – she has behaved exactly as you would have wished her to do; but not at all as I wished her. She has given me no encouragement. You have turned her out among you' – Frank was beginning to be very bitter now – 'but she has done nothing to deserve it. If there has been any fault it has been mine. But it is well that we should all understand each other. My intention is to marry Mary if I can.' And, so speaking, certainly without due filial respect, he turned towards the door.

'Frank,' said his mother, raising herself up with energy to make one last appeal. 'Frank, do you wish to see me die of a broken heart?'

'You know, mother, I would wish to make you happy, if I could.'

'If you wish to see me ever happy again, if you do not wish to see me sink broken-hearted to my grave, you must give up this mad idea, Frank,' – and now all Lady Arabella's energy came out. 'Frank, there is but one course left open to you. You MUST *marry money*.' And then Lady Arabella stood up before her son as Lady Macbeth might have stood, had Lady Macbeth lived to have a son of Frank's years.

'Miss Dunstable, I suppose,' said Frank, scornfully. 'No, mother; I made an ass, and worse than an ass of myself once in that way, and I won't do it again. I hate money.'

'Oh, Frank!'

'I hate money.'

'But, Frank, the estate?'

'I hate the estate – at least I shall hate it if I am expected to buy it as such a price as that. The estate is my father's.'

'Oh, no, Frank; it is not.'

'It is in the sense I mean. He may do with it as he pleases; he will never have a word of complaint from me. I am ready to go into a profession tomorrow. I'll be a lawyer, or a doctor, or an engineer; I don't care what.' Frank, in his enthusiasm, probably overlooked some of the preliminary difficulties. 'Or I'll take a farm under him, and earn my bread that way; but, mother, don't talk to me any more about marrying money.' And, so saying, Frank left the room.

Frank, it will be remembered, was twenty-one when he was first introduced to the reader; he is now twenty-two. It may be said that there was a great difference between his character then and now. A year at that period will make a great difference; but the change has been, not in his character, but in his feelings.

Frank went out from his mother and immediately ordered his black horse to be got ready for him. He would at once go over to Boxall Hill. He went himself to the stables to give his orders; and as he returned to get his gloves and whip he met Beatrice in the corridor.

'Beatrice,' said he, 'step in here,' and she followed him into his room. 'I'm not going to bear this any longer; I'm going to Boxall Hill.'

'Oh, Frank! how can you be so imprudent?'

'You, at any rate, have some decent feeling for Mary. I believe you have some regard for her; and therefore I tell you. Will you send her any message?'

'Oh, yes; my best, best love; that is if you will see her; but Frank, you are very foolish, very; and she will be infinitely distressed.'

'Do not mention this, that is, not at present; not that I mean to make any secret of it. I shall tell my father everything. I'm off now!' and then, paying no attention to her remonstrance, he turned down the stairs and was soon on horseback.

He took the road to Boxall Hill, but he did not ride very fast: he did not go jauntily as a jolly, thriving wooer;* but musingly, and often with diffidence, meditating every now and then whether it would not be better for him to turn back: to turn back – but not from fear of his mother; not from prudential motives; not because that often-repeated lesson as to marrying money was beginning to take effect; not from such causes as these; but because he doubted how he might be received by Mary.

He did, it is true, think something about his worldly prospects. He had talked rather grandiloquently to his mother as to his hating money, and hating the estate. His mother's never-ceasing worldly cares on such subjects perhaps demanded that a little grandiloquence should be opposed to them. But Frank did not hate the estate; nor did he at all hate the position of an English country gentleman. Miss Dunstable's eloquence, however, rang in his ears. For Miss Dunstable had an eloquence of her own, even in her letters. 'Never let them talk you out of your own true, honest, hearty feelings,' she had said. 'Greshamsbury is a very nice place, I am sure; and I hope I shall see it some day; but all its green knolls are not half so nice, should not be half so precious, as the pulses of your own heart. That is your own estate, your own, your very own – your own and another's; whatever may go to the money-lenders, don't send that there. Don't mortgage that, Mr Gresham.'

'No,' said Frank, pluckily, as he put his horse into a faster trot, 'I won't mortgage that. They may do what they like with the estate; but my heart's my own,' and so speaking to himself, almost aloud, he turned a corner of the road rapidly and came at once upon the doctor.

'Hallo, doctor! is that you?' said Frank, rather disgusted.

'What! Frank! I hardly expected to meet you here,' said Dr Thorne, not much better pleased.

They were now not above a mile from Boxall Hill, and the

doctor, therefore, could not but surmise whither Frank was going. They had repeatedly met since Frank's return from Cambridge, both in the village and in the doctor's house; but not a word had been said between them about Mary beyond what the merest courtesy had required. Not that each did not love the other sufficiently to make a full confidence between them desirable to both; but neither had had the courage to speak out.

Nor had either of them the courage to do so now. 'Yes,' said Frank, blushing, 'I am going to Lady Scatcherd's. Shall I find the ladies at home?'

'Yes; Lady Scatcherd is there; but Sir Louis is there also – an invalid: perhaps you would not wish to meet him.'

'Oh! I don't mind,' said Frank, trying to laugh; 'he won't bite, I suppose?'

The doctor longed in his heart to pray Frank to return with him; not to go and make further mischief; not to do that which might cause a more bitter estrangement between himself and the squire. But he had not the courage to do it. He could not bring himself to accuse Frank of being in love with his niece. So after a few more senseless words on either side, words which each knew to be senseless as he uttered them, they both rode on their own ways.

And then the doctor silently, and almost unconsciously, made such a comparison between Louis Scatcherd and Frank Gresham as Hamlet made between the dead and live king. It was Hyperion to a satyr.* Was it not as impossible that Mary should not love the one, as that she should love the other? Frank's offer of his affections had at first probably been but a boyish ebullition of feeling; but if it should now be, that this had grown into a manly and disinterested love, how could Mary remain unmoved? What could her heart want more, better, more beautiful, more rich than such a love as his? Was he not personally all that a girl could like? Were not his disposition, mind, character, acquirements, all such as women most delight to love? Was it not impossible that Mary should be indifferent to him?

So meditated the doctor as he rode along, with only too true a knowledge of human nature. Ah! it was impossible, it was quite impossible that Mary should be indifferent. She had never been indifferent since Frank had uttered his first half-joking word of love. Such things are more important to women than

they are to men, to girls than they are to boys. When Frank had
first told her that he loved her; aye, months before that, when
he merely looked his love, her heart had received the whisper,
had acknowledged the glance, unconscious as she was herself,
and resolved as she was to rebuke his advances. When, in her
hearing, he had said soft nothings to Patience Oriel, a hated,
irrepressible tear had gathered in her eye. When he had pressed
in his warm, loving grasp the hand which she had offered him
as a token of mere friendship, her heart had forgiven him the
treachery, nay, almost thanked him for it, before her eyes or her
words had been ready to rebuke him. When the rumour of his
liaison with Miss Dunstable reached her ears, when she heard
of Miss Dunstable's fortune, she had wept, wept outright, in her
chamber − wept, as she said to herself, to think that he should
be so mercenary; but she had wept, as she should have said to
herself, at finding that he was so faithless. Then, when she knew
at last that this rumour was false, when she found that she was
banished from Greshamsbury for his sake, when she was forced
to retreat with her friend Patience, how could she but love him,
in that he was not mercenary? How could she not love him in
that he was so faithful?

It was impossible that she should not love him. Was he not
the brightest and the best of men* that she had ever seen, or
was like to see? − that she could possibly ever see, she would
have said to herself, could she have brought herself to own the
truth? And then, when she heard how true he was, how he
persisted against father, mother, and sisters, how could it be
that that should not be a merit in her eyes which was so great a
fault in theirs? When Beatrice, with would-be solemn face, but
with eyes beaming with feminine affection, would gravely talk
of Frank's tender love as a terrible misfortune, as a misfortune
to them all, to Mary herself as well as others, how could Mary
do other than love him? 'Beatrice is his sister,' she would say
within her own mind, 'otherwise she would never talk like this;
were she not his sister, she could not but know the value of such
love as this.' Ah! yes; Mary did love him; love him with all the
strength of her heart; and the strength of her heart was very
great. And now by degrees, in those lonely donkey-rides at
Boxall Hill, in those solitary walks, she was beginning to own
to herself the truth.

And now that she did own it, what should be her course?

What should she do, how should she act if this loved one persevered in his love? And, ah! what should she do, how should she act if he did not persevere? Could it be that there should be happiness in store for her? Was it not too clear that, let the matter go how it would, there was no happiness in store for her? Much as she might love Frank Gresham, she could never consent to be his wife unless the squire would smile on her as his daughter-in-law. The squire had been all that was kind, all that was affectionate. And then, too, Lady Arabella! As she thought of the Lady Arabella a sterner form of thought came across her brow. Why should Lady Arabella rob her of her heart's joy? What was Lady Arabella that she, Mary Thorne, need quail before her? Had Lady Arabella stood only in her way, Lady Arabella, flanked by the De Courcy legion, Mary felt that she could have demanded Frank's hand as her own before them all without a blush of shame or a moment's hesitation. Thus, when her heart was all but ready to collapse within her, would she gain some little strength by thinking of the Lady Arabella.

'Please, my lady, here be young squire Gresham,' said one of the untutored servants at Boxall Hill, opening Lady Scatcherd's little parlour door as her ladyship was amusing herself by pulling down and turning, and refolding, and putting up again, a heap of household linen which was kept in a huge press for the express purpose of supplying her with occupation.

Lady Scatcherd, holding a vast counterpane in her arms, looked back over her shoulders and perceived that Frank was in the room. Down went the counterpane on the ground, and Frank soon found himself in the very position which that useful article had so lately filled.

'Oh, Master Frank! oh, Master Frank!' said her ladyship, almost in an hysterical fit of joy; and then she hugged and kissed him as she had never kissed and hugged her own son since that son had first left the parent nest.

Frank bore it patiently and with a merry laugh. 'But, Lady Scatcherd,' said he, 'what will they all say? you forget I am a man now,' and he stooped his head as she again pressed her lips upon his forehead.

'I don't care what none of 'em say,' said her ladyship, quite going back to her old days; 'I will kiss my own boy; so I will. Eh, but, Master Frank, this is good of you. A sight of you is good for sore eyes; and my eyes have been sore enough too since I saw you;' and she put her apron up to wipe away a tear.

'Yes,' said Frank, gently trying to disengage himself, but not successfully; 'yes, you have had a great loss, Lady Scatcherd. I was so sorry when I heard of your grief – '

'You always had a soft, kind heart, Master Frank; so you had, God's blessing on you! What a fine man you have grown! Deary me! Well, it seems as though it were only just t'other day like.' And she pushed him a little off from her, so that she might look the better into his face.

'Well. Is it all right? I suppose you would hardly know me again now I've got a pair of whiskers?'

'Know you! I should know you well if I saw but the heel of your foot. Why, what a head of hair you have got, and so dark too! but it doesn't curl as it used once.' And she stroked his hair, and looked into his eyes, and put her hand to his cheeks. 'You'll think me an old fool, Master Frank: I know that; but you may think what you like. If I live for the next twenty years you'll always be my own boy; so you will.'

By degrees, slow degrees, Frank managed to change the conversation, and to induce Lady Scatcherd to speak on some topic other than his own infantine perfections. He affected an indifference as he spoke of her guest, which would have deceived no one but Lady Scatcherd; but her it did deceive; and then he asked where Mary was.

'She's just out on her donkey – somewhere about the place. She rides on a donkey mostly every day. But you'll stop and take a bit of dinner with us? Eh, now do 'ee, Master Frank!'

But Master Frank excused himself. He did not choose to pledge himself to sit down to dinner with Mary. He did not know in what mood they might return with regard to each other at dinner-time. He said, therefore, that he would walk out and, if possible, find Miss Thorne; and that he would return to the house again before he went.

Lady Scatcherd then began making apologies for Sir Louis. He was an invalid; the doctor had been with him all the morning, and he was not yet out of his room.

These apologies Frank willingly accepted, and then made his way as he could on to the lawn. A gardener, of whom he inquired, offered to go with him in pursuit of Miss Thorne. This assistance, however, he declined, and set forth in quest of her, having learnt what were her most usual haunts. Nor was he directed wrongly; for after walking about twenty minutes, he saw through the trees the legs of a donkey moving on the greensward, at about two hundred yards from him. On that donkey doubtless sat Mary Thorne.

The donkey was coming towards him; not exactly in a straight line, but so much so as to make it impossible that Mary should not see him if he stood still. He did stand still, and soon emerging from the trees, Mary saw him all but close to her.

Her heart gave a leap within her, but she was so far mistress of herself as to repress any very visible sign of outward emotion. She did not fall from her donkey, or scream, or burst into tears. She merely uttered the words, 'Mr Gresham!' in a tone of not unnatural surprise.

'Yes,' said he, trying to laugh, but less successful than she had been in suppressing a show of feeling. 'Mr Gresham! I have come over at last to pay my respects to you. You must have thought me very uncourteous not to do so before.'

This she denied. 'She had not,' she said, 'thought him at all uncivil. She had come to Boxall Hill to be out of the way; and, of course, had not expected any such formalities.' As she uttered this she almost blushed at the abrupt truth of what she was saying. But she was taken so much unawares that she did not know how to make the truth other than abrupt.

'To be out of the way!' said Frank. 'And why should you want to be out of the way?'

'Oh! there were reasons,' said she, laughing. 'Perhaps I have quarrelled dreadfully with my uncle.'

Frank at the present moment had not about him a scrap of badinage. He had not a single easy word at his command. He could not answer her with anything in guise of a joke; so he walked on, not answering at all.

'I hope all my friends at Greshamsbury are well,' said Mary. 'Is Beatrice quite well?'

'Quite well,' said he.

'And Patience?'

'What, Miss Oriel; yes, I believe so. I haven't seen her this day or two.' How was it that Mary felt a little flush of joy, as Frank spoke in this indifferent way about Miss Oriel's health?

'I thought she was always a particular friend of yours,' said she.

'What! who? Miss Oriel? So she is! I like her amazingly; so does Beatrice.' And then he walked about six steps in silence, plucking up courage for the great attempt. He did pluck up his courage and then rushed at once to the attack.

'Mary!' said he, and as he spoke he put his hand on the donkey's neck and looked tenderly into her face. He looked tenderly, and, as Mary's ear at once told her, his voice sounded more soft than it had ever sounded before. 'Mary, do you remember the last time that we were together?'

Mary did remember it well. It was on that occasion when he had treacherously held her hand, on that day when, according to law, he had become a man; when he had outraged all the propriety of the De Courcy interest by offering his love to Mary in Augusta's hearing. Mary did remember it well; but how was she to speak of it? 'It was your birthday, I think,' said she.

'Yes. It was my birthday. I wonder whether you remember what I said to you then?'

'I remember that you were very foolish, Mr Gresham.'

'Mary, I have come to repeat my folly; – that is, if it be folly. I told you then that I loved you, and I dare say that I did so awkwardly, like a boy. Perhaps I may be just as awkward now; but you ought at any rate to believe me when you find that a year has not altered me.'

Mary did not think him at all awkward, and she did believe him. But how was she to answer him? She had not yet taught herself what answer she ought to make if he persisted in his suit. She had hitherto been content to run away from him; but she had done so because she would not submit to be accused of the indelicacy of putting herself in his way. She had rebuked him when he first spoke of his love; but she had done so because she looked on what he said as a boy's nonsense. She had schooled herself in obedience to the Greshamsbury doctrines. Was there any real reason, any reason founded on truth and honesty, why she should not be a fitting wife to Frank Gresham, – Francis Newbold Gresham, of Greshamsbury, though he was, or was to be?

He was well born – as well born as any gentleman in England. She was basely born – as basely born as any lady could be. Was this sufficient bar against such a match? Mary felt in her heart that some twelvemonth since, before she knew what little she did now know of her own story, she would have said it was so.

And would she indulge her own love by inveigling him she loved
into a base marriage? But then reason spoke again. What, after
all, was this blood of which she had taught herself to think so
much? Would she have been more honest, more fit to grace an
honest man's hearthstone, had she been the legitimate descendant of a score of legitimate duchesses? Was it not her first duty
to think of him – of what would make him happy? Then of her
uncle – what he would approve? Then of herself – what would
best become her modesty; her sense of honour? Could it be well
that she should sacrifice the happiness of two persons to a
theoretic love of pure blood?

So she had argued within herself; not now, sitting on the
donkey, with Frank's hand before her on the tame brute's neck;
but on other former occasions as she had ridden along demurely
among those trees. So she had argued; but she had never brought
her arguments to a decision. All manner of thoughts crowded
on her to prevent her doing so. She would think of the squire,
and resolve to reject Frank: and would then remember Lady
Arabella, and resolve to accept him. Her resolutions, however,
were most irresolute; and so, when Frank appeared in person
before her, carrying his heart in his hand, she did not know
what answer to make to him. Thus it was with her as with so
many other maidens similarly circumstanced; at last she left it
all to chance.

'You ought, at any rate, to believe me,' said Frank, 'when you
find that a year has not altered me.'

'A year should have taught you to be wiser,' said she.

'You should have learnt by this time, Mr Gresham, that your
lot and mine are not cast in the same mould; that our stations in
life are different. Would your father or mother approve of your
even coming here to see me?'

Mary, as she spoke these sensible words, felt that they were
'flat, stale, and unprofitable.'* She felt, also, that they were not
true in sense; that they did not come from her heart; that they
were not such as Frank deserved at her hands, and she was
ashamed of herself.

'My father I hope will approve of it,' said he. 'That my mother
should disapprove of it is a misfortune which I cannot help; but
on this point I will take no answer from my father or mother;
the question is one too personal to myself. Mary, if you say that
you will not, or cannot return my love, I will go away; – not

from here only, but from Greshamsbury. My presence shall not
banish you from all you hold dear. If you can honestly say that
I am nothing to you, can be nothing to you, I will then tell my
mother that she may be at ease, and I will go away somewhere
and get over it as I may.' The poor fellow got so far, looking
apparently at the donkey's ears, with hardly a gasp of hope in
his voice, and he so far carried Mary with him that she also had
hardly a gasp of hope in her heart. There he paused for a
moment, and then looking up into her face, he spoke but one
word more. 'But,' said he – and there he stopped. It was all
clearly told in that 'but.' Thus would he do if Mary would
declare that she did not care for him. If, however, she could not
bring herself so to declare, then was he ready to throw his father
and mother to the winds; then would he stand his ground; then
would he look all other difficulties in the face, sure that they
might finally be overcome. Poor Mary! the whole onus of
settling the matter was thus thrown upon her. She had only to
say that he was indifferent to her; – that was all.

If 'all the blood of all the Howards'* had depended upon it,
she could not have brought herself to utter such a falsehood.
Indifferent to her, as he walked there by her donkey's side,
talking thus earnestly of his love for her! Was he not to her like
some god come from the heavens to make her blessed? Did not
the sun shine upon him with a halo, so that he was bright as an
angel? Indifferent to her! Could the open unadulterated truth
have been practicable for her, she would have declared her
indifference in terms that would truly have astonished him. As
it was, she found it easier to say nothing. She bit her lips to keep
herself from sobbing. She struggled hard, but in vain, to prevent
her hands and feet from trembling. She seemed to swing upon
her donkey as though like to fall, and would have given much
to be upon her own feet upon the sward.

'Si la jeunesse savait. . . .'* There is so much in that wicked
old French proverb! Had Frank known more about a woman's
mind – had he, that is, been forty-two instead of twenty-two –
he would at once have been sure of his game, and have felt that
Mary's silence told him all he wished to know. But then, had he
been forty-two instead of twenty-two, he would not have been
so ready to risk the acres of Greshamsbury for the smiles of
Mary Thorne.

'If you can't say one word to comfort me, I will go,' said he, disconsolately. 'I made up my mind to tell you this, and so I came over. I told Lady Scatcherd I should not stay, – not even for dinner.'

'I did not know that you were so hurried,' said she, almost in a whisper.

On a sudden he stood still, and pulling the donkey's rein, caused him to stand still also. The beast required very little persuasion to be so guided, and obligingly remained meekly passive.

'Mary, Mary!' said Frank, throwing his arms round her knees as she sat upon her steed, and pressing his face against her body. 'Mary, you were always honest; be honest now. I love you with all my heart. Will you be my wife?'

But still Mary said not a word. She no longer bit her lips; she was beyond that, and was now using all her efforts to prevent her tears from falling absolutely on her lover's face. She said nothing. She could no more rebuke him now and send him from her than she could encourage him. She could only sit there shaking and crying and wishing she was on the ground. Frank, on the whole, rather liked the donkey. It enabled him to approach somewhat nearer to an embrace than he might have found practicable had they both been on their feet. The donkey himself was quite at his ease, and looked as though he was approvingly conscious of what was going on behind his ears.

'I have a right to a word, Mary; say "Go," and I will leave you at once.'

But Mary did not say 'Go.' Perhaps she would have done so had she been able; but just at present she could say nothing. This came from her having failed to make up her mind in due time as to what course it would best become her to follow.

'One word, Mary; one little word. There, if you will not speak, there is my hand. If you will have it, let it lie in yours; – if not, push it away.' So saying, he managed to get the end of his fingers on to her palm, and there it remained unrepulsed. 'La jeunesse' was beginning to get a lesson; experience when duly sought after sometimes comes early in life.

In truth, Mary had not strength to push the fingers away. 'My love, my own, my own!' said Frank, presuming on this very negative sign of acquiescence. 'My life, my own one, my own Mary!' and then the hand was caught hold of and was at his lips before an effort could be made to save it from such treatment.

'Mary, look at me; say one word to me.'

There was a deep sigh and then came the one word – 'Oh, Frank!'

'Mr Gresham, I hope I have the honour of seeing you quite well,' said a voice close to his ear. 'I beg to say that you are welcome to Boxall Hill.' Frank turned round and instantly found himself shaking hands with Sir Louis Scatcherd.

How Mary got over her confusion Frank never saw, for he had enough to do to get over his own. He involuntarily deserted Mary and began talking very fast to Sir Louis. Sir Louis did not once look at Miss Thorne, but walked back towards the house with Mr Gresham, sulky enough in temper, but still making some efforts to do the fine gentleman. Mary, glad to be left alone, merely occupied herself with sitting on the donkey; and the donkey, when he found that the two gentlemen went towards the house, for company's sake and for his stable's sake, followed after them.

Frank stayed but three minutes in the house; gave another kiss to Lady Scatcherd, getting three in return, and thereby infinitely disgusting Sir Louis, shook hands, anything but warmly, with the young baronet, and just felt the warmth of Mary's hand within his own. He felt also the warmth of her eyes' last glance, and rode home a happy man.

CHAPTER XXX

Post Prandial

Frank rode home a happy man, cheering himself, as successful lovers do cheer themselves, with the brilliancy of his late exploit: nor was it till he had turned the corner into the Greshamsbury stables that he began to reflect what he would do next. It was all very well to have induced Mary to allow his three fingers to lie half a minute in her soft hand; the having done so might certainly be sufficient evidence that he had overcome one of the lions in his path;* but it could hardly be said that all his difficulties were now smoothed. How was he to make further progress?

To Mary, also, the same ideas no doubt occurred – with many others. But, then, it was not for Mary to make any progress in the matter. To her at least belonged this passive comfort, that at present no act hostile to the De Courcy interest would be expected from her. All that she could do would be to tell her uncle so much as it was fitting that he should know. The doing this would doubtless be in some degree difficult; but it was not probable that there would be much difference, much of anything but loving anxiety for each other, between her and Dr Thorne. One other thing, indeed, she must do; Frank must be made to understand what her birth had been. 'This,' she said to herself, 'will give him an opportunity of retracting what he has done should he choose to avail himself of it. It is well he should have such opportunity.'

But Frank had more than this to do. He had told Beatrice that he would make no secret of his love, and he fully resolved to be as good as his word. To his father he owed an unreserved confidence; and he was fully minded to give it. It was, he knew, altogether out of the question that he should at once marry a portionless girl without his father's consent; probably out of the question that he should do so even with it. But he would, at any rate, tell his father, and then decide as to what should be done next. So resolving, he put his black horse into the stable and went in to dinner. After dinner he and his father would be alone.

Yes; after dinner he and his father would be alone. He dressed himself hurriedly, for the dinner-bell was almost on the stroke as he entered the house. He said this to himself once and again; but when the meats and the puddings, and then the cheese, were borne away, as the decanters were placed before his father, and Lady Arabella sipped her one glass of claret, and his sisters ate their portion of strawberries, his pressing anxiety for the coming interview began to wax somewhat dull.

His mother and sisters, however, rendered him no assistance by prolonging their stay. With unwonted assiduity he pressed a second glass of claret on his mother. But Lady Arabella was not only temperate in her habits, but also at the present moment very angry with her son. She thought that he had been to Boxall Hill, and was only waiting a proper moment to cross-question him sternly on the subject. Now she departed, taking her train of daughters with her.

'Give me one big gooseberry,' said Nina, as she squeezed

herself in under her brother's arm, prior to making her retreat.
Frank would willingly have given her a dozen of the biggest,
had she wanted them; but having got the one, she squeezed
herself out again and scampered off.

The squire was very cheery this evening; from what cause
cannot now be said. Perhaps he had succeeded in negotiating a
further loan, thus temporarily sprinkling a drop of water over
the ever-rising dust of his difficulties.

'Well, Frank, what have you been after today? Peter told me
you had the black horse out,' said he, pushing the decanter to
his son. 'Take my advice, my boy, and don't give him too much
summer road-work. Legs won't stand it, let them be ever so
good.'

'Why, sir, I was obliged to go out today, and therefore, it had
to be either the old mare or the young horse.'

'Why didn't you take Ramble?' Now Ramble was the squire's
own saddle hack, used for farm surveying, and occasionally for
going to cover.

'I shouldn't think of doing that, sir.'

'My dear boy, he is quite at your service; for goodness' sake
do let me have a little wine, Frank – quite at your service; any
riding I have now is after the haymakers, and that's all on the
grass.'

'Thank'ee, sir. Well, perhaps I will take a turn out of Ramble
should I want it.'

'Do, and pray, pray take care of that black horse's legs. He's
turning out more of a horse than I took him to be, and I should
be sorry to see him injured. Where have you been today?'

'Well, father, I have something to tell you.'

'Something to tell me!' and then the squire's happy and gay
look, which had been only rendered more happy and more gay
by his assumed anxiety about the black horse, gave place to that
heaviness of visage which acrimony and misfortune had made
so habitual to him. 'Something to tell me!' Any grave words like
these always presaged some money difficulty to the squire's ears.
He loved Frank with the tenderest love. He would have done so
under almost any circumstances; but, doubtless, that love had
been made more palpable to himself by the fact that Frank had
been a good son as regards money – not exigeant as was Lady
Arabella, or selfishly reckless as was his nephew, Lord Porlock.
But now Frank must be in difficulty about money. This was his

first idea. 'What is it, Frank; you have seldom had anything to say that has not been pleasant for me to hear?' And then the heaviness of visage again gave way for a moment as his eye fell upon his son.

'I have been to Boxall Hill, sir.'

The tenor of the father's thoughts was changed in an instant; and the dread of immediate temporary annoyance gave place to true anxiety for his son. He, the squire, had been no party to Mary's exile from his own domain; and he had seen with pain that she had now a second time been driven from her home: but he had never hitherto questioned the expediency of separating his son from Mary Thorne. Alas! it became too necessary – too necessary through his own default – that Frank should marry money!

'At Boxall Hill, Frank! Has that been prudent? Or, indeed, has it been generous to Miss Thorne, who has been driven there, as it were, by your imprudence?'

'Father, it is well that we should understand each other about this – '

'Fill your glass, Frank.' Frank mechanically did as he was bid, and passed the bottle.

'I should never forgive myself were I to deceive you, or keep anything from you.'

'I believe it is not in your nature to deceive me, Frank.'

'The fact is, sir, that I have made up my mind that Mary Thorne shall be my wife – sooner or later that is, unless, of course, she should utterly refuse. Hitherto, she has utterly refused me. I believe I may now say that she has accepted me.'

The squire sipped his claret, but at the moment said nothing. There was a quiet, manly, but yet modest determination about his son that he had hardly noticed before. Frank had become legally of age, legally a man, when he was twenty-one. Nature, it seems, had postponed the ceremony till he was twenty-two. Nature often does postpone the ceremony even to a much later age; – sometimes, altogether forgets to accomplish it.

The squire continued to sip his claret; he had to think over the matter for a while before he could answer a statement so deliberately made by his son.

'I think I may say so,' continued Frank, with perhaps unnecessary modesty. 'She is so honest that, had she not intended it, she would have said so honestly. Am I right, father, in thinking that, as regards Mary, personally, you would not object to her as a daughter-in-law?'

'Personally!' said the squire, glad to have the subject presented to him in a view that enabled him to speak out. 'Oh, no; personally, I should not object to her, for I love her dearly. She is a good girl; I do believe she is a good girl in every respect. I have always liked her; liked to see her about the house. But – '

'I know what you would say, father.' This was rather more than the squire knew himself. 'Such a marriage is imprudent.'

'It is more that that, Frank; I fear it is impossible.'

'Impossible! No, father; it is not impossible.'

'It is impossible, Frank, in the usual sense. What are you to live upon? What would you do with your children? You would not wish to see your wife distressed and comfortless.'

'No, I should not like to see that.'

'You would not wish to begin life as an embarrassed man and end it as a ruined man. If you were now to marry Miss Thorne such would, I fear, doubtless be your lot.'

Frank caught at the word 'now.' 'I don't expect to marry immediately. I know that would be imprudent. But I am pledged, father, and I certainly cannot go back. And now that I have told you all this, what is your advice to me?'

The father again sat silent, still sipping his wine. There was nothing in his son that he could be ashamed of, nothing that he could meet with anger, nothing that he could not love; but how should he answer him? The fact was, that the son had more in him than the father; that his mind and spirit were of a calibre not to be opposed successfully by the mind and spirit of the squire.

'Do you know Mary's history?' said Mr Gresham, at last; 'the history of her birth?'

'Not a word of it,' said Frank. 'I did not know she had a history.'

'Nor does she know it; at least, I presume not. But you should know it now. And, Frank, I will tell it you; not to turn you from her – not with that object, though I think that, to a certain extent, it should have that effect. Mary's birth was not such as would become your wife and be beneficial to your children.'

'If so, father, I should have known that sooner. Why was she brought in here among us?'

'True, Frank. The fault is mine; mine and your mother's.

Circumstances brought it about years ago, when it never occurred to us that all this would arise. But I will tell you her history. And, Frank, remember this, though I tell it you as a secret, a secret to be kept from all the world but one, you are quite at liberty to let the doctor know that I have told it you. Indeed, I shall be careful to let him know so myself should it ever be necessary that he and I should speak together as to this engagement.' The squire then told his son the whole story of Mary's birth, as it is known to the reader.

Frank sat silent, looking very blank; he also had, as had every Gresham, a great love for his pure blood. He had said to his mother that he hated money, that he hated the estate; but he would have been very slow to say, even in his warmest opposition to her, that he hated the roll of the family pedigree. He loved it dearly, though he seldom spoke of it; – as men of good family seldom do speak of it. It is one of those possessions which to have is sufficient. A man having it need not boast of what he has, or show it off before the world. But on that account he values it the more. He had regarded Mary as a cutting duly taken from the Ullathorne tree; not, indeed, as a grafting branch, full of flower, just separated from the parent stalk, but as being not a whit the less truly endowed with the pure sap of that venerable trunk. When, therefore, he heard her true history he sat awhile dismayed.

'It is a sad story,' said the father.

'Yes, sad enough,' said Frank, rising from his chair and standing with it before him, leaning on the back of it. 'Poor Mary, poor Mary! She will have to learn it some day.'

'I fear so, Frank;' and then there was again a few moments' silence.

'To me, father, it is told too late. It can now have no effect on me. Indeed,' said he, sighing as he spoke, but still relieving himself by the very sigh, 'it could have had no effect had I heard it ever so soon.'

'I should have told you before,' said the father; 'certainly I ought to have done so.'

'It would have done no good,' said Frank. 'Ah, sir, tell me this: who were Miss Dunstable's parents? What was that fellow Moffat's family?'

This was perhaps cruel of Frank. The squire, however, made no answer to the question. 'I have thought it right to tell you,' said he. 'I have all commentary to yourself. I need not tell you what your mother will think.'

'What did she think of Miss Dunstable's birth?' said he, again more bitterly than before. 'No, sir,' he continued, after a further pause. 'All that can make no change; none at any rate now. It can't make my love less, even if it could have prevented it. Nor, even, could it do so – which it can't the least, not in the least – but could it do so, it could not break my engagement. I am now engaged to Mary Thorne.'

And then he again repeated his question, asking for his father's advice under the present circumstances. The conversation was a very long one, so long as to disarrange all Lady Arabella's plans. She had determined to take her son most stringently to task that very evening; and with this object had ensconced herself in the small drawing-room which had formerly been used for a similar purpose by the august countess herself. Here she now sat, having desired Augusta and Beatrice, as well as the twins, to beg Frank to go to her as soon as he should come out of the dining-room. Poor lady! there she waited till ten o'clock, – tealess. There was not much of the Bluebeard about the squire;* but he had succeeded in making it understood through the household that he was not to be interrupted by messages from his wife during the post-prandial hour, which, though no toper, he loved so well.

As a period of twelve months will now have to be passed over, the upshot of this long conversation must be told in as few words as possible. The father found it impracticable to talk his son out of his intended marriage; indeed, he hardly attempted to do so by any direct persuasion. He explained to him that it was impossible that he should marry at once, and suggested that he, Frank, was very young.

'You married, sir, before you were one-and-twenty,' said Frank. Yes, and repented before I was two-and-twenty. So did *not* say the squire.

He suggested that Mary should have time to ascertain what would be her uncle's wishes, and ended by inducing Frank to promise, that after taking his degree in October he would go abroad for some months, and that he would not indeed return to Greshamsbury till he was three-and-twenty.

'He may perhaps forget her,' said the father to himself, as this agreement was made between them.

'He thinks that I shall forget her,' said Frank to himself at the same time; 'but he does not know me.'

When Lady Arabella at last got hold of her son she found that the time for her preaching was utterly gone by. He told her, almost with *sang-froid*, what his plans were; and when she came to understand them, and to understand also what had taken place at Boxall Hill, she could not blame the squire for what he had done. She also said to herself, more confidently than the squire had done, that Frank would quite forget Mary before the year was out. 'Lord Buckish,' said she to herself, rejoicingly, 'is now with the ambassador at Paris' – Lord Buckish was her nephew – 'and with him Frank will meet women that are really beautiful – women of fashion. When with Lord Buckish he will soon forget Mary Thorne.'

But not on this account did she change her resolve to follow up to the further point her hostility to the Thornes. She was fully enabled now to do so, for Dr Fillgrave was already reinstalled at Greshamsbury as her medical adviser.

One other short visit did Frank pay to Boxall Hill, and one interview had he with Dr Thorne. Mary told him all she knew of her own sad history, and was answered only by a kiss, a kiss absolutely not in any way by her to be avoided; the first, the only one, that had ever yet reached her lips from his. And then he went away.

The doctor told him all the story. 'Yes,' said Frank, 'I knew it all before. Dear Mary, dearest Mary! Don't you, doctor, teach yourself to believe that I shall forget her.' And then also he went his way from him – went his way also from Greshamsbury, and was absent for the full period of his alloted banishment – twelve months, namely, and a day.

END OF VOLUME II

CHAPTER XXXI

The Small End of the Wedge

Frank Gresham was absent from Greshamsbury twelve months and a day: a day is always added to the period of such absences, as shown in the history of Lord Bateman* and other noble heroes. We need not detail all the circumstances of his banishment, all the details of the compact that was made. One detail of course was this, that there should be no corresponding; a point to which the squire found some difficulty in bringing his son to assent.

It must not be supposed that Mary Thorne or the doctor were in any way parties to, or privy to these agreements. By no means. The agreements were drawn out, and made, and signed, and sealed at Greshamsbury, and were known of nowhere else. The reader must not imagine that Lady Arabella was prepared to give up her son, if only his love should remain constant for one year. Neither did Lady Arabella consent to any such arrangement, nor did the squire. It was settled rather in this wise: that Frank should be subjected to no torturing process, pestered to give no promises, should in no way be bullied about Mary – that is, not at present – if he would go away for a year. Then, at the end of the year, the matter should be again discussed. Agreeing to this, Frank took his departure, and was absent as per agreement.

What were Mary's fortunes immediately after his departure must be shortly told, and then we will again join some of our Greshamsbury friends at a period about a month before Frank's return.

When Sir Louis saw Frank Gresham standing by Mary's donkey, with his arms round Mary's knees, he began to fear that there must be something in it. He had intended that very day to throw himself at Mary's feet, and now it appeared to his inexperienced eyes as though somebody else had been at the same work before him. This not unnaturally made him cross; so, after having sullenly wished the visitor good-bye, he betook himself to his room, and there drank curaçoa alone, instead of coming down to dinner.

This he did for two or three days, and then, taking heart of grace, he remembered that, after all, he had very many advantages over young Gresham. In the first place, he was a baronet, and could make his wife a 'lady'. In the next place, Frank's father was alive and like to live, whereas, his own was dead. He possessed Boxall Hill in his own right, but his rival had neither house nor land of his own. After all, might it not be possible for him also to put his arm round Mary's knees; – her knees, or her waist, or, perhaps, even her neck? Faint heart never won fair lady. At any rate, he would try.

And he did try. With what result, as regards Mary, need hardly be told. He certainly did not get nearly so far as putting his hand even upon her knee before he was made to understand that it 'was no go,' as he graphically described it to his mother. He tried once and again. On the second, she was more determined, though less civil; and then she told him, that if he pressed her further he would drive her from his mother's house. There was something then about Mary's eye, a fixed composure round her mouth, and an authority in her face, which went far to quell him; and he did not press her again.

He immediately left Boxall Hill, and, returning to London, had more violent recourse to the curaçoa. It was not long before the doctor heard of him, and was obliged to follow him, and then again occurred those frightful scenes in which the poor wretch had to expiate, either in terrible delirium or more terrible prostration of spirits, the vile sin which his father had so early taught him.

Then Mary returned to her uncle's home. Frank was gone, and she therefore could resume her place at Greshamsbury. Yes, she came back to Greshamsbury; but Greshamsbury was by no means now the same place that it was formerly. Almost all intercourse was now over between the doctor and the Greshamsbury people. He rarely ever saw the squire, and then only on business. Not that the squire had purposely quarrelled with him; but Dr Thorne himself had chosen that it should be so, since Frank had openly proposed for his niece. Frank was now gone, and Lady

Arabella was in arms against him. It should not be said that he kept up any intimacy for the sake of aiding the lovers in their love. No one should rightfully accuse him of inveigling the heir to marry his niece.

Mary, therefore, found herself utterly separated from Beatrice. She was not even able to learn what Beatrice would think, or did think, of the engagement as it now stood. She could not even explain to her friend that love had been too strong for her, and endeavour to get some comfort from that friend's absolution from her sin. This estrangement was now carried so far that she and Beatrice did not even meet on neutral ground. Lady Arabella made it known to Miss Oriel that her daughter could not meet Mary Thorne, even as strangers meet; and it was made known to others also. Mrs Yates Umbleby, and her dear friend Miss Gushing, to whose charming tea-parties none of the Greshamsbury ladies went above once in a twelvemonth, talked through the parish of this distressing difficulty. They would have been so happy to have asked dear Mary Thorne, only the Greshamsbury ladies did not approve.

Mary was thus tabooed from all society in the place in which a twelvemonth since she had been, of all its denizens, perhaps the most courted. In those days, no bevy of Greshamsbury young ladies had fairly represented the Greshamsbury young ladyhood if Mary Thorne was not there. Now she was excluded from all such bevies. Patience did not quarrel with her, certainly; – came to see her frequently; – invited her to walk; – invited her frequently to the parsonage. But Mary was shy of acceding to such invitations, and at last frankly told her friend Patience, that she would not again break bread in Greshamsbury in any house in which she was not thought fit to meet the other guests who habitually resorted there.

In truth, both the doctor and his niece were very sore, but they were of that temperament that keeps all its soreness to itself. Mary walked out by herself boldly, looking at least as though she were indifferent to all the world. She was, indeed, hardly treated. Young ladies' engagements are generally matters of profoundest secrecy, and are hardly known of by their near friends till marriage is a thing settled. But all the world knew of Mary's engagement within a month of that day on which she had neglected to expel Frank's finger from her hand; it had been told openly through the country-side that she had confessed her love for the young squire. Now it is disagreeable for a young lady to walk about under such circumstances, especially so when she has no female friend to keep her in countenance, more especially so when the gentleman is of such importance in the neighbourhood as Frank was in that locality. It was a matter of moment to every farmer, and every farmer's wife, which bride Frank should marry of those two bespoken for him; Mary, namely, or Money. Every yokel about the place had been made to understand that, by some feminine sleight of hand, the doctor's niece had managed to trap Master Frank, and that Master Frank had been sent out of the way so that he might, if yet possible, break through the trapping. All this made life rather unpleasant for her.

One day, walking solitary in the lanes, she met that sturdy farmer to whose daughter she had in former days been so serviceable. 'God bless 'ee, Miss Mary,' said he – he always did bid God bless her when he saw her. 'And, Miss Mary, to say my mind out freely, thee be quite gude enough for un, quite gude enough; so thee be'st tho'f he were ten squoires.' There may, perhaps, have been something pleasant in the heartiness of this; but it was not pleasant to have this heart affair of hers thus publicly scanned and talked over: to have it known to every one that she had set her heart on marrying Frank Gresham, and that all the Greshams had set their heart on preventing it. And yet she could in nowise help it. No girl could have been more staid and demure, less demonstrative and boastful about her love. She had never yet spoken freely, out of her full heart, to one human being. 'Oh, Frank!' All her spoken sin had been contained in that.

But Lady Arabella had been very active. It suited her better that it should be known, far and wide, that a nameless pauper – Lady Arabella only surmised that her foe was nameless; but she did not scruple to declare it – was intriguing to catch the heir of Greshamsbury. None of the Greshams must meet Mary Thorne; that was the edict sent about the country; and the edict was well understood. Those, therefore, were bad days for Miss Thorne.

She had never yet spoken on the matter freely, out of her full heart, to one human being. Not to one? Not to him? Not to her uncle? No, not even to him, fully and freely. She had told him that that had passed between Frank and her which amounted, at any rate on his part, to a proposal.

'Well, dearest, and what was your answer?' said her uncle, drawing her close to him, and speaking in his kindest voice.

'I hardly made any answer, uncle.'

'You did not reject him, Mary?'

'No, uncle,' and then she paused; – he had never known her tremble as she now trembled. 'But if you say that I ought, I will,' she added, drawing every word from herself with difficulty.

'I say you ought, Mary! Nay; but this question you must answer yourself.'

'Must I?' said she, plaintively. And then she sat for the next half-hour with her head against his shoulder; but nothing more was said about it. They both acquiesced in the sentence that had been pronounced against them, and went on together more lovingly than before.

The doctor was quite as weak as his niece; nay, weaker. She hesitated fearfully as to what she ought to do: whether she should obey her heart or the dictates of Greshamsbury. But he had other doubts than hers, which nearly set him wild when he strove to bring his mind to a decision. He himself was now in possession – of course as trustee only – of the title-deeds of the estate; more of the estate, much more belonged to the heirs under Sir Roger Scatcherd's will than to the squire. It was now more than probable that that heir must be Mary Thorne. His conviction became stronger and stronger that no human efforts would keep Sir Louis in the land of the living till he was twenty-five. Could he, therefore, wisely or honestly, in true friendship to the squire, to Frank, or to his niece, take any steps to separate two persons who loved each other, and whose marriage would in all human probability be so suitable?

And yet he could not bring himself to encourage it then. The idea of 'looking after dead men's shoes'* was abhorrent to his mind, especially when the man whose death he contemplated had been so trusted to him as had been Sir Louis Scatcherd. He could not speak of the event, even to the squire, as being possible. So he kept his peace from day to day, and gave no counsel to Mary in the matter.

And then he had his own individual annoyances, and very aggravating annoyances they were. The carriage – or rather post-chaise – of Dr Fillgrave was now frequent in Greshamsbury, passing him constantly in the street, among the lanes, and on the high roads. It seemed as though Dr Fillgrave could never get to his patients at the big house without showing himself to his beaten rival, either on his way thither or on his return. This alone would, perhaps, not have hurt our doctor much; but it did hurt him to know that Dr Fillgrave was attending the squire for a little incipient gout, and that dear Nina was in measles under those unloving hands.

And then, also, the old-fashioned phaeton of old-fashioned old Dr Century was seen to rumble up to the big house, and it became known that Lady Arabella was not very well. 'Not very well,' when pronounced in a low, grave voice about Ladies Arabella, always means something serious. And, in this case, something serious was meant. Lady Arabella was not only ill, but frightened. It appeared, even to her, that Dr Fillgrave himself hardly knew what he was about, that he was not so sure in his opinion, so confident in himself, as Dr Thorne used to be. How should he be, seeing that Dr Thorne had medically had Lady Arabella in his hands for the last ten years?

If sitting with dignity in his hired carriage, and stepping with authority up the big front steps, would have done anything, Dr Fillgrave might have done much. Lady Arabella was greatly taken with his looks when he first came to her, and it was only when she by degrees perceived that the symptoms, which she knew so well, did not yield to him that she began to doubt those looks.

After a while Dr Fillgrave himself suggested Dr Century. 'Not that I fear anything, Lady Arabella,' said he, – lying hugely, for he did fear; fear both for himself and for her. 'But Dr Century has great experience, and in such a matter, when the interests are so important, one cannot be too safe.'

So Dr Century came and toddled slowly into her ladyship's room. He did not say much; he left the talking to his learned brother, who certainly was able to do that part of the business. But Dr Century, though he said little, looked very grave, and by no means quieted Lady Arabella's mind. She, as she saw the two putting their heads together, already felt misgivings that she had done wrong. She knew that she could not be safe without Dr Thorne at her bedside, and she already felt that she had exercised a most injudicious courage in driving him away.

'Well, doctor?' said she, as soon as Dr Century had toddled downstairs to see the squire.

'Oh! we shall be all right, Lady Arabella; all right, very soon.

But we must be careful, very careful; I am glad I've had Century here, very; but there's nothing to alter; little or nothing.'

There were but few words spoken between Dr Century and the squire; but few as they were, they frightened Mr Gresham. When Dr Fillgrave came down the grand stairs, a servant waited at the bottom to ask him also to go to the squire. Now there never had been much cordiality between the squire and Dr Fillgrave, though Mr Gresham had consented to take a preventative pill from his hands, and the little man therefore swelled himself out somewhat more than ordinarily as he followed the servant.

'Dr Fillgrave,' said the squire, at once beginning the conversation, 'Lady Arabella is, I fear, in danger.'

'Well, no; I hope not in danger, Mr Gresham. I certainly believe I may be justified in expressing a hope that she is not in danger. Her state is, no doubt, rather serious – rather serious – as Dr Century has probably told you;' and Dr Fillgrave made a bow to the old man, who sat quiet in one of the dining-room armchairs.

'Well, doctor,' said the squire, 'I have not any grounds on which to doubt your judgement.'

Dr Fillgrave bowed, but with the stiffest, slightest inclination which a head could possibly make. He rather thought that Mr Gresham had no ground for doubting his judgement.

'Nor do I.'

The doctor bowed, and a little, a very little less stiffly.

'But, doctor, I think that something ought to be done.'

The doctor this time did his bowing merely with his eyes and mouth. The former he closed for a moment, the latter he pressed; and then decorously rubbed his hands one over the other.

'I am afraid, Dr Fillgrave, that you and my friend Thorne are not the best friends in the world.'

'No, Mr Gresham, no; I may go as far as to say we are not.'

'Well, I am sorry for it – '

'Perhaps, Mr Gresham, we need hardly discuss it; but there have been circumstances – '

'I am not going to discuss anything, Dr Fillgrave; I say I am sorry for it, because I believe that prudence will imperatively require Lady Arabella to have Doctor Thorne back again. Now, if you would not object to meet him – '

'Mr Gresham, I beg pardon; I beg pardon, indeed; but you must really excuse me. Doctor Thorne has, in my estimation – '

'But, Doctor Fillgrave – '

'Mr Gresham, you really must excuse me; you really must, indeed. Anything else that I could do for Lady Arabella, I should be most happy to do; but after what has passed, I cannot meet Doctor Thorne; I really cannot. You must not ask me to do so, Mr Gresham. And, Mr Gresham,' continued the doctor, 'I did understand from Lady Arabella that his – that is, Doctor Thorne's – conduct to her ladyship had been such – so very outrageous, I may say, that – that – that – of course, Mr Gresham, you know best; but I did think that Lady Arabella herself was quite unwilling to see Doctor Thorne again;' and Dr Fillgrave looked very big, and very dignified, and very exclusive.

The squire did not again ask him. He had no warrant for supposing that Lady Arabella would receive Dr Thorne if he did come; and he saw that it was useless to attempt to overcome the rancour of a man so pigheaded as the little Galen now before him. Other propositions were then broached, and it was at last decided that assistance should be sought for from London, in the person of the great Sir Omicron Pie.

Sir Omicron came, and Drs Fillgrave and Century were there to meet him. When they all assembled in Lady Arabella's room, the poor woman's heart almost sank within her, – as well it might, at such a sight. If she could only reconcile it with her honour, her consistency, with her high De Courcy principles, to send once more for Dr Thorne. Oh, Frank! Frank! to what misery has your disobedience brought your mother!

Sir Omicron and the lesser provincial lights had their consultation, and the lesser lights went their way to Barchester and Silverbridge, leaving Sir Omicron to enjoy the hospitality of Greshamsbury.

'You should have Thorne back here, Mr Gresham,' said Sir Omicron, almost in a whisper, when they were quite alone. 'Doctor Fillgrave is a very good man, and so is Dr Century; very good, I am sure. But Thorne has known her ladyship so long.' And then, on the following morning, Sir Omicron also went his way.

And then there was a scene between the squire and her ladyship. Lady Arabella had given herself credit for great good generalship when she found that the squire had been induced to take that pill. We have all heard of the little end of the wedge and we have most of us an idea that the little end is the difficulty. That pill had been the little end of Lady Arabella's wedge. Up to that period she had been struggling in vain to make a severance between her husband and her enemy. That pill should do the business. She well knew how to make the most of it; to have it published in Greshamsbury that the squire had put his gouty toe into Dr Fillgrave's hands; how to let it be known – especially at that humble house in the corner of the street – that Fillgrave's prescriptions now ran current through the whole establishment. Dr Thorne did hear of it, and did suffer. He had been a true friend to the squire, and he thought the squire should have stood to him more staunchly.

'After all,' said he himself, 'perhaps it's as well – perhaps it will be best that I should leave this place altogether.' And then he thought of Sir Roger and his will, and of Mary and her lover. And then of Mary's birth, and of his own theoretical doctrines as to pure blood. And so his troubles multiplied, and he saw no present daylight through them.

Such had been the way in which Lady Arabella had got in the little end of the wedge. And she would have triumphed joyfully had not her incessant doubts and fears as to herself then come in to check her triumph and destroy her joy. She had not yet confessed to any one her secret regret for the friend she had driven away. She hardly yet acknowledged to herself that she did regret him; but she was uneasy, frightened, and in low spirits.

'My dear,' said the squire, sitting down by her bedside, 'I want to tell you what Sir Omicron said as he went away.'

'Well?' said her ladyship, sitting up and looking frightened.

'I don't know how you may take it, Bell; but I think it very good news:' the squire never called his wife Bell, except when he wanted her to be on particularly good terms with him.

'Well?' said she, again. She was not over-anxious to be gracious, and did not reciprocate his familiarity.

'Sir Omicron says that you should have Thorne back again, and upon my honour, I cannot but agree with him. Now, Thorne is a clever man, a very clever man; nobody denies that; and then, you know – '

'Why did not Sir Omicron say that to me?' said her ladyship, sharply, all her disposition in Dr Thorne's favour becoming wonderfully damped by her husband's advocacy.

'I suppose he thought it better to say it to me,' said the squire, rather curtly.

'He should have spoken to myself,' said Lady Arabella, who, though she did not absolutely doubt her husband's word, gave him credit for having induced and led on Sir Omicron to the uttering of this opinion. 'Doctor Thorne has behaved to me in so gross, so indecent a manner! And then, as I understand, he is absolutely encouraging that girl – '

'Now, Bell, you are quite wrong – '

'Of course I am; I always am quite wrong.'

'Quite wrong in mixing up two things; Doctor Thorne as an acquaintance, and Dr Thorne as a doctor.'

'It is dreadful to have him here, even standing in the room with me. How can one talk to one's doctor openly and confidentially when one looks upon him as one's worst enemy?' And Lady Arabella, softening, almost melted into tears.

'My dear, you cannot wonder that I should be anxious for you.'

Lady Arabella gave a little snuffle, which might be taken as a not very eloquent expression of thanks for the squire's solicitude, or as an ironical jeer at his want of sincerity.

'And, therefore, I have not last a moment in telling you what Sir Omicron said "You should have Thorne back here;" those were his very words. You can think it over, my dear. And remember this, Bell; if he is to do any good no time should be lost.'

And then the squire left the room, and Lady Arabella remained alone, perplexed by many doubts.

CHAPTER XXXII

Mr Oriel

I must now, shortly – as shortly as is in my power to do it – introduce a new character to my reader. Mention has been made of the rector of Greshamsbury; but, hitherto, no opportunity has offered itself for the Rev Caleb Oriel to come upon the boards.

Mr Oriel was a man of family and fortune, who, having gone to Oxford with the usual views of such men, had become inoculated there with very High-Church principles, and had gone into orders influenced by a feeling of enthusiastic love for the priesthood. He was by no means an ascetic – such men, indeed, seldom are – nor was he a devotee. He was a man well able, and certainly willing, to do the work of a parish clergyman; and when he became one, he was efficacious in his profession. But it may perhaps be said of him, without speaking slander-ously, that his original calling, as a young man, was rather to the outward and visible signs of religion than to its inward and spiritual graces.

He delighted in lecterns and credence-tables,* in services at dark hours of winter mornings when no one would attend, in high waistcoats and narrow white neckties, in chanted services and intoned prayers, and in all the paraphernalia of Anglican formalities which have given such offence to those of our brethren who live in daily fear of the scarlet lady.* Many of his friends declared that Mr Oriel would sooner or later deliver himself over body and soul to that lady; but there was no need to fear for him: for though sufficiently enthusiastic to get out of bed at five a.m. on winter mornings – he did so, at least, all through his first winter at Greshamsbury – he was not made of that stuff which is necessary for a staunch, burning, self-denying convert. It was not in him to change his very sleek black coat for a Capuchin's filthy cassock,* nor his pleasant parsonage for some dirty hole in Rome. And it was better so both for him and others. There are but few, very few, to whom it is given to be a Huss, a Wickcliffe, or a Luther;* and a man gains but little by being a false Huss, or a false Luther, and his neighbours gain less.

But certain lengths in self-privation Mr Oriel did go; at any rate, for some time. He eschewed matrimony, imagining that it became him as a priest to do so; he fasted rigorously on Fridays; and the neighbours declared that he scourged himself.

Mr Oriel was, as it has been said, a man of fortune; that is to say, when he came of age he was master of thirty thousand pounds. When he took it into his head to go into the Church, his friends bought for him the next presentation to the living of

Greshamsbury; and, a year after his ordination, the living falling in, Mr Oriel brought himself and his sister to the rectory.

Mr Oriel soon became popular. He was a dark-haired, good-looking man, of polished manners, agreeable in society, not given to monkish austerities – except in the matter of Fridays* nor yet to the Low-Church severity of demeanour. He was thoroughly a gentleman, good-humoured, inoffensive, and sociable. But he had one fault: he was not a marrying man.

On this ground there was a feeling against him so strong as almost at one time to throw him into serious danger. It was not only that he should be sworn against matrimony in his individual self – he whom fate had made so able to sustain the weight of a wife and family; but what an example was he setting! If other clergymen all around should declare against wives and families, what was to become of the country? What was to be done with the rural districts? The religious observances, as regards women, of a Brigham Young* were hardly so bad as this!

There were around Greshamsbury very many unmarried ladies – I believe there generally are so round most such villages. From the great house he did not receive much annoyance. Beatrice was then only just on the verge of being brought out, and was not perhaps inclined to think very much of a young clergyman; and Augusta certainly intended to fly at higher game. But there were the Miss Athelings, the daughters of a neighbouring clergyman, who were ready to go all lengths with him in High-Church matters, except as to that one tremendously papal step of celibacy; and the two Miss Hesterwells, of Hesterwell Park, the younger of whom boldly declared her purpose of civilising the savage; and Miss Opie Green, a very pretty widow, with a very pretty jointure, who lived in a very pretty house about a mile from Greshamsbury, and who declared her opinion that Mr Oriel was quite right in his view of a clergyman's position. How could a woman, situated as she was, have the comfort of a clergyman's attention if he were to be regarded just as any other man? She could now know in what light to regard Mr Oriel, and would be able without scruple to avail herself of his zeal. So she did avail herself of his zeal, – and that without any scruple.

And then there was Miss Gushing, – a young thing. Miss Gushing had a great advantage over the other competitors for the civilisation of Mr Oriel, namely, in this – that she was able to attend his morning services. If Mr Oriel was to be reached in any way, it was probable that he might be reached in this way. If anything could civilise him, this would do it. Therefore, the young thing, through all one long, tedious winter, tore herself from her warm bed, and was to be seen – no, not seen, but heard – entering Mr Oriel's church at six o'clock. With indefatigable assiduity the responses were made, uttered from under a close bonnet, and out of a dark corner, in an enthusiastically feminine voice, through the whole winter.

Nor did Miss Gushing altogether fail in her object. When a clergyman's daily audience consists of but one person, and that person is a young lady, it is hardly possible that he should not become personally intimate with her; hardly possible that he should not be in some measure grateful. Miss Gushing's responses came from her with such fervour, and she begged for ghostly advice with such eager longing to have her scruples satisfied, that Mr Oriel had nothing for it but to give way to a certain amount of civilisation.

By degrees it came to pass that Miss Gushing could never get her final prayer said, her shawl and boa adjusted, and stow away her nice new Prayer-Book with the red letters inside, and the cross on the back, till Mr Oriel had been into his vestry and got rid of his surplice. And then they met at the church-porch, and naturally walked together till Mr Oriel's cruel gateway separated them. The young thing did sometimes think that, as the parson's civilisation progressed, he might have taken the trouble to walk with her as far as Mr Yates Umbleby's hall door; but she had hope to sustain her, and a firm resolve to merit success, even though she might not attain it.

'Is it not ten thousand pities,' she once said to him, 'that none here should avail themselves of the inestimable privilege which your coming has conferred upon us? Oh, Mr Oriel, I do so wonder at it! To me it is so delightful! The morning service in the dark church is so beautiful, so touching!'

'I suppose they think it is a bore getting up so early,' said Mr Oriel.

'Ah, a bore!' said Miss Gushing, in an enthusiastic tone of depreciation. 'How insensate they must be! To me it gives a new charm to life. It quiets one for the day; makes one so much fitter for one's daily trials and daily troubles. Does it not, Mr Oriel?'

'I look upon morning prayer as an imperative duty, certainly.'

'Oh, certainly, a most imperative duty; but so delicious at the same time. I spoke to Mrs Umbleby about it, but she said she could not leave the children.'

'No: I dare say not,' said Mr Oriel.

'And Mr Umbleby said his business kept him up so late at night.'

'Very probably. I hardly expect the attendance of men of business.'

'But the servants might come, mightn't they, Mr Oriel?'

'I fear that servants seldom can have time for daily prayers in church.'

'Oh, ah, no; perhaps not.' And then Miss Gushing began to bethink herself of whom should be composed the congregation which it must be presumed Mr Oriel wished to see around him. But on this matter he did not enlighten her.

Then Miss Gushing took to fasting on Fridays, and made some futile attempts to induce her priest to give her the comfort of confessional absolution. But, unfortunately, the zeal of the master waxed cool as that of the pupil waxed hot; and, at last, when the young thing returned to Greshamsbury from an autumn excursion which she had made with Mrs Umbleby to Weston-super-Mare, she found that the delicious morning services had died a natural death. Miss Gushing did not on that account give up the game, but she was bound to fight with no particular advantage in her favour.

Miss Oriel, though a good Churchwoman, was by no means a convert to her brother's extremist views, and perhaps gave but scanty credit to the Gushings, Athelings, and Opie Greens for the sincerity of their religion. But, nevertheless, she and her brother were staunch friends; and she still hoped to see the day when he might be induced to think that an English parson might get through his parish work with the assistance of a wife better than he could do so without such feminine encumbrance. The girl whom she selected for his bride was not the young thing, but Beatrice Gresham.

And at last it seemed probable to Mr Oriel's nearest friends that he was in a fair way to be overcome. Not that he had begun to make love to Beatrice, or committed himself by the utterance of any opinion as to the propriety of clerical marriages; but he daily became looser about his peculiar tenets, raved less immoderately than heretofore as to the atrocity of the Greshamsbury church pews, and was observed to take some opportunities of conversing alone with Beatrice. Beatrice had always denied the imputation – this had usually been made by Mary in their happy days – with vehement asseverations of anger; and Miss Gushing had tittered, and expressed herself as supposing that great people's daughters might be as barefaced as they pleased.

All this had happened previous to the great Greshamsbury feud. Mr Oriel gradually got himself into a way of sauntering up to the great house, sauntering into the drawing-room for the purpose, as I am sure he thought, of talking to Lady Arabella, and then of sauntering home again, having usually found an opportunity for saying a few words to Beatrice during the visit. This went on all through the feud up to the period of Lady Arabella's illness; and then one morning, about a month before the date fixed for Frank's return, Mr Oriel found himself engaged to Miss Beatrice Gresham.

From the day that Miss Gushing heard of it – which was not however for some considerable time after this – she became an Independent Methodist. She could no longer, she said at first, have any faith in any religion; and for an hour or so she was almost tempted to swear that she could no longer have any faith in any man. She had nearly completed a worked cover for a credence-table when the news reached her, as to which, in the young enthusiasm of her heart, she had not been able to remain silent; it had already been promised to Mr Oriel; that promise she swore should not be kept. He was an apostate, she said, from his principles; an utter pervert; a false, designing man, with whom she would never have trusted herself alone on dark mornings had she known that he had such grovelling, worldly inclinations. So Miss Gushing became an Independent Methodist; the credence-table covering was cut up into slippers for the preacher's feet; and the young thing herself, more happy in this direction than she had been in the other, became the arbiter of that preacher's domestic happiness.

But this little history of Miss Gushing's future life is premature. Mr Oriel became engaged demurely, nay, almost silently, to Beatrice, and no one out of their own immediate families was at the time informed of the matter. It was arranged very differently from those two other matches – embryo, or not embryo, those, namely, of Augusta with Mr Moffat, and Frank with Mary Thorne. All Barsetshire had heard of them; but that of Beatrice and Mr Oriel was managed in a much more private manner.

'I do think you are a happy girl,' said Patience to her one morning.

'Indeed I am.'

'He is so good. You don't know how good he is as yet; he never thinks of himself, and thinks so much of those he loves.'

Beatrice took her friend's hand in her own and kissed it. She was full of joy. When a girl is about to be married, when she may lawfully talk of her love, there is no music in her ears so sweet as the praises of her lover.

'I made up my mind from the first that he should marry you.'

'Nonsense, Patience.'

'I did, indeed. I made up my mind that he should marry; and there were only two to choose from.'

'Me and Miss Gushing,' said Beatrice, laughing.

'No; not exactly Miss Gushing. I had not many fears for Caleb there.'

'I declare she's very pretty,' said Beatrice, who could afford to be good-natured. Now Miss Gushing certainly was pretty; and would have been very pretty had her nose not turned up so much, and could she have parted her hair in the centre.

'Well, I am very glad you chose me; – if it was you who chose,' said Beatrice, modestly; having, however, in her own mind a strong opinion that Mr Oriel had chosen for himself, and had never had any doubt in the matter. 'And who was the other?'

'Can't you guess?'

'I won't guess any more; perhaps Mrs Green.'

'Oh no; certainly not a widow. I don't like widows marrying. But of course you could guess if you would; of course it was Mary Thorne. But I soon saw Mary would not do, for two reasons; Caleb would never have liked her well enough nor would she ever have liked him.'

'Not like him! oh, I hope she will; I do so love Mary Thorne.'

'So do I, dearly; and so does Caleb; but he could never have loved her as he does you.'

'But, Patience, have you told Mary?'

'No, I have told no one, and shall not without your leave.'

'Ah, you must tell her. Tell it her with my best, and kindest, warmest love. Tell her how happy I am, and how I long to talk to her. Tell her that I will have her for my bridesmaid. Oh! I do hope that before that all this horrid quarrel will be settled.'

Patience undertook the commission, and did tell Mary; did give her also the message which Beatrice had sent. And Mary was rejoiced to hear it; for though, as Patience had said of her, she had never herself felt any inclination to fall in love with Mr Oriel, she believed him to be one in whose hands her friend's happiness would be secure. Then, by degrees, the conversation changed from the loves of Mr Oriel and Beatrice to the troubles of Frank Gresham and herself.

'She says, that let what will happen you shall be one of her bridesmaids.'

'Ah, yes, dear Trichy! that was settled between us in auld lang syne; but those settlements are all unsettled now, must all be broken. No, I cannot be her bridesmaid; but I shall yet hope to see her once before her marriage.'

'And why not be her bridesmaid? Lady Arabella will hardly object to that.'

'Lady Arabella!' said Mary, curling her lip with deep scorn. 'I do not care that for Lady Arabella,' and she let her silver thimble fall from her fingers on to the table. 'If Beatrice invited me to her wedding, she might manage as to that; I should ask no question as to Lady Arabella.'

'Then why not come to it?'

She remained silent for awhile, and then boldly answered, 'Though I do not care for Lady Arabella, I do care for Mr Gresham: – and I do care for his son.'

'But the squire always loved you.'

'Yes, and therefore I will not be there to vex his sight. I will tell you the truth, Patience. I can never be in that house again till Frank Gresham is a married man, or till I am about to be a married woman. I do not think they have treated me well, but I will not treat them ill.'

'I am sure you will not do that,' said Miss Oriel.

'I will endeavour not to do so; and, therefore, will go to none of their fêtes! No, Patience.' And then she turned her head to the arm of the sofa, and silently, without audible sobs, hiding her face, she endeavoured to get rid of her tears unseen. For one moment she had all but resolved to pour out the whole truth of her love into her friend's ears; but suddenly she changed her mind. Why should she talk of her own unhappiness? Why should she speak of her own love when she was fully determined not to speak of Frank's promises?

'Mary, dear Mary.'

'Anything but pity, Patience; anything but that,' said she, convulsively, swallowing down her sobs, and rubbing away her tears. 'I cannot bear that. Tell Beatrice from me, that I wish her every happiness; and, with such a husband, I am sure she will be happy. I wish her every joy; give her my kindest love; but tell her I cannot be at her marriage. Oh, I should so like to see her; not there, you know, but here, in my own room, where I still have liberty to speak.'

'But why should you decide now? She is not to be married yet, you know.'

'Now, or this day twelvemonth, can make no difference. I will not go into that house again, unless – but never mind; I will not go into it all; never, never again. If I could forgive her for myself, I could not forgive her for my uncle. But tell me, Patience, might not Beatrice now come here? It is so dreadful to see her every Sunday in church and never to speak to her, never to kiss her. She seems to look away from me as though she too had chosen to quarrel with me.'

Miss Oriel promised to do her best. She could not imagine, she said, that such a visit could be objected to on such an occasion. She would not advise Beatrice to come without telling her mother; but she could not think that Lady Arabella would be so cruel as to make any objection, knowing, as she could not but know, that her daughter, when married, would be at liberty to choose her own friends.

'Good-bye, Mary,' said Patience. 'I wish I knew how to say more to comfort you.'

'Oh, comfort! I don't want comfort. I want to be let alone.'

'That's just it: you are so ferocious in your scorn, so unbending, so determined to take all the punishment that comes in your way.'

'What I do take, I'll take without complaint,' said Mary; and then they kissed each other and parted.

CHAPTER XXXIII

A Morning Visit

It must be remembered that Mary, among her miseries, had to suffer this: that since Frank's departure, now nearly twelve months ago, she had not heard a word about him; or rather, she had only heard that he was very much in love with some lady in London. This news reached her in a manner so circuitous, and from such a doubtful source; it seemed to her to savour so strongly of Lady Arabella's precautions, that she attributed it at once to malice, and blew it to the winds. It might not improbably be the case that Frank was untrue to her; but she would not take it for granted because she was now told so. It was more than probable that he should amuse himself with some one; flirting was his prevailing sin; and if he did flirt, the most would of course be made of it.

But she found it to be very desolate to be thus left alone without a word of comfort or a word of love; without being able to speak to any one of what filled her heart; doubting, nay, more than doubting, being all but sure that her passion must terminate in misery. Why had she not obeyed her conscience and her better instinct in that moment when the necessity for deciding had come upon her? Why had she allowed him to understand that he was master of her heart? Did she not know that there was everything against such a marriage as that which he proposed? Had she not done wrong, very wrong, even to think of it? Had she not sinned deeply against Mr Gresham, who had ever been so kind to her? Could she hope, was it possible, that a boy like Frank should be true to his first love? And, if he were true, if he were ready to go to the altar with her tomorrow, ought she to allow him to degrade himself by such a marriage?

There was, alas! some truth about the London lady. Frank had taken his degree, as arranged, and had then gone abroad for the winter, doing the fashionable things, going up the Nile, crossing over to Mount Sinai, thence over the long desert to Jerusalem, and home by Damascus, Beirut, and Constantinople,* bringing back a long beard, a red cap, and a chibook,* just as our fathers used to go through Italy and Switzerland, and our grandfathers to spend a season in Paris. He had then remained for a couple of months in London, going through all the society which the De Courcys were able to open to him. And it was true that a certain belle of the season, of that season and some others, had been captivated – for the tenth time – by the silken sheen of his long beard. Frank had probably been more demonstrative, perhaps even more susceptible, than he should have been; and hence the rumour, which had all too willingly been forwarded to Greshamsbury.

But young Gresham had also met another lady in London, namely, Miss Dunstable. Mary would indeed have been grateful to Miss Dunstable, could she have known all that lady did for her. Frank's love was never allowed to flag. When he spoke of the difficulties in his way, she twitted him by being overcome by straws; and told him that no one was worth having who was afraid of every lion that he met in his path.* When he spoke of money, she bade him earn it; and always ended by offering to smooth for him any real difficulty which want of means might put in his way.

'No,' Frank used to say to himself, when these offers were made, 'I never intended to take her and her money together; and, therefore, I certainly will never take the money alone.'

A day or two after Miss Oriel's visit, Mary received the following note from Beatrice.

'Dearest, dearest Mary,

'I shall be so happy to see you, and will come tomorrow at twelve. I have asked mamma, and she says that, for once, she has no objection. You know it is not my fault that I have never been with you; don't you? Frank comes home on the 12th. Mr Oriel wants the wedding to be on the 1st of September; but that seems to be so very, very soon; doesn't it? However, mamma and papa are all on his side. I won't write about this though, for we shall have such a delicious talk. Oh, Mary! I have been so unhappy without you.

'Ever your own affectionate,
'Trichy.'

'Monday.'

Though Mary was delighted at the idea of once more having her friend in her arms, there was, nevertheless, something in this letter which oppressed her. She could not put up with the idea that Beatrice should have permission given to come to her – just for once. She hardly wished to be seen by permission. Nevertheless, she did not refuse the proffered visit, and the first sight of Beatrice's face, the first touch of the first embrace, dissipated for the moment all her anger.

And then Beatrice fully enjoyed the delicious talk which she had promised herself. Mary let her have her way, and for two hours all the delights and all the duties, all the comforts and all the responsibilities, of a parson's wife were discussed with almost equal ardour on both sides. The duties and responsibilities were not exactly those which too often fall to the lot of the mistress of an English vicarage. Beatrice was not doomed to make her husband comfortable, to educate her children, dress herself like a lady, and exercise open-handed charity on an income of two hundred pounds a year. Her duties and responsibilities would have to spread themselves over seven or eight times that amount of worldly burden. Living also close to Greshamsbury, and not far from Courcy Castle, she would have the full advantages and all the privileges of county society. In fact, it was all *couleur de rose*, and so she chatted deliciously with her friend.

But it was impossible that they should separate without something having been said as to Mary's own lot. It would, perhaps, have been better that they should do so; but this was hardly within the compass of human nature.

'And Mary, you know, I shall be able to see you as often as I like; – you and Dr Thorne, too, when I have a house of my own.'

Mary said nothing, but essayed to smile. It was but a ghastly attempt.

'You know how happy that will make me,' continued Beatrice. 'Of course mamma won't expect me to be led by her then: if he likes it, there can be no objection; and he will like it, you may be sure of that.'

'You are very kind, Trichy,' said Mary; but she spoke in a tone very different from that she would have used eighteen months ago.

'Why, what is the matter, Mary? Shan't you be glad to come to see us?'

'I do not know, dearest; that must depend on circumstances.

To see you, yourself, your own dear, sweet, loving face must always be pleasant to me.'

'And shan't you be glad to see him?'

'Yes, certainly, if he loves you.'

'Of course he loves me.'

'All that alone would be pleasant enough, Trichy. But what if there should be circumstances which should still make us enemies; should make your friends and my friends – friend, I should say, for I have only one – should make them opposed to each other?'

'Circumstances! What circumstances?'

'You are going to be married, Trichy, to the man you love; are you not?'

'Indeed, I am!'

'And is it not pleasant? is it not a happy feeling?'

'Pleasant! happy! yes, very pleasant; very happy. But, Mary, I am not at all in such a hurry as he is,' said Beatrice, naturally thinking of her own little affairs.

'And, suppose I should wish to be married to the man that I love?' Mary said this slowly and gravely, and as she spoke she looked her friend full in the face.

Beatrice was somewhat astonished, and for the moment hardly understood. 'I am sure I hope you will, some day.'

'No, Trichy; no, you hope just the other way. I love your brother; I love Frank Gresham; I love him quite as well, quite as warmly, as you love Caleb Oriel.'

'Do you?' said Beatrice, staring with all her eyes, and giving one long sigh, as this new subject for sorrow was so distinctly put before her.

'Is that so odd?' said Mary. 'You love Mr Oriel, though you have been intimate with him hardly more than two years. Is it so odd that I should love your brother, whom I have known almost all my life?'

'But, Mary, I thought it was always understood between us that – that – I mean that you were not to care about him; not in the way of loving him, you know – I thought you always said so – I have always told mamma so as if it came from yourself.'

'Beatrice, do not tell anything to Lady Arabella as though it came from me; I do not want anything to be told to her, either of me or from me. Say what you like to me yourself; whatever you will say will not anger me. Indeed, I know what you would say – and yet I love you. Oh, I love you, Trichy – Trichy, I do love you so much! Don't turn away from me!'

There was such a mixture in Mary's manner of tenderness and almost ferocity, that poor Beatrice could hardly follow her. 'Turn away from you, Mary! no never; but this does make me unhappy.'

'It is better you should know it all, and then you will not be led into fighting my battles again. You cannot fight them so that I should win: I do love your brother; love him truly, fondly, tenderly. I would wish to have him for my husband as you wish to have Mr Oriel.'

'But, Mary, you cannot marry him!'

'Why not?' said she, in a loud voice. 'Why can I not marry him? If the priest says a blessing over us, shall we not be married as well as you and your husband?'

'But you know he cannot marry unless his wife shall have money.'

'Money – money; and he is to sell himself for money! Oh, Trichy do not you talk about money. It is horrible. But, Trichy, I will grant it – I cannot marry him; but still, I love him. He has a name, a place in the world, and fortune, family, high blood, position, everything. He has all this, and I have nothing. Of course I cannot marry him. But yet I love him.'

'Are you engaged to him, Mary?'

'He is not engaged to me; but I am to him.'

'Oh, Mary, that is impossible!'

'It is not impossible: it is the case – I am pledged to him; but he is not pledged to me.'

'But, Mary, don't look at me in that way. I do not quite understand you. What is the good of your being engaged if you cannot marry him?'

'Good! there is no good. But can I help it, if I love him? Can I make myself not love him by just wishing it? Oh, I would do it if I could. But now you will understand why I shake my head when you talk of my coming to your house. Your ways and my ways must be different.'

Beatrice was startled, and, for a time, silenced. What Mary said of the difference of their ways was quite true. Beatrice had dearly loved her friend, and had thought of her with affection through all this long period in which they had been separated; but she had given her love and her thoughts on the understand-

ing, as it were, that they were in unison as to the impropriety of
Frank's conduct.

She had always spoken, with a grave face, of Frank and his
love as of a great misfortune, even to Mary herself; and her pity
for Mary had been founded on the conviction of her innocence.
Now all those ideas had to be altered. Mary owned her fault,
confessed herself to be guilty of all that Lady Arabella so
frequently laid to her charge, and confessed herself anxious to
commit that very crime as to which Beatrice had been ever so
ready to defend her.

Had Beatrice up to this dreamed that Mary was in love with
Frank, she would doubtless have sympathized with her more or
less, sooner or later. As it was, it was beyond all doubt that she
would soon sympathise with her. But, at the moment, the
suddenness of the declaration seemed to harden her heart, and
she forgot, as it were, to speak tenderly to her friend.

She was silent, therefore, and dismayed; and looked as though
she thought that her ways and Mary's ways must be different.

Mary saw all that was passing in the other's mind: no, not all;
all the hostility, the disappointment, the disapproval, the unhappiness, she did see; but not the undercurrent of love, which was
strong enough to well up and drown all these, if only time could
be allowed for it to do so.

'I am glad I have told you,' said Mary, curbing herself, 'for
deceit and hypocrisy are detestable.'

'It was a misunderstanding, not deceit,' said Beatrice.

'Well, now we understand each other; now you know that I
have a heart within me, which like those of some others has not
always been under my own control. Lady Arabella believes that
I am intriguing to be the mistress of Greshamsbury. You, at any
rate, will not think that of me. If it could be discovered
tomorrow that Frank were not the heir, I might have some
chance of happiness.'

'But, Mary – '

'Well?'

'You say you love him.'

'Yes: I do say so.'

'But if he does not love you, will you cease to do so?'

'If I have a fever, I will get rid of it if I can; in such case I must
do so, or die.'

'I fear,' continued Beatrice, 'you hardly know, perhaps do not think, what is Frank's real character. He is not made to settle down early in life; even now, I believe he is attached to some lady in London, whom, of course, he cannot marry.'

Beatrice said this in perfect trueness of heart. She had heard of Frank's new love-affair, and believing what she had heard, thought it best to tell the truth. But the information was not of a kind to quiet Mary's spirit.

'Very well,' said she, 'let it be so. I have nothing to say against it.'

'But are you not preparing wretchedness and unhappiness for yourself?'

'Very likely.'

'Oh, Mary, do not be so cold with me! you know how delighted I should be to have you for a sister-in-law, if only it were possible.'

'Yes, Trichy; but it is impossible, is it not? Impossible that Francis Gresham of Greshamsbury should disgrace himself by marrying such a poor creature as I am. Of course, I know it; of course, I am prepared for unhappiness and misery. He can amuse himself as he likes with me or others – with anybody. It is his privilege. It is quite enough to say that he is not made for settling down. I know my own position; – and yet I love him.'

'But, Mary, has he asked you to be his wife? If so – '

'You ask home-questions, Beatrice. Let me ask you one; has he ever told you that he has done so?'

At this moment, Beatrice was not disposed to repeat all that Frank had said. A year ago, before he went away, he had told his sister a score of times that he meant to marry Mary Thorne if she would have him; but Beatrice now looked on all that as idle, boyish vapouring. The pity was, that Mary should have looked on it differently.

'We will each keep our secret,' said Mary. 'Only remember this: should Frank marry tomorrow, I shall have no ground for blaming him. He is free as far as I am concerned. He can take the London lady if he likes. You may tell him so from me But, Trichy, what else I have told you, I have told to you only.'

'Oh, yes!' said Beatrice sadly; 'I shall say nothing of it to anybody. It is very sad, very, very; I was so happy when I came here, and now I am so wretched.' This was the end of that delicious talk to which she had looked forward with so much eagerness.

'Don't be wretched about me, dearest; I shall get through it. I sometimes think I was born to be unhappy, and that unhappiness agrees with me best. Kiss me now, Trichy, and don't be wretched any more. You owe it to Mr Oriel to be as happy as the day is long.'

And then they parted.

Beatrice, as she went out, saw Dr Thorne in his little shop on the right-hand side of the passage, deeply engaged in some derogatory branch of an apothecary's mechanical trade; mixing a dose, perhaps, for a little child. She would have passed him without speaking if she could have been sure of doing so without notice, for her heart was full, and her eyes were red with tears; but it was so long since she had been in his house that she was more than ordinarily anxious not to appear uncourteous or unkind to him.

'Good morning, doctor,' she said, changing her countenance as best she might, and attempting a smile.

'Ah, my fairy!' said he, leaving his villainous compounds, and coming out to her; 'and you, too, are about to become a steady old lady.'

'Indeed, I am not, doctor; I don't mean to be either steady or old for the next ten years. But who has told you? I suppose Mary has been a traitor.'

'Well, I will confess, Mary was the traitor. But hadn't I a right to be told, seeing how often I have brought you sugar-plums in my pocket? But I wish you joy with all my heart, – with all my heart. Oriel is an excellent, good fellow.'

'Is he not, doctor?'

'An excellent, good fellow. I never heard but of one fault that he had.'

'What was that one fault, Doctor Thorne?'

'He thought that clergymen should not marry. But you have cured that, and now he's perfect.'

'Thank you, doctor. I declare that you say the prettiest things of all my friends.'

'And none of your friends wish prettier things for you. I do congratulate you, Beatrice, and hope you may be happy with the man you have chosen;' and taking both her hands in his, he pressed them warmly, and bade God bless her.

'Oh, doctor! I do so hope the time will come when we shall all be friends again.'

'I hope it as well, my dear. But let it come, or let it not come, my regard for you will be the same:' and then she parted from him also, and went her way.

Nothing was spoken of that evening between Dr Thorne and his niece excepting Beatrice's future happiness; nothing, at least, having reference to what had passed that morning. But on the following morning circumstances led to Frank Gresham's name being mentioned.

At the usual breakfast-hour the doctor entered the parlour with a harassed face. He had an open letter in his hand, and it was at once clear to Mary that he was going to speak to her on some subject that vexed him.

'That unfortunate fellow is again in trouble. Here is a letter from Greyson.' Greyson was a London apothecary, who had been appointed as medical attendant to Sir Louis Scatcherd, and whose real business consisted in keeping a watch on the baronet, and reporting to Dr Thorne when anything was very much amiss. 'Here is a letter from Greyson; he has been drunk for the last three days, and is now laid up in a terribly nervous state.'

'You won't go to town again; will you, uncle?'

'I hardly know what to do. No, I think not. He talks of coming down here to Greshamsbury.'

'Who, Sir Louis?'

'Yes, Sir Louis. Greyson says that he will be down as soon as he can get out of his room.'

'What! to this house?'

'What other house can he come to?'

'Oh, uncle! I hope not. Pray, pray do not let him come here.'

'I cannot prevent it, my dear. I cannot shut my door on him.'

They sat down to breakfast, and Mary gave him his tea in silence. 'I am going over to Boxall Hill before dinner,' said he. 'Have you any message to send to Lady Scatcherd?'

'Message! no, I have no message; not especially: give her my love, of course,' she said, listlessly. And then, as though a thought had suddenly struck her, she spoke with more energy. 'But, couldn't I go to Boxall Hill again? I should be so delighted.'

'What! to run away from Sir Louis? No, dearest, we will have no more running away. He will probably also go to Boxall Hill, and he could annoy you much more there than he can here.'

'But, uncle, Mr Gresham will be at home on the 12th,' she said, blushing.

'What! Frank?'

'Yes. Beatrice said he was to be here on the 12th.'

'And would you run away from him too, Mary?'

'I do not know: I do not know what to do.'

'No; we will have no more running away; I am sorry that you ever did so. It was my fault, altogether my fault; but it was foolish.'

'Uncle, I am not happy here.' As she said this, she put down the cup which she had held, and leaning her elbows on the table, rested her forehead on her hands.

'And would you be happier at Boxall Hill? It is not the place makes the happiness.'

'No, I know that; it is not the place. I do not look to be happy in any place; but I should be quieter, more tranquil elsewhere than here.'

'I also sometimes think that it will be better for us to take up our staves and walk away out of Greshamsbury; – leave it altogether, and settle elsewhere; miles, miles, miles away from here. Should you like that, dearest?'

Miles, miles, miles away from Greshamsbury! There was something in the sound that fell very cold on Mary's ears, unhappy as she was. Greshamsbury had been so dear to her; in spite of all that had passed, was still so dear to her! Was she prepared to take up her staff, as her uncle said, and walk forth from the place with the full understanding that she was to return to it no more; with a mind resolved that there should be an inseparable gulf between her and its inhabitants? Such she knew was the proposed nature of that walking away of which her uncle spoke. So she sat there, resting on her arms, and gave no answer to the question that had been asked her.

'No, we will stay a while yet,' said her uncle. 'It may come to that, but this is not the time. For one season longer let us face – I will not say our enemies; I cannot call anybody my enemy who bears the name of Gresham.' And then he went on for a moment with his breakfast. 'So Frank is to be here on the 12th?'

'Yes, uncle.'

'Well, dearest, I have no questions to ask you; no directions to give. I know how good you are, and how prudent; I am anxious only for your happiness; not at all – '

'Happiness, uncle, is out of the question.'

'I hope not. It is never out of the question, never can be out of the question. But, as I was saying, I am quite satisfied your conduct will be good, and, therefore, I have no questions to ask. We will remain here; and, whether good or evil come, we will not be ashamed to show our faces.'

She sat for a while again silent; collecting her courage on the subject that was nearest her heart. She would have given the world that he should ask her questions; but she could not bid him to do so; and she found it impossible to talk openly to him about Frank unless he did so. 'Will he come here?' at last she said, in a low-toned voice.

'Who? he, Louis? Yes, I think that in all probability he will.'

'No; but Frank,' she said, in a still lower voice.

'Ah! my darling, that I cannot tell; but will it be well that he should come here?'

'I do not know,' she said. 'No, I suppose not. But, uncle, I don't think he will come.'

She was now sitting on a sofa away from the table, and he got up, sat down beside her, and took her hands in his. 'Mary,' said he, 'you must be strong now; strong to endure, not to attack. I think you have that strength; but, if not, perhaps it will be far better that we should go away.'

'I will be strong,' said she, rising up and going towards the door. 'Never mind me, uncle; don't follow me; I will be strong. It will be base, cowardly, mean, to run away; very base in me to make you do so.'

'No, dearest, not so; it will be the same to me.'

'No,' said she, 'I will not run away from Lady Arabella. And, as for him – if he loves this other one, he shall hear no reproach from me. Uncle, I will be strong;' and running back to him, she threw her arms round him and kissed him. And, still restraining her tears, she got safely to her bedroom. In what way she may there have shown her strength, it would not be well for us to inquire.

CHAPTER XXXIV

A Barouche and Four Arrives
at Greshamsbury

During the last twelve months Sir Louis Scatcherd had been very efficacious in bringing trouble, turmoil, and vexation upon Greshamsbury. Now that it was too late to take steps to save himself, Dr Thorne found that the will left by Sir Roger was so made as to entail upon him duties that he would find it almost impossible to perform. Sir Louis, though his father had wished to make him still a child in the eye of the law, was no child. He knew his own rights and was determined to exact them; and before Sir Roger had been dead three months, the doctor found himself in continual litigation with a low Barchester attorney, who was acting on behalf of his, the doctor's, own ward.

And if the doctor suffered so did the squire, and so did those who had hitherto had the management of the squire's affairs. Dr Thorne soon perceived that he was to be driven into litigation, not only with Mr Finnie, the Barchester attorney, but with the squire himself. While Finnie harassed him, he was compelled to harass Mr Gresham. He was no lawyer himself; and though he had been able to manage very well between the squire and Sir Roger, and had perhaps given himself some credit for his lawyer-like ability in so doing, he was utterly unable to manage between Sir Louis and Mr Gresham.

He had, therefore, to employ a lawyer on his own account, and it seemed probable that the whole amount of Sir Roger's legacy to himself would by degrees be expended in this manner. And then, the squire's lawyers had to take up the matter; and they did so greatly to the detriment of poor Mr Yates Umbleby, who was found to have made a mess of the affairs entrusted to him. Mr Umbleby's accounts were incorrect; his mind was anything but clear, and he confessed, when put to it by the very sharp gentleman that came down from London, that he was 'bothered;' and so, after a while, he was suspended from his duties, and Mr Gazebee, the sharp gentleman from London, reigned over the diminished rent-roll of the Greshamsbury estate.

Thus everything was going wrong at Greshamsbury with the

one exception of Mr Oriel and his love-suit. Miss Gushing attributed the deposition of Mr Umbleby to the narrowness of the victory which Beatrice had won in carrying off Mr Oriel. For Miss Gushing was a relation of the Umblebys, and had been for many years one of their family. 'If she had only chosen to exert herself as Miss Gresham had done, she could have had Mr Oriel, easily; oh, too easily! but she had despised such work,' so she said. 'But though she had despised it, the Greshams had not been less irritated, and, therefore, Mr Umbleby had been driven out of his house.' We can hardly believe this, as victory generally makes men generous. Miss Gushing, however, stated it as a fact so often that it is probable she was induced to believe it herself.

Thus everything was going wrong at Greshamsbury, and the squire himself was especially a sufferer. Umbleby had at any rate been his own man, and he could do what he liked with him. He could see him when he liked, and where he liked, and how he liked; could scold him if in an ill-humour, and laugh at him when in a good humour. All this Mr Umbleby knew, and bore. But Mr Gazebee was a very different sort of gentleman; he was the junior partner in the firm of Gumption, Gazebee & Gazebee, of Mount Street, a house that never defiled itself with any other business than the agency business, and that in the very highest line. They drew out leases, and managed property both for the Duke of Omnium and Lord de Courcy; and ever since her marriage, it had been one of the objects dearest to Lady Arabella's heart, that the Greshamsbury acres should be superintended by the polite skill and polished legal ability of that all but elegant firm in Mount Street.

The squire had long stood firm, and had delighted in having everything done under his own eye by poor Mr Yates Umbleby. But now, alas! he could stand it no longer. He had put off the evil day as long as he could; he had deferred the odious work of investigation till things had seemed resolved on investigating themselves; and then, when it was absolutely necessary that Mr Umbleby should go, there was nothing for him left but to fall into the ready hands of Messrs Gumption, Gazebee & Gazebee.

It must not be supposed that Messrs Gumption, Gazebee & Gazebee were in the least like the ordinary run of attorneys. They wrote no letters for six-and-eightpence each:* they collected no debts, filed no bills, made no charge per folio for 'whereases' and 'as aforesaids;' they did no dirty work, and probably were as ignorant of the interior of a court of law as any young lady living in their Mayfair vicinity. No; their business was to manage the property of great people, draw up leases, make legal assignments, get the family marriage settlements made, and look after the wills. Occasionally, also, they had to raise money; but it was generally understood that this was done by proxy.

The firm had been going on for a hundred and fifty years, and the designation had often been altered; but it always consisted of Gumptions and Gazebees differently arranged, and no less hallowed names had ever been permitted to appear. It had been Gazebee, Gazebee & Gumption; then Gazebee & Gumption; then Gazebee, Gumption & Gumption; then Gumption, Gumption & Gazebee; and now it was Gumption, Gazebee & Gazebee.

Mr Gazebee, the junior member of this firm, was a very elegant young man. While looking at him riding in Rotten Row, you would hardly have taken him for an attorney; and had he heard that you had so taken him, he would have been very much surprised indeed. He was rather bald; not being, as people say, quite so young as he was once. His exact age was thirty-eight. But he had a really remarkable pair of jet-black whiskers, which fully made up for any deficiency as to his head; he had also dark eyes, and a beaked nose, what may be called a distinguished mouth, and was always dressed in fashionable attire. The fact was, that Mr Mortimer Gazebee, junior partner in the firm of Gumption, Gazebee & Gazebee, by no means considered himself to be made of that very disagreeable material which mortals call small beer.

When this great firm was applied to, to get Mr Gresham through his difficulties, and when the state of his affairs was made known to them, they at first expressed rather a disinclination for the work. But at last, moved doubtless by their respect for the De Courcy interest, they assented; and Mr Gazebee, junior, went down to Greshamsbury. The poor squire passed many a sad day after that before he again felt himself to be master even of his own domain.

Nevertheless, when Mr Mortimer Gazebee visited Greshamsbury, which he did on more than one of two occasions, he was always received *en grand seigneur*. To Lady Arabella he was by no means an unwelcome guest, for she had found herself able, for the first time in her life, to speak confidentially on her husband's pecuniary affairs with the man who had the management of her husband's property. Mr Gazebee also was a pet with Lady de Courcy; and being known to be a fashionable man in London, and quite a different sore of person from poor Mr Umbleby, he was always received with smiles. He had a hundred little ways of making himself agreeable, and Augusta declared to her cousin, the Lady Amelia, after having been acquainted with him for a few months, that he would be a perfect gentleman, only, that his family had never been anything but attorneys. The Lady Amelia smiled in her own peculiarly aristocratic way, shrugged her shoulders slightly, and said, 'that Mr Mortimer Gazebee was a very good sort of person, very.' Poor Augusta felt herself snubbed, thinking perhaps of the tailor's son; but as there was never any appeal against the Lady Amelia, she said nothing more at that moment in favour of Mr Mortimer Gazebee.

All these evils – Mr Mortimer Gazebee being the worst of them – had Sir Louis Scatcherd brought down on the poor squire's head. There may be those who will say that the squire had brought them on himself, by running into debt; and so, doubtless, he had; but it was not the less true that the baronet's interference was unnecessary, vexatious and one might also say, malicious. His interests would have been quite safe in the doctor's hands, and he had, in fact, no legal right to meddle; but neither the doctor nor the squire could prevent him. Mr Finnie knew very well what he was about, if Sir Louis did not; and so the three went on, each with his own lawyer, and each of them distrustful, unhappy, and ill at ease. This was hard upon the doctor, for he was not in debt, and had borrowed no money.

There was not much reason to suppose that the visit of Sir Louis to Greshamsbury would much improve matters. It must be presumed that he was not coming with any amicable views, but with the object rather of looking after his own; a phrase which was now constantly in his mouth. He might probably find it necessary, while looking after his own at Greshamsbury, to say some very disagreeable things to the squire; and the doctor, therefore, hardly expected that the visit would go off pleasantly.

When last we saw Sir Louis, now nearly twelve months since, he was intent on making a proposal of marriage to Miss Thorne. This intention he carried out about two days after Frank

Gresham had done the same thing. He had delayed doing so until he had succeeded in purchasing his friend Jenkins's Arab pony, imagining that such a present could not but go far in weaning Mary's heart from her other lover. Poor Mary was put to the trouble of refusing both the baronet and the pony, and a very bad time she had of it while doing so. Sir Louis was a man easily angered, and not very easily pacified, and Mary had to endure a good deal of annoyance; from any other person, indeed, she would have called it impertinence. Sir Louis, however, had to bear his rejection as best he could, and, after a perseverance of three days, returned to London in disgust; and Mary had not seen him since.

Mr Greyson's first letter was followed by a second; and the second was followed by the baronet in person. He also required to be received *en grand seigneur*,* perhaps more imperatively than Mr Mortimer Gazebee himself. He came with four posters from the Barchester Station, and had himself rattled up to the doctor's door in a way that took the breath away from all Greshamsbury. Why! the squire himself for many a long year had been contented to come home with a pair of horses; and four were never seen in the place, except when the De Courcys came to Greshamsbury, or Lady Arabella with all her daughters returned from her hard-fought metropolitan campaigns.

Sir Louis, however, came with four, and very arrogant he looked, leaning back in the barouche belonging to the George and Dragon, and wrapped up in fur, although it was now midsummer. And up in the dicky behind was a servant, more arrogant, if possible, than his master – the baronet's own man, who was the object of Dr Thorne's especial detestation and disgust. He was a little fellow, chosen originally on account of his light weight on horseback; but if that may be considered a merit, it was the only one he had. His out-door show dress was a little tight frockcoat, round which a polished strap was always buckled tightly, a stiff white choker, leather breeches, top-boots, and a hat, with a cockade, stuck on one side of his head. His name was Jonah, which his master and his master's friends shortened into Joe; none, however, but those who were very intimate with his master were allowed to do so with impunity.

This Joe was Dr Thorne's especial aversion. In his anxiety to take every possible step to keep Sir Louis from poisoning himself, he had at first attempted to enlist the baronet's 'own man' in the cause. Joe had promised fairly, but had betrayed the doctor at once, and had become the worst instrument of his master's dissipation. When, therefore, his hat and the cockade were seen, as the carriage dashed up to the door, the doctor's contentment was by no means increased.

Sir Louis was now twenty-three years old, and was a great deal too knowing to allow himself to be kept under the doctor's thumb. It had, indeed, become his plan to rebel against his guardian in almost everything. He had at first been decently submissive, with the view of obtaining increased supplies of ready money; but he had been sharp enough to perceive that, lest his conduct be what it would, the doctor would keep him out of debt; but that the doing so took so large a sum that he could not hope for any further advances. In this respect, Sir Louis was perhaps more keen-witted than Dr Thorne.

Mary, when she saw the carriage, at once ran up to her own bedroom. The doctor, who had been with her in the drawing-room, went down to meet his ward, but as soon as he saw the cockade he darted almost involuntarily into his shop and shut the door. This protection, however, lasted only for a moment; he felt that decency required him to meet his guest, and so he went forth and faced the enemy.

'I say,' said Joe, speaking to Janet, who stood curtsying at the gate, with Bridget, the other maid, behind her, 'I say, are there any chaps about the place to take these things – eh? come, look sharp here.'

It so happened that the doctor's groom was not on the spot, and 'other chaps' the doctor had none.

'Take those things, Bridget,' he said, coming forward and offering his hand to the baronet. Sir Louis, when he saw his host, roused himself slowly from the back of his carriage. 'How do, doctor?' said he. 'What terrible bad roads you have here! and, upon my word, it's as cold as winter:' and, so saying, he slowly proceeded to descend.

Sir Louis was a year older than when we last saw him, and, in his generation, a year wiser.* He had then been somewhat humble before the doctor; but now he was determined to let his guardian see that he knew how to act the baronet; that he had acquired the manners of a great man; and that he was not to be put upon. He had learnt some lessons from Jenkins, in London, and other friends of the same sort, and he was about to profit by them.

The doctor showed him to his room, and then proceeded to ask after his health. 'Oh, I'm right enough,' said Sir Louis. 'You mustn't believe all that fellow Greyson tells you: he wants me to take his salts and senna, opodeldoc,* and all that sort of stuff; looks after his bill, you know – eh? like all the rest of you. But I won't have it; – not at any price; and then he writes to you.'

'I'm glad to see you able to travel,' said Dr Thorne, who could not force himself to tell his guest that he was glad to see him at Greshamsbury.

'Oh, travel; yes, I can travel well enough. But I wish you had some better sort of trap down in these country parts. I'm shaken to bits. And, doctor, would you tell your people to send that fellow of mine up here with hot water.'

So dismissed, the doctor went his way, and met Joe swaggering in one of the passages, while Janet and her colleague dragged along between them a heavy article of baggage.

'Janet,' said he, 'go downstairs and get Sir Louis some hot water, and Joe, do you take hold of your master's portmanteau.'

Joe sulkily did as he was bid. 'Seems to me,' said he, turning to the girl, and speaking before the doctor was out of hearing, 'seems to me, my dear, you be rather short-handed here; lots of work and nothing to get; that's about the ticket, ain't it?' Bridget was too demurely modest to make any answer upon so short an acquaintance; so, putting her end of the burden down at the strange gentleman's door, she retreated into the kitchen.

Sir Louis, in answer to the doctor's inquiries, had declared himself to be all right; but his appearance was anything but all right. Twelve months since, a life of dissipation, or rather, perhaps, a life of drinking, had not had upon him so strong an effect but that some of the salt of youth was still left; some of the freshness of young years might still be seen in his face. But this was now all gone; his eyes were sunken and watery, his cheeks were hollow and wan, his mouth was drawn and his lips dry; his back was even bent, and his legs were unsteady under him, so that he had been forced to step down from his carriage as an old man would do. Alas, alas! he had no further chance now of ever being all right again.

Mary had secluded herself in her bedroom as soon as the carriage had driven up to the door, and there she remained till dinner-time. But she could not shut herself up altogether. It would be necessary that she should appear at dinner; and, therefore, a few minutes before the hour, she crept out into the drawing-room. As she opened the door, she looked in timidly, expecting to see Sir Louis there; but when she saw that her uncle was the only occupant of the room, her brow cleared, and she entered with a quick step.

'He'll come down to dinner; won't he, uncle?'

'Oh, I suppose so.'

'What's he doing now?'

'Dressing, I suppose; he's been at it this hour.'

'But, uncle – '

'Well?'

'Will he come up after dinner, do you think?'

Mary spoke of him as though he were some wild beast, whom her uncle insisted on having in his house.

'Goodness knows what he will do! Come up? Yes. He will not stay in the dining-room all night.'

'But, dear uncle, do be serious.'

'Serious!'

'Yes; serious. Don't you think I might go to bed, instead of waiting?'

The doctor was saved the trouble of answering by the entrance of the baronet. He was dressed in what he considered the most fashionable style of the day. He had on a new dress-coat lined with satin, new dress-trousers, a silk waistcoat covered with chains, a white cravat, polished pumps, and silk stockings, and he carried a scented handkerchief in his hand; he had rings on his fingers, and carbuncle studs in his shirt, and he smelt as sweet as patchouli could make him. But he could hardly do more than shuffle into the room, and seemed almost to drag one of his legs behind him.

Mary, in spite of her aversion, was shocked and distressed when she saw him. He, however, seemed to think himself perfect, and was no whit abashed by the unfavourable reception which twelve months since had been paid to his suit. Mary came up and shook hands with him, and he received her with a compliment which no doubt he thought must be acceptable. 'Upon my word, Miss Thorne, every place seems to agree with you; one better than another. You were looking charming at

Boxall Hill; but, upon my word, charming isn't half strong enough now.'

Mary sat down quietly, and the doctor assumed a face of unutterable disgust. This was the creature for whom all his sympathies had been demanded, all his best energies put in requisition; on whose behalf he was to quarrel with his oldest friends, lose his peace and quietness of life, and exercise all the functions of a loving friend. This was his self-invited guest, whom he was bound to foster, and whom he could not turn from his door.

Then dinner came, and Mary had to put her hand upon his arm. She certainly did not lean upon him, and once or twice felt inclined to give him some support. They reached the dining-room, however, the doctor following them, and then sat down, Janet waiting in the room, as was usual.

'I say, doctor,' said the baronet, 'hadn't my man better come in and help? He's got nothing to do, you know. We should be more cosy, shouldn't we?'

'Janet will manage pretty well,' said the doctor.

'Oh, you'd better have Joe; there's nothing like a good servant at table. I say, Janet, just send that fellow in, will you?'

'We shall do very well without him,' said the doctor, becoming rather red about the cheek-bones, and with a slight gleam of determination about the eye. Janet, who saw how matters stool made no attempt to obey the baronet's order.

'Oh, nonsense, doctor; you think he's an uppish sort of fellow, I know, and you don't like to trouble him; but when I'm near him, he's all right; just send him in, will you?'

'Sir Louis,' said the doctor, 'I'm accustomed to none but my own old woman here in my own house, and if you will allow me, I'll keep my old ways. I shall be sorry if you are not comfortable.' The baronet said nothing more, and the dinner passed off slowly and wearily enough.

When Mary had eaten her fruit and escaped, the doctor got into one arm-chair and the baronet into another, and the latter began the only work of existence of which he knew anything.

'That's good port,' said he; 'very fair port.'

The doctor loved his port wine, and thawed a little in his manner. He loved it not as a toper, but as a collector loves his pet pictures. He liked to talk about it, and think about it; to praise it, and hear it praised; to look at it turned towards the light, and to count over the years it had lain in his cellar.

'Yes,' said he, 'it's pretty fair wine. It was, at least, when I got it, twenty years ago, and I don't suppose time has hurt it;' and he held the glass up to the window, and looked at the evening light through the ruby tint of the liquid. 'Ah, dear, there's not much of it left; more's the pity.'

'A good thing won't last for ever. I'll tell you what now; I wish I'd brought down a dozen or two of claret. I've some prime stuff in London; got it from Muzzle & Drug, at ninety-six shillings; it was a great favour, though. I'll tell you what now, I'll send up for a couple of dozen tomorrow. I mustn't drink you out of house, high and dry; must I, doctor?'

The doctor froze again immediately.

'I don't think I need trouble you,' said he: 'I never drink claret, at least not here; and there's enough of the old bin left to last some little time longer yet.'

Sir Louis drank two or three glasses of wine very quickly after each other, and they immediately began to tell upon his weak stomach. But before he was tipsy, he became more impudent and more disagreeable.

'Doctor,' said he, 'when are we to see any of this Greshamsbury money? That's what I want to know.'

'Your money is quite safe, Sir Louis; and the interest is paid to the day.'

'Interest, yes; but how do I know how long it will be paid? I should like to see the principal. A hundred thousand pounds, or something like it, is a precious large stake to have in one man's hands, and he preciously hard up himself. I'll tell you what, doctor – I shall look the squire up myself.'

'Look him up?'

'Yes; look him up; ferret him out; tell him a bit of my mind. I'll thank you to pass the bottle. D— me, doctor; I mean to know how things are going on.'

'Your money is quite safe,' repeated the doctor, 'and, to my mind, it could not be better invested.'

'That's all very well; d— well, I dare say, for you and Squire Gresham – '

'What do you mean, Sir Louis?'

'Mean! why I mean that I'll sell the squire up; that's what I mean – hallo – beg pardon. I'm blessed if I haven't broken the

water-jug. That comes of having water on the table. Oh, d—
me, it's all over me.' And then, getting up, to avoid the flood he
himself had caused, he nearly fell into the doctor's arms.

'You're tired with your journey, Sir Louis; perhaps you'd
better go to bed.'

'Well, I am a bit seedy or so. Those cursed roads of yours
shake a fellow so.'

The doctor rang the bell, and, on this occasion, did request
that Joe might be sent for. Joe came in, and, though he was
much steadier than his master, looked as though he also had
found some bin of which he had approved.

'Sir Louis wishes to go to bed,' said the doctor; 'you had
better give him your arm.'

'Oh, yes; in course I will,' said Joe, standing immovable about
half-way between the door and the table.

'I'll just take one more glass of the old port – eh, doctor?' said
Sir Louis, putting out his hand and clutching the decanter.

It is very hard for any man to deny his guest in his own house,
and the doctor, at the moment, did not know how to do it; so
Sir Louis got his wine, after pouring half of it over the table.

'Come in, sir, and give Sir Louis your arm,' said the doctor,
angrily.

'So I will, in course, if my master tells me; but, if you please,
Dr Thorne' – and Joe put his hand up to his hair in a manner
that had a great deal more of impudence than reverence in it –
'I just want to ax one question: where be I to sleep?'

Now this was a question which the doctor was not prepared
to answer on the spur of the moment, however well Janet or
Mary might have been able to do so.

'Sleep!' said he, 'I don't know where you are to sleep, and
don't care; ask Janet.'

'That's all very well, master – '

'Hold your tongue, sirrah!' said Sir Louis. 'What the devil do
you want of sleep? – come here,' and then, with his servant's
help, he made his way up to his bedroom, and was no more
heard of that night.

'Did he get tipsy?' asked Mary, almost in a whisper, when her
uncle joined her in the drawing-room.

'Don't talk of it,' said he. 'Poor wretch! poor wretch! Let's
have some tea now, Molly, and pray don't talk any more about

him tonight.' Then Mary did make the tea, and did not talk any more about Sir Louis that night.

What on earth were they to do with him? He had come there self-invited; but his connexion with the doctor was such, that it was impossible he should be told to go away, either he himself, or that servant of his. There was no reason to disbelieve him when he declared that he had come down to ferret out the squire. Such was, doubtless, his intention. He would ferret out the squire. Perhaps he might ferret out Lady Arabella also. Frank would be home in a few days; and he, too, might be ferreted out.

But the matter took a very singular turn, and one quite unexpected on the doctor's part. On the morning following the little dinner of which we have spoken, one of the Greshamsbury grooms rode up to the doctor's door with two notes. One was addressed to the doctor in the squire's well-known large hand-writing, and the other was for Sir Louis. Each contained an invitation to dinner for the following day; and that to the doctor was in this wise:–

'Dear Doctor,

'Do come and dine here tomorrow, and bring Sir Louis Scatch-erd with you. If you're the man I take you to be, you won't refuse me. Lady Arabella sends a note for Sir Louis. There will be nobody here but Oriel, and Mr Gazebee, who is staying in the house.

'Yours ever,
'F. N. Gresham.

'*Greshamsbury, July*, 185–.

'P.S. – I make a positive request that you'll come, and I think you will hardly refuse me.'

The doctor read it twice before he could believe it, and then ordered Janet to take the other note up to Sir Louis. As these invitations were rather in opposition to the then existing Greshamsbury tactics, the cause of Lady Arabella's special civility must be explained.

Mr Mortimer Gazebee was now at the house, and therefore, it must be presumed, that things were not allowed to go on after their old fashion. Mr Gazebee was an acute as well as a fashionable man; one who knew what he was about, and who, moreover, had determined to give his very best efforts on behalf of the Greshamsbury property. His energy, in this respect, will explain itself hereafter. It was not probable that the arrival in the village of such a person as Sir Louis Scatcherd should escape attention. He had heard of it before dinner, and, before the evening was over, had discussed it with Lady Arabella.

Her ladyship was not at first inclined to make much of Sir Louis, and expressed herself as but little inclined to agree with Mr Gazebee when that gentleman suggested that he should be treated with civility at Greshamsbury. But she was at last talked over. She found it pleasant enough to have more to do with the secret management of the estate than Mr Gresham himself; and when Mr Gazebee proved to her, by sundry nods and winks, and subtle allusions to her own infinite good sense, that it was necessary to catch this obscene bird which had come to prey upon the estate, by throwing a little salt upon his tail, she also nodded and winked, and directed Augusta to prepare the salt according to order.

'But won't it be odd, Mr Gazebee, asking him out of Doctor Thorne's house?'

'Oh, we must have the doctor too, Lady Arabella; by all means ask the doctor also.'

Lady Arabella's brow grew dark. 'Mr Gazebee,' she said, 'you can hardly believe how that man has behaved to me.'

'He is altogether beneath your anger,' said Mr Gazebee, with a bow.

'I don't know: in one way he may be, but not in another. I really do not think I can sit down to table with Doctor Thorne.'

But, nevertheless, Mr Gazebee gained his point. It was now about a week since Sir Omicron Pie had been at Greshamsbury, and the squire had, almost daily, spoken to his wife as to that learned man's last advice. Lady Arabella always answered in the same tone: 'You can hardly know, Mr Gresham, how that man has insulted me.' But, nevertheless, the physician's advice had not been disbelieved: it tallied too well with her own inward convictions. She was anxious enough to have Doctor Thorne back at her bedside, if she could only get him there without damage to her pride. Her husband, she thought, might probably send the doctor there without absolute permission from herself, in which case she would have been able to scold, and show that she was offended; and, at the same time, profit by what had been done. But Mr Gresham never thought of taking so violent a step as this, and, therefore, Dr Fillgrave still came, and her ladyship's *finesse* was wasted in vain.

But Mr Gazebee's proposition opened a door by which her point might be gained. 'Well,' said she, at last, with infinite self-denial, 'if you think it is for Mr Gresham's advantage, and if he chooses to ask Dr Thorne, I will not refuse to receive him.'

Mr Gazebee's next task was to discuss the matter with the squire. Nor was this easy, for Mr Gazebee was no favourite with Mr Gresham. But the task was at last performed successfully. Mr Gresham was so glad at heart to find himself able, once more, to ask his old friend to his own house; and, though it would have pleased him better that this sign of relenting on his wife's part should have reached him by other means, he did not refuse to take advantage of it; and so he wrote the above letter to Dr Thorne.

The doctor, as we have said, read it twice; and he at once resolved stoutly that he would not go.

'Oh, do, do, go!' said Mary. She well knew how wretched this feud had made her uncle. 'Pray, pray go!'

'Indeed, I will not,' said he. 'There are some things a man should bear, and some he should not.'

'You must go,' said Mary, who had taken the note from her uncle's hand, and read it. 'You cannot refuse him when he asks you like that.'

'It will greatly grieve me; but I must refuse him.'

'I also am angry, uncle; very angry with Lady Arabella; but for him, for the squire, I would go to him on my knees if he asked me in that way.'

'Yes; and had he asked you, I also would have gone.'

'Oh! now I shall be so wretched. It is his invitation, not hers: Mr Gresham could not ask me. As for her, do not think of her; but do, do go when he asks you like that. You will make me so miserable if you do not. And then Sir Louis cannot go without you,' – and Mary pointed upstairs – 'and you may be sure that he will go.'

'Yes; and make a beast of himself.'

This colloquy was cut short by a message praying the doctor to go up to Sir Louis's room. The young man was sitting in his dressing-gown, drinking a cup of coffee at his toilet-table, while Joe was preparing his razor and hot water. The doctor's nose immediately told him that there was more in the coffee-cup than had come out of his own kitchen, and he would not let the offence pass unnoticed.

'Are you taking brandy this morning, Sir Louis?'

'Just a little *chasse-café*,'* said he, not exactly understanding the word he used. 'It's all the go now; and a capital thing for the stomach.'

'It's not a capital thing for your stomach; – about the least capital thing you can take; that is, if you wish to live.'

'Never mind that now, doctor, but look here. This is what we call the civil thing – eh?' and he showed the Greshamsbury note. 'Not but what they have an object, of course. I understand all that. Lots of girls there – eh?'

The doctor took the note and read it. 'It is civil,' said he; 'very civil.'

'Well; I shall go, of course. I don't bear malice because he can't pay me the money he owes me. I'll eat his dinner, and look at the girls. Have you an invite too, doctor?'

'Yes; I have.'

'And you'll go?'

'I think not; but that need not deter you. But, Sir Louis – '

'Well! eh! what is it?'

'Step downstairs a moment,' said the doctor, turning to the servant, 'and wait till you are called for. I wish to speak to your master.' Joe, for a moment, looked up at the baronet's face, as though he wanted but the slightest encouragement to disobey the doctor's orders; but not seeing it, he slowly retired, and placed himself, of course, at the keyhole.

And then the doctor began a long and very useless lecture. The first object of it was to induce his ward not to get drunk at Greshamsbury; but having got so far, he went on, and did succeed in frightening his unhappy guest. Sir Louis did not possess the iron nerves of his father – nerves which even brandy had not been able to subdue. The doctor spoke strongly, very strongly; spoke of quick, almost immediate death in case of further excesses; spoke to him of the certainty there would be that he could not live to dispose of his own property if he could not refrain. And thus he did frighten Sir Louis. The father he had never been able to frighten. But there are men who, though they fear death hugely, fear present suffering more; who, indeed, will not bear a moment of pain if there be any mode of escape. Sir Louis was such: he had no strength of nerve, no courage, no ability to make a resolution and keep it. He promised the doctor that he would refrain; and, as he did so, he swallowed down his cup of coffee and brandy, in which the two articles bore about equal proportions.

The doctor did, at last, make up his mind to go. Whichever way he determined, he found that he was not contented with himself. He did not like to trust Sir Louis by himself, and he did not like to show that he was angry. Still less did he like the idea of breaking bread in Lady Arabella's house till some amends had been made to Mary. But his heart would not allow him to refuse the petition contained in the squire's postscript, and the matter ended in his accepting the invitation.

This visit of his ward's was, in every way, pernicious to the doctor. He could not go about his business, fearing to leave such a man alone with Mary. On the afternoon of the second day, she escaped to the parsonage for an hour or so, and then walked away among the lanes, calling on some of her old friends among the farmers' wives. But even then, the doctor was afraid to leave Sir Louis. What could such a man do, left alone in a village like Greshamsbury? So he stayed at home, and the two together went over their accounts. The baronet was particular about his accounts, and said a good deal as to having Finnie over to Greshamsbury. To this, however, Dr Thorne positively refused his consent.

The evening passed off better than the preceding one; at least, the early part of it. Sir Louis did not get tipsy: he came up to tea, and Mary, who did not feel so keenly on the subject as her uncle, almost wished that he had done so. At ten o'clock he went to bed.

But after that new troubles came on. The doctor had gone downstairs into his study to make up some of the time which he had lost, and had just seated himself at his desk, when Janet, without announcing herself, burst into the room; and Bridget, dissolved in hysterical tears, with her apron to her eyes, appeared behind the senior domestic.

'Please, sir,' said Janet, driven by excitement much beyond her usual pace of speaking, and becoming unintentionally a little less respectful than usual, 'please sir, that 'ere young man must go out of this here house; or else no respectable young 'ooman can't stop here; no, indeed, sir; and we be sorry to trouble you, Dr Thorne; so we be.'

'What young man? Sir Louis?' asked the doctor.

'Oh, no! he abides mostly in bed, and don't do nothing amiss; least way not to us. 'Tan't him, sir; but his man.'

'Man!' sobbed Bridget from behind. 'He an't no man, nor nothing like a man. If Tummas had been here, he wouldn't have dared; so he wouldn't.' Thomas was the groom, and, if all Greshamsbury reports were true, it was probable, that on some happy, future day, Thomas and Bridget would become one flesh and one bone.

'Please, sir,' continued Janet, 'there'll be bad work here if that 'ere young man doesn't quit this here house this very night, and I'm sorry to trouble you, doctor; and so I am. But Tom, he be given to fight a'most for nothin'. He's hout now; but if that there young man be's here when Tom comes home, Tom will be punching his head; I know he will.'

'He wouldn't stand by and see a poor girl put upon; no more he wouldn't,' said Bridget, through her tears.

After many futile inquiries, the doctor ascertained, that Mr Jonah had expressed some admiration for Bridget's youthful charms, and had, in the absence of Janet, thrown himself at the lady's feet in a manner which had not been altogether pleasing to her. She had defended herself stoutly and loudly, and in the middle of the row Janet had come down.

'And where is he now?' said the doctor.

'Why, sir,' said Janet, 'the poor girl was so put about that she did give him one touch across the face with the rolling-pin, and he be all bloody now, in the back kitchen.' At hearing this achievement of hers thus spoken of, Bridget sobbed more hysterically than ever; but the doctor, looking at her arm as she held the apron to her face, thought in his heart that Joe must have had so much the worst of it, that there could be no possible need for the interference of Thomas the groom.

And such turned out to be the case. The bridge of Joe's nose was broken; and the doctor had to set it for him in a little bedroom at the village public-house, Bridget having positively refused to go to bed in the same house with so dreadful a character.

'Quiet now, or I'll be serving thee the same way; thee see I've found the trick of it.' The doctor could not but hear so much as he made his way into his own house by the back door, after finishing his surgical operation. Bridget was recounting to her champion the fracas that had occurred; and he, as was so natural, was expressing his admiration at her valour.

CHAPTER XXXV

Sir Louis Goes Out to Dinner

The next day Joe did not make his appearance, and Sir Louis, with many execrations, was driven to the terrible necessity of dressing himself. Then came an unexpected difficulty: how were they to get up to the house? Walking out to dinner, though it was merely through the village and up the avenue, seemed to Sir Louis to be a thing impossible. Indeed, he was not well able to walk at all, and positively declared that he should never be able to make his way over the gravel in pumps. His mother would not have thought half as much of walking from Boxall Hill to Greshamsbury and back again. At last, the one village fly was sent for, and the matter was arranged.

When they reached the house, it was easy to see that there was some unwonted bustle. In the drawing-room there was no one but Mr Mortimer Gazebee, who introduced himself to them both. Sir Louis, who knew that he was only an attorney, did not take much notice of him, but the doctor entered into conversation.

'Have you heard that Mr Gresham has come home?' said Mr Gazebee.

'Mr Gresham; I did not know that he had been away.'

'Mr Gresham, junior, I mean.' No, indeed; the doctor had not heard. Frank had returned unexpectedly just before dinner, and he was now undergoing his father's smiles, his mother's embraces, and his sisters' questions.

'Quite unexpectedly,' said Mr Gazebee. 'I don't know what has brought him back before his time. I suppose he found London too hot.'

'Deuced hot,' said the baronet. 'I found it so, at lease. I don't know what keeps men in London when it's so hot; except those fellows who have business to do; they're paid for it.'

Mr Mortimer Gazebee looked at him. He was managing an

estate which owed Sir Louis an enormous sum of money, and, therefore, he could not afford to despise the baronet; but he thought to himself, what a very abject fellow the man would be if he were not a baronet, and had not a large fortune!

And then the squire came in. His broad, honest face was covered with a smile when he saw the doctor.

'Thorne,' he said, almost in a whisper, 'you're the best fellow breathing; I have hardly deserved this.' The doctor, as he took his old friend's hand, could not but be glad that he had followed Mary's counsel.

'So Frank has come home?'

'Oh, yes; quite unexpectedly. He was to have stayed a week longer in London. You would hardly know him if you met him. Sir Louis, I beg your pardon.' And the squire went up to his other guest, who had remained somewhat sullenly standing in one corner of the room. He was the man of highest rank present, or to be present, and he expected to be treated as such.

'I am happy to have the pleasure of making your acquaintance, Mr Gresham,' said the baronet, intending to be very courteous. 'Though we have not met before, I very often see your name in my accounts – ha! ha! ha!' and Sir Louis laughed as though he had said something very good.

The meeting between Lady Arabella and the doctor was rather distressing to the former; but she managed to get over it. She shook hands with him graciously, and said that it was a fine day. The doctor said that it was fine, only perhaps a little rainy. And then they went into different parts of the room.

When Frank came in, the doctor hardly did know him. His hair was darker than it had been, and so was his complexion; but his chief disguise was in a long silken beard, which hung down over his cravat. The doctor had hitherto not been much in favour of long beards,* but he could not deny that Frank looked very well with the appendage.

'Oh, doctor, I am so delighted to find you here,' said he, coming up to him; 'so very, very glad:' and, taking the doctor's arm, he led him away into a window, where they were alone. 'And how is Mary?' said he, almost in a whisper. 'Oh, I wish she were here! But, doctor, it shall all come in time. But tell me, doctor, there is no news about her, is there?'

'News – what news?'

'Oh, well; no news is good news: you will give her my love, won't you?'

The doctor said that he would. What else could he say? It appeared quite clear to him that some of Mary's fears were groundless.

Frank was again very much altered. It has been said, that though he was a boy at twenty-one, he was a man at twenty-two. But now, at twenty-three, he appeared to be almost a man of the world. His manners were easy, his voice under his control, and words were at his command: he was no longer either shy or noisy; but, perhaps, was open to the charge of seeming, at least, to be too conscious of his own merits. He was, indeed, very handsome; tall, manly, and powerfully built, his form was such as women's eyes have ever loved to look upon. 'Ah, if he would but marry money!' said Lady Arabella to herself, taken up by a mother's natural admiration for her son. His sisters clung round him before dinner, all talking to him at once. How proud a family of girls are of one big, tall, burly brother!

'You don't mean to tell me, Frank, that you are going to eat soup with that beard?' said the squire, when they were seated round the table. He had not ceased to rally his son as to this patriarchal adornment; but, nevertheless, any one could have seen, with half an eye, that he was as proud of it as were the others.

'Don't I, sir? All I require is a relay of napkins for every course:' and he went to work, covering it with every spoonful, as men with beards always do.

'Well, if you like it.' said the squire, shrugging his shoulders.

'But I do like it,' said Frank.

'Oh, papa, you wouldn't have him cut it off,' said one of the twins. 'It is so handsome.'

'I should like to work it into a chair-back instead of floss-silk,' said the other twin.

'Thank'ee, Sophy; I'll remember you for that.'

'Doesn't it look nice, and grand, and patriarchal?' said Beatrice, turning to her neighbour.

'Patriarchal, certainly,' said Mr Oriel. 'I should grow one myself if I had not the fear of the archbishop before my eyes.'

What was next said to him was in a whisper, audible only to himself.

'Doctor, did you know Wildman, of the 9th? He was left as

surgeon at Scutari* for two years. Why, my beard to his is only a little down.'

'A little way down, you mean,' said Mr Gazebee.

'Yes,' said Frank, resolutely set against laughing at Mr Gazebee's pun. 'Why, his beard descends to his ankles, and he is obliged to tie it in a bag at night, because his feet get entangled in it when he is asleep!'

'Oh, Frank!' said one of the girls.

This was all very well for the squire, and Lady Arabella, and the girls. They were all delighted to praise Frank, and talk about him. Neither did it come amiss to Mr Oriel and the doctor, who had both a personal interest in the young hero. But Sir Louis did not like it at all. He was the only baronet in the room, and yet nobody took any notice of him. He was seated in the post of honour, next to Lady Arabella; but even Lady Arabella seemed to think more of her own son than of him. Seeing how he was ill-used, he meditated revenge; but not the less did it behove him to make some effort to attract attention.

'Was your ladyship long in London, this season?' said he.

Lady Arabella had not been in London at all this year, and it was a sore subject with her. 'No,' said she, very graciously; 'circumstances have kept us at home.'

Sir Louis only understood one description of 'circumstances.' Circumstances, in his idea, meant the want of money, and he immediately took Lady Arabella's speech as a confession of poverty.

'Ah, indeed! I am very sorry for that; that must be very distressing to a person like your ladyship. But things are mending, perhaps?'

Lady Arabella did not in the least understand him. 'Mending!' she said, in her peculiar tone of aristocratic indifference; and then turned to Mr Gazebee, who was on the other side of her.

Sir Louis was not going to stand for this. He was the first man in the room, and he knew his own importance. It was not to be borne that Lady Arabella should turn to talk to a dirty attorney, and leave him, a baronet, to eat his dinner without notice. If nothing else would move her, he would let her know who was the real owner of the Greshamsbury title-deeds.

'I think I saw your ladyship out today, taking a ride.' Lady Arabella had driven through the village in her pony-chair.

'I never ride,' said she, turning her head for one moment from Mr Gazebee.

'In the one-horse carriage, I mean, my lady. I was delighted with the way you whipped him up round the corner.'

Whipped him up round the corner! Lady Arabella could make no answer to this; so she went on talking to Mr Gazebee. Sir Louis, repulsed, but not vanquished – resolved not to be vanquished by any Lady Arabella – turned his attention to his plate for a minute or two, and then recommenced.

'The honour of a glass of wine with you, Lady Arabella,' said he.

'I never take wine at dinner,' said Lady Arabella. The man was becoming intolerable to her, and she was beginning to fear that it would be necessary for her to fly the room, to get rid of him.

The baronet was again silent for a moment; but he was determined not to be put down.

'This is a nice-looking country about here,' said he.

'Yes; very nice,' said Mr Gazebee, endeavouring to relieve the lady of the mansion.

'I hardly know which I like best; this, or my own place at Boxall Hill. You have the advantage here in trees, and those sort of things. But, as to the house, why, my box there is very comfortable, very. You'd hardly know the place now, Lady Arabella, if you haven't seen it since my governor bought it. How much do you think he spent about the house and grounds, pineries included, you know, and those sort of things?'

Lady Arabella shook her head.

'Now guess, my lady,' said he. But it was not to be supposed that Lady Arabella should guess on such a subject.

'I never guess,' said she, with a look of ineffable disgust.

'What do you say, Mr Gazebee?'

'Perhaps a hundred thousand pounds.'

'What! for a house? You can't know much about money, nor yet about building, I think, Mr Gazebee.'

'Not much,' said Mr Gazebee, 'as to such magnificent places as Boxall Hill.'

'Well, my lady, if you won't guess, I'll tell you. It cost twenty-two thousand four hundred and nineteen pounds four shillings and eightpence. I've all the accounts exact. Now, that's a tidy lot of money for a house for a man to live in.'

Sir Louis spoke thus in a loud tone, which at least commanded the attention of the table. Lady Arabella, vanquished, bowed her head, and said that it was a large sum; Mr Gazebee went on sedulously eating his dinner; the squire was struck momentarily dumb in the middle of a long chat with the doctor; even Mr Oriel ceased to whisper; and the girls opened their eyes with astonishment. Before the end of his speech, Sir Louis's voice had become very loud.

'Yes, indeed,' said Frank; 'a very tidy lot of money. I'd have generously dropped the four and eightpence if I'd been the architect.'

'It wasn't all one bill; but that's the tot. I can show the bills:' and Sir Louis, well pleased with his triumph, swallowed a glass of wine.

Almost immediately after the cloth was removed, Lady Arabella escaped, and the gentlemen clustered together. Sir Louis found himself next to Mr Oriel, and began to make himself agreeable.

'A very nice girl, Miss Beatrice; very nice.'

Now Mr Oriel was a modest man, and, when thus addressed as to his future wife, found it difficult to make any reply.

'You parsons always have your own luck,' said Sir Louis. 'You get all the beauty, and generally all the money, too. Not much of the latter in this case, though – eh?'

Mr Oriel was dumbfounded. He had never said a word to any creature as to Beatrice's dowry; and when Mr Gresham had told him, with sorrow, that his daughter's portion must be small, he had at once passed away from the subject as one that was hardly fit for conversation, even between him and his future father-in-law; and now he was abruptly questioned on the subject by a man he had never before seen in his life. Of course, he could make no answer.

'The squire has muddled his matters most uncommonly,' continued Sir Louis, filling his glass for the second time before he passed the bottle. 'What do you suppose now he owes me, alone; just at one lump, you know?'

Mr Oriel had nothing for it but to run. He could make no answer, nor would he sit there to hear tidings as to Mr Gresham's embarrassments. So he fairly retreated, without having said one word to his neighbour, finding such discretion to be the only kind of valour left to him.*

'What, Oriel! off already?' said the squire. 'Anything the matter?'

'Oh, no; nothing particular. I'm not just quite – I think I'll go out for a few minutes.'

'See what it is to be in love,' said the squire, half whispering to Dr Thorne. 'You're not in the same way, I hope?'

Sir Louis then shifted his seat again, and found himself next to Frank. Mr Gazebee was opposite to him, and the doctor opposite to Frank.

'Parson seems peekish, I think,' said the baronet.

'Peekish?' said the squire, inquisitively.

'Rather down on his luck. He's decently well off himself, isn't he?'

There was another pause, and nobody seemed inclined to answer the question.

'I mean, he's got something more than his bare living.'

'Oh, yes,' said Frank, laughing. 'He's got what will buy him bread and cheese when the Rads shut up the Church: – unless, indeed, they shut up the Funds* too.'

'Ah, there's nothing like land,' said Sir Louis: 'nothing like the dirty acres; is there, squire?'

'Land is a very good investment, certainly,' said Mr Gresham.

'The best going,' said the other, who was now, as people say when they mean to be good-natured, slightly under the influence of liquor. 'The best going – eh, Gazebee?'

Mr Gazebee gathered himself up, and turned away his head, looking out of the window.

'You lawyers never like to give an opinion without money, ha! ha! ha! Do they, Mr Gresham? You and I have had to pay for plenty of them, and will have to pay for plenty more before they let us alone.'

Here Mr Gazebee got up, and followed Mr Oriel out of the room. He was not, of course, on such intimate terms in the house as was Mr Oriel; but he hoped to be forgiven by the ladies in consequence of the severity of the miseries to which he was subjected. He and Mr Oriel were soon to be seen through the dining-room window, walking about the grounds with the two eldest Miss Greshams. And Patience Oriel, who had also been of the party, was also to be seen with the twins. Frank looked at his father with almost a malicious smile, and began to think that he too might be better employed out among the walks. Did he think then of a former summer evening, when he had half broken Mary's heart by walking there too lovingly with Patience Oriel?

Sir Louis, if he continued his brilliant career of success, would soon be left the cock of the walk. The squire, to be sure, could not bolt, nor could the doctor very well; but they might be equally vanquished, remaining there in their chairs. Dr Thorne, during all this time, was sitting with tingling ears. Indeed, it may be said that his whole body tingled. He was in a manner responsible for this horrid scene; but what could he do to stop it? He could not take Sir Louis up bodily and carry him away. One idea did occur to him. The fly had been ordered for ten o'clock. He could rush out and send for it instantly.

'You're not going to leave me?' said the squire, in a voice of horror, as he saw the doctor rising from his chair.

'Oh, no, no, no,' said the doctor; and then he whispered the purpose of his mission. 'I will be back in two minutes.' The doctor would have given twenty pounds to have closed the scene at once; but he was not the man to desert his friend in such a strait as that.

'He's a well-meaning fellow, is the doctor,' said Sir Louis, when his guardian was out of the room, 'very; but he's not up to trap* – not at all.'

'Up to trap – well, I should say he was; that is, if I know what trap means,' said Frank.

'Ah, but that's just the ticket. Do you know? Now I say Dr Thorne's not a man of the world.'

'He's about the best man I know, or ever heard of,' said the squire. 'And if any man ever had a good friend, you have got one in him; and so have I:' and the squire silently drank the doctor's health.

'All very true, I dare say; but yet he's not up to trap. Now look here, squire – '

'If you don't mind, sir,' said Frank, 'I've got something very particular – perhaps, however – '

'Stay till Thorne returns, Frank.'

Frank did stay till Thorne returned, and then escaped.

'Excuse me, doctor,' said he, 'but I've something very particular to say; I'll explain tomorrow.' And then the three were left alone.

Sir Louis was now becoming almost drunk, and was knocking

his words together. The squire had already attempted to stop the bottle; but the baronet had contrived to get hold of a modicum of Madeira, and there was no preventing him from helping himself; at least none at that moment.

'As we were saying about lawyers,' continued Sir Louis. 'Let's see, what were we saying? Why, squire, it's just here. Those fellows will fleece us both if we don't mind what we are after.'

'Never mind about lawyers now,' said Dr Thorne, angrily.

'Ah, but I do mind; most particularly. That's all very well for you, doctor; you've nothing to lose. You've no great stake in the matter. Why, now, what sum of money of mine do you think those d— doctors are handling?'

'D— doctors!' said the squire in a tone of dismay.

'Lawyers, I mean, of course. Why, now, Gresham; we're all totted now, you see; you're down in my books, I take it, for pretty near a hundred thousand pounds.'

'Hold your tongue, sir!' said the doctor, getting up.

'Hold my tongue!' said Sir Louis.

'Sir Louis Scatcherd,' said the squire, slowly rising from his chair, 'we will not, if you please, talk about business at the present moment. Perhaps we had better go to the ladies.'

This latter proposition had certainly not come from the squire's heart: going to the ladies was the very last thing for which Sir Louis was now fit. But the squire had said it as being the only recognised formal way he could think of for breaking up the symposium.

'Oh, very well,' hiccupped the baronet, 'I'm always ready for the ladies,' and he stretched out his hand to the decanter to get a last glass of Madeira.

'No,' said the doctor, rising stoutly, and speaking with a determined voice. 'No; you will have no more wine:' and he took the decanter from him.

'What's all this about?' said Sir Louis, with a drunken laugh.

'Of course he cannot go into the drawing-room, Mr Gresham. If you will leave him here with me, I will stay with him till the fly comes. Pray tell Lady Arabella from me, how sorry I am that this has occurred.'

'Lady Arabella! why, what's the matter with her?' said Sir Louis.

The squire would not leave his friend, and they sat together till the fly came. It was not long, for the doctor had dispatched his messenger with much haste.

'I am so heartily ashamed of myself,' said the doctor, almost with tears.

The squire took him by the hand, affectionately. 'I've seen a tipsy man before tonight,' said he.

'Yes,' said the doctor, 'and so have I, but – ' He did not express the rest of his thoughts.

CHAPTER XXXVI

Will He Come Again?

Long before the doctor returned home after the little dinner-party above described, Mary had learnt that Frank was already at Greshamsbury. She had heard nothing of him or from him, not a word, nothing in the shape of a message, for twelve months; and at her age twelve months is a long period. Would he come and see her in spite of his mother? Would he send her any tidings of his return, or notice her in any way? If he did not, what would she do? and if he did, what then would she do? It was so hard to resolve; so hard to be deserted; and so hard to dare to wish that she might not be deserted! She continued to say to herself, that it would be better that they should be strangers; and she could hardly keep herself from tears in the fear that they might be so. What chance could there be that he should care for her, after an absence spent in travelling over the world? No; she would forget that affair of his hand; and then, immediately after having so determined, she would confess to herself that it was a thing not to be forgotten, and impossible of oblivion.

On her uncle's return, she would hear some word about him; and so she sat alone, with a book before her, of which she could not read a line. She expected them about eleven, and was, therefore, rather surprised when the fly stopped at the door before nine.

She immediately heard her uncle's voice, loud and angry, calling for Thomas. Both Thomas and Bridget were unfortunately out, being, at this moment, forgetful of all sublunary cares, and seated in happiness under a beechtree in the park. Janet flew to the little gate, and there found Sir Louis insisting that he would be taken at once to his own mansion at Boxall Hill, and positively swearing that he would no longer submit to the insult of the doctor's surveillance.

In the absence of Thomas, the doctor was forced to apply for assistance to the driver of the fly. Between them the baronet was dragged out of the vehicle, the windows suffered much, and the doctor's hat also. In this way, he was taken upstairs, and was at last put to bed, Janet assisting; nor did the doctor leave the room till his guest was asleep. Then he went into the drawing-room to Mary. It may easily be conceived that he was hardly in a humour to talk much about Frank Gresham.

'What am I to do with him?' said he, almost in tears: 'what am I to do with him?'

'Can you not send him to Boxall Hill?' asked Mary.

'Yes; to kill himself there But it is no matter; he will kill himself somewhere. Oh! what that family have done for me!' And then suddenly remembering a portion of their doings, he took Mary in his arms, and kissed and blessed her; and declared that, in spite of all this, he was a happy man.

There was no word about Frank that night. The next morning, the doctor found Sir Louis very weak, and begging for stimulants. He was worse than weak; he was in such a state of wretched misery and mental prostration; so low in heart, in such collapse of energy and spirit, that Dr Thorne thought it prudent to remove his razors from his reach.

'For God's sake do let me have a little *chasse-café*; I'm always used to it; ask Joe if I'm not! You don't want to kill me, do you?' And the baronet cried piteously, like a child, and, when the doctor left him for the breakfast-table, abjectly implored Janet to get him some curaçoa which he knew was in one of his portmanteaus. Janet, however, was true to her master.

The doctor did give him some wine; and then, having left strict orders as to his treatment – Bridget and Thomas being now both in the house – went forth to some of his too much neglected patients.

Then Mary was again alone, and her mind flew away to her lover. How should she be able to compose herself when she should first see him? See him she must. People cannot live in the same village without meeting. If she passed him at the church-door, as she so often passed Lady Arabella, what should she do? Lady Arabella always smiled a peculiar, little, bitter smile, and this, with half a nod of recognition, carried off the meeting. Should she try the bitter smile, the half-nod with Frank? Alas! she knew it was not in her to be so much mistress of her own heart's blood.

As she thus thought, she stood at the drawing-room window, looking out into her garden; and, as she leant against the sill, her head was surrounded by the sweet creepers. 'At any rate, he won't come here,' she said: and so, with a deep sigh, she turned from the window into the room.

There he was, Frank Gresham himself, standing there in her immediate presence, beautiful as Apollo. Her next thought was how she might escape from out of his arms. How it happened that she had fallen into them, she never knew.

'Mary! my own, own love! my own one! sweetest! dearest! best! Mary! dear Mary! have you not a word to say to me?'

No; she had not a word, though her life had depended on it. The exertion necessary for not crying was quite enough for her. This, then, was the bitter smile and the half-nod that was to pass between them; this was the manner in which estrangement was to grow into indifference; this was the mode of meeting by which she was to prove that she was mistress of her conduct, if not her heart! There he held her close bound to his breast, and she could only protect her face, and that all ineffectually, with her hands. 'He loves another,' Beatrice had said. 'At any rate, he will not love me,' her own heart had said, also. Here was now the answer.

'You know you cannot marry him,' Beatrice had said, also. Ah! if that really were so, was not this embrace deplorable for them both? And yet how could she not be happy? She endeavoured to repel him; but with what a weak endeavour! Her pride had been wounded to the core, not by Lady Arabella's scorn, but by the conviction which had grown on her, that though she had given her own heart absolutely away, had parted with it wholly and for ever, she had received nothing in return. The world, her world, would know that she had loved, and loved in vain. But here now was the loved one at her feet; the first moment that his enforced banishment was over, had brought him there. How could she not be happy?

They all said that she could not marry him. Well, perhaps it might be so; nay, when she thought of it, must not that edict too probably be true? But if so, it would not be his fault. He was true to her, and that satisfied her pride. He had taken from her, by surprise, a confession of her love. She had often regretted her weakness in allowing him to do so; but she could not regret it now. She could endure to suffer; nay, it would not be suffering while he suffered with her.

'Not one word, Mary? Then, after all my dreams, after all my patience, you do not love me at last?'

Oh, Frank! notwithstanding what has been said in thy praise, what a fool thou art! Was any word necessary for thee? Had not her heart beat against thine? Had she not borne thy caresses? Had there been one touch of anger when she warded off thy threatened kisses? Bridget, in the kitchen, when Jonah became amorous, smashed his nose with the rolling-pin. But when Thomas sinned, perhaps as deeply, she only talked of doing so. Miss Thorne, in the drawing-room, had she needed self protection, could doubtless have found the means, though the process would probably have been less violent.

At last Mary succeeded in her efforts at enfranchisement, and she and Frank stood at some little distance from each other. She could not but marvel at him. That long, soft beard, which just now had been so close to her face, was all new; his whole look was altered; his mien, and gait, and very voice were not the same. Was this, indeed, the very Frank who had chattered of his boyish love, two years since, in the gardens at Greshamsbury?

'Not one word of welcome, Mary?'

'Indeed, Mr Gresham, you are welcome home.'

'Mr Gresham! Tell me, Mary – tell me, at once – has anything happened? I could not ask up there.'

'Frank,' she said, and then stopped; not being able at the moment to get any further.

'Speak to me honestly, Mary; honestly and bravely. I offered you my hand once before; there it is again. Will you take it?'

She looked wistfully up in his eyes; she would fain have taken it. But though a girl may be honest in such a case, it is so hard for her to be brave.

He still held out his hand. 'Mary,' said he, 'if you can value it, it shall be yours through good fortune or ill fortune. There may be difficulties; but if you can love me, we will get over them. I am a free man; free to do as I please with myself, except so far as I am bound to you. There is my hand. Will you have it?' And then he, too, looked into her eyes, and waited composedly, as though determined to have an answer.

She slowly raised her hand, and, as she did so, her eyes fell to the ground. It then drooped again, and was again raised; and, at last, her light tapering fingers rested on his broad open palm.

They were soon clutched, and the whole hand brought absolutely into his grasp. 'There, now you are my own!' he said, 'and none of them shall part us; my own Mary, my own wife!'

'Oh, Frank, is not this imprudent? Is it not wrong?'

'Imprudent! I am sick of prudence. I hate prudence. And as for wrong – no. I say it is not wrong; certainly not wrong if we love each other. And you do love me, Mary – eh? You do! don't you?'

He would not excuse her, or allow her to escape from saying it in so many words; and when the words did come at last, they came freely. 'Yes, Frank, I do love you; if that were all you would have no cause for fear.'

'And I will have no cause for fear.'

'Ah; but your father, Frank, and my uncle. I can never bring myself to do anything that shall bring either of them to sorrow.'

Frank, of course, ran through all his arguments. He would go into a profession, or take a farm and live in it. He would wait; that is, for a few months. 'A few months, Frank!' said Mary. 'Well, perhaps six.' 'Oh Frank!' But Frank would not be stopped. He would do anything that his father might ask him. Anything but the one thing. He would not give up the wife he had chosen. It would not be reasonable, or proper, or righteous that he should be asked to do so; and here he mounted a somewhat high horse.

Mary had no arguments which she could bring from her heart to offer in opposition to all this. She could only leave her hand in his, and feel that she was happier than she had been at any time since the day of that donkey-ride at Boxall Hill.

'But, Mary,' continued he, becoming very grave and serious. 'We must be true to each other, and firm in this. Nothing that any of them can say shall drive me from my purpose; will you say as much?'

Her hand was still in his, and so she stood, thinking for a moment before she answered him. But she could not do less for him than he was willing to do for her. 'Yes,' said she – said in a very low voice, and with a manner perfectly quiet – 'I will be firm. Nothing that they can say shall shake me. But, Frank, it cannot be soon.'

Nothing further occurred in this interview which needs recording. Frank had been three times told by Mary that he had better go before he did go; and, at last, she was obliged to take the matter into her own hands, and lead him to the door.

'You are in a great hurry to get rid of me,' said he.

'You have been here two hours, and you must go now; what will they all think?'

'Who cares what they think? Let them think the truth: that after a year's absence, I have much to say to you.' However, at last, he did go, and Mary was left alone.

Frank, although he had been so slow to move, had a thousand other things to do, and went about them at once. He was very much in love, no doubt; but that did not interfere with his interest in other pursuits. In the first place, he had to see Harry Baker, and Harry Baker's stud. Harry had been specially charged to look after the black horse during Frank's absence, and the holiday doings of that valuable animal had to be inquired into. Then the kennel of the hounds had to be visited, and – as a matter of second-rate importance – the master. This could not be done on the same day; but a plan for doing so must be concocted with Harry – and then there were two young pointer pups.

Frank, when he left his betrothed, went about these things quite as vehemently as though he were not in love at all; quite as vehemently as though he had said nothing as to going into some profession which must necessarily separate him from horses and dogs. But Mary sat there at her window, thinking of her love, and thinking of nothing else. It was all in all to her now. She had pledged herself not to be shaken from her troth by anything, by any person; and it would behove her to be true to this pledge. True to it, though all the Greshams but one should oppose her with all their power; true to it, even though her own uncle should oppose her.

And how could she have done any other than so pledge herself, invoked to it as she had been? How could she do less for him that he was so anxious to do for her? They would talk to her of maiden delicacy, and tell her that she had put a stain

upon that snow-white coat of proof, in confessing her love for
one whose friends were unwilling to receive her. Let them so
talk. Honour, honesty, and truth, out-spoken truth, self-denying
truth, and fealty from man to man, are worth more than maiden
delicacy; more, at any rate, than the talk of it. It was not for
herself that this pledge had been made. She knew her position,
and the difficulties of it; she knew also the value of it. He had
much to offer, much to give; she had nothing but herself. He
had name, and old repute, family, honour, and what eventually
would at least be wealth to her. She was nameless, fameless,
portionless. He had come there with all his ardour, with the
impulse of his character, and asked for her love. It was already
his own. He had then demanded her troth, and she acknowledged that he had a right to demand it. She would be his if ever
it should be in his power to take her.

But there let the bargain end. She would always remember,
that though it was in her power to keep her pledge, it might too
probably not be in his power to keep his. That doctrine, laid
down so imperatively by the great authorities of Greshamsbury,
that edict, which demanded that Frank should marry money,
had come home also to her with a certain force. It would be sad
that the fame of Greshamsbury should perish, and that the glory
should depart from the old house. It might be, that Frank also
should perceive that he must marry money. It would be a pity
that he had not seen it sooner; but she, at any rate, would not
complain.

And so she stood, leaning on the open window, with her book
unnoticed lying beside her. The sun had been in the mid-sky
when Frank had left her, but its rays were beginning to stream
into the room from the west before she moved from her position.
Her first thought in the morning had been this: Would he come
to see her? Her last now was more soothing to her, less full of
absolute fear: Would it be right that he should come again?

The first sounds she heard were the footsteps of her uncle, as
he came up to the drawing-room, three steps at a time. His steps
was always heavy; but when he was disturbed in spirit, it was
slow; when merely fatigued in body by ordinary work, it was
quick.

'What a broiling day!' he said, and he threw himself into a
chair. 'For mercy's sake give me something to drink.' Now the
doctor was a great man for summer-drinks. In his house,

lemonade, currant-juice, orange-mixtures, and raspberry-vin-
egar were used by the quart. He frequently disapproved of these
things for his patients, as being apt to disarrange the digestion;
but he consumed enough himself to throw a large family into
such difficulties.

'Ha – a!' he ejaculated, after a draught; 'I'm better now. Well,
what's the news?'

'You've been out, uncle; you ought to have the news. How's
Mrs Green?'

'Really as bad as ennui and solitude can make her.'

'And Mrs Oaklerath?'

'She's getting better, because she has ten children to look
after, and twins to suckle. What has he been doing?' And the
doctor pointed towards the room occupied by Sir Louis.

Mary's conscience struck her that she had not even asked. She
had hardly remembered, during the whole day, that the baronet
was in the house. 'I do not think he has been doing much,' she
said. 'Janet has been with him all day.'

'Has he been drinking?'

'Upon my word, I don't know, uncle. I think not, for Janet
has been with him. But, uncle – '

'Well, dear – but just give me a little more of that tipple.'

Mary prepared the tumbler, and, as she handed it to him, she
said, 'Frank Gresham has been here today.'

The doctor swallowed his draught, and put down the glass
before he made any reply, and even then he said but little.

'Oh! Frank Gresham.'

'Yes, uncle.'

'You thought him looking pretty well?'

'Yes, uncle; he was very well, I believe.'

Dr Thorne had nothing more to say, so he got up and went to
his patient in the next room.

'If he disapproves of it, why does he not say so?' said Mary,
to herself. 'Why does he not advise me?'

But it was not so easy to give advice while Sir Louis Scatcherd
was lying there in that state.

CHAPTER XXXVII

Sir Louis Leaves Greshamsbury

Janet had been sedulous in her attentions to Sir Louis, and had not troubled her mistress; but she had not had an easy time of it. Her orders had been, that either she or Thomas should remain in the room the whole day, and those orders had been obeyed.

Immediately after breakfast, the baronet had inquired after his own servant. 'His confounded nose must be right by this time, I suppose?'

'It was very bad, Sir Louis,' said the old woman, who imagined that it might be difficult to induce Jonah to come into the house again.

'A man in such a place as his has no business to be laid up,' said the master, with a whine. 'I'll see and get a man who won't break his nose.'

Thomas was sent to the inn three or four times, but in vain. The man was sitting up, well enough, in the taproom; but the middle of his face was covered with streaks of plaster, and he could not bring himself to expose his wounds before his conqueror.

Sir Louis began by ordering the woman to bring him *chasse-café*. She offered him coffee, as much as he would; but no *chasse*. 'A glass of port wine,' she said, 'at twelve o'clock, and another at three had been ordered for him.'

'I don't care a – for the orders,' said Sir Louis; 'send me my own man.' The man was again sent for; but would not come. 'There's a bottle of stuff that I take, in that portmanteau, in the left-hand corner – just hand it to me.'

But Janet was not to be done. She would give him no stuff, except what the doctor had ordered, till the doctor came back. The doctor would then, no doubt, give him anything that was proper.

Sir Louis swore a good deal, and stormed as much as he could. He drank, however, his two glasses of wine, and he got no more. Once or twice he essayed to get out of bed and dress; but, at every effort, he found that he could not do it without

Joe: and there he was, still under the clothes when the doctor returned.

'I'll tell you what it is,' said he, as soon as his guardian entered the room, 'I'm not going to be made a prisoner of here.'

'A prisoner! no, surely not.'

'It seems very much like it at present. Your servant here – that old woman – takes it upon her to say she'll do nothing without your orders.'

'Well; she's right there.'

'Right! I don't know what you call right; but I won't stand it. You are not going to make a child of me, Dr Thorne; so you need not think it.'

And then there was a long quarrel between them, and but an indifferent reconciliation. The baronet said that he would go to Boxall Hill, and was vehement in his intention to do so because the doctor opposed it. He had not, however, as yet ferreted out the squire, or given a bit of his mind to Mr Gazebee, and it behoved him to do this before he took himself off to his own country mansion. He ended, therefore, by deciding to go on the next day but one.

'Let it be so, if you are well enough,' said the doctor.

'Well enough!' said the other, with a sneer. 'There's nothing to make me ill that I know of. It certainly won't be drinking too much here.'

On the next day, Sir Louis was in a different mood, and in one more distressing for the doctor to bear. His compelled abstinence from intemperate drinking had, no doubt, been good for him; but his mind had so much sunk under the pain of the privation, that his state was piteous to behold. He had cried for his servant, as a child cries for its nurse, till at last the doctor, moved to pity, had himself gone out and brought the man in from the public-house. But when he did come, Joe was of but little service to his master, as he was altogether prevented from bringing him either wine or spirits; and when he searched for the liqueur-case, he found that even that had been carried away.

'I believe you want me to die,' he said, as the doctor, sitting by his bedside, was trying, for the hundredth time, to make him understand that he had but one chance of living.

The doctor was not the least irritated. It would have been as wise to be irritated by the want of reason in a dog.

'I am doing what I can to save your life,' he said calmly; 'but, as you said just now, I have no power over you. As long as you are unable to move and remain in my house, you certainly shall not have the means of destroying yourself. You will be very wise to stay here for a week or ten days: a week or ten days of healthy living might, perhaps, bring you round.'

Sir Louis again declared that the doctor wished him to die, and spoke even of sending for his attorney, Finnie, to come to Greshamsbury to look after him.

'Send for him if you choose,' said the doctor. 'His coming will cost you three or four pounds, but can do no other harm.'

'And I will send for Fillgrave,' threatened the baronet. 'I'm not going to die here like a dog.'

It was certainly hard upon Dr Thorne that he should be obliged to entertain such a guest in his house; – to entertain him, and foster him, and care for him, almost as though he were a son. But he had no alternative; he had accepted the charge from Sir Roger, and he must go through with it. His conscience, moreover, allowed him no rest in this matter: it harassed him day and night, driving him on sometimes to great wretchedness. He could not love this incubus that was on his shoulders; he could not do other than be very far from loving him. Of what use or value was he to any one? What could the world make of him that would be good, or he of the world? Was not an early death his certain fate? The earlier it might be, would it not be the better?

Were he to linger on yet for two years longer – and such a space of life was possible for him – how great would be the mischief that he might do; nay, certainly would do! Farewell then to all hopes for Greshamsbury, as far as Mary was concerned. Farewell then to that dear scheme which lay deep in the doctor's heart, that hope that he might, in his niece's name, give back to the son the lost property of the father. And might not one year – six months be as fatal. Frank, they all said, must marry money; and even he – he the doctor himself, much as he despised the idea for money's sake – even he could not but confess that Frank, as the heir to an old, but grievously embarrassed property, had no right to marry, at his early age, a girl without a shilling. Mary, his niece, his own child, would probably be the heiress of this immense wealth; but he could not tell this to Frank; no, nor to Frank's father while Sir Louis was yet alive. What, if by so doing he should achieve this marriage for his niece, and that then Sir Louis should live to dispose of his own? How then would he face the anger of Lady Arabella?

'I will never hanker after a dead man's shoes, neither for myself nor for another,' he had said to himself a hundred times; and as often did he accuse himself of doing so. One path, however, was plainly open before him. He would keep his peace as to the will; and would use such efforts as he might use for a son of his own loins to preserve the life that was so valueless. His wishes, his hopes, his thoughts, he could not control; but his conduct was at his own disposal.

'I say, doctor, you don't really think I'm going to die?' Sir Louis said, when Dr Thorne again visited him.

'I don't think at all; I am sure you will kill yourself if you continue to live as you have lately done.'

'But suppose I go all right for a while, and live – live just as you tell me, you know?'

'All of us are in God's hands, Sir Louis. By so doing you will, at any rate, give yourself the best chance.'

'Best chance? Why, d——n, doctor! there are fellows have done ten times worse than I; and they are not going to kick. Come, now, I know you are trying to frighten me; ain't you, now?'

'I am trying to do the best I can for you.'

'It's very hard on a fellow like me; I have nobody to say a kind word to me; no, not one.' And Sir Louis, in his wretchedness, began to weep. 'Come, doctor; if you'll put me once more on my legs, I'll let you draw on the estate for five hundred pounds; by G——, I will.'

The doctor went away to his dinner, and the baronet also had his in bed. He could not eat much, but he was allowed two glasses of wine, and also a little brandy in his coffee. This somewhat invigorated him, and when Dr Thorne again went to him, in the evening, he did not find him so utterly prostrated in spirit. He had, indeed, made up his mind to a great resolve; and thus unfolded his final scheme for his own reformation:–

'Doctor,' he began again, 'I believe you are an honest fellow; I do, indeed.'

Dr Thorne could not but thank him for his good opinion.

'You ain't annoyed at what I said this morning, are you?'

The doctor had forgotten the particular annoyance to which

Sir Louis alluded; and informed him that his mind might be at rest on any such matter.

'I do believe you'd be glad to see me well; wouldn't you, now?'

The doctor assured him that such was in very truth the case.

'Well, now, I'll tell you what: I've been thinking about it a great deal today; indeed, I have, and I want to do what's right. Mightn't I have a little drop more of that stuff, just in a cup of coffee?'

The doctor poured him out a cup of coffee, and put about a teaspoonful of brandy in it. Sir Louis took it with a disconsolate face, not having been accustomed to such measures in the use of his favourite beverage.

'I do wish to do what's right – I do, indeed; only, you see, I'm so lonely. As to those fellows up in London, I don't think that one of them cares a straw about me.'

Dr Thorne was of the same way of thinking, and he said so. He could not but feel some sympathy with the unfortunate man as he thus spoke of his own lot. It was true that he had been thrown on the world without any one to take care of him.

'My dear friend, I will do the best I can in every way; I will, indeed. I do believe that your companions in town have been too ready to lead you astray. Drop them, and you may yet do well.'

'May I though, doctor? Well, I will drop them. There's Jenkins; he's the best of them; but even he is always wanting to make money of me. Not but what I'm up to the best of them in that way.'

'You had better leave London, Sir Louis, and change your old mode of life. Go to Boxall Hill for a while; for two or three years or so; live with your mother there and take to farming.'

'What! farming?'

'Yes; that's what all country gentlemen do: take the land there into your own hand, and occupy your mind upon it.'

'Well, doctor, I will – upon one condition.'

Dr Thorne sat still and listened. He had no idea what the condition might be, but he was not prepared to promise acquiescence till he heard it.

'You know what I told you once before,' said the baronet.

'I don't remember at this moment.'

'About my getting married, you know.'

The doctor's brow grew black, and promised no help to the poor wretch. Bad in every way, wretched, selfish, sensual, unfeeling, purse-proud, ignorant as Sir Louis Scatcherd was, still, there was left to him the power of feeling something like sincere love. It may be presumed that he did love Mary Thorne, and that he was at the time earnest in declaring, that if she could be given to him, he would endeavour to live according to her uncle's counsel. It was only a trifle he asked; but, alas, that trifle could not be vouchsafed.

'I should much approve of your getting married, but I do not know how I can help you.'

'Of course, I mean to Miss Mary: I do love her; I really do, Dr Thorne.'

'It is quite impossible, Sir Louis; quite. You do my niece much honour; but I am able to answer for her, positively, that such a proposition is quite out of the question.'

'Look here now, Dr Thorne; anything in the way of settlements – '

'I will not hear a word on the subject: you are very welcome to the use of my house as long as it may suit you to remain here; but I must insist that my niece shall not be troubled on this matter.'

'Do you mean to say she's in love with that young Gresham?'

This was too much for the doctor's patience. 'Sir Louis,' said he, 'I can forgive you much for your father's sake. I can also forgive something on the score of your own ill health. But you ought to know, you ought by this time to have learnt, that there are some things which a man cannot forgive. I will not talk to you about my niece; and remember this, also, I will not have her troubled by you:' and, so saying, the doctor left him.

On the next day the baronet was sufficiently recovered to be able to resume his braggadocio airs. He swore at Janet; insisted on being served by his own man; demanded in a loud voice, but in vain, that his liqueur-case should be restored to him; and desired that post-horses might be ready for him on the morrow. On that day he got up and ate his dinner in his bedroom. On the next morning he countermanded the horses, informing the doctor that he did so because he had a little bit of business to transact with Squire Gresham before he left the place! With some difficulty, the doctor made him understand that the squire would not see him on business; and it was at last decided, that

Mr Gazebee should be invited to call on him at the doctor's house; and this Mr Gazebee agreed to do, in order to prevent the annoyance of having the baronet up at Greshamsbury.

On this day, the evening before Mr Gazebee's visit, Sir Louis condescended to come down to dinner. He dined, however, *tête à tête* with the doctor. Mary was not there, nor was anything said as to her absence. Sir Louis Scatcherd never set eyes upon her again.

He bore himself very arrogantly on that evening, having resumed the airs and would-be dignity which he thought belonged to him as a man of rank and property. In his periods of low spirits, he was abject and humble enough; abject, and fearful of the lamentable destiny which at these moments he believed to be in store for him. But it was one of the peculiar symptoms of his state, that as he partially recovered his bodily health, the tone of his mind recovered itself also, and his fears for the time were relieved.

There was very little said between him and the doctor that evening. The doctor sat guarding the wine, and thinking when he should have his house to himself again. Sir Louis sat moody, every now and then uttering some impertinence as to the Greshams and the Greshamsbury property, and, at an early hour, allowed Joe to put him to bed.

The horses were ordered on the next day for three, and, at two, Mr Gazebee came to the house. He had never been there before, nor had he ever met Dr Thorne except at the squire's dinner. On this occasion he asked only for the baronet.

'Ah! ah! I'm glad you're come, Mr Gazebee; very glad;' said Sir Louis; acting the part of the rich, great man with all the power he had. 'I want to ask you a few questions so as to make it clear sailing between us.'

'As you have asked to see me, I have come, Sir Louis,' said the other, putting on much dignity as he spoke. 'But would it not be better that any business there may be should be done among the lawyers?'

'The lawyers are very well, I dare say; but when a man has so large a stake at interest as I have in this Greshamsbury property, why, you see, Mr Gazebee, he feels a little inclined to look after it himself. Now, do you know, Mr Gazebee, how much it is that Mr Gresham owes me?'

Mr Gazebee, of course, did know very well, but he was not going to discuss the subject with Sir Louis, if he could help it.

'Whatever claim your father's estate may have on that of Mr Gresham is, as far as I understand, vested in Dr Thorne's hands as trustee. I am inclined to believe that you have not yourself at present any claim on Greshamsbury. The interest, as it becomes due, is paid to Dr Thorne; and if I may be allowed to make a suggestion, I would say that it will not be expedient to make any change in that arrangement till the property shall come into your own hands.'

'I differ from you entirely, Mr Gazebee; *in toto*, as we used to say at Eton. What you mean to say is this – I can't go to law with Mr Gresham; I'm not so sure of that; but perhaps not. But I can compel Dr Thorne to look after my interests. I can force him to foreclose. And, to tell you the truth, Gazebee, unless some arrangement is proposed to me which I shall think advantageous, I shall do so at once. There is near a hundred thousand pounds owing to me; yes, to me. Thorne is only a name in the matter. The money is my money; and, by ——, I mean to look after it.'

'Have you any doubt, Sir Louis, as to the money being secure?'

'Yes, I have. It isn't so easy to have a hundred thousand pounds secured. The squire is a poor man, and I don't choose to allow a poor man to owe me such a sum as that. Besides, I mean to invest it in land. I tell you fairly, therefore, I shall foreclose.'

Mr Gazebee, using all the perspicuity which his professional education had left to him, tried to make Sir Louis understand that he had no power to do anything of the kind.

'No power! Mr Gresham shall see whether I have no power. When a man has a hundred thousand pounds owing to him he ought to have some power; and, as I take it, he has. But we will see. Perhaps you know Finnie; do you?'

Mr Gazebee, with a good deal of scorn in his face, said that he had not that pleasure. Mr Finnie was not in his line.

'Well, you will know him then, and you'll find he's sharp enough; that is, unless I have some offer made to me that I may choose to accept.' Mr Gazebee declared that he was not instructed to make any offer, and so he took his leave.

On that afternoon, Sir Louis went off to Boxall Hill, transferring the miserable task of superintending his self-destruction from the shoulders of the doctor to those of his mother. Of Lady Scatcherd, the baronet took no account in his proposed sojourn in the country, nor did he take much of the doctor in leaving Greshamsbury. He again wrapped himself in his furs, and, with tottering steps, climbed up into the barouche which was to carry him away.

'Is my man up behind?' he said to Janet, while the doctor was standing at the little front garden-gate, making his adieux.

'No, sir, he's not up yet,' said Janet, respectfully.

'Then send him out, will you? I can't lose my time waiting here all day.'

'I shall come over to Boxall Hill and see you,' said the doctor, whose heart softened towards the man, in spite of his brutality, as the hour of his departure came.

'I shall be happy to see you if you like to come, of course; that is, in the way of visiting, and that sort of thing. As for doctoring, if I want any I shall send for Fillgrave.' Such were his last words as the carriage, with a rush, went off from the door.

The doctor, as he re-entered the house, could not avoid smiling, for he thought of Dr Fillgrave's last patient at Boxall Hill. 'It's a question to me,' said he to himself, 'whether Dr Fillgrave will ever be induced to make another visit to that house, even with the object of rescuing a baronet out of my hands.'

'He's gone; isn't he, uncle?' said Mary, coming out of her room.

'Yes, my dear; he's gone, poor fellow!'

'He may be a poor fellow, uncle; but he's a very disagreeable inmate in a house. I have not had any dinner these two days.'

'And I haven't had what can be called a cup of tea since he's been in the house. But I'll make up for that tonight.'

CHAPTER XXXVIII

De Courcy Precepts and
De Courcy Practice

There is a mode of novel-writing which used to be much in vogue, but which has now gone out of fashion. It is, nevertheless, one which is very expressive when in good hands, and which enables the author to tell his story, or some portion of his story, with more natural trust than any other, I mean that of familiar letters. I trust I shall be excused if I attempt it as regards this one chapter; though, it may be, that I shall break down and fall into commonplace narrative, even before the one chapter be completed. The correspondents are the Lady Amelia de Courcy and Miss Gresham. I, of course, give precedence to the higher rank, but the first epistle originated with the latter-named young lady. Let me hope that they will explain themselves.

'*Miss Gresham to Lady Amelia de Courcy*

'GRESHAMSBURY HOUSE, June, 185-.
'My dearest Amelia,

'I wish to consult you on a subject which, as you will perceive, is of a most momentous nature. You know how much reliance I place in your judgement and knowledge of what is proper, and, therefore, I write to you before speaking to any other living person on the subject: not even to mamma; for, although her judgement is good too, she has so many cares and troubles, that it is natural that it should be a little warped when the interests of her children are concerned. Now that it is all over, I feel that it may possibly have been so in the case of Mr Moffat.

'You are aware that Mr Mortimer Gazebee is now staying here, and that he has been here for nearly two months. He is engaged in managing poor papa's affairs, and mamma, who likes him very much, says that he is a most excellent man of business. Of course, you know that he is the junior partner in the very old firm of Gumption, Gazebee, & Gazebee, who I understand, do not undertake any business at all, except what comes to them from peers, or commoners of the very highest class.

'I soon perceived, dearest Amelia, that Mr Gazebee paid me more than ordinary attention, and I immediately became very guarded in my manner. I certainly liked Mr Gazebee from the first. His manners are quite excellent, his conduct to mamma is charming, and, as regards myself, I must say that there has been nothing in his behaviour of which even you could complain. He has never attempted the slightest familiarity, and I will do him the justice to say, that, though he has been very attentive, he has also been very respectful.

'I must confess that, for the last three weeks, I have thought that he meant something. I might, perhaps, have done more to repel him; or I might have consulted you earlier as to the propriety of keeping altogether out of his way. But you know, Amelia, how often these things lead to nothing, and though I thought all along that Mr Gazebee was in earnest, I hardly liked to say anything about it even to you till I was quite certain. If you had advised me, you know, to accept his offer, and if, after that, he had never made it, I should have felt so foolish.

'But now he has made it. He came to me yesterday just before dinner, in the little drawing-room, and told me, in the most delicate manner, in words that even you could not but have approved, that his highest ambition was to be thought worthy of my regard, and that he felt for me the warmest love, and the most profound admiration, and the deepest respect. You may say, Amelia, that he is only an attorney, and I believe that he is an attorney; but I am sure you would have esteemed him had you heard the very delicate way in which he expressed his sentiments.

'Something had given me a presentiment of what he was going to do when I saw him come into the room, so that I was on my guard. I tried very hard to show no emotion; but I suppose I was a little flurried, as I once detected myself calling him Mr Mortimer: his name, you know, is Mortimer Gazebee. I ought not to have done so, certainly; but it was not so bad as if I had called him Mortimer without the Mr, was it? I don't think there could possibly be a prettier Christian name than Mortimer. Well, Amelia, I allowed him to express himself without interruption. He once attempted to take my hand; but even this was done without any assumption of familiarity; and when he saw that I would not permit it, he drew back, and fixed his eyes on the ground as though he were ashamed even of that.

'Of course, I had to give him an answer; and though I had expected that something of this sort would take place, I had not made up my mind on the subject. I would not certainly, under any circumstances, accept him without consulting you. If I really disliked him, of course there would be no doubt; but I can't say, dearest Amelia, that I do absolutely dislike him; and I really think that we should make each other very happy, if the marriage were suitable as regarded both our positions.

'I collected myself as well as I could, and I really do think that you would have said that I did not behave badly, though the position was rather trying I told him that, of course, I was flattered by his sentiments, though much surprised at hearing them; that since I knew him, I had esteemed and valued him as an acquaintance, but that, looking on him as a man of business, I had never expected anything more. I then endeavoured to explain to him, that I was not perhaps privileged, as some other girls might be, to indulge my own feelings altogether: perhaps that was saying too much, and might make him think that I was in love with him; but, from the way I said it, I don't think he would, for I was very much guarded in my manner, and very collected; and then I told him, that in any proposal of marriage that might be made to me, it would be my duty to consult my family as much, if not more than myself.

'He said, of course; and asked whether he might speak to papa. I tried to make him understand, that in talking of my family, I did not exactly mean papa, or even mamma. Of course, I was thinking of what was due to the name of Gresham. I know very well what papa would say. He would give his consent in half a minute; he is so brokenhearted by these debts. And, to tell you the truth, Amelia, I think mamma would too. He did not seem quite to comprehend what I meant; but he did say that he knew it was a high ambition to marry into the family of the Greshams. I am sure you would confess that he has most proper feelings; and as for expressing them no man could do it better.

'He owned that it was ambition to ally himself with a family above his own rank of life, and that he looked to doing so as a means of advancing himself. Now this was at any rate honest. That was one of his motives, he said; though, of course, not his first: and then he declared how truly attached he was to me. In answer to this, I remarked, that he had known me only a very short time. This, perhaps, was giving him too much encouragement; but, at that moment, I hardly knew what to say, for I did not wish to hurt his feelings. He then spoke of his income. He has fifteen hundred a year from the business, and that will be greatly increased when his father leaves it; and his father is much older than Mr Gumption, though he is only the second partner. Mortimer Gazebee will be the senior partner himself before very long; and perhaps that does alter his position a little.

'He has a very nice place down somewhere in Surrey; I have heard mamma say it is quite a gentleman's place. It is let now; but he will live there when he is married. And he has property of his own besides which he can settle. So, you see, he is quite as well off as Mr Oriel; better, indeed; and if a man is in a profession, I believe it is considered that it does not much matter what. Of course, a clergyman can be a bishop; but then, I think I have heard that one attorney did once become Lord Chancellor. I should have my carriage, you know; I remember his saying that, especial, though I cannot recollect how he brought it in.

'I told him, at last, that I was so much taken by surprise that I could not give him an answer then. He was going up to London, he said, on the next day, and might he be permitted to address me on the same subject when he returned? I could not refuse him, you know; and so now I have taken the opportunity of his absence to write to you for your advice. You understand the world so very well, and know so exactly what one ought to do in such a strange position!

'I hope I have made it all intelligible, at least, as to what I have written about. I have said nothing as to my own feelings, because I wish you to think on the matter without consulting them. If it would be derogatory to accept Mr Gazebee, I certainly would not do so because I happen to like him. If we were to act in that way, what would the world come to, Amelia? Perhaps my ideas may be overstrained; if so, you will tell me.

'When Mr Oriel proposed for Beatrice, nobody seemed to make any objection. It all seemed to go as a matter of course. She says that his family is excellent; but as far as I can learn, his grandfather was a general in India, and came home very rich. Mr Gazebee's grandfather was a member of the firm, and so, I believe, was his great-grandfather. Don't you think this ought to count for something? Besides, they have no business except with the most aristocratic persons, such as uncle De Courcy, and the Marquis of Kensington Gore, and that sort. I mention the marquis, because Mr Mortimer Gazebee is there now. And I know that one of the Gumptions was once in Parliament; and I don't think that any of the Oriels ever were. The name of attorney is certainly very bad, is it not, Amelia? but they certainly do not seem to be all the same, and I do think that this ought to make a difference. To hear Mortimer Gazebee talk of some attorney at Barchester, you would say that there is quite as much difference between them as between a bishop and a curate. And so I think there is.

'I don't wish at all to speak of my own feelings; but if he were not an attorney, he is, I think, the sort of man that I should like. He is very nice in every way, and if you were not told, I don't think you'd know he was an attorney. But, dear Amelia, I will be guided by you altogether. He is certainly much nicer than Mr Moffat, and has a great deal more to say for himself. Of course, Mr Moffat having been in Parliament, and having been taken up by uncle De Courcy, was in a different sphere; but I really felt almost relieved when he behaved in that way. With Mortimer Gazebee, I think it would be different.

'I shall wait so impatiently for your answer, so do pray write at once. I hear some people say that these sort of things are not so much thought of now as they were once, and that all manner of marriages are considered to be *comme il faut*.* I do not want, you know, to make myself foolish by being too particular. Perhaps all these changes are bad, and I rather think they are; but if the world changes, one must change too; one can't go against the world.

'So do write and tell me what you think. Do not suppose that I dislike the man, for I really cannot say that I do. But I would not for anything make an alliance for which any one bearing the name of De Courcy would have to blush.

> 'Always, dearest Amelia,
> 'Your most affectionate cousin,
> 'Augusta Gresham.

'PS. – I fear Frank is going to be very foolish with Mary Thorne. You know it is absolutely important that Frank should marry money.

'It strikes me as quite possible that Mortimer Gazebee may be in Parliament some of these days. He is just the man for it.'

Poor Augusta prayed very hard for her husband; but she prayed to a bosom that on this subject was as hard as a flint, and she prayed in vain. Augusta Gresham was twenty-two, Lady Amelia de Courcy was thirty-four; was it likely that Lady Amelia would permit Augusta to marry, the issue having thus been left in her hands? Why should Augusta derogate from her position by marrying beneath herself, seeing that Lady Amelia had spent so many more years in the world without having found it necessary to do so? Augusta's letter was written on two sheets of notepaper, crossed* all over; and Lady Amelia's answer was almost equally formidable.

'*Lady Amelia de Courcy to Miss Augusta Gresham*

COURCY CASTLE, June, 185–.

'My dear Augusta,

'I received your letter yesterday morning, but I have put off answering it till this evening, as I have wished to give it very mature consideration. The question is one which concerns, not only your character, but happiness for life, and nothing less than very mature consideration would justify me in giving a decided opinion on the subject.

'In the first place, I may tell you, that I have not a word to say against Mr Mortimer Gazebee.' (When Augusta had read as far as this, her heart sank within her; the rest was all leather and prunella;* she saw at once that the fiat had gone against her, and that her wish to become Mrs Mortimer Gazebee was not to be indulged.) 'I have known him for a long time, and I believe him to be a very respectable person, and I have no doubt a good man of business. The firm of Messrs Gumption & Gazebee stands probably quite among the first attorneys in London, and I know that papa has a very high opinion of them.

'All these would be excellent arguments to use in favour of Mr Gazebee as a suitor, had his proposals been made to any one in his own rank of life. But you, in considering the matter, should, I think, look on it in a very different light. The very fact that you pronounce him to be so much superior to other attorneys, shows in how very low esteem you hold the profession in general. It shows also, dear Augusta, how well aware you are that they are a class of people among whom you should not seek a partner for life.

'My opinion is, that you should make Mr Gazebee understand – very courteously, of course – that you cannot accept his hand. You observe that he himself confesses, that in marrying you he would seek a wife in a rank above his own. Is it not, therefore, clear, that in marrying him, you would descend to a rank below your own?

'I shall be very sorry if this grieves you; but still it will be better that you should bear the grief of overcoming a temporary fancy, than take a step which may so probably make you unhappy; and which some of your friends would certainly regard as disgraceful.

'It is not permitted to us, my dear Augusta, to think of ourselves in such matters. As you truly say, if we were to act in that way, what would the world come to? It has been God's pleasure that we should be born with high blood in our veins. This is a great boon which we both value, but the boon has its responsibilities as well as its privileges. It is established by law, that the royal family shall not intermarry with subjects. In our case there is no law, but the necessity is not the less felt; we should not intermarry with those who are probably of a lower rank. Mr Mortimer Gazebee is, after all, only an attorney; and, although you speak of his great-grandfather, he is a man of no blood whatsoever. You must acknowledge that such an admixture should be looked on by a De Courcy, or even by a Gresham, as a pollution.' (Here Augusta got very red, and she felt almost inclined to be angry with her cousin.) 'Beatrice's marriage with Mr Oriel is different; though, remember, I am by no means defending that; it may be good or bad, and I have had no opportunity of inquiring respecting Mr Oriel's family. Beatrice, moreover, has never appeared to me to feel what was due to herself in such matters; but, as I said, her marriage with Mr Oriel is very different. Clergymen – particularly the rectors and vicars of country parishes – do become privileged above other professional men. I could explain why, but it would be too long in a letter.

'Your feelings on the subject altogether do you great credit. I have no doubt that Mr Gresham, if asked, would accede to the match; but that is just the reason why he should not be asked. It would not be right that I should say anything against your father to you; but it is impossible for any of us not to see that all through life he has thrown away every advantage, and sacrificed his family. Why is he now in debt, as you say? Why is he not holding the family seat in Parliament? Even though you are his daughter, you cannot but feel that you would not do right to consult him on such a subject.

'As to dear aunt, I feel sure, that were she in good health, and left to exercise her own judgement, she would not wish to see you married to the agent for the family estate. For, dear Augusta, that is the real truth. Mr Gazebee often comes here in the way of business; and though papa always receives him as a gentleman –

that is, he dines at table and all that – he is not on the same footing in the house as the ordinary guests and friends of the family. How would you like to be received at Courcy Castle in the same way?

'You will say, perhaps, that you would still be papa's niece; so you would. But you know how strict in such matters papa is, and you must remember, that the wife always follows the rank of the husband. Papa is accustomed to the strict etiquette of a court, and I am sure that no consideration would induce him to receive the estate-agent in the light of a nephew. Indeed, were you to marry Mr Gazebee, the house to which he belongs would, I imagine, have to give up the management of this property.

'Even were Mr Gazebee in Parliament – and I do not see how it is probable that he should get there – it would not make any difference. You must remember, dearest, that I never was an advocate for the Moffat match. I acquiesced in it, because mamma did so. If I could have had my own way, I would adhere to all our old prescriptive principles. Neither money nor position can atone to me for low birth. But the world, alas! is retrograding; and, according to the new-fangled doctrines of the day, a lady of blood is not disgraced by allying herself to a man of wealth, and what may be called quasi-aristocratic position. I wish it were otherwise; but so it is. And, therefore, the match with Mr Moffat was not disgraceful, though it could not be regarded as altogether satisfactory.

'But with Mr Gazebee the matter would be altogether different. He is a man earning his bread; honestly, I dare say, but in a humble position. You say he is very respectable: I do not doubt it; and so is Mr Scraggs, the butcher in Courcy. You see, Augusta, to what such arguments reduce you.

'I dare say he may be nicer than Mr Moffat, in one way. That is, he may have more small-talk at his command, and be more clever in all those little pursuits and amusements which are valued by ordinary young ladies. But my opinion is, that neither I nor you would be justified in sacrificing ourselves for such amusements. We have high duties before us. It may be that the performance of those duties will prohibit us from taking a part in the ordinary arena of the feminine world. It is natural that girls should wish to marry; and, therefore, those who are weak, take the first that come. Those who have more judgement, make some sort of selection. But the strongest-minded are, perhaps, those who are able to forgo themselves and their own fancies, and to refrain from any alliance that does not tend to the maintenance of high principles. Of course, I speak of those who have blood in their veins. You and I need not dilate as to the conduct of others.

'I hope what I have said will convince you. Indeed, I know that it only requires that you and I should have a little cousinly talk on this matter to be quite in accord. You must now remain at Greshamsbury till Mr Gazebee shall return. Immediately that he does so, seek an interview with him; do not wait till he asks for it; then tell him, that when he addressed you, the matter had taken you so much by surprise, that you were not at the moment able to answer him with that decision that the subject demanded. Tell him, that you are flattered – in saying this, however, you must keep a collected countenance, and be very cold in your manner – but that family reasons would forbid you to avail yourself of his offer, even did no other cause prevent it.

'And then, dear Augusta, come to us here. I know you will be a little downhearted after going through this struggle; but I will endeavour to inspirit you. When we are both together, you will feel more sensibly the value of that high position which you will preserve by rejecting Mr Gazebee, and will regret less acutely whatever you may lose.

'Your very affectionate cousin,
'Amelia de Courcy

'PS. – I am greatly grieved about Frank; but I have long feared that he would do some very silly thing. I have heard lately that Miss Mary Thorne is not even the legitimate niece of your Dr Thorne, but is the daughter of some poor creature who was seduced by the doctor, in Barchester. I do not know how true this may be, but I think your brother should be put on his guard: it might do good.'

Poor Augusta! She was in truth to be pitied, for her efforts were made with the intention of doing right according to her lights. For Moffat she had never cared a straw; and then, therefore, she lost the piece of gilding for which she had been instructed by her mother to sell herself, it was impossible to pity her. But Mr Gazebee she would have loved with that sort of love which it was in her power to bestow. With him she would have been happy, respectable, and contented.

She had written her letter with great care. When the offer was made to her, she could not bring herself to throw Lady Amelia to the winds and marry the man, as it were, out of her own head. Lady Amelia had been the tyrant of her life, and so she strove hard to obtain her tyrant's permission. She used all her little cunning in showing that, after all, Mr Gazebee was not so very plebeian. All her little cunning was utterly worthless. Lady Amelia's mind was too strong to be caught with such chaff. Augusta could not serve God and Mammon. She must either be true to the god of her cousin's idolatry, and remain single, or serve the Mammon of her own inclinations, and marry Mr Gazebee.

When refolding her cousin's letter, after the first perusal, she did for a moment think of rebellion. Could she not be happy at the nice place in Surrey, having, as she would have, a carriage, even though all the De Courcys should drop her? It had been put to her that she would not like to be received at Courcy Castle with the scant civility which would be considered due to a Mrs Mortimer Gazebee: but what if she could put up without being received at Courcy Castle at all? Such ideas did float through her mind, dimly.

But her courage failed her. It is so hard to throw off a tyrant; so much easier to yield, when we have been in the habit of yielding. This third letter, therefore, was written; and it is the end of the correspondence.

'*Miss Augusta Gresham to Lady Amelia de Courcy*

'GRESHAMSBURY HOUSE, July, 185–.

'My dearest Amelia,

'I did not answer your letter before, because I thought it better to delay doing so till Mr Gazebee had been here. He came the day before yesterday, and yesterday I did, as nearly as possible, what you advised. Perhaps, on the whole, it will be better. As you say, rank has its responsibilities as well as its privileges.

'I don't quite understand what you mean about clergymen, but we can talk that over when we meet. Indeed, it seems to me that if one is to be particular about family – and I am sure I think we ought – one ought to be so without exception. If Mr Oriel be a *parvenu*, Beatrice's children won't be well born merely because their father was a clergyman, even though he is a rector. Since my former letter, I have heard that Mr Gazebee's great-great-great-grandfather established the firm; and there are many people who were nobodies then who are thought to have good blood in their veins now.

'But I do not say this because I differ from you. I agree with you so fully, that I at once made up my mind to reject the man; and, consequently, I have done so.

'When I told him I could not accept him from family consider-ations, he asked me whether I had spoken to papa. I told him, no; and that it would be no good, as I had made up my own mind. I don't think he quite understood me; but it did not perhaps much matter. You told me to be very cold, and I think that perhaps he thought me less gracious than before. Indeed, I fear that when he first spoke, I may seem to have given him too much encourage-ment. However, it is all over now; quite over!' (As Augusta wrote this, she barely managed to save the paper beneath her hand from being moistened with the tear which escaped from her eye.)

'I do not mind confessing now,' she continued, 'at any rate to you, that I did like Mr Gazebee a little. I think his temper and disposition would have suited me. But I am quite satisfied that I have done right. He tried very hard to make me change my mind. That is, he said a great many things as to whether I would not put off my decision. But I was quite firm. I must say that he behaved very well, and that I really do think he liked me honestly and truly; but, of course, I could not sacrifice family considerations on that account.

'Yes, rank has its responsibilities as well as its privileges. I will remember that. It is necessary to do so, as otherwise one would be without consolation for what one has to suffer. For I find that one has to suffer, Amelia. I know papa would have advised me to marry this man; and so, I dare say, mamma would, and Frank, and Beatrice, if they knew that I liked him. It would not be so bad if we all thought alike about it; but it is hard to have the responsibilities all on one's own shoulder; is it not?

'But I will go over to you, and you will comfort me. I always feel stronger on this subject at Courcy than at Greshamsbury. We will have a long talk about it, and then I shall be happy again. I purpose going on next Friday, if that will suit you and dear aunt. I have told mamma that you all wanted me, and she made no objection. Do write at once, dearest Amelia, for to hear from you now will be my only comfort.

'Yours, ever most affectionately and obliged,
'Augusta Gresham.

'PS. – I told mamma what you said about Mary Thorne, and she said, "Yes; I suppose all the world knows it now; and if all the world did know it, it makes no difference to Frank." She seemed very angry; so you see it was true.'

Though by so doing, we shall somewhat anticipate the end of our story, it may be desirable that the full tale of Mr Gazebee's loves should be told here. When Mary is breaking her heart on her death-bed in the last chapter, or otherwise accomplishing her destiny, we shall hardly find a fit opportunity of saying much about Mr Gazebee and his aristocratic bride.

For he did succeed at last in obtaining a bride in whose veins ran the noble ichor of De Courcy blood, in spite of the high doctrine preached so eloquently by the Lady Amelia. As Augusta had truly said, he had failed to understand her. He was led to think, by her manner of receiving his first proposal – and justly so, enough – that she liked him, and would accept him; and he was, therefore, rather perplexed by his second interview. He tried again and again, and begged permission to mention the matter to Mr Gresham; but Augusta was very firm, and he at last retired in disgust. Augusta went to Courcy Castle, and received from her cousin that consolation and re-strengthening which she so much required.

Four years afterwards – long after the fate of Mary Thorne had fallen? like a thunderbolt, on the inhabitants of Greshamsbury; when Beatrice was preparing for her second baby, and each of the twins had her accepted lover – Mr Mortimer Gazebee went down to Courcy Castle; of course, on matters of business. No doubt he dined at the table, and all that. We have the word of Lady Amelia, that the earl, with his usual good-nature, allowed him such privileges. Let us hope that he never encroached on them.

But on this occasion, Mr Gazebee stayed a long time at the castle, and singular rumours as to the cause of his prolonged visit became current in the little town. No female scion of the present family of Courcy had, as yet, found a mate. We may imagine that eagles find it difficult to pair when they become scarce in their localities; and we all know how hard it has sometimes been to get *comme il faut* husbands when there has been any number of Protestant princesses on hand.

Some such difficulty had, doubtless, brought it about that the

countess was still surrounded by her full bevy of maidens. Rank
has its responsibilities as well as its privileges, and these young
ladies' responsibilities seemed to have consisted in rejecting any
suitor who may have hitherto kneeled to them. But now it was
told through Courcy, that one suitor had kneeled, and not in
vain; from Courcy the rumour flew to Barchester, and thence
came down to Greshamsbury, startling the inhabitants, and
making one poor heart to throb with a violence that would have
been piteous had it been known. The suitor, so named, was Mr
Mortimer Gazebee.

Yes; Mr Mortimer Gazebee had now awarded to him many
other privileges than those of dining at the table, and all that.
He rode with the young ladies in the park, and they all talked to
him very familiarly before company; all except the Lady Amelia.
The countess even called him Mortimer, and treated him quite
as one of the family.

At last came a letter from the countess to her dear sister
Arabella. It should be given at length, but that I fear to introduce
another epistle. It is such an easy mode of writing, and facility is
always dangerous. In this letter it was announced with much
preliminary ambiguity, that Mortimer Gazebee – who had been
found to be a treasure in every way; quite a paragon of men –
was about to be taken into the De Courcy bosom as a child of
that house. On that day fortnight, he was destined to lead to the
altar – the Lady Amelia.

The countess then went on to say, that dear Amelia did not
write herself, being so much engaged by her coming duties – the
responsibilities of which she doubtless fully realised, as well as
the privileges; but she had begged her mother to request that the
twins should come and act as bridesmaids on the occasion. Dear
Augusta, she knew, was too much occupied in the coming event
in Mr Oriel's family to be able to attend.

Mr Mortimer Gazebee was taken into the De Courcy family,
and did lead the Lady Amelia to the altar; and the Gresham
twins did go there and act as bridesmaids. And, which is much
more to say for human nature, Augusta did forgive her cousin,
and, after a certain interval, went on a visit to that nice place in
Surrey which she had once hoped would be her own home. It
would have been a very nice place, Augusta thought, had not
Lady Amelia Gazebee been so very economical.

We must presume that there was some explanation between

them. If so, Augusta yielded to it, and confessed it to be satisfactory. She had always yielded to her cousin, and loved her with that sort of love which is begotten between fear and respect. Anything was better than quarrelling with her cousin Amelia.

And Mr Mortimer Gazebee did not altogether make a bad bargain. He never received a shilling of dowry, but that he had not expected. Nor did he want it. His troubles arose from the overstrained economy of his noble wife. She would have it, that as she had married a poor man – Mr Gazebee, however, was not a poor man – it behoved her to manage her house with great care. Such a match as that she had made – this she told in confidence to Augusta – had its responsibilities as well as its privileges.

But, on the whole, Mr Gazebee did not repent his bargain; when he asked his friends to dine, he could tell them that Lady Amelia would be very glad to see them; his marriage gave him some éclat at his club, and some additional weight in the firm to which he belonged; he gets his share of the Courcy shooting, and is asked about to Greshamsbury and other Barsetshire houses, not only 'to dine at table and all that,' but to take his part in whatever delights country society there has to offer. He lives with the great hope that his noble father-in-law may some day be able to bring him into Parliament.

CHAPTER XXXIX

What the World Says About Blood

'Beatrice,' said Frank, rushing suddenly into his sister's room, 'I want you to do me one especial favour.' This was three or four days after Frank had seen Mary Thorne. Since that time he had spoken to none of his family on the subject; but he was only postponing from day to day the task of telling his father. He had now completed his round of visits to the kennel, master huntsman, and stables of the county hunt, and was at liberty to attend to his own affairs. So he had decided on speaking to the squire that very day; but he first made his request to his sister.

'I want you to do me one especial favour.' The day for Beatrice's marriage had now been fixed, and it was not to be very distant. Mr Oriel had urged that their honeymoon trip would lose half its delights if they did not take advantage of the fine weather; and Beatrice had nothing to allege in answer. The day had just been fixed, and when Frank ran into her room with his special request, she was not in a humour to refuse him anything.

'If you wish me to be at your wedding, you must do it,' said he.

'Wish you to be there! You *must* be there, of course. Oh, Frank! what do you mean? I'll do anything you ask; if it is not to go to the moon, or anything of that sort.'

Frank was too much in earnest to joke. 'You must have Mary for one of your bridesmaids,' he said. 'Now, mind; there may be some difficulty, but you must insist on it. I know what has been going on; but it is not to be borne that she should be excluded on such a day as that. You that have been like sisters all your lives till a year ago!'

'But, Frank – '

'Now, Beatrice, don't have any buts; say that you will do it, and it will be done: I am sure Oriel will approve, and so will my father.'

'But, Frank, you won't hear me.'

'Not if you make objections; I have set my heart on your doing it.'

'But I had set my heart on the same thing.'

'Well?'

'And I went to Mary on purpose; and told her just as you tell me now, that she must come. I meant to make mamma understand that I could not be happy unless it were so; but Mary positively refused.'

'Refused! What did she say?'

'I could not tell you what she said; indeed, it would not be right if I could; but she positively declined. She seemed to feel, that after all that had happened, she never could come to Greshamsbury again.'

'Fiddlestick!'

'But, Frank, those are her feelings; and, to tell the truth, I could not combat them. I know she is not happy; but time will cure that. And, to tell you the truth, Frank – '

'It was before I came back that you asked her, was it not?'

'Yes; just the day before you came, I think.'

'Well, it's all altered now. I have seen her since that.'

'Have you, Frank?'

'What do you take me for? Of course, I have. The very first day I went to her. And now, Beatrice, you may believe me or not, as you like; but if ever I marry, I shall marry Mary Thorne; and if ever she marries, I think I may say, she will marry me. At any rate, I have her promise. And now, you cannot be surprised that I should wish her to be at your wedding; or that I should declare, that if she is absent, I will be absent. I don't want any secrets, and you may tell my mother if you like it – and all the De Courcys too, for anything I care.'

Frank had ever been used to command his sisters: and they especially Beatrice, had ever been used to obey. On this occasion, she was well inclined to do so, if she only knew how. She again remembered how Mary had once sworn to be at her wedding, to be near her, and to touch her – even though all the blood of the De Courcys should be crowded before the altar railings.

'I should be so happy that she should be there; but what am I to do, Frank, if she refuses? I have asked her, and she has refused.'

'Go to her again; you need not have any scruples with her. Do not I tell you she will be your sister? Not come again to Greshamsbury! Why, I tell you that she will be living here while you are living there at the parsonage, for years and years to come.'

Beatrice promised that she would go to Mary again, and that she would endeavour to talk her mother over if Mary would consent to come. But she could not yet make herself believe that Mary Thorne would ever be mistress of Greshamsbury. It was so indispensably necessary that Frank should marry money! Besides, what were those horrid rumours which were now becoming rife as to Mary's birth; rumours more horrid than any which had yet been heard?

Augusta had said hardly more than the truth when she spoke of her father being broken-hearted by his debts. His troubles were becoming almost too many for him; and Mr Gazebee, though no doubt he was an excellent man of business, did not seem to lessen them Mr Gazebee, indeed, was continually pointing out how much he owed, and in what a quagmire of difficulties he had entangled himself. Now, to do Mr Yates Umbleby justice, he had never made himself disagreeable in this manner.

Mr Gazebee had been doubtless right, when he declared that Sir Louis Scatcherd had not himself the power to take any steps hostile to the squire; but Sir Louis had also been right, when he boasted that, in spite of his father's will, he could cause others to move in the matter. Others did move, and were moving, and it began to be understood that a moiety, at least, of the remaining Greshamsbury property must be sold. Even this, however, would by no means leave the squire in undisturbed possession of the other moiety. And thus, Mr Gresham was nearly broken-hearted.

Frank had now been at home a week, and his father had not as yet spoken to him about the family troubles; nor had a word as yet been said between them as to Mary Thorne. It had been agreed that Frank should go away for twelve months, in order that he might forget her. He had been away the twelvemonth, and had now returned, not having forgotten her.

It generally happens, that in every household, one subject of importance occupies it at a time. The subject of importance now mostly thought of in the Greshamsbury household, was the marriage of Beatrice. Lady Arabella had to supply the trousseau for her daughter; the squire had to supply the money for the trousseau; Mr Gazebee had the task of obtaining the money for the squire. While this was going on, Mr Gresham was not anxious to talk to his son, either about his own debts or his son's love. There would be time for these things when the marriage-feast should be over.

So thought the father, but the matter was precipitated by Frank. He also had put off the declaration which he had to make, partly from a wish to spare the squire, but partly also with a view to spare himself. We have all some of that cowardice which induces us to postpone an inevitably evil day. At this time the discussions as to Beatrice's wedding were frequent in the house, and at one of them Frank had heard his mother repeat the names of the proposed bridesmaids. Mary's name was not among them, and hence had arisen his attack on his sister.

Lady Arabella had had her reason for naming the list before her son; but she overshot her mark. She wished to show to him how totally Mary was forgotten at Greshamsbury; but she only inspired him with a resolve that she should not be forgotten. He accordingly went to his sister; and then, the subject being full on his mind, he resolved at once to discuss it with his father.

'Sir, are you at leisure for five minuses?' he said, entering the room in which the squire was accustomed to sit majestically, to receive his tenants, scold his dependents, and in which, in former happy days, he had always arranged the meets of the Barsetshire hunt.

Mr Gresham was quite at leisure: when was he not so? But had he been immersed in the deepest business of which he was capable, he would gladly have put it aside at his son's instance.

'I don't like to have any secret from you, sir,' said Frank; 'nor, for the matter of that, from anybody else' – the anybody else was intended to have reference to his mother – 'and, therefore, I would rather tell you at once what I have made up my mind to do.'

Frank's address was very abrupt, and he felt it was so. He was rather red in the face, and his manner was fluttered. He had quite made up his mind to break the whole affair to his father; but he had hardly made up his mind as to the best mode of doing so.

'Good heavens, Frank! what do you mean? you are not going to do anything rash? What is it you mean, Frank?'

'I don't think it is rash,' said Frank.

'Sit down, my boy; sit down. What is it that you say you are going to do?'

'Nothing immediately, sir,' said he, rather abashed; 'but as I have made up my mind about Mary Thorne, – quite made up my mind, I think it right to tell you.'

'Oh, about Mary,' said the squire, almost relieved.

And then Frank, in voluble language, which he hardly, however, had quite under his command, told his father all that had passed between him and Mary. 'You see, sir,' said he, 'that it is fixed now, and cannot be altered. Nor must it be altered. You asked me to go away for twelve months, and I have done so. It has made no difference, you see. As to our means of living, I am quite willing to do anything that may be best and most prudent. I was thinking, sir of taking a farm somewhere near here, and living on that.'

The squire sat quite silent for some moments after this communication had been made to him. Frank's conduct, as a son, had been such that he could not find fault with it; and, in this special matter of his love, how was it possible for him to find fault? He himself was almost as fond of Mary as of a daughter; and, though he too would have been desirous that his son should relieve the estate from its embarrassments by a rich marriage, he did not at all share Lady Arabella's feelings on the subject. No Countess de Courcy had ever engraved it on the tablets of his mind that the world would come to ruin if Frank did not marry money. Ruin there was, and would be, but it had been brought about by no sin of Frank's.

'Do you remember about her birth, Frank?' he said, at last.

'Yes, sir; everything. She told me all she knew; and Dr Thorne finished the story.'

'And what do you think of it?'

'It is a pity, and a misfortune. It might, perhaps, have been a reason why you or my mother should not have had Mary in the house many years ago; but it cannot make any difference now.'

Frank had not meant to lean heavily on his father; but he did do so. The story had never been told to Lady Arabella; was not even known to her now, positively, and on good authority. But Mr Gresham had always known it. If Mary's birth was so great a stain upon her, why had he brought her into his house among his children?

'It is a misfortune, Frank; a very great misfortune. It will not do for you and me to ignore birth; too much of the value of one's position depends upon it.'

'But what was Mr Moffat's birth?' said Frank, almost with scorn; 'or what Miss Dunstable's?' he would have added, had it not been that his father had not been concerned in that sin of wedding him to the oil of Lebanon.

'True, Frank. But yet, what you would mean to say is not true. We must take the world as we find it. Were you to marry a rich heiress, were her birth even as low as that of poor Mary –'

'Don't call her poor Mary, father; she is not poor. My wife will have a right to take rank in the world, however she was born.'

'Well, – poor in that way. But were she an heiress, the world would forgive her birth on account of her wealth.'

'The world is very complaisant, sir.'

'You must take it as you find it, Frank. I only say that such is the fact. If Porlock were to marry the daughter of a shoeblack, without a farthing, he would make a *mésalliance*; but if the daughter of the shoeblack had half a million of money, nobody would dream of saying so. I am stating no opinion of my own: I am only giving you the world's opinion.'

'I don't care a straw for the world.'

'That is a mistake, my boy; you do care for it, and would be very foolish if you did not. What you mean is, that, on this particular point, you value your love more than the world's opinion.'

'Well, yes, that is what I mean.'

But the squire, though he had been very lucid in his definition, had got no nearer to his object; had not even yet ascertained what his own object was. This marriage would be ruinous to Greshamsbury; and yet, what was he to say against it, seeing that the ruin had been his fault, and not his son's?

'You could let me have a farm; could you not, sir? I was thinking of about six or seven hundred acres. I suppose it could be managed somehow?'

'A farm?' said the father, abstractedly.

'Yes, sir. I must do something for my living. I should make less of a mess of that than of anything else. Besides, it would take such a time to be an attorney, or a doctor, or anything of that sort.'

Do something for his living! And was the heir of Greshamsbury come to this – the heir and only son? Whereas, he, the squire, had succeeded at an earlier age than Frank's to an unembarrassed income of fourteen thousand pounds a year! The reflection was very hard to bear.

'Yes: I dare say you could have a farm:' and then he threw himself back in his chair, closing his eyes. Then, after a while, he rose again, and walked hurriedly about the room. 'Frank,' he said, at last, standing opposite to his son, 'I wonder what you think of me?'

'Think of you, sir!' ejaculated Frank.

'Yes; what you think of me, for having thus ruined you. I wonder whether you hate me?'

Frank, jumping up from his chair, threw his arms round his father's neck. 'Hate you, sir! How can you speak so cruelly? You know well that I love you. And, father, do not trouble yourself about the estate for my sake. I do not care for it; I can be just as happy without it. Let the girls have what is left, and I will make my own way in the world, somehow. I will go to Australia; yes, sir, that will be best. I and Mary will both go. Nobody will care about her birth there. But, father, never say, never think, that I do not love you!'

The squire was too much moved to speak at once, so he sat down again, and covered his face with his hands. Frank went on pacing the room, till, gradually, his first idea recovered possession of his mind, and the remembrance of his father's grief faded away. 'May I tell Mary,' he said, at last, 'that you consent to our marriage? It will make her so happy.'

But the squire was not prepared to say this. He was pledged to his wife to do all that he could to oppose it; and he himself thought, that if anything could consummate the family ruin, it would be this marriage.

'I cannot say that, Frank; I cannot say that. What would you both live on? It would be madness.'

'We would go to Australia,' answered he, bitterly. 'I have just said so.'

'Oh, no, my boy; you cannot do that. You must not throw the old place up altogether. There is no other one but you, Frank; and we have lived here now for so many, many years.'

'But if we cannot live here any longer, father?'

'But for this scheme of yours, we might do so. I will give up everything to you, the management of the estate, the park, all the land we have in hand, if you will give up this fatal scheme. For, Frank, it is fatal. You are only twenty-three; why should you be in such a hurry to marry?'

'You married at twenty-one, sir.'

Frank was again severe on his father, but unwittingly. 'Yes, I did,' said Mr Gresham; 'and see what has come of it! Had I waited ten years longer, how different would everything have been! No, Frank, I cannot consent to such a marriage; nor will your mother.'

'It is your consent I ask, sir; and I am asking for nothing but your consent.'

'It would be sheer madness; madness for you both. My own Frank, my dear, dear boy, do not drive me to distraction! Give it up for four years.'

'Four years!'

'Yes; for four years. I ask it as a personal favour; as an

obligation to myself, in order that we may be saved from ruin; you, your mother, and sisters, your family name, and the old house. I do not talk about myself; but were such a marriage to take place, I should be driven to despair.'

Frank found it very hard to resist his father, who now had hold of his hand and arm, and was thus half retaining him, and half embracing him. 'Frank, say that you will forget this for four years – say for three years.'

But Frank would not say so. To postpone his marriage for four years, or for three, seemed to him to be tantamount to giving up Mary altogether; and he would not acknowledge that any one had a right to demand of him to do that.

'My word is pledged, sir,' he said.

'Pledged! Pledged to whom?'

'To Miss Thorne.'

'But I will see her, Frank; – and her uncle. She was always reasonable. I am sure she will not wish to bring ruin on her old friends at Greshamsbury.'

'Her old friends at Greshamsbury have done but little lately to deserve her consideration. She has been treated shamefully. I know it has not been by you, sir; but I must say so. She has already been treated shamefully; but I will not treat her falsely.'

'Well, Frank, I can say no more to you. I have destroyed the estate which should have been yours, and I have no right to expect you should regard what I say.'

Frank was greatly distressed. He had not any feeling of animosity against his father with reference to the property, and would have done anything to make the squire understand this, short of giving up his engagement to Mary. His feeling rather was, that, as each had a case against the other, they should cry quits; that he should forgive his father for his bad management, on condition that he himself was to be forgiven with regard to his determined marriage. Not that he put it exactly in that shape, even to himself; but could he have unravelled his own thoughts, he would have found that such was the web on which they were based.

'Father, I do regard what you say; but you would not have me be false. Had you doubled the property instead of lessening it, I could not regard what you say any more.'

'I should be able to speak in a very different tone; I feel that, Frank.'

'Do not feel it any more, sir; say what you wish, as you would have said it under other circumstances; and pray believe this, the idea never occurs to me, that I have ground of complaint as regards the property; never. Whatever troubles we may have, do not let that trouble you.'

Soon after this Frank left him. What more was there that could be said between them? They could not be of one accord; but even yet it might not be necessary that they should quarrel. He went out, and roamed by himself through the grounds, rather more in meditation than was his wont.

If he did marry, how was he to live? He talked of a profession; but had he meant to do as others do, who make their way in professions, he should have thought of that a year or two ago! – or, rather, have done more than think of it. He spoke also of a farm, but even that could not be had in a moment; nor, if it could, would it produce a living. Where was his capital? Where his skill? and he might have asked also, where the industry so necessary for such a trade? He might set his father at defiance, and if Mary were equally headstrong with himself, he might marry her. But, what then?

As he walked slowly about, cutting off the daisies with his stick, he met Mr Oriel, going up to the house, as was now his custom, to dine there and spend the evening, close to Beatrice.

'How I envy you, Oriel!' he said. 'What would I not give to have such a position in the world as yours!'

'Thou shalt not covet a man's house, nor his wife,'* said Mr Oriel; 'perhaps it ought to have been added, nor his position.'

'It wouldn't have made much difference. When a man is tempted, the Commandments, I believe, do not go for much.'

'Do they not, Frank? That's dangerous doctrine; and one which, if you had my position, you would hardly admit. But what makes you so much out of sorts? Your own position is generally considered about the best which the world has to give.'

'Is it? Then let me tell you that the world has very little to give. What can I do? Where can I turn? Oriel, if there be an empty, lying humbug in the world, it is the theory of high birth and pure blood which some of us endeavour to maintain. Blood, indeed! If my father had been a baker, I should know by this time where to look for my livelihood. As it is, I am told of nothing but my blood. Will my blood ever get me half a crown?'

And then the young democrat walked on again in solitude,

leaving Mr Oriel in doubt as to the exact line of argument which
he had meant to inculcate.

CHAPTER XL

The Two Doctors Change Patients

Dr Fillgrave still continued his visits to Greshamsbury, for Lady
Arabella had not yet mustered the courage necessary for swallowing her pride and sending once more for Dr Thorne. Nothing
pleased Dr Fillgrave more than those visits.

He habitually attended grander families, and richer people;
but then, he had attended them habitually. Greshamsbury was a
prize taken from the enemy; it was his rock of Gibraltar, of
which he thought much more than of any ordinary Hampshire
or Wiltshire which had always been within his own kingdom.

He was just starting one morning with his post-horses for
Greshamsbury, when an impudent-looking groom, with a
crooked nose, trotted up to his door. For Joe still had a crooked
nose, all the doctor's care having been inefficacious to remedy
the evil effects of Bridget's little tap with the rolling-pin. Joe had
no written credentials, for his master was hardly equal to
writing, and Lady Scatcherd had declined to put herself into
further personal communication with Dr Fillgrave; but he had
effrontery enough to deliver any message.

'Be you Dr Fillgrave?' said Joe, with one finger just raised to
his cockaded hat.

'Yes,' said Dr Fillgrave, with one foot on the step of the
carriage, but pausing at the sight of so well-turned-out a servant.
'Yes; I am Dr Fillgrave.'

'Then you be to go to Boxall Hill immediately; before
anywhere else.'

'Boxall Hill!' said the doctor, with a very angry frown.

'Yes, Boxall Hill: my master's place – my master is Sir Louis
Scatcherd, baronet. You've heard of him, I suppose?'

Dr Fillgrave had not his mind quite ready for such an
occasion. So he withdrew his foot from the carriage step, and
rubbing his hands one over another, looked at his own hall door

for inspiration. A single glance at his face was sufficient to show that no ordinary thoughts were being turned over within his breast.

'Well!' said Joe, thinking that his master's name had not altogether produced the magic effect which he had expected; remembering, also, how submissive Greyson had always been, who, being a London doctor, must be supposed to be a bigger man than this provincial fellow. 'Do you know as how my master is dying, very like, while you stand there?'

'What is your master's disease?' said the doctor, facing Joe, slowly, and still rubbing his hands. 'What ails him? What is the matter with him?'

'Oh; the matter with him? Well, to say it out at once then, he do take a drop too much at times, and then he has the horrors – what is it they call it? delicious beam-ends, or something of that sort.'

'Oh, ah, yes; I know; and tell me, my man, who is attending him?'

'Attending him? why, I do, and his mother, that is, her ladyship.'

'Yes; but what medical attendant: what doctor?'

'Why, there was Greyson, in London, and – '

'Greyson!' and the doctor looked as though a name so medicinally humble had never before struck the tympanum of his ear.

'Yes; Greyson. And then, down at what's the name of the place, there was Thorne.'

'Greshamsbury?'

'Yes; Greshamsbury. But he and Thorne didn't hit it off; and so since that he has had no one but myself.'

'I will be at Boxall Hill in the course of the morning,' said Dr Fillgrave; 'or, rather, you may say, that I will be there at once: I will take it in my way.' And having thus resolved, he gave his orders that the post-horses should make such a detour as would enable him to visit Boxall Hill on his road. 'It is impossible,' said he to himself, 'that I should be twice treated in such a manner in the same house.'

He was not, however, altogether in a comfortable frame of mind as he was driven up to the hall door. He could not but remember the smile of triumph with which his enemy had regarded him in that hall; he could not but think how he had returned fee-less to Barchester, and how little he had gained in the medical world by rejecting Lady Scatcherd's bank-note. However, he also had had his triumphs since that. He had smiled scornfully at Dr Thorne when he had seen him in the Greshamsbury street; and had been able to tell, at twenty houses through the county, how Lady Arabella had at last been obliged to place herself in his hands. And he triumphed again when he found himself really standing by Sir Louis Scatcherd's bedside. As for Lady Scatcherd, she did not even show herself. She kept in her own little room, sending out Hannah to ask him up the stairs; and she only just got a peep at him through the door as she heard the medical creak of his shoes as he again descended.

We need say but little of his visit to Sir Louis. It mattered nothing now, whether it was Thorne, or Greyson, or Fillgrave. And Dr Fillgrave knew that it mattered nothing: he had skill at least for that – and heart enough also to feel that he would fain have been relieved from this task; would fain have left this patient in the hands even of Dr Thorne.

The name which Joe had given to his master's illness was certainly not a false one. He did find Sir Louis 'in the horrors.' If any father have a son whose besetting sin is a passion for alcohol, let him take his child to the room of a drunkard when possessed by 'the horrors.' Nothing will cure him if not that.

I will not disgust my reader by attempting to describe the poor wretch in his misery: the sunken, but yet glaring eyes; the emaciated cheeks; the fallen mouth; the parched, sore lips; the face, now dry and hot, and then suddenly clammy with drops of perspiration; the shaking hand, and all but palsied limbs; and worse than this, the fearful mental efforts, and the struggles for drink; struggles to which it is often necessary to give way.

Dr Fillgrave soon knew what was to be the man's fate; but he did what he might to relieve it. There, in one big, best bedroom, looking out to the north, lay Sir Louis Scatcherd, dying wretchedly. There, in the other big, best bedroom, looking out to the south, had died the other baronet about a twelvemonth since, and each a victim to the same sin. To this had come the prosperity of the house of Scatcherd!

And then Dr Fillgrave went on to Greshamsbury. It was a long day's work, both for himself and the horses; but then, the triumph of being dragged up that avenue compensated for both the expense and the labour. He always put on his sweetest smile as he came near the hall door, and rubbed his hands in the most complaisant manner of which he knew. It was seldom that he saw any of the family but Lady Arabella; but then he desired to see none other, and when he left her in a good humour, was quite content to take his glass of sherry and eat his lunch by himself.

On this occasion, however, the servant at once asked him to go into the dining-room, and there he found himself in the presence of Frank Gresham. The fact was, that Lady Arabella, having at last decided, had sent for Dr Thorne; and it had become necessary that some one should be intrusted with the duty of informing Dr Fillgrave. That some one must be the squire, or Frank. Lady Arabella would doubtless have preferred a messenger more absolutely friendly to her own side of the house; but such messenger there was none: she could not send Mr Gazebee to see her doctor, and so, of two evils, she chose the least.

'Dr Fillgrave,' said Frank, shaking hands with him very cordially as he came up, 'my mother is so much obliged to you for all your care and anxiety on her behalf! and, so indeed, are we all.'

The doctor shook hands with him very warmly. This little expression of a family feeling on his behalf was the more gratifying, as he had always thought that the males of the Greshamsbury family were still wedded to that pseudo-doctor, that half-apothecary who lived in the village.

'It has been awfully troublesome to you, coming over all this way, I am sure. Indeed, money could not pay for it; my mother feels that. It must cut up your time so much.'

'Not at all, Mr Gresham; not at all,' said the Barchester doctor, rising up on his toes proudly as he spoke. 'A person of your mother's importance, you know! I should be happy to go any distance to see her.'

'Ah! but, Dr Fillgrave, we cannot allow that.'

'Mr Gresham, don't mention it.'

'Oh, yes; but I must,' said Frank, who thought that he had done enough for civility, and was now anxious to come to the point. 'The fact is, doctor, that we are very much obliged for what you have done; but, for the future, my mother thinks she can trust to such assistance as she can get here in the village.'

Frank had been particularly instructed to be very careful how he mentioned Dr Thorne's name, and, therefore, cleverly avoided it.

Get what assistance she wanted in the village. What words were those that he heard? 'Mr Gresham, eh – hem – perhaps I do not completely –' Yes, alas! he had completely understood what Frank had meant that he should understand. Frank desired to be civil, but he had no idea of beating unnecessarily about the bush on such an occasion as this.

'It's by Sir Omicron's advice, Dr Fillgrave. You see, this man here' – and he nodded his head towards the doctor's house, being still anxious not to pronounce the hideous name – 'has known my mother's constitution for so many years.'

'Oh, Mr Gresham; of course, if it is wished.'

'Yes, Dr Fillgrave, it is wished. Lunch is coming directly:' and Frank rang the bell.

'Nothing, I thank you, Mr Gresham.'

'Do take a glass of sherry.'

'Nothing at all, I am very much obliged to you.'

'Won't you let the horses get some oats?'

'I will return at once, if you please, Mr Gresham.' And the doctor did return, taking with him, on this occasion, the fee that was offered to him. His experience had at any rate taught him so much.

But though Frank could do this for Lady Arabella, he could not receive Dr Thorne on her behalf. The bitterness of that interview had to be borne by herself. A messenger had been sent for him, and he was upstairs with her ladyship while his rival was receiving his *congé** downstairs. She had two objects to accomplish, if it might be possible: she had found that high words with the doctor were of no avail; but it might be possible that Frank could be saved by humiliation on her part. If she humbled herself before this man, would he consent to acknowledge that his niece was not the fit bride for the heir of Greshamsbury?

The doctor entered the room where she was lying on her sofa, and walking up to her with a gentle, but yet not constrained step, took the seat beside her little table, just as he had always been accustomed to do, and as though there had been no break in their intercourse.

'Well, doctor, you see that I have come back to you,' she said, with a faint smile.

'Or, rather, I have come back to you. And, believe me, Lady Arabella, I am very happy to do so. There need be no excuses. You were, doubtless, right to try what other skill could do; and I hope it has not been tried in vain.'

She had meant to have been so condescending; but now all that was put quite beyond her power. It was not easy to be condescending to the doctor: she had been trying it all her life, and had never succeeded.

'I have had Sir Omicron Pie,' she said.

'So I was glad to hear. Sir Omicron is a clever man, and has a good name. I always recommend Sir Omicron myself.'

'And Sir Omicron returns the compliment,' said she, smiling gracefully, 'for he recommends you. He told Mr Gresham that I was very foolish to quarrel with my best friend. So now we are friends again, are we not? You see how selfish I am.' And she put out her hand to him.

The doctor took her hand cordially, and assured her that he bore her no ill-will; that he fully understood her conduct – and that he had never accused her of selfishness. This was all very well and very gracious; but, nevertheless, Lady Arabella felt that the doctor kept the upper hand in those sweet forgivenesses. Whereas, she had intended to keep the upper hand, at least for a while, so that her humiliation might be the more effective when it did come.

And then the doctor used his surgical lore, as he well knew how to use it. There was an assured confidence about him, and an air which seemed to declare that he really knew what he was doing. These were very comfortable to his patients, but they were wanting in Dr Fillgrave. When he had completed his examinations and questions, and she had completed her little details and made her answer, she certainly was more at ease than she had been since the doctor had last left her.

'Don't go yet for a moment,' she said. 'I have one word to say to you.'

He declared that he was not the least in a hurry. He desired nothing better, he said, than to sit there and talk to her. 'And I owe you a most sincere apology, Lady Arabella.'

'A sincere apology!' said she, becoming a little red. Was he going to say anything about Mary? Was he going to own that he, and Mary, and Frank had all been wrong?

'Yes, indeed. I ought not to have brought Sir Louis Scatcherd here: I ought to have known that he would have disgraced himself.'

'Oh! it does not signify,' said her ladyship, in a tone almost of disappointment. 'I had forgotten it. Mr Gresham and you had more inconvenience than we had.'

'He is an unfortunate, wretched man – most unfortunate; with an immense fortune which he can never live to possess.'

'And who will the money go to, doctor?'

This was a question for which Dr Thorne was hardly prepared. 'Go to?' he repeated. 'Oh, some member of the family, I believe. There are plenty of nephews and nieces.'

'Yes; but will it be divided, or all go to one?'

'Probably to one, I think. Sir Roger had a strong idea of leaving it all in one hand.' If it should happen to be a girl, thought Lady Arabella, what an excellent opportunity would that be for Frank to marry money!

'And now, doctor, I want to say one word to you: considering the very long time that we have known each other, it is better that I should be open with you. This estrangement between us and dear Mary has given us all so much pain. Cannot we do anything to put an end to it?'

'Well, what can I say, Lady Arabella? That depends so wholly on yourself.'

'If it depends on me, it shall be done at once.'

The doctor bowed; and though he could hardly be said to do so stiffly, he did it coldly. His bow seemed to say, 'Certainly; if you choose to make a proper *amende** it can be done; but I think it is very unlikely that you will do so.'

'Beatrice is just going to be married, you know that, doctor.' The doctor said that he did know it. 'And it will be so pleasant that Mary should make one of us. Poor Beatrice; you don't know what she has suffered!'

'Yes,' said the doctor, 'there has been suffering, I am sure; suffering on both sides.'

'You cannot wonder that we should be anxious about Frank, Dr Thorne; an only son, and the heir to an estate that has been so very long in the family:' and Lady Arabella put her handkerchief to her eyes, as though these facts were in themselves melancholy, and not to be thought of by a mother without some soft tears. 'Now I wish you could tell me what your views are, in a friendly manner, between ourselves. You won't find me unreasonable.'

'My views, Lady Arabella?'

'Yes, doctor; about your niece, you know: you must have views of some sort; that's of course. It occurs to me, that perhaps we are all in the dark together. If so, a little candid speaking between you and me may set it all right.'

Lady Arabella's career had not hitherto been conspicuous for candour, as far as Dr Thorne had been able to judge of it; but that was no reason why he should not respond to so very becoming an invitation on her part. He had no objection to a little candid speaking; at least, so he declared. As to his views with regard to Mary, they were merely these: that he would make her as happy and comfortable as he could while she remained with him; and that he would give her his blessing – for he had nothing else to give her – when she left him; – if ever she should do so.

Now, it will be said that the doctor was not very candid in this; not more so, perhaps, than was Lady Arabella herself. But when one is specially invited to be candid, one is naturally set upon one's guard. Those who by disposition are most open, are apt to become crafty when so admonished. When a man says to you, 'Let us be candid with each other,' you feel instinctively that he desires to squeeze you without giving a drop of water himself.

'Yes; but about Frank,' said Lady Arabella

'About Frank!' said the doctor, with an innocent look, which her ladyship could hardly interpret.

'What I mean is this: can you give me your word that these young people do not intend to do anything rash? One word like that from you will set my mind quite at rest. And then we could all be so happy together again.'

'Ah! who is to answer for what rash things a young man will do?' said the doctor, smiling.

Lady Arabella got up from the sofa, and pushed away the little table. The man was false, hypocritical, and cunning. Nothing could be made of him. They were all in a conspiracy together to rob her of her son; to make him marry without money! What should she do? Where should she turn for advice or counsel? She had nothing more to say to the doctor; and he, perceiving that this was the case, took his leave. This little attempt to achieve candour had not succeeded.

Dr Thorne had answered Lady Arabella as had seemed best to him on the spur of the moment; but he was by no means satisfied with himself. As he walked away through the gardens, he bethought himself whether it would be better for all parties if he could bring himself to be really candid. Would it not be better for him at once to tell the squire what were the future prospects of his niece, and let the father agree to the marriage, or not agree to it, as he might think fit. But then, if so, if he did do this, would he not in fact say, 'There is my niece, there is this girl of whom you have been talking for the last twelve-month, indifferent as to what agony of mind you may have occasioned to her; there she is, a probable heiress! It may be worth your son's while to wait a little time, and not cast her off till he shall know whether she be an heiress or no. If it shall turn out that she is rich, let him take her; if not, why, he can desert her then as well as now.' He could not bring himself to put his niece into such a position as this. He was anxious enough that she should be Frank Gresham's wife, for he loved Frank Gresham; he was anxious enough, also, that she should give to her husband the means of saving the property of his family. But Frank, though he might find her rich, was bound to take her while she was poor.

Then, also, he doubted whether he would be justified in speaking of this will at all. He almost hated the will for the trouble and vexation it had given him, and the constant stress it had laid on his conscience. He had spoken of it as yet to no one, and he thought that he was resolved not to do so while Sir Louis should yet be in the land of the living.

On reaching home, he found a note from Lady Scatcherd, informing him that Dr Fillgrave had once more been at Boxall Hill, and that, on this occasion, he had left the house without anger.

'I don't know what he has said about Louis,' she added, 'for, to tell the truth, doctor, I was afraid to see him. But he comes again tomorrow, and then I shall be braver. But I fear that my poor boy is in a bad way.'

CHAPTER XLI

Doctor Thorne Won't Interfere

At this period there was, as it were, a truce to the ordinary little skirmishes which had been so customary between Lady Arabella and the squire. Things had so fallen out, that they neither of them had much spirit for a contest; and, moreover, on that point which at the present moment was most thought of by both of them, they were strangely in unison. For each of them was anxious to prevent the threatened marriage of their only son.

It must, moreover, be remembered, that Lady Arabella had carried a great point in ousting Mr Yates Umbleby and putting the management of the estate into the hands of her own partisan. But then the squire had not done less in getting rid of Fillgrave and reinstating Dr Thorne in possession of the family invalids. The losses, therefore, had been equal; the victories equal; and there was a mutual object.

And it must be confessed, also, that Lady Arabella's taste for grandeur was on the decline. Misfortune was coming too near to her to leave her much anxiety for the gaieties of a London season. Things were not faring well with her. When her eldest daughter was going to marry a man of fortune, and a member of Parliament, she had thought nothing of demanding a thousand pounds or so for the extraordinary expenses incident to such an occasion. But now, Beatrice was to become the wife of a parish parson, and even that was thought to be a fortunate event; she had, therefore, no heart for splendour.

'The quieter we can do it the better,' she wrote, to her countess-sister. 'Her father wanted to give him at least a thousand pounds; but Mr Gazebee has told me confidentially that it literally cannot be done at the present moment. Ah, my dear Rosina! how things have been managed. If one or two of the girls will come over, we shall all take it as a favour. Beatrice would think it very kind of them. But I don't think of asking you or Amelia.' Amelia was always the grandest of the De Courcy family, being almost on an equality with – nay, in some respects superior to – the countess herself. But this, of course, was before the days of the nice place in Surrey.

Such, and so humble being the present temper of the lady of

Greshamsbury, it will not be thought surprising that she and Mr Gresham should at last come together in their efforts to reclaim their son.

At first Lady Arabella urged upon the squire the duty of being very peremptory and very angry. 'Do as other fathers do in such cases. Make him understand that he will have no allowance to live on.' 'He understands that well enough,' said Mr Gresham.

'Threaten to cut him off with a shilling,' said her ladyship, with spirit. 'I haven't a shilling to cut him off with,' answered the squire, bitterly.

But Lady Arabella herself soon perceived that this line would not do. As Mr Gresham himself confessed, his own sins against his son had been too great to allow of his taking a high hand with him. Besides, Mr Gresham was not a man who could be severe with a son whose individual conduct had been so good as Frank's. This marriage was, in his view, a misfortune to be averted if possible, – to be averted by any possible means; but, as far as Frank was concerned, it was to be regarded rather as a monomania than a crime.

'I did feel so certain that he would have succeeded with Miss Dunstable,' said the mother, almost crying.

'I thought it impossible but that at his age a twelve-month's knocking about the world would cure him,' said the father.

'I never heard of a boy being so obstinate about a girl,' said the mother. 'I'm sure he didn't get it from the De Courcys:' and then, again, they talked it over in all its bearings.

'But what are they to live upon?' said Lady Arabella, appealing, as it were, to some impersonation of reason. 'That's what I want him to tell me. What are they to live upon?'

'I wonder whether De Courcy could get him into some embassy?' said the father. 'He does talk of a profession.'

'What! with the girl and all?' asked Lady Arabella with horror, alarmed at the idea of such an appeal being made to her noble brother.

'No; but before he marries. He might be broken of it that way.'

'Nothing will break him,' said the wretched mother; 'nothing – nothing. For my part, I think that he is possessed. Why was she brought here? Oh, dear! oh, dear! Why was she ever brought into the house?'

This last question Mr Gresham did not think it necessary to

answer. That evil had been done, and it would be useless to dispute it. 'I'll tell you what I'll do,' said he. 'I'll speak to the doctor himself.'

'It's not the slightest use,' said Lady Arabella. 'He will not assist us. Indeed, I firmly believe it's all his own doing.'

'Oh, nonsense that really is nonsense, my love.'

'Very well, Mr Gresham. What I say is always nonsense, I know; you have always told me so. But yet, see how things have turned out. I knew how it would be when she was first brought into the house.' This assertion was rather a stretch on the part of Lady Arabella.

'Well, it is nonsense to say that Frank is in love with the girl at the doctor's bidding.'

'I think you know, Mr Gresham, that I don't mean that. What I say is this, that Dr Thorne, finding what an easy fool Frank is – '

'I don't think he's at all easy, my love; and he certainly is not a fool.'

'Very well, have it your own way. I'll not say a word more. I'm struggling to do my best, and I'm browbeaten on every side. God knows I am not in a state of health to bear it!' And Lady Arabella bowed her head into her pocket-handkerchief.

'I think, my dear, if you were to see Mary herself it might do some good,' said the squire, when the violence of his wife's grief had somewhat subsided.

'What! go and call upon this girl?'

'Yes; you can send Beatrice to give her notice, you know. She never was unreasonable, and I do not think that you would find her so. You should tell her, you know – '

'Oh, I should know very well what to tell her, Mr Gresham.'

'Yes, my love; I'm sure you would; nobody better. But what I mean is, that if you are to do any good, you should be kind in your nature. Mary Thorne has a spirit that you cannot break. You may perhaps lead, but nobody can drive her.'

As this scheme originated with her husband, Lady Arabella could not, of course, confess that there was much in it. But, nevertheless, she determined to attempt it, thinking that if anything could be efficacious for good in their present misfortunes, it would be her own diplomatic powers. It was, therefore, at last settled between them, that he should endeavour to talk over the doctor, and that she would do the same with Mary.

'And then I will speak to Frank,' said Lady Arabella. 'As yet he has never had the audacity to open his mouth to me about Mary Thorne, though I believe he declares his love openly to every one else in the house.'

'And I will get Oriel to speak to him,' said the squire.

'I think Patience might do more good. I did once think he was getting fond of Patience, and I was quite unhappy about it then. Ah, dear I should be almost pleased at that now.'

And thus it was arranged that all the artillery of Greshamsbury was to be brought to bear at once on Frank's love, so as to crush it, as it were, by the very weight of metal.

It may be imagined that the squire would have less scruple in addressing the doctor on this matter than his wife would feel; and that his part of their present joint undertaking was less difficult than hers. For he and the doctor had ever been friends at heart. But, nevertheless, he did feel much scruple, as, with his stick in hand, he walked down to the little gate which opened out near the doctor's house.

This feeling was so strong, that he walked on beyond this door to the entrance, thinking of what he was going to do, and then back again. It seemed to be his fate to be depending always on the clemency or consideration of Dr Thorne. At this moment the doctor was imposing the only obstacle which was offered to the sale of a great part of his estate. Sir Louis, through his lawyer, was pressing the doctor to sell, and the lawyer was loudly accusing the doctor of delaying to do so. 'He has the management of your property,' said Mr Finnie; 'but he manages it in the interest of his own friend. It is quite clear, and we will expose it.' 'By all means,' said Sir Louis. 'It is a d— shame, and it shall be exposed.' Of all this the squire was aware.

When he reached the doctor's house, he was shown into the drawing-room, and found Mary there alone. It had always been his habit to kiss her forehead when he chanced to meet her about the house at Greshamsbury. She had been younger and more childish then; but even now she was but a child to him, so he kissed her as he had been wont to do. She blushed slightly as she looked up into his face, and said: 'Oh, Mr Gresham, I am so glad to see you here again.'

As he looked at her he could but not acknowledge that it was natural that Frank should love her. He had never before seen that she was attractive; – had never had an opinion about it. She had grown up as a child under his eye; and as she had not had the name of being especially a pretty child, he had never thought on the subject. Now he saw before him a woman whose every feature was full of spirit and animation; whose eye sparkled with more than mere brilliancy; whose face was full of intelligence; whose very smile was eloquent. Was it to be wondered at that Frank should have learned to love her?

Miss Thorne wanted one attribute which many consider essential to feminine beauty. She had no brilliancy of complexion, no pearly whiteness, no vivid carnation; nor, indeed, did she possess the dark brilliance of a brunette. But there was a speaking earnestness in her face; an expression of mental faculty which the squire now for the first time perceived to be charming.

And then he knew how good she was. He knew well what was her nature; how generous, how open, how affectionate, and yet how proud! Her pride was her fault; but even that was not a fault in his eyes. Out of his own family there was no one whom he had loved, and could love, as he loved her. He felt, and acknowledged that no man could have a better wife. And yet he was there with the express object of rescuing his son from such a marriage!

'You are looking very well, Mary,' he said, almost involuntarily. 'Am I?' she answered, smiling. 'It's very nice at any rate to be complimented. Uncle never pays me any compliments of that sort.'

In truth, she was looking well. She would say to herself over and over again, from morning to night, that Frank's love for her would be, must be, unfortunate; could not lead to happiness. But, nevertheless, it did make her happy. She had before his return made up her mind to be forgotten, and it was so sweet to find that he had been so far from forgetting her. A girl may scold a man in words for rashness in his love, but her heart never scolds him for such offence as that. She had not been slighted, and her heart, therefore, still rose buoyant within her breast.

The doctor soon entered the room. As the squire's visit had been expected by him, he had of course not been out of the house. 'And now I suppose I must go,' said Mary; 'for I know you are going to talk about business. But, uncle, Mr Gresham says I'm looking very well. Why have you not been able to find that out?'

'She's a dear good girl,' said the squire, as the door shut behind her; 'a dear good girl;' and the doctor could not fail to see that his eyes were filled with tears.

'I think she is,' said he, quietly. And then they both sat silent, as though each was waiting to hear whether the other had anything more to say on that subject. The doctor, at any rate, had nothing more to say.

'I have come here specially to speak to you about her,' said the squire.

'About Mary?'

'Yes, doctor; about her and Frank: something must be done, some arrangement made: if not for our sakes, at least for theirs.'

'What arrangement, squire?'

'Ah! that is the question. I take it for granted that either Frank or Mary has told you that they have engaged themselves to each other.'

'Frank told me so twelve months since.'

'And has not Mary told you?'

'Not exactly that. But never mind; she has, I believe, no secret from me. Though I have said but little to her, I think I know it all.'

'Well, what then?'

The doctor shook his head and put up his hands. He had nothing to say; no proposition to make; no arrangement to suggest. The thing was so, and he seemed to say that, as far as he was concerned, there was an end of it.

The squire sat looking at him, hardly knowing how to proceed. It seemed to him, that the fact of a young man and a young lady being in love with each other was not a thing to be left to arrange itself, particularly, seeing the rank of life in which they were placed. But the doctor seemed to be of a different opinion.

'But, Dr Thorne, there is no man on God's earth who knows my affairs as well as you do; and in knowing mine, you know Frank's. Do you think it possible that they should marry each other?'

'Possible; yes, it is possible. You mean, will it be prudent?'

'Well, take it in that way; would it not be most imprudent?'

'At present, it certainly would be. I have never spoken to either of them on the subject; but I presume they do not think of such a thing for the present.'

'But doctor – ' The squire was certainly taken aback by the coolness of the doctor's manner. After all, he, the squire, was Mr Gresham of Greshamsbury, generally acknowledged to be the first commoner in Barsetshire; after all, Frank was his heir, and, in process of time, he would be Mr Gresham of Greshamsbury. Crippled as the estate was, there would be something left, and the rank at any rate remained. But as to Mary, she was not even the doctor's daughter. She was not only penniless, but nameless, fatherless, worse than motherless! It was incredible that Dr Thorne, with his generally exalted ideas as to family, should speak in this cold way as to a projected marriage between the heir of Greshamsbury and his brother's bastard child!

'But, doctor,' repeated the squire.

The doctor put one leg over the other, and began to rub his calf. 'Squire,' said he, 'I think I know all that you would say, all that you mean. And you don't like to say it, because you would not wish to pain me by alluding to Mary's birth.'

'But, independently of that, what would they live on?' said the squire, energetically. 'Birth is a great thing, a very great thing. You and I think exactly alike about that, so we need have no dispute. You are quite as proud of Ullathorne as I am of Greshamsbury.'

'I might be if it belonged to me.'

'But you are. It is no use arguing. But, putting that aside altogether, what would they live on? If they were to marry, what would they do? Where would they go? You know what Lady Arabella thinks of such things; would it be possible that they should live up at the house with her? Besides, what a life would that be for both of them! Could they live here? Would that be well for them?'

The squire looked at the doctor for an answer; but he still went on rubbing his calf. Mr Gresham, therefore, was constrained to continue his expostulation.

'When I am dead there will still, I hope, be something; – something left for the poor fellow. Lady Arabella and the girls would be better off, perhaps, than now, and I sometimes wish, for Frank's sake, that the time had come.'

The doctor could not now go on rubbing his leg. He was moved to speak, and declared that, of all events, that was the one which would be furthest from Frank's heart. 'I know no son,' said he, 'who loves his father more dearly than he does.'

'I do believe it,' said the squire; 'I do believe it. But yet, I cannot but feel that I am in his way.'

'No, squire, no; you are in no one's way. You will find yourself happy with your son yet, and proud of him. And proud of his wife, too. I hope so, and I think so: I do, indeed, or I should not say so, squire; we will have many a happy day yet together, when we shall talk of all these things over the dining-room fire at Greshamsbury.'

The squire felt it kind in the doctor that he should thus endeavour to comfort him; but he could not understand, and did not inquire, on what basis these golden hopes were founded. It was necessary, however, to return to the subject which he had come to discuss. Would the doctor assist him in preventing this marriage? That was now the one thing necessary to be kept in view.

'But, doctor, about the young people; of course they cannot marry, you are aware of that.'

'I don't know that exactly.'

'Well, doctor, I must say I thought you would feel it.'

'Feel what, squire?'

'That, situated as they are, they ought not to marry.'

'That is quite another question. I have said nothing about that either to you or to anybody else. The truth is, squire, I have never interfered in this matter one way or the other; and I have no wish to do so now.'

'But should you not interfere? Is not Mary the same to you as your own child?'

Dr Thorne hardly knew how to answer this. He was aware that his argument about not interfering was in fact absurd; Mary could not marry without his interference; and had it been the case that she was in danger of making an improper marriage, of course he would interfere. His meaning was, that he would not at the present moment express any opinion; he would not declare against a match which might turn out to be in every way desirable; nor, if he spoke in favour of it, could he give his reasons for doing so. Under these circumstances, he would have wished to say nothing, could that only have been possible.

But as it was not possible, and as he must say something, he answered the squire's last question by asking another. 'What is your objection, squire?'

'Objection! Why, what on earth would they live on?'

'Then I understand, that if that difficulty were over, you would not refuse your consent merely because of Mary's birth?'

This was a manner in which the squire had by no means expected to have the affair presented to him. It seemed so impossible that any sound-minded man should take any but his view of the case, that he had not prepared himself for argument. There was every objection to his son and heir marrying Miss Thorne; but the fact of their having no income whatever between them, did certainly justify him in alleging that first.

'But that difficulty can't be got over, doctor. You know, however, that it would be cause of grief to us all to see Frank marry much beneath his station; that is, I mean in family. You should not press me to say this, for you know that I love Mary dearly.'

'But, my dear friend, it is necessary. Wounds sometimes must be opened in order that they may be healed. What I mean is this; – and, squire, I'm sure I need not say to you that I hope for an honest answer, – were Mary Thorne an heiress; had she, for instance, such wealth as that Miss Dunstable that we hear of; in that case would you object to the match?'

When the doctor declared that he expected an honest answer the squire listened with all his ears; but the question, when finished, seemed to have no bearing on the present case.

'Come, squire, speak your mind faithfully. There was some talk once of Frank's marrying Miss Dunstable; did you mean to object to that match?'

'Miss Dunstable was legitimate; at least, I presume so.'

'Oh, Mr Gresham has it come to that? Miss Dunstable, then, would have satisfied your ideas of high birth?'

Mr Gresham was rather posed, and regretted, at the moment, his allusion to Miss Dunstable's presumed legitimacy. But he soon recovered himself. 'No,' said he, 'it would not. And I am willing to admit, as I have admitted before, that the undoubted advantages arising from wealth are taken by the world as atoning for what would otherwise be a *mésalliance*. But – '

'You admit that, do you? You acknowledge that as your conviction on the subject?'

'Yes. But – ' The squire was going on to explain the propriety of this opinion, but the doctor uncivilly would not hear him.

'Then, squire, I will not interfere in this matter in one way or the other.'

'How on earth can such an opinion – '

'Pray excuse me, Mr Gresham; but my mind is now quite made up. It was very nearly so before. I will do nothing to encourage Frank, nor will I say anything to discourage Mary.'

'That is the most singular resolution that a man of sense like you ever came to.'

'I can't help it, squire; it is my resolution.'

'But what has Miss Dunstable's fortune to do with it?'

'I cannot say that it has anything; but, in this matter, I will not interfere.'

The squire went on for some time, but it was all to no purpose; and at last he left the house, considerably in dudgeon. The only conclusion to which he could come was, that Dr Thorne had thought the chance on his niece's behalf too good to be thrown away, and had, therefore, resolved to act in this very singular way.

'I would not have believed it of him, though all Barsetshire had told me,' he said to himself as he entered the great gates; and he went on repeating the same words till he found himself in his own room. 'No, not if all Barsetshire had told me!'

He did not, however, communicate the ill result of his visit to the Lady Arabella.

CHAPTER XLII

What Can You Give in Return?

In spite of the family troubles, these were happy days for Beatrice. It so seldom happens that young ladies on the eve of their marriage have their future husbands living near them. This happiness was hers, and Mr Oriel made the most of it. She was constantly being coaxed down to the parsonage by Patience, in order that she might give her opinion, in private, as to some domestic arrangement, some piece of furniture, or some new carpet; but this privacy was always invaded. What Mr Oriel's parishioners did in these halcyon days, I will not ask. His morning services, however, had been altogether given up, and he had provided himself with a very excellent curate.

But one grief did weigh heavily on Beatrice.' She continually heard her mother say things which made her feel that it would be more than ever impossible that Mary should be at her wedding; and yet she had promised her brother to ask her. Frank had also repeated his threat, that if Mary were not present, he would absent himself.

Beatrice did what most girls do in such a case; what all would do who are worth anything: she asked her lover's advice.

'Oh! but Frank can't be in earnest,' said the lover. 'Of course he'll be at our wedding.'

'You don't know him, Caleb. He is so changed that no one hardly would know him. You can't conceive how much in earnest he is, how determined and resolute. And then, I should like to have Mary so much if mamma would let her come.'

'Ask Lady Arabella,' said Caleb.

'Well, I suppose I must do that; but I know what she'll say, and Frank will never believe that I have done my best.' Mr Oriel comforted her with such little whispered consolations as he was able to afford, and then she went away on her errand to her mother.

She was indeed surprised at the manner in which her prayer was received. She could hardly falter forth her petition; but when she had done so, Lady Arabella answered in this wise:–

'Well, my dear, I have no objection, none the least; that is, of course, if Mary is disposed to behave herself properly.'

'Oh, mamma! of course she will,' said Beatrice; 'she always did and always does.'

'I hope she will, my love. But, Beatrice, when I say that I shall be glad to see her, of course I mean under certain conditions. I never disliked Mary Thorne, and if she would only let Frank understand that she will not listen to his mad proposals, I should be delighted to see her at Greshamsbury just as she used to be.'

Beatrice could say nothing in answer to this; but she felt very sure that Mary, let her intention be what it might, would not undertake to make Frank understand anything at anybody's bidding.

'I will tell you what I will do, my dear,' continued Lady Arabella; 'I will call on Mary myself.'

'What! at Dr Thorne's house?'

'Yes; why not? I have been at Dr Thorne's house before now.' And Lady Arabella could not but think of her last visit thither, and the strong feeling she had, as she came out, that she would never again enter those doors. She was, however, prepared to do anything on behalf of her rebellious son.

'Oh, yes! I know that, mamma.'

'I will call upon her, and if I can possibly manage it, I will ask her myself to make one of your party. If so, you can go to her afterwards and make your own arrangements. Just write her a note, my dear, and say that I will call tomorrow at twelve. It might fluster her if I were to go in without notice.'

Beatrice did as she was bid, but with a presentiment that no good would come of it. The note was certainly unnecessary for the purpose assigned by Lady Arabella, as Mary was not given to be flustered by such occurrences; but, perhaps, it was as well that it was written, as it enabled her to make up her mind steadily as to what information should be given, and what should not be given to her coming visitor.

On the next morning, at the appointed hour, Lady Arabella walked down to the doctor's house. She never walked about the village without making some little disturbance among its inhabitants. With the squire, himself, they were quite familiar, and he could appear and reappear without creating any sensation; but her ladyship had not made herself equally common in men's sight. Therefore, when she went in at the doctor's little gate, the fact was known through all Greshamsbury in ten minutes, and before she had left the house, Mrs Umbleby and Miss Gushing had quite settled between them what was the exact cause of the very singular event.

The doctor, when he had heard what was going to happen, carefully kept out of the way: Mary, therefore, had the pleasure of receiving Lady Arabella alone. Nothing could exceed her ladyship's affability. Mary thought that it perhaps might have savoured less of condescension; but then, on this subject, Mary was probably prejudiced. Lady Arabella smiled and simpered, and asked after the doctor, and the cat, and Janet, and said everything that could have been desired by any one less unreasonable than Mary Thorne.

'And now, Mary, I'll tell you why I have called.' Mary bowed her head slightly, as much as to say, that she would be glad to receive any information which Lady Arabella could give her on that subject. 'Of course you know that Beatrice is going to be married very shortly.'

Mary acknowledged that she had heard so much.

'Yes: we think it will be in September – early in September – and that is coming very soon now. The poor girl is anxious that you should be at her wedding.' Mary turned slightly red; but she merely said, and that somewhat too coldly, that she was much indebted to Beatrice for her kindness.

'I can assure you, Mary, that she is very fond of you, as much so as ever; and so, indeed, am I, and all of us are so. You know that Mr Gresham was always your friend.'

'Yes, he always was, and I am grateful to Mr Gresham,' answered Mary. It was well for Lady Arabella that she had her temper under command, for had she spoken her mind out there would have been very little chance left for reconciliation between her and Mary.

'Yes, indeed he was; and I think we all did what little we could to make you welcome at Greshamsbury, Mary, till those unpleasant occurrences took place.'

'What occurrences, Lady Arabella?'

'And Beatrice is so very anxious on this point,' said her ladyship, ignoring for the moment Mary's question. 'You two have been so much together, that she feels she cannot be quite happy if you are not near her when she is being married.'

'Dear Beatrice!' said Mary, warmed for the moment to an expression of genuine feeling.

'She came to me yesterday, begging that I would waive any objection I might have to your being there. I have made her no answer yet. What answer do you think I ought to make her?'

Mary was astounded at this question, and hesitated in her reply. 'What answer ought you to make her?' she said.

'Yes, Mary. What answer do you think I ought to give? I wish to ask you the question, as you are the person the most concerned.'

Mary considered for a while, and then gave her opinion on the matter in a firm voice. 'I think you should tell Beatrice; that as you cannot at present receive me cordially in your house, it will be better that you should not be called on to receive me at all.'

This was certainly not the sort of answer that Lady Arabella expected, and she was now somewhat astounded in her turn. 'But, Mary,' she said, 'I should be delighted to receive you cordially if I could do so.'

'But is seems you cannot, Lady Arabella; and so there must be an end of it.'

'Oh, but I do not know that:' and she smiled her sweetest smile. 'I do not know that. I want to put an end to all this ill-feeling if I can. It all depends upon one thing, you know.'

'Does it, Lady Arabella?'

'Yes, upon one thing. You won't be angry if I ask you another question – eh, Mary?'

'No; at least, I don't think I will.'

'Is there any truth in what we hear about your being engaged to Frank?'

Mary made no immediate answer to this, but sat quite silent, looking Lady Arabella in the face; not but that she had made up her mind as to what answer she would give, but the exact words failed her at the moment.

'Of course you must have heard of such a rumour,' continued Lady Arabella.

'Oh, yes, I have heard of it.'

'Yes, and you have noticed it, and I must say very properly. When you went to Boxall Hill, and before that with Miss Oriel to her aunt's, I thought you behaved extremely well.' Mary felt herself glow with indignation, and began to prepare words that should be sharp and decisive. 'But, nevertheless, people talk; and Frank, who is still quite a boy' (Mary's indignation was not softened by this allusion to Frank's folly), 'seems to have got some nonsense in his head. I grieve to say it, but I feel myself in justice bound to do so, that in this matter he has not acted as well as you have done. Now, therefore, I merely ask you whether there is any truth in the report. If you tell me that there is none, I shall be quite contented.'

'But it is altogether true, Lady Arabella; I am engaged to Frank Gresham.'

'Engaged to be married to him?'

'Yes; engaged to be married to him.'

What was she to say or to do now? Nothing could be more plain, more decided, or less embarrassed with doubt than Mary's declaration. And as she made it she looked her visitor full in the face, blushing indeed, for her cheeks were now suffused as well as her forehead; but boldly, and, as it were, with defiance.

'And you tell me so to my face, Miss Thorne?'

'And why not? Did you not ask me the question; and would

you have me answer with a falsehood? I am engaged to him. As you would put the question to me, what other answer could I make? The truth is, that I am engaged to him.'

The decisive abruptness with which Mary declared her own iniquity almost took away her ladyship's breath. She had certainly believed that they were engaged, and had hardly hoped that Mary would deny it; but she had not expected that the crime would be acknowledged, or, at any rate, if acknowledged, that the confession would be made without some show of shame. On this Lady Arabella could have worked; but there was no such expression, nor was there the slightest hesitation. 'I am engaged to Frank Gresham,' and having so said, Mary looked her visitor full in the face.

'Then it is indeed impossible that you should be received at Greshamsbury.'

'At present, quite so, no doubt: in saying so, Lady Arabella, you can only repeat the answer I made to your first question. I can now go to Greshamsbury only in one light: that of Mr Gresham's accepted daughter-in-law.'

'And that is perfectly out of the question; altogether out of the question, now and for ever.'

'I will not dispute with you about that; but, as I said before, my being at Beatrice's wedding is not to be thought of.'

Lady Arabella sat for a while silent, that she might meditate, if possible, calmly as to what line of argument she had now better take. It would be foolish in her, she thought, to return home, having merely expressed her anger. She had now an opportunity of talking to Mary which might not again occur: the difficulty was in deciding in what special way she should use the opportunity. Should she threaten, or should she entreat? To do her justice, it should be stated, that she did actually believe that the marriage was all but impossible; she did not think that it could take place. But the engagement might be the ruin of her son's prospects, seeing how he had before him one imperative, one immediate duty – that of marrying money.

Having considered all this as well as her hurry would allow her, she determined first to reason, then to entreat, and lastly, if necessary, to threaten.

'I am astonished! you cannot be surprised at that, Miss Thorne: I am astonished at hearing so singular a confession made.'

'Do you think my confession singular, or is it the fact of my being engaged to your son?'

'We will pass over that for the present. But do let me ask you, do you think it possible, I say possible, that you and Frank should be married?'

'Oh, certainly; quite possible.'

'Of course you know that he has not a shilling in the world.'

'Nor have I, Lady Arabella.'

'Nor will he have were he to do anything so utterly hostile to his father's wishes. The property, you are aware, is altogether at Mr Gresham's disposal.'

'I am aware of nothing about the property, and can say nothing about it except this, that it has not been, and will not be inquired after by me in this matter. If I marry Frank Gresham, it will not be for the property. I am sorry to make such an apparent boast, but you force me to do it.'

'On what then are you to live? You are too old for love in a cottage,* I suppose?'

'Not at all too old; Frank, you know, is "still quite a boy."'

Impudent hussy! forward, ill-conditioned, saucy minx! such were the epithets which arose to Lady Arabella's mind; but she politely suppressed them.

'Miss Thorne, this subject is of course to me very serious; very ill-adapted for jesting. I look upon such a marriage as absolutely impossible.'

'I do not know what you mean by impossible, Lady Arabella.'

'I mean, in the first place, that you two could not get yourselves married.'

'Oh, yes; Mr Oriel would manage that for us. We are his parishioners, and he would be bound to do it.'

'I beg your pardon; I believe that under all the circumstances it would be illegal.'

Mary smiled; but she said nothing. 'You may laugh, Miss Thorne, but I think you will find that I am right. There are still laws to prevent such fearful distress as would be brought about by such a marriage.'

'I hope that nothing I shall do will bring distress on the family.'

'Ah, but it would; don't you know that it would? Think of it, Miss Thorne. Think of Frank's state, and of his father's state. You know enough of that, I am sure, to be well aware that

Frank is not in a condition to marry without money. Think of the position which Mr Gresham's only son should hold in the county; think of the old name, and the pride we have in it; you have lived among us enough to understand this; think of these things, and then say whether it is possible such a marriage should take place without family distress of the deepest kind. Think of Mr Gresham; if you truly love my son, you could not wish to bring on him all this misery and ruin.'

Mary now was touched, for there was truth in what Lady Arabella said. But she had no power of going back; her troth was plighted, and nothing that any human being could say should shake her from it. If he, indeed, chose to repent, that would be another thing.

'Lady Arabella,' she said, 'I have nothing to say in favour of this engagement, except that he wishes it.'

'And is that a reason, Mary?'

'To me it is; not only a reason, but a law. I have given him my promise.'

'And you will keep your promise even to his own ruin?'

'I hope not. Our engagement, unless he shall choose to break it off, must necessarily be a long one; but the time will come – '

'What! when Mr Gresham is dead?'

'Before that, I hope.'

'There is no probability of it. And because he is headstrong, you, who have always had credit for so much sense, will hold him to this mad engagement?'

'No, Lady Arabella; I will not hold him to anything to which he does not wish to be held. Nothing that you can say shall move me: nothing that anybody can say shall induce me to break my promise to him. But a word from himself will do it. One look will be sufficient. Let him give me to understand, in any way, that his love for me is injurious to him – that he has learnt to think so – and then I will renounce my part in this engagement as quickly as you could wish it.'

There was much in this promise, but still not so much as Lady Arabella wished to get. Mary, she knew, was obstinate, but yet reasonable; Frank, she thought, was both obstinate and unreasonable. It might be possible to work on Mary's reason, but quite impossible to touch Frank's irrationality. So she persevered – foolishly.

'Miss Thorne – that is, Mary, for I still wish to be thought your friend –'

'I will tell you the truth, Lady Arabella: for some considerable time past I have not thought you so.'

'Then you have wronged me. But I will go on with what I was saying. You quite acknowledge that this is a foolish affair?'

'I acknowledge no such thing.'

'Something very much like it. You have not a word in its defence.'

'Not to you: I do not choose to be put on my defence by you.'

'I don't know who has more right; however, you promise that if Frank wishes it, you will release him from his engagement.'

'Release him! It is for him to release me; that is, if he wishes it.'

'Very well; at any rate, you give him permission to do so. But will it not be more honourable for you to begin?'

'No; I think not.'

'Ah, but it would. If he, in his position, should be the first to speak, the first to suggest that this affair between you is a foolish one, what would people say?'

'They would say the truth.'

'And what would you yourself say?'

'Nothing.'

'What would he think of himself?'

'Ah, that I do not know. It is according as that may be, that he will or will not act at your bidding.'

'Exactly; and because you know him to be high-minded, because you think that he, having so much to give, will not break his word to you – to you who have nothing to give in return – it is, therefore, that you say that the first step must be taken by him. Is that noble?'

Then Mary rose from her seat, for it was no longer possible for her to speak what it was in her to say, sitting there leisurely on her sofa. Lady Arabella's worship of money had not hitherto been so brought forward in the conversation as to give her unpardonable offence; but now she felt that she could no longer restrain her indignation. 'To you who have nothing to give in return!' Had she not given all that she possessed? Had she not emptied her store into his lap? that heart of hers, beating with such genuine life, capable of such perfect love, throbbing with so grand a pride; had she not given that? And was not that, between him and her, more than twenty Greshamsburys, nobler than any pedigree? 'To you who have nothing to give,' indeed! This to her who was so ready to give everything!

'Lady Arabella,' she said, 'I think that you do not understand me, and that it is not likely that you should. If so, our further talking will be worse than useless. I have taken no account of what will be given between your son and me in your sense of the word giving. But he has professed to – to love me' – as she spoke, she still looked on the lady's face, but her eyelashes for a moment screened her eyes, and her colour was a little heightened – 'and I have acknowledged that I also love him, and so we were engaged. To me my promise is sacred. I will not be threatened into breaking it. If, however, he shall wish to change his mind, he can do so. I will not upbraid him; will not, if I can help it, think harshly of him. So much you may tell him if it suits you; but I will not listen to your calculations as to how much or how little each of us may have to give to the other.'

She was still standing when she finished speaking, and so she continued to stand. Her eyes were fixed on Lady Arabella, and her position seemed to say that sufficient words had been spoken, and that it was time that her ladyship should go; and so Lady Arabella felt it. Gradually she also rose; slowly, but tacitly, she acknowledged that she was in the presence of a spirit superior to her own; and so she took her leave.

'Very well,' she said, in a tone that was intended to be grandiloquent, but which failed grievously; 'I will tell him that he has your permission to think a second time on this matter. I do not doubt but that he will do so.' Mary would not condescend to answer, but curtsied low as her visitor left the room. And so the interview was over.

The interview was over, and Mary was alone. She remained standing as long as she heard the footsteps of Frank's mother on the stairs; not immediately thinking of what had passed, but still buoying herself up with her hot indignation, as though her work with Lady Arabella was not yet finished; but when the footfall was no longer heard, and the sound of the closing door told her that she was in truth alone, she sank back in her seat, and, covering her face with her hands, burst into bitter tears.

All that doctrine about money was horrible to her; that insolent pretence, that she had caught at Frank because of his worldly position, made her all but ferocious; but Lady Arabella had not the less spoken much that was true. She did think of the position which the heir of Greshamsbury should hold in the county, and of the fact that a marriage would mar that position so vitally; she did think of the old name, and the old Gresham pride; she did think of the squire and his deep distress: it was true that she had lived among them long enough to understand these things, and to know that it was not possible that this marriage should take place without deep family sorrow.

And then she asked herself whether, in consenting to accept Frank's hand, she had adequately considered this; and she was forced to acknowledge that she had not considered it. She had ridiculed Lady Arabella for saying that Frank was still a boy; but was it not true that his offer had been made with a boy's energy, rather than a man's forethought? If so, if she had been wrong to accede to that offer when made, would she not be doubly wrong to hold him to it now that she saw their error?

It was doubtless true that Frank himself could not be the first to draw back. What would people say of him? She could now calmly ask herself the question that had so angered her when asked by Lady Arabella. If he could not do it, and if, nevertheless, it behoved them to break off this match, by whom was it to be done if not by her? Was not Lady Arabella right throughout, right in her conclusions, though so fully wrong in her manner of drawing them?

And then she did think for one moment of herself. 'You who have nothing to give in return!' Such had been Lady Arabella's main accusation against her. Was it in fact true that she had nothing to give? Her maiden love, her feminine pride, her very life, and spirit, and being – were these things nothing? Were they to be weighed against pounds sterling per annum? and, when so weighed, were they ever to kick the beam like feathers?*
All these things had been nothing to her when, without reflection, governed wholly by the impulse of a moment, she had first allowed his daring hand to lie for an instant in her own. She had thought nothing of these things when that other suitor came, richer far than Frank, to love whom it was as impossible to her as it was not to love him.

Her love had been pure from all such thoughts; she was conscious that it ever would be pure from them. Lady Arabella was unable to comprehend this, and, therefore, was Lady Arabella so utterly distasteful to her.

Frank had once held her close to his warm breast; and her very soul had thrilled with joy to feel that he so loved her, – with a joy which she had hardly dared to acknowledge. At that moment, her maidenly efforts had been made to push him off, but her heart had grown to his. She had acknowledged him to be master of her spirit; her bosom's lord; the man whom she had been born to worship; the human being to whom it was for her to link her destiny. Frank's acres had been of no account; nor had his want of acres. God had brought them two together that they should love each other; that conviction had satisfied her, and she had made it a duty to herself that she would love him with her very soul. And now she was called upon to wrench herself asunder from him because she had nothing to give in return!

Well, she would wrench herself asunder, as far as such wrenching might be done compatibly with her solemn promise. It might be right that Frank should have an opportunity offered him, so that he might escape from his position without disgrace. She would endeavour to give him this opportunity. So, with one deep sigh, she arose, took to herself pen, ink, and paper, and sat herself down again so that the wrenching might begin.

And then, for a moment, she thought of her uncle. Why had he not spoken to her of all this? Why had he not warned her? He who had ever been so good to her, why had he now failed her so grievously? She had told him everything, had had no secret from him; but he had never answered her a word. 'He also must have known,' she said to herself, piteously, 'he also must have known that I could give nothing in return.' Such accusation, however, availed her not at all, so she sat down and slowly wrote her letter.

'Dearest Frank,' she began. She had at first written 'dear Mr Gresham;' but her heart revolted against such useless coldness. She was not going to pretend she did not love him.

'Dearest Frank,
    'Your mother has been here talking to me about our engagement. I do not generally agree with her about such matters; but she has said some things today which I cannot but acknowledge to be true. She says, that our marriage would be distressing to your father, injurious to all your family, and ruinous to yourself. If this be so, how can I, who love you, wish for such a marriage?

'I remember my promise, and have kept it. I would not yield to your mother when she desired me to disclaim our engagement. But I do think it will be more prudent if you will consent to forget all that has passed between us – not, perhaps, to forget it; that may not be possible for us – but to let it pass by as though it had never been. If so, if you think so, dear Frank, do not have scruples on my account. What will be best for you, must be best for me. Think what a reflection it would ever be to me, to have been the ruin of one that I love so well!

'Let me have but one word to say that I am released from my promise, and I will tell my uncle that the matter between us is over. It will be painful for us at first; those occasional meetings which must take place will distress us, but that will wear off. We shall always think well of each other, and why should we not be friends? This, doubtless, cannot be done without inward wounds; but such wounds are in God's hands, and He can cure them.

'I know what your first feelings will be on reading this letter; but do not answer it in obedience to first feelings. Think over it, think of your father, and all you owe him, of your old name, your old family, and of what the world expects from you.' (Mary was forced to put her hand to her eyes, to save her paper from her falling tears, as she found herself thus repeating, nearly word for word, the arguments that had been used by Lady Arabella.) 'Think of these things, coolly, if you can, but, at any rate, without passion: and then let me have one word in answer. One word will suffice.

'I have but to add this: do not allow yourself to think that my heart will ever reproach you. It cannot reproach you for doing that which I myself suggest.' (Mary's logic in this was very false; but she was not herself aware of it.) 'I will never reproach you either in word or thought; and as for all others, it seems to me that the world agrees that we have hitherto been wrong. The world, I hope, will be satisfied when we have obeyed it.

'God bless you, dearest Frank! I shall never call you so again; but it would be a pretence were I to write otherwise in this letter. Think of this, and then let me have one line.

'Your affectionate friend,
'Mary Thorne.

'PS. – Of course I cannot be at dear Beatrice's marriage; but when they come back to the parsonage, I shall see her. I am sure

they will both be happy, because they are so good. I need hardly
say that I shall think of them on their wedding day.'

When she had finished her letter, she addressed it plainly, in
her own somewhat bold handwriting, to Francis N. Gresham,
Jun., Esq., and then took it herself to the little village post-office.
There should be nothing underhand about her correspondence:
all the Greshamsbury world should know of it – that world of
which she had spoken in her letter – if that world so pleased.
Having put her penny label on it, she handed it, with an open
brow and an unembarrassed face, to the baker's wife, who was
Her Majesty's postmistress at Greshamsbury; and, having so
finished her work, she returned to see the table prepared for her
uncle's dinner. 'I will say nothing to him,' said she to herself,
'till I get the answer. He will not talk to me about it, so why
should I trouble him?'

CHAPTER XLIII

The Race of Scatcherd Becomes Extinct

It will not be imagined, at any rate by feminine readers, that
Mary's letter was written off at once, without alterations and
changes, or the necessity for a fair copy. Letters from one young
lady to another are doubtless written in this manner, and even
with them it might sometimes be better if more patience had
been taken; but with Mary's first letter to her lover – her first
love-letter, if love-letter it can be called – much more care was
used. It was copied and re-copied, and when she returned from
posting it, it was read and re-read.

'It is very cold,' she said to herself; 'he will think I have no
heart, that I have never loved him!' And then she all but resolved
to run down to the baker's wife, and get back her letter, that
she might alter it. 'But it will be better so,' she said again. 'If I
touched his feelings now, he would never bring himself to leave
me. It is right that I should be cold to him. I should be false to
myself if I tried to move his love – I, who have nothing to give

him in return for it.' And so she made no further visit to the
post-office, and the letter went on its way.

We will follow its fortunes for a short while, and explain how
it was that Mary received no answer for a week; a week, it may
well be imagined, of terrible suspense to her. When she took it
to the post-office, she doubtless thought that the baker's wife
had nothing to do but to send it up to the house at Greshamsbury, and that Frank would receive it that evening, or at latest,
early on the following morning. But this was by no means so.
The epistle was posted on a Friday afternoon, and it behoved
the baker's wife to send it into Silverbridge – Silverbridge being
the post-town – so that all due formalities, as ordered by the
Queen's Government, might there be perfected. Now, unfortunately, the post-boy had taken his departure before Mary
reached the shop, and it was not, therefore, dispatched till
Saturday. Sunday was always a *dies non** with the Greshamsbury Mercury, and, consequently, Frank's letter was not delivered at the house till Monday morning; at which time Mary had
for two long days been waiting with weary heart for the
expected answer.

Now Frank had on that morning gone up to London by early
train, with his future brother-in-law, Mr Oriel. In order to
accomplish this, they had left Greshamsbury for Barchester
exactly   as   the   postboy   was   leaving   Silverbridge   for
Greshamsbury.

'I should like to wait for my letters,' Mr Oriel had said, when
the journey was being discussed.

'Nonsense,' Frank had answered. 'Who ever got a letter that
was worth waiting for?' and so Mary was doomed to a week of
misery.

When the post-bag arrived at the house on Monday morning,
it was opened as usual by the squire himself at the breakfast-
table. 'Here is a letter for Frank,' said he, 'posted in the village.
You had better send it to him:' and he threw the letter across
the table to Beatrice.

'It's from Mary,' said Beatrice, out loud, taking the letter up
and examining the address. And having said so, she repented
what she had done, as she looked first at her father and then at
her mother.

A cloud came over the squire's brow as for a minute he went

on turning over the letters and newspapers. 'Oh, from Mary Thorne, is it?' he said. 'Well, you had better send it to him.'

'Frank said, that if any letters came they were to be kept,' said his sister Sophy. 'He told me so particularly. I don't think he likes having letters sent after him.'

'You had better send that one,' said the squire.

'Mr Oriel is to have all his letters addressed to Long's Hotel, Bond Street, and this one can very well be sent with them,' said Beatrice, who knew all about it, and intended herself to make a free use of the address.

'Yes, you had better send it,' said the squire; and then nothing further was said at the table. But Lady Arabella, though she said nothing, had not failed to mark what had passed. Had she asked for the letter before the squire, he would probably have taken possession of it himself; but as soon as she was alone with Beatrice, she did demand it. 'I shall be writing to Frank myself,' she said, 'and will send it to him.' And so Beatrice, with a heavy heart, gave it up.

The letter lay before Lady Arabella's eyes all that day, and many a wistful glance was cast at it. She turned it over and over, and much she desired to know its contents; but she did not dare to break the seal of her son's letter. All that day it lay upon her desk, and all the next, for she could hardly bring herself to part with it; but on the Wednesday it was sent – sent with these lines from herself:–

'Dearest, dearest Frank, I send you a letter which has come by the post from Mary Thorne. I do not know what it may contain; but before you correspond with her, pray, pray think of what I said to you. For my sake, for your father's, for your own, pray think of it!'

That was all, but it was enough to make her word to Beatrice true. She did send it to Frank enclosed in a letter from herself. We must reserve to the next chapter what had taken place between Frank and his mother; but, for the present, we will return to the doctor's house.

Mary said not a word to him about the letter; but, keeping silent on the subject, she felt wretchedly estranged from him. 'Is anything the matter, Mary?' he said to her on the Sunday afternoon.

'No, uncle,' she answered, turning away her head to hide her tears.

'Ah, but there is something; what is it, dearest?'

'Nothing – that is, nothing that one can talk about.'

'What, Mary! Be unhappy and not talk about it to me? That's something new, is it not?'

'One has presentiments sometimes, and is unhappy without knowing why. Besides, you know – '

'I know! What do I know? Do I know anything that will make my pet happier?' and he took her in his arms as they sat together on the sofa. Her tears were now falling fast, and she no longer made an effort to hide them. 'Speak to me, Mary; this is more than a presentiment. What is it?'

'Oh, uncle – '

'Come, love, speak to me; tell me why you are grieving.'

'Oh, uncle, why have you not spoken to me? Why have you not told me what to do? Why have you not advised me? Why are you always so silent?'

'Silent about what?'

'You know, uncle, you know; silent about him; silent about Frank!'

Why, indeed? What was he to say to this? It was true that he had never counselled her; never shown her what course she should take; had never even spoken to her about her lover. And it was equally true that he was not now prepared to do so, even in answer to such an appeal as this. He had a hope, a strong hope, more than a hope, that Mary's love would yet be happy; but he could not express or explain his hope; nor could he even acknowledge to himself a wish that would seem to be based on the death of him whose life he was bound, if possible, to preserve.

'My love,' he said, 'it is a matter in which you must judge for yourself. Did I doubt your conduct, I should interfere; but I do not.'

'Conduct! Is conduct everything? One may conduct oneself excellently, and yet break one's heart.'

This was too much for the doctor; his sternness and firmness instantly deserted him. 'Mary,' he said, 'I will do anything that you would have me. If you wish it, I will make arrangements for leaving this place at once.'

'Oh, no,' she said, plaintively.

'When you tell me of a broken heart, you almost break my own. Come to me, darling; do not leave me so. I will say all that

I can say. I have thought, do still think, that circumstances will admit of your marriage with Frank if you both love each other, and can both be patient.'

'You think so,' said she, unconsciously sliding her hand into his, as though to thank him by its pressure for the comfort he was giving her.

'I do think so now more than ever. But I only think so; I have been unable to assure you. There, darling, I must not say more; only that I cannot bear to see you grieving, I would not have said this:' and then he left her, and nothing more was spoken on the subject.

If you can be patient! Why, a patience of ten years would be as nothing to her. Could she but live with the knowledge that she was first in his estimation, dearest in his heart; could it be also granted to her to feel that she was regarded as his equal, she could be patient for ever. What more did she want than to know and feel this? Patient, indeed!

But what could these circumstances be to which her uncle had alluded? 'I do think circumstances will admit of your marriage.' Such was his opinion, and she had never known him to be wrong. Circumstances! What circumstances? Did he perhaps mean that Mr Gresham's affairs were not so bad as they had been thought to be? If so, that alone would hardly alter the matter, for what could she give in return? 'I would give him all the world for one word of love,' she said to herself, 'and never think that he was my debtor. Ah! how beggarly the heart must be that speculates on such gifts as those!'

But there was her uncle's opinion: he still thought that they might be married. Oh, why had she sent her letter? and why had she made it so cold? With such a letter as that before him, Frank could not do other than consent to her proposal. And then, why did he not at least answer it?

On the Sunday afternoon there arrived at Greshamsbury a man and a horse from Boxall Hill, bearing a letter from Lady Scatcherd to Dr Thorne, earnestly requesting the doctor's immediate attendance. 'I fear everything is over with poor Louis,' wrote the unhappy mother. 'It has been very dreadful. Do come to me; I have no other friend, and I am nearly worn through with it. The man from the city' – she meant Dr Fillgrave – 'comes every day, and I dare say he is all very well, but he has never done much good. He has not had spirit enough to keep the bottle from him; and it was that, and that only, that most behoved to be done. I doubt you won't find him in this world when you arrive here.'

Dr Thorne started instantly. Even though he might have to meet Dr Fillgrave, he could not hesitate, for he went not as a doctor to the dying man, but as the trustee under Sir Roger's will. Moreover, as Lady Scatcherd had said, he was her only friend, and he could not desert her at such a moment for an army of Fillgraves. He told Mary he should not return that night; and taking with him a small saddle-bag, he started at once for Boxall Hill.

As he rode up to the hall door, Dr Fillgrave was getting into his carriage. They had never met so as to speak to each other since that memorable day, when they had their famous passages of arms in the hall of that very house before which they both now stood. But, at the present moment, neither of them was disposed to renew the fight.

'What news of your patient, Dr Fillgrave?' said our doctor, still seated on his sweating horse, and putting his hand lightly to his hat.

Dr Fillgrave could not refrain from one moment of supercilious disdain: he gave one little chuck to his head, one little twist to his neck, one little squeeze to his lips, and then the man within him overcame the doctor. 'Sir Louis is no more,' he said.

'God's will be done!' said Dr Thorne.

'His death is a release; for his last days have been very frightful. Your coming, Dr Thorne, will be a comfort to Lady Scatcherd.' And then Dr Fillgrave, thinking that even the present circumstances required no further condescension, ensconced himself in the carriage.

'His last days have been very dreadful! Ah me, poor fellow! Dr Fillgrave before you go, allow me to say this: I am quite aware that when he fell into your hands, no medical skill in the world could save him.'

Dr Fillgrave bowed low from the carriage, and after this unwonted exchange of courtesies, the two doctors parted, not to meet again – at any rate, in the pages of this novel. Of Dr Fillgrave, let it now be said, that he grows in dignity as he grows in years, and that he is universally regarded as one of the celebrities of the city of Barchester.

Lady Scatcherd was found sitting alone in her little room on the ground-floor. Even Hannah was not with her, for Hannah was now occupied upstairs. When the doctor entered the room, which he did unannounced, he found her seated on a chair, with her back against one of the presses, her hands clasped together over her knees, gazing into vacancy. She did not even hear him or see him as he approached, and his hand had slightly touched her shoulder before she knew that she was not alone. Then, she looked up at him with a face so full of sorrow, so worn with suffering, that his own heart was racked to see her.

'It is all over, my friend,' said he. 'It is better so; much better so.'

She seemed at first hardly to understand him, but still regarding him with that wan face, shook her head slowly and sadly. One might have thought that she was twenty years older than when Dr Thorne last saw her.

He drew a chair to her side, and sitting by her, took her hand in his. 'It is better so, Lady Scatcherd; better so,' he repeated. 'The poor lad's doom had been spoken, and it is well for him, and for you, that it should be over.'

'They are both gone now,' said she, speaking very low; 'both gone now. Oh, doctor! To be left alone here, all alone!'

He said some few words trying to comfort her; but who can comfort a widow bereaved of her child? Who can console a heart that has lost all that it possessed? Sir Roger had not been to her a tender husband; but still he had been the husband of her love. Sir Louis had not been to her an affectionate son; but still he had been her child, her only child. Now they were both gone. Who can wonder that the world should be a blank to her?

Still the doctor spoke soothing words, and still he held her hand. He knew that his words could not console her; but the sounds of kindness at such desolate moments are, to such minds as hers, some alleviation of grief. She hardly answered him, but sat there staring out before her, leaving her hand passively to him, and swaying her head backwards and forwards as though her grief were too heavy to be borne.

At last, her eye rested on an article which stood upon the table, and she started up impetuously from her chair. She did this so suddenly, that the doctor's hand fell beside him before he knew that she had risen. The table was covered with all those implements which become so frequent about a house when severe illness is an inhabitant there. There were little boxes and apothecaries' bottles, cups and saucers standing separate, and bowls, in which messes have been prepared with the hope of suiting a sick man's failing appetite. There was a small saucepan standing on a plate, a curiously shaped glass utensil left by the doctor, and sundry pieces of flannel, which had been used in rubbing the sufferer's limbs. But in the middle of the debris stood one black bottle, with head erect, unsuited to the companionship in which it was found.

'There,' said she, rising up, and seizing this in a manner that would have been ridiculous had it not been so truly tragic. 'There, that has robbed me of everything – of all that I ever possessed; of husband and child; of the father and son; that has swallowed them both – murdered them both! Oh, doctor! that such a thing as that should cause such bitter sorrow! I have hated it always, but now – Oh, woe is me! weary me!' And she let the bottle drop from her hand as though it were too heavy for her.

'This comes of their barro-niting,' she continued. 'If they had let him alone, he would have been here now, and so would the other one. Why did they do it? why did they do it? Ah, doctor, people such as us should never meddle with them above us. See what has come of it; see what has come of it!'

The doctor could not remain with her long, as it was necessary that he should take upon himself the direction of the household, and give orders for the funeral. First of all, he had to undergo the sad duty of seeing the corpse of the deceased baronet. This, at any rate, may be spared to my readers. It was found to be necessary that the interment should be made very quickly, as the body was already nearly destroyed by alcohol. Having done all this, and sent back his horse to Greshamsbury, with directions that clothes for a journey might be sent to him, and a notice that he should not be home for some days, he again returned to Lady Scatcherd.

Of course he could not but think much of the immense property which was now, for a short time, altogether in his own hands. His resolution was soon made to go at once to London and consult the best lawyer he could find – or the best dozen lawyers should such be necessary – as to the validity of Mary's claims. This must be done before he said a word to her or to any of the Gresham family; but it must be done instantly, so that all suspense might be at end as soon as possible. He must, of course, remain with Lady Scatcherd till the funeral should be over; but when that office should be complete, he would start instantly for London.

In resolving to tell no one as to Mary's fortune till after he had fortified himself with legal warranty, he made one exception. He thought it rational that he should explain to Lady Scatcherd who was now the heir under her husband's will; and he was the more inclined to do so, from feeling that the news would probably be gratifying to her. With this view, he had once or twice endeavoured to induce her to talk about the property, but she had been unwilling to do so. She seemed to dislike all allusions to it, and it was not till she had incidentally mentioned the fact that she would have to look for a home, that he was able to fix her to the subject. This was on the evening before the funeral; on the afternoon of which day he intended to proceed to London.

'It may probably be arranged that you may continue to live here,' said the doctor.

'I don't wish it at all,' said she, rather sharply. 'I don't wish to have any arrangements made. I would not be indebted to any of them for anything. Oh, dear! if money could make it all right, I should have enough of that.'

'Indebted to whom, Lady Scatcherd? Who do you think will be the owner of Boxall Hill?'

'Indeed, then, Dr Thorne, I don't much care: unless it be yourself, it won't be any friend of mine, or any one I shall care to make a friend of. It isn't so easy for an old woman like me to make new friends.'

'Well, it certainly won't belong to me.'

'I wish it did, with all my heart. But even then, I would not live here. I have had too many troubles here to wish to see more.'

'That shall be just as you like, Lady Scatcherd; but you will be surprised to hear that the place will – at least I think it will – belong to a friend of yours: to one to whom you have been very kind.'

'And who is he, doctor? Won't it go to some of those Americans? I am sure I never did anything kind to them; though, indeed, I did love poor Mary Scatcherd. But that's years upon years ago, and she is dead and gone now. Well, I begrudge nothing to Mary's children. As I have none of my own, it is right they should have the money. It has not made me happy; I hope it may do so to them.'

'The property will, I think, go to Mary Scatcherd's eldest child. It is she whom you have known as Mary Thorne.'

'Doctor!' And then Lady Scatcherd, as she made the exclamation, put both her hands down to hold her chair, as though she feared the weight of her surprise would topple her off her seat.

'Yes; Mary Thorne – my Mary – to whom you have been so good, who loves you so well; she, I believe, will be Sir Roger's heiress. And it was so that Sir Roger intended on his deathbed, in the event of poor Louis's life being cut short. If this be so, will you be ashamed to stay here as the guest of Mary Thorne? She has not been ashamed to be your guest.'

But Lady Scatcherd was now too much interested in the general tenor of the news which she had heard to care much about the house which she was to inhabit in future. Mary Thorne, the heiress of Boxall Hill! Mary Thorne, the still living child of that poor creature who had so nearly died when they were all afflicted with their early grief! Well; there was consolation, there was comfort in this. There were but three people left in the world that she could love: her foster-child, Frank Gresham – Mary Thorne, and the doctor. If the money went to Mary, it would of course go to Frank, for she now knew that they loved each other; and if it went to them, would not the doctor have his share also; such share as he might want? Could she have governed the matter, she would have given it all to Frank; and now it would be as well bestowed.

Yes; there was consolation in this. They both sat up more than half the night talking over it, and giving and receiving explanations. If only the council of lawyers would not be adverse! That was now the point of suspense.

The doctor, before he left her, bade her hold her peace, and say nothing of Mary's fortune to any one till her rights had been absolutely acknowledged. 'It will be nothing not to have it,' said the doctor; 'but it would be very bad to hear that it was hers, and then to lose it.'

On the next morning, Dr Thorne deposited the remains of Sir Louis in the vault prepared for the family in the parish church. He laid the son where a few months ago he had laid the father,

– and so the title of Scatcherd became extinct. Their race of honour had not been long.

After the funeral, the doctor hurried up to London, and there we will leave him.

CHAPTER XLIV

Saturday Evening and Sunday Morning

We must now go back a little and describe how Frank had been sent off on special business to London. The household at Greshamsbury was at this time in but a doleful state. It seemed to be pervaded, from the squire down to the scullery-maid, with a feeling that things were not going well; and men and women, in spite of Beatrice's coming marriage, were grim-visaged, and dolorous. Mr Mortimer Gazebee, rejected though he had been, still went and came, talking much to the squire, much also to her ladyship, as to the ill-doings which were in the course of projection by Sir Louis; and Frank went about the house with clouded brow, as though finally resolved to neglect his one great duty.

Poor Beatrice was robbed of half her joy: over and over again her brother asked her whether she had yet seen Mary, and she was obliged as often to answer that she had not. Indeed, she did not dare to visit her friend, for it was hardly possible that they should sympathise with each other. Mary was, to say the least, stubborn in her pride; and Beatrice, though she could forgive her friend for loving her brother, could not forgive the obstinacy with which Mary persisted in a course which, as Beatrice thought, she herself knew to be wrong.

And then Mr Gazebee came down from town, with an intimation that it behoved the squire himself to go up that he might see certain learned pundits, and be badgered in his own person at various dingy, dismal chambers in Lincoln's Inn Fields, the Temple, and Gray's Inn Lane. It was an invitation exactly of that sort which a good many years ago was given to a certain duck.

'Will you, will you – will you, will you – come and be killed?'*

Although Mr Gazebee urged the matter with such eloquence, the squire remained steady to his objection, and swam obstinately about his Greshamsbury pond in any direction save that which seemed to lead towards London.

This occurred on the very evening of that Friday which had witnessed Lady Arabella's last visit to Dr Thorne's house. The question of the squire's necessary journey to the great fountains of justice was, of course, discussed between Lady Arabella and Mr Gazebee; and it occurred to the former, full as she was of Frank's iniquity and of Mary's obstinacy, that if Frank were sent up in lieu of his father, it would separate them at least for a while. If she could only get Frank away without seeing his love, she might yet so work upon him, by means of the message which Mary had sent, as to postpone, if not break off, this hateful match it was inconceivable that a youth of twenty-three, and such a youth as Frank, should be obstinately constant to a girl possessed of no great beauty – so argued Lady Arabella to herself – and who had neither wealth, birth, nor fashion to recommend her.

And thus it was at last settled – the squire being a willing party to the agreement – that Frank should go up and be badgered in lieu of his father. At his age it was possible to make it appear a thing desirable, if not necessary – on account of the importance conveyed – to sit day after day in the chambers of Messrs Slow & Bideawhile, and hear musty law talk, and finger dusty law parchments. The squire had made many visits to Messrs Slow & Bideawhile, and he knew better. Frank had not hitherto been there on his own bottom, and thus he fell easily into the trap.

Mr Oriel was also going to London, and this was another reason for sending Frank. Mr Oriel had business of great importance, which it was quite necessary that he should execute before his marriage. How much of this business consisted in going to his tailor, buying a wedding-ring, and purchasing some other more costly present for Beatrice, we need not here inquire. But Mr Oriel was quite on Lady Arabella's side with reference to this mad engagement, and as Frank and he were now fast friends, some good might be done in that way. 'If we all caution him against it, he can hardly withstand us all!' said Lady Arabella to herself.

The matter was broached to Frank on the Saturday evening,

and settled between them all the same night. Nothing, of course, was at that moment said about Mary; but Lady Arabella was too full of the subject to let him go to London without telling him that Mary was ready to recede if he only would allow her to do so. About eleven o'clock, Frank was sitting in his own room, conning over the difficulties of his situation – thinking of his father's troubles, and his own position – when he was roused from his reverie by a slight tap at the door.

'Come in,' said he, somewhat loudly. He thought it was one of his sisters, who were apt to visit him at all hours and for all manner of reasons; and he, though he was usually gentle to them, was not at present exactly in a humour to be disturbed.

The door gently opened, and he saw his mother standing hesitating in the passage.

'Can I come in, Frank?' said she.

'Oh, yes, mother; by all means:' and then, with some surprise marked in his countenance, he prepared a seat for her. Such a visit as this from Lady Arabella was very unusual; so much so, that he had probably not seen her in his own room since the day when he first left school. He had nothing, however, to be ashamed of; nothing to conceal, unless it were an open letter from Miss Dunstable which he had in his hand when she entered, and which he somewhat hurriedly thrust into his pocket.

'I wanted to say a few words to you, Frank, before you start for London about this business.' Frank signified by a gesture, that he was quite ready to listen to her.

'I am so glad to see your father putting the matter into your hands. You are younger than he is; and then – I don't know why, but somehow your father has never been a good man of business – everything has gone wrong with him.'

'Oh, mother! do not say anything against him.'

'No, Frank, I will not; I do not wish it. Things have been unfortunate, certainly. Ah, me! I little thought when I married – but I don't mean to complain – I have excellent children, and I ought to be thankful for that.'

Frank began to fear that no good could be coming when his mother spoke in that strain. 'I will do the best I can,' said he, 'up in town. I can't help thinking myself that Mr Gazebee might have done as well, but – '

'Oh, dear, no; by no means. In such cases the principal must show himself. Besides, it is right you should know how matters stand. Who is so much interested in it as you are? Poor Frank! I so often feel for you when I think how the property has dwindled.'

'Pray do not mind me, mother. Why should you talk of it as my matter while my father is not yet forty-five? His life, so to speak, is as good as mine. I can do very well without it; all I want is to be allowed to settle to something.'

'You mean a profession.'

'Yes; something of that sort.'

'They are so slow, dear Frank. You, who speak French so well – I should think my brother might get you in as attaché to some embassy.'

'That wouldn't suit me at all,' said Frank.

'Well, we'll talk about that another time. But I came about something else, and I do hope you will hear me.'

Frank's brow again grew black, for he knew that his mother was about to say something which it would be disagreeable for him to hear.

'I was with Mary, yesterday.'

'Well, mother?'

'Don't be angry with me, Frank; you can't but know that the fate of an only son must be a subject of anxiety to a mother.' Ah! how singularly altered was Lady Arabella's tone since first she had taken upon herself to discuss the marriage prospects of her son! Then how autocratic had she been as she sent him away, bidding him, with full command, to throw himself into the golden embraces of Miss Dunstable! But how, how humble, as she came suppliantly to his room, craving that she might have leave to whisper into his ears a mother's anxious fears! Frank had laughed at her stern behests, though he had half obeyed them; but he was touched to the heart by her humility.

He drew his chair nearer to her, and took her by the hand. But she, disengaging hers, parted the hair from off his forehead, and kissed his brow. 'Oh, Frank,' she said, 'I have been so proud of you, am still so proud of you. It will send me to my grave if I see you sink below your proper position. Not that it will be your fault. I am sure it will not be your fault. Only circumstanced as you are, you should be doubly, trebly careful. If your father had not – '

'Do not speak against my father.'

'No, Frank; I will not – no, I will not; not another word. And now, Frank – '

Before we go on we must say one word further as to Lady Arabella's character. It will probably be said that she was a consummate hypocrite; but at the present moment she was not hypocritical. She did love her son; was anxious – very, very anxious for him; was proud of him, and almost admired the very obstinacy which so vexed her to her inmost soul. No grief would be to her so great as that of seeing him sink below what she conceived to be his position. She was as genuinely motherly, in wishing that he should marry money, as another woman might be in wishing to see her son a bishop; or as the Spartan matron, who preferred that her offspring should return on his shield, to hearing that he had come back whole in limb but tainted in honour.* When Frank spoke of a profession, she instantly thought of what Lord de Courcy might do for him. If he would not marry money, he might, at any rate, be an attaché at an embassy. A profession – hard work, as a doctor, or as an engineer – would, according to her ideas, degrade him; cause him to sink below his proper position; but to dangle at a foreign court, to make small talk at the evening parties of a lady ambassadress, and occasionally, perhaps, to write demi-official notes containing demi-official tittle-tattle; this would be in proper accordance with the high honour of a Gresham of Greshamsbury.

We may not admire the direction taken by Lady Arabella's energy on behalf of her son, but that energy was not hypocritical.

'And now, Frank – ' She looked wistfully into his face as she addressed him, as though half afraid to go on, and begging that he would receive with complaisance whatever she found herself forced to say.

'Well, mother?'

'I was with Mary, yesterday.'

'Yes, yes; what then? I know what your feelings are with regard to her.'

'No, Frank; you wrong me. I have no feelings against her – none, indeed; none but this: that she is not fit to be your wife.'

'I think her fit.'

'Ah, yes; but how fit? Think of your position, Frank, and what means you have of keeping her. Think what you are. Your father's only son; the heir to Greshamsbury. If Greshamsbury be ever again more than a name, it is you that must redeem it. Of all men living you are the least able to marry a girl like Mary Thorne.'

'Mother, I will not sell myself for what you call my position.'

'Who asks you! I do not ask you; nobody asks you. I do not want you to marry any one. I did think once – but let that pass. You are now twenty-three. In ten years' time you will still be a young man. I only ask you to wait. If you marry now, that is, marry such a girl as Mary Thorne – '

'Such a girl! Where shall I find such another?'

'I mean as regards money, Frank; you know I mean that; how are you to live? Where are you to go? And then, her birth. Oh, Frank! Frank!'

'Birth! I hate such pretence. What was – but I won't talk about it. Mother, I tell you my word is pledged, and on no account will I be induced to break it.'

'Ah, that's just it; that's just the point. Now, Frank, listen to me. Pray listen to me patiently for one minute. I do not ask much of you.'

Frank promised that he would listen patiently; but he looked anything but patient as he said so.

'I have seen Mary, as it was certainly my duty to do. You cannot be angry with me for that.'

'Who said that I was angry, mother?'

'Well, I have seen her, and I must own, that though she was not disposed to be courteous to me, personally, she said much that marked her excellent good sense. But the gist of it was this; that as she had made you a promise, nothing should turn her from that promise but your permission.'

'And do you think – '

'Wait a moment, Frank, and listen to me. She confessed that this marriage was one which would necessarily bring distress on all your family; that it was the one which would probably be ruinous to yourself; that it was a match which could not be approved of: she did, indeed; she confessed all that. "I have nothing," she said – those were her own words – "I have nothing to say in favour of this engagement, except that he wishes it." That is what she thinks of it herself. "His wishes are not a reason; but a law," she said – '

'And, mother, would you have me desert such a girl as that?'

'It is not deserting, Frank: it would not be deserting: you would be doing that which she herself approves of. She feels the impropriety of going on; but she cannot draw back because of her promise to you. She thinks that she cannot do it, even though she wishes it.'

'Wishes it! Oh, mother!'

'I do believe she does, because she has sense to feel the truth of all that your friends say. Oh, Frank, I will go on my knees to you if you will listen to me.'

'Oh, mother! mother! mother!'

'You should think twice, Frank, before you refuse the only request your mother ever made you. And why do I ask you? why do I come to you thus? Is it for my own sake? Oh, my boy! my darling boy! will you lose everything in life, because you love the child with whom you have played as a child?'

'Whose fault is it that we were together as children? She is now more than a child. I look on her already as my wife.'

'But she is not your wife, Frank; and she knows that she ought not to be. It is only because you hold her to it that she consents to be so.'

'Do you mean to say that she does not love me?'

Lady Arabella would probably have said this, also, had she dared; but she felt, that in so doing, she would be going too far. It was useless for her to say anything that would be utterly contradicted by an appeal to Mary herself.

'No, Frank; I do not mean to say that you do not love her. What I do mean is this: that it is not becoming in you to give up everything – not only yourself, but all your family – for such a love as this; and that she, Mary herself, acknowledges this. Every one is of the same opinion. Ask your father: I need not say that he would agree with you about everything if he could. I will not say ask the De Courcys.'

'Oh, the De Courcys!'

'Yes, they are my relations; I know that.' Lady Arabella could not quite drop the tone of bitterness which was natural to her in saying this. 'But ask your sisters; ask Mr Oriel, whom you esteem so much; ask your friend Harry Baker.'

Frank sat silent for a moment or two while his mother, with a look almost of agony, gazed into his face. 'I will ask no one,' at last he said.

'Oh, my boy! my boy!'

'No one but myself can know my own heart.'

'And you will sacrifice all to such a love as that, all; her, also, whom you say that you so love? What happiness can you give her as your wife? Oh, Frank! is that the only answer you will make your mother on her knees?'

'Oh, mother! mother!'

'No, Frank, I will not let you ruin yourself; I will not let you destroy yourself. Promise this, at least, that you will think of what I have said.'

'Think of it! I do think of it.'

'Ah, but think of it in earnest. You will be absent now in London; you will have the business of the estate to manage; you will have heavy cares upon your hands. Think of it as a man, and not as a boy.'

'I will see her tomorrow before I go.'

'No, Frank, no; grant me that trifle, at any rate. Think upon this without seeing her. Do not proclaim yourself so weak that you cannot trust yourself to think over what your mother says to you without asking her leave. Though you be in love, do not be childish with it. What I have told you as coming from her is true, word for word; if it were not, you would soon learn so. Think now of what I have said, and of what she says, and when you come back from London, then you can decide.'

To so much Frank consented after some further parley; namely, that he would proceed to London on the following Monday morning without again seeing Mary. And in the meantime, she was waiting with sore heart for his answer to that letter which was lying, and was still to lie for so many hours, in the safe protection of the Silverbridge post-mistress.

It may seem strange; but, in truth, his mother's eloquence had more effect on Frank than that of his father: and yet, with his father he had always sympathised. But his mother had been energetic; whereas, his father, if not lukewarm, had, at any rate, been timid. 'I will ask no one,' Frank had said in the strong determination of his heart; and yet the words were hardly out of his mouth before he bethought himself that he would talk the thing over with Harry Baker. 'Not,' said he to himself, 'that I have any doubt; I have no doubt; but I hate to have all the world against me. My mother wishes me to ask Harry Baker. Harry is a good fellow, and I will ask him.' And with this resolve he betook himself to bed.

The following day was Sunday. After breakfast Frank went with the family to church, as was usual; and there, as usual, he saw Mary in Dr Thorne's pew. She, as she looked at him, could not but wonder why he had not answered the letter which was still at Silverbridge; and he endeavoured to read in her face whether it was true, as his mother had told him, that she was quite ready to give him up. The prayers of both of them were disturbed, as is so often the case with the prayers of other anxious people.

There was a separate door opening from the Greshamsbury pew out into the Greshamsbury grounds, so that the family were not forced into unseemly community with the village multitude in going to and from their prayers; for the front door of the church led out into a road which had no connexion with the private path. It was not unusual with Frank and his father to go round, after the service, to the chief entrance, so that they might speak to their neighbours, and get rid of some of the exclusiveness which was intended for them. On this morning the squire did so; but Frank walked home with his mother and sisters, so that Mary saw no more of him.

I have said that he walked home with his mother and his sisters; but he rather followed in their path. He was not inclined to talk much, at least, not to them; and he continued asking himself the question – whether it could be possible that he was wrong in remaining true to his promise? Could it be that he owed more to his father and his mother, and what they chose to call his position, than he did to Mary?

After church, Mr Gazebee tried to get hold of him, for there was much still to be said, and many hints to be given, as to how Frank should speak, and, more especially, as to how he should hold his tongue among the learned pundits in and about Chancery Lane. 'You must be very wide awake with Messrs Slow & Bideawhile,' said Mr Gazebee. But Frank would not hearken to him just at that moment. He was going to ride over to Harry Baker, so he put Mr Gazebee off till the half-hour before dinner, – or else the half-hour after tea.

On the previous day he had received a letter from Miss Dunstable, which he had hitherto read but once. His mother had interrupted him as he was about to refer to it; and now, as his father's nag was being saddled – he was still prudent in saving the black horse – he again took it out.

Miss Dunstable had written in an excellent humour. She was in great distress about the oil of Lebanon, she said. 'I have been trying to get a purchaser for the last two years; but my lawyer won't let me sell it, because the would-be purchasers offer a thousand pounds or so less than the value. I would give ten to be rid of the bore; but I am as little able to act myself as Sancho was in his government.* The oil of Lebanon! Did you hear anything of it when you were in those parts? I thought of changing the name to 'London particular;'* but my lawyer says the brewers would bring an action against me.

'I was going down to your neighbourhood – to your friend the duke's, at least. But I am prevented by my poor doctor, who is so weak that I must take him to Malvern. It is a great bore; but I have the satisfaction that I do my duty by him!

'Your cousin George is to be married at last. So I hear, at least. He loves wisely, if not well; for his widow has the name of being prudent and fairly well to do in the world. She has also got over the caprices of her youth. Dear Aunt De Courcy will be so delighted. I might perhaps have met her at Gatherum Castle. I do so regret it.

'Mr Moffat has turned up again. We all thought you had finally extinguished him. He left a card the other day, and I have told the servant always to say that I am at home, and that you are with me. He is going to stand for some borough in the west of Ireland. He's used to shillelaghs by this time.

'By the by, I have a *cadeau** for a friend of yours. I won't tell you what it is, nor permit you to communicate the fact. But when you tell me that in sending it I may fairly congratulate her on having so devoted a slave as you, it shall be sent.

'If you have nothing better to do at present, do come and see my invalid at Malvern. Perhaps you might have a mind to treat for the oil of Lebanon. I'll give you all the assistance I can in cheating my lawyers.'

There was not much about Mary in this; but still, the little that was said made him again declare that neither father nor mother should move him from his resolution. 'I will write to her and say that she may send her present when she pleases. Or I will run down to Malvern for a day. It will do me good to see her.' And so resolved, he rode away to Mill Hill, thinking, as he went, how he would put the matter to Harry Baker.

Harry was at home; but we need not describe the whole interview. Had Frank been asked beforehand, he would have declared, that on no possible subject could he have had the slightest hesitation in asking Harry any question, or communicating to him any tidings. But when the time came, he found that he did hesitate much. He did not want to ask his friend if he should be wise to marry Mary Thorne. Wise or not, he was determined to do that. But he wished to be quite sure that his mother was wrong in saying that all the world would dissuade him from it. Miss Dunstable, at any rate, did not do so.

At last, seated on a stile at the back of the Mill Hill stables, while Harry stood close before him with both his hands in his pockets, he did get his story told. It was by no means the first time that Harry Baker had heard about Mary Thorne, and he was not, therefore, so surprised as he might have been, had the affair been new to him. And thus, standing there in the position we have described, did Mr Baker, junior, give utterance to such wisdom as was in him on this subject.

'You see, Frank, there are two sides to every question; and, as I take it, fellows are so apt to go wrong because they are so fond of one side, they won't look at the other. There's no doubt about it, Lady Arabella is a very clever woman, and knows what's what; and there's no doubt about this either, that you have a very ticklish hand of cards to play.'

'I'll play it straightforward; that's my game,' said Frank.

'Well and good, my dear fellow. That's the best game always. But what is straightforward? Between you and me, I fear there's no doubt that your father's property has got into a deuce of a mess.'

'I don't see that that has anything to do with it.'

'Yes, but it has. If the estate was all right, and your father could give you a thousand a year to live on without feeling it, and if your eldest child would be cock-sure of Greshamsbury, it might be very well that you should please yourself as to marrying at once. But that's not the case; and yet Greshamsbury is too good a card to be flung away.'

'I could fling it away tomorrow,' said Frank.

'Ah! you think so,' said Harry the Wise. 'But if you were to hear tomorrow that Sir Louis Scatcherd were master of the whole place, and be d— to him, you would feel very uncomfortable.' Had Harry known how near Sir Louis was to his last struggle, he would not have spoken of him in this manner. 'That's all very fine talk, but it won't bear wear and tear. You do care for Greshamsbury if you are the fellow I take you to be: care for it very much; and you care too for your father being Gresham of Greshamsbury.'

'This won't affect my father at all.'

'Ah, but it will affect him very much. If you were to marry Miss Thorne tomorrow, there would at once be an end to any hope of your saving the property.'

'And do you mean to say I'm to be a liar to her for such reasons as that? Why, Harry, I should be as bad as Moffat. Only it would be ten times more cowardly, as she has no brother.'

'I must differ from you there altogether; but mind, I don't mean to say anything. Tell me that you have made up your mind to marry her, and I'll stick to you through thick and thin. But if you ask my advice, why, I must give it. It is quite a different affair to that of Moffat's. He had lots of tin, everything he could want, and there could be no reason why he should not marry, – except that he was a snob, of whom your sister was well quit. But this is very different. If I, as your friend, were to put it to Miss Thorne, what do you think she would say herself?'

'She would say whatever she thought best for me.'

'Exactly: because she is a trump. And I say the same. There can be no doubt about it, Frank, my boy: such a marriage would be very foolish for you both; very foolish. Nobody can admire Miss Thorne more than I do; but you oughtn't to be a marrying man for the next ten years, unless you get a fortune. If you tell her the truth, and if she's the girl I take her to be, she'll not accuse you of being false. She'll peak for a while; and so will you, old chap. But others have had to do that before you. They have got over it, and so will you.'

Such was the spoken wisdom of Harry Baker, and who can say that he was wrong? Frank sat a while on his rustic seat, paring his nails with his penknife, and then looking up, he thus thanked his friend:–

'I'm sure you mean well, Harry; and I'm much obliged to you. I dare say you're right too. But, somehow, it doesn't come home to me. And what is more, after what has passed, I could not tell her that I wish to part from her. I could not do it. And besides, I have that sort of feeling, that if I heard she was to marry any one else, I am sure I should blow his brains out. Either his or my own.'

'Well, Frank, you may count on me for anything, except the last proposition:' and so they shook hands, and Frank rode back to Greshamsbury.

CHAPTER XLV

Law Business In London

On the Monday morning at six o'clock, Mr Oriel and Frank started together; but early as it was, Beatrice was up to give them a cup of coffee, Mr Oriel having slept that night in the house. Whether Frank would have received his coffee from his sister's fair hands had not Mr Oriel been there, may be doubted. He, however, loudly asserted that he should not have done so, when she laid claim to great merit for rising in his behalf.

Mr Oriel had been specially instigated by Lady Arabella to use the opportunity of their joint journey, for pointing out to Frank the iniquity as well as madness of the course he was pursuing; and he had promised to obey her ladyship's behests. But Mr Oriel was perhaps not an enterprising man, and was certainly not a presumptuous one. He did intend to do as he was bid; but when he began, with the object of leading up to the subject of Frank's engagement, he always softened down into some much easier enthusiasm in the matter of his own engagement with Beatrice. He had not that perspicuous, but not over-sensitive strength of mind which had enabled Harry Baker to express his opinion out at once; and boldly as he did it, yet to do so without offence.

Four times before the train arrived in London, he made some little attempt; but four times he failed. As the subject was matrimony, it was his easiest course to begin about himself; but he never could get any further.

'No man was ever more fortunate in a wife than I shall be,' he said, with a soft, euphemistic self-complacency, which would have been silly had it been adopted to any other person than the bride's brother. His intention, however, was very good, for he meant to show, that in his case marriage was prudent and wise, because his case differed so widely from that of Frank.

'Yes,' said Frank. 'She is an excellent good girl:' he had said it three times before, and was not very energetic.

'Yes, and so exactly suited to me; indeed, all that I could have dreamed of. How very well she looked this morning! Some girls only look well at night. I should not like that at all.'

'You mustn't expect her to look like that always at six o'clock a.m.,' said Frank, laughing. 'Young ladies only take that trouble on very particular occasions. She wouldn't have come down like that if my father or I had been going alone. No, and she won't do so for you in a couple of years' time.'

'Oh, but she's always nice. I have seen her at home as much almost as you could do; and then she's so sincerely religious.'

'Oh, yes, of course; that is, I am sure she is,' said Frank, looking solemn as became him.

'She's made to be a clergyman's wife.'

'Well, so it seems,' said Frank.

'A married life is, I'm sure, the happiest in the world – if people are only in a position to marry,' said Mr Oriel, gradually drawing near to the accomplishment of his design.

'Yes; quite so. Do you know, Oriel, I never was so sleepy in my life. What with all that fuss of Gazebee's, and one thing and another, I could not get to bed till one o'clock; and then I couldn't sleep. I'll take a snooze now, if you won't think it uncivil.' And then, putting his feet upon the opposite seat, he settled himself comfortably to his rest. And so Mr Oriel's last attempt for lecturing Frank in the railway-carriage faded away and was annihilated.

By twelve o'clock Frank was with Messrs Slow & Bideawhile. Mr Bideawhile was engaged at the moment, but he found the managing Chancery clerk to be a very chatty gentleman. Judging from what he saw, he would have said that the work to be done at Messrs Slow & Bideawhile's was not very heavy.

'A singular man that Sir Louis,' said the Chancery clerk.

'Yes; very singular,' said Frank.

'Excellent security, excellent; no better: and yet he will foreclose; but you see he has no power himself. But the question is, can the trustee refuse? Then, again, trustees are so circumstanced nowadays that they are afraid to do anything. There has been so much said lately, Mr Gresham, that a man doesn't know where he is, or what he is doing. Nobody trusts anybody. There have been such terrible things that we can't wonder at it. Only think of the case of those Hills!* How can any one expect that any one else will ever trust a lawyer again after that? But that's Mr Bideawhile's bell. How can any one expect it? He will see you now, I dare say, Mr Gresham.'

So it turned out, and Frank was ushered into the presence of Mr Bideawhile. He had got his lesson by heart, and was going to rush into the middle of his subject; such a course, however, was not in accordance with Mr Bideawhile's usual practice. Mr Bideawhile got up from his large wooden-seated Windsor chair, and, with a soft smile, in which, however, was mingled some slight dash of the attorney's acuteness, put out his hand to his young client; not, indeed, as though he were going to shake hands with him, but as though the hand were some ripe fruit all but falling, which his visitor might take and pluck if he thought proper. Frank took hold of the hand, which returned him no pressure, and then let it go again, not making any attempt to gather the fruit.

'I have come up to town, Mr Bideawhile, about this mortgage,' commenced Frank.

'Mortgage – ah, sit down, Mr Gresham; sit down. I hope your father is quite well.'

'Quite well, thank you.'

'I have a great regard for your father. So I had for your grandfather; a very good man indeed. You, perhaps, don't remember him, Mr Gresham?'

'He died when I was only a year old.'

'Oh, yes; no, you of course can't remember him; but I do, well: he used to be very fond of some port wine I had. I think it was "II"; and if I don't mistake, I have a bottle or two of it yet; but it is not worth drinking now. Port wine, you know, won't keep beyond a certain time. That was very good wine. I don't exactly remember what it stood me a dozen then; but such wine can't be had now. As for the Madeira, you know there's an end of that.* Do you drink Madeira, Mr Gresham?'

'No,' said Frank, 'not very often.'

'I'm sorry for that, for it's a fine wine; but then there's none of it left, you know. I have a few dozen. I'm told they're growing pumpkins where the vineyards were. I wonder what they do with all the pumpkins they grow in Switzerland! You've been in Switzerland, Mr Gresham?'

Frank said he had been in Switzerland.

'It's a beautiful country; my girls made me go there last year. They said it would do me good; but then, you know, they wanted to see it themselves; ha! ha! ha! However, I believe I shall go again this autumn. That is to Aix,* or some of those places; just for three weeks. I can't spare any more time, Mr Gresham. Do you like that dining at the *tables d'hôte*?'*

'Pretty well, sometimes.'

'One would get tired of it – eh! But they gave us capital dinners at Zurich. I don't think much of their soup. But they had fish, and about seven kinds of meats and poultry, and three or four puddings, and things of that sort. Upon my word, I thought we did very well, and so did my girls, too. You see a great many ladies travelling now.'

'Yes,' said Frank; 'a great many.'

'Upon my word, I think they are right; that is, if they can afford time. I can't afford time. I'm here every day till five, Mr Gresham; then I go out and dine in Fleet Street, and then back to work till nine.'

'Dear me! that's very hard.'

'Well, yes, it is hard work. My boys don't like it; but I manage it somehow. I get down to my little place in the country on Saturday. I shall be most happy to see you there next Saturday.'

Frank, thinking it would be outrageous on his part to take up much of the time of a gentleman who was constrained to work so unreasonably hard, began again to talk about his mortgages, and, in so doing, had to mention the name of Mr Yates Umbleby.

'Ah, poor Umbleby,' said Mr Bideawhile; 'what is he doing now? I am quite sure your father was right, or he wouldn't have done it; but I used to think that Umbleby was a decent sort of man enough. Not so grand, you know, as your Gazebees and Gumptions – eh, Mr Gresham? They do say young Gazebee is thinking of getting into Parliament. Let me see: Umbleby married – who was it he married? That was the way your father got hold of him; not your father, but your grandfather. I used to know all about it. Well, I was sorry for Umbleby. He has got something, I suppose – eh?'

Frank said that he believed Mr Yates Umbleby had something wherewith to keep the wolf from the door.

'So you have got Gazebee down there now? Gumption, Gazebee, & Gazebee: very good people, I'm sure; only, perhaps, they have a little too much on hand to do your father justice.'

'But about Sir Louis, Mr Bideawhile.'

'Well, about Sir Louis; a very bad sort of fellow, isn't he? Drinks – eh? I knew his father a little. He was a rough diamond, too. I was once down in Northamptonshire, about some railway business; let me see; I almost forget whether I was with him, or against him. But I know he made sixty thousand pounds by one hour's work; sixty thousand pounds! And then he got so mad with drinking that we all thought – '

And so Mr Bideawhile went on for two hours, and Frank found no opportunity of saying one word about the business which had brought him up to town. What wonder that such a man as this should be obliged to stay at his office every night till nine o'clock?

During these two hours, a clerk had come in three or four times, whispering something to the lawyer, who, on the last of such occasions, turned to Frank, saying, 'Well, perhaps that will do for today. If you'll manage to call tomorrow, say about two, I will have the whole thing looked up; or, perhaps, Wednesday or Thursday would suit you better.' Frank, declaring that the morrow would suit him very well, took his departure, wondering much at the manner in which business was done at the house of Messrs Slow & Bideawhile.

When he called the next day, the office seemed to be rather disturbed, and he was shown quickly into Mr Bideawhile's room. 'Have you heard this?' said that gentleman, putting a telegram into his hands. It contained tidings of the death of Sir Louis Scatcherd. Frank immediately knew that these tidings must be of importance to his father; but he had no idea how vitally they concerned his own more immediate interests.

'Dr Thorne will be up in town on Thursday evening after the funeral,' said the talkative clerk. 'And nothing of course can be done till he comes,' said Mr Bideawhile. And so Frank, pondering on the mutability of human affairs, again took his departure.

He could do nothing now but wait for Dr Thorne's arrival, and so he amused himself in the interval by running down to Malvern, and treating with Miss Dunstable in person for the oil of Lebanon. He went down on the Wednesday, and thus failed to receive, on the Thursday morning, Mary's letter, which reached London on that day. He returned, however, on the Friday, and then got it; and perhaps it was well for Mary's happiness that he had seen Miss Dunstable in the interval. 'I don't care what your mother says,' said she, with emphasis. 'I don't care for any Harry, whether it be Harry Baker, or old Harry himself. You made her a promise, and you are bound to keep it; if not on one day, then on another. What, because you cannot draw back yourself, get out of it by inducing her to do so! Aunt de Courcy herself could not improve upon that.' Fortified in this manner, he returned to town on the Friday morning, and then got Mary's letter. Frank also got a note from Dr Thorne, stating that he had taken up his temporary domicile at the Grey's Inn Coffee-house, so as to be near the lawyers.

It has been suggested that the modern English writers of fiction should among them keep a barrister, in order that they may be set right on such legal points as will arise in their little narratives, and thus avoid that exposure of their own ignorance of the laws, which now, alas! they too often make. The idea is worthy of consideration, and I can only say, that if such an arrangement can be made, and if a counsellor adequately skilful can be found to accept the office, I shall be happy to subscribe my quota; it would be but a modest tribute towards the cost.*

But as the suggestion has not yet been carried out, and as there is at present no learned gentleman whose duty would induce him to set me right, I can only plead for mercy if I be wrong in allotting all Sir Roger's vast possessions in perpetuity to Miss Thorne, alleging also, in excuse, that the course of my narrative absolutely demands that she shall be ultimately recognised as Sir Roger's undoubted heiress.

Such, after a not immoderate delay, was the opinion expressed to Dr Thorne by his law advisers; and such, in fact, turned out to be the case. I will leave the matter so, hoping that my very absence of defence may serve to protect me from severe attack. If under such a will as that described as having been made by Sir Roger, Mary would not have been the heiress, that will must have been described wrongly.

But it was not quite at once that those tidings made themselves absolutely certain to Dr Thorne's mind; nor was he able to express any such opinion when he first met Frank in London. At that time Mary's letter was in Frank's pocket; and Frank, though his real business appertained much more to the fact of Sir Louis's death, and the effect that would immediately have on his father's affairs, was much more full of what so much more nearly concerned himself. 'I will show it Dr Thorne himself,' said he, 'and ask him what he thinks.'

Dr Thorne was stretched fast asleep on the comfortless horse-hair sofa in the dingy sitting-room at the Gray's Inn Coffee-house when Frank found him. The funeral, and his journey to London, and the lawyers had together conquered his energies, and he lay and snored, with nose upright, while heavy London summer flies settled on his head and face, and robbed his slumbers of half their charms.

'I beg your pardon,' said he, jumping up as though he had been detected in some disgraceful act. 'Upon my word, Frank, I beg your pardon; but – well, my dear fellow, all well at Greshamsbury – eh?' and as he shook himself, he made a lunge at one uncommonly disagreeable fly that had been at him for the last ten minutes. It is hardly necessary to say that he missed his enemy.

'I should have been with you before, doctor, but I was down at Malvern.'

'At Malvern, eh? Ah! so Oriel told me. The death of poor Sir Louis was very sudden – was it not?'

'Very.'

'Poor fellow – poor fellow! His fate has for some time been past hope. It is a madness, Frank; the worst of madness. Only think of it – father and son! And such a career as the father had – such a career as the son might have had!'

'It has been very quickly run,' said Frank.

'May it be all forgiven him! I sometimes cannot but believe in a special Providence. That poor fellow was not able, never would have been able, to make proper use of the means which fortune had given him. I hope they may fall into better hands. There is no use in denying it, his death will be an immense relief to me, and a relief also to your father. All this law business will now, of course, be stopped. As for me, I hope I may never be a trustee again.'

Frank had put his hand four or five times into his breast-pocket, and had as often taken out and put back again Mary's letter before he could find himself able to bring Dr Thorne to the subject. At last there was a lull in the purely legal discussion, caused by the doctor intimating that he supposed Frank would now soon return to Greshamsbury.

'Yes; I shall go tomorrow morning.'

'What! so soon as that? I counted on having you one day in London with me.'

'No, I shall go tomorrow. I'm not fit company for any one. Nor am I fit for anything. Read that, doctor. It's no use putting it off any longer. I must get you to talk this over with me. Just read that, and tell me what you think about it. It was written a week ago, when I was there, but somehow I have only got it today.' And putting the letter into the doctor's hands, he turned away to the window, and looked out among the Holborn omnibuses. Dr Thorne took the letter and read it. Mary, after she had written it, had bewailed to herself that the letter was cold; but it had not seemed cold to her lover, nor did it appear so to her uncle. When Frank again turned round from the window, the doctor's handkerchief was up to his eyes; who, in order to hide the tears that were there, was obliged to go through a rather violent process of blowing his nose.

'Well,' he said, as he gave back the letter to Frank.

Well! what did well mean? Was it well? or would it be well, were he, Frank, to comply with the suggestion made to him by Mary?

'It is impossible,' he said, 'that matters should go on like that. Think what her sufferings must have been before she wrote that. I am sure she loves me.'

'I think she does,' said the doctor.

'And it is out of the question that she should be sacrificed; nor will I consent to sacrifice my own happiness. I am quite willing to work for my bread, and I am sure that I am able. I will not submit to – Doctor, what answer do you think I ought to give to that letter? There can be no person so anxious for her happiness as you are – except myself.' And, as he asked the question, he again put into the doctor's hand, almost unconsciously, the letter which he had still been holding in his own.

The doctor turned it over and over, and then opened it again.

'What answer ought I to make to it?' demanded Frank, with energy.

'You see, Frank, I have never interfered in this matter, otherwise than to tell you the whole truth about Mary's birth.'

'Oh, but you must interfere: you should say what you think.'

'Circumstanced as you are now – that is, just at the present moment – you could hardly marry immediately.'

'Why not let me take a farm? My father could, at any rate, manage a couple of thousand pounds or so for me to stock it. That would not be asking much. If he could not give it me, I would not scruple to borrow so much elsewhere.' And Frank bethought him of all Miss Dunstable's offers.

'Oh, yes; that could be managed.'

'Then why not marry immediately; say in six months or so? I am not unreasonable; though, Heaven knows, I have been kept in suspense long enough. As for her, I am sure she must be suffering frightfully. You know her best, and, therefore, I ask you what answer I ought to make: as for myself, I have made up my own mind; I am not a child, nor will I let them treat me as such.'

Frank, as he spoke, was walking rapidly about the room; and he brought out his different propositions, one after the other, with a little pause, while waiting for the doctor's answer. The doctor was sitting, with the letter still in his hands, on the head of the sofa, turning over in his mind the apparent absurdity of Frank's desire to borrow two thousand pounds for a farm, when, in all human probability, he might in a few months be in possession of almost any sum he should choose to name. And yet he would not tell him of Sir Roger's will. 'If it should turn out to be all wrong?' said he to himself.

'Do you wish me to give her up?' said Frank, at last.

'No. How can I wish it? How can I expect a better match for her? Besides, Frank, I love no man in the world so well as I do you.'

'Then you will help me?'

'What, against your father?'

'Against! no, not against anybody. But will you tell Mary that she has your consent?'

'I think she knows that.'

'But you have never said anything to her.'

'Look here, Frank; you ask me for my advice, and I will give it you: go home; though, indeed, I would rather you went anywhere else.'

'No, I must go home; and I must see her.'

'Very well, go home: as for seeing Mary, I think you had better put it off for a fortnight.'

'Quite impossible.'

'Well, that's my advice. But, at any rate, make up your mind to nothing for a fortnight. Wait for one fortnight, and I then will tell you plainly – you and her too – what I think you ought to do. At the end of a fortnight come to me, and tell the squire that I will take it as a great kindness if he will come with you. She has suffered, terribly, terribly; and it is necessary that something should be settled. But a fortnight more can make no great difference.'

'And the letter?'

'Oh! there's the letter.'

'But what shall I say? Of course I shall write tonight.'

'Tell her to wait a fortnight. And, Frank, mind you bring your father with you.'

Frank could draw nothing further from his friend save constant repetitions of this charge to him to wait a fortnight, – just one other fortnight.

'Well, I will come to you at any rate,' said Frank; 'and, if possible, I will bring my father. But I shall write to Mary tonight.'

On the Saturday morning, Mary, who was then nearly broken-hearted at her lover's silence, received this short note:–

'My own Mary,

'I shall be home tomorrow. I will by no means release you from your promise. Of course you will perceive that I only got your letter today.

'Your own dearest,
'Frank.

'PS. – You will have to call me so hundreds and hundreds of times yet.'

Short as it was, this sufficed to Mary. It is one thing for a young lady to make prudent, heart-breaking suggestions, but quite another to have them accepted. She did call him dearest Frank, even on that one day, almost as often as he had desired her.

CHAPTER XLVI

Our Pet Fox Finds a Tail*

Frank returned home, and his immediate business was of course with his father, and with Mr Gazebee, who was still at Greshamsbury.

'But who is the heir?' asked Mr Gazebee, when Frank had explained that the death of Sir Louis rendered unnecessary any immediate legal steps.

'Upon my word I don't know,' said Frank.

'You saw Dr Thorne,' said the squire. 'He must have known.'

'I never thought of asking him,' said Frank, naïvely.

Mr Gazebee looked rather solemn. 'I wonder at that,' said he; 'for everything now depends on the hands the property will go into. Let me see; I think Sir Roger had a married sister. Was not that so, Mr Gresham?' And then it occurred for the first time, both to the squire and to his son, that Mary Thorne was the eldest child of this sister. But it never occurred to either of them that Mary could be the baronet's heir.

Dr Thorne came down for a couple of days before the fortnight was over to see his patients, and then returned again to London. But during this short visit he was utterly dumb on the subject of the heir. He called at Greshamsbury to see Lady Arabella, and was even questioned by the squire on the subject. But he obstinately refused to say more than that nothing certain could be known for yet a few days.

Immediately after his return, Frank saw Mary, and told her all that happened. 'I cannot understand my uncle,' said she, almost trembling as she stood close to him in her own drawing-room. 'He usually hates mysteries, and yet now he is so mysterious. He told me, Frank – that was after I had written that unfortunate letter – '

'Unfortunate, indeed! I wonder what you really thought of me when you were writing it?'

'If you had heard what your mother said, you would not be surprised. But, after that, uncle said – '

'Said what?'

'He seemed to think – I don't remember what it was he said.

But he said, he hoped that things might yet turn out well; and then I was almost sorry that I had written the letter.'

'Of course you were sorry, and so you ought to have been. To say that you would never call me Frank again!'

'I didn't exactly say that.'

'I have told him I will wait a fortnight, and so I will. After that, I shall take the matter into my own hands.'

It may be well supposed that Lady Arabella was not well pleased to learn that Frank and Mary had been again together; and, in the agony of her spirit, she did say some ill-natured things before Augusta, who had now returned from Courcy Castle, as to the gross impropriety of Mary's conduct. But to Frank she said nothing.

Nor was there much said between Frank and Beatrice. If everything could really be settled at the end of that fortnight which was to witness the disclosure of the doctor's mystery, there would still be time to arrange that Mary should be at the wedding. 'It shall be settled then,' said he to himself; 'and if it be settled, my mother will hardly venture to exclude my affianced bride from the house.' It was now the beginning of August, and it wanted yet a month to the Oriel wedding.

But though he said nothing to his mother or to Beatrice, he did say much to his father. In the first place, he showed him Mary's letter. 'If your heart be not made of stone it will be softened by that,' he said. Mr Gresham's heart was not of stone, and he did acknowledge that the letter was a very sweet letter. But we know how the drop of water hollows the stone. It was not by the violence of his appeal that Frank succeeded in obtaining from his father a sort of half-consent that he would no longer oppose the match; but by the assiduity with which the appeal was repeated. Frank, as we have said, had more stubbornness of will than his father; and so, before the fortnight was over, the squire had been talked over, and had promised to attend at the doctor's bidding.

'I suppose you had better take the Hazlehurst farm,' said he to his son, with a sigh. 'It joins the park and the homefields, and I will give you up them also. God knows, I don't care about farming any more – or about anything else either.'

'Don't say that, father.'

'Well, well! But, Frank, where will you live? The old house is big enough for us all. But how would Mary get on with your mother?'

At the end of this fortnight, true to his time, the doctor returned to the village. He was a bad correspondent; and though he had written some short notes to Mary, he had said no word to her about his business. It was late in the evening when he got home, and it was understood by Frank and the squire that they were to be with him on the following morning. Not a word had been said to Lady Arabella on the subject.

It was late in the evening when he got home, and Mary waited for him with a heart almost sick with expectation. As soon as the fly had stopped at the little gate she heard his voice, and heard at once that it was quick, joyful, and telling much of inward satisfaction. He had a good-natured word for Janet, and called Thomas an old blunderhead in a manner that made Bridget laugh outright.

'He'll have his nose put out of joint some day; won't he?' said the doctor. Bridget blushed and laughed again, and made a sign to Thomas that he had better look to his face.

Mary was in his arms before he was yet within the door. 'My darling,' said he, tenderly kissing her. 'You are my own darling yet awhile.'

'Of course I am. Am I not always to be so?'

'Well, well; let me have some tea, at any rate, for I'm in a fever of thirst. They may call that tea at the Junction if they will; but if China were sunk under the sea it would make no difference to them.'

Dr Thorne always was in a fever of thirst when he got home from the railway, and always made complaint as to the tea at the Junction. Mary went about her usual work with almost more than her usual alacrity, and so they were soon seated in the drawing-room together.

She soon found that his manner was more than ordinarily kind to her; and there was moreover something about him which seemed to make him sparkle with contentment, but he said no word about Frank, nor did he make any allusion to the business which had taken him up to town.

'Have you gone through all your work?' she said to him once.

'Yes, yes; I think all.'

'And thoroughly?'

'Yes; thoroughly, I think. But I am very tired, and so are you too, darling, with waiting for me.'

'Oh, no, I am not,' said she, as she went on continually filling his cup; 'but I am so happy to have you home again. You have been away so much lately.'

'Ah, yes; well, I suppose I shall not go away any more now. It will be somebody else's turn now.'

'Uncle, I think you're going to take to writing mysterious romances, like Mrs Radcliffe's.'*

'Yes; and I'll begin tomorrow, certainly, with – But, Mary, I will not say another word tonight. Give me a kiss, dearest, and I'll go.'

Mary did kiss him, and he did go. But as she was still lingering in the room, now putting away a book, or a reel of thread, and then sitting down to think what the morrow would bring forth, the doctor again came into the room in his dressing-gown, and with his slippers on.

'What, not gone yet?' said he.

'No, not yet; I'm going now.'

'You and I, Mary, have always affected a good deal of indifference as to money, and all that sort of thing.'

'I won't acknowledge that it has been affectation at all,' she answered.

'Perhaps not; but we have often expressed it, have we not?'

'I suppose, uncle, you think that we are like the fox that lost its tail, or rather some unfortunate fox that might be born without one.'

'I wonder how we should either of us bear it if we found ourselves suddenly rich. It would be a great temptation – a sore temptation. I fear, Mary, that when poor people talk disdainfully of money, they often are like your fox, born without a tail. If nature suddenly should give that beast a tail, would he not be prouder of it than all the other foxes in the wood?'

'Well, I suppose he would. That's the very meaning of the story. But how moral you've become all of a sudden at twelve o'clock at night! Instead of being Mrs Radcliffe, I shall think you're Mr Æsop.'

He took up the article which he had come to seek, and kissing her again on the forehead, went away to his bedroom without further speech. 'What can he mean by all this about money?' said Mary to herself. 'It cannot be that by Sir Louis's death he will get any of all this property;' and then she began to bethink herself whether, after all, she would wish him to be a rich man. 'If he were very rich, he might do something to assist Frank; and then – '

There never was a fox yet without a tail who would not be delighted to find himself suddenly possessed of that appendage. Never; let the untailed fox have been ever so sincere in his advice to his friends! We are all of us, the good and the bad, looking for tails – for one tail, or for more than one; we do so too often by ways that are mean enough: but perhaps there is no tail-seeker more mean, more sneakingly mean, than he who looks out to adorn his bare back with a tail by marriage.

The doctor was up very early the next morning, long before Mary was ready with her teacups. He was up, and in his own study behind the shop, arranging dingy papers, pulling about tin boxes which he had brought down with him from London, and piling on his writing-table one set of documents in one place, and one in another. 'I think I understand it all,' said he; 'but yet I know I shall be bothered. Well, I never will be anybody's trustee again. Let me see!' and then he sat down, and with bewildered look recapitulated to himself sundry heavy items. 'What those shares are really worth I cannot understand, and nobody seems able to tell one. They must make it out among them as best they can. Let me see; that's Boxall Hill, and this is Greshamsbury. I'll put a newspaper over Greshamsbury, or the squire will know it!' and then, having made his arrangements, he went to his breakfast.

I know I am wrong, my much and truly honoured critic, about these title-deeds and documents. But when we've got that barrister in hand, then if I go wrong after that, let the blame be on my own shoulders – or on his.

The doctor ate his breakfast quickly, and did not talk much to his niece. But what he did say was of a nature to make her feel strangely happy. She could not analyse her own feelings, or give a reason for her own confidence; but she certainly did feel, and even trust, that something was going to happen after breakfast which would make her more happy than she had been for many months.

'Janet,' said he, looking at his watch, 'if Mr Gresham and Mr Frank call, show them into my study. What are you going to do with yourself, my dear?'

'I don't know, uncle; you are so mysterious, and I am in such a twitter, that I don't know what to do. Why is Mr Gresham coming here – that is, the squire?'

'Because I have business with him about the Scatcherd property. You know that he owed Sir Louis money. But don't go out, Mary. I want you to be in the way if I should have to call for you. You can stay in the drawing-room, can't you?'

'Oh, yes, uncle; or here.'

'No, dearest; go into the drawing-room.' Mary obediently did as she was bid; and there she sat, for the next three hours, wondering, wondering, wondering. During the greater part of that time, however, she well knew that Mr Gresham, senior, and Mr Gresham, junior, were both with her uncle, below.

At eleven o'clock the doctor's visitors came. He had expected them somewhat earlier, and was beginning to become fidgety. He had so much on his hands that he could not sit still for a moment till he had, at any rate, commenced it. The expected footsteps were at last heard on the gravel-path, and a moment or two afterwards Janet ushered the father and son into the room.

The squire did not look very well. He was worn and sorrowful, and rather pale. The death of his young creditor might be supposed to have given him some relief from his more pressing cares, but the necessity of yielding to Frank's wishes had almost more than balanced this. When a man has daily to reflect that he is poorer than he was the day before, he soon becomes worn and sorrowful.

But Frank was well; both in health and spirits. He also felt as Mary did, that the day was to bring forth something which should end his present troubles; and he could not but be happy to think that he could now tell Dr Thorne that his father's consent to his marriage had been given.

The doctor shook hands with them both, and then they sat down. They were all rather constrained in their manner; and at first it seemed that nothing but little speeches of compliment were to be made. At last, the squire remarked that Frank had been talking to him about Miss Thorne.

'About Mary?' said the doctor.

'Yes; about Mary,' said the squire, correcting himself. It was quite unnecessary that he should use so cold a name as the other, now that he had agreed to the match.

'Well!' said Dr Thorne.

'I suppose it must be so, doctor. He has set his heart upon it, and, God knows, I have nothing to say against her – against her personally. No one could say a word against her. She is a sweet, good girl, excellently brought up; and, as for myself, I have always loved her.' Frank drew near to his father, and pressed his hand against the squire's arm, by way of giving him, in some sort, a filial embrace for his kindness.

'Thank you, squire, thank you,' said the doctor. 'It is very good of you to say that. She is a good girl, and if Frank chooses to take her, he will, in my estimation, have made a good choice.'

'Chooses!' said Frank, with all the enthusiasm of a lover.

The squire felt himself perhaps a little ruffled at the way in which the doctor received his gracious intimation; but he did not show it as he went on. 'They cannot, you know, doctor, look to be rich people – '

'Ah! well, well,' interrupted the doctor.

'I have told Frank so, and I think that you should tell Mary. Frank means to take some land into his hand, and he must farm it as a farmer. I will endeavour to give him three, or perhaps four hundred a year. But you know better – '

'Stop, squire; stop a minute. We will talk about that presently. This death of poor Sir Louis will make a difference.'

'Not permanently,' said the squire, mournfully.

'And now, Frank,' said the doctor, not attending to the squire's last words, 'what do you say?'

'What do I say? I say what I said to you in London the other day. I believe Mary loves me; indeed, I won't be affected – I know she does. I have loved her – I was going to say always; and, indeed, I almost might say so. My father knows that this is no light fancy of mine. As to what he says about our being poor, why – '

The doctor was very arbitrary, and would hear neither of them on this subject.

'Mr Gresham,' said he, interrupting Frank, 'of course I am well aware how very little suited Mary is by birth to marry your only son.'

'It is too late to think about it now,' said the squire.

'It is not too late for me to justify myself,' replied the doctor. 'We have long known each other, Mr Gresham, and you said here the other day, that this is a subject as to which we have been both of one mind. Birth and blood are very valuable gifts.'

'I certainly think so,' said the squire; 'but one can't have everything.'

'No; one can't have everything.'

'If I am satisfied in that matter – ' began Frank.

'Stop a moment, my dear boy,' said the doctor. 'As your father says, one can't have everything. My dear friend – 'and he gave his hand to the squire – 'do not be angry if I allude for a moment to the estate. It has grieved me to see it melting away – the old family acres that have so long been the heritage of the Greshams.'

'We need not talk about that now, Dr Thorne,' said Frank, in an almost angry tone.

'But I must, Frank, for one moment, to justify myself. I could not have excused myself in letting Mary think that she could become your wife if I had not hoped that good might come of it.'

'Well; good will come of it,' said Frank, who did not quite understand at what the doctor was driving.

'I hope so. I have had much doubt about this, and have been sorely perplexed; but now I do hope so. Frank – Mr Gresham – ' and then Dr Thorne rose from his chair; but was, for a moment, unable to go on with his tale.

'We will hope that it is all for the best,' said the squire.

'I am sure it is,' said Frank.

'Yes; I hope it is. I do think it is; I am sure it is, Frank. Mary will not come to you empty-handed. I wish for your sake – yes, and for hers too – that her birth were equal to her fortune, as her worth is superior to both. Mr Gresham, this marriage will, at any rate, put an end to your pecuniary embarrassments – unless, indeed, Frank should prove a hard creditor. My niece is Sir Roger Scatcherd's heir.'

The doctor, as soon as he made the announcement, began to employ himself sedulously about the papers on the table; which, in the confusion caused by his own emotion, he transferred hither and thither in such a manner as to upset all his previous arrangements. 'And now,' he said, 'I might as well explain, as well as I can, of what that fortune consists. Here, this is – no – '

'But, Dr Thorne,' said the squire, now perfectly pale, and almost gasping for breath, 'what is it you mean?'

'There's not a shadow of doubt,' said the doctor. 'I've had Sir Abraham Haphazard, and Sir Rickety Giggs, and old Neversaye Die, and Mr Snilam; and they are all of the same opinion. There is not the smallest doubt about it. Of course, she must administer, and all that; and I'm afraid there'll be a very heavy sum to pay for the tax; for she cannot inherit as a niece, you know. Mr Snilam pointed that out particularly. But, after all that, there'll be – I've got it down on a piece of paper, somewhere – three grains of blue pill. I'm really so bothered, squire, with all these papers, and all those lawyers, that I don't know whether I'm sitting or standing. There's ready money enough to pay all the tax and all the debts. I know that, at any rate.'

'You don't mean to say that Mary Thorne is now possessed of all Sir Roger Scatcherd's wealth?' at last ejaculated the squire.

'But that's exactly what I do mean to say,' said the doctor, looking up from his papers with a tear in his eye, and a smile on his mouth; 'and what is more, squire, you owe her at the present moment exactly – I've got that down too, somewhere, only I'm so bothered with these papers. Come, squire, when do you mean to pay her? She's in a great hurry, as young ladies are when they want to get married.'

The doctor was inclined to joke if possible, so as to carry off, as it were, some of the great weight of obligation which it might seem that he was throwing on the father and son; but the squire was by no means in a state to understand a joke: hardly as yet in a state to comprehend what was so very serious in this matter.

'Do you mean that Mary is the owner of Boxall Hill?' said he.

'Indeed, I do,' said the doctor; and he was just going to add, 'and of Greshamsbury also,' but he stopped himself.

'What, the whole property there?'

'That's only a small portion,' said the doctor. 'I almost wish it were all, for then I should not be so bothered. Look here; these are the Boxall Hill title-deeds; that's the simplest part of the whole affair; and Frank may go and settle himself there tomorrow if he pleases.'

'Stop a moment, Dr Thorne,' said Frank. These were the only words which he had yet uttered since the tidings had been conveyed to him.

'And these, squire, are the Greshamsbury papers:' and the doctor, with considerable ceremony, withdrew the covering

newspapers. 'Look at them; there they all are once again. When
I suggested to Mr Snilam that I supposed they might now all go
back to the Greshamsbury muniment room, I thought he would
have fainted. As I cannot return them to you, you will have to
wait till Frank shall give them up.'

'But, Dr Thorne,' said Frank.

'Well, my boy.'

'Does Mary know all about this?'

'Not a word of it. I mean that you shall tell her.'

'Perhaps, under such very altered circumstances – '

'Eh?'

'The change is so great and so sudden, so immense in its
effects, that Mary may perhaps wish – '

'Wish! wish what? Wish not to be told of it at all?'

'I shall not think of holding her to her engagement – that is, if
– I mean to say, she should have time at any rate for
consideration.'

'Oh, I understand,' said the doctor. 'She shall have time for
consideration. How much shall we give her, squire? three
minutes? Go up to her, Frank: she is in the drawing-room.'

Frank went to the door, and then hesitated, and returned. 'I
could not do it,' said he. 'I don't think that I understand it all
yet. I am so bewildered that I could not tell her;' and he sat
down at the table, and began to sob with emotion.

'And she knows nothing of it?' asked the squire.

'Not a word. I thought that I would keep the pleasure of
telling her for Frank.'

'She should not be left in suspense,' said the squire.

'Come, Frank, go up to her,' again urged the doctor. 'You've
been ready enough with your visits when you knew that you
ought to stay away.'

'I cannot do it,' said Frank, after a pause of some moments;
'nor is it right that I should. It would be taking advantage of
her.'

'Go to her yourself, doctor; it is you that should do it,' said
the squire.

After some further slight delay, the doctor got up, and did go
upstairs. He, even, was half afraid of the task. 'It must be done,'
he said to himself, as his heavy steps mounted the stairs. 'But
how to tell it!'

When he entered, Mary was standing half-way up the room,

as though she had risen to meet him. Her face was troubled, and her eyes were almost wild. The emotion, the hopes, the fears of the morning had almost been too much for her. She had heard the murmuring of voices in the room below, and had known that one was that of her lover. Whether that discussion was to be for her good or ill she did not know; but she felt that further suspense would almost kill her. 'I could wait for years,' she thought to herself, 'if I did but know. If I lost him, I suppose I should bear it, if I did but know.' – Well; she was going to know.

Her uncle met her in the middle of the room. His face was serious, though not sad; too serious to confirm her hopes at that moment of doubt. 'What is it, uncle?' she said, taking one of his hands between both of her own. 'What is it? Tell me.' And as she looked up into his face with her wild eyes, she almost frightened him.

'Mary,' he said, gravely, 'you have heard much, I know, of Sir Roger Scatcherd's great fortune.'

'Yes, yes, yes!'

'Now that poor Sir Louis is dead – '

'Well, uncle, well?'

'It has been left – '

'To Frank! to Mr Gresham! to the squire!' exclaimed Mary, who felt, with an agony of doubt, that this sudden accession of immense wealth might separate her still further from her lover.

'No, Mary, not to the Greshams; but to yourself.'

'To me!' she cried, and putting both her hands to her forehead, she seemed to be holding her temples together. 'To me!'

'Yes, Mary; it is all your own now. To do as you like best with it all – all. May God, in His mercy, enable you to bear the burden, and lighten for you the temptation!'

She had so far moved as to find the nearest chair, and there she was now seated, staring at her uncle with fixed eyes. 'Uncle,' she said, 'what does it mean?' Then he came, and sitting beside her, explained, as best he could, the story of her birth, and her kinship with the Scatcherds. 'And where is he, uncle?' she said. 'Why does he not come to me?'

'I wanted him to come, but he refused. They are both there now, the father and son; shall I fetch them?'

'Fetch them! whom? The squire? No, uncle; but may we go to them?'

'Surely, Mary.'

'But, uncle – '

'Yes, dearest.'

'Is it true? are you sure? For his sake, you know; not for my own. The squire, you know – Oh, uncle! I cannot go.'

'They shall come to you.'

'No – no. I have gone to him such hundreds of times; I will never allow that he shall be sent to me. But, uncle, is it true?'

The doctor, as he went downstairs, muttered something about Sir Abraham Haphazard, and Sir Rickety Giggs; but these great names were much thrown away upon poor Mary. The doctor entered the room first, and the heiress followed him with downcast eyes and timid steps. She was at first afraid to advance, but when she did look up, and saw Frank standing alone by the window, her lover restored her courage, and rushing up to him, she threw herself into his arms. 'Oh Frank; my own Frank! my own Frank! we shall never be separated now.'

CHAPTER XLVII

How the Bride Was Received, and Who Were Asked to the Wedding

And thus after all did Frank perform his great duty; he did marry money; or rather, as the wedding has not yet taken place, and is, indeed, as yet hardly talked of, we should more properly say that he had engaged himself to marry money. And then, such a quantity of money! The Scatcherd wealth greatly exceeded the Dunstable wealth; so that our hero may be looked on as having performed his duties in a manner deserving the very highest commendation from all classes of the De Courcy connexion.

And he received it. But that was nothing. That *he* should be fêted by the De Courcys and Greshams, now that he was about to do his duty by his family in so exemplary a manner: that he should be patted on the back, now that he no longer meditated that vile crime which had been so abhorrent to his mother's soul; this was only natural; this is hardly worthy of remark. But there was another to be fêted, another person to be made a personage, another blessed human mortal about to do her duty by the family of Gresham in a manner that deserved, and should receive, Lady Arabella's warmest caresses.

Dear Mary! it was, indeed, not singular that she should be prepared to act so well, seeing that in early youth she had had the advantage of an education in the Greshamsbury nursery; but not on that account was it the less fitting that her virtue should be acknowledged, eulogised, nay, all but worshipped.

How the party at the doctor's got itself broken up, I am not prepared to say. Frank, I know, stayed and dined there, and his poor mother, who would not retire to rest till she had kissed him, and blessed him, and thanked him for all that he was doing for the family, was kept waiting in her dressing-room till a very unreasonable hour of the night.

It was the squire who brought the news up to the house. 'Arabella,' he said, in a low, but somewhat solemn voice, 'you will be surprised at the news I bring you. Mary Thorne is the heiress to all the Scatcherd property!'

'Oh, heavens! Mr Gresham.'

'Yes, indeed,' continued the squire. 'So it is; it is very, very – ' But Lady Arabella had fainted. She was a woman who generally had her feelings and her emotions much under her own control; but what she now heard was too much for her. When she came to her senses, the first words that escaped her lips were, 'Dear Mary!'

But the household had to sleep on the news before it could be fully realised. The squire was not by nature a mercenary man. If I have at all succeeded in putting his character before the reader, he will be recognised as one not over attached to money for money's sake. But things had gone so hard with him, the world had become so rough, so ungracious, so full of thorns, the want of means had become an evil so keenly felt in every hour, that it cannot be wondered at that his dreams that night should be of a golden elysium. The wealth was not coming to him. True. But his chief sorrow had been for his son. Now that son would be his only creditor. It was as though mountains of marble had been taken from off his bosom.

But Lady Arabella's dreams flew away at once into the seventh heaven. Sordid as they certainly were, they were not absolutely selfish. Frank would now certainly be the first commoner in Barsetshire; of course he would represent the county; of course there would be the house in town; it wouldn't be her house, but she was contented that the grandeur should be that of her child. He would have heaven knows what to spend per annum. And that it should come through Mary Thorne! What a blessing that she had allowed Mary to be brought into the Greshamsbury nursery! Dear Mary!

'She will of course be one now,' said Beatrice to her sister. With her, at the present moment, 'one' of course meant one of the bevy that was to attend her at the altar. 'Oh, dear! how nice! I shan't know what to say to her tomorrow. But I know one thing.'

'What is that?' asked Augusta.

'She will be as mild and as meek as a little dove. If she and the doctor had lost every shilling in the world, she would have been as proud as an eagle.' It must be acknowledged that Beatrice had the wit to read Mary's character aright.

But Augusta was not quite pleased with the whole affair. Not that she begrudged her brother his luck, or Mary her happiness. But her ideas of right and wrong – perhaps we should rather say Lady Amelia's ideas – would not be fairly carried out.

'After all, Beatrice, this does not alter her birth. I know it is useless saying anything to Frank.'

'Why, you wouldn't break both their hearts now?'

'I don't want to break their hearts, certainly. But there are those who put their dearest and warmest feelings under restraint rather than deviate from what they know to be proper.' Poor Augusta! she was the stern professor of the order of this philosophy; the last in the family who practised with unflinching courage its cruel behests; the last, always excepting the Lady Amelia.

And how slept Frank that night? With him, at least, let us hope, nay, let us say boldly, that his happiest thoughts were not of the wealth which he was to acquire. But yet it would be something to restore Boxall Hill to Greshamsbury; something to give back to his father those rumpled vellum documents, since the departure of which the squire had never had a happy day; nay, something to come forth again to his friends as a gay, young country squire, instead of as a farmer, clod-compelling for his bread. We would not have him thought to be better than he was, nor would we wish to make him of other stuff than nature generally uses. His heart did exult at Mary's wealth; but it leaped higher still when he thought of purer joys.

And what shall we say of Mary's dreams? With her, it was altogether what she should give, not at all what she should get. Frank had loved her so truly when she was so poor, such an utter castaway; Frank, who had ever been the heir of Greshamsbury! Frank, who with his beauty, and spirit, and his talents might have won the smiles of the richest, the grandest, the noblest! What lady's heart would not have rejoiced to be allowed to love her Frank? But he had been true to her through everything. Ah, how often she had thought of that hour, when suddenly appearing before her, he had strained her to his breast, just as she had resolved how best to bear the death-like chill of his supposed estrangements! She was always thinking of that time. She fed her love by recurring over and over to the altered feeling of that moment. And now she could pay him for his goodness. Pay him! No, that would be a base word, a base thought. Her payment must be made, if God would so grant it, in many, many years to come. But her store, such as it was, should be emptied into his lap. It was soothing to her pride that she would not hurt him by her love, that she would bring no injury to the old house. 'Dear, dear Frank,' she murmured, as her waking dreams, conquered at last by sleep, gave way to those of the fairy world.

But she thought not only of Frank; dreamed not only of him. What had he not done for her, that uncle of hers, who had been more loving to her than any father! How was he, too, to be paid? Paid, indeed! Love can only be paid in its own coin: it knows of no other legal tender. Well, if her home was to be Greshamsbury, at any rate she would not be separated from him.

What the doctor dreamed of that night, neither he nor any one ever knew. 'Why, uncle, I think you've been asleep,' said Mary to him that evening, as he moved for a moment uneasily on the sofa. He had been asleep for the last three-quarters of an hour; – but Frank, his guest, had felt no offence. 'No, I've not been exactly asleep,' said he; 'but I'm very tired. I wouldn't do it all again, Frank, to double the money. You haven't got any more tea, have you, Mary?'

On the following morning, Beatrice was of course with her friend. There was no awkwardness between them in meeting. Beatrice had loved her when she was poor, and though they had not lately thought alike on one very important subject, Mary was too gracious to impute that to Beatrice as a crime.

'You will be one now, Mary; of course you will.'

'If Lady Arabella will let me come.'

'Oh, Mary; let you! Do you remember what you once said about coming, and being near me? I have so often thought of it. And now, Mary, I must tell you about Caleb;' and the young lady settled herself on the sofa, so as to have a comfortable, long talk. Beatrice had been quite right. Mary was as meek with her, and as mild as a dove.

And then Patience Oriel came. 'My fine, young, darling, magnificent, overgrown heiress,' said Patience, embracing her. 'My breath deserted me, and I was nearly stunned when I heard of it. How small we shall all be, my dear! I am quite prepared to toady you immensely; but pray be a little gracious to me, for the sake of auld lang syne.'

Mary gave her a long, long kiss. 'Yes, for auld lang syne, Patience; when you took me away under your wing to Richmond.' Patience also had loved her when she was in her trouble, and that love, too, should never be forgotten.

But the great difficulty was Lady Arabella's first meeting with her. 'I think I'll go down to her after breakfast,' said her ladyship to Beatrice, as the two were talking over the matter while the mother was finishing her toilet.

'I am sure she will come up if you like it, mamma.'

'She is entitled to every courtesy – as Frank's accepted bride, you know,' said Lady Arabella. 'I would not for worlds fail in any respect to her for his sake.'

'He will be glad enough for her to come, I am sure,' said Beatrice. 'I was walking with Caleb this morning, and he says – '

The matter was of importance, and Lady Arabella gave it her most mature consideration. The manner of receiving into one's family an heiress whose wealth is to cure all one's difficulties, disperse all one's troubles, give a balm to all the wounds of misfortune, must, under any circumstances, be worthy of much care. But when that heiress has been already treated as Mary had been treated!

'I must see her, at any rate, before I go to Courcy,' said Lady Arabella.

'Are you going to Courcy, mamma?'

'Oh, certainly; yes, I must see my sister-in-law now. You don't seem to realise the importance, my dear, of Frank's marriage. He will be in a great hurry about it, and, indeed, I cannot blame him. I expect that they will all come here.'

'Who, mamma? the De Courcys?'

'Yes, of course. I shall be very much surprised if the earl does not come now. And I must consult my sister as to asking the Duke of Omnium.'

Poor Mary!

'And I think it will perhaps be better,' continued Lady Arabella, 'that we should have a larger party than we intended at your affair. The countess, I'm sure, would come now. We couldn't put it off for ten days; could we, dear?'

'Put it off for ten days!'

'Yes; it would be convenient.'

'I don't think Mr Oriel would like that at all, mamma. You know he has made all his arrangements for his Sundays –'

Pshaw! The idea of the parson's Sundays being allowed to have any bearing on such matter as Frank's wedding would now become! Why, they would have – how much? Between twelve and fourteen thousand a year! Lady Arabella, who had made her calculations a dozen times during the night, had never found it to be much less than the larger sum. Mr Oriel's Sundays, indeed!

After much doubt, Lady Arabella acceded to her daughter's suggestion, that Mary should be received at Greshamsbury instead of being called on at the doctor's house. 'If you think she won't mind the coming up first,' said her ladyship, 'I certainly could receive her better here. I should be more – more – more able, you know, to express what I feel. We had better go into the big drawing-room today, Beatrice. Will you remember to tell Mrs Richards?'

'Oh, certainly,' was Mary's answer, when Beatrice, with a voice a little trembling, proposed to her to walk up to the house. 'Certainly, I will, if Lady Arabella will receive me; – only one thing, Trichy.'

'What's that, dearest?'

'Frank will think that I come after him.'

'Never mind what he thinks. To tell you the truth, Mary, I often call upon Patience for the sake of finding Caleb. That's all fair now, you know.'

Mary very quietly put on her straw bonnet, and said she was ready to go up to the house. Beatrice was a little fluttered, and showed it. Mary was, perhaps, a good deal fluttered, but she did not show it. She had thought a good deal of her first interview with Lady Arabella, of her first return to the house; but she had resolved to carry herself as though the matter were easy to her. She would not allow it to be seen that she felt that she brought with her to Greshamsbury, comfort, ease, and renewed opulence.

So she put on her straw bonnet and walked up with Beatrice. Everybody about the place had already heard the news. The old woman at the lodge curtsied low to her; the gardener, who was mowing the lawn. The butler, who opened the front door – he must have been watching Mary's approach – had manifestly put on a clean white neckcloth for the occasion.

'God bless you once more, Miss Thorne!' said the old man, in a half-whisper. Mary was somewhat troubled, for everything seemed, in a manner, to bow down before her. And why should not everything bow down before her, seeing that she was in very truth the owner of Greshamsbury?

And then a servant in livery would open the big drawing-room door. This rather upset both Mary and Beatrice. It became almost impossible for Mary to enter the room just as she would have done two years ago; but she got through the difficulty with much self-control.

'Mamma, here's Mary,' said Beatrice.

Nor was Lady Arabella quite mistress of herself, although she had studied minutely how to bear herself.

'Oh Mary, my dear Mary; what can I say to you?' and then, with a handkerchief to her eyes, she ran forward and hid her face on Miss Thorne's shoulders. 'What can I say – can you forgive me my anxiety for my son?'

'How do you do, Lady Arabella?' said Mary.

'My daughter! my child! my Frank's own bride! Oh, Mary! oh, my child! If I have seemed unkind to you, it has been through love to him.'

'All these things are over now,' said Mary. 'Mr Gresham told me yesterday that I should be received as Frank's future wife;

and so, you see, I have come.' And then she slipped through Lady Arabella's arms and sat down, meekly down on a chair. In five minutes she had escaped with Beatrice into the school-room, and was kissing the children, and turning over the new trousseau. They were, however, soon interrupted, and there was, perhaps, some other kissing besides that of the children.

'You have no business in here at all, Frank,' said Beatrice. 'Has he, Mary?'

'None in the world, I should think.'

'See what he has done to my poplin; I hope you won't have your things treated so cruelly. He'll be careful enough about them.'

'Is Oriel a good hand at packing up finery – eh, Beatrice?' asked Frank.

'He is, at any rate, too well behaved to spoil it.' Thus Mary was again made at home in the household of Greshamsbury.

Lady Arabella did not carry out her little plan of delaying the Oriel wedding. Her idea had been to add some grandeur to it, in order to make it a more fitting precursor of that other greater wedding which was to follow so soon in its wake. But this, with the assistance of the countess, she found herself able to do without interfering with poor Mr Oriel's Sunday arrangements. The countess herself, with the Ladies Alexandrina and Margaretta, now promised to come, even to this first affair; and for the other, the whole De Courcy family would turn out, count and countess, lords and ladies, Honourable Georges and Honourable Johns. What honour, indeed, could be too great to show to a bride who had fourteen thousand a year in her own right, or to a cousin who had done his duty by securing such a bride to himself!

'If the duke be in the country, I am sure he will be happy to come,' said the countess. 'Of course, he will be talking to Frank about politics. I suppose the squire won't expect Frank to belong to the old school now.'

'Frank, of course, will judge for himself, Rosina; – with his position, you know!' And so things were settled at Courcy Castle.

And then Beatrice was wedded and carried off to the Lakes. Mary, as she had promised, did stand near her; but not exactly in the gingham frock of which she had once spoken. She wore on that occasion – But it will be too much, perhaps, to tell the reader what she wore as Beatrice's bridesmaid, seeing that a couple of pages, at least, must be devoted to her own marriage-dress, and seeing, also, that we have only a few pages to finish everything; the list of visitors, the marriage settlements, the dress, and all included.

It was in vain that Mary endeavoured to repress Lady Arabella's ardour for grand doings. After all, she was to be married from the doctor's house, and not from Greshamsbury, and it was the doctor who should have invited the guests; but, in this matter, he did not choose to oppose her ladyship's spirit, and she had it all her own way.

'What can I do?' said he to Mary. 'I have been contradicting her in everything for the last two years. The least we can do is to let her have her own way now in a trifle like this.'

But there was one point on which Mary would let nobody have his or her own way; on which the way to be taken was very manifestly to be her own. This was touching the marriage settlements. It must not be supposed, that if Beatrice were married on a Tuesday, Mary could be married on the Tuesday week following. Ladies with twelve thousand a year cannot be disposed of in that way: and bridegrooms who do their duty by marrying money often have to be kept waiting. It was spring, the early spring, before Frank was made altogether a happy man.

But a word about the settlements. On this subject the doctor thought he would have been driven mad. Messrs Slow & Bideawhile, as the lawyers of the Greshamsbury family – it will be understood that Mr Gazebee's law business was of quite a different nature, and his work, as regarded Greshamsbury, was now nearly over – Messrs Slow & Bideawhile declared that it would never do for them to undertake alone to draw out the settlements. An heiress, such as Mary, must have lawyers of her own; half a dozen at least, according to the apparent opinion of Messrs Slow & Bideawhile. And so the doctor had to go to other lawyers, and they had again to consult Sir Abraham, and Mr Snilam on a dozen different heads.

If Frank became tenant in tail,* in right of his wife, but under his father, would he be able to grant leases for more than twenty-one years? and, if so, to whom would the right of trover belong? As to flotsam and jetsam'* there was a little property, Mr Critic, on the seashore – that was a matter that had to be left unsettled at the last. Such points as these do take a long time to consider. All this bewildered the doctor sadly, and Frank himself began to make accusations that he was to be done out of his wife altogether.

But, as we have said, there was one point on which Mary would have her own way. The lawyers might tie up as they would on her behalf all the money, and shares, and mortgages which had belonged to the late Sir Roger, with this exception, all that had ever appertained to Greshamsbury should belong to Greshamsbury again; not in perspective, not to her children, or to her children's children, but at once. Frank should be lord of Boxall Hill in his own right; and as to those other *liens* on Greshamsbury, let Frank manage that with his father as he might think fit. She would only trouble herself to see that he was empowered to do as he did think fit.

'But,' argued the ancient, respectable family attorney to the doctor, 'that amounts to two-thirds of the whole estate. Two-thirds, Dr Thorne! It is preposterous; I should almost say impossible.' And the scanty hairs on the poor man's head almost stood on end as he thought of the outrageous manner in which the heiress prepared to sacrifice herself.

'It will all be the same in the end,' said the doctor, trying to make things smooth. 'Of course, their joint object will be to put the Greshamsbury property together again.'

'But, my dear sir,' – and then, for twenty minutes, the lawyer went on proving that it would by no means be the same thing; but, nevertheless, Mary Thorne did have her own way.

In the course of the winter, Lady de Courcy tried very hard to induce the heiress to visit Courcy Casde, and this request was so backed by Lady Arabella, that the doctor said he thought she might as well go there for three or four days. But here, again, Mary was obstinate.

'I don't see it at all,' she said. 'If you make a point of it, or Frank, or Mr Gresham, I will go; but I can't see any possible reason.' The doctor, when so appealed to, would not absolutely say that he made a point of it, and Mary was tolerably safe as regarded Frank or the squire. If she went, Frank would be expected to go, and Frank disliked Courcy Castle almost more than ever. His aunt was now more than civil to him, and, when they were together, never ceased to compliment him on the desirable way in which he had done his duty by his family.

And soon after Christmas a visitor came to Mary, and stayed a fortnight with her: one whom neither she nor the doctor had expected, and of whom they had not much more than heard. This was the famous Miss Dunstable. 'Birds of a feather flock together,' said Mrs Rantaway – late Miss Gushing – when she heard of the visit. 'The railway man's niece – if you can call her a niece – and the quack's daughter will do very well together, no doubt.'

'At any rate, they can count their money-bags,' said Mrs Umbleby.

And, in fact, Mary and Miss Dunstable did get on very well together; and Miss Dunstable made herself quite happy at Greshamsbury, although some people – including Mrs Rantaway – contrived to spread a report, that Dr Thorne, jealous of Mary's money, was going to marry her.

'I shall certainly come and see you turned off,' said Miss Dunstable, taking leave of her new friend. Miss Dunstable, it must be acknowledged, was a little too fond of slang; but then, a lady with her fortune, and of her age, may be fond of almost whatever she pleases.

And so by degrees the winter wore away – very slowly to Frank, as he declared often enough; and slowly, perhaps, to Mary also, though she did not say so. The winter wore away, and the chill, bitter, windy, early spring came round.

The comic almanacs give us dreadful pictures of January and February; but, in truth, the months which should be made to look gloomy in England are March and April. Let no man boast himself that he has got through the perils of winter till at least the seventh of May.

It was early in April, however, that the great doings were to be done at Greshamsbury. Not exactly on the first. It may be presumed, that in spite of the practical, common-sense spirit of the age, very few people do choose to have themselves united on that day. But some day in the first week of that month was fixed for the ceremony, and from the end of February all through March, Lady Arabella worked and strove in a manner that entitled her to profound admiration.

It was at last settled that the breakfast should be held in the large dining-room at Greshamsbury. There was a difficulty about it which taxed Lady Arabella to the utmost, for, in making the proposition, she could not but seem to be throwing some slight on the house in which the heiress had lived. But when the affair was once opened to Mary, it was astonishing how easy it became.

'Of course,' said Mary, 'all the rooms in our house would not hold half the people you are talking about – if they must come.'

Lady Arabella looked so beseechingly, nay, so piteously, that Mary had not another word to say. It was evident that they must all come: the De Courcys to the fifth generation;* the Duke of Omnium himself, and others in concatenation accordingly.

'But will your uncle be angry if we have the breakfast up here? He has been so very handsome to Frank, that I wouldn't make him angry for all the world.'

'If you don't tell him anything about it, Lady Arabella, he'll think that it is all done properly. He will never know, if he's not told, that he ought to give the breakfast, and not you.'

'Won't he, my dear?' And Lady Arabella looked her admiration for this very talented suggestion. And so that matter was arranged. The doctor never knew, till Mary told him some year or so afterwards, that he had been remiss in any part of his duty.

And who was asked to the wedding? In the first place, we have said that the Duke of Omnium was there. This was, in fact, the one circumstance that made this wedding so superior to any other that had ever taken place in that neighbourhood. The Duke of Omnium never went anywhere; and yet he went to Mary's wedding! And Mary, when the ceremony was over, absolutely found herself kissed by a duke. 'Dearest Mary!' exclaimed Lady Arabella, in her ecstasy of joy, when she saw the honour that was done to her daughter-in-law.

'I hope we shall induce you to come to Gatherum Castle soon,' said the duke to Frank. 'I shall be having a few friends there in the autumn. Let me see; I declare, I have not seen you since you were good enough to come to my collection. Ha! ha! ha! It wasn't bad fun, was it?' Frank was not very cordial with his answer. He had not quite reconciled himself to the difference of his position. When he was treated as one of the 'collection' at Gatherum Castle, he had not married money.

It would be vain to enumerate all the De Courcys that were there. There was the earl, looking very gracious, and talking to the squire about the county. And there was Lord Porlock, looking very ungracious, and not talking to anybody about anything. And there was the countess, who for the last week past had done nothing but pat Frank on the back whenever she could catch him. And there were the Ladies Alexandrina, Margaretta, and Selina, smiling at everybody. And the Honourable George, talking in whispers to Frank about his widow – 'Not such a catch as yours, you know; but something extremely snug; – and have it all my own way, too, old fellow, or I shan't come to the scratch.'* And the Honourable John prepared to toady Frank about his string of hunters; and the Lady Amelia, by herself, not quite contented with these democratic nuptials – 'After all, she is so absolutely nobody; absolutely, absolutely,' she said confidentially to Augusta, shaking her head. But before Lady Amelia had left Greshamsbury, Augusta was quite at a loss to understand how there could be need for so much conversation between her cousin and Mr Mortimer Gazebee.

And there were many more De Courcys, whom to enumerate would be much too long.

And the bishop of the diocese, and Mrs Proudie were there. A hint had been given, that his lordship would himself condescend to perform the ceremony, if this should be wished; but that work had already been anticipated by a very old friend of the Greshams. Archdeacon Grantly, the rector of Plumstead Episcopi, had long since undertaken this part of the business; and the knot was eventually tied by the joint efforts of himself and Mr Oriel. Mrs Grantly came with him, and so did Mrs Grantly's sister, the new dean's wife. The dean himself was at the time unfortunately absent at Oxford.*

And all the Bakers and the Jacksons were there. The last time they had all met together under the squire's roof, was on the occasion of Frank's coming of age. The present gala doings were carried on in a very different spirit. That had been a very poor affair, but this was worthy of the best days of Greshamsbury.

Occasion also had been taken of this happy moment to make up, or rather to get rid of the last shreds of the last feud that had so long separated Dr Thorne from his own relatives. The Thornes of Ullathorne had made many overtures in a covert way. But our doctor had contrived to reject them. 'They would not receive Mary as their cousin,' said he, 'and I will go nowhere that she cannot go.' But now all this was altered. Mrs Gresham would certainly be received in any house in the county. And thus, Mr Thorne of Ullathorne, an amiable, popular old bachelor, came to the wedding; and so did his maiden sister, Miss Monica Thorne, than whose no kinder heart glowed through all Barsetshire.

'My dear,' said she to Mary, kissing her, and offering her some little tribute, 'I am very glad to make your acquaintance; very. It was not her fault,' she added, speaking to herself. 'And now that she will be a Gresham, that need not be any longer thought of.' Nevertheless, could Miss Thorne have spoken her inward thoughts out loud, she would have declared, that Frank would have done better to have borne his poverty than marry wealth without blood. But then, there are but few so stanch as Miss Thorne; perhaps none in that county – always excepting Lady Amelia.

And the Oriels were there, of course: the rector and his young wife, and Patience again enacting bridesmaid. It was pretty to see how Beatrice came out as a matron, and gave all manner of matured counsel to her still maiden friend. A month or two of married life does make such a difference

And Miss Dunstable, also, was a bridesmaid. 'Oh, no said she, when asked; 'you should have them young and pretty.' But she gave way when she found that Mary did not flatter her by telling her that she was either the one or the other. 'The truth is,' said Miss Dunstable, 'I have always been a little in love with your Frank, and so I shall do it for his sake.' There were but four: the other two were the Gresham twins. Lady Arabella exerted herself greatly in framing hints to induce Mary to ask some of the De Courcy ladies to do her so much honour; but Mary on this head would please herself. 'Rank,' said she to Beatrice, with a curl on her lip, 'has its drawbacks – and must put up with them.'

And now I find that I have not one page – not half a page – for the wedding-dress. But what matters? Will it not be all found written in the columns of the *Morning Post*?*

And thus Frank married money, and became a great man. Let us hope that he will be a happy man. As the time of the story has been brought down so near to the present era, it is not practicable for the novelist to tell much of his future career. When I last heard from Barsetshire, it seemed to be quite settled that he is to take the place of one of the old members at the next general election; and they say, also, that there is no chance of any opposition. I have heard, too, that there have been many very private consultations between him and various gentlemen of the county, with reference to the hunt; and the general feeling is said to be that the hounds shall go to Boxall Hill.

At Boxall Hill the young people established themselves on their return from the Continent. And that reminds me that one word must be said of Lady Scatcherd.

'You will always stay there with us,' said Mary to her, caressing her ladyship's rough hand, and looking kindly into that kind face.

But Lady Scatcherd would not consent to this. 'I will come and see you sometimes, and then I shall enjoy myself. Yes, I will come and see you, and my own dear boy.' The affair was ended by her taking Mrs Opie Green's cottage, in order that she might be near the doctor; Mrs Opie Green having married – somebody.

And of whom else must we say a word? Patience, also, of course, got a husband – or will do so. Dear Patience! it would be a thousand pities that so good a wife should be lost to the world. Whether Miss Dunstable will ever be married, or Augusta Gresham, or Mr Moffat, or any of the tribe of the De Courcys – except Lady Amelia – I cannot say. They have all of them still their future before them. That Bridget was married to Thomas – that I am able to assert; for I know that Janet was much put out by their joint desertion.

Lady Arabella has not yet lost her admiration for Mary, and Mary, in return, behaves admirably. Another event is expected, and her ladyship is almost as anxious about that as she was about the wedding. 'A matter, you know, of such importance in the county!' she whispered to Lady de Courcy.

Nothing can be more happy than the intercourse between the squire and his son. What their exact arrangements are, we need not specially inquire; but the demon of pecuniary embarrassment has lifted his black wings from the demesne of Greshamsbury.

And now we have but one word left for the doctor. 'If you don't come and dine with me,' said the squire to him, when they found themselves both deserted, 'mind, I shall come and dine with you.' And on this principle they seem to act. Dr Thorne continues to extend his practice, to the great disgust of Dr Fillgrave; and when Mary suggested to him that he should retire, he almost boxed her ears. He knows the way, however, to Boxall Hill as well as ever he did, and is willing to acknowledge, that the tea there is almost as good as it ever was at Greshamsbury.

NOTES

---

p. 3 Goshen: the land of plenty given by Joseph to his brothers: 'And thou shalt dwell in the land of Goshen, and thou shalt be near unto me, thou, and thy children, and thy children's children, and thy flocks, and thy herds, and all that thou hast. And there will I nourish thee, (for yet there are five years of famine;) lest thou, and thy household, and all that thou hast, come to poverty.' (Genesis 45:10–11.)

p. 3 which return members . . . land magnate: the Reform Act of 1832 redistributed parliamentary seats in accordance with the increasing urban population disenfranchising 143 English seats, and creating new ones in England (125), Wales (5), Scotland (8) and Ireland (5). In addition the creation of a £10 household voting qualification enfranchised another 300,000 people (an increase in the electorate of 50 per cent).

p. 3 a beadle: a parish officer with the power of punishing petty offenders.

p. 4 Peelism: repeal, in 1846, of the Corn Laws (which, through keeping the price of imported corn artificially high, had benefited the predominantly Tory agricultural interest) split Sir Robert Peel's Conservative Party into protectionists and Peelites (either free-traders or personal supporters of Peel).

p. 4 Fate . . . and the Duke of Wellington: In 1832, the Duke of Wellington (who had resigned as prime minister in 1828 because of his opposition to electoral reform), fearing the creation of sufficient Whig peers to enable the passage of the Reform Bill through the Lords, publicly withdrew his personal opposition to the Bill.

p. 4 St Stephen's: St Stephen's Chapel, the Palace of Westminster, destroyed by fire in 1834.

p. 5 fight the good fight: proverbial, but see 1 Timothy 6:12: 'Fight the good fight of faith . . .'

p. 6 blue books: parliamentary reports.

p. 8 that bourne ... made: cf. Hamlet's description of '... death,/The undiscover'd country, from whose bourn/No traveller returns...' (*Hamlet*, III.i.78–80).

p. 11 Longleat ... Hatfield: Longleat House, Wiltshire, designed by its owner Sir John Thynne, was completed in 1580; Hatfield House, Hertfordshire, rebuilt by its owner, Robert Cecil, earl of Salisbury, was completed in 1612. Both were seen at the time as 'gothic' rather than 'modern'.

p. 15 'The beards wagged all': one of Trollope's favourite allusions, from 'August's Abstract' in *Five Hundred Points of Good Husbandry* (1573), by Thomas Tusser (1524–80): "Tis merry in hall/When beards wag all.'

p. 17 the Reverend Caleb Oriel, the high-church rector: Oriel's High Church affinities can be inferred from his name. The Oxford Movement, which called for the Church of England to regain the Catholicity lost after its cessation from Rome, and which flourished in Oxford during the 1830s and 1840s, had at its heart the theologians of Oriel College.

p. 18 Mr Thorne of Ullathorne ... in the county: The extreme reactionary tendencies of Squire Thorne of Ullathorne are detailed in *Barchester Towers* (1857), in which he and his sister are prominent characters.

p. 19 Galen: Greek physician and philosopher of the second century AD, the epitome of medical wisdom.

p. 24 God tempered the wind to the shorn lamb: a favourite literary tag of Trollope, from the rendering of a French proverb ('A brebis tondue Dieu mesure le vent') in the section 'Maria', in Sterne's *A Sentimental Journey* (1768).

p. 26 ichor: in Greek mythology, the ethereal juice in the veins of the gods.

p. 28 the business of a dispensing apothecary to that of physician: When reading *Doctor Thorne*, one has to be mindful of the different social status each different branch of the medical profession possessed. For much of the early nineteenth century, apothecaries (dispensing chemists who treated patients, but who also sold toothbrushes, hairbrushes, etc.) had been generally regarded as little better than lower-class shopkeepers; physicians were significantly more respectable, practising and administering medicine, but not tending to dispense their own drugs; surgeons (those who effected cures by manual operations) did not enjoy anywhere near the same prestige they do now; and, finally, 'general practitioners' (those who combined elements of all three branches of the profession) were regarded as little better than quacks. The issue of the regulation and professionalisation of the practice of medicine was of great moment during the mid-1850s, when the novel is set: throughout the decade the issue of medical reform had been a fraught one, and in 1857 W. F. Cowper, President of the Board of Health, proposed a Bill that would legally define what constituted a qualified medical practitioner, and establish a national register of medics. The Bill was finally introduced, under a new government, in March 1858, and on becoming an Act of Parliament finally established a new, self-governing General Council of Medical Education and Registration. The importance of the Act, as Noel and José Parry have noted, 'was that it provided the basis for the unification of the medical profession through the concept of the equal recognition of all registered practitioners before the law' (Noel and José Parry, *The Rise of the Medical Profession: A Study of Collective Social Mobility* (London: Croom Helm, 1976), p. 126). Prior to such regulation, of course, the uncertainty of the social status of the individual practitioner gave way to precisely the sort of scramble for respectability that constitutes Dr Fillgrave's feud with Dr Thorne in this novel.

p. 29 *en règle*: in due order [Fr.].

p. 29 *de trop*: unwanted, in the way [Fr.].

p. 29 *Æsculapius*: Latin form of the Greek *Asklepios*, the god of medicine and healing.

p. 30 **If there was ... combativeness**: referring to the practice of phrenology, the pseudo-science that had widespread respectability in the early part of the nineteenth century; it held that various mental faculties were located in different parts of the skull, investigable by feeling the bumps on the outside of the head. By the time Trollope was writing *Doctor Thorne*, the practice had been largely discredited.

p. 32 *The Lancet ... Scalping Knife*: *The Lancet* was founded in 1823 by the surgeon and radical politician Thomas Wakley (1795–1862). Its reformist tendencies would have been likely to have supported Doctor Thorne's bid to collapse the distinction between 'apothecary' and 'physician'. The other journals mentioned are, as far as I can establish, fictional. ('Chirurgeon' is the old form of 'surgeon'.)

p. 33 **the world was his oyster ... all at once**: one of Trollope's favourite Shakespearian (and semi-proverbial) expressions. See *The Merry Wives of Windsor*, II.ii.2–3:

> Why then the world's mine oyster,
> Which I with sword will open.

p. 34 the tenor of the doctor's ways: cf. Gray's *Elegy in a Country Churchyard* (1742–50), stanza 19:

> Far from the madding crowd's ignoble strife
> Their sober wishes never learn'd to stray;
> Along the cool sequester'd vale of life
> They keep the noiseless tenor of their way.

p. 37 the precepts of Solomon: see Proverbs 23:24: 'He that spareth his rod hateth his son: but he that loveth him chasteneth him betimes.'

p. 49 translating the undertaker's mottoes: More conventional translations are 'I shall rise again' and 'Rest in peace'.

p. 50 beating the devil's tattoo: Presumably Squire Gresham is starting to irritate Doctor Thorne: according to *Brewer's Dictionary of Phrase and Fable*, 'beating the devil's tattoo' is the 'drumming on the table with one's fingers a wearisome number of times, or on the floor with one's foot; repeating any rhythmical mechanical sound with annoying persistence.'

p. 51 Sufficient for the day is the evil thereof: see Matthew 6:34: 'Take therefore no thought for the morrow: for the morrow shall take thought for the things of itself. Sufficient unto the day is the evil thereof.'

p. 59 not only humble but umble: presumably recalling the hypocritically 'umble' Uriah Heep, in Dickens's *David Copperfield* (1849–50).

p. 60 as ugly as the veiled prophet ... as beautiful as Zuleika: referring to 'The Veiled Prophet of Khorassan', one of the narrative poems in *Lalla Rookh* (1817), a series of oriental verse-tales linked by a prose narrative, by the Irish writer Thomas Moore (1779–1852). Trollope makes a small error here: in the poem, the beautiful maiden's name is actually 'Zelica'.

p. 63 Malthusians ... meaning that they drink beer: a rather laboured pun: Malthusians were followers of Thomas Malthus (1766–1834), the economist who advocated population-control on the grounds that the population tended to outgrow the rate of food-production.

p. 63 wasting fragrance on the desert air: cf. Gray's *Elegy*, stanza 14:

> Full many a flower is born to blush unseen
> And waste its sweetness on the desert air.

p. 68 a Monsoon: As David Skilton tells us, Frank's horse has been sired by Monsoon: 'Monsoon is listed in the General Stud Book as bred in Ireland by R. Caldwell, and was a brown colt foaled in 1850 by Simoon out of Miss Charlotte by Turcoman. He was therefore too young to have sired Frank's horse.' (See *World's Classics* edition, 1980.)

p. 73 he was not a marrying man ... profession: Oriel's neo-Catholic tendencies are again evident: clearly he believes in the celibacy of the priesthood.

p. 74 Orlando: hero of Shakespeare's *As You Like It*.

p. 74 'that which is sport to you, may be death to me': This reference has remained stubbornly unidentifiable.

p. 74 if you act thus, in the green leaf, what will you do in the dry: cf. Luke 23:21: 'For if they do these things in a green tree, what shall be done in the dry?' See also p. 78.

p. 75 In maiden meditation, fancy free: Lady Amelia has not been hit by Cupid's dart. See *A Midsummer Night's Dream*, II.i.160–64:

> But I might see young Cupid's fiery shaft
> Quench'd in the chaste beams of the watery moon;
> And the imperial votaress passèd on,
> In maiden meditation, fancy-free.

p. 77 ointment: Miss Dunstable's father has made his fortune from patent medicine, the disreputable and brazen marketing of which was a common feature of the nineteenth century. For an account of the patent-medicine trade and its appearance in nineteenth-century fiction (including *Framley Parsonage*), see Richard D. Altick's *The Presence of the Present: Topics of the Day in the Victorian Novel* (Columbus: Ohio State University Press, 1991), pp. 547–61.

p. 78 off with the new love and again on with the old: one of Trollope's favourite quotations, from the Scot's ballad 'Here's a health to them that's awa'':

> It's gude to be merry and wise;
>   It's gude to be honest and true;
> It's gude to be off with the old love,
>   Before you are on with the new.

p. 78 'Women grow on the sunny side of the wall': a quotation from one of Trollope's favourite texts, *Philip Van Artevelde* (1834), a verse-drama in no less than ten acts, by Sir Henry Taylor (1800–86).

p. 83 We are inclined to think ... ought to be hallowed: Victoria Glendinning, in her recent biography of Trollope (London: Hutchinson,

1992), argues that Trollope here recounts his own proposal to Rose Heseltine, his future wife. Such argument is purely inferential, however, but may satisfy those desperate to read Trollope's novels as being in some way autobiographical.

p. 85 she had abruptly fallen into unpleasant places: an inverted rendering of one of Trollope's favourite biblical quotations. See Psalms 16:6: 'The lines are fallen unto me in pleasant places; yea I have a goodly heritage.'

p. 97 St Anthony: Saint Anthony the Great (*c.* 250–356), the ascetic whose resistance to temptation became proverbial.

p. 97 a quick spasmodic style of narrative: Presumably Trollope uses 'spasmodic' in the pejorative sense given currency by the Scottish poet W. E. Aytoun (1813–65) to describe a group of mid-nineteenth-century poets that included Sydney Dobell (1824–74) and Alexander Smith (?1830–67). Their works were initially immensely popular, but quickly fell into disfavour after the publication of Aytoun's parody *Firmilian; or, The Student of Badajoz* in 1854, which satirised mercilessly the spasmodic tendency for over-blown and violent language to express profound emotion. Dobell's dramatic poem *Balder* (1854), for instance, contains the memorable lines 'Ah! Ah! Ah! Ah! Ah! Ah! Ah! Ah! Ah! Ah! Ah! Ah! Ah!' The narrator's comment that were he 'spasmodic' enough he would be able to describe the scene 'in five words and half a dozen dashes and inverted commas' clearly recalls such stylistic excesses.

p. 97 Argus-eyed: in Greek mythology, the hundred-eyed giant Argus Panoptes was sent by Hera to watch over the priestess Io.

p. 105 one of those 'whom the king delighteth to honour': Esther 6:6: 'What shall be done unto the man whom the king delighteth to honour?'

p. 106 the rosy god: Dionysos (Bacchus), Greek (Roman) god of wine.

p. 106 Eleusinian mysteries: pertaining to the rites of Demeter, the Greek corn-goddess, which in ancient times were celebrated (by initiates only) at Eleusis, near Athens.

p. 106 posiums: Trollope's humorous coinage for solo drinking-sessions; a symposium is a drinking party.

p. 108 a canal . . . through the Isthmus of Panama: The long-proposed Panama Canal was not, in fact, completed until 1914.

p. 110 *ci-devant*: former [Fr.].

p. 113 Mentor: proverbial for a trusted and wise counsellor, after Odysseus's sage adviser in the *Odyssey*.

p. 121 **Louis Philippe ... the King of the French:** Louis-Philippe (1773–1850), the 'Citizen King', was elected sovereign by the people of Paris after the Revolution of 1830. His initial popularity with radicals in Britain corresponds with the time of Sir Roger's son's birth and christening.

p. 122 **ruffle:** to bluster; to swagger.

p. 126 **the cynosure of his eye:** 'Cynosure' refers either to the constellation of Ursa Minor, or to the North Star (which is within the constellation); hence, anything that strongly attracts attention or admiration. Cf. Milton's *L'Allegro* (?1613), ll. 79–80:

> Where perhaps some beauty lies
> The cynosure of neighbouring eyes

p. 133 **When Greek Meets Greek, Then Comes Tug of War:** a common misquotation from *The Rival Queens* (1677) by Nathaniel Lee (1653?–1692): 'When Greeks joined Greeks, then was the tug of war!' (IV.ii).

p. 134 **guerdon:** reward, recompense. Bearing in mind the regularity with which Trollope quotes from Milton's *Lycidas* (1637) in his fiction, and considering the outcome of Dr Fillgrave's visit to Boxall Hill, 'guerdon' may be used to connote the following well-known passage (ll. 70–76):

> Fame is the spur that the clear spirit doth raise
> (That last infirmity of noble mind)
> To scorn delights, and live laborious days:
> But the fair guerdon when we hope to find,
> And think to burst out into sudden blaze,
> Comes the blind Fury with th'abhorred shears
> And slits the thin-spun life.

p. 134 **the story of the frog and the ox:** in Aesop's fable, the frog explodes through trying to puff himself up to the same size as the ox.

p. 140 **Burley ... Bothwell ... mountain side:** combatants in Scott's tale of religious factionalism, *Old Mortality* (1816).

p. 140 **Achilles ... Hector:** warrior-heroes of the *Iliad*. The Greek Achilles slays the Trojan Hector in battle.

p. 140 **a black dose:** a laxative made from senna and Epsom salts.

p. 141 **Had I the pen of Molière ... medical anger:** Molière (1622–73) first penned and performed his medical comedies *L'Amour médecin*, *Le médecin malgré lui* and *Le Malade imaginaire* in 1665, 1666 and 1673 respectively.

p. 141 *quoad*: in the capacity of [Lat.].

p. 155 **Plutus ... Venus**: respectively, the Roman god of wealth, and the Roman goddess of beauty.

p. 159 **gudgeons**: easily caught carp-like freshwater fish; hence, people easily cheated.

p. 159 **at the feet of her lady Gamaliel**: Gamaliel was Paul's spiritual guide before the latter's conversion to the Christian faith. See Acts 22:3: 'I am verily a man which am a Jew, born in Tarsus, a city in Cicilia, yet brought up in this country at the feet of Gamaliel, and taught according to the perfect manner of the law of the fathers, and was zealous toward God, as ye all are this day.'

p. 169 **in the days of William III**: William III (1650–1702) reigned jointly with his wife Mary II (1662–94) from 1689 until her death; he held the throne for a further eight years.

p. 170 **the Freetraders, Tallyhoes and Royal Mails**: four-in-hand coaches and official mail coaches.

p. 171 **Come, my friend, and discourse with me ... our latter-days**: Trollope here lapses into a parody of the portentous style ('oh, my melancholy, care-ridden friend!') of Thomas Carlyle (1795–1881). Carlyle's *Past and Present* (1843) compared institutions of the past with those of the present, invariably to the detriment of the latter; while his *Latter-day Pamphlets* were gloomy anti-democratic rants against contemporary society. Trollope had earlier parodied Carlyle as 'Dr Pessimist Anticant' in *The Warden* (1855).

p. 171 **seise**: Those interested in the petty tribulations of editing and annotating nineteenth-century novels might be interested to know that this has proved to be the most troublesome word in the entire novel. Most recent editions I have consulted have acquired from somewhere the misprint 'sieve', even though such a rendering – 'he of the sieve' – makes no sense whatsoever (although it *could* just squeeze by as an example of Carlylean obscurantism). However, 'seise' (which appears in both the first and third editions), an old spelling of 'seize', carries the sense of 'to put in possession [of]', and doesn't make much sense in the context in which it is deployed here either. Nevertheless, after an extensive trawl back and forth through several volumes of the OED, I can reveal to an anxious world that 'seise' is also an obscure variant of 'seis', which is itself an obscure variant of 'sais' or more commonly 'syce', which is an obscure Anglo-Indian adaptation of an Arab word meaning 'groom', or 'one who attends to horses'.

p. 174 the bump of veneration: another phrenological reference. See note to p. 30.

p. 174 shibboleth: a cant phrase. See Judges 12: 5–6, where 'shibboleth' (Heb. for 'ear of corn' or 'stream') was the test-word employed by the Gileadites for detecting Ephraimites (who were unable to pronounce it correctly).

p. 174 the Manchester school: applied to the grouping of Radicals and free-traders, originating from businessmen of the Manchester Chamber of Commerce and sponsors of the Anti-Corn Law league (established in 1838), led by Richard Cobden (1804–65) and John Bright (1811–89). 'Manchester' politics came to signify two things: devotion to laissez-faire economic politics, and opposition to colonial expansion.

p. 175 Prince Consort: another topical reference: Albert had been made Prince Consort on 25 June 1857.

p. 175 The next arrival ... the magnates of the earth: Trollope here introduces into the novel two of the main protagonists of the earlier *Barchester Towers*.

p. 176 muff: a bungler; one who is awkward or unskilful.

p. 176 he didn't kiss any of them, did he: This conversation may be designed to convey to the reader that Frank and George view Barchester through metropolitan eyes; their jocular contempt at Moffat's inappropriate behaviour to three pretty women (that is, his failure to proposition them, even though one is the wife of a chorister) reflects the common contemporary assumption that milliners were possessed of lax morality, and were easily preyed upon. As Altick puts it, '[c]onventional wisdom held that, just as men in their unredeemed state were potential seducers, so young women in dressmakers' shops, yearning to bedeck themselves in the finery they made for the more fortunate members of their sex, were their natural prey' (Altick, *op. cit.*, p. 534). Altick quotes from an anonymous article in *Fraser's Magazine*, March 1846: 'It is inconceivable how many of those unfortunate beings who live on the wages of prostitution, might refer the first step taken towards the downward path to the house of the milliner or dressmaker'; while in 1859 Arthur Munby recorded that '[m]y impression is that the morality of the milliner class is lower than that of any other' (quoted in Derek Hudson, *Munby: Man of Two Worlds. The Life and Diaries of Arthur J. Munby 1828–1910* (London: John Murray, 1972; new edition London: Sphere Books, 1974), p. 19. Moreover, it was customary to hire pretty women to model the hats, hence the attractiveness of the assistants in the Barchester millinery; hence, also, the association, as far as milliners were concerned, between sexual attractiveness and sexual availability. In 1862, for instance, Henry Mayhew described 'genteel and beautiful girls in shops and working-rooms in the West End, milliners, dressmakers, and shopgirls ... flitting along Regent Street and Pall Mall, like bright birds of passage, to meet with some gentleman on the sly, and to obtain a few quickly-earned guineas to add to their scanty salaries' (quoted in Peter Quennell [ed.], *London's Underworld* [London: Spring Books, 1950] p. 44). Similarly, in Trollope's *The Small House at Allington* (1862–4), Trollope establishes both the sexual allure and the potential availability of the coarse Amelia Roper by stating that she had been 'first young lady [i.e. chief model] in a millinery establishment in Manchester' (ch. 4).

p. 177 that wonderful box ... top of a cab: a topical reference. On 22 January 1856, '[t]he elderly Countess of Ellesmere, on her way to visit at Windsor Castle, sent ahead of her to Paddington station a cab on whose roof was loosely secured a trunk containing £15,000-worth of 'her ladyship's grandeur' in clothing and jewels. Happening to notice this inviting cargo as it trundled through Grosvenor Square, a self-described house painter hopped aboard and, unobserved by the driver or the maids inside, delivered it into the willing arms of his mate, a 'labourer', and his wife. Embarrassed by the riches they discovered when they opened the trunk in the back parlour of a Shoreditch oil shop, they got rid of them at deep discounts, selling Lady Ellesmere's wardrobe for three pounds and some jewels to 'a Jew' for £300. They threw away other jewellery, including a pair of diamond earrings that landed in a field near Whitechapel. Detected and arrested, these incompetent practitioners were convicted of theft and received sentences of various lengths' (Altick, *op. cit.*, p. 558). The confession of one of the perpetrators was recounted in the *Illustrated London News*, 12 December 1857.

p. 189 some question ... all her energy: Britain and France declared war on Russia on 26 March 1854; the first landings took place in September, and the allied forces won the first engagement, the Battle of Alma, on 20 September.

p. 190 The last view ... advocated by Sir Roger: Sir Roger here displays his radical credentials. Both Cobden and Bright were members of the Peace Society, and vociferously denounced the Crimean War.

p. 190 goose: a tailor's smoothing-iron, so called because its handle resembles the neck of a goose.

p. 191 deaf to the voice of that charmer: cf. Psalms 58:3–5: 'The wicked are estranged from the womb: they go astray as soon as they be born, speaking lies. Their poison is like the poison of a serpent: they are like the deaf adder that stoppeth her ear; Which will not hearken to the voice of the charmers, charming never so wisely.'

p. 193 'would'st not . . . wrongly win?': *Macbeth*, I.v.22–4:

> What thou wouldst highly,
> Thou wouldst thou holily; wouldst not play false
> And yet wouldst wrongly win.

p. 195 ten-pound freeholders: One of the major provisions of the 1832 Reform Act was the enfranchisement of the ten-pound freeholder, one entitled to vote because his property had a yearly value of at least ten pounds.

p. 197 Sir Edwin Landseer: Sir Edwin Henry Landseer (1802–73), famous animal painter. His *Monarch of the Glen* was first exhibited in 1851; and he modelled the bronze lions at the foot of Nelson's Column (1859–66).

p. 197 cabbaging: a tailoring expression; 'cabbaging' is the practice of taking portions of a customer's cloth as a perquisite.

p. 199 from the ninth part of a man: another apt heckle; the proverbial lack of manliness that characterised tailors (the occupation not being thought conducive to sound physical development) gave rise to the expression 'Nine tailors make a man'.

p. 210 this bird, so rare in the land: a good example of how the classical education undergone by Victorian 'gentlemen' informs the text of so many of Trollope's novels. He here renders in English a stock Latin tag, from Juvenal's *Satire VI*, l. 165, 'Rara avis in terris nigroque simillima cycno' ('A rare bird on earth, something like a black swan').
To Trollope's classically educated readers, the use of the phrase might have served to underline the ironic portrayal of Moffat, as Juvenal's original use of the phrase is inherently ambiguous; the 'rara avis' in question is the hypothetically perfect woman, whom Juvenal rejects, after listing all her virtues, in favour of the whore. Just as Juvenal rejects the perfect woman, so Trollope may intend the reference to reinforce his readers' rejecting of Mr Moffat.

p. 214 tuft-hunters: people who search for influential friends. (Formerly, at Oxbridge, titled undergraduates wore gold tassels, or tufts, on their caps; hence 'tuft' came to signify a person of social consequence.)

p. 216 **Gatherum Castle:** the rather ponderous joke behind the Duke of Omnium's name is at last revealed: 'omnium gatherum' is mock-Latin for a gathering of all-sorts. Presumably the point of the joke is that the duke assembles a motley collection of politicians and political affiliates under the broad Whig banner.

p. 216 **tax-cart ... tandem-horse:** a two-wheeled light spring-cart, on which reduced tax was payable. Normally pulled by one horse, the De Courcy cart (possibly because of its four passengers) is pulled by two in tandem.

p. 216 **Italian in its style of architecture:** Skilton suggests that Gatherum recalls Blenheim Palace, designed for the Duke of Marlborough by Sir John Vanbrugh, and completed in 1719.

p. 217 **This portico ... Ionic columns:** Trollope's architectural knowledge is at best vague; strictly speaking, a portico is itself a range of columns along the front or side of a building.

p. 218 **an ordinary:** a meal provided at a fixed charge.

p. 220 **Dr Stanhope ... villa in Italy:** A brief mention of another character from *Barchester Towers*.

p. 221 **nones, complines, and vespers:** nones: a church office originally for the ninth hour (three o'clock), afterwards earlier; compline: the seventh and last service of the day; vespers: evensong.

p. 000 **where Finnie goes Bolus may go too:** Again the class-based perceptions of apothecaries are brought before the reader. Mr Athill is implicitly condemning Bolus's claims to be a 'gentleman' by linking him with the attorney Finnie: an attorney (one appointed to act for another in matters legal and financial) was considered not quite respectable by the Victorians, the OED telling us that 'attorneyism' was a common mid-nineteenth-century expression for 'unscrupulous cleverness'. In Chapter 10 of *Barchester Towers*, for example, the Barchester clergy are snobbishly surprised to find Finnie attending Mrs Proudie's first reception at the episcopal palace: 'Mr Finnie, the attorney, with his wife, was to be seen, much to the dismay of many who had never met him in a drawing-room before.'

p. 224 **the light of his countenance:** common biblical phraseology.

p. 227 **one who had already fought his battles, and ... glory:** An allusion to Horace, *Odes*, III, xxvi, ll. 1–2.

> Vixi puellis nuper idoneus
> et militavi non sine gloria;

(Trans: 'until recently I lived fit for young women, and served not without glory.')

p. 238 none but the brave deserves the fair: Dryden, *Alexander's Feast* (1697), l.15.

p. 238 off with Miss Gresham and . . . on with Miss Dunstable: see note to p. 78.

p. 241 a second Balaclava gallop: The disastrous charge of the Light Brigade took place on October 25, 1854.

p. 242 Sir Richard himself: referring to Sir Richard Mayne (1796–1868), Chief Commissioner of the Metropolitan Police from 1850.

p. 247 In these days of snow-white purity . . . venality at elections: The paragraphs that follow are an adaptation of a passage in Trollope's Carlylean critique of English institutions, *The New Zealander* (written in 1855, never published in Trollope's lifetime). 'The object of the work,' states the reader's report for Longman's, 'is to show how England may be saved from the ruin that now threatens her!! And how the realisation of Macaulay's famous prophecy of the "New Zealander standing on the ruins of London Bridge" may be indefinitely postponed.' The report goes on to advise Longman's 'not to publish the work on any terms', which advice Longman's accepted. Trollope, perhaps eager not to waste words in which he, at least, had some faith, responded by incorporating *verbatim* large chunks of *The New Zealander* into *The Three Clerks* (1857), his tale of the Civil Service and corruption in public life, as well as appropriating the following passage for use in *Doctor Thorne* (written immediately after *The Three Clerks*), which is reprinted here for purposes of comparison:

(Bold italics indicate text deleted from *The New Zealander*; the text in square brackets indicates additions to *Doctor Thorne*.)

In nothing is this pretended horror of political delinquency so strongly evinced by members of Parliament as in cases of bribery. The sin of bribery is damnable. It is the one sin for which[,] in the House of Commons[,] there can be no forgiveness. When discovered, it should render the culprit liable to political death without hope of pardon *or chance of mercy*. It is treason to a higher throne than that on which the [Queen] *Sovereign* sits. It is a heresy which requires an *auto-da-fé*. It is pollution to the whole [h]House, which can only be cleansed by a great sacrifice. Anathema,[-] maranatha! [o]Out with it from amongst us, even though [the] half of our heart's blood be poured forth in the

conflict! Out with it, and for ever! [new paragraph] Such is the
language of patriotic members with regard to bribery[;]. [a]And
doubtless, if sincere, they are in the right. It is a bad thing, certainly
that a rich man should [buy] *obtain* votes *by his riches*; bad also that
a poor man should [sell them] *so use a privilege allotted to him for a
very different purpose. By all means let us have strong laws against
bribery.*

[no new paragraph] By all means also let us repudiate the system
with heartfelt disgust. [new paragraph] With heartfelt disgust[,] if we
can do so, [by all means;] but not with disgust pretended only, and not
felt in the heart at all.

[no new paragraph] The laws against bribery at elections[s] are now
so stringent *in their different clauses* that an unfortunate candidate
may easily become guilty, even though actuated by the purest intentions. [But not the less on that account does any gentleman, ambitious
of the honour of serving his country in parliament, think it necessary
as a preliminary measure to provide a round sum of money at his
banker's.] *It is difficult to say what is not bribery.* A candidate must
[pay for no treating, no refreshments, no band of music;] *not only
hermetically seal his own breeches' pockets during his election, but he
must put a padlock, of which he himself must keep the key, on those
of all his friends.* [h]He must give neither ribbons to the girls, nor ale
to the men. *He must pay for no music, no refreshments, no band
of followers.* If a huzza be uttered in his favour, it is at his peril. It
may be necessary [for him] to prove before a committee that it was
the spontaneous result of British feeling in his favour, and not
the purchased result of British beer. He cannot safely ask anyone
to share his hotel dinner. Bribery [hides itself] *descends* now [in]
to the most impalpable shapes, and may be effected by the offer of a
glass of sherry. [But not the less on his account does a poor man find
that he is quite unable to overcome the difficulties of a contested
election.]

We strain at [our] gnats with a vengeance, but [we] swallow [our]
the camels with ease. [For what purpose is it that we employ those
peculiarly safe men of business – Messrs Nearthewinde and Closerstil
– when we wish to win our path through all obstacles into that sacred
recess, if all be so open, all so easy, all so much above-board?] *Is it not
still considered necessary for any gentleman who prepares himself for
a contested election to see that a considerable sum of money is also
prepared for the purpose? Except in some few isolated cases such
necessity undoubtedly exists.* [Alas!] the money is [still] necessary, is

[still] prepared, or at any rate *is* expended. The poor candidate of course knows nothing of the matter till the attorney's bill is laid before him[,] when all danger of petition[s] has passed away. He little dreamed till then, not he, that there had been banquetings and junket[t]ings, [secret doings, and deep drinkings] *deep drinkings and secret doings going on* at his expense. Poor candidate! Poor member! Who was so ignorant as he? 'Tis true he has paid such bills before; but 'tis equally true that he specially [begged] *desired* his managing friends[, Mr Nearthewinde] *Twistem and Twinum* to be very careful that all was [done] according to law.[!] He pays the bill, however, and on the next election will again employ [Mr Nearthewinde] *Messrs Twistem and Twinum.*

(The reader is referred to N. John Hall's excellent edition of *The New Zealander* [Oxford: Clarendon Press, 1972].)

p. 247 *auto-da-fé*: either the public declaration of the judgement passed on heretics in Spain and Portugal by the infliction of the punishment that immediately followed thereupon.

p. 248 Anathema maranatha!: see 1 Corinthians 16:22: 'If any man love not the Lord Jesus Christ, let him be Anathema Maranatha.' ('Anathema' means 'curse be upon him'; 'maranatha' is taken to mean 'our Lord cometh'.)

p. 248 We strain ... with ease: see Matthew 23:24: 'Ye blind guides, which strain at a gnat, and swallow a camel.'

p. 249 peri: in Persian mythology a beautiful (but evil) being with supernatural powers.

p. 249 *quidnunc*: a newsmonger, a gossip [Lat.].

p. 252 the curled darlings of the nation: see *Othello*, I.ii.66–7:

> So opposite to marriage that she shunn'd
> The wealthy curled darlings of our nation.

p. 256 O whistle and I'll come to you, my lad: a song by Burns (1759–96).

p. 258 'I am monarch of all I survey': the opening line of 'Verses Supposed To Be Written By Alexander Selkirk, During His solitary Abode In The Island of Juan Fernandez' (publ. 1782), by William Cowper (1731–1800). The rest of the stanza reveals the extent of Mary's irony:

> I am monarch of all I survey,
>   My right there is none to dispute;

> From the centre all round to the sea,
>   I am lord of the fowl and the brute.
> Oh, solitude! where the charms
>   That sages have seen in thy face?
> Better dwell in the midst of alarms,
>   Than reign in this horrible place.

p. 263 the power of heaping coals of fire ... so injured her: cf. Proverbs 25:21: 'If thine enemy be hungry, give him bread to eat; and if he be thirsty, give him water to drink: For thou shalt heap coals of fire upon his head, and the Lord shall reward thee.'

p. 267 the periporollida: Skilton establishes that this is a nonsense-word.

p. 268–9 a Xantippe ... Imogenes: Xanthippe, proverbial for a shrew, was the wife of Socrates; Imogen is the virtuous wife of Posthumus Leonatus in Shakespeare's *Cymbeline*.

p. 270 the *toga virilis*: the garb of manhood [Lat.]

p. 270 lords of the ascendant: Trollope here deploys metaphorically an astrological term. According to *Brewer*, '[t]he lord of the ascendant is any planet within the 'house of the Ascendant'. The house and lord of the ascendant at birth were said by astrologers to exercise great influence on the future of the child'.

p. 271 *alma mater*: literally, 'benign mother' [Lat.], applied by alumni to their school or university.

p. 272 sharpers and blacklegs: respectively, swindlers at card-games and race-meetings.

p. 278 His name ... ever industrious: Trollope is probably parodying Samuel Smiles's *Life of George Stephenson* (1857), which represented the great railway engineer's life as a moral *exemplum* for the industrial working classes. (Smiles, of course, made the genre of biography-as-moral-fable his own with the publication of the runaway bestseller *Self-Help*, in 1859.)

p. 281 to my own cheek: to/for my own satisfaction.

p. 283 a pearl of great price: cf. Matthew 18:45–6: 'Again, the kingdom of heaven is like unto a merchant-man, seeking goodly pearls; Who, when he had found one pearl of great price, went and sold all that he had, and bought it.'

p. 290 the baked meats ... funeral banquet: cf. *Hamlet*, I.ii.180–81:

> ... the funeral baked-meats
> Did coldly furnish forth the marriage tables.

p. 291 a Gordian knot, not to be cut: According to legend, the peasant Gordius, made King of Phrygia, preserved his wagon as a tribute to Jupiter, fastening it with a complicated knot. On being told that whoever undid the knot would rule over the East, Alexander the Great drew his sword and cut it.

p. 300 war to the knife: cf. Byron, *Childe Harold's Pilgrimage* (1812–18), Canto i, stanza 86: 'War, war, is still the cry, "War even to the knife!"'

p. 306 Bashaw: a wilful, haughty man, from the Turkish title *pasha*.

p. 313 cherry-bounce: cherry brandy.

p. 317 living cleanly and forswearing sack: cf. *I Henry IV*, v.iv.162–64: 'He that rewards me, God reward him! If I do grow great, I'll grow less; for I'll purge, and leave sack, and live cleanly, as a nobleman should do.'

p. 318 put money in your purse: a slight misquotation from *Othello*. Iago's repeated advice to Roderigo, in the former's long speech at the end of I.iii, is to 'Put money in thy purse.'

p. 324 The snake was so but scotched: cf. *Macbeth*, III.ii.13: 'We have scotch'd the snake, not kill'd it.'

p. 326 a jolly, thriving wooer: Richard's self-description, in *Richard III*, IV.iii.43.

p. 327 It was Hyperion to a satyr: a contrast unfavourable to the latter, from Hamlet's contrast between his dead father and his uncle Claudius (*Hamlet*, II.i.139–40). In Greco-Roman mythology Hyperion was the sun-god Helios, and the incarnation of light and beauty; a satyr was a Greek god of the woodlands, represented by the Romans as part goat.

p. 328 the brightest and the best of men: recalling one of the hymns of Bishop Reginald Heber (1783–1826): 'Brightest and best of the sons of the morning.'

p. 333 flat, stale, and unprofitable: an echo of *Hamlet*, I.ii.133–34:

> How weary, stale, flat, and unprofitable
> Seem to me all the uses of this world.

p. 334 'If all the blood of all the Howards': see Pope's *An Essay on Man*, Epistle IV (1734), ll.215–16:

What can ennoble sots, or slaves, or cowards?
Alas! not all the blood of all the Howards.

p. 334 'Si la jeunesse savait ...': si jeunesse savoit; si vieillesse pouvoit'
('If youth knew; if age could'), Épigramme CXCI in *Les Prémices*, by
Henri Estienne (1531–98).

p. 336 one of the lions in his path: see Proverbs, 26:13: 'The slothful
man saith, There is a lion in the way; a lion is in the streets.'

p. 342 not much of the Bluebeard about the squire: the wife-murderer
in the story 'La Barbe bleu', by Charles Perrault (1628–1703), in his
collection of fairy stories *Contes de ma mère l'oye* (*Tales of Mother
Goose*) (1697).

p. 345 a day ... Lord Bateman: referring to *The Loving Ballad of
Lord Bateman* (1839), supposedly 'transcribed' by Thackeray, with
illustrations by Cruikshank and mock-learned notes by Dickens. Trollope seems here to misremember the original: in *The Loving Ballad*, the
time spent by Lord Bateman away from his Turkish lover Sophia is
seven years and fourteen days:

Now sevin long years is gone and past,
   And fourteen days vell known to me;
She packed up all her gay clouthing,
   And swore Lord Bateman she would go see.

p. 349 'looking after dead men's shoes': looking out for a legacy;
anticipating such circumstances that would follow the death of another.

p. 355 credence-tables: the credence table is the small table beside the
altar on which the bread and wine are placed before being consecrated.

p. 355 the scarlet lady: pejorative Protestant term for the Roman
Catholic Church; a reference to the Whore of Babylon in Revelation 17
('... a woman ... arrayed in purple and scarlet colour, and decked
with gold and precious stones and pearls, having a golden cup in her
hand full of abominations and filthiness of her fornication.... And I
saw the woman drunken with the blood of saints, and with the blood
of the martyrs of Jesus ...')

p. 355 Capuchin's filthy cassock: the Order of Friars Minor Capuchin
began in 1525, taking its name from the *cappuccino* (pointed hood) of
the order's habit, which represented a return to a literal observance of
the rule of St Francis of Assissi. The 'filthy cassock' Trollope mentions
is a metonymic reference to the extreme austerity and poverty of the
order.

p. 355 a Huss, a Wickliffe, or a Luther: John Huss (c. 1369–1416),

Bohemian religious reformer, excommunicated in 1411, and burned at the stake in July 1416; John Wycliffe (c. 1329–84), first translator of the Bible into English, and a fervent believer in inner spirituality as taking precedence over the mechanics of the Church hierarchy; Martin Luther (1483–1546), German religious reformer and founder of the Reformation.

p. 356 **the matter of Fridays:** Presumably the High Church Oriel follows the Catholic convention of eating fish on Fridays.

p. 356 **Brigham Young:** Young (1801–77) was the second president of the Mormon church, and first State Governor of Utah (appointed in 1850, and again in 1854). Trollope here refers to the Mormon endorsement of polygamy; Young himself took over 20 wives and fathered 47 children. The reference to Young is highly topical: in 1857, President James Buchanan, frustrated at the continued friction between the Mormons and the federal judiciary, replaced Young as governor, and sent an army to Utah to enforce the principle of federal rule. (Trollope himself later had a none-too-successful encounter with Young in 1872, while visiting Utah: 'I did not achieve great intimacy with the great polygamist of the Salt Lake City. I called upon him, sending to him my card, apologising for doing so without an introduction, and excusing myself by saying that I did not like to pass through the territory without seeing a man of whom I had heard so much. He received me in his doorway, not asking me to enter, and inquired whether I were not a miner. When I told him that I was not a miner, he asked me whether I earned my bread. I told him I did. 'I guess you're a miner,' said he. Then he turned upon his heel, went back into the house, and closed the door. I was properly punished, as I had been vain enough to conceive that he would have heard my name.' [*An Autobiography*, ch. 19])

p. 363 **fashionable things . . . Constantinople:** As Trollope states, travel to the Holy Land became fashionable in the 1850s. Trollope himself visited Palestine in 1858 after his trip to Egypt on Post Office business, and *Doctor Thorne* was completed on the journey. His next novel, *The Bertrams* (1859) describes in some detail two trips to the Holy Land; Trollope also based several of his short stories ('An Unprotected Female at the Pyramids' (1860), 'A Ride Across Palestine' (1861) and 'George Walker at Suez' (1861) on the trip.

p. 363 **chibook:** a long straight-stemmed Turkish pipe.

p. 364 **afraid of every lion that he met in his path:** see note to p. 336.

p. 375 letters for six-and-eightpence each: one-third of a pound in imperial currency; the standard minimum fee for a legal transaction.

p. 378 en grand seigneur: like a great lord [Fr.].

p. 379 in his generation, a year wiser: see Luke 16:8: '. . .the children of this world are in their generation wiser than the children of light.'

p. 380 opodeldoc: name (given by Paracelsus) to various local applications, usually made from soap-liniment.

p. 388 chasse-café: properly, a dram or liqueur taken after coffee.

p. 392 in favour of long beards: Frank's beard is very much of the moment; during, and immediately after, the Crimean War, the returning veterans, sporting beards, made such facial appendages highly fashionable.

p. 394 Scutari: the site of Florence Nightingale's first military hospital, established in October 1854; now Üsküdor, a suburb of Istanbul.

p. 396 discretion ... the only kind of valour left to him: proverbial, but see *I Henry IV*, v.iv wherein Falstaff escapes being killed in battle by feigning death: 'The better part of valour is discretion; in the which better part I have saved my life.'

p. 397 when the Rads ... the Funds: the Rads: radicals; the Funds: government stock.

p. 398 up to trap: knowing; sly; crafty

p. 421 *comme il faut*: as it should be; approved by fashionable society; genteel [Fr.].

p. 422 crossed: 'Crossing' was the nineteenth-century practice of writing twice on a piece of paper, the second time at right angles to the first.

p. 422 leather and prunella: one of Trollope's favourite allusions, from Pope's *Essay on Man*, Ep. iv (1734), ll.203–4:

> Worth makes the man, and want of it the fellow;
> The rest is all but leather or prunella.

Pope is contrasting the cobbler with the parson, 'leather' signifying the former, and 'prunella' (the material from which clerical robes were made) the latter.

p. 439 'Thou shalt not covet a man's house, nor his wife': a paraphrase of the Tenth Commandment. See Exodus 20:17: 'Thou shalt not covet thy neighbour's house, thou shalt not covet thy neighbour's wife, nor his man-servant, nor his maid-servant, nor his ox, nor his ass, nor any thing that is thy neighbour's.'

NOTES

549

p. 444 *congé*: leave to depart [Fr.].

p. 446 *amende*: penalty; fine [Fr.].

p. 464 **love in a cottage:** proverbial for marriage without financial means to maintain one's social status. The *Oxford Dictionary of Quotations* cites George Colman (1732–94), *The Clandestine Marriage*, I, ii: 'Love and a cottage! Eh, Fanny! Ah give me indifference and a coach and six!'

p. 468 **kick the beam like feathers?:** According to *Brewer*, to 'kick the beam' is 'to be of light weight; to be of inferior consequence. When one scale-pan is weighted less than the other, it flies upwards and "kicks the beam" of the scales.'

p. 472 **a *dies non*:** a day on which judges do not sit, or one on which normal business is not transacted [Lat.].

p. 481 **'Will you ... come and be killed':** a variant of a line from the nursery rhyme 'Oh, what have you got for dinner, Mrs Bond?':

> Oh, what have you got for dinner, Mrs Bond?
> There's beef in the larder, and ducks in the pond;
> Dilly, dilly, dilly, dilly, come to be killed
> For you must be stuffed and my customers filled.

p. 485 **the Spartan matron ... whole in limb but tainted in honour:** Trollope seems to conflate two of the anecdotes from Plutarch's *Lacaenarum Apophthegmata* (*Sayings of Spartan Woman*), in Book III of the *Moralia*. 'Gyrtias' tells of the eponymous matron's concern for her grandson's honour: according to the Loeb translation, '[w]hen a messenger came from Crete bringing the news of the death of Acrotatus, she said, "When he had come to the enemy, was he not bound either to be slain by them or to slay them? It is more pleasing to hear that he died in a manner worthy of myself, his country, and his ancestors than if he had lived for all time a coward."' However, in the section 'Other Spartan Women to Fame Unknown', No. 16, a mother hands a shield to her son who is about to depart for battle, telling him, 'Come back either with your shield, or upon it.'

p. 490 **as Sancho was in his government:** in Cervantes' *Don Quixote de la Mancha* (1605–15), Sancho Panza is made governor of the isle of Barataria, but is constantly prevented from enjoying the privileges of his new position: for instance, he is continually prevented from eating the food put before him, as it is immediately taken away again.

p. 490 **'London particular':** either a type of beer (as it would seem to be here), or a brand of Madeira wine.

p. 490 *cadeau*: gift [Fr.].

p. 495 **the case of those Hills**: If a real case is referred to, 'Hills' may be a misprint for 'Halls', as no relevant cases concerning trusts and trustees, and involving litigants named Hill or Hills, were heard before the Court of Chancery in the ten years before Trollope was writing. A relevant case, Hall *v.* Franck (in which two individuals named Hall were concerned) was however heard on 9 March 1849. Hall and another successfully sued two trustees for having lost a payment of £1,200 on a mortgage, by putting the money into the wrong hands. Mr Bideawhile's clerk could be making this reference to point out to Frank Gresham the danger of dealing with only one of two co-trustees, particularly in the matter of a mortgage.

p. 495 **I think it was '11' . . . an end of that**: Trollope's original readers would have known that 1811 was an almost legendary year for the great and lasting quality of its vintages. 1811 ports, in particular, survived until the end of the century. The vineyards of Madeira had been devastated by an attack of the fungal disease grape-mildew, or oidium, in 1852.

p. 496 **Aix**: Perhaps Mr Bideawhile believes Aix-les-Bains, in the Savoy, to be in Switzerland. The Duchy of Savoy was not absorbed into France until Victor Emmanuel exchanged it for Napoleon III's support for his attempt to mount the throne of a united Italy.

p. 496 *tables d'hôtel*: fixed meals at set prices and times, the hotel guests often being served at a large table, presided over by the hotelier.

p. 498 **It has been suggested . . . towards the cost**: Trollope's response to a criticism made by the reviewer of *The Three Clerks* in the *Saturday Review*, 5 December 1857, 517–18: 'There is a legal portion of the story, and law is a pitfall from which few novelists can escape uninjured. . . . Why do not novelists consult some legal friend before they write about law? Is it impossible to find a barrister who has a hobby for criminal law, and also a hobby for criticising novels, and who would bring his skill in both lines to bear upon the correction of a layman's mistakes? We think that such a man might be found, and he would be invaluable to all fiction writers who evolve descriptions of English trials out of the depths of their consciousness, and square them to meet the principles of eternal justice.' Spurred on by Trollope's response, *The Saturday Review* was unable to resist repeating its criticism in its notice of *Doctor Thorne* (12 June 1858, 618–19), adding that Trollope's apology is a huge aesthetic mistake: 'The fault of the book throughout is its carelessness. . . . [C]arelessness occurs about the will on which the catastrophe depends. Mr Trollope states as a fact that it *had* the effect which he attributes to it, and that if it had not, the point has been misstated. He adds that he wishes that, in order to avoid the responsibility of legal mistakes, novelists could adopt a suggestion which we offered in our review of his last novel, that they should have their books settled by counsel. We are flattered by his readiness to take advice, and in return we will not discuss the question whether Sir Roger Scatcherd's will was not altered just before his death (though we rather think it was), but we must observe that Mr Trollope does not meet our point. The contract of the writer with the reader is to create and maintain a reasonably perfect illusion as to the reality of the events which he relates, and he breaks that contract if he wantonly points out the difficulties of his task, and says that there is a way out of them, but that he does not choose to take the trouble to find it.' Interestingly enough, Trollope followed the *Saturday Review*'s advice on at least one subsequent occasion: 'The legal opinion as to heirlooms in *The Eustace Diamonds* was written for me by Charles Merewether, the present Member for Northampton. I am told that it has become the ruling authority on the subject' (*An Autobiography*, ch. 6).

p. 503 **Our Pet Fox Finds a Tail:** referring to the fable by Æsop, in which the fox, after losing his tail in a trap, tries to persuade his peers that they too would be better off without tails. Eventually he discovers his old tail, and changes his mind.

p. 506 **mysterious romances, like Mrs Radcliffe's:** Ann Radcliffe (1764–1823), writer famous for her Gothic romances *The Castles of Athlin and Dunbayne* (1789), *A Sicilian Romance* (1790), *The Romance of the Forest* (1791), *The Italian* (1797) and, above all, *The Mysteries of Udolpho* (1794).

p. 522 **tenant in tail:** freeholder in the property for the term of his life, his son having the inheritance. A Victorian expert in property law explains: 'It is the almost universal practice, when lands are brought into strict settlement upon a marriage, to give an estate for life to the husband, followed by an estate tail to the eldest (unborn) son. Consequently the lands cannot be alienated until the son attains the age of twenty-one' (Kenelm Digby, *History of the Law of Real Property*, 2nd ed., 1876, p. 220n). This device was necessary at a time when married women were unable to own property independently of their husbands.

p. 522 **trover ... flotsam and jetsam:** Trollope is perhaps thinking of treasure-trove, since trover is a legal action taken to recover the value of personal property illegally acquired by another. Another minor

Trollopian misunderstanding occurs here, since flotsam and jetsam are respectively wreckage floating in the sea and goods thrown overboard from a ship. If these reach shore, they are called 'wreck'.

p. 525 the De Courcys to the fifth generation: cf. Exodus 20:5: '... I the Lord thy God am a jealous God, visiting the iniquity of the fathers upon the children unto the third and fourth generation of them that hate me.'

p. 526 I shan't come to the scratch: According to *Brewer*, '[u]nder the London Prize Ring Rules, introduced in 1839, a round in a prize fight ended when one of the fighters was knocked down. After a 30-second interval this fighter was allowed eight seconds in which to make his way unaided to a mark scratched in the centre of the ring; if he failed to do so, he "had not come up to scratch" and was declared beaten.'

p. 526 And the bishop ... absent at Oxford: Trollope rounds off his novel by introducing, belatedly, the main protagonists of *The Warden* and *Barchester Towers*, perhaps in order to cement the links between the three novels. In making an issue out of who is to conduct Frank and Mary's marriage, the novel recalls the feuding between the Grantly and Proudie factions that is the substance of *Barchester Towers*.

p. 527 *Morning Post*: the highly fashionable society paper.

Doctor Thorne received generally favourable reviews, although reviewers were not unanimous in what each found praiseworthy or detracting. The following extract, for example, from the Examiner, is cautiously appreciative of the novel, even as he finds it teetering towards caricature, especially in the case of Sir Roger Scatcherd:

> Mr Trollope in his new story quits his old cathedral town only to pass into its county, and to make acquaintance with some of the county families. He invites us, not to Barchester, but into Barsetshire. Perhaps the county families are over-hardly dealt with, but there is a good deal of shrewd and pleasant malice in the great debates on questions of blood and treasure. The scenes of rivalry among country practitioners of medicine are certainly not overcharged, though the particular turns sometimes given to them are not exactly true to nature. There is more exaggeration also in the picture of the brandy-drinking man of the day, Roger Scatcherd, than belongs fairly to one of the main characters in the story, and his gin-drinking clerk is an extravagant abortion. These objections we suggest to a novelist who has taken already a high position in his art, and who is able to confirm a very genuine success. The quiet touches of satire blended with the careful character-painting in the Warden and Barchester Towers gave promise of a success more permanent than can be achieved by the more showy strokes of caricature, for which we hope that Mr Trollope has not been emboldened to exchange them. There is plenty of the old grace and of the old sterling quality in Doctor Thorne; it is a novel that no sensible reader will confound with the mass of manufactured fiction that is only meant to last a day. There is sense in it, humour in it, now and then a touch of pathos; it is interesting, and is written in good English. But at the same time there is sign in it of the beginning of an evil that some day will eat away all that is soundest in the author's credit if it be not promptly checked. We

speak of Mr Trollope as of one from whom the public has it knows not what – but surely much – to hope.

(Unsigned notice, *Examiner*, 29 May 1858, p. 340)

By contrast, Geraldine Jewbury's unsigned review in the *Athenaeum*, finds elements of the tragic in the representation of Sir Roger, but finds the love interest between Mary and Frank tiresome:

There is genuine humour in 'Doctor Thorne,' not strained or ambitiously displayed, but arising from the natural play of the characters. The characters are real creatures of human nature, flesh and blood, vigorously and broadly drawn, but not caricatured, – they would be likenesses if they were not types. The grand family at De Courcy Castle, with their social motto, 'Rank has its drawbacks' – the grand Countess, the goddess and presiding genius of the family – the minor deities, Lady Amelia, Lady Margarhetta, and Lady Arabella, who had been spared to preside over the Greshams – they are all excellent, and their high mightiness, which somehow always bends to convenience, is a vein of genuine comedy; they are shown bare to the very heart of their small natures – their heartlessness, their meanness, their worldliness are brought into daylight; it is not done contemptuously, but with a shrewd good-nature that keeps the reader from being pained. It is this genial quality which marks the ripeness of Mr Trollope's faculties; there is nothing acrid in the flavour of his pleasantry; with the touch of nature which 'makes the whole world kin,' he makes us feel that even De Courcy Castle is not cut off from our sympathies – we do not disown the family, and that makes the secret of Mr Trollope's excellence. Miss Dunstable, the heiress of the 'ointment of Lebanon,' is charming, and the letter she writes in reply to the proposal of the Honourable John is delightful – and the reader feels good naturedly revenged for all the impertinence and small maliciousness of the Castle. Mr Moffat and his wooing, and the fate that befell him, will not the reader find it all written in the second volume of the chronicle? – and so we shall not say more. Sir Roger Scatcherd, the railway baronet, is a study, and as true to the life as the other characters, but he takes a deeper hold on our sympathies; there is a pathetic, tragic interest about him which moves to a pity deeper than tears. The interest is not worked up in scenes, it pervades the whole history of the man. The death-bed, however, is equal in its way to any of the three death-beds in 'Clarissa Harlowe.' Dr Thorne is the good genius of everybody in the book, and is repaid by being indispensable – whether loved or hated, nobody can do without him. The reader, however, perhaps cares less for him than for some of the other characters. Frank Gresham, the lover of the heroine, might, we are quite willing to believe, have been a fine young fellow, – but to speak candidly, and 'not to put too fine a point on it,' we have known heroes much better worth being miserable about. A man worth all the tears he cost would have set about to earn his living earlier, – and if Miss Mary Thorne had seen him with *our* eyes she would have looked at some one else; but everybody knows that those things go by favour, and not by merit. The fault of 'Doctor Thorne' is, that it is too long. The love affairs of Frank and Mary drag, – the difficulties and objections which beset them are said and re-said till they become wearisome. Two volumes would have afforded 'ample room and verge enough' to detail, unravel, and defeat all the machinations of the adverse party. Few tales are strong enough to hold out for three volumes without showing symptoms of distress. Nevertheless, 'Doctor Thorne' is an excellent novel, and as such we commend it to our readers.

Geraldine Jewbury [anon.], *Athenaeum*, 5 June 1858, p. 719)

The review in the *Spectator* has different reservations. While it gives its approval to the novel, it nevertheless suggests, implicitly, that the novel's ultimate endorsement of Mary's illegitimacy displays a morality 'of a questionable kind':

In Mr Trollope's first novel of 'The Warden' his satire took a wider yet a closer range than he has since attempted, embracing the law, the church, the press, especially the 'Thunderer' under the title of the 'Jupiter,' and several of what the author deemed the Reforming cants of the day. His story, however, was bald and purposeless, and constructed without regard to the commonest requirements of art, if, indeed, it could be said to have a structure. In 'Barchester Towers,' his satire was more limited, being mainly confined to Tractarianism, and High and Low Church; the Evangelicals, in their representative Mr Slope, receiving no mercy at his hands. In 'The Three Clerks' the civil service and competitive examinations were the aim of the satire, while the late misappropriations of other people's money through ill-regulated ambition, or a mere wish to shine beyond one's sphere, were also exhibited. Upon the whole, however, contemporary weaknesses and passing events were scarcely handled with so much pith and pungency as in the two earlier fictions; but there was a completer story, and a greater novel-interest. In the book before us, *Dr Thorne*, the satire or the hits at passing events are not perhaps so fully obvious, as in 'The Three Clerks'; though some may think they recognize traits in the great Whig noble the Duke of Omnium, and the great heiress Miss Dunstable; there is also the old subject of a contested election very well done, especially in the dinners and gatherings. The satire, however, is mainly directed against a rather worn matter – the formalities and jealousies of the medical profession; and one main source of the trouble consists in the pecuniary embarrassments of a country squire, caused by elections, hounds, and the expenses of a high-bred wife. There *is* a story, however, with characters not merely serving as vehicles for the author's fun or comments, but really interested in the events, and what is more to the purpose, interesting the reader. It may be true that the object of the author as it appears in his work is of a questionable kind, and that the main elements of the tale – family trouble arising from pecuniary embarrassment, love crossed by social ambition, and, as Mr Trollope would say, social prejudice – have been exhibited before. The elements, however, are well put together, and the story is narrated with that close observation of human manners, and of human nature as modified by human manners in this middle of the nineteenth century, which form the author's distinguishing characteristic; whilst the writing has the smartness, point, and pungency that always impart an interest to Mr Trollope's pages, not by mere style, but by the matter which that style displays.

(Unsigned review, *Spectator*, 29 May 1858, xxxi. 577–8)

Still on the subject of Mary's illegitimacy, a long essay in the *National Review* finds it central to what it takes to be the novel's central concern, the exposure of the folly of laying a stress on 'blood' over moral worth:

The main purpose of Mr Trollope's last novel is to ridicule the maxims which are supposed to prevail among a certain portion of the aristocracy of this country on the subject of birth and ancient blood. The author is far too good a Tory not to sympathize with the genuine pride of an old English family, whose pedigree dates back to the ages of chivalry, unstained by a single *mésalliance* for some thirty generations.... But nothing can exceed his bitter contempt for those who, while pluming themselves on purity of blood and illustrious lineage, consider that money can wipe out any taint; and that he who marries the daughter of a country apothecary commits a mortal sin, while he who allies himself with the heiress of a successful tradesman, so his success have enabled her to count her fortune by hundreds of thousands, merits the thanks of his family and the admiration of high-born neighbours. The heroine of his tale is the illegitimate child of the doctor's brother, who has seduced a poor and pretty girl in the neighbourhood. The victim's brother very righteously sets forth to chastise the villain; but his heavy stick does its work more effectually than perhaps he intended, and the avenger is found guilty of manslaughter and sent to prison for half a year. The child is born; and the mother disappears from the scene. The illegitimate girl is allowed, improbably enough, to become the playfellow of the squire's children, and eventually the beloved of his heir. Meantime her mother's brother, whose wife had nursed the 'young Squire Gresham,' rises in the world by dint of industry and genius, and is presented to us as the wealthy baronet Sir Roger Scatcherd. He and his wife are perhaps the most striking characters in the tale; and his terrible end, when he falls a victim to the intemperance of a life-time, is powerfully conceived. The niece of Dr Thorne, the child of Mary Scatcherd, becomes heiress to the wealth left by this great railway-contractor and former stonemason, when his son follows his father's fatal example, and drinks himself to death. Then the family who had scornfully repudiated her engagement to their heir are only too glad to accept what they can no longer resist, and the lovers are made happy. There are similar tales of sordidness and inconsistency interwoven with this, all illustrating the meanness which can so value money as to let it cover all defects of birth or character, and so despise love, and faith, and purity, as to hold them of no account when weighed against gold. The great Whig family of the county are, with pardonable partyspirit, made to furnish all the instances of this paltry huckstering tone which are presented to us; and a gentle hint is insinuated that the rival faction have at once more true reverence for birth and more respect for plebeian talent.

The low-born persons of the tale are very fairly treated. Mary

Thorne is as perfect as other novel-heroines; Sir Roger Scatcherd is an honest, clever, really generous-hearted man; his son Louis, and the tailor-descended Moffat, are as mean, pitiful, insignificant creatures as they well could be. Lady Scatcherd, again, once the wet-nurse of Frank Gresham, is a vulgar, honest, affectionate, womanly woman. Indeed, she and her husband inspire us with as much interest as any other personage in the tale. There is much truth and pathos in the picture of her desolate solitude of spirit, when left absolutely alone to bear 'the burden of an honour where unto she was not born.' . . .

And here, for the present, we take our leave of Mr Trollope. He has powers which, if used with due painstaking conscientiousness, may make him one of the most successful novelists of the day, as they always render him readable and entertaining. But above all, he has the gift of finishing his work to the most minute detail without becoming for an instant tedious or trivial; and this is a gift so rare that it should never be neglected. The author of *Barchester Towers* should never write so as to tempt his readers to 'skip'; and though few do so less often, yet there are symptoms in some passages of his later works of a somnolency, which we trust will not be allowed to grow upon him. The popularity which he has already earned should be a sufficient stimulus to induce him steadily and perseveringly to deserve it.

(Anon., 'Mr Trollope's Novels', *National Review*, October 1858, vii. 416–35)

Twentieth-century criticism of *Doctor Thorne* is not as widespread as it might be, given the novel's enduring popularity. Moreover, such criticism tends to be rather gushing in tone. The following extract, from Elizabeth Bowen's introduction to the Riverside edition of the novel, is included as an example of such overly appreciative criticism:

Yet there can, I believe, be an artistry which is inadvertent – more than unconscious, all but unwilling. To this Trollope was subject; one is aware of its unmistakable action in *Doctor Thorne*. I spoke, at the outset of this preface, of his scenes' having a certain glow and rotundity; and there are moments when they have more. Something idyllic, if not poetic, is added to their intense likeness; they become, if never piercingly beautiful, more nearly beautiful than is most reality – and when this happens there is a momentary transparency in his dense prose, as though by some magic the verbal sand reached a heat where it could run into glass. Elsewhere, at crisis of emotion between the characters, that emotion not only commands us but austerely seems to command him, giving anonymous authority to his pen. An artist transmits more than he knows: in that sense we find Trollope to be an artist. On a level below that, he is a great conveyor of that to which he greatly reacted: charm – whether of face, person or manner, landscape, the visage or environment of a house. Aesthetically and fondly he loved girls, bevy-in-muslins, swinging their bonnets by the ribbons, dispersing over lawns liquid with sunset – he depicts floating pleasures, whose spell is in their evanescence, their slipping by. Had he been a painter, he would have been an inland Boudin. Also he took pleasure in masculine upright bearing and open countenance. Honour was his darling; grace, where he was concerned, went with strength in reserve or courage in play. *Doctor Thorne* as a novel has sterling merits – some I have touched on, others you will discover. But it acts on us most, perhaps, through some inner quality that only a warm and gentle word can define. It endears itself to us. For many, this is enough.

(Elizabeth Bowen, 'Introduction' to Riverside Press edition [Cambridge, Mass: 1959], reprinted in Bareham [ed.] *The Barsetshire Novels* [London and Basingstoke: Macmillan, 1983], pp. 163–77, 176–7)

Finally, a more tough-minded approach to the novel can be found in Jane Nardin's feminist reading of the novel, which argues for its inherent conservatism:

Frank and Mary's marriage is ideally conservative in being free from any modern mercenary taint, and it is ideal as well in Mary's conservative refusal to use the leverage that her money might have given her to claim equality of power with her husband. Social mobility, which tends to unbalance the traditional power relations of marriage, is no threat when a wife is committed to traditional views of woman's place. And unlike many intelligent women in Trollope's later novels, Mary never resents her powerless position as a female. Asked to wait alone in the drawing room while Doctor Thorne and the Gresham men arrange her future, Mary 'obediently did as she was bid; and there she sat, for the next three hours, wondering, wondering' (46). She does not protest, or even regret, her exclusion. Mary proves her commitment to a conservative view of woman's place when she freely gives 'all that had ever appertained' (47) to the Greshamsbury estate back to Frank, refusing to tie it up legally on her own behalf. 'She would only trouble herself to see that [Frank] was empowered to do as he did think fit' (47). And because she is so deserving, Mary need not fear that her husband will deny her a wife's legitimate influence. Thus Frank and Mary's marriage redeems the failures of the older generation.

Marriage, in *Doctor Thorne*, is central both to the unity of society and to personal happiness. The Gresham estate is regenerated not just by Mary's money but also by the guidance she and Frank, as a perfect couple, will bring to it. Trollope never implies here, as he does in so many later novels, that Victorian marriage offers a wife insufficient scope for action. Lady Arabella is dissatisfied with domesticity, but her dissatisfaction is completely unjustified. The institution of marriage, at its best, is the moral center of the novel, the forces that cures – just as it was in *The Three Clerks*. In a materialistic, unstable world, the good marriage may be hard to achieve, but that is the fault of materialism and instability, not of marriage itself.

(Jane Nardin, *He Knew She Was Right: The Independent Woman in the Novels of Anthony Trollope* [Carbondale and Edwardsville: Southern Illinois University Press, 1989], pp.62-3)

SUGGESTIONS FOR FURTHER READING

Most major works on Trollope contain treatments of *Doctor Thorne*. Examples of general works on Trollope are Bradford A. Booth, *Anthony Trollope: Aspects of His Life and Art* (London, 1958), A. O. J. Cockshut, *Anthony Trollope* (London, 1955), P. D. Edwards, *Anthony Trollope: His Art and Scope* (St Lucia, Queensland, 1977), John Halperin, *Trollope and Politics: A Study of the Pallisers and Others* (London, 1977), Geoffrey Harvey, *The Art of Anthony Trollope* (London, 1980), Walter M. Kendrick, *The Novel-Machine: The Theory and Fiction of Anthony Trollope* (Baltimore, 1980), James R. Kincaid, *The Novels of Anthony Trollope* (Oxford, 1977), Coral Lansbury, *The Reasonable Man: Trollope's Legal Fiction* (Princeton, 1981), Robert M. Polhemus, *The Changing World of Anthony Trollope* (Berkeley and Los Angeles, 1968), Arthur Pollard, *Anthony Trollope* (London, 1978), Michael Sadleir, *Trollope: A Commentary* (London, 1927), L. P. and R. P. Stebbins, *The Trollopes: The Chronicle of a Writing Family* (London, 1946), R. C. Terry, *Anthony Trollope: The Artist in Hiding* (London 1977), Robert Tracy, *Trollope's Later Novels* (Berkeley Ca., 1978), and Stephen Wall, *Trollope and Character* (London, 1988).

Despite a number of serious bibliographical errors, Donald Smalley (ed.), *Anthony Trollope: The Critical Heritage* (London, 1969), contains a useful collected of Victorian Criticism of Trollope's fiction. Trollope's contemporary reception is analysed in David Skilton, *Anthony Trollope and His Contemporaries: A Study in the Theory and Conventions of Mid-Victorian Fiction* (London, 1972). An annotated bibliography of later criticism is found in J. C. Olmsted and J. E. Welsh, *The Reputation of Trollope: An Annotated Bibliography 1925–1975* (New York, 1978), and a fuller listing of Trollope editions as well as selected secondary works is found in *Anthony Trollope: A Collector's Catalogue 1847–1990* (London: the Trollope Society, 1992). The standard descriptive bibliography of Trollope's works in their original editions is Michael Sadleir, *Trollope: A Bibliography* (London, 1928).

The most scholarly biographies are N. John Hall, *Trollope: A Biography* (Oxford, 1991), and R. H. Super, *The Chronicler of*

Barsetshire: A Life of Anthony Trollope (Ann Arbor, 1988), while Richard Mullen, *Anthony Trollope: A Victorian in His World* (London, 1990), gives a more opinionated account. Victoria Glendinning's *Anthony Trollope* (London, 1992) is fascinating and exceptionally readable, and contains very plausible speculations about unknown aspects of the author's life, including his marriage. Trollope's letters are admirably collected in N. John Hall (ed.), *The Letters of Anthony Trollope* (Stanford, Ca., 1983). Also useful in the study of Trollope as a public and private figure is R. C. Terry (ed.), *Trollope: Interviews and Recollections* (London, 1987).

See also Ivan Melada, 'The Idea of a Gentleman: *Dr Thorne*', in his *The Captain of Industry in English Fiction 1821–1871*' (Albuquerque: University of New Mexico Press, 1970, pp. 166–71).

TEXT SUMMARY

Chapter 1: The Greshams of Greshamsbury
Descriptions of Squire Gresham and Lady Arabella, of Frank and his coming of age banquet.

Chapter 2: Long, Long Ago
Describing the murder of Henry Thorne, and Mary's adoption by the doctor.

Chapter 3: Dr Thorne
The rivalry between Thorne and Dr Fillgrave is described, as is the history of the former's becoming physician to the Gresham family.

Chapter 4: Lessons from Courcy Castle
Advice on the desirability of suitable marriages is given by the De Courcys to various members of the Gresham family, while the squire confesses his financial anxieties to Dr Thorne.

Chapter 5: Frank Gresham's First Speech
Describing the birthday dinner for Frank at Greshamsbury.

Chapter 6: Frank Gresham's Early Loves
Frank flirts with Patience Oriel; the De Courcy faction hatches a plan to marry Frank off to the millionairess Emily Dunstable; Frank proposes to Mary, who refuses him.

Chapter 7: The Doctor's Garden
Discussion between Mary and the Doctor over her forebears and the issue of rank leaves the doctor anxious about Mary's future.

Chapter 8: Matrimonial Prospects
Frank again seeks out Mary, but is advised by the De Courcys that, for the sake of the family, he must marry money.

Chapter 9: Sir Roger Scatcherd
Describing the baronet, his descent into alcohol, and his relationship with Dr Thorne. Sir Roger and the doctor quarrel.

Chapter 10: Sir Roger's Will
An ambiguous clause in Sir Roger's will raises the possibility that in the event of the deaths of both Sir Roger and his son Louis Philippe, Mary might inherit the Scatcherd fortune.

Chapter 11: The Doctor Drinks His Tea
The doctor realises he has forgotten to broach the subject of negotiating a new loan for the squire from Sir Roger. Mary asks to visit the Scatcherds.

Chapter 12: When Greek Meets Greek Then Comes Tug of War
Dr Fillgrave is unceremoniously turned out of Sir Roger's house.

Chapter 13: The Two Uncles
Dr Thorne confesses to Sir Roger that they are both uncles to Mary.

Chapter 14: Sentence of Exile
Squire Gresham is worried about Moffat's intentions towards Augusta. The doctor and Lady Arabella quarrel over her request that Mary should no longer visit Greshamsbury.

Chapter 15: Courcy
Describing Courcy, and the coming election in which Moffat and Sir Roger are to stand against one another.

Chapter 16: Miss Dunstable
. . . is introduced. The countess tries to prepare Frank for his coming proposal.

Chapter 17: The Election
Sir Roger wins the Barchester seat by two votes.

Chapter 18: The Rivals
Miss Dunstable refuses a proposal from George De Courcy, and outmanoeuvres Moffat in his similar project.

Chapter 19: The Duke of Omnium
Dinner at Gatherum Castle for the prominent Whigs of the county. Frank is unimpressed by the duke's behaviour.

Chapter 20: The Proposal
Frank half-heartedly proposes to Miss Dunstable. She refuses him, and they become good friends.

Chapter 21: Mr Moffat Falls into Trouble
Moffat jilts Augusta Gresham. He is thrashed by Frank on the steps of his club.

Chapter 22: Sir Roger is Unseated
... over allegations of bribery at the election. His drinking is near to killing him.

Chapter 23: Retrospective
Detailing the doctor's current round of anxieties about Mary. He is summoned to Sir Roger's.

Chapter 24: Louis Scatcherd
... is introduced. He is as dissipated as his father.

Chapter 25: Sir Roger Dies
The doctor beseeches Scatcherd to alter his will. He refuses. The baronet proposes that Louis and Mary should be man and wife. Sir Roger dies.

Chapter 26: War
Lady Arabella visits the doctor. They quarrel vehemently over Frank and Mary.

Chapter 27: Miss Thorne Goes on a Visit
... to Boxall Hill. In the meantime Lady Arabella instructs the Greshams that they are to have no further contact with the Thornes.

Chapter 28: The Doctor Hears Something to His Advantage
Sir Louis is beginning to fall in love with Mary, as well as to take an interest in the title-deeds of the Greshamsbury estate.

Chapter 29: The Donkey Ride
Frank quarrels with his mother and heads for Boxall Hill. He and Mary are interrupted by Sir Louis.

Chapter 30: Post Prandial
Frank confesses his love for Mary to his father, but agrees to leave Greshamsbury for one year.

Chapter 31: The Small End of the Wedge
Both the Thorne and Gresham households wonder at the prudence of their respective positions.

Chapter 32: Mr Oriel
... is introduced. His courtship of Beatrice Gresham is described.

Chapter 33: A Morning Visit
Beatrice visits Mary. They discuss Frank.

Chapter 34: A Barouche and Four Arrives at Greshamsbury
Sir Louis arrives, and stays with the doctor. His dissipation has increased.

Chapter 35: Sir Louis Goes Out to Dinner
. . . to the Greshams. His drunken behaviour and tactlessness about the Gresham debts causes great embarrassment.

Chapter 36: Will He Come Again?
Frank pays Mary a surprise visit.

Chapter 37: Sir Louis Leaves Greshamsbury
Sir Louis confesses his love for Mary, to the doctor's great disgust. The baronet steps up his claim to recover his debts.

Chapter 38: De Courcy Precepts and De Courcy Practice
Detailing how Lady Amelia dissuades Augusta from marrying Mr Gazebee, and marries him herself.

Chapter 39: What the World Says About Blood
Frank reaffirms to Dr Thorne and the squire his intent to marry Mary.

Chapter 40: The Two Doctors Change Patients
Lady Arabella swallows her pride and recalls Dr Thorne. In the meantime Fillgrave attends Sir Louis at Boxall Hill.

Chapter 41: Doctor Thorne Won't Interfere
. . . to break off Mary and Frank's engagement.

Chapter 42: What Can You Give in Return?
Lady Arabella tries to negotiate with Mary, but the latter's stubbornness forces a quarrel.

Chapter 43: The Race of Scatcherd Becomes Extinct
Sir Louis dies, and the doctor intimates to Lady Scatcherd that Mary will inherit the Scatcherd fortune.

Chapter 44: Saturday Evening and Sunday Morning
Frank ponders whether he should obey his mother.

Chapter 45: Law Business in London
. . . over the Greshamsbury estate. Frank tells Dr Thorne of his fixed resolve to wed Mary.

Chapter 46: Our Pet Fox Finds a Tail
The truth of Mary's inheritance is revealed: 'Oh Frank; my own Frank! . . . we shall never be separated now.'

Chapter 47: How the Bride Was Received, and Who Were Asked to the Wedding
Frank and Mary wed.

ACKNOWLEDGEMENTS

The editors and publishers wish to thank the following for permission to use copyright material in the *Trollope and His Critics* section of this volume:

Oxford University Press for material from N. John Hall, *Trollope: A Biography* (Clarendon Press, 1991);

Richard Sadler for material from Michael Sadler, *Trollope: A Commentary* (Constable & Co., 1927);

University of Chicago Press for material from Christopher Herbert, *Trollope and Comic Pleasure*, 1987.

Every effort has been made to trace the copyright holders but if any have been inadvertently overlooked the publishers will be pleased to make the necessary arrangement at the first opportunity.